THE WORKS

OF

THOMAS CARLYLE

(*COMPLETE*)

OLIVER CROMWELL'S
LETTERS AND SPEECHES WITH ELUCIDATIONS

THE LIFE OF
FRIEDRICH SCHILLER

COMPREHENDING AN

EXAMINATION OF HIS WORKS

ILLUSTRATED

Volume Nine

NEW YORK
PETER FENELON COLLIER, PUBLISHER
1897

CW01510129

KESSINGER PUBLISHING'S
RARE MYSTICAL REPRINTS

THOUSANDS OF SCARCE BOOKS
ON THESE AND OTHER SUBJECTS:

Freemasonry * Akashic * Alchemy * Alternative Health * Ancient Civilizations * Anthroposophy * Astrology * Astronomy * Aura * Bible Study * Cabalah * Cartomancy * Chakras * Clairvoyance * Comparative Religions * Divination * Druids * Eastern Thought * Egyptology * Esoterism * Essenes * Etheric * ESP * Gnosticism * Great White Brotherhood * Hermetics * Kabalah * Karma * Knights Templar * Kundalini * Magic * Meditation * Mediumship * Mesmerism * Metaphysics * Mithraism * Mystery Schools * Mysticism * Mythology * Numerology * Occultism * Palmistry * Pantheism * Parapsychology * Philosophy * Prosperity * Psychokinesis * Psychology * Pyramids * Qabalah * Reincarnation * Rosicrucian * Sacred Geometry * Secret Rituals * Secret Societies * Spiritism * Symbolism * Tarot * Telepathy * Theosophy * Transcendentalism * Upanishads * Vedanta * Wisdom * Yoga * *Plus Much More!*

DOWNLOAD A FREE CATALOG
AND
SEARCH OUR TITLES AT:

www.kessinger.net

LIST OF ILLUSTRATIONS.

PORTRAIT OF CHARLES I., FROM AN OLD ENGRAVING.

FRONTISPIECE—Carlyle, Vol. Nine.

CONTENTS.

OLIVER CROMWELL'S LETTERS AND SPEECHES.

APPENDIX.

CONTENTS.

EARLY KINGS OF NORWAY.

FRIEDRICH SCHILLER.

SUPPLEMENT OF 1872.
SAUPE'S "SCHILLER AND HIS FATHER'S HOUSEHOLD."

APPENDIX.

OLIVER CROMWELL'S LETTERS AND SPEECHES.

WITH ELUCIDATIONS.

THE First Session of this Parliament closed, last June, under such auspicious circumstances as we saw; leaving the People and the Lord Protector in the comfortable understanding that there was now a Settlement arrived at, a Government possible by Law; that irregular exercises of Authority, Major-Generals and such like, would not be needed henceforth for saving of the Commonwealth. Our Public Affairs, in the Netherlands and elsewhere, have prospered in the interim; nothing has misgone. Why should not this Second Session be as successful as the First was?—Alas, success, especially on such a basis as the humors and parliamentary talkings and self-developments of four hundred men, is very uncertain! And indeed this Second Session meets now under conditions somewhat altered.

For one thing, there is to be a new House of Lords: we know not how that may answer! For another thing, it is not now permissible to stop our Haselrigs, Scotts and Ashley Coopers at the threshold of the Parliament, and say, Ye shall not enter: if they choose to take the Oath prescribed by this new Instrument, they have power to enter, and only the Parliament itself can reject them. These, in this Second Session, are new elements; on which as we have seen, the generation of Plotters are already speculating; on which naturally his Highness too has his anxieties. His Highness, we find, as heretofore, struggles to *do* his best and wisest, not yielding much to anxieties: but the result is, this Session proved entirely unsuccessful; perhaps the unsuccessfulest of all Sessions or Parliaments on record hitherto!—

The new House of Lords was certainly a rather questionable adventure. You do not improvise a Peerage:—no, his Highness is well aware of that! Nevertheless "somewhat to stand between me and the House of Commons" has seemed a thing

(1)

desirable, a thing to be decided on: and this new House of Lords, this will be a "somewhat,"—the best that can be had in present circumstances. Very weak and small as yet, like a tree new-planted; but very certain to grow stronger, if it have real life in it, if there be in the nature of things a real necessity for it. Plant it, try it, this new Puritan Oliverian Peerage-of-Fact, such as it has been given us. The old Peerage-of-Descent, with its thousand years of strength, — what of the old Peerage has Puritan sincerity, and manhood and marrow in its bones, will, in the course of years, rally round an Oliver and his new Peerage-of-Fact, — as it is already, by many symptoms, showing a tendency to do. If the Heavens ordain that Oliver continue and succeed as hitherto, undoubtedly his new Peerage may succeed along with him, and gather to it whatever of the Old is worth gathering. In the mean while it has been enacted by the Parliament and him; his part is now, To put it in effect the best he can.

The List of Oliver's Lords can be read in many Books;[1] but issuing as that matter did, it need not detain us here. Puritan Men of Eminence, such as the Time had yielded: Skippon, Desborow, Whalley, Pride, Hewson, these are what we may call the *Napoleon-Marshals* of the business: Whitlocke, Haselrig, Lenthall, Maynard, old Francis Rouse, Scotch Warriston, Lockhart; Notabilities of Parliament, of Religious Politics, or Law. Montague, Howard are there; the Earls of Manchester, Warwick, Mulgrave —some six Peers; of whom only one, the Lord Eure from Yorkshire, would, for the present, take his seat. The rest of the six as yet stood aloof; even Warwick, as near as he was to the Lord Protector, could not think[2] of sitting with such a Napoleon-Marshal as Major-General Hewson, who, men say, started as a Shoemaker in early life. Yes; in that low figure did Hewson start; and has had to fight every inch of his way up hitherward, doing manifold

---

[1] Complete, in *Parliamentary History*, xxi. 167–169: incomplete, with angry contemporary glosses to each Name, which are sometimes curious, in *Harleian Miscellany*, vi. 460–471. An old Copy of the official *Summons* to these Lords is in Additional Ayscough MSS. no. 3246.

[2] Ludlow, ii. 596.

victorious battle with the Devil and the World as he went along, — proving himself a bit of right good stuff, thinks the Lord Protector! You, Warwicks and others, according to what sense of manhood you may have, you can look into this Hewson, and see if you find any manhood or worth in him ; — I have found some! The Protector's List, compiled under great difficulties,[1] seems, so far as we can now read it, very unexceptionable ; practical, substantial, with an eye for the New and for the Old ; doing between these two, with good insight, the best it can. There were some sixty-three summoned in all ; of whom some forty and upwards sat, mostly taken from the House of Commons : — the worst effect of which was, that his Highness thereby lost some forty favorable votes in that other House ; which, as matters went, proved highly detrimental there.

However, Wednesday, 20th January, 1657-8, has arrived. The Excluded Members are to have readmission, — so many of them as can take the Oath according to this New Instrument. His Highness hopes if they volunteer to swear this Oath, they will endeavor to keep it ; and seems to have no misgivings about them. He to govern and administer, and they to debate and legislate, in conformity with this Petition and Advice, not otherwise ; this is, in word and in essence, the thing they and he have mutually with all solemnity bargained to do. It may be rationally hoped that in all misunderstandings, should such arise, some good basis of agreement will and must unfold itself between parties so related to each other. The common dangers, as his Highness knows and will in due time make known, are again imminent ; Royalist Plottings once more rife, Spanish Charles-Stuart Invasion once more preparing itself.

But now the Parliament reassembling, on this Wednesday, the 20th, there begins, in the " Outer Court," since called the Lobby, an immense "administering of the Oath," the whole Parliament taking it ; Six Commissioners appearing " early in the morning," with due apparatus and solemnity, minutely

---

[1] Thurloe, vi. 648.

described in the Journals and Old Books;[1] and then laboring till all are sworn. That is the first great step. Which done, the Commons House constitutes itself; appoints "Mr. Smythe" Clerk, instead of Scobell, who has gone to the Lords, and with whom there is continual controversy thenceforth about "surrendering of Records" and the like. In a little while (hour not named) comes Black Rod; reports that his Highness is in the Lords House, waiting for this House. Whereupon, Shoulder Mace, — yes, let us take the Mace, — and march. His Highness, somewhat indisposed in health, leaving the main burden of the exposition to Nathaniel Fiennes of the Great Seal, who is to follow him, speaks to this effect; as the authentic Commons Journals yield it for us.

SPEECH XVI.

"MY LORDS, AND GENTLEMEN [OF] THE HOUSE OF COMMONS:

"I meet you here in this capacity by the Advice and Petition of this present Parliament. After so much expense of blood and treasure [we are now] to search and try what blessings God hath in store for these Nations. I cannot but with gladness of heart remember and acknowledge the labor and industry that is past [your past labor], which hath been spent upon a business worthy of the best men and the best Christians. [*May it prove fruitful!*]

"It is very well known unto you all what difficulties we have passed through, and what [issue] we are now arrived at. We hope we may say we have arrived if not [altogether] at what we aimed at, yet at that which is much beyond our expectations. The nature of this Cause, and the Quarrel, what that was at the first, you all very well know; I am persuaded most of you have been actors in it: It was the maintaining of the Liberty of these Nations; our Civil Liberties as men, our Spiritual Liberties as Christians. [*Have we arrived at that?*] I shall not much look back; but rather say one word concerning the state and condition we are all now in.

---

[1] *Commons Journals*, vii. 578; Whitlocke, p. 666; Burton, ii. 322.

"You know very well, the first Declaration,[1] after the beginning of this War, that spake to the life, was a sense held forth by the Parliament, That for some succession of time designs had been laid to innovate upon the Civil Rights of the Nations, [and] to innovate in matters of Religion. And those very persons who, a man would have thought, should have had the least hand in meddling with Civil things, did justify them all. [*Zealous sycophant Priests, Sibthorp, Manwaring, Montagu, of the Laud fraternity: forced-loans, monopolies, ship-moneys, all Civil Tyranny was right according to them!*] All the [Civil] transactions that were, — [they justified them] in their pulpits, presses, and otherwise! Which was verily thought [had they succeeded in it] would have been a very good shelter to them, to innovate upon us in matters of Religion also. And so to innovate as to eat out the core and power and heart and life of all Religion! By bringing on us a company of poisonous Popish Ceremonies [*Somewhat animated, your Highness!*], and imposing them upon those that were accounted 'the Puritans' of the Nation, and professors of religion among us, — driving them to seek their bread in an howling wilderness! As was instanced to our friends who were forced to fly for Holland, New England, almost any-whither, to find Liberty for their Consciences.

"Now if this thing hath been the state and sum of our Quarrel, and of those Ten Years of War wherein we were exercised; and if the good hand of God, for we are to attribute it to no other, hath brought this business thus home unto us as it is now settled in the Petition and Advice, — I think we have all cause to bless God, and the Nations have all cause to bless Him. [*If we were of thankful just heart, — yea!*]

"I well remember I did a little touch upon the Eighty-fifth Psalm when I spake unto you in the beginning of this Parliament.[2] Which expresseth well what *we* may say, as truly as

---

[1] Declaration, 2d August, 1642, went through the Lords House that day; it is in *Parliamentary History*, vi. 350. A thing of audacity reckoned almost impious at the time (see D'Ewes's MS. Journal, 23d July); corresponds in purport to what is said of it here.

[2] Antea, Speech VI., p. 117.

it was said of old by the Penman of that Psalm! The first verse is an acknowledgment to God that He 'had been favorable unto His land,' and 'brought back the captivity of His people; and [then] how that He had pardoned all their iniquities and covered all their sin, and taken away all His wrath;' — and indeed of these unspeakable mercies, blessings, and deliverances out of captivity, pardoning of national sins and national iniquities. Pardoning, as God pardoneth the man whom He justifieth! He breaks through, and overlooks iniquity; and pardoneth because He will pardon. And sometimes God pardoneth Nations also! — And if the enjoyment of our present Peace and other mercies may be witnesses for God [to *us*], — we feel and we see them every day.

" The greatest demonstration of His favor and love appears to us in this: That He hath given us *Peace;* — and the blessings of Peace, to wit, the enjoyment of our Liberties civil and spiritual! [*Were not our prayers, and struggles, and deadly wrestlings, all even for this; — and we in some measure have it!*] And I remember well, the Church [in that same Eighty-fifth Psalm] falls into prayer and into praises, great expectations of future mercies, and much thankfulness for the enjoyment of present mercies; and breaks into this expression: 'Surely salvation is nigh unto them that fear Him; that glory may dwell in our land.' In the beginning it is called His land; 'Thou hast been favorable to Thy land.' Truly I hope this is His land! In some sense it may be given out that it *is* God's land. And he that hath the weakest knowledge, and the worst memory, can easily tell that we are 'a Redeemed People,' — [from the time] when God was first pleased to look favorably upon us [to redeem us] out of the hands of Popery, in that never to be forgotten Reformation, that most significant and greatest [mercy] the Nation hath felt or tasted! I would but touch upon that, — but a touch: How God hath redeemed us, as we stand this day! Not from trouble and sorrow and anger only, but into a blessed and happy estate and condition, comprehensive of all Interests, of every member, of every individual; — [an imparting to *us*] of those mercies [there spoken of], as you very well see!

"And then in what sense it is 'our Land;' — through this grace and favor of God, That He hath vouchsafed unto us and bestowed upon us, with the Gospel, Peace, and rest out of Ten Years' War; and given us what we would desire! Nay, who could have forethought, when we were plunged into the midst of our troubles, That ever the people of God should have had liberty to worship God without fear of enemies? [*Strange: this "liberty" is to Oliver Cromwell a blessing almost too great for belief; to us it has become as common as the liberty to breathe atmospheric air, — a liberty not once worth thinking of. It is the way with all attainments and conquests in this world. Do I think of Cadmus, or the old unknown Orientals, while I write with* LETTERS? *The world is built upon the mere dust of Heroes: once earnest-wrestling, death-defying, prodigal of their blood; who now sleep well, forgotten by all their heirs. — "Without fear of enemies," he says*] Which is the very acknowledgment of the Promise of Christ that 'He would deliver His from the fear of enemies, that they might worship Him in holiness and in righteousness all the days of their life.'

"This is the portion that God hath given *us;* and I trust we shall forever heartily acknowledge it! — The Church goes on there [in that Psalm], and makes her boast yet farther; 'His salvation is nigh them that fear Him, that glory may dwell in our land.' *His* glory; not carnal, nor anything related thereto: this glory of a Free Possession of the Gospel; this is that which we may glory in! [*Beautiful, thou noble soul! — And very strange to see such things in the Journals of the English House of Commons. O Heavens, into what oblivion of the Highest have stupid, canting, cotton-spinning, partridge-shooting mortals fallen, since that January, 1658 !*] And it is said farther, 'Mercy and Truth are met together; Righteousness and Peace have kissed each other.' And [note], it shall be such righteousness as comes down from Heaven: 'Truth shall grow out of the Earth, and Righteousness shall come down from Heaven.' Here is the Truth of all [truths]; here is the righteousness of God, under the notion of righteousness confirming *our* abilities, — answerable to the truth which He hath in the Gospel revealed to us! [*According to Calvin and Paul.*]

And the Psalm closeth with this: 'Righteousness shall go before Him, and shall set us in the way of His steps;'—that righteousness, that mercy, that love, and that kindness which we have seen, and been made partakers of from the Lord, *it* shall be our Guide, to teach us to know the right and the good way; which is, To tread in the steps of mercy, righteousness and goodness that our God hath walked before us in. —

"We [too] have a Peace this day! I believe in my very heart, you all think the things that I speak to you this day. I am sure you have cause.

"And yet we are not without the murmurings of many people, who turn all this grace and goodness into wormwood; who indeed are disappointed by the works of God. And those men are of several ranks and conditions; great ones, lesser ones,—of all sorts. Men that are of the Episcopal spirit, with all the branches, the root and the branches;—who gave themselves a fatal blow in this Place,[1] when they would needs make a 'Protestation that no Laws were good, which were made by this House and the House of Commons in *their* absence;' and so without injury to others cut themselves off! [Men of an Episcopal spirit:] indeed men that know not God; that know not how to account upon the works of God, how to measure them out; but will trouble Nations for an Interest which is but *mixed*, at the best,—made up of iron and clay, like the feet of Nebuchadnezzar's Image: whether they were more Civil or Spiritual was hard to say. But their continuance was like to be known beforehand [*Yes, your Highness!*]; iron and clay make no good mixtures, they are not durable at all! —

"You have now a godly Ministry; you have a knowing Ministry; such a one as, without vanity be it spoken, the world has not. Men knowing the things of God, and able to search into the things of God,—by that only which can fathom those things in some measure. The spirit of a beast knows not the things of a man; nor doth the spirit of man know the

---

[1] In this same House of Lords, on the 10th of December, 1641. Busy Williams the Lincoln Decoy-duck, with his Eleven too hasty Bishops, leading the way in that suicide. (Antea, vol. xvii. p. 118.)

things of God! 'The things of God are known *by the Spirit.*'[1] — Truly I will remember but one thing of those [the misguided persons now cast out from us]: Their greatest persecution hath been of the People of God;—men really of the spirit of God, as I think very experience hath now sufficiently demonstrated!—

"But what's the reason, think you, that men slip in this age wherein we live? As I told you before, they understand not the works of God. They consider not the operation of His Laws. They consider not that God resisted and broke in pieces the Powers that were, that men might fear Him;—might have liberty to do and enjoy all that that we have been speaking of! Which certainly God has manifested to have been the end; and so hath He brought the things to pass! *Therefore* it is that men yet slip, and engage themselves against God. And for that very cause, saith David (*Psalm Twenty-eighth*), 'He shall break them down, and not build them up!'

"If, therefore, you would know upon what foundation you stand, own your foundation [to be] from God. He hath set you where you are: He hath set you in the enjoyment of your Civil and Spiritual Liberties.

"I deal clearly with you,[2] I have been under some infirmity [*His Highness still looks unwell*]; therefore dare not speak farther to you;—except to let you know thus much, That I have with truth and simplicity declared the state of our Cause, and our attainments in it by the industry and labor of this Parliament since they last met upon this foundation— You shall find I mean, Foundation of a Cause and Quarrel thus attained to, wherein we are thus estated.[3] I should be very glad to lay my bones with yours [*What a tone!*];—and would have done it, with all heartiness and cheerfulness, in the meanest capacity I ever yet was in, to serve the Parliament.

"If God give you, as I trust He will,—["*His blessing*"

---

[1] 1 Corinthians ii. 11.   [2] Means "Give me leave to say."

[3] This Parliament's "foundation," the ground *this* Parliament took its stand upon, was a recognition that our Cause had been so and so, that our "attainment" and "estate" in it were so and so; hence their *Petition and Advice,* and other very salutary labors.

or "strength:" but the Sentence is gone.] — He *hath* given it
you, for what have I been speaking of but what you have
done ? He hath given you strength to do what you have
done ! And if God should bless you in this work, and make
this Meeting happy on this account, you shall all be called the
Blessed of the Lord. [*Poor Oliver !*] — The generations to
come will bless us. You shall be the 'repairers of breaches,
and the restorers of paths to dwell in!'[1] and if there be
any higher work which mortals can attain unto in the world,
beyond this, I acknowledge my ignorance [of it].

"As I told you, I have some infirmities upon me. I have
not liberty to speak more unto you; but I have desired an
Honorable Person here by me — [*Glancing towards Nathaniel
Fiennes, him with the Purse and Seal*] to discourse, a little
more particularly, what may be more proper for this occasion
and this meeting."[2]

Nathaniel Fiennes follows in a long high-flown, ingenious
Discourse,[3] characterized by Dryasdust, in his Parliamentary
History and other Works, as false, canting, and little less than
insane; for which the Anti-dryasdust reader has by this time
learned to forgive that fatal Doctor of Darkness. Fiennes's
Speech is easily recognizable, across its Calvinistic dialect, as
full of sense and strength; broad manful thought and clear insight, couched in a gorgeous figurative style, which a friendly
judge might almost call poetic. It is the first time we thoroughly forgive the Honorable Nathaniel for surrendering
Bristol to Prince Rupert long ago; and rejoice that Prynne and
Independency Walker did not get him shot, by Court-Martial,
on that occasion.

Nathaniel compares the present state of England to the
rising of Cosmos out of Chaos as recorded in *Genesis:* Two
"firmaments" are made, two separate Houses of Parliament;
much is made, but much yet remains to be made. He is full

---

[1] Isaiah lviii. 12.

[2] *Commons Journals*, vii. 579 : that is the Original, — reported by Widdring-
ton next day. *Burton* (ii. 322), *Parliamentary History* (xxi. 170), are copies.

[3] Reported, *Commons Journals*, vii. 582-587, Monday, 25th Jan. 1657-8.

of figurative ingenuity : full of resolution, of tolerance, of discretion, and various other good qualities not very rife in the world. "What shall be done to our Sister that hath no breasts ? " he asks, in the language of Solomon's Song. What shall we do with those good men, friends to our Cause, who yet reject us, and sit at home on their estates ? We will soothe them, we will submit to them, we will in all ways invite them to us. Our little Sister, — " if she be a wall, we will build a palace of silver upon her; if she be a door, we will enclose her with boards of cedar: " — our little Sister shall not be estranged from us, if it please God ! —

There is, in truth, need enough of unanimity at present. One of these days, there came a man riding jogtrot through Stratford-at-the-Bow, with " a green glazed cover over his hat," a " nightcap under it," and " his valise behind him ; " a rustic-looking man; recognizable to *us*, amid the vanished populations who take no notice of him as he jogs along there, — for the Duke of Ormond, Charles Stuart's head man ! He sat up, at Colchester, the night before, " playing shuffleboard with some farmers, and drinking hot ale." He is fresh from Flanders, and the Ex-King; has arrived here to organize the Spanish Charles-Stuart Invasion, and see what Royalist Insurrection, or other domestic mischief there may be hopes of. Lodges now, " with dyed hair," in a much disguised manner, " at the house of a Papist Chirurgeon in Drury Lane; " communicating with the ringleaders here.[1]

The Spanish Charles-Stuart Invasion is again on foot, and no fable. He has Four English-Irish Regiments; the low-minded Dutch, we understand, have hired him two-and-twenty ships, which hope to escape our frigates some dark night; and Don John has promised a Spanish Army of six thousand or ten thousand, if the domestic Royalists will bestir themselves. Like the waves of the sea, that cannot rest; that have to go on throwing up mire and dirt ! Frantic-Anabaptists too are awakening; the general English Hydra is rallying itself again, as if to try it one other last time.

[1] Carte's *Ormond*, ii. 176–178.

Foreign Affairs also look altogether questionable to a Protestant man. Swede and Dane in open war; inextricable quarrels bewildering the King of Sweden, King of Denmark, Elector of Brandenburg, all manner of Foreign Protestants, whom Oliver never yet could reconcile; and the Dutch playing false; and the Spaniards, the Austrians, the Pope and Papists, too well united! — Need enough that this Parliament be unanimous.

The hopes of Oliver and Fiennes and all practicable Puritans may have naturally stood high at this meeting: — but if so, it was not many hours till they began fatally to sink. There exists also an *impracticable* set of Puritan men, — the old Excluded Members, introduced now, or now first admitted into this Parliament, — whom no beautifulest "two firmaments" seen overspanning Chaos, no Spanish Invasion threatening to bring Chaos back, no hopefulest and no fearfulest phenomenon of Nature or Constitutional Art, will ever divorce from their one Republican Idea. Intolerability of the Single Person: this, and this only, will Nature in her dumb changes, and Art in her spoken interpretations thereof, reveal to these men. It is their one Idea; which, in fact, they will carry with them to — the gallows at Charing Cross, when no Oliver any more is there to restrain it and them! Poor windy angry Haselrig, poor little peppery Thomas Scott — And yet these were not the poorest. Scott was only hanged: but what shall we say of a Luke Robinson, also very loud in this Parliament, who had to turn his coat that he might escape hanging? The history of this Parliament is not edifying to Constitutional men.

SPEECH XVII.

WE said, the Two Houses, at least the First House, very ill fulfilled his Highness's expectations. Hardly had they got into their respective localities after his Highness's Opening Speech, when the New House, sending the Old a simple message about requesting his Highness to have a day of Fasting, there arose a Debate as to What answer should be given; as to What "name," first of all, this said New House was to have, — otherwise what answer could you give ? Debate carried on with great vigor ; resumed, re-resumed day after day ; — and never yet terminated ; not destined to be terminated in this world ! How eloquent were peppery Thomas Scott and others, lest we should call them a House of *Lords*, — not, alas, lest he the peppery Constitutional Debater, and others such, should lose their own heads, and intrust their Cause with all its Gospels to a new very curious Defender of the Faith ! It is somewhat sad to see.

On the morning of Monday, January 25th, the Writer of the Diary called *Burton's*, — Nathaniel Bacon if that were he, — finds, on entering the House, Sir Arthur Haselrig on his feet there, saying, " Give me my Oath ! " Sir Arthur, as we transiently saw, was summoned to the Peers House ; but he has decided to sit *here*. It is an ominous symptom. After " Mr. Peters " has concluded his morning exercise,[1] the intemperate Sir Arthur again demands, " Give me my Oath ! " — " I dare not," answers Francis Bacon, the official person ; Brother of the Diarist. But at length they do give it him ; and he sits : Sir Arthur is henceforth here. And, on the whole, ought we not to call this pretented Peers House the " Other House " merely ? Sir Arthur, peppery Scott, Luke Robinson and Company, are clearly of that mind.

However, the Speaker has a Letter from his Highness, summoning us all to the Banqueting-House at Whitehall this afternoon at three ; both Houses shall meet him there. There accordingly does his Highness, do both Houses and all the Official world make appearance. Gloomy Rushworth, Bacon, and one " Smythe," with Note-books in their hands, are there. His Highness, in the following large manful manner, looking before and after, looking abroad and at home, with true nobleness if we consider all things, — speaks : —

" MY LORDS AND GENTLEMEN OF THE TWO HOUSES OF PAR-
     LIAMENT :
   " (For *so* I must own you,) in whom together with myself is vested the Legislative Power of these Nations ! — The impres-

---

[1] Burton, ii. 347.

sion of the weight of those affairs and interests for which we
are met together is such that I could not with a good conscience
satisfy myself, if I did not remonstrate to you somewhat of
my apprehensions of the State of the Affairs of these Nations;
together with the proposal of such remedy as may occur, to the
dangers now imminent upon us.

"I conceive the Well-being, yea the Being of these Nations
is now at stake. If God bless this Meeting, — our tranquillity
and peace may be lengthened out to us; if *otherwise*, — I shall
offer it to your judgments and considerations, by the time I
have done, whether there be, as to *men*,[1] [so much as] a possibility of discharging that Trust which is incumbent upon us
for the safety and preservation of these Nations! When I
have told you what occurs to my thoughts, I shall leave it
to such an operation on your hearts as it shall please God
Almighty to work upon you. [*His Highness, I think, looks earnest enough to-day. Oppressed with many things, and not in
good health either. In those deep mournful eyes, which are always full of noble silent sorrow, of affection and pity and valor,
what a depth to-day of thoughts that cannot be spoken! Sorrow
enough, depth enough, — and this deepest attainable depth, to rest
upon what "it shall please God Almighty" to do!*]

"I look upon this to be the great duty of my Place; as
being set on a watch-tower to see what may be for the good of
these Nations, and what may be for the preventing of evil;
that so, by the advice of so wise and great a Council as this,
which hath in it the life and spirit of these Nations, such
'good' may be attained, and such 'evil,' whatever it is, may
be obviated. [*Truly!*] We shall hardly set our shoulders to
this work, unless it shall please God to work some conviction
upon our hearts that *there is need* of our most serious and best
counsels at such a time as this is! —

"I have not prepared any such matter and rule of speech to
deliver myself unto you, as perhaps might have been fitter for
me to have done, and more serviceable for you in understanding me; — but shall only speak plainly and honestly to you out
of such conceptions as it hath pleased God to set upon me.

---

[1] humanly speaking.

"We have not been now four years and upwards in this Government, to be totally ignorant of what things may be of the greatest concernment to us. [*No mortal thinks so, your Highness !*] Your dangers — for that is the head of my speech — are either with respect to Affairs Abroad and their difficulties, or to Affairs at Home and their difficulties. You are come now, as I may say, into the end [*Which may but prove the new beginning !*] of as great difficulties and straits as, I think, ever Nation was engaged in. I had in my thoughts to have made this the method of my Speech : To have let you see the things which hazard your Being, and [those which hazard] your Well-being. But when I came seriously to consider better of it, I thought, as your affairs stand, all things would resolve themselves into very Being ! You are not a Nation, you will not be a Nation, if God strengthen you not to meet these evils that are upon us!

"First, from Abroad : What are the Affairs, I beseech you, abroad ? I thought the Profession of the Protestant Religion was a thing of 'Well-being;' and truly, in a good sense, so it is, and it is no more : though it be a very high thing, it is but a thing of 'Well-being.' [*A Nation can still* BE, *even without Protestantism.*] But take it with all the complications of it, with all the concomitants of it, with respect had to the Nations abroad, — I do believe, he that looks well about him, and considereth the estate of the Protestant Affairs all Christendom over ; he must needs say and acknowledge that the grand Design now on foot, in comparison with which all other Designs are but low things, is, Whether the Christian world shall be all Popery ? Or, whether God hath a love to, and we ought to have [a love to, and] a brotherly fellow-feeling of, the interests of all the Protestant Christians in the world? [*Yes, your Highness ; the raging sea shut out by your labor and valor and death-peril, — with what indifference do we now safe at two centuries' distance, look back upon it, hardly audible so far off, — ungrateful as we are !*] He that strikes at but one species of a general[1] to make it nothing, strikes at all.

"Is it not so now, that the Protestant Cause and Interest

---

[1] Means "one limb of a body :" metaphysical metaphor.

abroad is struck at; and is, in opinion and apprehension, quite
under foot, trodden down? Judge with me a little, I beseech
you, Whether it be so or no. And then, I will pray you, consider how far *we* are concerned in that danger, as to ⌊our
very⌋ Being!

"We have known very well, the Protestant Cause is accounted the honest and religious Interest of this Nation. It
was not trodden under foot all at once, but by degrees, — that
this Interest might be consumed as with a canker insensibly,
as Jonah's gourd was, till it was quite withered. It is at
another rate now! For certainly this, in the general [is the
fact]: The Papacy, and those that are upholders of it, they
have openly and avowedly trodden God's people under foot,
on this very motion and account, that they were Protestants.
The money you parted with in that noble Charity which was
exercised in this Nation, and the just sense you had of those
poor Piedmonts, was satisfaction enough to yourselves of this,[1]
That if all the Protestants in Europe had had but that head,
that head had been cut off, and so an end of the whole. But
is this [of Piedmont] all? No. Look how the House of
Austria, on both sides of Christendom [both in Austria Proper
and Spain], are armed and prepared to destroy the whole
Protestant Interest.

"Is not — to begin there — the King of Hungary, who
expecteth with his partisans to make himself Emperor of
Germany, and in the judgment of all men [with] not only a
possibility but a certainty of the acquisition of it, — is not he,
since he hath mastered the Duke of Brandenburg, one of the
Electors [as good as sure of the Emperorship]?[2] No doubt
but he will have three of the Episcopal Electors [on his side],

---

[1] proof enough that you believed.

[2] Emperor Ferdinand III., under whom the Peace of Westphalia was made,
had died this year · his second son, Leopold, on the death of the first son, had
been made King of Hungary in 1655; he was, shortly after this, electe
Emperor, Leopold I., and reigned till 1705. "Brandenburg" was Frederick
William; a distinguished Prince; father of the First King of Prussia;
Frederick the Great's great-grandfather; properly the Founder of the Prus
sian Monarchy.

and the Duke of Bavaria. [*There are but Eight Electors in all; Hanover not yet made.*] Whom will he then have to contest with him abroad, for taking the Empire of Germany out of his hands? Is not he the son of a Father whose principles, interest and personal conscience guided him to exile all the Protestants out of his own patrimonial country, — out of Bohemia, got with the sword; out of Moravia and Silesia? [*Ferdinand the Second, his Grandfather; yea, your Highness; — and brought the great Gustavus upon him in consequence. Not a good kindred, that!* — And] it is the daily complaint which comes over to us, — new reiterations of which we have but received within these two or three days, being conveyed by some godly Ministers of the City, That the Protestants are tossed out of Poland into the Empire; and out thence whither they can fly to get their bread; and are ready to perish for want of food.

"And what think you of the other side of Europe, Italy to wit, — if I may call it the other side of Europe, as I think I may, — [Italy,] Spain, and all those adjacent parts, with the Grisons, the Piedmonts before mentioned, the Switzers? They all, — what are they but a prey of the Spanish power and interest? And look to that that calls itself [*Neuter gender*] the Head of all this! A Pope fitted, — I hope indeed 'born' not '*in*' but out of 'due time,' to accomplish this bloody work; so that he may fill up his cup to the brim, and make himself ripe for judgment! [*Somewhat grim of look, your Highness!*] He doth as *he* hath always done. He influences all the Powers, all the Princes of Europe to this very thing [*Rooting out of the Protestants. — The sea which is now scarcely audible to us, two safe centuries off, how it roars and devouringly rages while this Valiant One is heroically bent to bank it in! — He prospers, he does it, flings his life into the gap, — that* WE *for all coming centuries may be safe and ungrateful!*]; — and no man like this present man.[1] So that, I beseech you, what is there in all the parts of Europe but a consent, a co-operating, at this very time and season [of all Popish Powers], to suppress everything that stands in their way? [*A grave epoch indeed.*]

[1] Alexander VII.; "an able Pope," Dryasdust informs me.

"But it may be said, 'This is a great way off, in the extremest parts of the world;[1] what is that to us?' — If it be nothing to you, let it be nothing to you! I have told you it is somewhat to you. It concerns all your religions, and all the good interests of England.

"I have, I thank God, considered, and I would beg of you to consider a little with me: What that resistance is that is likely to be made to this mighty current, which seems to be coming from all parts upon all Protestants? Who is there that holdeth up his head to oppose this danger? A poor Prince [*Charles X. King of Sweden: at present attacked by the King of Denmark; the Dutch also aiming at him*]; — indeed poor; but a man in his person as gallant, and truly I think I may say as good, as any these last ages have brought forth; a man that hath adventured his all against the Popish Interest in Poland, and made his acquisition still good [there] for the Protestant Religion. He is now reduced into a corner: and what addeth to the grief of all, — more grievous than all that hath been spoken of before (I wish it may not be too truly said!) — is, That men of our Religion forget this, and seek his ruin. [*Dutch and Danes: but do not some of us too forget? "I wish it may not be too truly said!"*]

"I beseech you consider a little; consider the consequences of all that! For what doth it all signify? Is it only a noise? Or hath it not withal an articulate sound in it? Men that are not true to the Religion we profess, — [profess] I am persuaded, with greater truth, uprightness and sincerity than it is [professed] by any collected body, so nearly gathered together as these Nations are, in all the world, — God will find them out! [*The low-minded Dutch: pettifogging for " Sound Dues," for " Possession of the Sound," and mere shopkeeper lucre!*] I beseech you consider how things do co-operate. [Consider,] If this may seem but a design against your Well-being? It is a design against your very Being; this artifice, and this complex design, against the Protestant Interest, — wherein so many Protestants are not so right as were to be wished! If they can shut us out of the Baltic Sea, and make themselves

[1] " parts of it " in orig.

masters of that, where is your Trade? Where are your materials to preserve your Shipping? Where will you be able to challenge any right by sea, or justify yourselves against a foreign invasion in your own soil? Think upon it; this is in design! I believe, if you will go and ask the poor mariner in his red cap and coat [*"Coat," I hope, is not "red:"* — *but we are in haste*], as he passeth from ship to ship, you will hardly find in any ship but they will tell you this is designed against you. So obvious is it, by this and other things, that you are the object. And in my conscience, I know not for what else [you are so] but because of the purity of the profession amongst you; who have not yet made it your trade to prefer your profit before your godliness [*Whatever certain Dutch and Danes may do!*], but reckon godliness the *greater* gain!

"But should it happen that, as contrivances stand, you should not be able to vindicate yourselves against all whomsoever, — I name no one state upon this head [*Do not name the Dutch, with their pettifoggings for the Sound: no!*], but I think all acknowledge States *are* engaged in the combination, — judge you where you were! You have accounted yourselves happy in being environed with a great Ditch from all the world beside. Truly you will not be able to keep your Ditch, nor your Shipping, — unless you turn your Ships and Shipping into Troops of Horse and Companies of Foot; and fight to defend yourselves on *terra firma!* —

"And these things stated, *liberavi animam meam ;* and if there be 'no danger' in [all] this, I am satisfied. I have told you; you will judge if no danger! If you shall think, We may discourse of all things at pleasure, — [*Debate for days and weeks, Whether it shall be "House of Lords" or "Other House ;" put the question, Whether this question shall be put; and say Ay, say No ; and thrash the air with idle jargon!*], — and that it is a time of sleep and ease and rest, without any due sense of these things, — I have this comfort to God-ward: I have told you of it. [*Yes, your Highness! — O intemperate vain Sir Arthur, peppery Thomas Scott, and ye other constitutional Patriots, is there no SENSE of truth in you, then ; no dis-*

cernment of what really is what?   Instead of belief and insight, have you nothing but whirlpools of old paper-clippings, and a gray waste of Parliamentary constitutional logic?   Such HEADS, *too common in the world, will run a chance in these times to get themselves — stuck up on Temple Bar!*]

"Really were it not that France (give me leave to say it) is a balance against that Party at this time—! Should there be a Peace made (which hath been, and is still labored and aimed at, 'a General Peace'), then will England be the 'general' object of all the fury and wrath of all the Enemies of God and our Religion in the world! I have nobody to accuse;—but do look on the other side of the water! You have neighbors there; some that you are in amity with; some that have professed malice enough against you. I think you are fully satisfied in that. I had rather you would trust your enemy than some friends,—that is, rather believe your enemy, and trust *him* that he means your ruin, than have confidence in some who perhaps may be in some alliance with you! [*We have watched the Dutch, and their dealings in the Baltic lately!*]—I perhaps could enforce all this with some particulars, nay I [certainly] could. For you know that your enemies be the same who have been accounted your enemies ever since Queen Elizabeth came to the crown. An avowed designed enemy [all along]; wanting nothing of counsel, wisdom and prudence, to root you out from the face of the Earth: and when public attempts [*Spanish Armadas and such like*] would not do, how have they, by the Jesuits and other their Emissaries, laid foundations to perplex and trouble our Government by taking away the lives of them whom they judged to be of any use for preserving our peace! [*Guy Faux and Jesuit Garnet were a pair of pretty men; to go no farther. Ravaillac in the Rue de la Ferronerie, and Stadtholder William's Jesuit; and the Night of St. Bartholomew: here and elsewhere they have not wanted "counsel," of a sort!*] And at this time I ask you, Whether you do not think they are designing as busily as ever any people were, to prosecute the same counsels and things to the uttermost?

"The business *then* was: The Dutch needed Queen Eliza-

beth of famous memory for their protection. They had it
[had protection from her]. I hope they will never ill requite
it! For if they should forget either the kindness that was
then shown them (which was their real safety), or the desires
this Nation hath had to be at peace with them, — truly I
believe whoever exercises any ingratitude in this sort will
hardly prosper in it. [*He cannot, your Highness: unless* GOD
and His TRUTH *be a mere Hearsay of the market, he never
can!*] But this may awaken you, howsoever. I hope you
will be awakened, upon all these considerations! It is certain,
they [*These Dutch*] have professed a principle which, thanks
be to God, we never knew. They will sell arms to their enemies, and lend their ships to their enemies. They will do so.
And truly that principle is not a matter of dispute at this
time [we are not here to argue with them about it] : only let
everything weigh with your spirits as it ought ; — let it do so.
And we must tell you, we do know that this [of their having
such a principle] is *true*. I dare assure you of it ; and I
think if but your Exchange here [in London] were resorted
to, it would let you know, as clearly as you can desire to
know, That they have hired — sloops, I think they call them,
or some other name, — they have hired sloops [let sloops on
hire] to transport upon you four thousand Foot and a thousand Horse, upon the pretended interest of that young man
that was the late King's Son. [*What a designation for
"Charles by the grace of God!" The "was" may possibly
have been "is" when spoken ; but we cannot afford to change
it.*] And this is, I think, a thing far from being reckonable
as a suggestion to any ill end or purpose : — a thing to no
other end than that it may awaken you to a just consideration of your danger, and to uniting for a just and natural
defence.

"Indeed I never did, I hope I never shall, use any artifice
with you to pray you to help us with money for defending ourselves : but if money be needful, I will tell you, 'Pray help us
with money, that the Interest of the Nation may be defended
abroad and at home.' I will use no arguments ; and thereby
will disappoint the artifice of bad men abroad who say, It is

for money.   Whosoever shall think to put things out of frame
upon such a suggestion — [*His fate may be guessed ; but the
Sentence is off*] — For you will find I will be very plain with
you before I have done; and that with all love and affection
and faithfulness to you and these Nations.

"If this be the condition of your affairs abroad, I pray a
little consider what is the estate of your affairs at home.   And
if both these considerations [of home affairs and foreign] have
but this effect, to *get* a consideration among you, a due and
just consideration, — let God move your hearts for the answering [1] of anything that shall be due unto the Nation, as He shall
please !   And I hope I shall not be solicitous [*The " artifice "
and " money " of the former paragraph still sounding somewhat
in his Highness's ears*]; I shall look up to Him who hath been
my God and my Guide hitherto.

"I say, I beseech you look to your own affairs at home, how
they stand !   I am persuaded you are all, I apprehend you are
all, honest and worthy good men; and that there is not a man
of you but would desire to be found a good patriot.   I know
you would !   We are apt to boast sometimes that we are Englishmen : and truly it is no shame for us that we are Englishmen ;
men ; — but it is a motive to us to do like Englishmen, and
seek the real good of this Nation, and the interest of it.
[*Truly !*] — But, I beseech you, what is our case at home ? —
I profess I do not well know where to begin on this head, or
where to end, — I do not.   But I must needs say, Let a man
begin where he will, he shall hardly be out of that drift I am
speaking to you [upon].   We are as full of calamities, and of
divisions among us in respect of the spirits of men [as we could
well be], — though, through a wonderful, admirable, and never
to be sufficiently admired providence of God, [still] in peace !
And the fighting we have had, and the success we have had —
yea, we that are here, we are an astonishment to the world !
And take us in that temper we are in, or rather in that distemper, it is the greatest miracle that ever befell the sons of
men [that we are got again to peace] —

[1] performing on such demand.

["Beautiful great Soul," exclaims a modern Commentator here, "Beautiful great Soul; to whom the Temporal is all irradiated with the Eternal, and God is everywhere divinely visible in the affairs of men, and man himself has as it were become divine! O ye eternal Heavens, have those days and those souls passed away without return? — Patience: intrinsically they can never pass away: intrinsically they remain with us; and will yet, in nobler unexpected form, reappear among us, — if it please Heaven! There *have been* Divine Souls in England; England too, poor moiling toiling heavy-laden thick-eyed England has been illuminated, though it were but once, by the Heavenly Ones; — and *once*, in a sense, is always!"]

— that we are got again to peace. And whoever shall seek to break it, God Almighty root that man out of this Nation! And He will do it, let the pretences be what they may! [*Privilege of Parliament, or whatever else, my peppery friends!*]

"[Peace-breakers, do they consider what it *is* they are driving towards? They should do it!] He that considereth not the 'woman with child,' — the sucking children of this Nation that know not the right hand from the left, of whom, for aught I know, it may be said this City is as full as Nineveh was said to be; — he that considereth not these, and the fruit that is like to come of the bodies of those now living added to these; he that considereth not these, must have the heart of a Cain; who was marked, and made to be an enemy to all men, and all men enemies to him! For the wrath and justice of God will prosecute such a man to his grave, if not to Hell! [*Where is Sam Cooper, or some "prince of limners," to take us that look of his Highness? I would give my ten best High-Art Paintings for it, gilt frames and twaddle-criticisms into the bargain!*] — I say, look on this Nation; look on it! Consider what are the varieties of Interests in this Nation, — if they be worthy the name of Interests. If God did not hinder, it would all but make up one confusion. We should find there would be but one Cain in England, if God did not restrain! We should have another more bloody Civil War than ever we had in England. For, I beseech you, what is the general spirit of this

Nation? Is it not that each sect of people,—if I may call them sects, whether sects upon a Religious account or upon a Civil account—[*Sentence gone; meaning left clear enough*]— Is not this Nation miserable in that respect? What is that which possesseth every sect? What is it? That every sect may be uppermost! That every sort of men may get the power into their hands, and 'they would use it well;'—that every sect may get the power into their hands! [*A reflection to make one wonder.—Let them thank God they have got a man able to bit and bridle them a little; the unfortunate, peppery, loud-babbling individuals, with so much good in them too, while "bitted"!*]

"It were a happy thing if the Nation would be content with rule. [Content with rule,] if it were but in Civil things, and with those that would rule *worst;*—because misrule is better than no rule; and an ill Government, a bad Government, is better than none!—Neither is this all: but we have an appetite to variety; to be not only making wounds [but widening those already made]. As if you should see one making wounds in a man's side, and eager only to be groping and grovelling with his fingers in those wounds! This is what [such] men would be at; this is the spirit of those who would trample on men's liberties in Spiritual respects. They will be making wounds, and rending and tearing, and making them wider than they were. Is not this the case? Doth there want anything —I speak not of sects in an ill sense; but the Nation is hugely made up of them,— and what is the want that prevents these things from being done to the uttermost, but that men have more anger than strength? They have not power to attain their ends. [There wants nothing else.] And, I beseech you, judge what such a company of men, of these sects, are doing, while they are contesting one with another! They are contesting in the midst of a generation of men (a malignant Episcopal Party, I mean); contesting in the midst of these *all united.* What must be the issue of such a thing as this? [So stands it;] it is *so.*—And do but judge what proofs have been made of the spirits of these men. [*Republican spirits: we took a "Standard" lately, a Painted one, and a Printed, with wondrous apparatus behind it!*] Summoning men to take up arms; and exhorting men, each sort of them, to fight for their notions; each sort thinking they are to try it out by the sword; and every sort thinking that *they* are truly under the banner of Christ, if they but come in, and bind themselves in such a project![1]

"Now do but judge what a hard condition this poor Nation is in. *This* is the state and condition we are in. Judge, I say, what a hard condition this poor Nation is in, and the Cause of God [is in], — amidst such a party of men as the Cavaliers are, and their participants! Not only with respect to what these — [*"Cavaliers and their Participants," both equally at first, but it becomes the latter chiefly, and at length exclusively, before the Sentence ends*] — are like to do of themselves: but some of these, yea some of these, they care not who carry the goal [*Frantic-Anabaptist Sexby, dead the other day, he was not very careful!*]: — some of these have invited the Spaniard himself to carry on the Cavalier Cause.

"And this is *true*. [This] and many other things that are not fit to be suggested unto you; because [so] we should betray the interest of our intelligence. [*Spy-Royalist Sir Richard Willis and the like ambiguous persons, if we show them in daylight, they vanish forever, — as Manning, when they shot him in Neuburg, did.*] I say, this is your condition! What is your defence? What hindereth the irruption of all this upon you, to your utter destruction? Truly, [that] you have an army in these parts, — in Scotland, in England and Ireland. Take *them* away to-morrow, would not all these Interests run into one another? — I know you are rational prudent men. Have you any Frame or Model of things that would satisfy the minds of men, if *this* be not the Frame, [this] which you are now called together upon, and engaged in, — I mean, the Two Houses of Parliament and myself? What hinders this Nation from being an Aceldama [a field of blood], if this doth not? It is, without doubt [this]: give the glory to God; for without this, it would prove[2] as great a plague as all that hath

---

[1] "and oblige upon this account" in orig.

[2] "it would prove" is an *impersonal* verb; such as "it will rain," and the like.

been spoken of. It is this, without doubt that keeps this Nation in peace and quietness. — And what is the case of your
Army [withal]? A poor unpaid Army; the soldiers going
barefoot at this time, in this city, this weather! [*Twenty-
fifth of January.*] And yet a peaceable people [these sol-
diers]; seeking to serve you with their lives; judging their
pains and hazards and all well bestowed, in obeying their
officers and serving you, to keep the Peace of these Nations!
Yea, he must be a man with a heart as hard as the weather
who hath not a due sense of this! [*A severe frost, though the
Almanacs do not mention it.*] —

"So that, I say, it is most plain and evident, this is your
outward and present defence. [*This frame of Government;
the Army is a part of that.*] And yet, at this day, — do but
you judge! The Cavalier Party, and the several humors of
unreasonable men [of other sorts], in those several ways,
having [continually] made battery at this defence ever since
you got to enjoy peace — [*Sentence catches fire*] — What have
they made their business but this, To spread libellous Books
[*Their "Standard," "Killing no Murder," and other little fid-
dling things belonging to that sort of Periodical Literature*];
yea and pretend the 'Liberty of the Subject' — [*Sentence
gone again*] — ? — which really wiser men than they may pretend! For let me say this to you at once : I never look to see
the People of England come into a just Liberty, if another
[Civil] War overtake us. I think, [I] at least, that the thing
likely to bring us into our 'Liberty' is a consistency and
agreement at this Meeting! — Therefore all I can say to you
is this : It will be your wisdom, I do think truly, and your
justice, to keep that concernment close to you; to uphold this
Settlement [now fallen upon]. Which I have no cause but to
think you are agreed to; and that you like it. For I assure
you I am very greatly mistaken else [for my own part]; having taken this which is now the Settlement among us as my
chief inducement to bear the burden I bear, and to serve the
Commonwealth in the place I am in!

"And therefore if you judge that all this be not argument
enough to persuade you to be sensible of your danger — ?

[A danger] which [all manner of considerations], besides good-nature and ingenuity [themselves], would move a stone to be sensible of! — Give us leave to consider a little, What will become of us, if our spirits should go *otherwise* [and break this Settlement]? If our spirits be dissatisfied, what will become of things? Here is an Army five or six months behind in pay; yea, an Army in Scotland near as much [behind]; an Army in Ireland much more. And if these things be considered, — I cannot doubt but they will be considered; — I say, judge what the state of Ireland is if free-quarter come upon the Irish People! [*Free-quarter must come, if there be no pay provided, and that soon!*] You have a company of Scots in the North of Ireland [forty or fifty thousand of them settled there]; who, I hope, are honest men. In the Province of Galway almost all the Irish, transplanted to the West.[1] You have the Interest of England newly begun to be planted. The people there [in these English settlements] are full of necessities and complaints. They bear to the uttermost. And should the soldiers run upon free-quarter there, — upon your English Planters, as they must, — the English Planters must quit the country through mere beggary: and thât which hath been the success of so much blood and treasure, to get that Country into your hands, what can become of it, but that the English must needs run away for pure beggary, and the Irish must possess the country [again] for a receptacle to the Spanish Interest? —

"And hath Scotland been long settled? [*Middleton's Highland Insurrection, with its Mosstroopery and misery, is not dead three years yet.*[2]] Have not they a like sense of poverty? I speak plainly. In good earnest, I do think the Scots Nation have been under as great a suffering, in point of livelihood and subsistence outwardly, as any People I have yet named to you. I do think truly they are a very ruined Nation. [*Torn to pieces with now near Twenty Years of continual War, and foreign and intestine worrying with themselves and with all the*

---

[1] "All the Irish;" all the Malignant Irish, the ringleaders of the Popish Rebellion: Galway is here called "Galloway."

[2] Feb. 1654-5 (Whitlocke, p. 599).

world.] — And yet in a way (I have spoken with some Gentlemen come from thence) hopeful enough; — it hath pleased
God to give that plentiful encouragement to the meaner sort
in Scotland. I must say, if it please God to encourage the
meaner sort — [*The consequences may be foreseen, but are not
stated here.*] — The meaner sort [in Scotland] live as well, and
are likely to come into as thriving a condition under your
Government, as when they were under their own great Lords,
who made them work for their living no better than the Peasants of France. I am loath to speak anything which may
reflect upon that Nation: but the middle sort of people do
grow up there into such a substance as makes their lives comfortable, if not better than they were before. [*Scotland is prospering; has fair-play and ready money; — prospering though
sulky.*]

"If now, after all this, we shall not be sensible of all those
designs that are in the midst of us: of the *united* Cavaliers;
of the designs which are animated every day from Flanders
and Spain; while we have to look upon ourselves as a *divided*
people — [*Sentence off*] — A man cannot certainly tell where
to find consistency anywhere in England! Certainly there is
no consistency in anything, that may be worthy of the name
of a body of consistency, but in this Company who are met
here! How can any man lay nis hand on his heart, and [per-
mit himself to] talk of things [*Roots of Constitutional Government*, " *Other House*," " *House of Lords* " *and such like*], neither
to be made out by the light of Scripture nor of Reason; and
draw one another off from considering of *these* things [which
are very palpable things]! I dare leave them with you, and
commit them to your bosom. They have a weight, — a greater
weight than any I have yet suggested to you, from abroad or
at home! If such be our case abroad and at home, That our
Being and Well-being, — our Well-being is not worth the naming comparatively, — I say, if such be our case, of our Being
at home and abroad, That through want to bear up our Honor
at Sea, and through want to maintain what is our Defence at
Home [we stand exposed to such dangers]; and if through our
mistake we shall be led off from the consideration of these

things; and talk of circumstantial things, and quarrel about circumstances; and shall not with heart and soul intend and carry on these things —! I confess I can look for nothing [other], I can say no other than what a foolish Book[1] expresseth, of one that having consulted everything, could hold to nothing; neither Fifth-Monarchy, Presbytery, nor Independency, nothing; but at length concludes, He is for nothing but an 'orderly confusion'! And for men that have wonderfully lost their consciences and their wits, — I speak of men going about who cannot tell *what* they would have, yet are willing to kindle coals to disturb others —! [*An " orderly confusion," and general fire-consummation : what else is possible?*]

"And now having said this, I have discharged my duty to God and to you, in making this demonstration, — and I profess, not as a rhetorician! My business was to prove the verity of the Designs from Abroad; and the still unsatisfied spirits of the Cavaliers at Home, — who from the beginning of our Peace to this day have not been wanting to do what they could to kindle a fire at home in the midst of us. And I say, if this be so, the truth, — I pray God affect your hearts with a due sense of it! [*Yea!*] And give you one heart and mind to carry on this work for which we are met together! If these things be so, — should you meet to-morrow, and accord in all things tending to your preservation and your rights and liberties, really it will be feared there is too much time elapsed [already] for your delivering yourselves from those dangers that hang upon you! —

"We have had now Six Years of Peace, and have had an interruption of Ten Years *War*. We have seen and heard and felt the evils of War; and now God hath given us a new taste of the benefits of Peace. Have you not had such a Peace in England, Ireland and Scotland, that there is not a man to lift up his finger to put you into distemper? Is not this a mighty blessing from the Lord of Heaven? [*Hah!*] Shall

---

[1] Now rotting probably, or rotten, among the other Pamphletary rubbish, in the crypts of Public Dryasdust Collections, — all but this one phrase of it, here kept alive.

we now be prodigal of time ?   Should any man, shall *we*, listen
to delusions, to break and interrupt this Peace ?   There is not
any man that hath been true to this Cause, as I believe you
have been all, who can look for anything but the greatest rending and persecution that ever was in this world !   [*Peppery
Scott's hot head will go up on Temple Bar, and Haselrig will do
well to die soon.*[1]] — I wonder how it can enter into the heart
of man to undervalue these things ; to slight Peace and the
Gospel, the greatest mercy of God.   We have Peace and the
Gospel !   [*What a tone !*]   Let us have one heart and soul ; one
mind to maintain the honest and just rights of this Nation ;
not to *pretend* to them, to the destruction of our Peace, to the
destruction of the Nation !   [*As yet there is one Hero-heart
among you, ye blustering contentious rabble ; one Soul blazing as
a light-beacon in the midst of Chaos, forbidding Chaos yet to be
supreme.   In a little while that too will be extinct ; and then !*]
Really, pretend what we will, if you run into *another* flood of
blood and War, the sinews of this Nation being wasted by the
last, it must sink and perish utterly.   I beseech you, and
charge you in the name and presence of God, and as before
Him, be sensible of these things and lay them to heart !   You
have a Day of Fasting coming on.   I beseech God touch your
hearts and open your ears to this truth ; and that you may be
as deaf adders to stop your ears to all Dissension !   And may
look upon them [who would sow dissension], whoever they
may be, as Paul saith to the Church of Corinth,[2] as I remember : '*Mark* such as cause divisions and offences,' and would
disturb you from that foundation of Peace you are upon, under
any pretence whatsoever ! —

"I shall conclude with this.   I was free, the last time of
our meeting, to tell you I would discourse upon a Psalm ; and
I did it.[3]   I am not ashamed of it at any time [*Why should you,
your Highness ?   A word that does speak to us from the eternal*

---

[1] He died in the *Annus Mirabilis* of 1660 itself, say the *Baronetages*.   Worn
to death, it is like, by the frightful vicissitudes and distracting excitement of
those sad months.

[2] Not "Corinth" properly, but Rome (Romans xvi. 17).

[3] The Eighty-fifth ; antea, pp. 239 et seqq.

heart of things, "word of God" as you well call it, is highly worth discoursing upon!] — especially when I meet with men of such consideration as you. There you have one verse which I forgot. 'I will hear what God the Lord will speak: for He will speak peace unto His people and to His saints; but let them not turn again to *folly.*' Dissension, division, destruction, in a poor Nation under a Civil War, — having all the effects of a Civil War upon it! Indeed if we return again to 'folly,' let every man consider, If it be *not* like turning to destruction? If God shall unite your hearts and bless you, and give you the blessing of union and love one to another; and tread down everything that riseth up in your hearts and tendeth to deceive your own souls with pretences of this thing or that, as we have been saying, — [*The Sentence began as a positive "if God shall;" but gradually turning on its axis, it has now got quite round into the negative side*], — and not prefer the keeping of Peace, that we may see the fruit of righteousness in them that love peace and embrace peace, — it will be said of this poor Nation, *Actum est de Anglia* [It is all over with England]!

"But I trust God will never leave it to such a spirit. And while I live, and am able, I shall be ready —

[Courage, my brave one! Thou hast but some Seven Months more of it, and then the ugly coil is all over; and thy part in it manfully done; manfully. and fruitfully, to all Eternity! Peppery Scott's hot head can mount to Temple Bar, whither it is bound; and England, with immense expenditure of liquor and tar-barrels, can call in its Nell-Gwynn Defender of the Faith, — and make out a very notable Two Hundred Years under *his* guidance; and, finding itself now nearly *got* to the Devil, may perhaps pause, and recoil, and remember: who knows? Nay who cares? may Oliver say. *He* is honorably quit of it, he for one; and the Supreme Powers will guide it farther according to their pleasure.]

— I shall be ready to stand and fall with you, in this seemingly promising Union [1] which God had wrought among you,

---

[1] The new Frame of Government.

which I hope neither the pride nor envy of men shall be able to make void. I have taken my Oath [*In Westminster Hall, Twenty-sixth of June last*] to govern 'according to the Laws' that are now made ; and I trust I shall fully answer it. And know, I sought not this place. [*Who would have "sought" it, that could have as nobly avoided it ? Very scurvy creatures only. The "place" is no great things, I think ; — with either Heaven or else Hell so close upon the rear of it, a man might do without the "place"! Know all men, Oliver Cromwell did not seek this place, but was sought to it, and led and driven to it, by the Necessities, the Divine Providences, the Eternal Laws.*] I speak it before God, Angels, and Men : I DID NOT. You sought me for it, you brought me to it ; and I took my Oath to be faithful to the Interest of these Nations, to be faithful to the Government. All those things were implied, in my eye, in the Oath 'to be faithful to this Government' upon which we have now met. And I trust, by the grace of God, as I have taken my Oath to serve this Commonwealth on such an account, I shall, — I must ! — see it done, according to the Articles of Government. That every just Interest may be preserved ; that a Godly Ministry may be upheld, and not affronted by seducing and seduced spirits ; that all men may be preserved in their just rights, whether civil or spiritual. Upon this account did I take oath, and swear to this Government ! — [*And mean to continue administering it withal.*] — And so having declared my heart and mind to you in this, I have nothing more to say, but to pray, God Almighty bless you."[1]

His Highness, a few days after, on occasion of some Reply to a Message of his "concerning the state of the Public Moneys," — was formally requested by the Commons to furnish them with a Copy of this Speech :[2] he answered that he did not remember four lines of it in a piece, and that he could not furnish a Copy. Some Copy would nevertheless have been got up, had the Parliament continued sitting. Rushworth, Smythe, and

---

[1] Burton, ii. 351–371.

[2] Thursday, 28th Jan. 1657–8 (*Parliamentary History,* xxi. 196; Burton, ii. 379).

"I" (the Writer of *Burton's Diary*), we, so soon as the Speech was done, went to York House; Fairfax's Town-house, where Historical John, brooding over endless Paper-masses, and doing occasional Secretary work, still lodges: here at York House we sat together till late, "comparing Notes of his Highness's Speech;" could not finish the business that night, our Notes being a little cramp. It was grown quite dark before his Highness had done; so that we could hardly see our pencils go, at the time.[1]

The Copy given here is from the *Pell Papers*, and in part from an earlier Original; first printed by Burton's Editor; and now reproduced, with slight alterations of the pointing &c., such as were necessary here and there to bring out the sense, but not such as could change anything that had the least title to remain unchanged.

SPEECH XVIII.

His Highness's last noble appeal, the words as of a strong great Captain addressed in the hour of imminent shipwreck, produced no adequate effect. The dreary Debate, supported chiefly by intemperate Haselrig, peppery Scott, and future-renegade Robinson, went on, trailing its slow length day after day; daily widening itself, too, into new dreariness, new questionability: a kind of pain to read even at this distance, and with view of the intemperate hot heads actually *stuck* on Temple Bar! For the man in "green oil-skin hat with night-cap under it," the Duke of Ormond namely, who lodges at the Papist Chirurgeon's in Drury Lane, is very busy all this while. And Fifth-Monarchy and other Petitions are getting concocted in the City, to a great length indeed; — and there are stirrings in the Army itself; — and, in brief, the English Hydra, cherished by the Spanish Charles-Stuart Invasion, will shortly hiss sky-high again, if this continue!

As yet, however, there stands one strong Man between us and that issue. The strong Man gone, that issue, we may

------

[1] Burton, ii. 351.

guess, will be inevitable; but he is not yet gone. For ten days more the dreary Debate has lasted. Various good Bills and Notices of Bills have been introduced; attempts on the part of well-affected Members to do some useful legislation here;[1] attempts which could not be accomplished. What could be accomplished was, to open the fountains of constitutional logic, and debate this question day after day. One or two intemperate persons, not excluded at the threshold, are of great moment in a Popular Assembly. The mind of which, if it have any mind, is one of the vaguest entities; capable, in a very singular degree, of being made to ferment, to freeze, to take fire, to develop itself in this shape or in that! The history of our Second Session, and indeed of these Oliverian Parliaments generally, is not exhilarating to the Constitutional mind!—

But now on the tenth day of the Debate, with its noise growing ever noisier, on the 4th of February, 1657–8, "about eleven in the morning,"—while peppery Scott is just about to attempt yelping out some new second speech, and there are cries of "Spoken! spoken!" which Sir Arthur struggles to argue down,—arrives the Black Rod.—"The Black Rod stays!" cry some, while Sir Arthur is arguing for Scott.— "What care I for the Black Rod?" snarls he: "The Gentleman [peppery Scott] ought to be heard."—Black Rod, however, is heard first; signifies that "His Highness is in the Lords House, and desires to speak with you." Under way therefore! "Shall we take our Mace?" By all means, if you consider it likely to be useful for you![2]

They take their Mace; range themselves in due mass, in the "Other House," Lords House, or whatever they call it; and his Highness, with a countenance of unusual earnestness, sorrow, resolution and severity, says:—

"My Lords, and Gentlemen of the House of Commons:

"I had very comfortable expectations that God would make the meeting of this Parliament a blessing; and, the Lord be

---

[1] *Parliamentary History*, xxi. 203, 204.

[2] Burton, ii. 462 et seqq.;—see also Tanner MSS. li. 1, for a more minute account.

my witness, *I* desired the carrying on the Affairs of the
Nation to these ends! The blessing which I mean, and
which we ever climbed at, was mercy, truth, righteousness
and peace, — which I desired might be improved.

"That which brought me into the capacity I now stand
in was the Petition and Advice given me by you; who, in
reference to the ancient Constitution [" *Which had Two
Houses and a King,*" — *though we do not in words mention
that!*], did draw me to accept the place of Protector. ["*I
was a kind of Protector already, I always understood; but let
that pass. Certainly you invited me to become the Protector I
now am, with Two Houses and other appendages, and there
lies the gist of the matter at present.*"] There is not a man
living can say I sought it; no, not a man nor woman tread-
ing upon English ground. But contemplating the sad condition of these Nations, relieved from an intestine War into
a six or seven years' Peace, I did think the Nation happy
therein! ["*I did think even my first Protectorate was a successful kind of thing!*"] But to be petitioned thereunto, and
advised by you to undertake such a Government, a burden
too heavy for any creature; and this to be done by the
House that then had the Legislative capacity: — certainly I
did look that the same men who made the Frame should make
it good unto me! I can say in the presence of God, in comparison with whom we are but like poor creeping ants upon
the earth, — I would have been glad to have lived under my
woodside, to have kept a flock of sheep — [*Yes, your Highness; it had been infinitely quieter, healthier, freer. But it is
gone forever: no woodsides now, and peaceful nibbling sheep,
and great still thoughts, and glimpses of God "in the cool of
the evening walking among the trees:" nothing but toil and
trouble, double, double, till one's discharge arrive, and the Eternal Portals open! Nay even there by your woodside, you had
not been happy; not you, — with thoughts going down to the
Death-kingdoms, and Heaven so near you on this hand, and
Hell so near you on that. Nay who would grudge a little temporary Trouble, when he can do a large spell of eternal Work?
Work that is true, and will last through all Eternity!* Com-

plain not, your Highness ! — His Highness does not complain.
" To have kept a flock of sheep," he says] — rather than undertaken such a Government as this.   But undertaking it by the
Advice and Petition of you, I did look that you who had
offered it unto me should make it good·

"I did tell you, at a Conference [1] concerning it, that I
would not undertake it, unless there might be some other
Persons to interpose between me and the House of Commons, who then had the power, and prevent tumultuary and
popular spirits : and it was granted I should name another
House.   I named it of men who shall meet you wheresoever
you go, and shake hands with you; and tell you it is not
Titles, nor Lords, nor Parties that they value, but a Christian and an English Interest!   Men of your own rank and
quality, who will not only be a balance unto you, but a new
force added to you,[2] while you love England and Religion.

"Having proceeded upon these terms ; — and finding such
a spirit as is too much predominant, everything being too
high or too low; where virtue, honesty, piety and justice are
omitted : — I thought I had been doing that which was my
duty, and thought it would have satisfied you!   But if everything must be too high or too low, you are not to be satisfied.
[*There is an innocency and childlike goodness in these poor sen-*
tences, which speaks to us in spite of rhetoric.]

"Again, I would not have accepted of the Government,
unless I knew there would be a just accord between the
Governor and Governed; unless they would take an Oath to
make good what the Parliament's Petition and Advice advised
me unto!   Upon that I took an Oath [*On the Twenty-sixth of*
June last], and they [*On the Twentieth of January last, at their*
long Table in the Anteroom] took another Oath upon their part
answerable to mine : — and did not every one know upon what
condition he swore ?   God knows, *I* took it upon the conditions
expressed in the [Act of] Government!   And I did think we
had been upon a foundation, and upon a bottom; and there-

---

[1] One of the Kingship Conferences of which there is no Report.
[2] " but to themselves," however helplessly, must mean this ; and a good
reporter would have substituted this.

upon I thought myself bound to take it, and to be 'advised by the Two Houses of Parliament.' And we standing unsettled till we arrived at that, the consequences would necessarily have been confusion, if that had not been settled. Yet there were not constituted 'Hereditary Lords,' nor 'Hereditary Kings;' [no,] the Power consisteth in the Two Houses and myself. — I do not say, that was the meaning of your Oath to *you*. That were to go against my own principles, to enter upon another man's conscience. God will judge between you and me! If there had been in you any intention of Settlement, you would have settled upon this basis, and have offered your judgment and opinion [as to minor improvements].

"God is my witness; I speak it; it is evident to all the world and people living, That a new business hath been seeking in the Army against this actual Settlement made by your consent. I do not speak to these Gentlemen ["*Pointing to his right hand,*" *says the Report*], or Lords, or whatsoever you will call them; I speak not this to them, but to *you*. — You advised me to come into this place, to be in a capacity [1] by your Advice. Yet instead of owning a thing, some must have I know not what; — and you have not only disjointed yourselves but the whole Nation, which is in likelihood of running into more confusion in these fifteen or sixteen days that you have sat, than it hath been from the rising of the last Session to this day. Through the intention of devising a Commonwealth again! That some people might be the men that might rule all! [*Intemperate Haselrig, peppery Scott, and such like: very inadequate they to "rule;" inadequate to keep their own heads on their shoulders, if they were not* RULED, *they!*] And they are endeavoring to engage the Army to carry that thing. — And hath that man been 'true to this Nation,' whosoever he be, especially that hath taken an Oath, thus to prevaricate? These designs have been made among the Army, to break and divide us. I speak this in the presence of some of the Army: That these things have not been according to God, nor according to truth, pretend what you will! [*No, your Highness; they have not.*] These things tend to nothing else but the play-

---

[1] "of authority" is delicately understood, but not expressed.

ing of the King of Scots' game (if I may so call him); and I think myself bound before God to do what I can to prevent it. [*" I, for my share:" Yea!*]

"That which I told you in the Banqueting-House [ten days ago] was true, That there are preparations of force to invade us. God is my witness, it hath been confirmed to me since, not a day ago, That the King of Scots hath an Army at the water's side, ready to be shipped for England. I have it from those who have been eye-witnesses of it. And while it is doing, there are endeavors from some who are not far from this place, to stir up the people of this Town into a tumulting — [*City Petitions are mounting very high, — as perhaps Sir Arthur and others know!*] — what if I said, Into a rebellion! And I hope I shall make it appear to be no better, if God assist me. [*Noble scorn and indignation is gradually getting the better of every other feeling in his Highness and us.*]

"It hath been not only your endeavor to pervert the Army while you have been sitting, and to draw them to state the question about a 'Commonwealth;' but some of you have been listing of persons, by commission of Charles Stuart, to join with any Insurrection that may be made. [*What a cold qualm in some conscious heart that listens to this! Let him tremble, every joint of him; — or not visibly tremble; but cower home to his place, and repent; and remember in whose hand his beggarly existence in this world lies!*] And what is like to come upon this, the Enemy being ready to invade us, but even present blood and confusion? — [*The next and final Sentence is partly on fire*] — And if this be so, I do assign [it] to this cause: Your not assenting to what you did invite me to by your Petition and Advice, as that which might prove the Settlement of the Nation. And if this be the end of your sitting, and this be your carriage — [*Sentence now all beautifully blazing*], I think it high time that an end be put to your sitting. And I DO DISSOLVE THIS PARLIAMENT! And let God be judge between you and me!"[1]

Figure the looks of Haselrig, Scott and Company! "The Mace was clapt under a cloak; the Speaker withdrew, and

[1] Burton, ii. 465–470.

exit Parliamentum," the Talking-Apparatus vanishes.[1] "God be judge between you and me!" — "Amen!" answered they,[2] thought they, indignantly; and sank into eternal silence.

It was high time; for in truth the Hydra, on every side, is stirring its thousand heads. "Believe me," says Samuel Hartlib, Milton's friend, writing to an Official acquaintance next week, "believe me, it was of such necessity, that if their Session had continued but two or three days longer, all had been in blood both in City and Country, upon Charles Stuart's account."[3]

His Highness, before this Monday's sun sets, has begun to lodge the Anarchic Ringleaders, Royalist, Fifth-Monarchist, in the Tower; his Highness is bent once more with all his faculty, the Talking-Apparatus being gone, to front this Hydra, and trample it down once again.[4] On Saturday he summons his Officers, his Acting-Apparatus, to Whitehall round him; explains to them "in a Speech two hours long" what kind of Hydra it is; asks, Shall it conquer us, involve us in blood and confusion? They answer from their hearts, No, it shall not! "We will stand and fall with your Highness, we will live and die with you!"[5] — It is the last duel this Oliver has with any Hydra fomented into life by a Talking-Apparatus; and he again conquers it, invincibly compresses it, as he has heretofore done.

One day, in the early days of March next, his Highness said to Lord Broghil: An old friend of yours is in Town, the Duke of Ormond, now lodged in Drury Lane, at the Papist Surgeon's there: you had better tell him to be gone![6] — Whereat his Lordship stared; found it a fact, however; and his Grace of Ormond did go with exemplary speed, and got again to Bruges and the Sacred Majesty, with report That Cromwell had many

[1] Burton, ii. 464.

[2] Tradition in various modern Books (*Parliamentary History*, xxi. 203; Note to Burton, ii. 470); not supported, that I can find, by any contemporary witness.

[3] Hartlib in London (11th Feb. 1657-8) to Moreland at Geneva; printed in *Parliamentary History*, xxi. 205.

[4] Appendix, No. 31.   [5] Hartlib's Letter, ubi suprà.

[6] Godwin, iv. 508; Budgel's *Lives of the Boyles*, p. 49; &c.

enemies, but that the rise of the Royalists was moonshine.
And on the 12th of the month his Highness had the Mayor
and Common Council with him in a body at Whitehall; and
"in a Speech at large" explained to them that his Grace of
Ormond was gone only "on Tuesday last;" that there were
Spanish Invasions, Royalist Insurrections and Frantic-Anabaptist Insurrections rapidly ripening; — that it would well
beseem the City of London to have its Militia in good order.
To which the Mayor and Common Council, "being very sensible
thereof," made zealous response [1] by speech and by act.   In a
word, the Talking-Apparatus being gone, and an Oliver Protector now at the head of the Acting-Apparatus, no Insurrection, in the eyes of reasonable persons, had any chance.   The
leading Royalists shrank close into their privacies again, —
considerable numbers of them had to shrink into durance in
the Tower.   Among which latter class, his Highness, justly
incensed, and "considering," as Thurloe says, "that it was not
fit there should be a Plot of this kind every winter," had determined that a High Court of Justice should take cognizance
of some.   High Court of Justice is accordingly nominated [2] as
the Act of Parliament prescribes: among the parties marked
for trial by it are Sir Henry Slingsby, long since prisoner for
Penruddock's business, and the Rev. Dr. Hewit, a man of
much forwardness in Royalism.   Sir Henry, prisoner in Hull
and acquainted with the Chief Officers there, has been treating
with them for betrayal of the place to his Majesty; has even,
to that end, given one of them a Majesty's commission; for
whose Spanish Invasion such a Haven and Fortress would
have been extremely convenient.   Rev. Dr. Hewit, preaching
by sufferance, according to the old ritual, "in St. Gregory's
Church near Paul's," to a select disaffected audience, has farther seen good to distinguish himself very much by secular
zeal in this business of the Royalist Insurrection and Spanish
Charles-Stuart Invasion; — which has now come to nothing,
and left poor Dr. Hewit in a most questionable position.   Of

[1] Newspapers (in *Cromwelliana*, p. 171).

[2] 27th April, 1658.   Act of Parliament, with List of the Names, is in Scobell, ii. 372–375 : see also *Commons Journals* vii. 427 (Sept. 1656).

these two, and of others, a High Court of Justice shall take cognizance.

The Insurrection having no chance in the eyes of reasonable Royalists, and they in consequence refusing to lead it, the large body of *un*reasonable Royalists now in London City or gathering thither decide, with indignation, That they will try it on their own score, and lead it themselves. Hands to work, then, ye unreasonable Royalists; pipe, All hands! Saturday, the 15th of May, that is the night appointed: To rise that Saturday night; beat drums for "Royalist Apprentices," "fire houses at the Tower," slay this man, slay that, and bring matters to a good issue. Alas, on the very edge of the appointed hour, as usual, we are all seized; the ringleaders of us are all seized, "at the Mermaid in Cheapside," — for Thurloe and his Highness have long known what we were upon! Barkstead Governor of the Tower "marches into the City with five drakes," at the rattle of which every Royalist Apprentice, and party implicated, shakes in his shoes: — and this also has gone to vapor, leaving only for result certain new individuals of the Civic class to give account of it to the High Court of Justice.

Tuesday, 25th May, 1658, the High Court of Justice sat; a formidable Sanhedrim of above a hundred and thirty heads, consisting of " all the Judges," chief Law Officials, and others named in the Writ according to Act of Parliament; — sat " in Westminster Hall, at Nine in the morning, for the Trial of Sir Henry Slingsby Knight, John Hewit Doctor of Divinity," and three others whom we may forget.[1] Sat day after day till all were judged. Poor Sir Henry, on the first day, was condemned; he pleaded what he could, poor gentleman, a very constant Royalist all along; but the Hull business was too palpable; he was condemned to die. Rev. Dr. Hewit, whose proceedings also had become very palpable, refused to plead at all; refused even "to take off his hat," says Carrion Heath, "till the officer was coming to do it for him:" "had a Paper of Demurrers prepared by the learned Mr. Prynne," who is now again doing business this way; — "conducted himself not very wisely," says Bulstrode. He likewise received sentence of death. The

---

[1] Newspapers (in *Cromwelliana,* p. 172).

others, by narrow missing, escaped; by good luck, or the Protector's mercy, suffered nothing.

As to Slingsby and Hewit the Protector was inexorable. Hewit has already taken a very high line: let him persevere in it! Slingsby was the Lord Fauconberg's Uncle, married to his Aunt Bellasis; but that could not stead him, — perhaps that was but a new monition to be strict with him. The Commonwealth of England and its Peace are not nothing! These Royalist Plots every winter, deliveries of garrisons to Charles Stuart, and reckless "usherings of us into blood," shall end! Hewit and Slingsby suffered on Tower Hill, on Monday, 8th June; amid the manifold rumor and emotion of men. Of the City Insurrectionists six were condemned; three of whom were executed, three pardoned. And so the High Court of Justice dissolved itself; and at this and not at more expense of blood, the huge Insurrectionary movement ended, and lay silent within its caves again.

Whether in any future year it would have tried another rising against such a Lord Protector, one does not know, — one guesses rather in the negative. The Royalist Cause, after so many failures, after such a sort of enterprises "on the word of a Christian King," had naturally sunk very low. Some twelvemonth hence, with a Commonwealth not now under Cromwell, but only under the impulse of Cromwell, a Christian King hastening down to the Treaty of the Pyrenees, where France and Spain were making Peace, found one of the coldest receptions. Cardinal Mazarin "sent his coaches and guards a day's journey to meet Lockhart the Commonwealth Ambassador;" but refused to meet the Christian King at all; would not even meet Ormond except as if by accident, "on the public road," to say that there was no hope. The Spanish Minister, Don Luis de Haro, was civiller in manner; but as to Spanish Charles-Stuart Invasions or the like, he also decisively shook his head.[1] The Royalist Cause was as good as desperate in England; a melancholy Reminiscence, fast fading away into the realm of shadows. Not till Puritanism sank of its own accord, could Royalism rise again. But Puritanism, the King

[1] Kennet, iii. 214; Clarendon, iii. 914.

of it once away, fell loose very naturally in every fibre, — fell
into *Kinglessness*, what we call Anarchy; crumbled down, ever
faster, for Sixteen Months, in mad suicide, and universal clashing and collision; proved, by trial after trial, that there lay
not in it either Government or so much as Self-government
any more; that a Government of England by *it* was henceforth
an impossibility.   Amid the general wreck of things, all Government threatening now to be impossible, the Reminiscence
of Royalty rose again, "Let us take refuge in the Past, the
Future is not possible!" — and Major-General Monk crossed the
Tweed at Coldstream, with results which are well known.

Results which we will not quarrel with, very mournful as
they have been! If it please Heaven, these Two Hundred
Years of universal Cant in Speech, with so much of Cotton-
spinning, Coal-boring, Commercing, and other valuable Sincerity of Work, going on the while, shall not be quite lost to us!
Our Cant will vanish, our whole baleful cunningly compacted
Universe of Cant, as does a heavy Nightmare Dream.   We
shall awaken; and find ourselves in a world greatly *widened*.
— Why Puritanism could not continue? My friend, Puritanism was *not* the Complete Theory of this immense Universe;
no, only a part thereof! To me it seems, in my hours of hope,
as if the Destinies meant something grander with England
than even Oliver Protector did! We will not quarrel with
the Destinies; we will work as we can towards fulfilment of
them.

But in these same June days of the year 1658, while Hewit
and Slingsby lay down their heads on Tower Hill, and the
English Hydra finds that its Master is still here, there arrive
the news of Dunkirk alluded to above: Dunkirk gloriously
taken, Spaniards gloriously beaten; victories and successes
abroad; which are a new illumination to the Lord Protector
in the eyes of England. Splendid Nephews of the Cardinal,
Manzinis, Ducs de Crequi, come across the Channel to congratulate "the most invincible of Sovereigns;" young Louis
Fourteenth himself would have come, had not the attack of
small-pox prevented.[1] With whom the elegant Lord Faucon-

---

[1] Newspapers (in *Cromwelliana*, pp. 172-173; 15th-21st June, 1658).

berg and others busy themselves: their pageantry and gilt coaches, much gazed at by the idler multitudes, need not detain us here.

The Lord Protector, his Parliament having been dismissed with such brevity, is somewhat embarrassed in his finances. But otherwise his affairs stand well; visibly in an improved condition. Once more he has saved Puritan England; once more approved himself invincible abroad and at home. He looks with confidence towards summoning a new Parliament, of juster disposition towards Puritan England and him.[1] With a Parliament, or if extremity of need arrive, without a Parliament and in spite of Parliaments, the Puritan Gospel Cause, sanctioned by a Higher than Parliaments, shall not sink while life remains in this Man. Not till Oliver Cromwell's head lie low, shall English Puritanism bend its head to any created thing. Erect, with its foot on the neck of Hydra Babylon, with its open Bible and drawn Sword, shall Puritanism stand, and with pious all-defiance victoriously front the world. That was Oliver Cromwell's appointed function in this piece of Sublunary Space, in this section of swift-flowing Time; that noble, perilous, painful function: and he has manfully done it, — and is now near ending it, and getting honorably relieved from it.

LETTER CCXXV.

THE poor Protestants of Piedmont, it appears, are again in a state of grievance, in a state of peril. The Lord Protector, in the thickest press of domestic anarchies, finds time to think of these poor people and their case. Here is a Letter to Ambassador Lockhart, who is now at Dunkirk Siege, in the French King and Cardinal's neighborhood: a generous pious Letter; dictated to Thurloe, partly perhaps of Thurloe's composition, but altogether of Oliver's mind and sense; — fit enough, since it so chances, to conclude our Series here.

[1] Thurloe, vii. 84, 99, 128, &c. (April, May, 1658).

Among the Lockhart Letters in *Thurloe*, which are full of Dunkirk in these weeks, I can find no trace of this new Piedmont business: but in Milton's Latin State-Letters, among the *Literæ Oliverii Protectoris*, there are Three, to the French King, to the Swiss Cantons, to the Cardinal, which all treat of it. The first of which, were it only as a sample of the Milton-Oliver Diplomacies, we will here copy, and translate that all may read it. An emphatic State-Letter; which Oliver Cromwell meant, and John Milton thought and wrote into words; not unworthy to be read. It goes by the same Express as the Letter to Lockhart himself; and is very specially referred to there:—

"*Serenissimo potentissimoque Principi, Ludovico Galliarum Regi.*

"SERENISSIME POTENTISSIMEQUE REX, AMICE AC FŒDERATE AUGUSTISSIME:

"Meminisse potest Majestas Vestra, quo tempore inter nos de renovando Fœdere agebatur (quod optimis auspiciis initum multa utriusque Populi commoda, multa Hostium communium exinde mala testantur), accidisse miseram illam Convallensium Occisionem; quorum causam undique desertam atque afflictam Vestræ misericordiæ atque tutelæ, summo cum ardore animi ac miseratione, commendavimus. Nec defuisse per se arbitramur Majestatem Vestram officio tam pio, immo verò tam humano, pro eâ quâ apud Ducem Sabaudiæ valere debuit vel auctoritate vel gratiâ: Nos certè aliique multi Principes ac Civitates, legationibus, literis, precibus interpositis, non defuimus.

"Post cruentissimam utriusque sexûs omnis ætatis Trucidationem, Pax tandem data est; vel potiùs inductæ Pacis nomine hostilitas quædam tectior. Conditiones Pacis vestro in oppido Pinarolii sunt latæ: duræ quidem illæ, sed quibus miseri atque inopes, dira omnia atque immania perpessi, facile acquiescerent, modò iis, duræ et iniquæ ut sint, staretur. Non statur; sed enim earum quoque singularum falsâ interpretatione variisque diverticulis, fides eluditur ac violatur. Antiquis sedibus multi dejiciuntur, Religio Patria multis interdicitur; Tributa nova exiguntur; Arx nova cervicibus imponitur, unde milites crebrò erumpentes obvios quosque vel diripiunt vel trucidant. Ad hæc nuper novæ copiæ clanculum contra eos parantur ; quique inter eos Romanam Religionem colunt, migrare ad tempus jubentur : ut omnia nunc rursùs videantur ad illorum inter-necionem miserorum spectare, quos illa prior laniena reliquos fecit.

"Quod ergò per dextram tuam, Rex Christianissime, quæ Fœdus nobiscum et amicitiam percussit, obsecro atque obtestor, per illud Christianissimi tituli decus sanctissimum, fieri ne siveris : nec tantam sæviendi licentiam, non dico Principi cuiquam (neque enim in ullum Principem, multò minus in ætatem illius Principis teneram, aut in muliebrem Matris animum, tanta sævitia cadere potest), sed sacerrimis illis Sicariis, ne permiseris. Qui cum Christi Servatoris nostri servos atque imitatores sese profiteantur, qui venit in hunc mundum ut peccatores servaret, Ejus mitissimi Nomine atque Institutis ad innocentium crudelissimas cædes abutuntur. Eripe qui potes, quique in tanto fastigio dignus es posse, tot supplices tuos homicidarum ex manibus, qui cruore nuper ebrii sanguinem rursùs sitiunt, suæque invidiam crudelitatis in Principes derivare consultissimum sibi ducunt. Tu verò nec Titulos tuos aut Regni fines istâ invidiâ, nec Evangelium Christi pacatissimum istâ crudelitate fœdari, te regnante pa-tiaris. Memineris hos ipsos Avi tui Henrici Protestantibus amicissimi Dedititios fuisse ; cùm Diguierius per ea Loca, quà etiam commodissimus in Italiam transitus est, Sabaudum trans Alpes cedentem victor est insecutus. Deditionis illius Instru-mentum in Actis Regni vestri Publicis etiamnum extat : in quo exceptum atque cautum inter alia est, ne cui posteà Convallenses traderentur, nisi iisdem conditionibus quibus eos Avus tuus invictissimus in fidem recepit. Hanc fidem nunc implorant, avitam abs te Nepote supplices requirunt. Tui esse quàm cujus nunc sunt, vel permutatione aliquâ si fieri possit, malint atque optârint : id si non licet, patrocinio sal-tem, miseratione atque perfugio.

"Sunt et rationes regni quæ hortari possint ut Convallenses ad te confugientes ne rejicias : sed nolim te, Rex tantus cum sis, aliis rationibus ad defensionem calamitosorum quàm fide à

Majoribus datâ, pietate, regiâque animi benignitate ac magnitudine permoveri. Ita pulcherrimi facti laus atque gloria illibata atque integra tua erit, et ipse Patrem Misericordiæ ejusque Filium Christum Regem, cujus Nomen atque Doctrinam ab immanitate nefariâ vindicaveris, eò magis faventem tibi et propitium per omnem vitam experieris.

"Deus Opt. Max. ad gloriam suam, tot innocentissimorum hominum Christianorum tutandam salutem, Vestrumque verum decus, Majestati Vestræ hanc mentem injiciat.

[Majestatis Vestræ Studiosissimus

OLIVERIUS PROTECTOR REIP. ANGLIÆ,] &c.

" *Westmonasterio, Maii* [26° *die*], *anno* 1658."[1]

Of which here is a Version the most literal we can make :—

" *To the most serene and potent Prince, Louis, King of France.*

"MOST SERENE AND POTENT KING, MOST CLOSE FRIEND AND ALLY:

"Your Majesty may recollect that during the negotiation between us for the renewing of our League[2] (which many advantages to both Nations, and much damage to their common Enemies, resulting therefrom, now testify to have been very wisely done), — there fell out that miserable Slaughter of the People of the Valleys; whose cause, on all sides deserted and trodden down, wo, with the utmost earnestness and pity, recommended to your mercy and protection. Nor do we think Your Majesty, for your own part, has been wanting in an office so pious and indeed so human, in so far as either by authority or favor you might have influence with the Duke of Savoy: we certainly, and many other Princes and States, by embassies, by letters, by entreaties directed thither, have not been wanting.

"After that most sanguinary Massacre, which spared no age nor either sex, there was at last a Peace given; or rather, under the specious name of Peace, a certain more disguised hostility. The terms of the Peace were settled in your Town

[1] *The Prose Works of John Milton* (London, 1833), p. 815.
[2] June, 1655: antea, vol. xviii. p. 491.

of Pignerol : hard terms ; but such as those poor People, indigent and wretched, after suffering all manner of cruelties
and atrocities, might gladly acquiesce in ; if only, hard and
unjust as the bargain is, it were adhered to. It is not adhered
to : those terms are broken ; the purport of every one of them
is, by false interpretation and various subterfuges, eluded and
violated. Many of these People *are* ejected from their Old
Habitations ; their Native Religion is prohibited to many :
new Taxes are exacted ; a new Fortress has been built over
them, out of which soldiers frequently sallying plunder or kill
whomsoever they meet. Moreover, new Forces have of late
been privily got ready against them ; and such as follow the
Romish Religion are directed to withdraw from among them
within a limited time : so that everything seems now again
to point towards the extermination of all among those unhappy
People, whom the former Massacre had left.

"Which now, O Most Christian King, I beseech and obtest
thee, by thy right-hand which pledged a League and Friendship with us, by the sacred honor of that Title of Most Christian, — permit not to be done : nor let such license of savagery,
I do not say to any Prince (for indeed no cruelty like this
could come into the mind of any Prince, much less into the
tender years of that young Prince, or into the woman's heart
of his Mother), but to those most accursed Assassins, be given.
Who while they profess themselves the servants and imitators
of Christ our Saviour, who came into this world that He
might save sinners, abuse His most merciful Name and Com-
mandments to the cruelest slaughterings. Snatch, thou who
art able, and who in such an elevation art worthy to be able,
those poor Suppliants of thine from the hands of Murderers,
who, lately drunk with blood, are again athirst for it, and
think convenient to turn the discredit of their own cruelty
upon their Prince's score. Suffer not either thy Titles and the
Environs of thy Kingdom to be soiled with that discredit, or
the peaceable Gospel of Christ by that cruelty, in thy Reign.
Remember that these very People became subjects of thy Ancestor, Henry, most friendly to Protestants ; when Lesdiguières
victoriously pursued him of Savoy across the Alps, through

those same Valleys,[1] where indeed the most commodious pass to Italy is. The Instrument of that their Paction and Surrender is yet extant in the Public Acts of your Kingdom: in which this among other things is specified and provided against, That these People of the Valleys should not thereafter be delivered over to any one except on the same conditions under which thy invincible Ancestor had received them into fealty. This promised protection they now implore; promise of thy Ancestor they now, from thee the Grandson, suppliantly demand. To be thine rather than his whose they now are, if by any means of exchange it could be done, they would wish and prefer: if that may not be, thine at least by succor, by commiseration and deliverance.

"There are likewise reasons of state which might give inducement not to reject these People of the Valleys flying for shelter to thee: but I would not have thee, so great a King as thou art, be moved to the defence of the unfortunate by other reasons than the promise of thy Ancestors, and thy own piety and royal benignity and greatness of mind. So shall the praise and fame of this most worthy action be unmixed and clear; and thyself shalt find the Father of Mercy, and His Son Christ the King, whose Name and Doctrine thou shalt have vindicated, the more favorable to thee, and propitious through the course of life.

"May the Almighty, for His own glory, for the safety of so many most innocent Christian men, and for your true honor, dispose Your Majesty to this determination.

"Your Majesty's most friendly

"OLIVER PROTECTOR OF THE COMMONWEALTH OF ENGLAND.

"WESTMINSTER, 26th May, 1658."

[*To Sir William Lockhart, our Ambassador at the French Court, These.*]

"[WHITEHALL,] 26th May, 1658.

"SIR, — The continual troubles and vexations of the poor People of Piedmont professing the Reformed Religion, —

---

[1] In 1592. Hénault, *Abrégé Chronologique* (Paris, 1774), ii. 597.

and that after so many serious instances of yours in the Court of France in their behalf, and after such hearty recommendations of their most deplorable condition to his Majesty in our name, who also has been pleased upon all such occasions to profess very deep resentments of their miseries, and to give us no small hopes of interposing his power and interest with the Duke of Savoy for the accommodating of those affairs, and for the restoring those poor distressed creatures to their ancient privileges and habitations, — are matter of so much grief to us, and lie so near our heart, that, notwithstanding we are abundantly satisfied with those many signal marks you have always hitherto given of your truly Christian zeal and tenderness on their regard, yet the present conjuncture of their affairs, and the misery that is daily added to their affliction begetting in us fresh arguments of pity towards them, not only as men, but as the poor distressed Members of Christ, — do really move us at present to recommend their sad condition to your special care. Desiring you to redouble your instances with the King, in such pathetic and affectionate expressions as may be in some measure suitable to the greatness of their present sufferings and grievances. Which, the truth is, are almost inexpressible. For so restless and implacable is the malice and fury of their Popish Adversaries, that, — as though they esteemed it but a light matter to have formerly shed the innocent blood of so many hundreds of souls, to have burned their houses, to have razed their churches, to have plundered their goods, and to have driven out the Inhabitants beyond the River Pelice, out of those their ancient Possessions which they had quietly enjoyed for so many ages and generations together, — they are now resolved to fill their cup of affliction up to the brim, and to heat the furnace yet seven times hotter than before. Amongst other things : —

" *First*, — They forcibly prohibit all manner of Public Exercises [1] at San Giovanni, which, notwithstanding, the Inhabitants have enjoyed time out of mind : and in case they yield not ready obedience to such most unrighteous orders, they are immediately summoned before their Courts of Justice,

---

[1] Means " Public Worship."

and there proceeded against in a most severe and rigorous manner, and some threatened to be wholly destroyed and exterminated.

"2. And forasmuch as, in the said Valleys, there are not found among the Natives men fitly qualified and of abilities for Ministerial Functions to supply so much as one half of their Churches, and upon this account they are necessitated to entertain some out of France and Geneva, which are the Duke of Savoy's friends and allies, — their Popish Enemies take hold of this advantage; and make use of this stratagem, namely, to banish and drive out the shepherds of the flocks, that so the wolves may the better come in and devour the sheep.

"3. To this we add, their strict prohibition of all Physicians and Chirurgeons of the Reformed Religion to inhabit in the Valleys. And thus they attempt not only to starve their souls for want of spiritual food and nourishment, but to destroy their bodies likewise for want of those outward conveniences and helps which God hath allowed to all mankind.

"4. And as a supplement to the former grievances, those of the Reformed Religion are prohibited all manner of Commerce and Trade with their Popish neighbors; that so they may not be able to subsist and maintain their families : and if they offend herein in the least, they are immediately apprehended as rebels.

"5. Moreover, to give the world a clear testimony what their main design in all these oppressions is, they have issued out Orders whereby to force the poor Protestants To sell their Lands and Houses to their Popish neighbors : whereas the Papists are prohibited upon pain of excommunication to sell any immovable to the Protestants.

"6. Besides, the Court of Savoy have rebuilt the Fort of La Torre; contrary to the formal and express promise made by them to the Ambassadors of the Evangelical Cantons. Where they have also placed Commanders, who commit the Lord knows how many excesses and outrages in all the neighboring parts; without being ever called to question, or compelled to make restitution for the same. If by chance any

murder be committed in the Valleys (as is too-too often practised) whereof the authors are not discovered, the poor Protestants are immediately accused as guilty thereof, to render
them odious to their neighbors.

"7. There are sent lately into the said Valleys several
Troops of Horse and Companies of Foot; which hath caused
the poor People, out of fear of a massacre, with great expense
and difficulty to send their wives and little ones, with all that
were feeble and sick amongst them, into the Valley of Perosa,
under the King of France his Dominions.

"These are, in short, the grievances, and this is the present
state and condition of those poor People even at this very day.
Whereof you are to use your utmost endeavors to make his
Majesty thoroughly sensible; and to persuade him to give
speedy and effectual orders [to] his Ambassador who resides
in the Duke's Court, To act vigorously in their behalf. Our
Letter,[1] which you shall present his Majesty for this end and
purpose, contains several reasons in it which we hope will
move his heart to the performance of this charitable and merciful work. And we desire you to second and animate the same
with your most earnest solicitations; representing unto him
how much his own interest and honor is concerned in the
making good that Accord of Henry the Fourth, his royal
predecessor, with the Ambassadors of those very People, in
the year 1592, by the Constable of Lesdiguières; which Accord
is registered in the Parliament of Dauphiné; and whereof you
have an authentic Copy in your own hands. Whereby the
Kings of France oblige themselves and their Successors To
maintain and preserve their ancient privileges and concessions.
Besides that the gaining to himself the hearts of that People,
by so gracious and remarkable a protection and deliverance,
might be of no little use another day, in relation to Pignerol
and the other adjacent places under his Dominions.

"One of the most effectual remedies, which we conceive
the fittest to be applied at present is, That the King of France
would be pleased to make an Exchange with the Duke of
Savoy for those Valleys; resigning over to him some other

---

[1] Milton's, given above.

part of his Dominions in lieu thereof, — as, in the reign of Henry the Fourth, the Marquisate of Saluces was exchanged with the Duke for La Bresse.[1] Which certainly could not but be of great advantage to his Majesty, as well for the safety of Pignerol, as for the opening of a Passage for his Forces into Italy, — which [Passage], if under the dominion, and in the hands of so powerful a Prince, joined with the natural strength of these places by reason of their situation, must needs be rendered impregnable.

"By what we have already said, you see our intentions; and therefore we leave all other particulars to your special care and conduct; and rest,

[Your friend,]

" OLIVER P." [2]

Lockhart, both General and Ambassador in these months, is, as we hinted, infinitely busy with his share in the Siege of Dunkirk, now just in its agony; and before this Letter can well arrive, has done his famous feat of Fighting, which brings Turenne and him their victory, among the sandhills there.[3] Much to the joy of Cardinal and King; who will not readily refuse him in any reasonable point at present. There came no new Massacre upon the poor People of the Valleys; their grievances were again "settled," scared away for a season, by negotiation.

———◆———

DEATH OF THE PROTECTOR.

THERE remain no more *Letters and Speeches of Oliver Cromwell* for us; the above is the last of them of either kind. As a Speaker to Men, he takes his leave of the world, in these final words addressed to his Second Parliament, on the 4th of February, 1657–8: "God be judge between you and me!" — So was it appointed by the Destinies and the Oblivions; these were his last public words.

---

[1] In 1601 (Hénault, ii. 612).   [2] Ayscough MSS., no. 4107, f. 89.

[3] Thursday, 3d June, 1658 (Thurloe, vii. 155, 156).

Other Speeches, in that crisis of Oliver's affairs, we have already heard of; "Speech of two hours" to his Officers in Whitehall; Speech to the Lord Mayor and Common Council, in the same place, on the same subject: but they have not been reported, or the report of them has not come down to us. There were domestic Letters also, as we still find, written in those same tumultuous weeks; Letters to the Earl of Warwick, on occasion of the death of his Grandson, the Protector's Son-in-law. For poor young Mr. Rich, whom we saw wedded in November last, is dead.[1] He died on the twelfth day after that Dissolution of the Parliament; while Oliver and the Commonwealth are wrestling against boundless Anarchies, Oliver's own Household has its visitations and dark days. Poor little Frances Cromwell, in the fourth month of her marriage, still only about seventeen, she finds herself suddenly a widow; and Hampton Court has become a house of mourning. Young Rich was much lamented. Oliver condoled with the Grandfather " in seasonable and sympathizing Letters;" for which the brave old Earl rallies himself to make some gratefulest Reply;[2] — " Cannot enough confess my obligation, much less discharge it, for your seasonable and sympathizing Letters; which, besides the value they derive from so worthy a hand, express such faithful affections, and administer such Christian advices as renders them beyond measure dear to me." Blessings, and noble eulogies, the outpouring of a brave old heart, conclude this Letter of Warwick's. He himself died shortly after;[3] a new grief to the Protector. — The Protector was delivering the Commonwealth from Hydras and fighting a world-wide battle, while he wrote those Letters on the death of young Rich. If by chance they still lie hidden in the archives of some kinsman of the Warwicks, they may yet be disimprisoned and made audible. Most probably they too are lost. And so we have now nothing more; — and Oliver has nothing more. His Speakings, and also his Actings, all his manifold Strug-

[1] 16th Feb. 1657-8 (Newspapers in *Cromwelliana*, p. 170).

[2] Earl of Warwick to the Lord Protector, date 11th March, 1657-8; printed in *Godwin*, iv. 528.

[3] 19th April, 1658 (Thurloe, vii. 85).

glings, more or less victorious, to utter the great God's-Message that was in him, — have here what we call ended. This Summer of 1658, likewise victorious after struggle, is his last in our World of Time. Thenceforth he enters the Eternities; and rests upon his arms *there*.

Oliver's look was yet strong; and young for his years,[1] which were fifty-nine last April. The "threescore and ten years," the Psalmist's limit, which probably was often in Oliver's thoughts and in those of others there, might have been anticipated for him: Ten Years more of Life; — which, we may compute, would have given another History to all the Centuries of England. But it was not to be so, it was to be otherwise. Oliver's health, as we might observe, was but uncertain in late times; often "indisposed" the spring before last. His course of life had not been favorable to health! "A burden too heavy for man!" as he himself, with a sigh, would sometimes say. Incessant toil; inconceivable labor, of head and heart and hand; toil, peril, and sorrow manifold, continued for near twenty years now, had done their part: those robust life-energies, it afterwards appeared,[2] had been gradually eaten out. Like a Tower strong to the eye, but with its foundations undermined; which has not long to stand; the fall of which, on any shock, may be sudden. —

The Manzinis and Ducs de Crequi, with their splendors, and congratulations about Dunkirk, interesting to the street-populations and general public, had not yet withdrawn, when at Hampton Court there had begun a private scene, of much deeper and quite opposite interest there. The Lady Claypole, Oliver's favorite Daughter, a favorite of all the world, had fallen sick we know not when; lay sick now, — to death, as it proved. Her disease was of internal female nature; the painfulest and most harassing to mind and sense, it is understood, that falls to the lot of a human creature. Hampton Court we can fancy once more, in those July days, a house of sorrow; pale Death knocking there, as at the door of the meanest hut. "She had great sufferings, great exercises of spirit." Yes: —

[1] Heath.   [2] Doctor Bates, on examination *post mortem*.

and in the depths of the old Centuries, we see a pale anxious Mother, anxious Husband, anxious weeping Sisters, a poor young Frances weeping anew in her weeds. "For the last fourteen days" his Highness has been by her bedside at Hampton Court, unable to attend to any public business whatever.[1] Be still, my Child; trust thou yet in God: in the waves of the Dark River, there too is He a God of help! — On the 6th day of August she lay dead; at rest forever. My young, my beautiful, my brave! She is taken from me; I am left bereaved of her. The Lord giveth, and the Lord taketh away; blessed be the Name of the Lord! —

"His Highness," says Harvey,[2] "being at Hampton Court, sickened a little before the Lady Elizabeth died. Her decease was on Friday, 6th August, 1658; she having lain long under great extremity of bodily pain, which, with frequent and violent convulsion-fits, brought her to her end. But as to his Highness, it was observed that his sense of her outward misery, in the pains she endured, took deep impression upon him; who indeed was ever a most indulgent and tender Father; — his affections" too "being regulated and bounded by such Christian wisdom and prudence, as did eminently shine in filling up not only that relation of a Father, but also all other relations; wherein he was a most rare and singular example. And no doubt but the sympathy of his spirit with his sorely afflicted and dying Daughter" did break him down at this time; "considering also," — innumerable other considerations of sufferings and toils, "which made me often wonder he was able to hold up so long; except" indeed "that he was borne up by a Supernatural Power at a more than ordinary rate. As a mercy to the truly Christian World, and to us of these Nations, had we been worthy of him!" —

<hr>

[1] Thurloe, vii. 295 (27th July, 1658).

[2] A Collection of several Passages concerning his late Highness Oliver Cromwell, in the Time of his Sickness; wherein is related many of his Expressions upon his Death-bed, together with his Prayer within two or three Days before his Death. Written by one that was then Groom of his Bedchamber. (King's Pamphlets, sm. 4to, no. 792, art. 22: London, 9th June, 1659.)

The same authority, who unhappily is not chronological, adds elsewhere this little picture, which we must take with us: "At Hampton Court, a few days after the death of the Lady Elizabeth, which touched him nearly, — being then himself under bodily distempers, forerunners of that Sickness which was to death, and in his bed-chamber, — he called for his Bible, and desired an honorable and godly person there, with others, present, To read unto him that passage in *Philippians* Fourth: '*Not that I speak in respect of want ; for I have learned in whatsoever state I am, therewith to be content. I know both how to be abased, and I know how to abound. Everywhere, and by all things, I am instructed ; both to be full and to be hungry, both to abound and to suffer need. I can do all things, through Christ which strengtheneth me.*'[1] Which read, — said he, to use his own words as near as I can remember them: 'This Scripture did once save my life; when my eldest Son [poor Robert[2]] died ; which went as a dagger to my heart, indeed it did.' And then repeating the words of the text himself, and reading the tenth and eleventh verses, of Paul's contentation, and submission to the will of God in all conditions, — said he: 'It's true, Paul, *you* have learned this, and attained to this measure of grace: but what shall *I* do? Ah poor creature, it is a hard lesson for me to take out! I find it so!' But reading on to the thirteenth verse, where Paul saith, '*I can do all things through Christ that strengtheneth me,*' — then faith began to work, and his heart to find support and comfort, and he said thus to himself, 'He that was Paul's Christ is my Christ too!' And so drew waters out of the well of Salvation."

In the same dark days, occurred George Fox's third and last interview with Oliver. Their first interview we have seen. The second, which had fallen out some two years ago, did not prosper quite so well. George, riding into Town "one evening," with some "Edward Pyot" or other broad-brimmed man, espied the Protector "at Hyde Park Corner among his Guards,"

---

[1] Philippians iv. 11, 12, 13.

[2] A blank in the Pamphlet here: not "Oliver" as hitherto supposed (see vol. xvii. p. 183), but "Robert" (ibid. p. 48): see vol. xvii. pp. 124, 183.

and made up to his carriage-window, in spite of opposition; and was altogether cordially welcomed there. But on the following day, at Whitehall, the Protector "spake lightly;" he sat down loosely "on a table," and "spake light things to me," in fact, rather quizzed me; finding my enormous sacred Self-confidence none of the least of my attainments![1] Such had been our second interview; here now is the third and last. — George dates nothing; and his facts everywhere lie round him like the leather-parings of his old shop: but we judge it may have been about the time when the Manzinis and Ducs de Crequi were parading in their gilt coaches, That George and two Friends "going out of Town," on a summer day, "two of Hacker's men" had met them, — taken them, brought them to the Mews. "Prisoners there a while:" — but the Lord's power was over Hacker's men; they had to let us go. Whereupon : —

"The same day, taking boat I went down [up] to Kingston, and from thence to Hampton Court, to speak with the Protector about the Sufferings of Friends. I met him riding into Hampton Court Park; and before I came to him, as he rode at the head of his Life-guard, I saw and felt a waft [whiff] of death go forth against him." — Or in favor of him, George? His life, if thou knew it, has not been a merry thing for this man, now or heretofore! I fancy he has been looking, this long while, to give it up, whenever the Commander-in-Chief required. To quit his laborious sentry-post; honorably lay up his arms, and be gone to his rest: — all Eternity to rest in, O George! Was thy own life merry, for example, in the hollow of the tree; clad permanently in leather? And does kingly purple, and governing refractory worlds instead of stitching coarse shoes, make it merrier? The waft of death is not against *him*, I think, — perhaps against thee, and me, and others, O George, when the Nell-Gwynn Defender and Two Centuries of all-victorious Cant have come in upon us! My unfortunate George — "a waft of death go forth against him; and when I came to him, he looked like a dead man. After I had laid the Sufferings of Friends before him, and had

[1] *Fox's Journal*, i. 381, 382.

warned him according as I was moved to speak to him, he bade me come to his house. So I returned to Kingston; and, the next day, went up to Hampton Court to speak farther with him. But when I came, Harvey, who was one that waited on him, told me the Doctors were not willing that I should speak with him. So I passed away, and never saw him more." [1]

Friday, the 20th of August, 1658, this was probably the day on which George Fox saw Oliver riding into Hampton Park with his Guards, for the last time. That Friday, as we find, his Highness seemed much better: but on the morrow a sad change had taken place; feverish symptoms, for which the Doctors rigorously prescribed quiet. Saturday to Tuesday the symptoms continued ever worsening: a kind of tertian ague, "bastard tertian" as the old Doctors name it; for which it was ordered that his Highness should return to Whitehall, as to a more favorable air in that complaint. On Tuesday accordingly he quitted Hampton Court; — never to see it more.

"His time was come," says Harvey; "and neither prayers nor tears could prevail with God to lengthen out his life and continue him longer to us. Prayers abundantly and incessantly poured out on his behalf, both publicly and privately, as was observed, in a more than ordinary way. Besides many a secret sigh, — secret and unheard by men, yet like the cry of Moses, more loud, and strongly laying hold on God, than many spoken supplications. All which — the hearts of God's People being thus mightily stirred up — did seem to beget confidence in some, and hopes in all; yea some thoughts in himself, that God would restore him."

"Prayers public and private:" they are worth imagining to ourselves. Meetings of Preachers, Chaplains, and Godly Persons; "Owen, Goodwin, Sterry, with a company of others, in an adjoining room;" in Whitehall, and elsewhere over religious London and England, fervent outpourings of many a loyal heart. For there were hearts to whom the nobleness of this man was known; and his worth to the Puritan Cause

[1] *Fox's Journal*, pp. 485, 486.

was evident. Prayers, — strange enough to us; in a dialect
fallen obsolete, forgotten now. Authentic wrestlings of ancient
Human Souls, — who were alive then, with their affections,
awe-struck pieties; with their Human Wishes, risen to be
transcendent, hoping to prevail with the Inexorable. All swallowed now in the depths of dark Time; which is full of such,
since the beginning! — Truly it is a great scene of World-
History, this in old Whitehall: Oliver Cromwell drawing nigh
to his end. The exit of Oliver Cromwell and of English Puritanism; a great Light, one of our few authentic Solar Lumi-
naries, going down now amid the clouds of Death. Like the
setting of a great victorious Summer Sun; its course now
finished. "*So stirbt ein Held*," says Schiller, "So dies a Hero!
Sight worthy to be worshipped!" — He died, this Hero Oliver,
in Resignation to God; as the Brave have all done. "We
could not be more desirous he should abide," says the pious
Harvey, "than he was content and willing to be gone." The
struggle lasted, amid hope and fear, for ten days. — Some
small miscellaneous traits, and confused gleanings of last-
words; and then our poor History ends.

Oliver, we find, spoke much of "the Covenants;" which
indeed are the grand axis of all, in that Puritan Universe of
his. Two Covenants; one of Works, with fearful Judgment
for our shortcomings therein; one of Grace and unspeakable
mercy; — gracious Engagements, "Covenants," which the Eternal God has vouchsafed to make with His feeble creature Man.
Two; and by Christ's Death they have become One: there for
Oliver is the divine solution of this our Mystery of Life.[1]
"They were Two," he was heard ejaculating: "Two, but put
into One before the Foundation of the World!" And again:
"It is holy and true, it is holy and true, it is holy and true!
— Who made it holy and true? The Mediator of the Covenant!" And again: "The Covenant is but One. Faith in
the Covenant is my only support. And if I believe not, He
abides faithful!" When his Children and Wife stood weeping

[1] Much intricate intense reasoning to this effect, on this subject, in Owen's
Works, among others.

round him, he said : "Love not this world. I say unto you, it is not good that you should love this world!" No. "Chil- dren, live like Christians :— I leave you the Covenant to feed upon!" Yea, my brave one; even so! The Covenant, and eternal Soul of Covenants, remains sure to all the faithful: deeper than the Foundations of this World; earlier than they, and more lasting than they!—

Look also at the following; dark hues and bright; immortal light-beams struggling amid the black vapors of Death. Look; and conceive a great sacred scene, the sacredest this world sees;— and think of it, do not speak of it, in these mean days which have no sacred word. "Is there none that says, Who will deliver me from the peril?" moaned he once. Many hearts are praying, O wearied one! "Man can do nothing," rejoins he; "God can do what He will."— Another time, again thinking of the Covenant, "Is there none that will come and praise God," whose mercies endure forever!—

Here also are ejaculations caught up at intervals, undated, in those final days : "Lord, Thou knowest, if I do desire to live, it is to show forth Thy praise and declare Thy works!" — Once he was heard saying, "It is a fearful thing to fall into the hands of the Living God!"[1] "This was spoken three times," says Harvey; "his repetitions usually being very weighty, and with great vehemency of spirit." Thrice over he said this; looking into the Eternal Kingdoms : "A fearful thing to fall into the hands of the Living God!"— But again : "All the promises of God are in *Him :* yes, and in Him Amen; to the glory of God by us, — by *us* in Jesus Christ."— "The Lord hath filled me with as much assurance of His pardon, and His love, as my soul can hold."— "I think I am the poorest wretch that lives : but I love God; or rather, am beloved of God."— "I am a conqueror, and more than a conqueror, through Christ that strengtheneth me!"[2]

So pass, in the sick-room, in the sick-bed, these last heavy uncertain days. "The Godly Persons had great assurances of a return to their Prayers :" transcendent Human Wishes find

[1] Hebrews x. 31.

[2] From Harvey; scattered over his Pamphlet.

in their own echo a kind of answer! They gave his Highness
also some assurance that his life would be lengthened. Hope
was strong in many to the very end.

On Monday, August 30th, there roared and howled all day
a mighty storm of wind. Ludlow, coming up to town from
Essex, could not start in the morning for wind; tried it in the
afternoon; still could not get along, in his coach, for head-
wind; had to stop at Epping.[1] On the morrow, Fleetwood
came to him in the Protector's name, to ask, What he wanted
here? — Nothing of public concernment, only to see my
Mother-in-law! answered the solid man. For indeed he did
not know that Oliver was dying; that the glorious hour of
Disenthralment, and immortal "Liberty" to plunge over precipices with one's self and one's Cause was so nigh! — It
came; and he took the precipices, like a strong-boned resolute
blind gin-horse rejoicing in the breakage of its halter, in a
very gallant constitutional manner. Adieu, my solid friend;
if I go to Vevay, I will read thy Monument there, perhaps not
without emotion, after all! —

It was on this stormy Monday, while rocking winds, heard
in the sick-room and everywhere, were piping aloud, that
Thurloe and an Official person entered to inquire, Who, in
case of the worst, was to be his Highness's Successor? The
Successor is named in a sealed Paper already drawn up, above
a year ago, at Hampton Court; now lying in such and such a
place. The paper was sent for, searched for; it could never
be found. Richard's is the name understood to have been
written in that Paper: not a good name; but in fact one does
not know. In ten years' time, had ten years more been
granted, Richard might have become a fitter man; might have
been cancelled, if palpably unfit. Or perhaps it was Fleetwood's name, — and the Paper, by certain parties, was stolen?
None knows. On the Thursday night following, "and not
till then," his Highness is understood to have formally named
"Richard;" — or perhaps it might only be some heavy-laden
"Yes, yes!" spoken, out of the thick death-slumbers, in answer to Thurloe's *question* "Richard?" The thing is a little

[1] Ludlow, ii. 610–612.

uncertain.[1] It was, once more, a matter of much moment; — giving color probably to all the subsequent Centuries of England, this answer! —

On or near the night of the same stormy Monday, "two or three days before he died," we are to place that Prayer his Highness was heard uttering; which, as taken down by his attendants, exists in many old Note-books. In the tumult of the winds, the dying Oliver was heard uttering this

PRAYER.

"Lord, though I am a miserable and wretched creature, I am in Covenant with Thee through grace. And I may, I will, come to Thee, for Thy People. Thou hast made me, though very unworthy, a mean instrument to do them some good, and Thee service; and many of them have set too high a value upon me, though others wish and would be glad of my death; Lord, however Thou do dispose of me, continue and go on to do good for them. Give them consistency of judgment, one heart, and mutual love; and go on to deliver them, and with the work of reformation; and make the Name of Christ glorious in the world. Teach those who look too much on Thy instruments, to depend more upon Thyself. Pardon such as desire to trample upon the dust of a poor worm, for they are Thy People too. And pardon the folly of this short Prayer: — Even for Jesus Christ's sake. And give us a good night, if it be Thy pleasure. Amen."

"Some variation there is," says Harvey, "of this Prayer, as to the account divers give of it; and something is here omitted. But so much is certain, that these were his requests. Wherein his heart was so carried out for God and His People, — yea indeed some who had added no little sorrow to him," the Anabaptist Republicans, and others, — "that at this time he seems to forget his own Family and nearest relations." Which indeed is to be remarked.

[1] Authorities in Godwin, iv. 572, 573. But see also *Thurloe*, vii. 375; Fauconberg's second Letter there.

Thursday night the Writer of our old Pamphlet was himself in attendance on his Highness; and has preserved a trait or two; with which let us hasten to conclude. To-morrow is September Third, always kept as a Thanksgiving day, since the Victories of Dunbar and Worcester. The wearied one "that very night before the Lord took him to his everlasting rest," was heard thus, with oppressed voice, speaking: —

"'Truly God is good; indeed He is; He will not—' Then his speech failed him, but as I apprehended, it was, 'He will not leave me.' This saying, 'God is good,' he frequently used all along; and would speak it with much cheerfulness, and fervor of spirit, in the midst of his pains. — Again he said: 'I would be willing to live to be farther serviceable to God and His People: but my work is done. Yet God will be with His People.'

"He was very restless most part of the night, speaking often to himself. And there being something to drink offered him, he was desired To take the same, and endeavor to sleep. — Unto which he answered: 'It is not my design to drink or sleep; but my design is, to make what haste I can to be gone.' —

"Afterwards, towards morning, he used divers holy expressions, implying much inward consolation and peace; among the rest he spake some exceeding self-debasing words, *annihilating* and judging himself. And truly it was observed, that a public spirit to God's Cause did breathe in him, — as in his lifetime, so now to his very last."

When the morrow's sun rose, Oliver was speechless; between three and four in the afternoon, he lay dead. Friday, 3d September, 1658. "The consternation and astonishment of all people," writes Fauconberg,[1] "are inexpressible; their hearts seem as if sunk within them. My poor Wife, — I know not what on earth to do with her. When seemingly quieted, she bursts out again into a passion that tears her very heart in pieces." — Husht, poor weeping Mary! Here is a Life-battle right nobly done. Seest thou not,

[1] To Henry Cromwell, 7th September, 1658 (*Thurloe*, vii. 375).

"The storm is changed into a calm,
    At His command and will;
So that the waves which raged before
    Now quiet are and still!

" Then are *they* glad, — because at rest
    And quiet now they be:
So to the haven He them brings
    Which they desired to see."

"Blessed are the dead that die in the Lord;" blessed are the valiant that have lived in the Lord. "Amen, saith the Spirit," — Amen. "They do rest from their labors, and their works follow them."

"Their works follow them." As, I think, this Oliver Cromwell's works have done and are still doing! We have had our "Revolutions of Eighty-eight," officially called "glorious;" and other Revolutions not yet called glorious; and somewhat has been gained for poor Mankind. Men's ears are not now slit off by rash Officiality; Officiality will, for long henceforth, be more cautious about men's ears. The tyrannous Starchambers, branding-irons, chimerical Kings and Surplices at All-hallowtide, they are gone, or with immense velocity going. Oliver's works do follow him! — The works of a man, bury them under what guano-mountains and obscene owl-droppings you will, do not perish, cannot perish. What of Heroism, what of Eternal Light was in a Man and his Life, is with very great exactness added to the Eternities; remains forever a new divine portion of the Sum of Things; and no owl's voice, this way or that, in the least avails in the matter. — But we have to end here.

Oliver is gone; and with him England's Puritanism, laboriously built together by this man, and made a thing far-shining, miraculous to its own Century, and memorable to all the Centuries, soon goes. Puritanism, without its King, is *kingless*, anarchic; falls into dislocation, self-collision; staggers, plunges into ever deeper anarchy; King, Defender of the Puritan Faith there can now none be found; — and nothing is left but to recall the old disowned Defender with the remnants of his Four Surplices, and Two Centuries of *Hypocrisis* (or Play-acting *not* so called), and put up with all that, the best we may. The Genius of England no longer soars Sunward, world-defiant, like an Eagle through the storms, "mewing her mighty youth," as John Milton saw her do : the Genius of England, much liker a greedy Ostrich intent on provender and a whole skin mainly, stands with its *other* extremity Sunward ; with its Ostrich head stuck into the readiest bush, of old Church-tippets, King-cloaks, or what other "sheltering Fallacy" there may be, and *so* awaits the issue. The issue has been slow ; but it is now seen to have been inevitable. No Ostrich, intent on gross terrene provender, and sticking its head into Fallacies, but will be awakened one day, — in a terrible *à-posteriori* manner, if not otherwise ! — Awake before it come to that ; gods and men bid us awake ! The Voices of our Fathers, with thousand-fold stern monition to one and all, bid us awake.

APPENDIX.

No. 1.

LETTER TO DOWNHALL.

[Vol. xvii. p. 54.]

THE stolen Letter of the Ashmole Museum has been found printed, and even reprinted. It is of the last degree of insignificance: a mere Note of Invitation to Downhall to stand "Godfather unto my Child." Man-child now ten days old,[1] who, as we may see, is christened " on Thursday next" by the name of RICHARD, — and had strange ups and downs as a Man when it came to that!

"*To my approved good Friend Mr. Henry Downhall, at his Chambers in St. John's College, Cambridge: These.*

"HUNTINGDON, 14th October, 1626.

" LOVING SIR, — Make me so much your servant as to be [2] Godfather unto my Child. I would myself have come over to have made a formal invitation; but my occasions would not permit me: and therefore hold me in that excused. The Day of your trouble is Thursday next. Let me entreat your company on Wednesday.

" By this time it appears, I am more apt to encroach upon you for new favors than to show my thankfulness for the love I have already found. But I know your patience and your goodness cannot be exhausted by

" Your friend and servant,

" OLIVER CROMWELL." [3]

Of this Downhall, sometimes written Down*hault*, and even Down*ett* and Down*tell*; who grounds his claim, such as it is, to human remem-

---

[1] Vol. xvii. p. 69. [2] " by being " in orig.
[3] Hearne's *Liber Niger Scaccarii* (London, 1771), i. 261 n.

brance on the above small Note from Oliver, — a helpful hand has, with unsubduable research, discovered various particulars, which might amount almost to an outline of a history of Downhall, were such needed. He was of Northamptonshire, come of gentlefolks in that County. Admitted Fellow of St. John's College, Cambridge, 12th April, 1614; — had known Oliver, and apparently been helpful and instructive to him, two years after that.   More interesting still, he this same Downhall was Vicar of St. Ives when Oliver came thither in 1635; still Vicar when Oliver left it, though with far other tendencies than Oliver's now; and had, alas, to be "ejected with his Curate, in 1642," as an Anti-Puritan Malignant:[1] — Oliver's course and his having altogether parted now!   Nay farther, the same Downhall, surviving the Restoration, became "Archdeacon of Huntingdon" in 1667: fifty-one years ago he had lodged there as Oliver Cromwell's Guest and Gossip; and now he comes as Archdeacon, — with a very strange set of *Annals* written in his old head, poor Downhall!   He died "at Cottingham in Northamptonshire, his native region, in the winter-time of 1669;"—and so, with his Ashmole Letter, ends.[2]

No. 2.

AT ELY.

[Vol. xvii. p. 92.]

THERE is at Ely a Charitable Foundation now above four centuries old; which in Oliver's time was named the *Ely Feoffees' Fund*, and is now known as *Parsons's Charity;* the old Records of which, though somewhat mutilated during those years, offer one or two faint but indubitable vestiges of Oliver, not to be neglected on the present occasion.

This *Charity* of ancient worthy Thomas *Parsons*, it appears, had, shortly before Oliver's arrival in Ely, been somewhat remodelled by a new Royal Charter: To be henceforth more specially devoted to the Poor of Ely; to be governed by Twelve Feoffees; namely, by Three

---

[1] Vol. xvii. p. 86.

[2] Cooper's *Annals of Cambridge*, iii. 187; and MS. communicated by Mr. Cooper, resting on the following formidable mass of documentary Authorities:

Cole MSS. (which is a Transcript of Baker's *History of St. John's College*), 166, 358; Rymer's *Fœdera*, xix. 261; Le Neve's *Fasti Ecclesiæ Anglicanæ*, p. 160; Kennet's *Register and Chronicle*, pp. 207, 251; Walker's *Sufferings*, ii. 129, 130; Wood's *Athenæ* (2d edition, passage wanting in both the 1st and 3d), ii. 1179.

Dignitaries of the Cathedral, and by Nine Townsmen of the better sort, who are permanent, and fill up their own vacancies,[1]— of which latter class, Oliver Cromwell Esquire, most likely elected in his Uncle's stead, was straightway made one. The old Books, as we say, are specially defective in those years; " have lost 40 or 50 leaves at the end of Book I., and 12 leaves at the beginning of Book II.,"—leaves cut out for the sake of Oliver's autograph, or as probably for other reasons. Detached Papers, however, still indicate that Oliver was one of the Feoffees, and a moderately diligent one, almost from his first residence there. Here, under date some six or seven months after his arrival, is a small Entry in certain loose Papers, labelled *" The Accompts of Mr. John Hand and Mr. Wm. Crauford, Collectors of the Revenewes belonging to the Towne of Ely"* (that is, to Parsons's Charity in Ely); and under this special head, *" The Disbursements of Mr. John Hand, from the — of August*, 1636, *unto the — of —* 1641 : —

" Given to divers Poore People at y⁰ Work-house, in the presence of Mr. Archdeacon of Ely,[2] Mr. Oliver Cromwell, Mr. John Goodricke and others, 10th February, 1636, as appeareth . . } £16 14 0."

And under this other head, *" The Disbursements of Mr. Crauford,"* which unluckily are not dated, and run vaguely from 1636 to 1641 :

" Item to Jones, by Mr. Cromwell's consent . . . £1 0 0."

Twice or thrice elsewhere the name of Cromwell is mentioned, but not as indicating activity on his part, indicating merely Feoffeeship and passivity;[3]— except in the following instance, where there is still extant a small Letter of his. " Mr. Hand," as we have soon, is one of the " Collectors," himself likewise a Feoffee or Governor, the Governors (it would appear) taking that office in turn.

[To Mr. Hand, at Ely : These.]

" [ELY,] 13th September, 1638.

" MR. HAND, — I doubt not but I shall be as good as my word for your Money. I desire you to deliver Forty Shillings of the Town Money

---

[1] *Report of the Commissioners concerning Charities* (London, 1837): distinct account of it there, § Cambridgeshire, pp. 218-220.

[2] One " Wigmore ; " the Dean was " William Fuller ; " the Bishop " Matthew Wren," very famous for his Popish Candles and other fripperies, who lay long in the Tower afterwards. These were the three Clerical Feoffees in Oliver's time.

[3] Excerpts of Documents obligingly communicated by the Dean of Ely, — now *penes* Mr. Cooper of Cambridge.

to this Bearer, to pay for the physic for Benson's cure. If the Gentlemen will not allow it at the time of account, keep this Note, and I will pay it out of my own purse. So I rest,

"Your loving friend,
"OLIVER CROMWELL."[1]

Poor "Benson" is an old invalid. Among Mr. Hand's Disbursements for the year 1636 is this : —

"For phisicke and surgery for old Benson   .   £2   7   4."

And among Crauford's, of we know not what year : —

"To Benson at divers times   .   .   .   .   £0 15   0."

Let him have forty shillings more, poor old man; and if the Gentlemen won't allow it, Oliver Cromwell will pay it out of his own purse.

———————◆———————

No. 3.

CAMBRIDGE : CORPORATION (1641) ; WHELOCKE (1643).

[Vol. xvii. pp. 115 ; — 130, 138.]

TWO vestiges of Oliver at Cambridge, in his parliamentary and in his military capacity, there still are.

1. The first, which relates to a once very public Affair, is his Letter (his and Lowry's) to the Cambridge Authorities, in May, 1641 ; Letter accompanying the celebrated "Protestation and Preamble" just sent forth by the House of Commons, with earnest invitation to all constituencies to adopt the same.

"*A Preamble, with the Protestation made by the whole House of Commons the 3d of May, 1641, and assented unto by the Lords of the Upper House the 4th of May.*

"We, the Knights, Citizens and Burgesses of the Commons House, in Parliament, finding, to the grief of our hearts, That the designs of

---

[1] *Memoirs of the Protector,* by Oliver Cromwell, a Descendant &c. (London, 1822), i. 351 ; where also (p. 350) is found, in a very indistinct state, the above-given Entry from *Hand's Accompts,* misdated "1641," instead of 10th February, 1636–7. The Letter to Hand "has not been among the Feoffees' Papers for several years ; " and is now (1846) none knows where.

the Priests and Jesuits, and other Adherents to the See of Rome, have been of late more boldly and frequently put in practice than formerly, to the undermining, and danger of ruin, of the True Reformed Religion in his Majesty's Dominions established: And finding also that there hath been, and having cause to suspect there still are even during the sitting in Parliament, endeavors to subvert the Fundamental Laws of England and Ireland, and to introduce the exercise of an Arbitrary and Tyrannical Government, by most pernicious and wicked counsels, plots and conspiracies: And that the long intermission, and unhappier breach, of Parliaments hath occasioned many illegal Taxations, whereupon the Subjects have been prosecuted and grieved: And that divers Innovations and Superstitions have been brought into the Church; multitudes driven out of his Majesty's dominions; jealousies raised and fomented between the King and People; a Popish Army levied in Ireland,[1] and Two Armies brought into the bowels of this Kingdom, to the hazard of his Majesty's royal Person, the consumption of the revenue of the Crown, and the treasure of this Realm: And lastly, finding great causes of jealousy that endeavors[2] have been and are used to bring the English Army into misunderstanding of this Parliament, thereby to incline that Army by force to bring to pass those wicked counsels, —

"Have therefore thought good to join ourselves in a declaration of our united affections and resolutions; and to make this ensuing

"PROTESTATION.

"I, A. B., do in the Presence of Almighty God promise, vow and protest, To maintain and defend as far as lawfully I may, with my life, power and estate, the True Reformed Protestant Religion, expressed in the Doctrine of the Church of England, against all Popery and Popish Innovations, and according to the duty of my allegiance to his Majesty's royal Person, Honor and Estate: as also the Power and Privilege of Parliament, the Lawful Rights and Liberties of the Subjects; and every Person that maketh this Protestation in whatsoever he shall do in the lawful pursuance of the same. And to my power, as far as lawfully I may, I will oppose, and by good ways and means endeavor to bring to condign punishment all such as shall, by force, practice, counsel, plots, conspiracies or otherwise, do anything to the contrary in this present Protestation contained.

[1] By Strafford lately, against the Scots and their enterprises.

[2] This is the important point, nearly shaded out of sight: "finding the great causes of jealousy, endeavors have" &c. is the tremulous, indistinct and even ungrammatical phrase in the original.

" And farther I shall, in all just and honorable ways, endeavor to preserve the union and peace betwixt the Three Kingdoms of England, Scotland and Ireland; and neither for hope, fear nor other respect, shall relinquish this Promise, Vow and Protestation." [1]

This is on Monday, 3d May, 1641, while the Apprentices are bellowing in Palace-yard : Cromwell is one of those that take the Protestation this same Monday, present in the House while the redacting of it goes on.   Long lists of Members take it, — not John Lowry, who I conclude must have been absent.   On Wednesday, 5th May, there is this Order : —

" *Ordered,* That the Protestation made by the Members of this House, with the Preamble, shall be together printed ; " Clerk to attest the copies ; all Members to send them down to the respective Sheriffs, Justices, to the respective Cities, Boroughs, and "intimate with what willingness the Members made this Protestation ; and that as they justify the taking of it in themselves, so they cannot but approve it in them that shall likewise take it."

Strict *Order,* at the same time, That all Members " now in Town and not sick shall appear here To-morrow at Eight of Clock," and take this Protestation : non-appearance to be " accounted a contempt of this House," and expose one to be expelled, or worse ; — in spite of which John Lowry still does not sign, not till Friday morning, after even " Philip Warwick " and " Endymion Porter " have signed : whence I infer he was out of Town or unwell. [2] — This Letter, which seems to be of Cromwell's writing, still stands on the Corporation Books of Cambridge ; read in Common Council there on the 11th May ; at which time, said Letter being read, the Town Authorities did one and all zealously accept the same, and signed the Protestation on the spot. The Letter is not dated ; but as Lowry signed on Friday, and the Corporation meeting is on Tuesday, the 11th, we may safely guess the Letter to have arrived on Monday, and to have been written on Saturday.

" To the Right Worshipful the Mayor and Aldermen of Cambridge, with the rest of that Body : Present these.

" [LONDON, 8th] May, 1641.

" GENTLEMEN, — We heartily salute you ; and herewith, according to the directions of the House of Commons in this present Parliament assembled, send unto you a Protestation ; — the contents whereof will

---

[1] *Commons Journals,* ii. 132 (3d May, 1641).

[2] *Ibid.* ii. 133, 5, 6, 7. Rushworth, iv. 241 et seqq.

best appear in the thing itself. The Preamble therewith printed doth declare the weighty reasons inducing them, in their own persons, to begin [making it].

" We shall only let you know that, with alacrity and willingness, the Members of that Body entered thereinto. It was in them a right honorable and necessary act; not unworthy your imitation. You shall hereby as the Body Represented avow the practice of the Representative. The conformity is in itself praiseworthy; and will be by them approved. The result may, through the Almighty's blessing, become stability and security to the whole Kingdom. Combination carries strength with it. It's dreadful to adversaries; especially when it's in order to the duty we owe to God, to the loyalty we owe to our King and Sovereign, and to the affection due to our Country and Liberties, — the main ends of this Protestation now herewith sent you.

" We say no more: but commit you to the protection of Him who is able to save you; desiring your prayers for the good success of our present affairs and endeavors, — which indeed are not ours, but the Lord's and yours. Whom we desire to serve in integrity: and bidding you heartily Farewell, rest,

" Your loving friends to be commanded,

" OLIVER CROMWELL.
JOHN LOWRY." [1]

2. The second is a small antiquarian relic (date, Spring, 1643); dim and of little worth in its detached form, but capable of lighting itself up, and the reader's fancy along with it, when set in the right combination.

" Mr. Abraham Whelocke," whose name and works are still well enough known, was, later in that century, " the celebrated Professor of Arabic at Oxford;" and is now, we perceive, in this Spring, 1643, a Student at Cambridge; of meditative peripatetic habits; often walking into the country with a little Arabic Volume in his pocket: — apt to be fluttered at the Town Gates by these new military arrangements. In this difficulty he calls on Colonel Cromwell; and — But his little Volume itself is still extant, and tells its own story and his. A thin duodecimo, in white hog-skin binding now grown very brown; size handy for the smallest coat-pocket: — and on the fly-leaf, in Oliver's hand, stands written (signed successively by three other Committee-men whom Whelocke would soon search out for the feat): —

---

[1] Cambridge Corporation Day-Book: in Cooper's *Annals of Cambridge*, iii. 311. Printed also, with errors, in O. Cromwell's *Memoirs of the Protector*, i. 406.

"4th APRIL, 1643.

"Suffer the Bearer hereof, Mr Abraham Whelocke, to pass your guards so often as he shall have occasion, into and out of Cambridge, towards Little Shelford or any other place; and this shall be your warrant.

"THO. COOKE.   OLIVER CROMWELL.[1]

EDW. CLENCHE.   JAMES THOMPSON."

No. 4.

EASTERN ASSOCIATION: THREATENED RISING OF PAPISTS IN NORFOLK.

[Vol. xvii. p. 126.]

TWO Committee-Letters, both of Oliver's writing; illustrations of his diligent procedure in the birth-time of the Eastern Association.

" *To our noble Friends, Sir John Hobart, Sir Thomas Richardson, Sir John Potts, Sir John Palgrave, [Sir] John Spelman, Knights and Baronets, and the rest of the Deputy-Lieutenants for the County of Norfolk: Present these.*

[CAMBRIDGE, 26th January, 1642.]

" GENTLEMEN, — The Parliament and the Lord General have taken into their care the peace and protection 'of these Eastern parts of the Kingdom; and to that end have sent down hither some part of their Forces, — as likewise a Commission, with certain Instructions to us and others directed; all which do highly concern the peace and safety of your County. Therefore we entreat that some of you would give us a meeting at Mildenhall[2] in Suffolk, on Tuesday, the 31st of this instant January. And in the mean time that you would make all possible

---

[1] Whelocke's Arabic Volume (a version into Arabic of one of Bellarmin's Books, by some Armenian Patriarch, for benefit of the Heathen, Rome, 1627, — with slight marks of Whelocke on the other fly-leaves): Volume now in the possession of Dr. Lee, Hartwell, Buckinghamshire, who has kindly given me sight of it. — Next year, under this Pass of Oliver's, lower half of the same fly-leaf, there is a Renewal of it, or Copy in almost precisely the same terms, written and signed by the Earl of Manchester (in ink now grown very pale, while Oliver's has changed to strong red-brown), of date "27th February, 1643"–4, when his Lordship again for a time (see vol. xvii. p. 177) had become chief Authority in Cambridge. (*Note of 1857.*)

[2] "Millnall" he writes.

speed to have in a readiness, against any notice shall be given, a considerable force of Horse and Foot to join with us, to keep any Enemy's force from breaking in upon your yet peaceable Country. For we have certain intelligence that some of Prince Rupert's forces are come as far as Wellingborough in Northamptonshire, and that the Papists in Norfolk are solicited to rise presently upon you.

"Thus presenting all our neighborly and loving respects, we rest,

"Your respective friends to serve you,

MILES SANDYS.

"TERRELL JOCELYN.   FRANC. RUSSELL.
WILLM. MARCHE.   OLIVER CROMWELL.
EDW. CLENCHE.   THOMAS SYMONS.
JAMES THOMPSON.   ROBERT CLERKE."[1]

"*To our worthy Friends, Sir John Hobart, Sir Thomas Richardson, Sir John Potts, Sir John Palgrave, Sir John Spelman, Knights and Baronets. Present these :*

"CAMBRIDGE, 27th January, 1642.

"GENTLEMEN, — The grounds of your Jealousies are real. They concur with our intelligences from Windsor; the sum whereof we give unto you : —

"From a prisoner taken by Sir Samuel Luke (one Mr. Gandy, a Captain of Dragooners) this confession was drawn, That the Papists by direction from Oxford should rise in Norfolk. Whereupon it was desired from thence That Sir Henry Benningfield and Mr. Gandy, their persons should be seized, and that we should do our endeavor to make stay of the Person and Letter which contained this encouragement to them, — he being described by his horse and clothes. But we believe [he] was past us before we had notice, for our Scouts could not light on him.

"As for the other consideration of his Majesty's forces being invited into these parts, we have confirmation thereof from all hands; — and there is this reason to doubt it will be so, Because his Majesty is weary of Oxford; there being little in those parts left to sustain his Army, — and surely the fulness of these parts and fitness of them for Horse are too-too good arguments to invite him hither. Thus we agree in the grounds of our doubt and fear.

"The next thought is of Remedy. And in this we account it our happiness to consult with you of common safety, to be had either by the

---

[1] Original in Tanner MSS. lxiv. 116.

Association you speak of, or by [1] any other consideration by communication of assistance, according to necessity.   Wherein I hope you shall find all readiness and cheerfulness in us, to assist you to break any strength that shall be gathered ; or to prevent it, if desired, — having timely notice given from you thereof.   The way will be best settled, if you give us a meeting, according to our desire by a Letter particularly prepared [2] before we received yours, and now sent unto you for that purpose together with these.

" This is all we can say for the present ; but that we are,
" Your friends and servants,
MILES SANDYS.

" THOM. MARTYN.   FRANC. RUSSELL.   TERRELL JOCELYN.
OLIVER CROMWELL.   THOS. SYMONS.
WILLM. MARCHE.   ROBERT CLERKE.
EDW. CLENCHE.   JAMES THOMPSON.

" [P.S.]   We sent to Sir William Spring to offer him our assistance for the apprehension of Sir H. Benningfield, &c.   We have not yet received any answer. — We knew not how to address ourselves to you. It's our desire to assist you in that or any other public service." [3]

———◆———

No. 5.

GAINSBOROUGH FIGHT.

[Vol. xvii. p. 153.]

HERE are other details concerning Gainsborough Fight; Two Letters upon it that have successively turned up.

1. The first is a Letter two days earlier in date ; evidently not written by Cromwell, though signed by him and two chief Lincolnshire Committee-men, as he passes through their City on his way to Huntingdon.   Sir Edward Ayscough, or " Ayscoghe " as he here signs himself, — probably a kinsman of Sir George the Sailor's, possibly the father of the " Captain Ayscoghe " mentioned here, — he and John Broxholme, Esq., both of the Lincolnshire Committee,[4] are clearly the writers of the present Letter.

[1] Comes to the end of the sheet, and turns to the margin.
[2] Preceding Letter, seemingly, or rather Copy of it.
[3] Original, in Cromwell's own hand throughout, in Tanner MSS. lxiv. 129.
[4] Husband, ii. 171.

"*For the Honorable William Lenthall, Esquire, Speaker of the Commons House of Parliament: These.*

"LINCOLN, 29th July, 1643 (Six o'clock at night).

" NOBLE SIR, — We, having solicited a conjunction of Forces towards the raising of the Siege of Gainsborough, did appoint a general rendezvous at North Scarle to be upon Thursday, the 27th of July. To the which place, Sir John Meldrum with about Three Hundred Horse and Dragoons, and Colonel Cromwell with about Six or Seven Troops of Horse and about One Hundred Dragoons, came. With these they marched towards Gainsborough; and meeting with a good party of the Enemy about a mile from the Town, beat them back, — but not with any commendations to our Dragoons. We advanced still towards the Enemy, all along under the Cony-Warren, which is upon a high Hill above Gainsborough. The Lincoln Troops had the van, two Northampton, and three small Troops of Nottingham the battle, and Colonel Cromwell the rear; the Enemy in the mean time with his body keeping the top of the Hill.

"Some of the Lincoln Troops began to advance up the Hill; which were opposed by a force of the Enemy; but our men repelled them, until all our whole body was got up the Hill. The Enemy kept his ground; which he chose for his best advantage, with a body of Horse of about Three Regiments of Horse, and a reserve behind them consisting of General Cavendish his Regiment, which was a very full regiment. We presently put our Horse in order; which we could hardly do by reason of the cony-holes and the difficult ascent up the Hill; the Enemy being within musket-shot of us, and advancing towards us before we could get ourselves into any good order. But with those Troops we could get up, we charged the greater body of the Enemy; came up to the sword's point; and disputed it so a little with them, that our men pressing heavily upon them, they could not bear it, but all their Body ran away, some on the one side of their Reserve, others on the other. Divers of our Troops pursuing had the chase about six miles.

"General Cavendish with his Regiment standing firm all the while, and facing some of our Troops that did not follow the chase, — Colonel Cromwell, with his Major Whalley and one or two Troops more, were following the chase, and were in the rear of that Regiment. When they saw the body stand unbroken, [they] endeavored, with much ado, to get into a body those three or four Troops which were divided. Which when they had done, — perceiving the Enemy to charge two or three of the Lincoln scattered Troops, and to make them retire by reason of their being many more than they in number; and the rest being elsewhere engaged and following the chase, — Colonel Cromwell with his three Troops followed them in the rear; brake this Regiment; and forced their General, with divers of their men, into a quagmire in the bottom of the Hill. Where one of Colonel Cromwell his men cut General Cavendish on the head; by reason whereof he fell off his horse; and the Colonel's[1] Captain-Lieutenant thrust him into the side, whereof within two hours he died; — the rest chasing his Regiment quite out of the field, having execution of them, so that the field was left wholly unto us, not a man appearing. Upon this, divers of our men went into the Town, carrying in to my Lord Willoughby some of the Ammunition we brought for him; — believing that our work was at an end; saving to take care how to bring farther provisions into the Town, to enable it to stand a siege in case my Lord Newcastle should draw up with his Army to attempt it.

"Whilst we were considering of these things, word was brought us That there was a small remainder of the Enemy's force not yet meddled with, about a mile beyond Gainsborough, with some Foot, and two pieces of Ordnance. We having no Foot, desired to have some out of the Town; which my Lord Willoughby granted, and sent us about Six Hundred Foot: with these we advanced towards the Enemy. When we came thither to the top of the hill, we beat divers Troops of the Enemy's Horse back: but at the bottom we saw a Regiment of Foot; after that another (my Lord Newcastle's own Regiment, consisting of nineteen colors) appearing also, and many Horse; — which indeed was his Army. Seeing these there so unexpectedly, we advised what to do.

"Colonel Cromwell was sent to command the Foot to retire, and to draw off the Horse. By the time he came to them, the Enemy was marching up the hill. The Foot did retire disorderly into the Town, which was not much above a quarter of a mile from them; upon whom the Enemy's Horse did some small execution. The Horse also did retire in some disorder, about half a mile, — until they came to the end of a field where a passage was; where, by the endeavor of Colonel Cromwell, [of] Major Whalley and Captain Ayscoghe, a body was drawn up. With these we faced the Enemy; stayed their pursuit; and opposed them with about four Troops of Colonel Cromwell's and four Lincoln Troops; the Enemy's body in the mean time increasing very much from the Army. But such was the goodness of God,

---

[1] Original has "his;" and for "General Cavendish" in the foregoing line "him."

giving courage and valor to our men and officers, that whilst Major
Whalley and Captain Ayscoghe, sometimes the one with four Troops
faced the Enemy, sometimes the other, to the exceeding glory of God be
it spoken, and the great honor of those two Gentlemen, they with this
handful forced the Enemy so, and dared them to their teeth in at the
least eight or nine several removes, — the Enemy following at their
heels; and they, though their horses were exceedingly tired, retreating
in order, near carbine-shot of the Enemy, who thus followed them,
firing upon them; Colonel Cromwell gathering up the main body and
facing them, behind those two lesser bodies, — that, in despite of the
Enemy, we brought off our Horse in this order, without the loss of two
men.

"Thus have you a true relation of this notable service: wherein God
is to have all the glory. And care must be taken speedily to relieve
this noble Lord from his and the State's Enemies, by a speedy force
sent unto us, — and that without any delay; or else he will be lost,
and that important Town, and all those parts; and way made for this
Army instantly to advance into the South. Thus resting upon your
care in speeding present Succors hither, we humbly take our leaves,
and remain,

"Your humble servants,

"EDW. AYSCOGHE.
JO. BROXOLME.
OLIVER CROMWELL."[1]

2. The Second Letter, the Original of which still exists, is of much
greater interest; being from Cromwell's own hand, and evidently thrown
off in a quite familiar and even hasty fashion. Written, as would appear, on the march from Lincoln to Huntingdon; no mention precisely
where; but probably at the Army's quarters on the evening of their
first day's march homewards. In the original the *surname* of the
"Sir John" to whom the Letter addresses itself has been, probably by
some royalist descendant (of mixed emotions), so industriously crossed
out with many strokes of the pen, that not only is it entirely illegible,
but the polite possessor of the Autograph cannot undertake to guess for
me how many letters may have been in the word. On other grounds
I pretty confidently undertake, nevertheless, to read *Wray*: Sir John
Wray of Glentworth, Member for Lincolnshire, and on the Committee
of that County; at present, I suppose, attending his duty in London.

---

[1] Tanner MSS. lxii. 194; and, with little or no variation, Baker MSS. xxviii.
434.

Glentworth House is almost within sight and sound of these trans-actions; the well-affected Knight of the Shire, for many reasons, may fitly hear a word of them, while we rest from our march. Sir John's Mother, I find by the Dryasdust records [1] was a Montague of Bough-ton; so that " your noble Kinsman " near the end of this Letter will mean my Lord of Manchester, " Sergeant-Major of the Association," a man well qualified to give information.

    " *To my noble Friend Sir John* [*Wraye*], *Knight and Baronet:*
               Present these.

               " [EASTERN ASSOCIATION,] 30th July, 1643.

    " SIR, —The particular respects I have received at your hands do much oblige me, but the great affection you bear to the public much more: for that cause I am bold to acquaint you with some late Passages wherein it hath pleased God to favor us ; — which, I am assured, will be welcome to you.

    " After Burleigh House was taken, we went towards Gainsborough to a general rendezvous, where met us Lincolnshire Troops ; so that we were Nineteen or Twenty Troops, when we were together, of Horse and Foot, and about Three or Four Troops of Dragooners. We marched with this Force to Gainsborough. Upon Friday morning, being the 28th of July, we met with a forlorn-hope of the Enemy, and with our men brake it in. We marched on to [2] the Town's end. The Enemy being upon the top of a very steep Hill over our heads, some of our men attempted to march up that Hill; the Enemy opposed; our men drove them up, and forced their passage. By the time [3] we came up, we saw the Enemy well set in two bodies: the foremost a large fair body, the other a reserve consisting of six or seven brave Troops. Before we could get our force into order, the great body of the Enemy advanced; they were within musket-shot of us when we came to the pitch of the Hill : we advanced likewise towards them; and both charged, each upon the other : Thus advancing, we came to pistol and sword's point, both in that close order that it was disputed very strongly who should break the other. But our men pressing a little heavily upon them, they began to give back; which our men per-ceiving, instantly forced them, — brake that whole body ; some of them flying on this side, some on the other side, of the reserve. Our men, pursuing them in great disorder, had the execution about four, or some

---

[1] Burke's *Extinct Baronetage*, § Wray.   [2] Means "towards."
[3] "that time " in orig.

say six miles. With much ado, this done, and all their force being gone, not one man standing, but all beaten out of the field,— we drew up our body together, and kept the field, — the half of our men being well worn in the chase of the Enemy.

"Upon this we endeavored the Business we came for; which was the relief of the Town with Ammunition. We sent in some Powder, which was the great want of that Town. Which done, word was brought us that the Enemy had about Six Troops of Horse, and Three Hundred Foot, a little on the other side of the Town. Upon this we drew some musketeers out of the Town, and with our body of horse marched towards them. We saw two Troops towards the Mill; which my men drove down into a little village at the bottom of the Hill: when *we* [*we* emphatic] came with our horse to the top of that Hill, we saw in the bottom a whole regiment of Foot, after that another and another, — and, as some counted, about Fifty Colors of Foot. Which indeed was my Lord Newcastle's Army; — with which he now besieges Gainsborough.

"My Lord Willoughby commanded me to bring off the Foot and Horse: which I endeavored; but the Foot (the Enemy pressing on with the Army) retreated in some disorder into the Town, being of that Garrison. Our Horse also, being wearied, and unexpectedly pressed by this new force, so great, — gave off, not being able to brave the charge. But, with some difficulty, we got our Horse into a body, and with them faced the Enemy; and retreated in such order that though the Enemy followed hard, they were not able to disorder us, but we got them off safe, to Lincoln, from this fresh force, and lost not one man. The honor of this retreat, equal to any of late times, is due to Major Whalley and Captain Ayscough, next under God.

"This Relation I offer you for the honor of God (to whom be all the praise); as also to let you know you have some servants faithful to you, to incite to action. I beseech you let this good success quicken your countrymen to this engagement! It's great evidence of God's favor. Let not your business be starved. I know, if all be of your mind, we shall have an honorable return. It's your own business :— a reasonable strength now raised speedily may do that which much more will not do after some time. Undoubtedly, if they succeed here, you will see them in the bowels of your Association! [As] for the time, you will hear it from your noble Kinsman and Colonel Palgrave: if we be not able in ten days to relieve Gainsborough, a noble Lord will be lost, many good Foot, and a considerable Pass over Trent in

these parts. — The Lord prosper your endeavors and ours. I beseech
you present my humble service to the high Honorable Lady. Sir,
I am

> " Your faithful servant,
>
> " OLIVER CROMWELL.

" P.S. — I stayed [from the chase after our first encounter] two of
my own Troops, and my Major stayed his; in all three. There were
in front of the Enemy's reserve three or four of the Lincoln Troops yet
unbroken: the Enemy charged those Troops; utterly broke and chased
them; so that none of the Troops on our part stood, but my three.
Whilst the Enemy was following our flying Troops, I charged him on
the rear with my three Troops; drove him down the Hill, brake him
all to pieces; forced Lieutenant-General Cavendish into a Bog, who
fought in this reserve: one Officer but him on the head; and, as he lay,
my Captain-Lieutenant Berry thrust him into the short ribs, of which
he died, about two hours after, in Gainsborough." [1]

By this Postscript is at last settled the question, Who killed Charles
Cavendish ? It was "my Captain-Lieutenant Berry;" he and no other,
if any one still wish to know. Richard Baxter's friend once; and
otherwise a known man.

————◆————

No. 6.

LETTER TWO DAYS PRIOR TO THAT CAMBRIDGE ONE.

[Vol. xvii. p. 177.]

[*To Sir Samuel Luke*, — *Member for Bedford, leading Committee-man,
&c.,* — *These.*]

" [No date of Place] 8 March, 1643.

" NOBLE SIR, — I beseech you cause Three Hundred Foot, under a
Captain, to march to Buckingham upon Monday morning, there to
quarter with Four Hundred Foot of Northampton, which Mr. Crew
sends thither upon Monday next. There will be the Major-General
[Crawford] to command them. I am going for a Thousand Foot more
at least to be sent from Cambridge and out of the Associations. If

[1] Original in the possession of Dawson Turner, Esq., Great Yarmouth; printed
in *Papers of Norfolk Archæological Society* (Norwich, Jan. 1848), pp. 45-50.

any man be come to you from Cambridge, I beseech you send him to me to Bedford with all speed; let him stay for me at the Swan. Sir, I am

"Your humble servant,

"OLIVER CROMWELL.

"Present my humble service to Colonel Aylife, and tell him he promised me his coat of mail." [1]

No. 7.

TWO LETTERS: ACTION AT ISLIP-BRIDGE AND BLETCHINGTON. DITTO AT BAMPTON-IN-THE-BUSH.

[Vol. xvii. pp. 197, 199.]

1. WRITTEN the night before that in the Text, on the same subject.

[*For the Right Honorable Sir Thomas Fairfax, General of the Army: These.*]

"[BLETCHINGTON,] 24th April, 1645.

" RIGHT HONORABLE, — I met at my rendezvous at Watlington, on Wednesday last; where I stayed somewhat long for the coming up of the Body of Horse, which your Honor was pleased to give me the command of. After the coming whereof, I marched with all expedition to Wheatley-Bridge; having sent before to Major-General Browne, for what intelligence he could afford me of the state of affairs in Oxford (I being not so well acquainted in those parts), — of the condition, and number, of the Enemy in Oxford. Who himself informed me by letters, That Prince Maurice his forces were not in Oxford, as I supposed; and that, — as he was informed by four very honest and faithful Gentlemen that came out of Oxford to him a little before the receipt of my letter, — there were Twelve pieces of Ordnance with their carriages and wagons, ready for their march; and in another place Five more pieces with their carriages, ready to advance with their Convoy.

" After I received this satisfaction from Major-General Browne, I advanced this morning, — being Thursday, the twenty-fourth of April, — near to Oxford. There I lay before the Enemy; who perceiving it at Oxford, and being in readiness to advance, sent out a party of Horse

---

[1] Ellis, *Original Letters illustrative of English History* (London, 1846), iv. 225.

against me : part of the Queen's Regiment, part of the Earl of North-ampton's Regiment, and part of the Lord Wilmot's Regiment ; — who made an infall upon me.

"Whereupon I drew forth your Honor's Regiment, — lately mine own, — against the Enemy (who had drawn themselves into several Squadrons, to be ready for action) ; — and commanded your Honor's own Troop therein, to charge a Squadron of the Enemy. Who performed it so gallantly that, after a short firing, they entered the whole Squadron, and put them to a confusion. And the rest of my Horse presently entering after them, they made a total rout of the Enemy ; and had the chase of them three or four miles ; — and killed two hundred ; took as many prisoners, and about four hundred Horses. [Also] the Queen's colors, richly embroidered, with the Crown in the midst, and eighteen flower-de-luces wrought all about in gold, with a golden cross on the top. Many escaped to Oxford, and divers were drowned.

"Part of them likewise betook themselves to a strong House in Bletchington ; where Colonel Windebank kept a Garrison, with near two hundred horse and foot therein. Which, after surrounding it, I summoned : — but they seemed very dilatory in their answer. At last, they sent out Articles to me of Surrender, — which I have sent your Honor enclosed : [1] — and after a large treaty thereupon, the Surrender was agreed upon between us. They left behind them between two and three hundred muskets, seventy horses ; besides other arms and ammunition. — I humbly rest,

"Your honor's humble servant,

"OLIVER CROMWELL." [2]

2. A few months since, in 1868, there has incidentally turned up, among the *Manuscripts of the House of Lords,* and been reawakened into daylight and publicity, from its dark sleep of 223 years, the " contemporaneous Copy " of a Letter by Oliver himself ; which curiously adjusts itself to its old combination here, completely elucidating for us those small Bletchington-Bampton transactions ; and is of itself otherwise worth reading. It is of date the day *before* that Farringdon Affair.

1 Given in Rushworth, vi. 24.
2 King's Pamphlets, small 4to, no. 203, § 7.

" To the Right Honorable the Committee of Both Kingdoms, at Derby House.

"[FARRINGDON,] April 28th, 1645.

"MY LORDS AND GENTLEMEN, — Since my last it has pleased God to bless me with more success in your service. In pursuance of your commands I marched from Bletchington to Middleton Stonies, and from thence towards Witney, as privately as I could, believing that to be a good place for interposing between the King and the West, whether he intended Goring and Grenville, or the two·Princes.

"In my march I was informed of a body of foot which were marching towards Farringdon; which indeed were a commanded party of three hundred, which came a day before from Farringdon, under Colonel Richard Vaughan, to strengthen Woodstock against me, and were now returning.

"I understood they were not above three hours' march before me. I sent after them. My forlorn overtook them as they had gotten into enclosures not far from Bampton Bush, and skirmished with them. They killed some of my horses, mine killed and got some of them; but they recovered the town [*Bampton*, i.e.] before my body came up, and my forlorn not being strong enough was not able to do more than they did. The Enemy presently barricaded up the town, got a pretty strong house: my body coming up about eleven in the night, I sent them a summons. They slighted it. I put myself in a posture that they should not escape me, hoping to deal with them in the morning. My men charged them up to their barricades in the night; but truly they were of so good resolution that we could not force them from it; and indeed they killed some of my horses, and I was forced to wait until the morning: besides they had got a pass over a brook. In the night they strengthened themselves as well as they could in the storehouse. In the morning I sent a drum to them; but their answer was, they would not quit except they might march out upon honorable terms. The terms I offered were to submit all to mercy. They refused with anger. I insisted upon them, and prepared to storm. I sent them word to desire them to deliver out the gentleman and his family; which they did; for they must expect extremity, if they put me to a storm. After some time spent, all was yielded to mercy. Arms I took, muskets near 200, besides other arms, about two barrels of powder, soldiers and officers near 200. Ninescore besides officers, the rest being scattered and killed before. The chief prisoners were Colonel Sir Richard Vaughan, Lieutenant-Colonel Littleton, and Major Lee, two or three Captains, and other Officers.

"As I was upon my march, I heard of some horse of the Enemy which crossed me towards Evesham. I sent Colonel Fiennes after them; whom God so blessed that he took about thirty prisoners, 100 horse, and three horse colors. Truly his diligence was great; and this I must testify, that I find no man more ready to all services than himself. I would not say so, if I did not find it: if his men were at all considered, I should hope you might expect very real service from them. I speak this the rather because I find him a gentleman of that fidelity to you, and so conscientious, that he would all his troop were as religious and civil as any, and makes it a great part of his care to get them so.

"In this march my men also got one of the Queen's troopers, and of them and others about 100 horses. This morning Colonel John Fiennes sent me in the gentleman that waits upon the Lord Digby in his chamber, who was going to General Goring about exchange of a prisoner. He tells me the King's forces were drawn out the last night to come to relieve Sir Richard Vaughan, and Legge commanded them; they were about 700 horse and 500 foot; but I believe they are gone back. He saith many of the horse were volunteer gentlemen; for I believe I have left him few others here.

"I looked upon his letters, and found them directed to Marlborough. He tells me Goring is about the Devizes. I asked him what farther orders he had to him. He tells me he was only to bid him follow former orders. I pressed him to know what they were; and all that I could get was, that it was to hasten with all he had up to the King to Oxford. He saith he has about 3000 horse and 1000 foot; that he is discontented that Prince Rupert commanded away his foot.

"I am now quartered up to Farringdon. I shall have an eye towards him. I have that which was my regiment, and a part of Colonel Sydney's five troops [that] were re-created, and a part of Colonel Vermuyden's, and five troops of Colonel Fiennes's; three whereof and Sir John [Browne's][1] and Captain Hammond's I sent with the first prisoners to Aylesbury. It's great pity we want dragoons. I believe most of their petty garrisons might have been taken in, and other services done; for the Enemy is in high fear. God does terrify them. It's good to take the season; and surely God delights that you have endeavored to reform your armies; and I beg it may be done more and more. Bad men and discontented say it's faction. I wish to be of the faction that desires to avoid the oppression of the poor people of this miserable Nation, upon whom who can look without a bleeding heart? Truly it grieves my soul, our men should still be upon free quarters, as they

---

[1] Orig. illegible.

are. I beseech you help it what and as soon as you can. My Lords, pardon me this boldness; it is because I find in these things wherein I serve you, that He does all. I profess His very hand has led me. I preconsulted none of these things.

"My Lords and Gentlemen, I wait your farther pleasure, subscribing myself,

"OLIVER CROMWELL." [1]

No. 8.

BATTLE OF NASEBY. BURIAL OF COLONEL PICKERING. TWO LETTERS CONCERNING ELY.

[Vol. xvii. pp. 91, 205, 225.]

(a.) THE following very rough Notes of a studious Tourist will perhaps be acceptable to some readers. Notes dashed down evidently in the most rough-and-ready manner, but with a vigilant eye both on the Old Books and on the actual Ground of Naseby; taken, as appears, in the year 1842.

"*Battle of Naseby*, 14th June, 1645: *From Sprigge* (London, 1647); *Rushworth*, vi. (London, 1701); *Old Pamphlets; and the Ground.*

"*Fairfax's Stages towards Naseby* (Sprigge, p. 30 et seqq.). Wednesday, 11th June, a rainy day: Marched 'from Stony Stratford to Wootton,'—three miles south of Northampton. Bad quarters there; 'but the Mayor came,' &c.—Thursday, 12th June: From Wootton to (not 'Guilsborough four miles west of Northampton,' as Sprigge writes, but evidently) Kislingbury and the Farmsteads round. The King 'lies encamped on Burrough Hill' (five miles off); has been 'hunting,' this day: 'his horses all at grass.' The night again wet; Fairfax, riding

---

[1] *Notes and Queries*, 8 Aug. 1868;—printed there, as I learn on inquiry, "from a contemporaneous Copy" found among the House of Lords MSS. in the course of some official examination going on there; corrected and investigated into clearness for me by the kindness of John Forster, Esq., most obliging of Friends, whose final remark on it is: "As to Farringdon [Letter xxvii. of Text], though Cromwell had now crossed the river, and was quartered up to the place, he was not in adequate force for reducing it. 'It's great pity we want dragoons,' is his remark in this Letter; and, according to Rushworth's statement, he had already sent to Abingdon for four or five companies of infantry. Burgess knew very well, there is little doubt, the real state of affairs." (*Note of* 1869.)

about, all night, ou the spy is stopped by one of his own sentries,. &c.:
'at Flower' (near Weedon), sees the King's Forces all astir on the
Burrough Hill, about four in the morning; 'firing their huts;' rapidly
making off, — Northward, as it proved. At six, a Council of War.
Cromwell, greatly to our joy, has just come in from the Associated
Counties, — 'received with shouts.' Major Harrison, with horse, is sent
towards Daventry to explore; Ireton, also with horse, to the Northward, after the King's main body. 'We,' Fairfax's main body, now
set forward 'towards Harborough,' flanking the King; and that night,
— Friday, 13th June, — arrive (not at 'Gilling,' as Sprigge has it, —
is there any such place? — but) at Guilsborough.[1] Which is the last
of the *Stages*.

"The King's van is now, this Friday night, at Harborough; his rear
is quartered in Naseby, — where Ireton beats them up (probably about
half-past nine), 'taking prisoners,' &c.: and so the fugitives rouse the
King out of his bed 'at Lubenham;'[2] — who thereupon drives off to
Prince Rupert at Harborough; arrives about midnight; calls a Council
('resting himself in a chair in a low room,' till Rupert and the rest get
on their clothes); and there, after debate,[3] determines on turning back
to beat the Roundheads for this affront. — Ireton lies at Naseby, therefore; 'we' (Fairfax and the Army), at Guilsborough, all this night.

"*Battle of Naseby*. Saturday, 14th June, 1645. Starting at three in
the morning, we arrive about five at Naseby. King 'reported to be at
Harborough,' uncertain whitherward next; behold, 'great bodies of his
troops are *seen* coming over the Hill from Harborough towards us;'
— he has turned, and is for fighting us, then! We put our Army in
order, — 'large fallow field northwest of Naseby,' 'the brow of the Hill
running east and west' 'for something like a mile:' King has sunk out
of sight in a hollow; but comes up again nearer us,[4] and now evidently
drawn out for battle. We fall back, 'about a hundred paces, from the
brow of the Hill,' to hide ourselves and our plans: he rushes on the
faster, thinking we run ('much of his ordnance left behind'): the Battle
joins on the very brow of the Hill. Their word, *Queen Mary*; ours,
God is our Strength.

"About three hundred Musketeers of ours on the Left Wing, are advanced a little, as a forlorn, down the *steep* of the Hill; they retire firing,
as Rupert charges up: Ireton and Skippon command in this quarter;

---

[1] Rushworth, vi. 46 (Despatch from the Parliament Commissioners).
[2] See *Iter Carolinum* too.   [3] See Clarendon, &c.
[4] "At Sibbertoft" (Rushworth).

'Lantford Hedges,' a kind of thicket which runs right down the Hill, is lined with Colonel Okey and his dragoons, — all on *foot* at present, and firing lustily on Rupert as he gallops past. — Cromwell is on the extreme Right (easternmost part of the Hill) : he, especially Whalley under him, dashes down *before* the Enemy's charge upwards (which is led by Langdale) can take effect ; scatters said charge to the winds ; not without hard cutting : a good deal impeded ' by furze-bushes ' and ' a cony-warren.' *These* Royalist Horse, Langdale's, fled all behind their own Foot, ' a quarter of a mile from the Battle-ground,' — *i.e.* near to the present Farm of Dust Hill, or between that and Clipstow ; — and never fought again. So that Cromwell had only to keep *them* in check ; and aid his own Main battle to the left of him : which he diligently did.

"Our Right Wing, then, has beaten Langdale. But Rupert, on the other side of the field, beats back our Left : — over ' Rutput Hill,' ' Fenny Hill ' (*Fanny* Hill, as the Old Books call it) ; towards Naseby Hamlet ; on to our Baggage train (which stands on the *northwest side* of the Hamlet, *eastward* of said ' Rutput ' and ' Fenny,' but northward of ' Leane Leafe Hill,' very sober ' Hills,' I perceive !). Our extreme Left was ' hindered by pits and ditches ' in charging ; at any rate, it lost the charge ; fled : and Rupert now took to attacking the Baggage and its Guard, — in vain, and with very wasteful delay. For our Main battle too was in a critical state ; and might have been overset, at this moment. Our Main battle, — our Horse on the Left of it giving way ; and the King's Foot ' coming up into sight,' over the brow of the Hill, ' with one terrible volley,' and then with swords and musket-butts, — ' mostly all fled.' Mostly all : except the Officers, who ' snatched the colors,' ' fell into the Reserves with them,' &c. And then, said Reserves now rushing on, and the others rallying to them ; and Cromwell being victorious and diligent on the Right, and Rupert idle among the Baggage on the Left, — the whole business was ere long *retrieved ;* and the King's Foot and other Force were all driven pell-mell down the Hill : towards Dust Hill (or *eastward* of the present Farm-house, I think). There the King still stood, — joined at last by Rupert, and struggling to rally his Horse for another brush ; but the Foot would not halt, the Foot were all off : and the Horse too, seeing Cromwell with all *our* Horse and victorious Foot now again ready for a second charge, would not stand it ; but broke ; and dissipated, towards Harborough, Leicester, and Infinite Space.

" The Fight began at ten o'clock ;[1] lasted three hours :[2] there were some five thousand Prisoners ; how many Slain I cannot tell."

---

[1] Clarendon.   [2] Cromwell's Letter.

(*b.*) Colonel Pickering, a distinguished Officer, whose last notable exploit was at the storm of Basing House, has caught the epidemic, " new disease " as they call it, some ancient *influenza* very prevalent and fatal during those wet winter-operations; and after a few days' illness, " at Autree " (St. Mary *Ottery*) where the head-quarter was, is dead. Sir Gilbert, his brother, is a leading man in Parliament, with much service yet before him; — Cousin Dryden, one day to be Poet Dryden, is in Northamptonshire, a lad of fourteen at present. Sprigge (p. 156) has a pious copy of " sorrowful verse over dear Colonel Pickering's hearse ; " and here is a Note concerning his funeral.

" *To Colonel Cicely, at Pendennis Castle : These.*

" TIVERTON, 10th December. 1645.

" SIR, — It's the desire of Sir Gilbert Pickering that his deceased Brother, Colonel Pickering, should be interred in your Garrison; and to the end his Funeral may be solemnized with as much honor as his memory calls for, you are desired to give all possible assistance therein. The particulars will be offered to you by his Major. Major Jubbs,[1] with whom I desire you to concur herein.

" And believe it, Sir, you will not only lay a huge obligation upon myself and all the Officers of this Army, but I dare assure you the General himself will take it for an especial favor, and will not let it go without a full acknowledgment. — But what need I prompt him to so honorable an action whose own ingenuity will be argument sufficient herein ? Wherefore rests assured

" Your humble servant,

" OLIVER CROMWELL." [2]

(*c.*) A Couple of very small Letters, which have now (May, March, 1846) accidentally turned up, too late for insertion in the Text, may find their corner here.

1. The First, which is fully dated (just eight days before the Battle of Naseby), but has lost its specific Address, may without much doubt be referred to Ely and the " Fortifications " going on there.[3]

[1] " Gubbs " he writes.

[2] Polwhele's *Traditions and Recollections* (London, 1826), i. 22: with a Note on Cicely, and reference to " the Original among the Family Papers of the Rev. G. Moore, of Grampound."

[3] *Commons Journals,* iv. 161, 165 ; *Cromwelliana,* p. 16.

[To Captain Underwood, at Ely : These.]

"HUNTINGDON, 6th June, 1645.

"CAPTAIN UNDERWOOD, — I desire the guards may be very well strengthened and looked unto. Let a new breastwork be made about the gravel,[1] and a new work half-musket-shot behind the old work ; all storm-ground [1] stuff. Tell Colonel Fothergill to take care of keeping strong guards. — Not having more, I rest,

"Yours,

"OLIVER CROMWELL."[2]

2. "Sir Dudley North," Baronet, of Catlidge Hall near Newmarket, is Member for Cambridgeshire ; sits too, there is small doubt, in the Ely Committee at London ; — is wanted now for a small County business.

The "30th of March," as we know, is but the fifth day of the then New Year : Oliver, — I find after some staggering, for his date will not suit with other things, — takes the cipher of the Old Year, as one is apt to do, and for 1647 still writes "1646." As this Entry, abridged from the Commons Journals,[3] will irrefragably prove, to readers of his Letter : "John Hobart Esq. dismissed from being Sheriff of Cambridge and Huntingdon Shires, and *Tristram Dyamond Esq. appointed in his place,* 1st January, 1646," which, for us, and for Cromwell too on the 30th of March following, means 1647.

"*For the Honorable Sir Dudley North : These.*

"[LONDON,] 30th March, 1646 [*error for* 1647].

"SIR, — It being desired to have the Commission of the Peace renewed in the Isle of Ely, — with some addition, as you may perceive ; none left out ; only Mr. Diamond, now High Sheriff of the County, and my Brother Desborow, added, there being great want of one in that part of the Isle where I live, — I desire you to join with me in a Certificate ; and rest,

"Your humble servant,

"OLIVER CROMWELL."[4]

---

[1] Word uncertain to the Copyist.
[2] Original now (May, 1846) in the Baptist College, Bristol.
[3] v. 36 (1st Jan. 1646-7).
[4] Original in the possession of the Rev. W. S. Spring Casborne, of Pakenham, Suffolk ; a descendant of the North Family.

No. 9.

LANGPORT BATTLE (10th July, 1645).   SUMMONS TO WINCHESTER.

[Vol. xvii. p. 223.]

HERE is Oliver's own account of the Battle of Langport, mentioned in our Text : —

[*To* —— ——.]

[LANGPORT, —·July, 1645.]

"DEAR SIR, — I have now a double advantage upon you, through the goodness of God, who still appears for us. And as for us, we have seen good things in this last mercy, — it is not inferior to any we have had ; — as followeth.

"We were advanced to Long-Sutton, near a very strong place of the Enemy's, called Langport ; far from our Garrisons, without much ammunition, in a place extremely wanting in provisions, — the Malignant Clubmen interposing, who are ready to take all advantages against our parties, and would undoubtedly take them against our Army, if they had opportunity. — Goring stood upon the advantage of strong passes, staying until the rest of his recruits came up to his Army, with a resolution not to engage until Grenville and Prince Charles his men were come up to him. We could not well have necessitated him to an Engagement, nor have stayed one day longer without retreating to our ammunition and to conveniency of victual.

"In the morning, word was brought us, That the Enemy drew out. He did so, with a resolution to send most of his cannon and baggage to Bridgewater, — which he effected, — but with a resolution not to fight, but, trusting to his ground, thinking he could make away at pleasure.

"The pass was strait between him and us; he brought two cannons to secure his, and laid his Musketeers strongly in the hedges. We beat off his cannon, fell down upon his Musketeers, beat them off from their strength, and, where our Horse could scarcely pass two abreast, I commanded Major Bethel to charge them with two Troops of about one hundred and twenty Horse. Which he performed with the greatest gallantry imaginable ; — beat back two bodies of the Enemy's Horse, being Goring's own Brigade ; brake them at sword's-point. The Enemy charged him with near 400 fresh Horse ; set them all going, — until, oppressed with multitudes, he brake through them, with the loss not of above three or four men. Major Desborow seconded him, with some other of those Troops, which were about three. Bethel faced about; and they both routed, at sword's-point, a great body of the Enemy's Horse. Which gave such an unexpected terror to the Enemy's Army, that it set them all a-running. Our Foot, in the mean time, coming on bravely, and beating the Enemy from their strength, we presently had the chase to Langport and Bridgewater. We took and killed about 2000, — brake all his Foot. We have taken very many Horses, and considerable Prisoners. What are slain we know not. We have the Lieutenant-General of the Ordnance; Colonel Preston, Colonel Heveningham, Colonel Slingsby, we know of, besides very many other Officers of quality. All Major-General Massey's party was with him [Massey], seven or eight miles from us, — and about twelve hundred of our Foot, and three Regiments of our Horse. So that we had but Seven Regiments with us.

" Thus you see what the Lord hath wrought for us. Can any creature ascribe anything to itself? Now can we give the glory to God, and desire all may do so, for it is all due unto Him! — Thus you have Long-Sutton mercy added to Naseby mercy. And to see this, is it not to see the face of God! You have heard of Naseby: it was a happy victory. As in this, so in that, God was pleased to use His servants; and if men will be malicious, and swell with envy, we know Who hath said, If they will not see, yet they shall see, and be ashamed for their envy at His People. — I can say this of Naseby, That when I saw the Enemy draw up and march in gallant order towards us, and we a company of poor ignorant men, to seek how to order our battle, — the General having commanded me to order all the Horse, — I could not, riding alone about my business, but smile out to God in praises, in assurance of victory, because God would, by things that are not, bring to naught things that are. Of which I had great assurance; and God did it. Oh that men would therefore praise the Lord, and declare the wonders that He doth for the children of men!

" I cannot write more particulars now. I am going to the rendezvous of all our Horse, three miles from Bridgewater; we march that way. — It is a seasonable mercy. I cannot better tell you than write, That God will go on! — We have taken two guns, three carriages of ammunition. In the chase, the Enemy quitted Langport; when they ran out of one end of the Town, we entered the other. They fired that at which we should chase; which hindered our pursuit: but we overtook many of them. I believe we got near fifteen hundred Horse.

" Sir, I beg your prayers. Believe, and you shall be established.
I rest,

" Your servant,

[OLIVER CROMWELL.] " [1]

A couple of months after this battle, Oliver is before Winchester, and
makes this Summons : —

" *To the Mayor of the City of Winchester.*

" [BEFORE WINCHESTER,] 28th September, 1645,
5 o'clock at night.

" SIR, — I come not to this City but with a full resolution to save it,
and the Inhabitants thereof, from ruin.

" I have commanded the soldiers, upon pain of death, That no wrong
be done : — which I shall strictly observe ; only I expect you give me
Entrance into the City, without necessitating me to force my way ; which
if I do, then it will not be in my power to save you or it.   I expect your
Answer within half an hour ; and rest,

" Your humble servant,

" OLIVER CROMWELL." [2]

———•———

No. 10.

ARMY TROUBLES IN 1647.

[Vol. xvii. p. 262.]

THE Vote " that Field-Marshal Skippon, Lieutenant-General Cromwell, Commissary-General Ireton and Colonel Fleetwood," all Members
of this House, " shall proceed to their charges in the Army," and endeavor to quiet all distempers there, — was passed on the 30th of April :
day of the Three Troopers and Army-Letter, and directly on the back
of that occurrence.[3] They went accordingly, perhaps on the morrow,
and proceeded to business ; but as nothing specific came of them, or could
come, till the 8th of May, that day is taken as the date of the Deputa-
tion. — Here are Three Letters from them ; one prior and one posterior ;
which, copied from the Tanner MSS., have got into print, but cannot
throw much light on the affair.

[1] Pamphlet in Lincoln College, Oxford ; no. 10, " Battles and Sieges," — title of
it, " The Copy of Lieutenant-General Cromwell's Letter to a worthy Member of the
House of Commons ; published by Authority, London, 1645."

[2] *History and Antiquities of Winchester* (London, 1773), ii. 127.

[3] *Commons Journals*, v. 158 : see antea, vol. xvii. p. 260.

1. [*To the Honorable William Lenthall, Esquire, Speaker of the Commons House : These.*]

"[SAFFRON WALDEN,] 3d May, 1647.

" SIR, — We have sent out orders to summon the Officers of the several Regiments to appear before us on Thursday next; to the end we may understand from them the true condition and temper of the Soldiers in relation to the discontents lately represented; and the better to prepare and enable them, — by speaking with them, and acquainting them with your Votes,[1] — to allay any Discontents that may be among the Soldiers.

" We judged this way most likely to be effectual to your service; though it asks some time, by reason of the distance of the quarters. When we shall have anything worthy of your knowledge, we shall represent it; — and in the mean time study to approve ourselves,

" Your most humble servants,

" PH. SKIPPON.
OLIVER CROMWELL.
H. IRETON." [2]

---

2. [*To the Honorable William Lenthall, Esquire, Speaker of the Commons House : These.*]

" SAFFRON WALDEN, 8th May, 1647

" SIR, — According to our orders sent out to the Officers of the Army, many of them appeared at the time appointed. The greatest failing was of Horse Officers; who, by reason of the great distance of their quarters from this place (being some of them above threescore miles off), could not be here: yet there were, accidentally, some of every Regiment except Colonel Whalley's present at our Meeting; — which was upon Friday morning,[3] about ten of the clock.

" After some discourse offered unto them, About the occasion of the Meeting, together with the deep sense the Parliament had of some Discontents which were in the Army, and of our great trouble also that it should be so, — we told them, We were sent down to communicate the

---

[1] Votes passed that same 30th of April: That the Soldiers shall have Indemnity; that they shall have Pay, — and in short, Justice (*Commons Journals*, v. 158). "Thursday next" is the 6th of May.

[2] " A Letter from Major-General [elsewhere called Field-Marshal] Skippon, Lieutenant-General Cromwell and Commissary-General Ireton, was this day read " (*Commons Journals*, 4th May, 1647).

[3] Friday, yesterday; not "Thursday," as at first proposed.

House of Commons' Votes unto them ; whereby their [the Parliament's] care of giving the Army satisfaction might appear : desiring them [furthermore] To use their utmost diligence with all good conscience and effect, by improving their interests in the Soldiers, *for* their satisfaction ; and that they would communicate to their Soldiers the Votes, together with such informations as they received then from us, to the end their distemper might be allayed. — After this had been said, and a Copy of the Votes delivered to the Chief Officer of every respective Regiment, to be communicated as aforesaid, we desired them To give us a speedy account of the success of their endeavors ; and if in anything they needed our advice or assistance for furthering the work, we should be ready here at Saffron Walden to give it them, upon notice from them.

"We cannot give you a full and punctual account of the particular distempers, with the grounds of them: because the Officers were desirous to be spared therein by us, until they might make a farther inquiry amongst the Soldiers, and see what effect your Votes and their endeavors might have with them. We desire as speedy an account of this business as might well be ; but, upon the desire of the Officers, thought it necessary for the service to give them until Saturday next[1] to bring us an account of their business, by reason the Regiments were so far distant.

"As anything falls out worthy of your knowledge, we shall represent it ; and in the mean time study to approve ourselves,

"Your most humble servants,

"PH. SKIPPON.

OLIVER CROMWELL.

H. IRETON.

CHARLES FLEETWOOD."[2]

3. [*To the Honorable William Lenthall, Esquire, Speaker of the Commons House: These.*]

"WALDEN, 17th May, 1647.

"SIR, — We having made some progress in the Business you commanded us upon, we are bold to give you this account. Which, although it come not with that expedition you may expect and your other affairs require, yet we hope you will be pleased to excuse us with the weight of the Affair : in comparison whereof nothing that ever yet we under-

[1] This day week ; the 15th.

[2] "Letter from the General Officers," "from Walden, of 8th Maii, 1647, was this day read" (*Commons Journals*, Tuesday, 11th May, 1647). The Letter seems to be of Cromwell's writing.

took was, at least to our apprehension, equal; and wherein, whatever the issue prove, our greatest comfort is, That our consciences bear us witness we have, according to our abilities, endeavored faithfully to serve you and the Kingdom.

" The Officers repaired to us at Saffron Walden upon Saturday last, according to appointment, to give us a return of [1] what they had in charge from us at our last Meeting; which was, To read your Votes to the Soldiers under their respective commands for their satisfaction, and to improve their interest faithfully and honestly with them to that end; and [then] to give us a perfect account of the effect of their endeavors, and a true representation of the temper of the Army.

" At this Meeting we received what they had to offer to us. Which they delivered to us in writing, by the hands of some chosen by the rest of the Officers then present, and in the name of the rest of the Officers and of the Soldiers under their commands. Which was not done till Sunday in the evening. At which time, and likewise before upon Saturday, we acquainted them all with a Letter from the Earl of Manchester, expressing that an Act of Indemnity, large and full, had passed the House of Commons; [2] and that two weeks' pay more was voted to those that were disbanded, as also to them that undertook the service of Ireland. And, thinking fit to dismiss the Officers to their several commands, — all but some that were to stay here about farther business, — we gave them in charge To communicate these last Votes to their Soldiers, and to improve their utmost diligence and interest for their best satisfaction.

" We must acknowledge, we found the Army under a deep sense of some sufferings, and the common Soldiers much unsettled; whereof, that which we have to represent to you will give you a more perfect view. Which, because it consists of many papers, and needs some more method in the representation of them to you than can be done by letter, and forasmuch as we were sent down by you to our several charges *to do our best to keep the Soldiers in order,* — we are not well satisfied, any of us, to leave the place nor duty you sent us to, until we have the signification of your pleasure to us. To which we shall most readily conform; and rest,

" Your most humble servants,

" Ph. Skippon.
Oliver Cromwell.
H. Ireton.
Charles Fleetwood." [3]

[1] Means "response to." [2] *Commons Journals,* v. 174 (14th May, 1647).
[3] Tanner MSS. (in Cary, i. 205-216).

No. 11.

Welsh Disturbances in 1648.

[Vol. xvii. p. 315.]

1. Some charge of Welsh misbehavior, perhaps treachery, in the late May revolt; charge which, if founded, ought to be made good against "Edwards"! Colonel Hughes has been Governor of Chepstow, from the time when it was first taken, in autumn, 1645;[1] and, we may infer, has returned to his post since Ewers (25th May, 1648) retook the Castle. Of Edwards, and his misdeeds, and his accusers, no other clear trace has occurred to me. But in Moyne's Court, Monmouthshire, the seat of this Colonel Thomas Hughes, the following old Note had turned up, and was printed in 1791.

[*To Colonel Hughes, Chepstow Castle.*]

"[Before Pembroke,] 26th June, 1648.

"Colonel Hughes, — It's of absolute necessity that Collington and Ashe do attend the Council of War, to make good what they say of Edwards. Let it be your especial care to get them into Monmouthshire thereunto. What Mr. Herbert and Mrs. Cradock hath (*sic*) promised to them in point of indemnity, I will endeavor to have it performed; and I desire you to certify as much to them for their encouragement. I pray do this speedily after receipt hereof, and I shall remain

"Your servant,

"Oliver Cromwell."[2]

2. A short Letter to the Committee of Carmarthen. The ancient "Iron-furnaces" at Carmarthen, the "Committee" sitting there, the "Paper" or Proclamation from the Leaguer: these, and the other points of this Letter, will be intelligible to the reader.

"*For my noble Friends the Committee of Carmarthen: These.*

"The Leaguer before Pembroke, 9th June, 1648.

"Gentlemen, — I have sent this Bearer to you to desire we may have your furtherance and assistance in procuring some necessaries to be cast in the Iron-furnaces in your county of Carmarthen, which will the better enable us to reduce the Town and Castle of Pembroke.

[1] *Commons Journals*, iv. 321 and v. 115.

[2] The *Topographer*, edited by Sir E. Brydges (London, March, 1791), iv. 125-129

"The principal things are: Shells for our Mortar-piece; the depth of them we desire may be of fourteen inches and three-quarters of an inch. That which I desire at your hands is, To cause the service to be performed, and that with all possible expedition; that so, if it be the will of God, the service being done, these poor wasted countries may be freed from the burden of the Army.

"In the next place, we desire some D cannon-shot, and some culverin-shot, may with all possible speed be cast for us, and hasted to us also.

"We give you thanks for your care in helping us with bread and [*word lost*]. You do herein a very special service to the State; and I do most earnestly desire you to continue herein, according to our desire in the late Letters. I desire that copies of this Paper[1] may be published throughout your county, and the effects thereof observed; for the ease of the county, and to avoid the wronging of the country men.

"Not doubting the continuance of your care to give assistance to the Public in the services we have in hand, I rest,

"Your affectionate servant,

"O. CROMWELL."[2]

3. Letter found, some years ago, among the lumber of "St. Jillian's [Julian's] old castle of the Lords Herbert in Monmouthshire:" Address gone, and not conjecturable with any certainty; Letter evidently genuine, — and still hanging curiously as postscript to Letter LX. (vol. **xvii.** p. 314) of date the day before.

[*For the Honorable Richard Herbert, at St. Jillian's: These.*]

"LEAGUER BEFORE PEMBROKE, 18th June, 1648.

"SIR, — I would have you to be informed that I have good report of your secret practices against the public advantage; by means whereof that arch-traitor Sir Nicholas Kemeys, with his Horse, did surprise the Castle of Chepstow: but we have notable discovery, from the papers taken by Colonel Ewer[3] on recovering the Castle, That Sir Trevor Williams of Llangibby was the Malignant who set on foot the plot.

"Now I give you this plain warning by Captain Nicholas and Cap-

---

[1] Some *Proclamation* seemingly, — of the conceivable sort.

[2] Brayley's *Graphic and Historical Illustrator* (London, 1834), p. 355. "Original in the hands of Richard Williams, Esq., Stapleton Hall, Hornsey."

[3] "Hewer" he spells.

tain Burges, That if you harbor or conceal either of the parties or abet their misdoings, I will cause your treasonable nest to be burnt about your ears.

" OLIVER CROMWELL." [1]

---

4. In the Town Archives of Haverfordwest, Pembrokeshire, are the following three Papers ; footmarks, still visible, of Oliver's transit through those parts. Twelfth July, date of the first Paper, is the morrow after Pembroke surrendered.

(a.) " To the Mayor and Aldermen of Haverfordwest.

" WE being authorized by Parliament to view and consider what Garrisons and Places of Strength are fit to be demolished ; and we finding that the Castle of Haverford is not tenable for the services of the State, and yet that it may be possessed by ill-affected persons, to the prejudice of the peace of these parts : These are to authorize you to summon in the Hundred of Roose and the inhabitants of the Town and County of Haverfordwest ; and that they forthwith demolish the several walls and towers of the said Castle, so as that the said Castle may not be possessed by the Enemy, to the endangering of the peace of these parts.

" Given under our hands this 12th of July, 1648.

" ROGER LORT.   JOHN LORT.

SAMSON LORT.   THOMAS BARLOWE.

" We expect an account of your proceedings, with effect, in this business, by Saturday, being the 15th of July instant."

To which Oliver appends : —

" IF a speedy course be not taken to fulfil the commands of this Warrant, I shall be necessitated to consider of settling a Garrison.

" OLIVER CROMWELL."

---

[1] " *Monmouthshire Merlin* [Welsh Newspaper] for September, 1845." Inserted there, it would appear, along with other antiquarian fractions, in very ignorant condition, by one Mr. W. M. Townshend, an Attorney in Newport, who is now (1858) dead some years since. — " St. Jillian's," now a farm-house near Caerleon, Monmouthshire, was the mansion of the Lords Herbert, of the celebrated Lord Edward of Cherbury for one, — to whom (or to his successor, as the Attorney thinks) this Note was addressed. Note picked up in converting the old Manor-house into a Farm-house (which it still is), and published, along with other antiquarian tagraggeries in a very dim and helpless manner, by the Attorney who had been in charge of that operation.

(b.) "*For the Honorable Lieutenant-General Cromwell, at Pembroke.*

"HAVERFORDWEST, 13th July, 1648.

"HONORED SIR, — We received an Order from your Honor and the Committee, for the demolishing of the Castle of Haverfordwest. According to which we have this day set some workmen about it: but we find the work so difficult to be brought about without powder to blow it by, that it will exhaust an [huge] sum of money, and will not in a long time be effected.

"Wherefore we become suitors of your Honor that there may a competent quantity of Powder be spared out of the Ships, for the speedy effecting the work, and the County paying for the same. And we likewise desire that your Honor and the Committee be pleased that the whole County may join with us in the work; and that an Order be considered for the levying of a competent sum of money on the several Hundreds of the County, for the paying for the Powder, and defraying the rest of the charge.

"Thus being over-bold to be troublesome to your Honor; desiring to know your Honor's resolves, — we rest,

"Your Honor's humble servants,

"JOHN PRYNNE, *Mayor.*

JENKIN HOWELL.	WILLIAM WILLIAMS.
WILLIAM BOWEN.	JOB DAVIES.
ROGER BEVANS.	ETHELDRED DAVIES."

Gunpowder cannot be spared on light occasion; and "levying of competent sums" have had their difficulties before now: here is the handier method: —

(c.) "*To the Mayor and Aldermen of Haverfordwest.*

"Whereas upon view and consideration with Mr. Roger Lort, Mr. Samson Lort, and the Mayor and Aldermen of Haverfordwest, it is thought fit, for the preserving of the peace of this County, that the Castle of Haverfordwest should be speedily demolished:

"These are to authorize you to call unto your assistance, in the performance of this exercise (?), the Inhabitants of the Hundreds of Dungleddy, Dewisland, Kemis, Roose and Kilgerran; who are hereby required to give you assistance.

"Given under our hands this 14th of July, 1648.

"OLIVER CROMWELL

[and the two Lorts in a corner of the Paper]."[1]

---

[1] Printed in *Welshman* Newspaper (Carmarthen, 29th Dec. 1848).

No. 12.

LETTER TO THE DERBY-HOUSE COMMITTEE AFTER PRESTON BATTLE.

[Vol. xvii. p. 344.]

SAME day with that Letter in the Text, urging the York Committee to help in pursuit of Duke Hamilton, Oliver writes home for Supplies.

" *To the Right Honorable the Committee of Lords and Commons, at Derby House : These.   Haste, haste.*

"WIGAN, 23d August, 1648.

"MY LORDS AND GENTLEMEN, — I did not (being straitened with time) send you an Account of the great blessing of God upon your Army : — I trust it is satisfactory to your Lordships that the House had it so fully presented to them.[1]

"My Lords, it cannot be imagined that so great a business as this could be without some loss ; — although I [confess] very little compared with the weightiness of the Engagement ; there being on our part not an Hundred Slain, yet many Wounded.   And to our little it is a real weakening, for indeed we are but a handful.   I submit to your Lordships, whether you will think fit or no To recruit our Loss; we having but Five poor Regiments of foot, and our horse so exceedingly battered as I never saw them in all my life.

"It is not to be doubted but your Enemy's designs are deep : this Blow will make them very angry: the principles they went on were such as should a little awaken Englishmen ; for I have heard it from very good hands of their own party, that the Duke made this the argument to his Army, That the Lands of the Country and — [*illegible the next line or two, from ruin of the paper ; the words lost mean clearly,* " *That the Scots were to share our lands among them, and come to inhabit the conquered country:* " *a very high figure of rumor indeed !*] — which accordingly is done in part, there being a Transplantation of many women and children and of whole families in Westmoreland and Cumberland, as I am credibly informed [*for the moment!*] — Much more might be said ; but I forbear.   I offer it to your Lordships that Money

---

[1] In Letter LXIV. (suprà, vol. xvii. pp. 335–342.)

may be [sent] to pay the foot and horse to some equality. Some of those that are here seventy days before I marched from Windsor into Wales have not had any pay ; and amongst the horse, my own Regiment and some others are much behind. I wish your Lordships may manage it for the best advantage, and not be wanting to yourselves in what is necessary: which is the end of my offering these things to you. My Lords, Money is not for Contingencies so as were to be wished ; we have very many things to do which might be better done if we had where-withal. · Our Foot want Clothes, Shoes and Stockings ; these ways and weather have shattered them all to pieces : that which was the great blow to our Horse was (beside the weather and incessant marches) our March ten miles to fight with the Enemy, and a Fight continuing four hours in as dirty a place as ever I saw horse stand in, and, upon the matter, the continuance of this Fight two days more together in our following the Enemy, and lying close by him in the mire — [*moths again and mildew* . . . until at length we broke him at a near . . . a great party of our horse having . . . miles towards Lancaster ; who came up . . . to us, and were with us in all the Action]. — These things I thought fit to intimate, not knowing what is fit to ask, because I know not how your Affairs stand, nor what you can supply.

"I have sent Major-General Lambert, upon the day I received the Enclosed, with above two thousand horse and dragoons and about fourteen thousand foot in prosecution of the Duke and the Nobility of Scotland with him ; who will, I doubt not, have the blessing of God with him in the business. But indeed his horse are exceeding weak and weary. — I have sent to Yorkshire and to my Lord Grey to alarm all parts to a prosecution : and if they be not wanting to the work, I see not how many can escape. I am marched myself back to Preston ; — and so on towards Monro or otherwise, as God shall direct.

"As things fall out, I shall represent them to you ; and rest, my Lords and Gentlemen,

"Your most humble [servant],

"OLIVER CROMWELL."[1]

---

[1] Tanner MSS. lvii. (1.) 229. Original, signed inside and out by Cromwell: much injured by mildew and moths.

No. 13.

LETTER TO THE DERBY-HOUSE COMMITTEE IN 1648.

[Vol. xvii. p. 367.]

RECAPITULATING what is already known in the Text ; finds its place here.

" To the Right Honorable the Committee of Lords and Commons, at Derby House.

"NORHAM, 20th Sept. 1648.

" MY LORDS AND GENTLEMEN, — I did, from Alnwick, write to Sir William Armyn[1] an account of our condition ; and recommended to him divers particular considerations about your affairs here in the North, — with a desire of particular things to be done by your Lordships' appointment, in order to the carrying on of your affairs.   I send you here a copy of the Summons that was sent to Berwick[2] when I was come as far as Alnwick ; as also of a Letter written to the Committee of Estates of Scotland :[3] — I mean those who we did presume were convened as Estates, and were the men that managed the business of the War.   But there being, as I learned since, none such; the Earl of Roxburgh and some others having deserted, so that they are not able to make a Committee ; — I believe the said Letter is suppressed,[4] and retained in the hands of Colonel Bright and Mr. William Rowe.   For whom we [had] obtained a safe Convoy to go to the Estates of that Kingdom with our said Letter ; the Governor of Berwick's Answer to our Summons leading us thereunto.   By advantage whereof we did instruct them to give all assurances to the Marquis of Argyle and the Honest Party in Scotland, — who we heard were gathered together in a considerable Body about Edinburgh, to make opposition to the Earl of Lanark, Monro, and their Armies, — of our good affection to them.   Wherewith they went the 16th of this month.

" Upon the 17th of this month Sir Andrew Ker and Major Strahan, with divers other Scots Gentlemen, brought me this enclosed Letter, signed by the Lord Chancellor of Scotland, as your Lordships will

[1] Original Member for Grantham ; one of the Committee, and from of old busy in those International concerns.

[2] Letter LXX. (vol. xvii. p. 355).   [3] Letter LXXII. (vol. xvii. p. 358).

[4] Not "suppressed; " though it cannot be received except unofficially (vol. xvii. p. 359).

see. They also showed me their Instructions, and a Paper containing the matter of their Treaty with Lanark and Monro; as also an Expostulation upon Lanark's breach with them, — in falling upon Argyle and his men, contrary to agreement, wherein the Marquis hardly escaped, they having hold of him, but seven hundred of his men were killed and taken.[1] These Papers I also send here enclosed to your Lordships.

" So soon as those Gentlemen came to me, I called a Council of War; the result whereof was the Letter directed to the Lord Chancellor;[2] a Copy whereof your Lordships have here enclosed. Which I delivered to Sir Andrew Ker and Major Strahan; with which they returned upon the 18th, being the next day.

" Upon private discourse with these Gentlemen, I do find the condition of their Affairs and their Army to be thus: The Earl of Lanark, the Earl of Crawford and Lindsay, Monro, and their Army, hearing of our advance, and understanding the condition and endeavors of their Adversaries, — marched with all speed to get possession of Stirling-Bridge; that so they might have three parts in four of Scotland at their backs, to raise men, and to enable themselves to carry on their designs. They were about 5,000 Foot, and 2,500 Horse. The Earl of Leven, who is chosen General; the Marquis of Argyle, with the Honest Lords and Gentlemen, David Lesley being the Lieutenant-General: [these] having about 7,000 Foot, but very weak in Horse, — lie about six miles this side the Enemy. I hear that their Infantry consists of men who come to them out of conscience; and are generally of the Godly People of that Nation, which they express by their piety and devotion in their quarters; and indeed I hear they are a very godly and honest body of men.

" I think it is not unknown to your Lordships what directions I have received from you for the prosecution of our late Victory. Whereof I shall be bold to remember a clause of your Letter; which was, ' That I should prosecute the remaining Party in the North, and not leave any of them, wheresoever they go, to be a beginning of a new Army; nor cease to pursue the Victory till I finish and fully complete it with the rendition of those Towns of Berwick and Carlisle, which most unjustly, and against all obligations, and the Treaties then in force, they surprised and garrisoned against us.'

" In order whereunto, I marched to the Borders of Scotland: where I found the whole Country so harassed and impoverished by Monro and

---

[1] Bishop Guthry's *Memoirs*.   [2] Letter LXXIII. (vol. xvii. p. 360).

the Forces with him, that the Country was no way able to bear us on the English side ; but we must necessarily have ruined both your Army and the Subjects of this Kingdom, who would not have had bread for a day if we had continued among them. In prosecution of your Orders, and in answer to the necessities of your friends in Scotland, and their desires; and considering the necessity of marching into Scotland, to prevent the Governor of Berwick from putting of provisions into his Garrisons on the Scots side, whereof he is at present in some want, as we are informed, — I marched a good part of the Army over Tweed yesterday about noon, the residue being to come after as conveniently as we may.

" Thus have I given your Lordships an account of our present condition and engagement. And having done so, I must discharge my duty in remembering to your Lordships the Desires formerly expressed in my Letters to Sir William Armyn and Sir John Evelyn, for supplies ; and in particular for that of Shipping to be upon these Coasts, who may furnish us with Ammunition or other necessaries wheresoever God shall lead us ; there being extreme difficulty to supply us by land, without great and strong convoys, which will weary out and destroy our Horse, and cannot well come to us if the Tweed be up, without going very far about.

" Having laid these things before you, I rest,
" Your Lordships' most humble servant,
" OLIVER CROMWELL.

" P.S. Whilst we are here, I wish there be no neglect of the Business in Cumberland and Westmoreland. I have sent Orders both into Lancashire and to the Horse before Pontefract. I should be glad your Lordships would second them, and those other considerations expressed in my Desires to Sir William Armyn thereabouts." [1]

[1] Old Pamphlet (in *Parliamentary History*, xvii. 481).

No. 14.

LETTER ON BEHALF OF YOUNG CHOLMELY.

[Vol. xvii. p. 379.]

WRITTEN on the march from Carlisle to Pontefract.

" *To the Honorable William Lenthall, Esquire, Speaker of the House of Commons : These.*

" BOROUGHBRIDGE, 28th October, 1648.

" SIR, — I do not often trouble you in particular businesses ; but I shall be bold now, upon the desire of a worthy Gentleman, Lieutenant-Colonel Cholmely, to entreat your favor in his behalf.

" The case stands thus. His son Major Cholmely, who was bold in the Fight against the Scots at Berwick,[1] was Custom-master at Carlisle ; — the Gentleman [had] merited well from you. Since his death, his aged Father, having lost this his Eldest Son in your service, did resolve to use his endeavors to procure the place for a Younger Son, who had likewise been in your service. And resolving to obtain my Letter to some friends about it, did acquaint an *undertenant* of the place for his Son with this his purpose To come to me to the borders of Scotland to obtain the said Letter ; — which the said servant [or undertenant] did say, Was very well.

" And when the said Lieutenant-Colonel was come for my Letter, this tenant immediately hastens away to London ; where he, in a very circumventing and deceitful way, prefers a Petition to the House of Commons ; gets a reference to the Committee of the Navy ; who approve of the said man [the undertenant] by the mediation of some gentlemen : — but I hear there is a stop of it in the House.

" My humble suit to you is, That if Colonel Morgan do wait upon you about this business, — I having given you this true information of the state of it, as I have received it, — you would be pleased to further his desire concerning Lieutenant-Colonel Cholmely's youngest Son, that *he* may have the place conferred upon him; and that you would acquaint some of my friends herewith.

" By which you will very much oblige,

" Your most humble servant,

" OLIVER CROMWELL." [2]

[1] Against Monro, I suppose, when he ended his maraudings in that quarter (vol. xvii. p. 351).

[2] Tanner MSS. (in Cary, ii. 46).

No. 15.

CORRESPONDENCE WITH THE MAYOR OF WATERFORD.

[Vol. xvii. p. 498.]

PRESERVED in the anonymous Fragment of a Narrative, more than once referred to, are these Letters and Replies : —

LETTER 1. " *To the Mayor and Aldermen of the City of Waterford.*

"KILBARRY, NEAR WATERFORD, 21st Nov. 1649.

" GENTLEMEN, — I have received information that you hitherto refuse a Garrison of the Enemy to be imposed upon you ; as also that some Factions in the Town are very active still, notwithstanding your refusal, to persuade you to the contrary.

" Being come into these parts, not to destroy people and places, but to save them, that men may live comfortably and happily by their trade, if the fault be not in themselves ; and purposing also, by God's assistance, to reduce this City of Waterford to its due obedience, as He shall dispose the matter, by Force, or by Agreement with you upon Terms wherein your own good and happiness, and that of your wives, children and families may consist, notwithstanding [what] some busy-headed persons may pretend to the contrary ; [and] knowing that if after all this you shall receive a Garrison, it will probably put you out of a capacity to make any such Accord for yourselves, which was the cause of the ruin of the Town and people of Wexford, — I thought fit to lay these things before you ; leaving you to use your own judgment therein.

" And if any shall have so much power upon you as to persuade you that these are the counsels of an enemy, I doubt it will hardly prove, in the end, that *they* gave you better. You did once live flourishingly under the power (*sic*) and in commerce with England. It shall be your own faults if you do not so again. I send these intimations timeously to you : weigh them well ; it so behooves you. I rest,

"Your loving friend,

" OLIVER CROMWELL."

REPLY 1. " *For General Cromwell, General of the Parliament Forces in Ireland.*

"WATERFORD, 23d November, 1649.

"MY LORD, — Your Letter of the 21st, directed to me and my Aldermen, we have, by your Trumpet, received. Your Lordship's advice, as we do all others, we weigh with the condition of our safety; and so far shall make use thereof as it contributes to the same.

" For your intentions of reducing this City, by Force or Agreement: —as we will by all possible means endeavor our natural defence against the first, so happily will we not be averse to the latter, — if we shall find it not dishonorable nor destructive. And for that purpose [we] do desire your Lordship will grant us a Cessation, for fifteen days, from all acts of hostility; and send us Safe-conducts, with blanks for the men we shall employ, to treat with your Lordship; and iu the interim bring your Army no nearer this City than now it is.

" We have learned not to slight advice, if we find it wholesome, even from an enemy's hand; nor to deny him such thanks as it merits. And if your Lordship should deny us the time we look for, we doubt not, — with the men we have already in Town, though we should receive no more, — to make good this Place, till the Power of the Kingdom relieves us.

" To signify which to your Lordship, the Council and Commons have laid their commands on me, my Lord,

" Your very loving friend, ·

" JOHN LYVETT, *Mayor of Waterford.*"

LETTER 2. " *For the Mayor, Aldermen, or other Governor or Governors of the City of Waterford.*

" FROM MY CAMP BEFORE WATERFORD,
24th November, 1649.

" GENTLEMEN, — I expected to have heard from you before this, by my Trumpet; but he not coming to me, I thought fit to send, That I might have an account given me, how you have disposed of him. And to save farther trouble, I have thought fit —

" Hereby to summon you To surrender the City and Fort into my hands, to the use of the State of England.

" I expect to receive your answer to these things; and rest,

" Your servant,

" OLIVER CROMWELL."

REPLY 2. " *For the Lieutenant-General Cromwell.*

" WATERFORD, 24th November, 1649.

" MY LORD, — Your Letter of the 24th I have received even now; in which you desire an account of your Lordship's Trumpeter, sent with a former Letter to us; and summon us to deliver your Lordship this City and Fort.

"Your Lordship's former Letter by your Trumpeter we have answered yesterday morning; and do doubt, by the Trumpeter's not coming to you, he might have suffered some mischance by going the County-of-Kilkenny way. We therefore now send you a Copy of that Answer;[1] to which we desire your Lordship's resolution. Before we receive which, we cannot make farther answer to the rest of your Letter.

"We therefore desire you will despatch the Safe-conduct desired, and forbear acts of hostility during the Treaty; — and you shall be very soon attended by Commissioners from, my Lord,

"Your Lordship's servant,
"JOHN LYVETT, Mayor of Waterford."

LETTER 3. "*To the Mayor and Aldermen of the City of Waterford.*

"[BEFORE WATERFORD,] 24th November, 1649.

"SIRS, — My first Trumpet not being yet come to me, makes me suspect that, as you say, he has suffered some mischance going by the way of the County of Kilkenny.

"If I had received your Letter sooner, I should nevertheless, by the help of God, have marched up to this place as I have done. And as for your desire of a Treaty, I am more willing to that way, for the prevention of blood and ruin, than to the other of Force; — although if necessitated thereunto, you and we are under the overruling Power of God, who will dispose of you and us as He pleaseth.

"As to a Cessation for Fifteen Days, I shall not agree thereunto; because a far shorter time may bring this Business to a conclusion as well. But for Four or Five Days I am content that there be a Cessation of all acts of hostility betwixt your City and this Army: — provided you give me assurance That, in the mean time, no soldiers not now in your City be received into it, during the Cessation, nor for twenty-four hours after.

"I expect to have your present answer hereto: because, if this be agreed to, I shall forbear any nearer approach during the said Cessation.

"Your servant,
"OLIVER CROMWELL.

"I have by this Bearer returned a Safe-convoy, as you desire, for what Commissioners you think fit to send out to me. [2]

---

[1] Reply 1; already given.

[2] Fragment of Narrative; in Ayscough MSS. no. 4769, pp. 95 et seqq.

No. 16.

EXCHANGE OF PRISONERS: RENEGADO WOGAN.

[Vol. xvii. p. 503.]

THE Narrative Fragment above cited has these words, in reference to the affair at Passage and its consequences: "At that time, there being one Captain Caufield a prisoner at Clonmel, a stranger to the General, but being a prisoner on an English account, the Army concerned themselves for him, and at a Council of War certain Votes were passed," which we shall soon read: —

"*For Lieutenant-General Farrell, Governor of Clonmel.*

[CORK, 4th January, 1649.]

" At the Council of War held at the City of Cork, the fourth day of January, Anno Domini, 1649, whereat the Lord-Lieutenant of Ireland, the Lord President of Munster,[1] Sir Hardress Waller knight, and divers other chief Officers of the Army were present, it was resolved as followeth: —

"1. That a Letter be sent, by Lieutenant-General Farrell's Trumpet, to let him know, That for every private Foot-soldier of our party, prisoner with him, whom he shall release, he shall have so many of his private soldiers, prisoners with us, released for them; and for every Trooper of ours which he shall release, he shall have Two private Foot-soldiers released for him.

"2. That the Lord-Lieutenant is ready to release Officers of like quality for such Officers of ours as are in their power; and that he will deliver a Major of Foot for a Captain of Horse, and two Captains of Foot for a Captain of Horse; and so proportionably.

"3. Or that he will deliver Major-General Butler, the Earl of Ormond's Brother, for those Officers of ours now in their custody."

" SIR, — Having lately received an advertisement, that some of the principal Officers of the Irish Army did send menacing Orders to the Governor of Clonmel, to be communicated to the Lord Broghil, That if we did put to death Colonel Wogan, they were ready to put Captain Caufield to death, — I thought fit to offer to you the equal Exchanges before mentioned; leaving you to your election. Which when you perform, there shall be just and honest performance on my part. And withal to

---

[1] Ireton.

let you know, That if any shall think to put such conditions on me that I may not execute a Person so obnoxious as Wogan, — who did not only betray his trust in England, but counterfeited the General's hand, thereby to carry his men (whom he had seduced) into a Foreign Nation,[1] to invade England, under whom he had taken pay, and from whose service he was not discharged; and with the said Nation did invade England; and hath since, contrary to the said trust, taken up arms here: — That [then, I say] as I am willing to the Exchanges aforesaid; so [if] that equality be denied me, I would that all concerned should understand, That I am resolved to deal with Colonel Wogan as I shall see cause, and be satisfied in my conscience and judgment to do. And if anything thereupon shall be done to Captain Caufield as is menaced, I think fit to let you know, That I shall, as God shall enable me, put all those that are with me at mercy for life, into the same condition.

" Your servant,

" OLIVER CROMWELL." [2]

No. 17.

IRELAND: ARRANGEMENTS FOR THE ADMINISTRATION OF JUSTICE THERE.

[Vol. xvii. p. 504.]

" *For my very worthy Friend John Sadler, Esq., one of the Masters of the Chancery in England : These.*

" CORK, 31st December, 1649.

" SIR, — To put a business of weight suddenly to your consideration may perhaps beget so much prejudice as may cause you either not to think of it at all, or to incline to the worser part when you resolve. The thing I have to offer hath been thought upon by us, as you will perceive by the reasons wherewith we enforce it; and we do willingly tender it to you ; desiring God, not you, may give us the answer.

" That a Divine Presence hath gone along with us in the late great transactions in this Nation, I believe most good men are sensible of, and thankful to God for ; and are persuaded that He hath a farther end ; and that as by this dispensation He hath manifested His severity and justice, so there will be a time wherein He will manifest grace and mercy, in

---

[1] Scotland: to join Hamilton and his *Engagement.*

[2] Fragment of Narrative : in Ayscough MSS. no. 4769, ubi suprà.

which He so much delights.   To us who are employed as instruments
in this work the contentment that appears is, That we are doing our
Master's work; that we have His presence and blessing with us; — and
that we live in hope to see Him cause wars to cease, and bringing in
that Kingdom of Glory and Peace which He hath promised.   This being so, as the hope thereof occasions our comfort, so the seeing some way
made already cannot but [raise] hope that goodness and mercy intends
to visit this poor Island.   Therefore in what we may as poor instruments, [we] cannot but be endeavoring to answer the mind of God as
any opportunity offers itself.

" First let me tell you, in divers places where we come, we find the
people very greedy after the Word, and flocking to Christian meetings;
much of that prejudice that lies upon poor people in England being a
stranger to their minds.   And truly we have hoped much of it is done
in simplicity; and I mind you the rather of this because it is a sweet
symptom, if not an earnest, of the good we expect.

" In the next place, our condition was such at our arrival here, — by
reason of the War, and prevalency of the Enemy, — that there was a
dissolution of the whole frame of Government; there being no visible
authority residing in persons intrusted to act according to the forms of
law, except in two corporations [*Dublin and Derry at our arrival*], in
this whole Land.   And although it hath pleased God to give us much
territory, yet how to fall suddenly into that way again, I see not; nor is
it for the present practicable.   Wherefore I am constrained, of my own
authority, to issue out Commissions to persons to hear and determine
the present controversies that do arise, as they may.

" Sir, it seems to me we have a great opportunity to set up, until the
Parliament shall otherwise determine, a way of doing justice amongst
these poor people, which, for the uprightness and cheapness of it, may
exceedingly gain upon them, — who have been accustomed to as much
injustice, tyranny and oppression from their landlords, the great men,
and those that should have done them right, as (I believe) any people
in that which we call Christendom.   And indeed [they] are accounted
the bribing'st [*so to speak!*] people that are; they having been inured
thereto.   Sir, if justice were freely and impartially administered here,
the foregoing darkness and corruption would make it look so much the
more glorious and beautiful; and draw more hearts after it! — I am
loath to write what the consequences might be, or what may be said
upon this subject; — and therefore I shall let you know my desire in
a word.

" There uses to be a Chief-Justice in the Province of Munster, who
having some others with him in assistance uses to hear and determine

Causes depending there : you are desired by me to accept of that employment. I do believe that nothing will suit your mind better than having a standing Salary for the same ; that so you may not be troubled within common allowances, which have been to others (I doubt) but a color to their covetous practices. I dare assure you [of] £1,000 a year, half-yearly, to be paid by even parts, as your allowance ; — and although this be more than hath usually been allowed, yet shall we have wherewith readily to make performance, if you accept.

" I know not how far this desire of mine will be interpreted by you as a call : but sure I am I have not done anything with a clearer breast, nor wherein I do more approve my heart to the Lord and His people in sincerity and uprightness ; — the Lord direct you what to do. I desire a few things of you : let my Letter be as little seen as you may ; — you know what constructions are usually put upon some men's actings ; and (were it fit to be committed to paper) would [be] if I should say That this business, by the blessing of God, might be so managed as might abate much superfluity. I desire you not to discourse of the allowance but to some choice friends. Next I could desire, if you have any acquaintance with Mr. Graves the Lawyer, you would move him to the acceptance of a place here, which should be honorable, and not to his outward disadvantage. And any other godly and able man you know of. Let me have your mind so soon as conveniently you may ; and whether you have tried any as is desired, and whom, and what return they make.

" Desiring your prayers, I rest,
" Your affectionate friend and servant,
" OLIVER CROMWELL." [1]

Sadler did not go ; John Cook, Advocate famed in the King's trial, went. Of Graves I know nothing. Sadler has left some Books ; indicating a strange corner of dreamy imaginativeness in his otherwise solid, lucid and pious mind. A man much esteemed by Hartlib, Milton's friend, and by the world legal and other. He continued one of the Masters in Oliver's new Chancery, when the number was reduced to six.

[1] General Dictionary (by Birch, Bernard, &c. London, 1739), vol. ix. pp. 19, 20, § Sadler (materials furnished by " Thos. Sadler, Deputy Clerk of the Pells," a descendant of this Sadler's).

No. 18.

IRELAND: OPERATIONS IN TIPPERARY.

[Vol. xviii. p. 28.]

COLONEL PHAYR is in Cork, "with near five hundred foot," since November last; Broghil, Fenton, and their relation to him, were also indicated in the Text.[1]

"For Colonel Phayr, Governor of Cork: These. Haste, haste.

"FETHARD, 9th February, 1649.

"SIR, — It hath pleased God to be very gracious to us hitherto, in the possessing of Cashel, Fethard and Roghill Castle, without any blood. Callan cost us at least four or five men; but we are possessed of it also, and of divers other places of good importance. We are in the very bowels of Tipperary; and hope, will lie advantageously (by the blessing of God) for farther attempts.

"Many places take up our men: wherefore I must needs be earnest with you to spare us what you can. If you can send Two Companies more of your Regiment to Mallow,[2] do it. If not, one at the least; that so my Lord Broghil may spare us two or three of Colonel Ewers's, to meet him with the rest of his[3] Regiment at Fermoy.

"Give Colonel Ewers what assistance you can in the Business I have sent to him about. Salute all my Friends with you. My service to Sir William Fenton. Pray for us. I rest,

"Your very loving friend,

"OLIVER CROMWELL.

"[P.S.] Sir, if you think that we draw you too low in men whilst we are inactive, — I presume you are in no danger; however, I desire you would make this use of it, To rid the Town of Cork of suspicious and ill-affected persons as fast as you can. And herein deal with effect."[4]

---

[1] Letters CXIV. CXV. vol. xvii. pp. 488, 489.

[2] "Mayallo" in orig.   [3] i.e. Colonel Ewers's.

[4] *Gentleman's Magazine* for March, 1843, p. 266. Endorsed, by Phayr, "The Lo. Leu't Letter to mee the ninth of Feb¹ 1649; About sending men." By another hand there is also written on the outside "Mallo posest," — meaning, probably for Phayr's information, *Mallow possessed* (got, laid hold of).

No. 19.

Haselrig and Dunbar Battle.

[Vol. xviii. p. 125.]

Here, by the kindness of R. Ormston, Esq., Newcastle-on-Tyne, are now (for our *Third* and all other *Editions*) the Letters themselves. This Gentleman, Grandson of the "Steward of the Haselrigs" mentioned in vol. xviii. p. 142, possesses all the Four Cromwell Letters alluded to by Brand; and has now (May, 1847) beneficently furnished an exact copy of them, privately printed. Letter CXXXIX. alone is autograph; the other Three are in a Clerk's hand. Letter CXXXIX., Letter CXLI., these and the Two which follow here, it appears, Mr. O.'s Grandfather "begged from the fire, on a day when much destruction of old Letters and waste Papers was going on at Nosely Hall,"— Letter CXXXIX. and all England are somewhat obliged to him! Here are the other Two :—

1. "*For the Honorable Sir Arthur Haselrig, Governor of Newcastle :
     These.*

"Dunbar, 5th September, 1650.

"Sir, — After much deliberation, we can find no way how to dispose of these Prisoners that will be consisting with these two ends (to wit, the not losing them and the not starving them, neither of which would we willingly incur) but by sending them into England; where the Council of State may exercise their wisdom and better judgment in so dispersing and disposing of them, as that they may not suddenly return to your prejudice.

"We have despatched away near 5,000 poor wretches of them; very many of which, it's probable, will die of their wounds, or be rendered unserviceable for time to come by reason thereof. I have written to the Council of State, desiring them to direct how they shall be disposed of: and I make no question but you will hasten the Prisoners up Southwards, and second my desires with your own to the Council. I know you are a man of business. This, not being every-day's work, will willingly be performed by you; especially considering you have the commands of your Superior.

"Sir, I judge it exceeding necessary you send us up what Horse and Foot you can, with all possible expedition; especially considering that indeed our men fall very sick ; and if the Lord shall please to enable us effectually to prosecute this Business, to the which He hath opened so gracious a way, no man knows but that it may produce a Peace to England, and much security and comfort to God's People. Wherefore I pray you, continue to give what furtherance you can to this Work, by speeding such supplies to us as you can possibly spare. — Not having more at present, I rest,

"Your affectionate friend and servant,

"OLIVER CROMWELL."[1]

2. "*For the Honorable Sir Arthur Haselrig, Governor of Newcastle: These. Haste, haste.*

"EDINBURGH, 9th September, 1650.

" SIR, — I cannot but hasten you in sending up what Forces possibly you can. This enclosed was intended to you on Saturday, but could not come.

" We are not able to carry on our business as we would, until we have wherewith to keep Edinburgh and Leith, — until we attempt, and are acting, forwards. We have not, in these parts [at such a season of the year], above two months to keep the field. Therefore expedite what you can ! And I desire you to send us free Masons ; — you know not the importance of Leith.

" I hope your Northern Guests are come to you, by this time. I pray you let humanity be exercised towards them ; I am persuaded it will be comely. Let the Officers be kept at Newcastle, some sent to Lynn, some to Chester.

" I have no more ; but rest,

" Your affectionate servant,

" OLIVER CROMWELL.

" I desire, as forces come up, I may hear from time to time what they are, how their marches are laid, and when I may expect them.

" My service to the dear Lady."[2]

---

[1] Original in the possession of R. Ormston, Esq., Newcastle-on-Tyne.

[2] Original in the possession of R. Ormston, Esq., Newcastle-on-Tyne. Besides the Signature, "My service to the dear Lady" is also autograph.

No. 20.

Four Letters to the Speaker, in Behalf of individual Military Gentlemen, and their Claims.

Letter 1st, in behalf of Colonel Maleverer's Family.

[*To the Right Honorable William Lenthall, Esquire, Speaker of the Parliament of England: These.*]

"Edinburgh, 28th Dec., 1650.

"Right Honorable, — It having pleased God to take away by death Colonel John Maleverer, a very useful member of this Army, I thought it requisite to move you on the behalf of his sad Widow and seven small Children.

"I need not say much. His faithfulness in your service, and his cheerfulness to be spent in the same, is very well known. And truly, he had a spirit very much beyond his natural strength of body, having undergone many fits of sickness during this hard service in your field, where he was constant and diligent in his charge ; and, notwithstanding the weakness of his body, thought himself bound in conscience to continue to the utmost, preferring the Public service before his private relations. And (as I have been credibly informed) his losses by the Royal and Malignant Party have been very great ; being occasioned by his appearing with the first in his Country for the Parliament.

"I have therefore made bold to represent these things before you, that you may timely consider of those that he hath left behind him, and bestow some mark of favor and respect upon them towards their comfortable subsistence. I rest,

"Your most humble servant,

"Oliver Cromwell." [1]

Letter 2d, in behalf of John Arundel of Trerice.

Oliver is now in Scotland, busy enough with great matters ; must not neglect the small either. Military Gentlemen, Ex-Royalist even, applying to the Lord-General in their distress, seem to be a frequent item just now. To whom how can he be deaf, if it is undeserved distress ? — "This Enclosed" [2] is from an Ex-Royalist Gentleman, Mr. John

---

[1] Tanner MSS. (in Cary, ii. 243).   [2] Ibid. ii. 258.

Arundel of Trerice in Cornwall; and relates to what is now an old story, the Surrender of Pendennis Castle to Fairfax's people (August, 1646); in which Mr. John, by the arbitrary conduct of a certain Parliamentary Official, suffers huge damage at this time, — a fine of no less than £10,000, "quite ruinous to my poor estate," and clear against bargain at the rendition of Pendennis, being now laid upon him by the arbitrary Parliamentary Official in those parts. As not only human justice, but the honor of the Army is concerned, Mr. John has written to the Lord-General, — the Trerice Arundels, he alleges furthermore, having once "had the honor to stand in some friendship, or even kinship, with your noble family." Oliver, during that hurried first visit to Glasgow, writes in consequence : —

[To the Right Honorable William Lenthall, Esquire, Speaker of the Parliament of England: These.]

"GLASGOW, 25th April, 1651.

" SIR, — Receiving this Enclosed, and finding the contents of it to expostulate for justice and faith-keeping, and the direction not improper to myself from the Party interested, forasmuch as it is the word and the faith of the Army engaged unto a performance ; and understanding by what steps it hath proceeded, which this enclosed Letter of the Gentleman's will make manifest unto you : — I make bold humbly to present the Business to the Parliament.

" If he desires that which is not just and honorable for you to grant, I shall willingly bear blame for this trouble, and be glad to be denied : but if it be just and honorable, and tends to make good the faith of your servants, I take the boldness then to pray he may stand or fall according to that. And this desire, I hope, is in faithfulness to you; and will be so judged. I take leave ; and rest, Sir,

" Your most humble servant,

" OLIVER CROMWELL." [1]

Letter 3d, in behalf of Colonel Clayton.

[To the Right Honorable William Lenthall, Esquire, Speaker of the Parliament of England: These.]

"EDINBURGH, 10th May, 1651.

" SIR, — I am very desirous to make an humble motion unto you on the behalf of Colonel Randall Clayton ; — who, being taken prisoner [2]

---

[1] Tanner MSS. (in Cary, ii. 270).
[2] Supra, vol. xviii. p. 45. and Whitlocke, p. 432.

when I was in Ireland, was with some other Officers judged to die, as those that had formerly served the Parliament, but were then partakers with the Lord Inchiquin in his Revolt: and although the rest suffered, according to the sentence passed upon them, yet, with the advice of the chief Officers, I thought meet to give him, the said Colonel Randall Clayton, his life, as one that is furnished with large abilities for the service of his Country: and indeed there was the appearance of such remorse, and of a work of grace upon his spirit, that I am apt to believe he will hereafter prove an useful member unto the State, upon the best account.

"Having thus given him his release, and observing his Christian candor, I then promised him to negotiate with the Parliament for the taking off the sequestration that is upon his estate, which indeed is but very small. I do therefore humbly entreat you To pass such a special act of favor towards him, whereby he will be engaged and enabled to improve his interest the more vigorously, in his place, for the advantage of the Public.

"I would not address such an overture to you, did I not suppose that the placing of this favor upon this person will be of very good use, and an act of much charity and tenderness. I rest, Sir,

"Your most humble servant,

"OLIVER CROMWELL." [1]

Letter written (what may be noted) just in the beginning of that dangerous Fit of Sickness; — following Letter just about the end of it.

Letter 4th, in behalf of Colonel Borlace.

[*To the Right Honorable William Lenthall, Esquire, Speaker of the Parliament of England: These.*]

"EDINBURGH, 13th June, 1651.

"SIR, — Having received the enclosed Petition and Letter from the Officers of a Court of War at Whitehall, representing unto me that the faith of the Army concerning the Articles of Truro,[2] in the particular case of Colonel Nicholas Borlace, is violated; and the Petitioner himself having come hither to Scotland, desiring me to be instrumental that the said Articles be performed, and that the faith of the Army thereupon

---

[1] Tanner MSS. (in Cary, ii. 272).

[2] Hopton's Surrender, 14th March, 1645-6 (antea, vol. xvii. p. 223); a hurried Treaty, which gave rise to much doubting and pleading, in other instances than this.

given might be made good: — I do therefore humbly desire That the Parliament will take his case into consideration, and that his Business may receive a speedy hearing (he being already almost quite exhausted in the prosecution thereof) ; that so justice may be done unto him, and that the faith of the Army may be preserved.

"I crave pardon for this trouble ; and rest, Sir,

"Your most humble servant,

"OLIVER CROMWELL." [1]

No. 20*.

[Vol. xviii. p. 228.]

GENERAL HARRISON, with some force, is on the Border, keeping open our communications. Along with that Letter to Mrs. Cromwell goes another, dated the same day.

"*For the Honorable Major-General Harrison : These.*

"EDINBURGH, May 3d, 1651.

"DEAR HARRISON, — I received thine of the 23d of April. Thy Letters are always very welcome to me.

"Although your new militia forces are so bad as you mention, yet I am glad that you are in the head of them; because I believe God will give you a heart to reform them; a principal means whereof will bo, by placing good Officers over them, and putting out the bad; whereunto you will not want my best furtherance and concurrence. I have had much such stuff to deal withal, in those sent to me into Scotland; but, blessed be the Lord, we have [been] and are reforming them daily, finding much encouragement from the Lord therein; only we do yet want some honest men to come to us to make Officers. And this is the grief, that this being the cause of God and of His people, so many saints should be in their security and ease, and not come out to the work of the Lord in this great day of the Lord.

"I hear nothing of the men you promised me. Truly I think you should do well to write to friends in London and elsewhere, to quicken their sense in this great business. I have written this week to Sir Henry Vane, and given him a full account of your affairs. I hope it will not be in vain.

[1] Tanner MSS. (in Cary, ii. 276).

"I think it will be much better for you to draw nigher to Carlisle, where [are] twelve troops of horse; whereof six are old troops, and five or six of dragoons. Besides, the troops you mention upon the Borders will be ready upon a day's notice to fall into conjunction with you; so that if any parties should think to break into England (which, through the mercy of God, we hope to have an eye to), you will be, upon that conjunction, in a good posture to obviate [them]. Truly I think that if you could be at Penrith and those parts, it would do very well. And I do therefore desire you, as soon as you can, to march thither. Whereby also you and we shall have the more frequent and constant correspondency one with another. And it will be better, if a party of the enemy should happen to make such an attempt, to fight him before he hath an opportunity to get far into our country.

"I have offered a consideration also to our friend at London, that you might have two regiments of foot sent too, [of] which I am not without hope.

"The Lord bless you and keep you, and increase the number of His faithful ones. Pray for us, and for him who assures you he is

"Your affectionate faithful Friend,

"OLIVER CROMWELL."[1]

───────◆───────

No. 21.

MARCH TO WORCESTER.

[Vol. xviii. p. 244.]

OLIVER, in his swift March from Scotland towards Worcester, takes Ripon and Doncaster as stages : Provision for us must be "in readiness against our coming."

[*To the Mayor and Corporation of Doncaster : These.*]

"RIPON, 18th August, 1651.

"GENTLEMEN, — I intend, God willing, to be at Doncaster with the Army on Wednesday[2] night or Thursday morning; and forasmuch as the Soldiers will need a supply of victual, I desire you to give notice

---

[1] Letter in possession of B. S. Elcock, Esq., of Prior-Park Buildings, Bath (*Note of* 1869).

[2] Wednesday is 20th.

to the country, and to use your best endeavors to cause bread, butter, cheese and flesh to be brought in, and to be in readiness there against our coming; for which the country shall receive ready money. Not doubting of your care herein, I rest,

" Your very loving friend,

" OLIVER CROMWELL." [1]

No. 22.

AFTER WORCESTER BATTLE : LETTERS TO THE SPEAKER.

[Vol. xviii. p. 254.]

[*To the Right Honorable William Lenthall, Esquire, Speaker of the Parliament of England : These.*]

"EVESHAM, 8th September, 1651.

" SIR, — The late most remarkable, seasonable, and signal Victory, which our good God (to whom alone be ascribed all the glory) was pleased to vouchsafe your servants against the Scottish Army at Worcester, doth, as I conceive, justly engage me humbly to present in reference thereunto this consideration : That as the Lord appeared so wonderfully in His mercies towards you, so it will be very just to extend mercy to His people, our Friends that suffered in these parts upon this occasion ; and that some reparation may be made them out of the Sequestration or Estates of such as abetted this Engagement against you. The town being entered by storm, some honest men, promiscuously and without distinction, suffered by your Soldier ; — which could not at that time possibly be prevented, in the fury and heat of the battle.

" I also humbly present to your charity the poor distressed Wife and Children of one William Guise, of the City of Worcester, who was barbarously put to death by the Enemy for his faithfulness to the Parliament. The man (as I am credibly informed) feared the Lord ; and upon that account likewise deserveth more consideration. Really, Sir, I am abundantly satisfied, that divers honest men, both in city and country, suffered exceedingly (even to the ruin of their families), by these parts being the seat of the War : and it will be an encouragement

---

[1] Original in the possession of Pudsey Dawson, Esq., Hornby Castle, Lancashire (communicated, 19th October, 1850).

to honest men, when they are not given over to be swallowed up in the same destruction with enemies.

"I hope the Commissioners of the Militia will be very careful and discerning in the distribution of your charity. I cannot but double my desires, that some speedy course may be taken herein.

"I have sent the Mayor and Sheriff of Worcester to Warwick Castle, there to attend the pleasure of Parliament concerning their Trial; I having not opportunity to try them by Court Martail. I have also taken security of the other Aldermen who remained in the city, to be forthcoming when I shall require them.

"It may be well worthy your consideration, That some severity be shown to some of those of this Country, as well of quality as meaner ones, who, having been engaged in the former War, did now again appear in arms against you. I rest, Sir,

"Your most humble servant,

"OLIVER CROMWELL." [1]

[*To the Right Honorable William Lenthall, Esquire, Speaker of the Parliament of England: These.*]

"CHIPPING NORTON, 8th September, 1651.

" SIR, — I have sent this Bearer, Captain Orpyn, with the Colors taken in the late Fight; — at least as many of them as came to my hands, for I think very many of them have miscarried. I believe the number of these sent will be about an Hundred; the remainder also being Forty or Fifty, which were taken at the Engagement in Fife.[2] I ask pardon for troubling you herewith; and rest, Sir,

"Your most humble servant,

"OLIVER CROMWELL." [8]

* * *

No. 23.

LETTER TO SISTER ELIZABETH.

[Vol. xvii. p. 21 note: xviii. 274.]

BY accident, another curious glimpse into the Cromwell family. "Sister Elizabeth," of whom, except the date of her birth and that she died

---

[1] Tanner MSS. (in Cary, ii. 378).

[2] Inverkeithing Fight in July: see Letter CLXXV.

[8] Tanner MSS. (in Cary, ii. 380).

unmarried,[1] almost nothing is known, comes visibly to light here; "living at Ely," in very truth (as Noble had guessed she did); quietly boarded at some friendly Doctor's there, in the scene and among the people always familiar to her. She is six years older than Oliver; now and then hears from him, we are glad to see, and receives "small tokens of his love" of a substantial kind. For the rest, sad news in this Letter! Son Ireton is dead of fever in Ireland; the tidings reached London just a week ago.

" For my dear Sister Mrs. Elizabeth Cromwell, at Doctor Richard Stand[2] *his house at Ely : These.*

"[COCKPIT,] 15th December, 1651.

"DEAR SISTER, — I have received divers Letters from you; I must desire you to excuse my not writing so often as you expect: my burden is not ordinary, nor are my weaknesses a few to go through therewith; but I have hope in a better Strength. — I have herewith sent you Twenty Pounds as a small token of my love. I hope I shall be mindful of you. I wish you and I may have our rest and satisfaction where all saints have theirs. What is of this world will be found transitory; a clear evidence whereof is my Son Ireton's death. I rest, dear Sister,

"Your affectionate Brother,

"OLIVER CROMWELL.[3]

" [P.S.][4] My Mother, Wife, and your friends here remember their loves."

────◆────

No. 24.

LETTER TO THE COMMITTEE FOR SEQUESTRATIONS, IN BEHALF OF MR. AND MRS. FINCHAM.

[Vol. xviii. p. 278.]

THOMAS FINCHAM, Esquire, of Oatwell, Isle of Ely, is on the List of Delinquents : Oliver, as an old friend or at least neighbor, will do what he can for him.

---

[1] Vol. xvii. p. 21.   [2] Query, not *Hand !*

[3] Original shown me, and copied for me (26th October, 1853), by Mr. Puttick, Auctioneer, 191 Piccadilly, — who sold it, with another (Letter to *Dick*, 2d April, 1650, *Carrick*, our Letter CLXXXII.), next day, " for 9 guineas, to Mr. Holloway, Bedford Street :" the *Dick*, a long letter, in very good keeping, went " for 26 guineas, to Mr. John Young, 6 Size Lane, Bucklersbury."

[4] On the margin.

" To the Commissioners for Sequestration, at Goldsmiths' Hall: These.

"COCKPIT, — December, 1651.

"GENTLEMEN, — I formerly recommended unto you the Petition of one Mr. Fincham and his Wife, desiring that if it were in your power to give remedy in their case, you would be pleased to hear them, according to the equity of their case. And forasmuch as they have waited long in Town for a hearing, to their great charge and expenses, which their present condition will not well bear, I again earnestly desire that you will grant them your favor of a speedy hearing of their business, and to relieve them according to the merits and justice of their case: whereby you will very much oblige, Gentlemen,

"Your very loving friend,

"OLIVER CROMWELL." [1]

No. 25.

To OXFORD AND CAMBRIDGE.

[Vol. xviii. p. 280.]

FROM those nine months of 1652 remain certain other small vestiges or waymarks; relating, as it happens, to the Universities, of one of which Oliver was Chancellor. The first is a Letter to Oxford.

"Greenwood" we have already seen: "Goodwin" is the famed Independent, at this time President of Magdalen College. Of "Zachary Maine," and his wishes and destinies, the reader can find an adequate account in Wood, with express allusion to the Letter which follows.[2] Zachary's desire was complied with. A godly young man from Exeter City; not undeserving such a favor; who lived seven years in profitable communion with Goodwin, Owen and the others; then, at the Restoration, fell into troubles, into waverings; but ended peaceably as Master of the Free School of Exeter, the Mayor and Chamber favoring him there.

1. *" To the Reverend my very loving Friend Dr. Greenwood, Vice-Chancellor of the University of Oxford.*

"[COCKPIT,] 12th April, 1652.

"SIR, — Mr. Thomas Goodwin hath recommended unto me one Zachary Maine, Demy of Magdalen College, to have the favor To be

---

[1] Composition Papers, in State-Paper Office.　　[2] *Athenæ,* iv. 411.

dispensed with for the want of two or three terms in the taking of his Degree of Bachelor. I am assured that he is eminently godly, of able parts, and willing to perform all his exercises. Upon which account (if it will not draw along with it too great an inconvenience) I desire that he may have the particular favor to be admitted to the said Degree. Which I intend not to draw into a precedent, but shall be very sparing therein. I remain, Sir,

" Your very loving friend,

" OLIVER CROMWELL." [1]

The Second an official Protection to Cambridge : —

2. " *To all Officers, Soldiers under my command, and others whom it may concern.*

" These are to charge and require you, upon sight hereof: Not to quarter any Officers or Soldiers in any of the Colleges, Halls or other Houses belonging to the University of Cambridge ; Nor to offer any injury or violence to any of the Students or Members of any of the Colleges or Houses of the said University. As you shall answer the contrary at your peril.

" Given under my hand and seal, the First of July, 1652.

" OLIVER CROMWELL." [2]

Note. In the Archives of Trinity College Cambridge is a Patent duly signeted, and superscribed " Oliver P.," of date " Whitehall, 21st October, 1654 ; " appointing Richard Pratt, " who, as we are informed, is very poor and necessitous," a *Bedesman* (small pensioner for life) of that College. Which merely official Piece, as Richard Pratt too, except this of being poor, is without physiognomy for us, we do not insert here. [3]

The Third and Fourth are for Oxford again : —

3. " *By his Excellency the Lord General Cromwell, Chancellor of the University of Oxford.*

" Whereas divers applications have been made unto me, from several of the Members of the University of Oxford, concerning differences

---

[1] From the Archives of Oxford University. Communicated by the Rev. Dr. Bliss.
[2] Cooper's *Annals of Cambridge*, iii. 452.   [3] Copy *penes me.*

which have arisen between the Members of the said University about divers matters which fall under my cognizance as Chancellor: And forasmuch as differences and complaints of the like nature may [again] happen and arise between them: And considering that it would be very troublesome and chargeable to the parties concerned to attend me at this distance about the same: And the present burden of public affairs not permitting me so fully to hear and understand the same as to be able to give my judgment and determination therein:

"I do hereby desire and authorize Mr. John Owen, now Vice-chancellor of the University, and the Heads of the several Colleges and Halls there, or any Five or more of them (whereof the said Vice-chancellor to be one), To hear and examine all such differences and complaints which have [arisen,] or shall arise, between any of the said Members; giving them as full power and authority as in me lies to order and determine therein as, in their judgments, they shall think meet and agreeable to justice and equity. And this Power and Commission to continue during the space of Six Months now next ensuing.

"Given under my hand and seal, the 16th day of October, 1652.

"OLIVER CROMWELL."

---

4. "*By his Excellency the Lord General Cromwell, Chancellor of the University of Oxford.*

"Whereas within the University of Oxford there frequently happen several things to be disposed, granted and confirmed, wherewith the Vice-chancellor, Doctors-Regent, Masters and others of the said University, in their Delegacies and Convocations, cannot by their statutes dispense, grant or confirm, without the assent of their Chancellor: And forasmuch as the present weighty affairs of the Commonwealth do call for and engage me to reside, and give my personal attendance, in or near London; so that the Scholars of the said University and others are put to much charge and trouble by coming to London to obtain my assent in the cases before mentioned: Therefore, taking the premises into consideration, For the more ease and benefit of the said Scholars and University, and that I may with less avocation and diversion attend the councils and service of the Commonwealth:

"I do by these presents ordain, authorize, appoint and delegate Mr. John Owen, Dean of Christchurch and Vice-chancellor of the said University; Dr. Wilkins, Warden of Wadham College; Dr. Jonathan Goddard, Warden of Merton College; Mr. Thomas Goodwin, President of Magdalen College; and Mr. Peter French, Prebend of Christchurch, or any Three or more of them, To take into consideration all and every matter of dispensation, grant or confirmation whatsoever which requires my assent as Chancellor to the said University, and thereupon to dispense, grant, confirm, or otherwise dispose thereof, as to them shall seem meet; and to certify the same to the Convocation. And all and every such dispensation, grant, confirmation or disposition made by the aforesaid Mr. John Owen, Dr. Wilkins, Dr. Jonathan Goddard, Mr. Thomas Goodwin, and Mr. Peter French, or any Three or more of them, shall be to all intents and purposes firm and valid, in as full, large and ample manner as if to every such particular act they had my assent in writing under my hand and seal, or I had been personally present and had given my voice and suffrage thereunto.

"In witness whereof I have hereunto set my hand and seal, the 16th day of October, 1652.

"OLIVER CROMWELL."[1]

---------•---------

No. 26.

LETTER TO LORD WHARTON ABOUT HENRY CROMWELL'S MARRIAGE.

[Vol. xviii. p. 246.]

"Poor foolish Mall," whom we guessed in the Text to be on a visit at Winchington, was then busy there, it would seem, and is now again busy, on a very important matter: scheme of marriage between her brother Henry, now in Ireland, and her fair Friend here, Lord Wharton's Daughter, — the Lady Elizabeth, his eldest, as may be clearly inferred from the genealogies.[2] The Lord General approves; match most honorable; shall not fail for want of money on his part. Unless, indeed, "the just scruples of the Lady" prove unsurmountable? Which, apparently, they did. Both parties afterwards married: the Lady Elizabeth to "the third Earl Lindsay;" Henry Cromwell a "Russel of Chippenham;" on which latter event, the "Dalby and Broughton," here mentioned, were actually settled upon Henry. Burleigh and Oakham went to his brother Richard.

---

[1] From the Archives of Oxford University. Communicated by the Rev. Dr. Bliss.

[2] Lipscomb's *History and Antiquities of Buckinghamshire* (London, 1847), i. 544.

[For the Right Honorable the Lord Wharton: These.]

"[COCKPIT,] 30th June, 1652.

" MY DEAR LORD, — Indeed I durst not suddenly make up any judgment what would be fit for me to do or desire, in the Business you know of.   But being engaged to give you an account upon our last conference, I shall be bold to do that, and add a word or two therewith.

" For the Estate I mentioned, I cannot now (by reason my Steward is not here) be so exact as I would : but the Lands I design for this occasion are Burleigh, Oakham, and two other little things not far distant; in all about £1,900 per annum.   Moreover Dalby [and] Broughton, £1,600 per annum.   Burleigh hath some charge upon it, which will in convenient time be removed.   This is near twice as much as I intended my Son : yet all is unworthy of the honorable Person.

" My Lord, give me leave to doubt that the Lady hath so many just scruples, which if not very freely reconciled may be too great a tentation to her spirit, and also have after-inconveniences.   And although I know your Lordship so really,[1] yet I believe you may have your share of difficulties to conflict with; which may make the Business uneasy : — wherefore, good my Lord, I beg it, If there be not freedom and cheerfulness in the noble Person, let this Affair slide easily off, and not a word more be spoken about it, — as your Lordship's [own] thoughts are.   So hush all, and save the labor of little Mall's fooling, — lest she incur the loss of a good Friend indeed.   My Lord, I write my heart plainly to you, as becomes, my Lord,

" Your most affectionate servant,

"OLIVER CROMWELL."[2]

———◆———

No. 27.

SCRAPS FROM 1653.

[Vol. xviii. p. 331.]

1. IN a volume of the *Annual Register* are given certain Letters or Petitions concerning the printing of Dr. Walton's Polyglot Bible.   At the end of the Petitions is the following : —

[1] "reallilye" in orig.
[2] Original in Bodleian Library; endorsed by Lord Wharton, "My Lord Generall to mee about his Sonne." Printed in *Illustrated London News*, 7th November, 1856.

"[WHITEHALL,] 16th May, 1653.

"I THINK fit that this work of printing the Bible in the Original and other Languages go on without any let or interruption.

"OLIVER CROMWELL." [1]

"By favor of whose Government," as Walton in his Preface furthermore records, "we had our paper free of duty, *quorum favore chartam a vectigalibus immunem habuimus*," — with perhaps other furtherances. See Irwell's *Life of Pocock* (reprint, London, 1816), pp. 209–211.

---

2. Here, lest any one should be again sent hunting through "Pegge's Manuscripts," take the following highly insignificant Official Note. Date, four weeks after the Dismissal of the Rump; when the "Committee of the Army," and Oliver "Commander of all the Forces raised and to be raised," are naturally desirous to know the state of the Army-Accounts. Where Mitchell commands at present, I do not know; nor whether he might be the "Captain Mitchell" who was known some years ago in a disagreeable transaction with the Lord-General's Secretary,[2] and whose Accounts may be rather specially a matter of interest.

"*For Lieutenant-Colonel Mitchell.*

"WHITEHALL, 18th May, 1653.

"SIR, — You are desired with all expedition to prepare and send to the Committee for the Army an Account of all Moneys by you received upon their Warrants between the Fifteenth of January, 1647, and the Twentieth of October, 1651, for the use of the Forces within the time aforesaid under your command, or for the use of any other Regiment, Troop or Company, by or for whom you were intrusted or appointed to receive any money.

"And in case you cannot perfect your Account, and send the same, as you are hereby directed, before the Seventh of June next, you are desired by that time at the farthest to send in writing under your hand to the said Committee, What Moneys by you received as aforesaid do remain in your hands.

"Hereof you are not to fail.

"OLIVER CROMWELL." [3]

[1] *Annual Register*, xxxvi. 373, 374.
[2] Newspapers (in *Cromwelliana*, p. 61), 22d–29th June, 1649.
[3] Pegge's MSS. (in the College of Arms, London), vii. 425.

3. Among the State-Papers in Paris there have lately been found Three small Notes to Mazarin, not of much, if indeed of almost any moment, but worth preserving since they are here. Two of them belong to this Section. The first, which exists only in French, apparently as translated for Mazarin's reading, would not be wholly without significance if we had it in the original. It is dated just three days after that Summons to the Puritan Notables ;[1] — and the Lord General, we see, struggles to look upon himself as a man that has done with Political Affairs.

[*A Son Eminence, Monsieur le Cardinal Mazarin.*]

"DE WESTMINSTER, ce 9-19 Juin, 1653.

" MONSIEUR, — J'ai été surpris de voir que votre Eminence ait voulu penser à une personne si peu considérable que moi, vivant en quelque façon rétiré du reste du monde. Cet honneur a fait avec juste raison une si forte impression sur moi, que je me sens obligé de servir votre Eminence en toutes occasions ; et comme je m'estimerai heureux de les pouvoir rencontrer, j'espère que M. de Bourdeaux en facilitera les moyens à celui qui est, Monsieur,

"De votre Eminence
" Le très-humble serviteur,
" OLIVER CROMWELL."[2]

Of which take this Version : —

"WESTMINSTER, 9th June, 1653.

" SIR, — I have been surprised that your Eminency was pleased to remember a person so inconsiderable as myself, living, as it were, withdrawn from the rest of the world. This honor has justly such a resentment with me that I feel myself bound, by all opportunities, to be serviceable to your Eminency; and as I shall be happy to meet with such, so I hope M. de Bourdeaux [the Ambassador] will help to procure them to, Sir,

"Your Eminency's most humble servant,
" OLIVER CROMWELL."

Nay here now (*Edition* 1857) is the Original itself; politely forwarded to me, three years ago, by the Translator of M. Guizot's *English Commonwealth*, where doubtless it has since appeared in print : —

[1] Antea, vol. xviii. p. 297.
[2] From the Archives du Ministère des Affaires Etrangères at Paris. Communicated by Thomas Wright, Esq. F.S.A. &c.

"WESTMINSTER, the 9th June, 1653.

"IT's surprise to me that your Eminence should take notice of a person so inconsiderable as myself, living, as it were, separate from the world. This honor has, as it ought, [made] a very deep impression upon me, and does oblige [me] to serve your Eminency upon all occasions: and as I shall be happy to find out [such], so I trust that very honorable person, Monsieur Burdoe, will therein be helpful to,

"Your Eminency's thrice-humble servant,

"O. CROMWELL."

---

4. The negotiations with Whitlocke for going on that perilous Embassy to Sweden have left for us the following offhand specimen of an Official Note from Oliver. Oliver and Pickering had already been earnestly dealing with the learned man that he would go: at their subsequent interview, Oliver observed to Whitlocke, "Sir Gilbert" Pickering "would needs write a very fine Letter; and when he had done, did not like it himself. I then took pen and ink and straightway wrote that to you:"—

[*To Sir Bulstrode Whitlocke, Lord Commissioner of the Great Seal.*]

"WHITEHALL, 2d September, 1653.

"MY LORD, — The Council of State having thoughts of putting your Lordship to the trouble of being Extraordinary Ambassador to the Queen of Swedeland, did think fit not to impose that service upon you without first knowing your own freedom thereunto. Wherefore they were pleased to command our service to make this address to your Lordship; and hereby we can assure you of a very large confidence in your honor and abilities for this employment. To which we begging your answer, do rest, my Lord,·

"Your humble servants,

"OLIVER CROMWELL.
GILBERT PICKERING." [1]

---

5. The Little Parliament has now dismissed itself, and Oliver has henceforth a new Signature.

[1] From Whitlocke's Account of his Embassy (quoted in Forster. IV. 319).

[To his Eminency Cardinal Mazarin.]

"[WHITEHALL,] 26th January, 1653.

"MY LORD,— Monsieur de Baas[1] hath delivered me the Letter which your Eminency hath been pleased to write to me; and also communicated by word of mouth your particular affections and good disposition towards me, and the affairs of these Nations as now constituted. Which I esteem a very great honor; and hold myself obliged, upon the return of this Gentleman to you, to send my thanks to your Eminency for so singular a favor; my just resentment whereof I shall upon all occasions really demonstrate; and be ready to express the great value I have of your person and merits, as your affairs and interest shall require from,

"Your very affectionate friend to serve you,

"OLIVER P."[2]

---

6. "The Corporation of Lynn Regis," it appears, considered that the navigation of their Port would be injured by the works now going on for Draining the great Bedford Level of the Fens. They addressed the Protector on the subject; and this is his Letter in answer thereto. Nothing came of it farther.

"*To the Mayor and Aldermen of Lynn Regis.*

"WHITEHALL, 30th January, 1653.

"GENTLEMEN,— I received yours; and cannot but let you know the good resentments I have of your respects;— assuring you that I shall be always ready to manifest a tender love and care of you and your welfare, and in particular of that concernment of yours relating to navigation.

"Commending you to the grace of God, I remain,

"Your loving friend,

"OLIVER P."[3]

[1] The new Envoy, or Agent; of whom in the next No.

[2] From the Archives du Ministère des Affaires Etrangères, at Paris. Communicated by Thomas Wright, Esq. F.S.A. &c.

[3] *History of the Ancient and Present State of the Navigation of the Port of King's Lynn and of Cambridge* (London, fol. 1766), p. 55.

No. 28.

From 1654–1655: Vowel's Plot; Rectory of Houghton Conquest; Penruddock's Plot; Letter to the Poet Waller;
New England.

[Vol. xviii. pp. 394, 486; antea, p. 5.]

1. ANOTHER wholly insignificant Official Note to Mazarin, in regard
to Vowel's Plot, and the dismissal of M. De Baas for his complicity in it.
De Baas, whom some call Le Baas, or rightly Le Bas, was a kind of subsidiary Agent despatched by Mazarin early in the Spring of 1653–4 " to
congratulate the new Protector,"— that is, to assist Bourdeaux, who soon
after got the regular title of Ambassador, in ascertaining how a Treaty
could be made with the new Protector, or, on the whole, what was to be
done with England and him. Hitherto, during the Dutch War and other
vicissitudes, there had been a mixed undefinable relation between the two
Countries, rather hostile than neutral. The " Treaty and firm Amity,"
as we know, had its difficulties, its delays ; in the course of which it
occurred to M. Le Bas that perhaps the Restoration of Charles Stuart,
by Vowel and Company, might be a shorter cut to the result. Examination of Witnesses in consequence ; examination of Le Bas himself
by the Protector and Council, in consequence ; mild hint to Le Bas that
he must immediately go home again.[1]

[*Eminentissimo Cardinali Mazarino.*]

" EMINENTISSIME CARDINALIS, — In Litteris Nostris ad Regem da-
tis, causas et rationes recensuimus quare Dominum De Baas ex hâc Re-
publicâ excedere jussimus, et Majestatcm Suam certam fecimus, Nos,
non obstante hâc dicti De Baas machinationé, cujus culpam ei solum-
modo imputamus, in eâdem adhuc sententiâ perstare, firmam arctamque
Pacem et Amicitiam cum Galliâ colendi et paciscendi. Atque hâc occasione gratum nobis est priora illa propensæ nostræ erga vos et res vcs-
tras voluntatis indicia et testimonia renovare ; quam etiam, datâ subinde
occasione, palam facere et luculenter demonstrare parati erimus. Interea
Eminentiam vestram Divinæ benignitatis præsidio commendamus.

" Dab. ex Albâ Aulâ, vicesimo nono Junii an. 1654.

" OLIVERIUS P."[2]

[1] Depositions concerning him (April, May, 1654), Thurloe, ii. 309, 351–353:
notice of his first arrival (February, 1653–4), ib. 113. See also ib. 379, 437.

[2] From the Archives du Ministère des Affaires Etrangères, at Paris. Communicated by Thomas Wright, Esq., F.S.A. &c.

Of which, if it be worth translating, this is the English : —

" MOST EMINENT CARDINAL, — In our Letter to the King we have set forth the grounds and occasions moving us to order M. de Baas to depart from this Commonwealth ; and have assured his Majesty, that notwithstanding this deceit of the said De Baas, the blame of which is imputed to him alone, we persist as heretofore in the same purpose of endeavoring and obtaining a firm and intimate Peace and Amity with France.   And it gives us pleasure, on this occasion, to renew those former testimonies of our good inclination towards you and your interests ; which also, as opportunity offers, we shall in future be ready to manifest and clearly demonstrate.   In the mean while, we commend your Eminency to the keeping of the Almighty,

" OLIVER P.

" WHITEHALL, 29th June, 1654."

----

2. PRESENTATION TO THE RECTORY OF HOUGHTON CONQUEST.

[*Communicated to me — Thomas Baker, the Cambridge Antiquary — by my worthy friend Brown Willis, Esq., of Whaddon Hall in Com. Bucks, from the original Presentation, in the hands of a friend of his.*]

" OLIVER P.

" Oliver, Lord Protector of the Commonwealth of England, Scotland and Ireland, and the Dominions thereunto belonging, to the Commissioners authorized by a late Ordinance for Approbation of Public Preachers, or [to] any five of them, greeting.   We present John Pointer to the Rectory of Houghton Conquest in the County of Bedford, void by the death of the late Incumbent, and to our presentation belonging ; to the end he may be approved of by them, and admitted thereunto, with all its rights, members and appurtenances whatsoever, according to the tenor of the aforesaid Ordinance.

" Given at Whitehall, the 29th of September, 1654."[1]

[1] Harl. MSS. no. 7053, f. 158.

3. Design against the Spanish West Indies.

[Vol. xviii. pp. 450; antea, p. 3.]

Our great Design against the Spaniards in the West Indies is still called only " a Design by Sea," and kept very secret. Proper, however, as the rumors probably are loud, to give the Parliament, now sitting, some hint of it. Hence this Letter; of no moment otherwise. Unluckily " the right-hand border of the Paper is now much worn away ; " so that several words are wanting, — conjecturally supplied here, *in italics.*

" *To Our right trusty and well-beloved William Lenthall, Esquire, Speaker of the Parliament.*

" Whitehall, 22d September, 1654.

" Mr. Speaker, — I have, by advice of the Council, undertaken a Design by Sea, very much (as we hope and judge) for the honor and advantage of the Commonwealth ; and have already made the preparations requisite for such an undertaking. But before I proceed to the execution thereof, the Parliament being now convened, I thought it agreeable to my trust to communicate to them the aforesaid resolution, and not to desire the delay thereof any longer (although I suppose you may be engaged, at the present, in matters of greater weight) ; because many *miscarriages* will fall out in this Business through delay, as well in *providing* of the charge as otherwise ; the well-timing of such a *Design* being as considerable as anything about it. And the*refore I* desire you to take your first opportunity to acquaint *the House* with the contents of this Letter, wherein I have *forborne* to be more particular, because there are severed *persons* in Parliament who know this whole Business, and *can inform* the House of all particulars, if the House do judge *it to be* consistent with the nature of the Design to have it *offered* to them particularly : — which I refer to their consideration ; and rest,

" Your assured friend,

" Oliver P." [1]

---

[1] " Autograph Letter throughout." Copy *penes me ;* reference (Tanner MSS. no doubt) is unfortunately lost. See *Commons Journals,* vii. 369 (22d September, 1654), for the Return made.

4. New Appointments; Announcement of them to the Parliament.

"OLIVER P.

" To Our right trusty and right well-beloved William Lenthall, Esquire, Speaker of the Parliament.

"RIGHT TRUSTY AND RIGHT WELL-BELOVED, — We greet you well. It being expressed in the Thirty-fourth Article of the Government, That the Chancellor, Keeper or Commissioners of the Great Seal, the Treasurer, Admiral, Chief Governors of Ireland and Scotland, and the Chief Justices of both the Benches, shall be chosen by the approbation of Parliament, and in the intervals of Parliament by the approbation of the major part of the Council, — to be afterwards approved by the Parliament; and several Persons of integrity and ability having been appointed by Me (with the Council's approbation) for some of those Services before the meeting of the Parliament; — I have thought it necessary to transmit unto you, in the enclosed Schedule, the names of those Persons, to the end that the resolution of the Parliament may be known concerning them: which I desire may be with such speed as the other public occasions of the Commonwealth will admit. And so I bid you heartily farewell.

" Given at Whitehall, this Fifth day of October, 1654." [1]

Enclosure is endorsed: " The Schedule inclosed in his Highnes Letter of ye 5th of October, 1654." — " Read October 5th, 1654; and again, 6th Oct."

CHARLES FLEETWOOD, Esquire . .	Deputy of Ireland.
BULSTRODE WHITLOCKE, Esquire . SIR THOMAS WIDDRINGTON, Knt. . JOHN LISLE, Esquire	Commissioners of the Great Seal of England.
The Three Commissioners of the Great Seal above named . . . . THE LORD CHIEF JUSTICE ROLLE . THE LORD CHIEF JUSTICE ST. JOHN EDWARD MONTAGUE, Esquire . . . WILLIAM SYDENHAM, Esquire . . .	Commissioners of the Treasury.
HENRY ROLLE	Chief Justice of the Court of Upper Bench.
OLIVER ST. JOHN	Chief Justice of the Court of Common Pleas.

[1] Original, with the Great Seal attached, in Tanner MSS., lii. 135. See *Commons Journals*, vii. 378 (24th October, 1654).

5 and 6. The following Two Letters, one of which is clearly of Thurloe's composition, have an evident reference to Penruddock's affair; they find their place here.

Sergeant Wilde, now more properly Lord Chief Baron Wilde, is a Worcester man; sat in the Long Parliament for that City, very prominent all along in Law difficulties and officialities, — in particular, directly on the heel of the Second Civil War, Autumn, 1648, he rode circuit, and did justice on offenders, without asking his Majesty's opinion on the subject; which was thought a great feat on his part.[1] Shortly after which he was made Chief Baron, and so continues, — holding even now the Spring Assizes at Worcester, I think. Thurloe, as we said, appears to have shaped this Letter into words; only the signature and meaning can be taken as Oliver's. Unluckily too, either Mrs. Warner the Editress must have misread the date "25th" for 24th, or else Thurloe himself in his haste have miswritten, forgetting that it was New Year's Day overnight, that it is not now 1654 but 1655. We will take the former hypothesis; and correct Mrs. Warner's "25th," which in this case makes a whole year of difference.

" For Sir John Wilde, Sergeant-at-Law, and the rest of the Justices of Peace for the County of Worcester, or any of them, to be communicated to the rest; or, in his absence, to Nicholas Lechmere, Esq., Worcester.

"WHITEHALL, 24th March, 1654.

" GENTLEMEN, — We doubt not but you have heard before this time of the hand of God going along with us, in defeating the late rebellious Insurrection. And we hope that, through His blessing upon our labors, an effectual course will be taken for the total disappointment of the whole Design. Yet knowing the resolution of the common Enemy to involve this Nation in new calamities, we conceive ourselves, and all others intrusted with preserving the peace of the Nation, obliged to endeavor in their places to prevent and defeat the Enemy's intentions: and therefore, as a measure especially conducing to that end,

" We do earnestly recommend to you To take order that diligent Watches (such as the Law hath appointed) be daily kept, for taking a strict account of all strangers in the Country. Which will not only be a means to suppress all loose and idle persons; but may probably cause some of those who come from abroad to kindle fires here, to be apprehended and seized upon, — especially if care be taken to secure

[1] Thanked by the Parliament (*Commons Journals*, v. 49, 10th October, 1648).

all them that cannot give a good account of their business; — and may also break all dangerous meetings and assemblings together. Herein we do require, and shall expect, your effectual endeavors; knowing that, if what by Law ought to be done were done with diligence in this respect, the contrivance of such dangerous Designs as these would be frustrated in their bud, or kept from growing to a maturity. I rest,

"Your affectionate friend,

"Oliver P."[1]

This second Letter, to the Gloucester Authorities, on the same subject, we judge by the style of it to be mostly or altogether the Protector's own.

"For Major Wade, Major Creed, and the Mayor and Aldermen of the City of Gloucester.

"Whitehall, 24th March, 1654.

"Gentlemen, — We doubt not but you have heard before this time of the good hand of God going along with us in defeating the late rebellious Insurrection; so that, as we have certain intelligence from all parts, the Risings are everywhere suppressed and dissolved, and some hundreds of prisoners in custody, and daily more are discovered and secured. And we hope that, through the blessing of God upon our labors, an effectual course will be taken for the total disappointment of the whole Design.

"The readiness of the Honest People to appear hath been a great encouragement to us, and of no less discouragement to the Enemy; who, had he prevailed, would, without doubt, have made us the most miserable and harassed Nation in the world. And therefore we hold ourselves obliged to return you our hearty thanks for your zeal and forwardness in so readily appearing and contributing your assistance; wherein, although your Country and your own particular as to outward and inward happiness were concerned, yet we are fully persuaded that a more general Principle respecting the glory of God, and the good of all these Nations, hath been the motive to incite you: and therefore your action goes upon the higher and more noble account.

"You have desired that we would consider of ways how to find money to carry on this work. If the Business had not been allayed, we *must* have found out a way and means to allay that want. But otherwise indeed we make it, as we hope we ever shall, our design to ease this

[1] Rebecca Warner's *Epistolary Curiosities*, First Series (Bath, 1818), pp. 51-53.

Nation, and not to burden it; and are tender, — as we conceive yourselves have been, — of putting the good people thereof to any unnecessary charge. And therefore, as you shall have fitting opportunity, you may recommend our thankfulness to your honest willing Countrymen, as we hereby do to yourselves, for this their forwardness; and let them know That when any danger shall approach, as we shall be watchful to observe the Enemy's stirrings, we will give you timely notice thereof: and we trust those good hearts will be ready, [on] being called out by you, to appear upon all such occasions. In the mean time they may continue at their homes, blessing God for His mercy, and enjoying the fruit and comfort of this happy deliverance, and the other benefits of Peace.

" And I do hereby let you know that Letters are directed to the Justices of Peace of several Counties,[1] That Watches be kept, such as the Law hath appointed for taking a strict account of all strangers, especially near the Coast. Which will not only be a means to suppress all loose and idle persons, but may probably cause some of those that come from abroad [in order] to kindle fires here, to be apprehended and seized, — especially if care be taken to secure all them that cannot give a good account; and may also break all dangerous meetings and assemblings together. And indeed if what by Law ought to be done were done with diligence in this respect, the continuance of such dangerous Designs as these would be frustrated in the birth, or kept from growing to maturity.

" Having said this, — with remembrance of my hearty love to you, I rest,

" Your very affectionate friend,

" OLIVER P."[2]

Of the same date, the same Letter (with insignificant variations), bearing the address, *For Colonel Humphrey Brewster and the rest of the Commissioners for the Militia for the County of Suffolk*, and dated as well as signed in Oliver's hand, is now in the possession of Charles Meadows, Esq., Great Bealings, Woodbridge, a kinsman or representative of this Humphrey Brewster.

The one considerable variation is as follows. Paragraph second, of the Copy given here, and the first two sentences of paragraph third, are suppressed in Brewster's Copy, and there stands instead, — after " Design: " " And now forasmuch as it hath pleased God thus to allay this

---

[1] Foregoing Letter, To Wilde, for one.

[2] *Bibliotheca Gloucestrensis* (Gloucester, 1825; — see antea, vol. xvii. p. 160), p. 418; — from the City Records of Gloucester.

Business ; and making it, as we hope we soon (*sic*) shall, our design to ease this Nation :" &c. — after and before which the two Copies almost exactly correspond. (MS. *penes me*.)

By the City Records just cited from, it appears that, on the eve of the Battle of Worcester, in 1651, "Eighteen Gloucester Bakers had sent to Tewkesbury for the Lord General Cromwell's Army, thirteen hundred and odd Dozens of Bread at a Shilling the dozen, amounting to £66 5*s*. ; and that the Mayor and others, on the 1st September, 1651, sent Forty barrels of strong Beer to the Lord General, ' praying your favorable acceptance thereof, as an argument of the good affection of this Corporation, who doth congratulate your seasonable coming into these parts, for the relief thereof against the violence of the common Enemy, and wish prosperous success to you and your Army.'"[1]

Furthermore, that on the 11th October, 1651, directly after the said Battle, Gloucester did itself the honor of appointing the Lord General Oliver Cromwell, "in consideration of the singular favor and benevolence which his Excellency hath manifested to us and to this City," High Steward of the same, "with an annual rent of 100 shillings, issuing out of our Manors ; " — for at least one payment of which there exists the Lord General's receipt, in this form : —

"23 Novemb 1652.

"Recd of the Maior and Burg[s] of Glouc[r] by the hands of Mr. Dorney Townclerke of the said City, the day and year above[d] the some of ffive pounds as being a fee due to me as Lord High Steward of the said Citty, I say Recd

$$£\ s.\ d.$$
$$05\ 00\ 00$$

" O. CROMWELL."[2]

---

7. The following brief Note to the Poet Waller, which has latterly turned up, has a certain peculiar interest, on two grounds: *first*, to all readers, as offering some momentary glimpse, momentary but unique and indisputable, of Oliver's feeling on reading the Poet's noble "*Panegyric to my Lord Protector;* " and *secondly*, to antiquarian people, as fixing what was hitherto left vague, the approximate date of that celebrated

---

[1] *Bibliotheca Gloucestrensis*, p. 406.　　　　[2] Ib. p. 411.

Piece.[1] To an audacious guesser it might almost seem, these Verses had reached Oliver, by messenger, a day or two before; and the "unhappy mistake" were Oliver's, in sending, on the morrow, to have an Interview with Waller, and finding him to be at Northampton instead!

"For my very loving Friend Edmund [2] Waller, Esq., Northampton: Haste, haste.

" [WHITEHALL,] 13th June, 1655.

" SIR, — Let it not trouble you that, by so unhappy a mistake, you are, as I hear, at Northampton. Indeed I am passionately affected with it.

" I have no guilt upon me unless it be to be revenged for your so willingly mistaking me in your Verses.[3] This action [of mine] will put you to redeem me from yourself, as you have already from the world. Ashamed, I am,

" Your friend and servant,

" OLIVER P."[4]

---

8 and 9. Two poor American scraps, which our New England friends ought to make more lucent for us; worth their paper and ink in this place.

" To Our trusty and well-beloved the President, Assistants and Inhabitants of Rhode Island, together with the rest of the Providence Plantations, in the Narragansett Bay in New England.

"[WHITEHALL,] 29th March, 1655.

" GENTLEMEN, — Your Agent here hath presented unto us some particulars concerning your Government, which you judge necessary to be settled by us here. But by reason of the other great and weighty affairs of this Commonwealth, we have been necessitated to defer the consideration of them to a farther opportunity.

" In the mean while we were willing to let you know, That you are to proceed in your Government according to the tenor of your Charter formerly granted on that behalf; taking care of the peace and safety of

---

1 Fenton, *Works of Edmund Waller* (London, 1730), gives the *Panegyric* (pp. 113-121); and (ib. p. cix) his Note upon it, in which all he can say as to date is, "about the year 1654."

2 Copy has "Edward " as yet.

3 Fenton's *Waller*, pp. 113 and cix.

4 In the *Waller* Archives, Beaconsfield; copied by a "Rev. L. B. Larking," Cousin of the now Waller; — printed in *Notes-and-Queries* Newspaper, 2d Jan. 1858. (*Note of 1869.*)

these Plantations, that neither through any intestine commotions, or foreign invasions, there do arise any detriment or dishonor to this Commonwealth or yourselves, as far as you by your care and diligence can prevent. And as for the things which are before us, they shall, as soon as the other occasions will permit, receive a just and fitting determination.

"And so we bid you farewell; and rest,

"Your very loving friend,

"OLIVER P."[1]

Towards the end of the Dutch War, during that undefinable relation with France, "hostile rather than neutral," which did not end in Treaty till October, 1655,[2] Oliver's Major Sedgwick, whom we have since known in Jamaica, had laid hold of certain "French Forts," and indeed of a whole French region, the region now called *Nova Scotia*, then called *Acadie;* of which Forts and of the region they command, it is Oliver's purpose, for the behoof of his New-Englanders, to retain possession;[3]— as the following small document will testify: —

" To Captain John Leverett, Commander of the Forts lately taken from the French in America.

"We have received an account from Major Sedgwick of his taking several Forts from the French in America, and that he hath left you to command and secure them for Us and this Commonwealth: And although We make no doubt of your fidelity and diligence in performance of your trust, yet We have thought it necessary to let you know of how great consequence it is, that you use your utmost care and circumspection, as well to defend and keep the Forts abovesaid, as also to improve the regaining of them into Our hands to the advantage of Us and this State, by such ways and means as you shall judge conducible thereunto. And as We shall understand from you the state and condition of those places, We shall from time to time give such directions as shall be necessary.

"Given at Whitehall, this 3d of April, 1655.

"OLIVER P."[4]

[1] Original in the Rhode Island Archives: Printed in Hutchinson's *Collection*, and elsewhere.

[2] Thurloe, iv. 75.

[3] In Bancroft's *History of the United States* (Boston, 1837), i. 445, is some faint and not very exact notice of the affair.

[4] Original in the possession of the Massachusetts Historical Society: Printed in their *Third Series*, vii. 121. — In vol. ii. of the same Work (Boston, 1820),

To which there are now, from this side of the Water, the following small Excerpts to be added : —

Grant of Privy Seal: "6th June, 1655, to Major Robert Sedgwick, £1,793 7s. 8d., in full of his Account for service done against the French." And

Ditto, "28th July, 1656, to Captain John Leverett, £4,482 3s. 11½d., in full satisfaction of all sums of money due to him upon Account of his receipts and disbursements about the Forts taken from the French in America, and of his Salary for 760 days, at 15s. *per diem.*" [1]

Oliver kept his Forts and his *Acadie,* through all French Treaties, for behoof of his New-Englanders : not till after the Restoration did the country become French again, and continue such for a century or so.

———

10. Is a small domestic matter : —

"*For Colonel Alban Cox, in Hertfordshire.*

"WHITEHALL, 24th April, 1655.

"SIR, — Having occasion to speak with you upon some Affairs relating to the Public, I would have you, as soon as this comes to your hands, to repair up hither; and upon your coming, you shall be acquainted with the particular reasons of my sending for you. I rest,

"Your loving friend,

"OLIVER P." [2]

———

At Blackdown House in Sussex, now and for long past the residence of a family named Yaldwin, are preserved two Letters Patent signed "Oliver P.," of date 3d December, 1656, appointing "William Yaldwin Esq." High Sheriff of Sussex. Printed in Dallaway's *Rape of Arundel* (p. 363) ; need not be reprinted here.

pp. 323–364, is an elaborate Notice of certain fragmentary MS. *Records of the Long Parliament* still extant at New York, — which Notice ought to be cancelled in subsequent editions! The amazingly curious "Records" at New York turn out to be nothing but some odd volumes of the *Commons Journals* of that period; the entire Set of which, often enough copied in *manuscript,* was *printed* here about fifty years ago, and is very common indeed, in the Buttershops and elsewhere!

[1] *Fourth Report of Deputy Keeper of the Public Records* (London, 1843), Appendix ii. p. 192 ; *Fifth Report* (London, 1844), Appendix ii. p. 260.

[2] *Gentleman's Magazine* (London, 1788), lviii. 379.

No. 29.

SUFFOLK YEOMANRY.

THE Suffolk Commission for a select mounted County-Militia, still remains; one remaining out of many that have perished. Addressed to the Humphrey Brewster whom we have occasionally met with before.[1]

" Instructions unto Colonel Humphrey Brewster, commissionated by his Highness the Lord Protector to be Captain of a Troop of Horse to be raised within the County of Suffolk, for the service of his Highness and the Commonwealth.

" 1. You shall forthwith raise, enlist, and have in readiness under your command as Captain, and such Lieutenant, Cornet and Quarter-Master as his Highness shall commissionate for that purpose, one hundred able Soldiers, the three Corporals included, well mounted for service, and armed with one good sword and case of pistols, holsters, saddle, bridle, and other furniture fit for war, to serve as a Troop of Horse in the service of the Commonwealth, as is hereafter required.

" 2. You shall use your utmost endeavor that the said Troops shall be men of good life and conversation; and before their being listed shall promise that they will be true and faithful to his Highness the Lord Protector and the Commonwealth, against all who shall design or attempt anything against his Highness's Person, or endeavor to disturb the Public Peace. And the like engagement shall be taken by the Lieutenant, Cornet and Quarter-Master of the said Troop.

" 3. You shall be ready to draw forth and muster the said Troop, armed and fitted as aforesaid, upon the 25th day of December next ensuing, from which time the said Troop, Officers and Soldiers, shall be deemed to be in the actual service of his Highness and the Commonwealth, and be paid ·accordingly. And you shall also draw forth the said Troops four times in every year within the county of Suffolk, completely furnished as before mentioned, to be raised and mustered by such persons as shall from time to time be appointed by the Protector.

" 4. You shall also at all other times have the said Troops in all readiness as aforesaid at forty-eight hours' warning, or sooner if it may

[1] Antea, p. 375.

be, whensoever his Highness, or such as he shall appoint for that purpose, shall require the same for the suppressing of any invasion, rebellion, insurrection, or tumult, or performing of any other service within England and Wales. And in case that any of the said service shall continue above the space of twenty-eight days in one year, the said Officers and Soldiers shall, after the expiration of the said twenty-eight days, be paid according to the establishment of the Army then in force, over and besides what is agreed to be paid unto them by these presents, for so long as they shall continue in the said service.

"5. That in case any shall make default in appearance, without just and sufficient cause, or shall not be mounted, armed and provided as aforesaid, or shall offend against good manners or the laws of war; that every person so offending shall be liable to such punishment as the Captain or chief Officer present with the Troops, with advice of the persons appointed to take the said musters, shall think fit: provided the said punishment extends no farther than loss of place or one year's pay.

"6. That in consideration of the service to be performed as aforesaid, you shall receive for the use of the said Troop the sum of one thousand pounds per annum, to be paid out of the public revenue by quarterly payments, to be distributed according to the proportions following: To yourself, as Captain, one hundred pounds per annum; to the Lieutenant fifty pounds per annum; to the Cornet twenty-five pounds per annum; to the Quarter-Master thirteen pounds six shillings and eightpence per annum; to each of the three Corporals, two pounds [additional] per annum; one Trumpet, five pounds six shillings and fourpence per annum; and to each Soldier eight pounds per annum.

"OLIVER P.[1]

"WHITEHALL, 26th October, 1655."

———◆———

No. 30.

SPEECH SHOULD BE "XV."

[Antea, p. 217.]

FINAL Speech on that matter of the Kingship (concerning *which* it is gracefully altogether silent); that is to say, Speech on *accepting* the Humble Petition and Advice, with the Title of King withdrawn, and

---

[1] In the possession of Charles Meadows, Esq., Great Bealings, Woodbridge; a descendant of Brewster's.

that of Protector substituted as he had required: Painted Chamber, Monday, 25th May, 1657.[1]

" MR. SPEAKER, — I desire to offer a word or two unto you; which shall be but a word. I did well bethink myself, before I came hither this day, that I came not as to a triumph, but with the most serious thoughts that ever I had in all my life, to undertake one of the greatest tasks that ever was laid upon the back of a human creature. And I make no question but you will, and so will all men, readily agree with me that without the support of the Almighty I shall necessarily sink under the burden of it; not only with shame and reproach to myself, but with that that is more a thousand times, and in comparison of which I and my family are not worthy to be mentioned, — with the loss and prejudice of these Three Nations. And, that being so, I must ask your help, and the help of all those that fear God, that by their prayers I may receive assistance from the hand of God. His presence, going along, will enable to the discharge of so great a duty and trust as this is : and nothing else [will].

" Howbeit, I have some other things to desire you, I mean of the Parliament: — That seeing this is but, as it were, an introduction to the carrying on of the government of these Nations, and forasmuch as there are many things which cannot be supplied, for the enabling to the carrying on of this work, without your help and assistance, I think it is my duty to ask your help in them. Not that I doubted; for I believe the same spirit that hath led you to this will easily suggest the rest to you. The truth is, and I can say [it] in the presence of God, that nothing would have induced me to have undertaken this insupportable burden to flesh and blood, had it not been that I have seen in this Parliament all along a care of doing all those things that might truly and really answer the ends that have been engaged: for you have satisfied [2] your forwardness and readiness therein very fully already.

" I thought it my duty, when your Committee which you were pleased to send to me to give the grounds and reasons of your proceedings to help my conscience and judgment, — I was then bold to offer to them several considerations : which were received by them, and have been presented to you. In answer to which, the Committee did bring several resolves of yours, which I have by me. I think those are not yet made so authentic and authoritative as was desired; and therefore, though I cannot doubt it, yet I thought it my duty to ask it of you, that there

---

[1] *Commons Journals*, vii. 539, 537 (last entry there).
[2] Query, testified ?

may be a perfecting of those things. Indeed, as I said before, I have my witness in the sight of God, that nothing would· have been an argument to me, howsoever desirable great places may seem to be to other men ; I say, nothing would have been an argument to me to have undertaken this ; but, as I said before, I saw such things determined by you as makes clearly for the liberty of the Nations, and for the liberty and interest and preservation of all such as fear God, — of all that fear God under various forms. And if God make not these Nations thankful to you for your care therein, it will fall as a sin on their heads. And therefore I say, that hath been one main encouragement.

" I confess there are other things that tend to reformation, to the discountenancing of vice, to the encouragement of good men and virtue, and the completing of those things also, — concerning some of which you have not yet resolved anything ; save to let me know by your Committee that you would not be wanting in anything for the good of these Nations. Nor do I speak it as in the least doubting it ; but I do earnestly and heartily desire, to the end God may crown your work and bless you and this Government, that in your own time, and with what speed you judge fit, these things may be provided for." [1]

No. 31.

From 1657. LAST ROYALIST PLOT.

[Antea, p. 273.]

1. " *To Our trusty and well-beloved the Vice-chancellor and Convocation of our University of Oxford.*

"OLIVER P.

" TRUSTY AND WELL-BELOVED, — We greet you well. Amongst the many parts of that Government which is intrusted to us, we do look upon the Universities as meriting very much of our care and thoughts : And finding that the place of Chancellor of our University of Oxford is at present in Ourself ; and withal judging that the continuance thereof in our hands may not be so consistent with the present constitution of affairs, —

" We have therefore thought fit to resign the said Office, as we hereby

[1] *Commons Journals*, vii. 439, 440.

do ; and to leave you at freedom to elect some such other person thereunto, as you shall conceive meet for the execution thereof.

" Our will and pleasure therefore is, That you do proceed to the election of a Chancellor with your first conveniency. Not doubting but you will, in your choice, have a just regard to the advancement and encouragement of Piety and Learning, and to the continuing and farther settling of good Order and Government amongst you ; which you may easily find yourselves obliged to have principally in your consideration and design, whether you respect the University itself, or the good of the Commonwealth upon which it hath so great an influence. And although our relation to you may by this means in some sort be changed, yet you may be confident we shall still retain a real affection to you, and be ready upon all occasions to seek and promote your good.

" Given at Whitehall, this 3d day of July, 1657."[1]

2. " *To Our trusty and well-beloved the Bailiffs and Free Burgesses of our Town of Oswestry : These.*

" OLIVER P.

" Trusty and Well-beloved, — We, being informed that the Free School of our Town of Oswestry is now void of a Head Schoolmaster settled there, by reason of the delinquency and ejection of Edward Paine late Schoolmaster thereof,

" Have thought fit to recommend unto you Mr. John Evans, the son of Matthew Evans late of Penegos in the County of Montgomery, as a fit person, both for piety and learning, to be Head Schoolmaster of the said School ; and That, so far as in yourselves [is], the said Mr. Evans may be forthwith settled and invested there accordingly.

" Which Act of yours we shall be ready to confirm, if it be adjudged requisite and proper for us. And not doubting of the performance of this our pleasure, we commit you to God.

" Given at Whitehall, this 13th day of July, 1657."[2]

---

[1] Archives of Oxford University. Communicated by the Rev. Dr. Bliss.

[2] *Endowed Grammar-Schools*, by N. Carlisle (London, 1818), ii. 369, art. Salop.

3. " *To Our trusty and well-beloved the Mayor, Aldermen, and Common Council of our City of Gloucester : These.*

" OLIVER P.

" Trusty and Well-beloved, — We greet you well. I do hear on all hands that the Cavalier party are designing to put us into blood. We are, I hope, taking the best care we can, by the blessing of God, to obviate this danger ; but our intelligence on all hands being, that they have a design upon your City, we could not but warn you thereof, and give you authority, as we do hereby,

" To put yourselves into the best posture you can for your own defence, by raising your Militia by virtue of your Commissioners formerly sent to you, and putting them in a readiness for the purpose aforesaid. Letting you also know that, for your better encouragement herein, you shall have a troop of horse sent you to quarter in or near your Town.

" We desire you to let us hear from you, from time to time, what occurs to you touching the Malignant party : and so we bid you farewell.

" Given at Whitehall, this 2d of December, 1657." [1]

A Paper of the same date, of precisely the same purport, directed to the Authorities at Bristol, has come to us ; another out of many then sent ; but of course only one, if even one, requires to be inserted here.

---

4. Letter written directly on dissolving the Parliament ; probably one of many, to the like effect, despatched that day : —

" *For Colonel Fox, Captain of the Militia Troop in our County of Hertford : These. For our special service.*

" *To be left with the Postmaster of St. Albans : to be speedily sent.*

" Whitehall, 4th February, 1657.

" Sir, — By our last Letters to you, we acquainted you what danger the Commonwealth was then in from the old Cavalier Party (who were designing new insurrections within us, whilst their Head and Master was contriving to invade us from abroad) ; — and thereupon desired

---

[1] City Records of Gloucester (in *Bibliotheca Gloucestrensis*, p. 419).

your care and vigilancy for preserving the peace, and apprehending all dangerous persons.

" Our intelligence of that kind still continues. And we are more assured of their resolutions to put in execution their designs aforesaid within a very short time ; [they] being much encouraged from some late actings of some turbulent and unquiet spirits, as well in this Town as elsewhere, who, to frustrate and render vain and fruitless all those good hopes of Settlement which we had conceived from the proceedings of Parliament before their Adjournment in June last, framed a treasonable Petition to the House of Commons, by the name of the ' Parliament of the Commonwealth of England ; ' designing thereby not only the over-throw of the late *Petition and Advice* of the Parliament, but of all that hath been done these seven years ; hoping thereby to bring all things into confusion ; — and were in a very tumultuous manner procuring subscriptions thereunto, giving out that they were encouraged to it by some Members of the House of Commons.

" And the truth is, the Debates that have been in that House since their last meeting have had a tendency to the stirring up and cherish-ing such humors ; — having done nothing in fourteen days but debate Whether they should own the Government of these Nations, as it is contained in the *Petition and Advice,* which the Parliament at their former sitting had invited us to accept of, and had sworn us unto ; they themselves also having taken an Oath upon it before they went into the House. And we, judging these things to have in them very dangerous consequences to the Peace of this Nation, and to the loosening all the bonds of Government ; and being hopeless of obtaining supplies of money, for answering the exigencies of the Nation, from such men as are not satisfied with the Foundation we stand upon, — thought it of absolute necessity to dissolve this present Parliament ; — which I have done this day : — And to give you notice thereof ; that you, with your Troop, may be most vigilant for the suppressing of any disturbance which may arise from any party whatsoever. And if you can hear of any persons who have been active to promote the aforesaid treasonable Petition, that you apprehend them, and give an account thereof to us forthwith. And we do farther let you know, That we are sensible of your want of pay for yourself and Troop ; and do assure you that effectual care shall be taken therein, and that without delay. And so I rest,

" Your loving friend,

" OLIVER P."[1]

1 *Gentleman's Magazine* (London, 1788), lviii. 313.

5. *"For the Commanders of the Militia of the City of Gloucester :*
These.

"WHITEHALL, 11th March, 1657.

"GENTLEMEN, — We are informed that the Enemy from Flanders intend to invade us very suddenly, and to that purpose have Twenty-two Ships of War ready in the Harbor of Ostend, and are preparing others also which they have bought in Holland, and some men are ready to be put on board them. And at the same time an Insurrection is intended in this Nation. And the time for the executing these designs is intended by them to be very sudden.

"We have therefore thought fit to give you notice hereof; and to signify to you our pleasure, That you put yourselves into the best posture you can for the securing the City of Gloucester, and put the arms into such hands as are true and faithful to us and this Commonwealth. We desire you to be very careful, and to let us hear from you of the receipt of this, and what you shall do in pursuance of this Letter. I rest,

"Your very assured friend,

"OLIVER P." [1]

———•———

No. 32.

TWO MANDATES TO CAMBRIDGE UNIVERSITY.

1. THAT John Castle be made Master of Arts : ——

" To Our trusty and well-beloved the Vice-chancellor and Senate of
Our University of Cambridge.

"OLIVER P.

"TRUSTY AND WELL-BELOVED, — Whereas by our appointment several Students in our University of Cambridge have been invited abroad to preach the Gospel in our Fleet, and for their encouragement have been by us assured that they should not suffer any prejudice in the University by reason of their absence in the said service : And whereas a petition hath been exhibited on the behalf of Mr. John Castle

[1] City Records of Gloucester (in *Bibliotheca Gloucestrensis*, p. 421).

of Trinity College, showing that whilst he was abroad as Minister in the Newcastle Frigate, he was disappointed of taking his degree of Master of Arts (as by course he ought), and that he cannot now, since his return, commence without the loss of one year's seniority, by reason of a statute of the University denying degrees to any non-resident:

" In performance of our said promise, and for the future encouragement of others in the like service, We do hereby signify unto you, That it is our will and pleasure that the said John Castle be by you created Master of Arts, and allowed the same seniority which, according to the custom of your University, he had enjoyed had he been resident at the usual time of taking degrees.

" Given at Whitehall, the 22d day of June, 1658." [1]

Castle, the Books indicate, had entered Trinity at the same time, and been under the same Tutor, with a very famous person, " *John Driden Northampt. admissus Pens.*" — both, namely, were admitted " Pensioners," in Sept., 1649.

------

2. That Benjamin Rogers. be made Bachelor of Music, — " a Form of Oliver Cromwell's Mandats," says Baker, who has excerpted this one.

" *To Our trusty and well-beloved the Vice-chancellor and Senate of Our University of Cambridge.*

" OLIVER P.

" TRUSTY AND WELL-BELOVED, — We greet you well. Whereas we are informed that you cannot, by the statutes and according to the customs of your University, admit any to the degree of Bachelor of Music unless he had some years before [been] admitted in a college : And whereas we are also certified that Benjamin Rogers hath attained to eminency and skill in that faculty : — We, willing to give all encouragement to the studies and abilities of men in that or any other ingenuous faculty, have thought fit to declare our will and pleasure, by these our letters, that, notwithstanding your statutes and customs, you cause Benjamin Rogers to be admitted and created Bachelor in Music, in some one or more of your congregations assembled in that our University ; he

[1] Cambridge Archives, " Grace-Book H. p. 181." Communicated by Rev. J. Edleston, Fellow of Trinity College.

paying such dues as are belonging to that degree, and giving some proof of his accomplishments and skill in music. And for so doing, these our letters shall be your warrant.

" Given at Whitehall, the 28th day of May, 1658." [1]

[1] Copy in Harl. MSS. no. 7053, f. 152 (Baker MSS. x. 373) ; — and as before, in " Grace-Book H. p. 180." — The Originals will never turn up. In the same Register of " Graces," or Decrees of Senate. is one (of date 1661) for *burning* whatsoever Mandates or Missives there are from Cromwell ; whereby doubtless the Originals (with small damage to *them*, and some satisfaction to the Heads of Houses) were destroyed.

EARLY KINGS OF NORWAY.

The Icelanders, in their long winter, had a great habit of writing; and were, and still are, excellent in penmanship, says Dahlmann. It is to this fact, that any little history there is of the Norse Kings and their old tragedies, crimes and heroisms, is almost all due. The Icelanders, it seems, not only made beautiful letters on their paper or parchment, but were laudably observant and desirous of accuracy; and have left us such a collection of narratives (*Sagas*, literally "Says") as, for quantity and quality, is unexampled among rude nations. Snorro Sturleson's History of the Norse Kings is built out of these old Sagas; and has in it a great deal of poetic fire, not a little faithful sagacity applied in sifting and adjusting these old Sagas; and, in a word, deserves, were it once well edited, furnished with accurate maps, chronological summaries, &c., to be reckoned among the great history-books of the world. It is from these sources, greatly aided by accurate, learned and unwearied Dahlmann,[1] the German Professor, that the following rough notes of the early Norway Kings are hastily thrown together. In Histories of England (Rapin's excepted) next to nothing has been shown of the many and strong threads of connection between English affairs and Norse.

[1] J. G. Dahlmann, *Geschichte von Dännemark*, 3 vols. 8vo. Hamburg, 1840-1843.

EARLY KINGS OF NORWAY.

———◆———

CHAPTER I.

HARALD HAARFAGR.

TILL about the Year of Grace 860 there were no kings in Norway, nothing but numerous jarls, — essentially kinglets, — each presiding over a kind of republican or parliamentary little territory; generally striving each to be on some terms of human neighborhood with those about him, but, — in spite of *"Fylke Things"* (Folk Things, little parish parliaments), and small combinations of these, which had gradually formed themselves, — often reduced to the unhappy state of quarrel with them. Harald Haarfagr was the first to put an end to this state of things, and become memorable and profitable to his country by uniting it under one head and making a kingdom of it; which it has continued to be ever since. His father, Halfdan the Black, had already begun this rough but salutary process, — inspired by the cupidities and instincts, by the faculties and opportunities, which the good genius of this world, beneficent often enough under savage forms, and diligent at all times to diminish anarchy as the world's *worst* savagery, usually appoints in such cases, — *conquest*, hard fighting, followed by wise guidance of the conquered; — but it was Harald the Fairhaired, his son, who conspicuously carried it on and completed it. Harald's birth-year, death-year, and chronology in general, are known only by inference and computation; but, by the latest reckoning, he died about the year 933 of our era, a man of eighty-three.

(159)

The business of conquest lasted Harald about twelve years (A.D. 860–872 ?), in which he subdued also the vikings of the out-islands, Orkneys, Shetlands, Hebrides, and Man. Sixty more years were given him to consolidate and regulate what he had conquered, which he did with great judgment, industry and success. His reign altogether is counted to have been of over seventy years.

The beginning of his great adventure was of a romantic character, — youthful love for the beautiful Gyda, a then glorious and famous young lady of those regions, whom the young Harald aspired to marry. Gyda answered his embassy and prayer in a distant, lofty manner: "Her it would not beseem to wed any Jarl or poor creature of that kind; let him do as Gorm of Denmark, Eric of Sweden, Egbert of England, and others had done, — subdue into peace and regulation the confused, contentious bits of jarls round him, and become a king; then, perhaps, she might think of his proposal: till then, not." Harald was struck with this proud answer, which rendered Gyda tenfold more desirable to him. He vowed to let his hair grow, never to cut or even to comb it till this feat were done, and the peerless Gyda his own. He proceeded accordingly to conquer, in fierce battle, a Jarl or two every year, and, at the end of twelve years, had his unkempt (and almost unimaginable) head of hair clipt off, — Jarl Rögnwald (*Reginald*) of Möre, the most valued and valuable of all his subject-jarls, being promoted to this sublime barber function; — after which King Harald, with head thoroughly cleaned, and hair grown, or growing again to the luxuriant beauty that had no equal in his day, brought home his Gyda, and made her the brightest queen in all the north. He had after her, in succession, or perhaps even simultaneously in some cases, at least six other wives; and by Gyda herself one daughter and four sons.

Harald was not to be considered a strict-living man, and he had a great deal of trouble, as we shall see, with the tumultuous ambition of his sons; but he managed his government, aided by Jarl Rögnwald and others, in a large, quietly potent,

and successful manner; and it lasted in this royal form till
his death, after sixty years of it.

These were the times of Norse colonization; proud Norsemen flying into other lands, to freer scenes, — to Iceland, to
the Faröe Islands, which were hitherto quite vacant (tenanted
only by some mournful hermit, Irish Christian *fakir*, or so);
still more copiously to the Orkney and Shetland Isles, the
Hebrides and other countries where Norse squatters and settlers already were. Settlement of Iceland, we say; settlement of the Faröe Islands, and, by far the notablest of all,
settlement of Normandy by Rolf the Ganger (A.D. 876 ?).[1]

Rolf, son of Rögnwald,[2] was lord of three little islets far
north, near the Fjord of Folden, called the Three Vigten
Islands; but his chief means of living was that of sea-
robbery; which, or at least Rolf's conduct in which, Harald
did not approve of. In the Court of Harald, sea-robbery was
strictly forbidden as between Harald's own countries, but as
against foreign countries it continued to be the one profession
for a gentleman; thus, I read, Harald's own chief son, King
Eric that afterwards was, had been at sea in such employments
ever since his twelfth year. Rolf's crime, however, was that
in coming home from one of these expeditions, his crew having fallen short of victual, Rolf landed with them on the
shore of Norway, and in his strait, drove in some cattle there
(a crime by law) and proceeded to kill and eat; which, in a
little while, he heard that King Harald was on foot to inquire
into and punish; whereupon Rolf the Ganger speedily got
into his ships again, got to the coast of France with his sea-
robbers, got infeftment by the poor King of France in the
fruitful, shaggy desert which is since called Normandy, land
of the Northmen; and there, gradually felling the forests,
banking the rivers, tilling the fields, became, during the next
two centuries, Wilhelmus Conquæstor, the man famous to England, and momentous at this day, not to England alone, but to all

---

[1] "Settlement," dated 912, by Munch, Hénault, &c. The Saxon Chronicle
says (anno 876): "In this year Rolf overran Normandy with his army, and
he reigned fifty winters."

[2] Dahlmann, ii. 87.

speakers of the English tongue, now spread from side to side of
the world in a wonderful degree.   Tancred of Hauteville and
his Italian Normans, though important too, in Italy, are not
worth naming in comparison.   This is a feracious earth, and
the grain of mustard-seed will grow to miraculous extent in
some cases.

Harald's chief helper, counsellor, and lieutenant was the
above-mentioned Jarl Rögnwald of Möre, who had the honor
to cut Harald's dreadful head of hair.   This Rögnwald was
father of Turf-Einar, who first invented peat in the Orkneys,
finding the wood all gone there; and is remembered to this
day.   Einar, being come to these islands by King Harald's
permission, to see what he could do in them, — islands in-
habited by what miscellany of Picts, Scots, Norse squatters
we do not know, — found the indispensable fuel all wasted.
Turf-Einar too may be regarded as a benefactor to his kind.
He was, it appears, a bastard; and got no coddling from his
father, who disliked him, partly perhaps, because "he was
ugly and blind of an eye," — got no flattering even on his
conquest of the Orkneys and invention of peat.   Here is the
parting speech his father made to him on fitting him out with
a "long-ship" (ship of war, "dragon-ship," ancient seventy-
four), and sending him forth to make a living for himself in
the world: "It were best if thou never camest back, for I
have small hope that thy people will have honor by thee;
thy mother's kin throughout is slavish."

Harald Haarfagr had a good many sons and daughters;
the daughters he married mostly to jarls of due merit who
were loyal to him; with the sons, as remarked above, he had
a great deal of trouble.   They were ambitious, stirring fellows, and grudged at their finding so little promotion from
a father so kind to his jarls; sea-robbery by no means an
adequate career for the sons of a great king,   Two of them,
Halfdan Haaleg (Long-leg), and Gudröd Ljome (Gleam), jealous of the favors won by the great Jarl Rögnwald, surrounded
him in his house one night, and burnt him and sixty men to
death there.   That was the end of Rögnwald, the invaluable
jarl, always true to Haarfagr; and distinguished in world

history by producing Rolf the Ganger, author of the Norman Conquest of England, and Turf-Einar, who invented peat in the Orkneys. Whether Rolf had left Norway at this time there is no chronology to tell me. As to Rolf's surname, "Ganger," there are various hypotheses; the likeliest, perhaps, that Rolf was so weighty a man no horse (small Norwegian horses, big ponies rather) could carry him, and that he usually walked, having a mighty stride withal, and great velocity on foot.

One of these murderers of Jarl Rögnwald quietly set himself in Rögnwald's place, the other making for Orkney to serve Turf-Einar in like fashion. Turf-Einar, taken by surprise, fled to the mainland; but returned, days or perhaps weeks after, ready for battle, fought with Halfdan, put his party to flight, and at next morning's light searched the island and slew all the men he found. As to Halfdan Long-leg himself, in fierce memory of his own murdered father, Turf-Einar "cut an eagle on his back," that is to say, hewed the ribs from each side of the spine and turned them out like the wings of a spread-eagle: a mode of Norse vengeance fashionable at that time in extremely aggravated cases!

Harald Haarfagr, in the mean time, had descended upon the Rögnwald scene, not in mild mood towards the new jarl there; indignantly dismissed said jarl, and appointed a brother of Rögnwald (brother, notes Dahlmann), though Rögnwald had left other sons. Which done, Haarfagr sailed with all speed to the Orkneys, there to avenge that cutting of an eagle on the human back on Turf-Einar's part. Turf-Einar did not resist; submissively met the angry Haarfagr, said he left it all, what had been done, what provocation there had been, to Haarfagr's own equity and greatness of mind. Magnanimous Haarfagr inflicted a fine of sixty marks in gold, which was paid in ready money by Turf-Einar, and so the matter ended.

CHAPTER II.

ERIC BLOOD-AXE AND BROTHERS.

IN such violent courses Haarfagr's sons, I know not how
many of them, had come to an untimely end; only Eric, the
accomplished sea-rover, and three others remained to him.
Among these four sons, rather impatient for property and
authority of their own, King Harald, in his old days, tried to
part his kingdom in some eligible and equitable way, and
retire from the constant press of business, now becoming bur-
densome to him.   To each of them he gave a kind of kingdom; Eric, his eldest son, to be head king, and the others to
be feudatory under him, and pay a certain yearly contribution;
an arrangement which did not answer well at all.   Head-King
Eric insisted on his tribute; quarrels arose as to the payment,
considerable fighting and disturbance, bringing fierce destruction from King Eric upon many valiant but too stubborn
Norse spirits, and among the rest upon all his three brothers,
which got him from the Norse populations the surname of
Blod-axe, "Eric Blood-axe," his title in history.   One of his
brothers he had killed in battle before his old father's life
ended; this brother was Bjorn, a peaceable, improving, trading, economic Under-king, whom the others mockingly called
"Bjorn the Chapman."   The great-grandson of this Bjorn
became extremely distinguished by and by as *Saint* Olaf.
Head-King Eric seems to have had a violent wife, too.   She
was thought to have poisoned one of her other brothers-in-law.
Eric Blood-axe had by no means a gentle life of it in this
world, trained to sea-robbery on the coasts of England, Scotland, Ireland and France, since his twelfth year.

Old King Fairhair, at the age of seventy, had another son,
to whom was given the name of Hakon.   His mother was a
slave in Fairhair's house; slave by ill-luck of war, though

nobly enough born. A strange adventure connects this Hakon
with England and King Athelstan, who was then entering upon
his great career there. Short while after this Hakon came into
the world, there entered Fairhair's palace, one evening as Fairhair sat feasting, an English ambassador or messenger, bearing
in his hand, as gift from King Athelstan, a magnificent sword,
with gold hilt and other fine trimmings, to the great Harald,
King of Norway. Harald took the sword, drew it, or was half
drawing it, admiringly from the scabbard, when the English
excellency broke into a scornful laugh, "Ha, ha; thou art now
the feudatory of my English king; thou hast accepted the
sword from him, and art now his man!" (acceptance of a
sword in that manner being the symbol of investiture in those
days.) Harald looked a trifle flurried, it is probable; but held
in his wrath, and did no damage to the tricksy Englishman.
He kept the matter in his mind, however, and next summer
little Hakon, having got his weaning done, — one of the pret-
tiest, healthiest little creatures, — Harald sent him off, under
charge of "Hauk" (*Hawk* so called), one of his principal warriors, with order, "Take him to England," and instructions
what to do with him there. And accordingly, one evening,
Hauk, with thirty men escorting, strode into Athelstan's high
dwelling (where situated, how built, whether with logs like
Harald's, I cannot specifically say), into Athelstan's high presence, and silently set the wild little cherub upon Athelstan's
knee. "What is this?" asked Athelstan, looking at the little
cherub. "This is King Harald's son, whom a serving-maid
bore to him, and whom he now gives thee as foster-child!"
Indignant Athelstan drew his sword, as if to do the gift a
mischief; but Hauk said, "Thou hast taken him on thy knee
[common symbol of adoption]; thou canst kill him if thou
wilt; but thou dost not thereby kill all the sons of Harald."
Athelstan straightway took milder thoughts; brought up, and
carefully educated Hakon; from whom, and this singular adventure, came, before very long, the first tidings of Christianity
into Norway.

Harald Haarfagr, latterly withdrawn from all kinds of business, died at the age of eighty-three — about A.D. 933, as is

computed; nearly contemporary in death with the first **Danish King, Gorm the Old,** who had done a corresponding feat in reducing Denmark under one head.   Remarkable old men, these two first kings; and possessed of gifts for bringing Chaos a little nearer to the form of Cosmos; possessed, in fact, of loyalties to Cosmos, that is to say, of authentic virtues in the savage state, such as have been needed in all societies at their incipience in this world; a kind of "virtues" hugely in discredit at present, but not unlikely to be needed again, to the astonishment of careless persons, before all is done !

CHAPTER III.

HAKON THE GOOD.

ERIC BLOOD-AXE, whose practical reign is counted to have begun about A.D. 930, had by this time, or within a year or so of this time, pretty much extinguished all his brother kings, and crushed down recalcitrant spirits, in his violent way; but had naturally become entirely unpopular in Norway, and filled it with silent discontent and even rage against him.   Hakon Fairhair's last son, the little foster-child of Athelstan in England, who had been baptized and carefully educated, was come to his fourteenth or fifteenth year at his father's death; a very shining youth, as Athelstan saw with just pleasure.   So soon as the few preliminary preparations had been settled, Hakon, furnished with a ship or two by Athelstan, suddenly appeared in Norway; got acknowledged by the Peasant Thing in Trondhjem; "the news of which flew over Norway, like fire through dried grass," says an old chronicler.   So that Eric, with his Queen Gunhild, and seven small children, had to run; no other shift for Eric.   They went to the Orkneys first of all, then to England, and he "got Northumberland as earldom," I vaguely hear, from Athelstan.   But Eric soon died, and his queen, with her children, went back to the Orkneys in search of refuge or help; to little purpose there or elsewhere.   **From**

Orkney she went to Denmark, where Harald Blue-tooth took her poor eldest boy as foster-child; but I fear did not very faithfully keep that promise. The Danes had been robbing extensively during the late tumults in Norway; this the Christian Hakon, now established there, paid in kind, and the two countries were at war; so that Gunhild's little boy was a welcome card in the hand of Blue-tooth.

Hakon proved a brilliant and successful king; regulated many things, public law among others (*Gule-Thing* Law, *Froste-Thing* Law: these are little codes of his accepted by their respective Things, and had a salutary effect in their time); with prompt dexterity he drove back the Blue-tooth foster-son invasions every time they came; and on the whole gained for himself the name of Hakon the Good. These Danish invasions were a frequent source of trouble to him, but his greatest and continual trouble was that of extirpating heathen idolatry from Norway, and introducing the Christian Evangel in its stead. His transcendent anxiety to achieve this salutary enterprise was all along his grand difficulty and stumbling-block; the heathen opposition to it being also rooted and great. Bishops and priests from England Hakon had, preaching and baptizing what they could, but making only slow progress; much too slow for Hakon's zeal. On the other hand, every Yule-tide, when the chief heathen were assembled in his own palace on their grand sacrificial festival, there was great pressure put upon Hakon, as to sprinkling with horse-blood, drinking Yule-beer, eating horse-flesh, and the other distressing rites; the whole of which Hakon abhorred, and with all his steadfastness strove to reject utterly. Sigurd, Jarl of Lade (Trondhjem), a liberal heathen, not openly a Christian, was ever a wise counsellor and conciliator in such affairs; and proved of great help to Hakon. Once, for example, there having risen at a Yule-feast, loud, almost stormful demand that Hakon, like a true man and brother, should drink Yule-beer with them in their sacred hightide, Sigurd persuaded him to comply, for peace's sake, at least, in form. Hakon took the cup in his left hand (excellent *hot beer*), and with his right cut the sign of the cross above it, then drank a draught. " Yes;

but what is this with the king's right hand ?" cried the company. "Don't you see?" answered shifty Sigurd; "he makes the sign of Thor's hammer before drinking!" which quenched the matter for the time.

Horse-flesh, horse-broth, and the horse ingredient generally, Hakon all but inexorably declined. By Sigurd's pressing exhortation and entreaty, he did once take a kettle of horse-broth by the handle, with a good deal of linen-quilt or towel interposed, and did open his lips for what of steam could insinuate itself. At another time he consented to a particle of horse-liver, intending privately, I guess, to keep it outside the gullet, and smuggle it away without *swallowing ;* but farther than this not even Sigurd could persuade him to go. At the Things held in regard to this matter Hakon's success was always incomplete; now and then it was plain failure, and Hakon had to draw back till a better time. Here is one specimen of the response he got on such an occasion; curious specimen, withal, of antique parliamentary eloquence from an Anti-Christian Thing.

At a Thing of all the Fylkes of Trondhjem, Thing held at Froste in that region, King Hakon, with all the eloquence he had, signified that it was imperatively necessary that all Bonders and sub-Bonders should become Christians, and believe in one God, Christ the Son of Mary; renouncing entirely blood sacrifices and heathen idols ; should keep every seventh day holy, abstain from labor that day, and even from food, devoting the day to fasting and sacred meditation. Whereupon, by way of universal answer, arose a confused universal murmur of entire dissent. "Take away from us our old belief, and also our time for labor !" murmured they in angry astonishment; "how can even the land be got tilled in that way ?" "We cannot work if we don't get food," said the hand laborers and slaves. "It lies in King Hakon's blood," remarked others ; "his father and all his kindred were apt to be stingy about food, though liberal enough with money." At length, one Osbjörn (or Bear of the Åsen or Gods, what we now call Osborne), one Osbjörn of Medalhusin Gulathal, stept forward, and said, in a distinct manner, "We Bonders (peasant proprietors) thought, King Hakon, when thou heldest thy first Thing-day here in Trondhjem, and we took thee for our king, and received our hereditary lands from thee again, that we had got heaven itself. But now we know not how it is, whether we have won freedom, or whether thou intendest anew to make us slaves, with this wonderful proposal that we should renounce our faith, which our fathers before us have held, and all our ancestors as well, first in the age of burial by burning, and now in that of earth burial; and yet these departed ones were much our superiors, and their faith, too, has brought prosperity to us! Thee, at the same time, we have loved so much that we raised thee to manage all the laws of the land, and speak as their voice to us all. And even now it is our will and the vote of all Bonders to keep that paction which thou gavest us here on the Thing at Froste, and to maintain thee as king so long as any of us Bonders who are here upon the Thing has life left, provided thou, king, wilt go fairly to work, and demand of us only such things as are not impossible. But if thou wilt fix upon this thing with so great obstinacy, and employ force and power, in that case, we Bonders have taken the resolution, all· of us, to fall away from thee, and to take for ourselves another head, who will so behave that we may enjoy in freedom the belief which is agreeable to us. Now shalt thou, king, choose one of these two courses before the Thing disperse." "Where-upon," adds the Chronicle, "all the Bonders raised a mighty shout, ' Yes, we will have it so, as has been said.'" So that Jarl Sigurd had to intervene, and King Hakon to choose for the moment the milder branch of the alternative.[1] At other Things Hakon was more or less successful. All his days, by such methods as there were, he kept pressing forward with this great enterprise; and on the whole did thoroughly shake asunder the old edifice of heathendom, and fairly introduce some foundation for the new and better rule of faith and life among his people. Sigurd, Jarl of Lade, his wise counsellor in all these matters, is also a man worthy of notice.

Hakon's arrangements against the continual invasions of Eric's sons, with Danish Blue-tooth backing them, were mani-

---

[1] Dahlmann, ii. 93.

fold, and for a long time successful. He appointed, after consultation and consent in the various Things, so many war-ships, fully manned and ready, to be furnished instantly on the King's demand by each province or fjord; watch-fires, on fit places, from hill to hill all along the coast, were to be carefully set up, carefully maintained in readiness, and kindled on any alarm of war. By such methods Blue-tooth and Co.'s invasions were for a long while triumphantly, and even rapidly, one and all of them, beaten back, till at length they seemed as if intending to cease altogether, and leave Hakon alone of them. But such was not their issue after all. The sons of Eric had only abated under constant discouragement, had not finally left off from what seemed their one great feasibility in life. Gunhild, their mother, was still with them: a most contriving, fierce-minded, irreconcilable woman, diligent and urgent on them, in season and out of season; and as for King Blue-tooth, he was at all times ready to help, with his good-will at least.

That of the alarm-fires on Hakon's part was found troublesome by his people; sometimes it was even hurtful and provoking (lighting your alarm-fires and rousing the whole coast and population, when it was nothing but some paltry viking with a couple of ships); in short, the alarm-signal system fell into disuse, and good King Hakon himself, in the first place, paid the penalty. It is counted, by the latest commentators, to have been about A.D. 961, sixteenth or seventeenth year of Hakon's pious, valiant, and worthy reign. Being at a feast one day, with many guests, on the Island of Stord, sudden announcement came to him that ships from the south were approaching in quantity, and evidently ships of war. This was the biggest of all the Blue-tooth foster-son invasions; and it was fatal to Hakon the Good that night. Eyvind the Skald-aspillir (annihilator of all other Skalds), in his famed *Hakon's Song*, gives account, and, still more pertinently, the always practical Snorro. Danes in great multitude, six to one, as people afterwards computed, springing swiftly to land, and ranking themselves; Hakon, nevertheless, at once deciding not to take to his ships and run, but to fight there, one to six; fighting, accordingly, in his most splendid manner, and at last gloriously prevailing; routing and scattering back to their ships and flight homeward these six-to-one Danes. "During the struggle of the fight," says Snorro, "he was very conspicuous among other men; and while the sun shone, his bright gilded helmet glanced, and thereby many weapons were directed at him. One of his henchmen, Eyvind Finnson (*i.e.* Skaldaspillir, the poet), took a hat, and put it over the king's helmet. Now, among the hostile first leaders were two uncles of the Ericsons, brothers of Gunhild, great champions both; Skreya, the elder of them, on the disappearance of the glittering helmet, shouted boastfully, 'Does the king of the Norsemen hide himself, then, or has he fled? Where now is the golden helmet?' And so saying, Skreya, and his brother Alf with him, pushed on like fools or madmen. The king said, 'Come on in that way, and you shall find the king of the Norsemen.'" And in a short space of time braggart Skreya did come up, swinging his sword, and made a cut at the king; but Thoralf the Strong, an Icelander, who fought at the king's side, dashed his shield so hard against Skreya, that he tottered with the shock. On the same instant the king takes his sword "quernbiter" (able to cut *querns* or millstones) with both hands, and hews Skreya through helm and head, cleaving him down to the shoulders. Thoralf also slew Alf. That was what they got by such over-hasty search for the king of the Norsemen.[1]

Snorro considers the fall of these two champion uncles as the crisis of the fight; the Danish force being much disheartened by such a sight, and King Hakon now pressing on so hard that all men gave way before him, the battle on the Ericson part became a whirl of recoil; and in a few minutes more a torrent of mere flight and haste to get on board their ships, and put to sea again; in which operation many of them were drowned, says Snorro; survivors making instant sail for Denmark in that sad condition.

This seems to have been King Hakon's finest battle, and the most conspicuous of his victories, due not a little to his own grand qualities shown on the occasion. But, alas! it was his last also. He was still zealously directing the chase of that

[1] Laing's *Snorro*, i. 344.

mad Danish flight, or whirl of recoil towards their ships, when an arrow, shot most likely at a venture, hit him under the left armpit; and this proved his death.

He was helped into his ship, and made sail for Alrekstad, where his chief residence in those parts was; but had to stop at a smaller place of his (which had been his mother's, and where he himself was born) — a place called Hella (the Flat Rock), still known as "Hakon's Hella," faint from loss of blood, and crushed down as he had never before felt. Having no son and only one daughter, he appointed these invasive sons of Eric to be sent for, and if he died to become king; but to "spare his friends and kindred." "If a longer life be granted me," he said, "I will go out of this land to Christian men, and do penance for what I have committed against God. But if I die in the country of the heathen, let me have such burial as you yourselves think fittest." These are his last recorded words. And in heathen fashion he was buried, and besung by Eyvind and the Skalds, though himself a zealously Christian king. Hakon the *Good;* so one still finds him worthy of being called. The sorrow on Hakon's death, Snorro tells us, was so great and universal, "that he was lamented both by friends and enemies; and they said that never again would Norway see such a king."

CHAPTER IV.

HARALD GREYFELL AND BROTHERS.

ERIC's sons, four or five of them, with a Harald at the top, now at once got Norway in hand, all of it but Trondhjem, as king and under-kings; and made a severe time of it for those who had been, or seemed to be, their enemies. Excellent Jarl Sigurd, always so useful to Hakon and his country, was killed by them; and they came to repent that before very long. The slain Sigurd left a son, Hakon, as Jarl, who became famous in the northern world by and by. This Hakon, and him only, would the Trondhjemers accept as sovereign. "Death to him, then," said the sons of Eric, but only in secret, till they had got their hands free and were ready; which was not yet for some years. Nay, Hakon, when actually attacked, made good resistance, and threatened to cause trouble. Nor did he by any means get his death from these sons of Eric at this time, or till long afterwards at all, from one of their kin, as it chanced. On the contrary, he fled to Denmark now, and by and by managed to come back, to their cost.

Among their other chief victims were two cousins of their own, Tryggve and Gudröd, who had been honest under-kings to the late head-king, Hakon the Good; but were now become suspect, and had to fight for their lives, and lose them in a tragic manner. Tryggve had a son, whom we shall hear of. Gudröd, son of worthy Bjorn the Chapman, was grandfather of Saint Olaf, whom all men have heard of, — who has a church in Southwark even, and another in Old Jewry, to this hour. In all these violences, Gunhild, widow of the late king Eric, was understood to have a principal hand. She had come back to Norway with her sons; and naturally passed for the secret adviser and Maternal President in whatever of violence went on; always reckoned a fell, vehement, relentless personage where her own interests were concerned. Probably as things settled, her influence on affairs grew less. At least one hopes so; and, in the Sagas, hears less and less of her, and before long nothing.

Harald, the head-king in this Eric fraternity, does not seem to have been a bad man, — the contrary indeed; but his position was untowardly, full of difficulty and contradictions. Whatever Harald could accomplish for behoof of Christianity, or real benefit to Norway, in these cross circumstances, he seems to have done in a modest and honest manner. He got the name of *Greyfell* from his people on a very trivial account, but seemingly with perfect good humor on their part. Some Iceland trader had brought a cargo of furs to Trondhjem (Lade) for sale; sale being slacker than the Icelander wished, he presented a chosen specimen, cloak, doublet, or whatever it was, to Harald; who wore it with acceptance in public, and rapidly brought disposal of the Icelander's stock, and the surname of *Greyfell* to himself. His under-kings and he were certainly not popular, though I almost think Greyfell himself, in absence of his mother and the under-kings, might have been so. But here they all were, and had wrought great trouble in Norway. "Too many of them," said everybody; "too many of these courts and court people, eating up any substance that there is." For the seasons withal, two or three of them in succession, were bad for grass, much more for grain; no *herring* came either; very cleanness of teeth was like to come in Eyvind Skaldaspillir's opinion. This scarcity became at last their share of the great Famine of A.D. 975, which desolated Western Europe (see the poem in the Saxon Chronicle). And all this by Eyvind Skaldaspillir, and the heathen Norse in general, was ascribed to anger of the heathen gods. Discontent in Norway, and especially in Eyvind Skaldaspillir, seems to have been very great.

Whereupon exile Hakon, Jarl Sigurd's son, bestirs himself in Denmark, backed by old King Blue-tooth, and begins invading and encroaching in a miscellaneous way; especially intriguing and contriving plots all round him. An unfathomably cunning kind of fellow, as well as an audacious and strong-handed! Intriguing in Trondhjem, where he gets the under-king, Greyfell's brother, fallen upon and murdered; intriguing with Gold Harald, a distinguished cousin or nephew of King Blue-tooth's, who had done fine viking work, and gained such wealth that he got the epithet of "Gold," and who now was infinitely desirous of a share in Blue-tooth's kingdom as the proper finish to these sea-rovings. He even ventured one day to make publicly a distinct proposal that way to King Harald Blue-tooth himself; who flew into thunder and lightning at the mere mention of it; so that none durst speak to him for several days afterwards. Of both these Haralds Hakon was confidential friend; and needed all his skill to walk without immediate annihilation between such a pair of dragons, and work out Norway for himself withal. In the end he found he must take solidly to Blue-tooth's side of the question; and

that they two must provide a recipe for Gold Harald and
Norway both at once.

"It is as much as your life is worth to speak again of shar-
ing this Danish kingdom," said Hakon very privately to Gold
Harald; "but could not you, my golden friend, be content with
Norway for a kingdom, if one helped you to it?"

"That could I well," answered Harald.

"Then keep me those nine war-ships you have just been
rigging for a new viking cruise; have these in readiness when
I lift my finger!"

That was the recipe contrived for Gold Harald; recipe for
King Greyfell goes into the same vial, and is also ready.

Hitherto the Hakon-Blue-tooth disturbances in Norway had
amounted to but little. King Greyfell, a very active and valiant man, has constantly, without much difficulty, repelled
these sporadic bits of troubles; but Greyfell, all the same,
would willingly have peace with dangerous old Blue-tooth
(ever anxious to get his clutches over Norway on any terms)
if peace with him could be had. Blue-tooth, too, professes
every willingness; inveigles Greyfell, he and Hakon do, to
have a friendly meeting on the Danish borders, and not only
settle all these quarrels, but generously settle Greyfell in certain fiefs which he claimed in Denmark itself; and so swear
everlasting friendship. Greyfell joyfully complies, punctually appears at the appointed day in Lymfjord Sound, the
appointed place. Whereupon Hakon gives signal to Gold
Harald, "To Lymfjord with these nine ships of yours, swift!"
Gold Harald flies to Lymfjord with his ships, challenges
King Harald Greyfell to land and fight; which the undaunted
Greyfell, though so far outnumbered, does; and, fighting his
very best, perishes there, he and almost all his people. Which
done, Jarl Hakon, who is in readiness, attacks Gold Harald,
the victorious but the wearied; easily beats Gold Harald,
takes him prisoner, and instantly hangs and ends him, to the
huge joy of King Blue-tooth and Hakon; who now make
instant voyage to Norway; drive all the brother under-kings
into rapid flight to the Orkneys, to any readiest shelter; and
so, under the patronage of Blue-tooth, Hakon, with the title

of Jarl, becomes ruler of Norway. This foul treachery done on the brave and honest Harald Greyfell is by some dated about A.D. 969, by Munch, 965, by others, computing out of Snorro only, A.D. 975. For there is always an uncertainty in these Icelandic dates (say rather, rare and rude attempts at dating, without even an "A.D." or other fixed "year one" to go upon in Iceland), though seldom, I think, so large a discrepancy as here.

———•———

CHAPTER V.

HAKON JARL.

HAKON JARL, such the style he took, had engaged to pay some kind of tribute to King Blue-tooth, "if he could;" but he never did pay any, pleading always the necessity of his own affairs; with which excuse, joined to Hakon's readiness in things less important, King Blue-tooth managed to content himself, Hakon being always his good neighbor, at least, and the two mutually dependent. In Norway, Hakon, without the title of king, did in a strong-handed, steadfast, and at length successful way, the office of one; governed Norway (some count) for above twenty years; and, both at home and abroad, had much consideration through most of that time; specially amongst the heathen orthodox, for Hakon Jarl himself was a zealous heathen, fixed in his mind against these chimerical Christian innovations and unsalutary changes of creed, and would have gladly trampled out all traces of what the last two kings (for Greyfell, also, was an English Christian after his sort) had done in this respect. But he wisely discerned that it was not possible, and that, for peace's sake, he must not even attempt it, but must strike preferably into "perfect toleration," and that of "every one getting to heaven or even to the other goal in his own way." He himself, it is well known, repaired many heathen temples (a great "church builder" in his way!), manufactured many splendid idols, with much gilding and such artistic ornament as there was, — in particular, one huge image of Thor, not forgetting the hammer and appendages, and such a collar (supposed of solid gold, which it was not quite, as we shall hear in time) round the neck of him as was never seen in all the North. How he did his own Yule festivals, with what magnificent solemnity, the horse-eatings, blood-sprinklings, and other sacred rites, need not be told. Something of a "Ritualist," one may perceive; perhaps had Scandinavian Puseyisms in him, and other desperate heathen notions. He was universally believed to have gone into magic, for one thing, and to have dangerous potencies derived from the Devil himself. The dark heathen mind of him struggling vehemently in that strange element, not altogether so unlike our own in some points.

For the rest, he was evidently, in practical matters, a man of sharp, clear insight, of steadfast resolution, diligence, promptitude; and managed his secular matters uncommonly well. Had sixteen Jarls under him, though himself only Hakon Jarl by title; and got obedience from them stricter than any king since Haarfagr had done. Add to which that the country had years excellent for grass and crop, and that the herrings came in exuberance; tokens, to the thinking mind, that Hakon Jarl was a favorite of Heaven.

His fight with the far-famed Jomsvikings was his grandest exploit in public rumor. Jomsburg, a locality not now known, except that it was near the mouth of the River Oder, denoted in those ages the impregnable castle of a certain body corporate, or "Sea Robbery Association (limited)," which, for some generations, held the Baltic in terror, and plundered far beyond the Belt, — in the ocean itself, in Flanders and the opulent trading havens there, — above all, in opulent anarchic England, which, for forty years from about this time, was the pirates' Goshen; and yielded, regularly every summer, slaves, Danegelt, and miscellaneous plunder, like no other country Jomsburg or the viking-world had ever known. Palnatoke, Bue, and the other quasi-heroic heads of this establishment are still remembered in the northern parts. *Palnatoke* is the title of a tragedy by Oehlenschläger, which had its run of immortality in Copenhagen some sixty or seventy years ago.

I judge the institution to have been in its floweriest state, probably now in Hakon Jarl's time. Hakon Jarl and these pirates, robbing Hakon's subjects and merchants that frequented him, were naturally in quarrel; and frequent fightings had fallen out, not generally to the profit of the Jomsburgers, who at last determined on revenge, and the rooting out of this obstructive Hakon Jarl. They assembled in force at the Cape of Stad, — in the Firda Fylke; and the fight was dreadful in the extreme, noise of it filling all the north for long afterwards. Hakon, fighting like a lion, could scarcely hold his own, — Death or Victory, the word on both sides; when suddenly, the heavens grew black, and there broke out a terrific storm of thunder and hail, appalling to the human mind, — universe swallowed wholly in black night; only the momentary forked-blazes, the thunder-pealing as of Ragnarök, and the battering hail-torrents, hailstones about the size of an egg. Thor with his hammer evidently acting; but in behalf of whom? The Jomsburgers in the hideous darkness, broken only by flashing thunder-bolts, had a dismal apprehension that it was probably not on their behalf (Thor having a sense of justice in him); and before the storm ended, thirty-five of their seventy ships sheered away, leaving gallant Bue, with the other thirty-five, to follow as they liked, who reproachfully hailed these fugitives, and continued the now hopeless battle. Bue's nose and lips were smashed or cut away; Bue managed, half-articulately, to exclaim, "Ha! the maids ('mays') of Fünen will never kiss me more. Overboard, all ye Bue's men!" And taking his two sea-chests, with all the gold he had gained in such life-struggle from of old, sprang overboard accordingly, and finished the affair. Hakon Jarl's renown rose naturally to the transcendent pitch after this exploit. His people, I suppose chiefly the Christian part of them, whispered one to another, with a shudder, "That in the blackest of the thunder-storm, he had taken his youngest little boy, and made away with him; sacrificed him to Thor or some devil, and gained his victory by art-magic, or something' worse." Jarl Eric, Hakon's eldest son, without suspicion of art-magic, but already a distinguished viking, became thrice distinguished by his style of sea-fighting in this battle; and awakened great expectations in the viking public; of him we shall hear again.

The Jomsburgers, one might fancy, after this sad clap went visibly down in the world; but the fact is not altogether so. Old King Blue-tooth was now dead, died of a wound got in battle with his *un*natural (so-called "natural") son and successor, Otto Svein of the Forked Beard, afterwards king and conqueror of England for a little while; and seldom, perhaps never, had vikingism been in such flower as now. This man's name is Sven in Swedish, Svend in German, and means *boy* or *lad*,—the English "swain." It was at old "Father Blue-tooth's funeral-ale" (drunken burial-feast), that Svein, carousing with his Jomsburg chiefs and other choice spirits, generally of the robber class, all risen into height of highest robber enthusiasm, pledged the vow to one another; Svein that he would conquer England (which, in a sense, he, after long struggling, did); and the Jomsburgers that they would ruin and root out Hakon Jarl (which, as we have just seen, they could by no means do), and other guests other foolish things which proved equally unfeasible. Sea-robber volunteers so especially abounding in that time, one perceives how easily the Jomsburgers could recruit themselves, build or refit new robber fleets, man them with the pick of crews, and steer for opulent, fruitful England; where, under Ethelred the Unready, was such a field for profitable enterprise as the viking public never had before or since.

An idle question sometimes rises on me, — idle enough, for it never can be answered in the affirmative or the negative, Whether it was not these same refitted Jomsburgers who appeared some while after this at Red Head Point, on the shore of Angus, and sustained a new severe beating, in what the Scotch still faintly remember as their "Battle of Loncarty"? Beyond doubt a powerful Norse-pirate armament dropt anchor at the Red Head, to the alarm of peaceable mortals, about that time. It was thought and hoped to be on its way for

England, but it visibly hung on for several days, deliberating (as was thought) whether they would do this poorer coast the honor to land on it before going farther.   Did land, and vigorously plunder and burn southwestward as far as Perth; laid siege to Perth; but brought out King Kenneth on them, and produced that "Battle of Loncarty" which still dwells in vague memory among the Scots.   Perhaps it might be the Jomsburgers; perhaps also not; for there were many pirate associations, lasting not from century to century like the Jomsburgers, but only for very limited periods, or from year to year; indeed, it was mainly by such that the splendid thief-harvest of England was reaped in this disastrous time.   No Scottish chronicler gives the least of exact date to their famed victory of Loncarty, only that it was achieved by Kenneth III., which will mean some time between A.D. 975 and 994; and, by the order they put it in, probably soon after A.D. 975, or the beginning of this Kenneth's reign.   Buchanan's narrative, carefully distilled from all the ancient Scottish sources, is of admirable quality for style and otherwise; quiet, brief, with perfect clearness, perfect credibility even, — except that semi-miraculous appendage of the Ploughmen, Hay and Sons, always hanging to the tail of it; the grain of possible truth in which can now never be extracted by man's art![1]   In brief, what we know is, fragments of ancient human bones and armor have occasionally been ploughed up in this locality, proof-positive of ancient fighting here; and the fight fell out not long after Hakon's beating of the Jomsburgers at the Cape of Stad. And in such dim glimmer of wavering twilight, the question whether these of Loncarty were refitted Jomsburgers or not, must be left hanging.   Loncarty is now the biggest bleach-field in Queen Victoria's dominions; no village or hamlet there, only the huge bleaching-house and a beautiful field, some six or seven miles northwest of Perth, bordered by the beautiful Tay river on the one side, and by its beautiful tributary Almond on the other; a Loncarty fitted either for bleaching linen, or for a bit of fair duel between nations, in those simple times.

[1] G. Buchanani *Opera Omnia*, i. 103, 104 (Curante Ruddimano, Edinburgi, 1715).

Whether our refitted Jomsburgers had the least thing to do with it is only matter of fancy, but if it were they who here again got a good beating, fancy would be glad to find herself fact. The old piratical kings of Denmark had been at the founding of Jomsburg, and to Svein of the Forked Beard it was still vitally important, but not so to the great Knut, or any king that followed; all of whom had better business than mere thieving; and it was Magnus the Good, of Norway, a man of still higher anti-anarchic qualities, that annihilated it, about a century later.

Hakon Jarl, his chief labors in the world being over, is said to have become very dissolute in his elder days, especially in the matter of women; the wretched old fool, led away by idleness and fulness of bread, which to all of us are well said to be the parents of mischief. Having absolute power, he got into the habit of openly plundering men's pretty daughters and wives from them, and, after a few weeks, sending them back; greatly to the rage of the fierce Norse heart, had there been any means of resisting or revenging. It did, after a little while, prove the ruin and destruction of Hakon the Rich, as he was then called. It opened the door, namely, for entry of Olaf Tryggveson upon the scene, — a very much grander man; in regard to whom the wiles and traps of Hakon proved to be a recipe, not on Tryggveson, but on the wily Hakon himself, as shall now be seen straightway.

CHAPTER VI.

OLAF TRYGGVESON.

HAKON, in late times, had heard of a famous stirring person, victorious in various lands and seas, latterly united in sea-robbery with Svein, Prince Royal of Denmark, afterwards King Svein of the Double-beard ("*Zvae Skiaeg,*" *Twa Shag*) or fork-beard, both of whom had already done transcendent feats in the viking way during this copartnery. The fame of

Svein, and this stirring personage, whose name was "Ole," and, recently, their stupendous feats in plunder of England, siege of London, and other wonders and splendors of viking glory and success, had gone over all the North, awakening the attention of Hakon and everybody there. The name of "Ole" was enigmatic, mysterious, and even dangerous-looking to Hakon Jarl; who at length sent out a confidential spy to investigate this "Ole;" a feat which the confidential spy did completely accomplish, — by no means to Hakon's profit! The mysterious "Ole" proved to be no other than *Olaf*, son of Tryggve, destined to blow Hakon Jarl suddenly into destruction, and become famous among the heroes of the Norse world.

Of Olaf Tryggveson one always hopes there might, one day, some real outline of a biography be written ; fished from the abysses where (as usual) it welters deep in foul neighborhood for the present. Farther on we intend a few words more upon the matter. But in this place all that concerns us in it limits itself to the two following facts : first, that Hakon's confidential spy "found Ole in Dublin ; " picked acquaintance with him, got him to confess that he was actually Olaf, son of Tryggve (the Tryggve, whom Blood-axe's fierce widow and her sons had murdered); got him gradually to own that perhaps an expedition into Norway might have its chances; and finally that, under such a wise and loyal guidance as his (the confidential spy's, whose friendship for Tryggveson was so indubitable), he (Tryggveson) would actually try it upon Hakon Jarl, the dissolute old scoundrel. Fact second is, that about the time they two set sail from Dublin on their Norway expedition, Hakon Jarl removed to Trondhjem, then called Lade ; intending to pass some months there.

Now just about the time when Tryggveson, spy, and party had landed in Norway, and were advancing upon Lade, with what support from the public could be got, dissolute old Hakon Jarl had heard of one Gudrun, a Bonder's wife, unparalleled in beauty, who was called in those parts, " Sunbeam of the Grove " (so inexpressibly lovely); and sent off a couple of thralls to bring her to him. " Never," answered Gudrun; "never," her

indignant husband; in a tone dangerous and displeasing to
these Court thralls; who had to leave rapidly, but threatened
to return in better strength before long. Whereupon, instantly,
the indignant Bonder and his Sunbeam of the Grove sent out
their war-arrow, rousing all the country into angry promptitude, and more than one perhaps into greedy hope of revenge
for their own injuries. The rest of Hakon's history now
rushes on with extreme rapidity.

Sunbeam of the Grove, when next demanded of her Bonder,
has the whole neighborhood assembled in arms round her;
rumor of Tryggveson is fast making it the whole country.
Hakon's insolent messengers are cut in pieces; Hakon finds he
cannot fly under cover too soon. With a single slave he flies
that same night; — but whitherward? Can think of no safe
place, except to some old mistress of his, who lives retired in
that neighborhood, and has some pity or regard for the wicked
old Hakon. Old mistress does receive him, pities him, will do
all she can to protect and hide him. But how, by what uttermost stretch of female artifice hide him here; every one will
search here first of all! Old mistress, by the slave's help,
extemporizes a cellar under the floor of her pig-house; sticks
Hakon and slave into that, as the one safe seclusion she can
contrive. Hakon and slave, begrunted by the pigs above them,
tortured by the devils within and about them, passed two days
in circumstances more and more horrible. For they heard,
through their light-slit and breathing-slit, the triumph of
Tryggveson proclaiming itself by Tryggveson's own lips, who
had mounted a big boulder near by and was victoriously speaking to the people, winding up with a promise of honors and
rewards to whoever should bring him wicked old Hakon's head.
Wretched Hakon, justly suspecting his slave, tried to at least
keep himself awake. Slave did keep himself awake till Hakon
dozed or slept, then swiftly cut off Hakon's head, and plunged
out with it to the presence of Tryggveson. Tryggveson, detest-
ing the traitor, useful as the treachery was, cut off the slave's
head too, had it hung up along with Hakon's on the pinnacle
of the Lade Gallows, where the populace pelted both heads
with stones and many curses, especially the more important of

the two. "Hakon the Bad" ever henceforth, instead of Hakon the Rich.

This was the end of Hakon Jarl, the last support of heathenry in Norway, among other characteristics he had: a strong-handed, hard-headed, very relentless, greedy and wicked being. He is reckoned to have ruled in Norway, or mainly ruled, either in the struggling or triumphant state, for about thirty years (965–995 ?). He and his seemed to have formed, by chance rather than design, the chief opposition which the Haarfagr posterity throughout its whole course experienced in Norway. Such the cost to them of killing good Jarl Sigurd, in Greyfell's time! For "curses, like chickens," do sometimes visibly "come home to feed," as they always, either visibly or else invisibly, are punctually sure to do.

Hakon Jarl is considerably connected with the *Faröer Saga;* often mentioned there, and comes out perfectly in character; an altogether worldly-wise man of the roughest type, not without a turn for practicality of kindness to those who would really be of use to him. His tendencies to magic also are not forgotten.

Hakon left two sons, Eric and Svein, often also mentioned in this Saga. On their father's death they fled to Sweden, to Denmark, and were busy stirring up troubles in those countries against Olaf Tryggveson; till at length, by a favorable combination, under their auspices chiefly, they got his brief and noble reign put an end to. Nay, furthermore, Jarl Eric left sons, especially an elder son, named also Eric, who proved a sore affliction, and a continual stone of stumbling to a new generation of Haarfagrs, and so continued the curse of Sigurd's murder upon them.

Towards the end of this Hakon's reign it was that the discovery of America took place (985). Actual discovery, it appears, by Eric the Red, an Icelander; concerning which there has been abundant investigation and discussion in our time. *Ginnungagap* (Roaring Abyss) is thought to be the mouth of Behring's Straits in Baffin's Bay; *Big Helloland*, the coast from Cape Walsingham to near Newfoundland; *Little Helloland*, Newfoundland itself. *Markland* was Lower Canada, New

Brunswick, and Nova Scotia. Southward thence to Chesapeake Bay was called *Wine Land* (wild grapes still grow in Rhode Island, and more luxuriantly further south). *White Man's Land*, called also *Great Ireland*, is supposed to mean the two Carolinas, down to the Southern Cape of Florida. In Dahlmann's opinion, the Irish themselves might even pretend to have probably been the first discoverers of America; they had evidently got to Iceland itself before the Norse exiles found it out. It appears to be certain that, from the end of the tenth century to the early part of the fourteenth, there was a dim knowledge of those distant shores extant in the Norse mind, and even some straggling series of visits thither by roving Norsemen; though, as only danger, difficulty, and no profit resulted, the visits ceased, and the whole matter sank into oblivion, and, but for the Icelandic talent of writing in the long winter nights, would never have been heard of by posterity at all.

CHAPTER VII.

REIGN OF OLAF TRYGGVESON.

OLAF TRYGGVESON (A.D. 995–1000) also makes a great figure in the *Faröer Saga*, and recounts there his early troubles, which were strange and many. He is still reckoned a grand hero of the North, though his *vates* now is only Snorro Sturleson of Iceland. Tryggveson had indeed many adventures in the world. His poor mother, Astrid, was obliged to fly, on murder of her husband by Gunhild, — to fly for life, three months before he, her little Olaf, was born. She lay concealed in reedy islands, fled through trackless forests; reached her father's with the little baby in her arms, and lay deep-hidden there, tended only by her father himself; Gunhild's pursuit being so incessant, and keen as with sleuth-hounds. Poor Astrid had to fly again, deviously to Sweden, to Esthland (Esthonia), to Russia. In Esthland she was sold as a slave, quite parted from her boy, — who also was sold, and again sold; but did at last fall in with a kinsman high in the Russian service; did from him find redemption and help, and so rose, in a distinguished manner, to manhood, victorious self-help, and recovery of his kingdom at last. He even met his mother again, he as king of Norway, she as one wonderfully lifted out of darkness into new life and happiness still in store.

Grown to manhood, Tryggveson, — now become acquainted with his birth, and with his, alas, hopeless claims, — left Russia for the one profession open to him, that of sea-robbery; and did feats without number in that questionable line in many seas and scenes, — in England latterly, and most conspicuously of all. In one of his courses thither, after long labors in the Hebrides, Man, Wales, and down the western shores to the very Land's End and farther, he paused at the Scilly Islands for a little while. He was told of a wonderful Christian hermit living strangely in these sea-solitudes; had the curiosity to seek him out, examine, question, and discourse with him; and, after some reflection, accepted Christian baptism from the venerable man. In *Snorro* the story is involved in miracle, rumor, and fable; but the fact itself seems certain, and is very interesting; the great, wild, noble soul of fierce Olaf opening to this wonderful gospel of tidings from beyond the world, tidings which infinitely transcended all else he had ever heard or dreamt of! It seems certain he was baptized here; date not fixable; shortly before poor heart-broken Dunstan's death, or shortly after; most English churches, monasteries especially, lying burnt, under continual visitation of the Danes. Olaf, such baptism notwithstanding, did not quit his viking profession; indeed, what other was there for him in the world as yet?

We mentioned his occasional copartneries with Svein of the Double-beard, now become King of Denmark, but the greatest of these, and the alone interesting at this time, is their joint invasion of England, and Tryggveson's exploits and fortunes there some years after that adventure of baptism in the Scilly Isles. Svein and he "were above a year in England together," this time: they steered up the Thames with three hundred ships and many fighters; siege, or at least furious assault, of London was their first or main enterprise, but it did not succeed. The Saxon Chronicle gives date to it, A.D. 994, and names expressly, as Svein's co-partner, "Olaus, king of Norway,"—which he was as yet far from being; but in regard to the Year of Grace the Saxon Chronicle is to be held indisputable, and, indeed, has the field to itself in this matter. Famed Olaf Tryggveson, seen visibly at the siege of London, year 994, it throws a kind of momentary light to us over that disastrous whirlpool of miseries and confusions, all dark and painful to the fancy otherwise! This big voyage and furious siege of London is Svein Double-beard's first real attempt to fulfil that vow of his at Father Blue-tooth's "funeral ale," and conquer England,—which it is a pity he could not yet do. Had London now fallen to him, it is pretty evident all England must have followed, and poor England, with Svein as king over it, been delivered from immeasurable woes, which had to last some two-and-twenty years farther, before this result could be arrived at. But finding London impregnable for the moment (no ship able to get athwart the bridge, and many Danes perishing in the attempt to do it by swimming), Svein and Olaf turned to other enterprises; all England in a manner lying open to them, turn which way they liked. They burnt and plundered over Kent, over Hampshire, Sussex; they stormed far and wide; world lying all before them where to choose. Wretched Ethelred, as the one invention he could fall upon, offered them Danegelt (£16,000 of silver this year, but it rose in other years as high as £48,000); the desperate Ethelred, a clear method of quenching fire by pouring *oil* on it! Svein and Olaf accepted; withdrew to Southampton,—Olaf at least did,—till the money was got ready. Strange to think of, fierce Svein of the Double-beard, and conquest of England by him; this had at last become the one salutary result which remained for that distracted, down-trodden, now utterly chaotic and anarchic country. A conquering Svein, followed by an ably and earnestly administrative, as well as conquering, Knut (whom Dahlmann compares to Charlemagne), were thus by the mysterious destinies appointed the effective saviors of England.

Tryggveson, on this occasion, was a good while at Southampton; and roamed extensively about, easily victorious over everything, if resistance were attempted, but finding little or none; and acting now in a peaceable or even friendly capacity. In the Southampton country he came in contact with the then Bishop of Winchester, afterwards Archbishop of Canterbury, excellent Elphegus, still dimly decipherable to us as a man of great natural discernment, piety, and inborn veracity; a hero soul, probably of real brotherhood with Olaf's own. He even made court visits to King Ethelred; one visit to him at Andover of a very serious nature. By Elphegus, as we can discover, he was introduced into the real depths of the Christian faith. Elphegus, with due solemnity of apparatus, in presence of the king, at Andover, baptized Olaf anew, and to him Olaf engaged that he would never plunder in England any more; which promise, too, he kept. In fact, not long after, Svein's conquest of England being in an evidently forward state, Tryggveson (having made, withal, a great English or Irish marriage, — a dowager Princess, who had voluntarily fallen in love with him, — see *Snorro* for this fine romantic fact!) mainly resided in our island for two or three years, or else in Dublin, in the precincts of the Danish Court there in the Sister Isle. Accordingly it was in Dublin, as above noted, that Hakon's spy found him; and from the Liffey that his squadron sailed, through the Hebrides, through the Orkneys, plundering and baptizing in their strange way, towards such success as we have seen.

Tryggveson made a stout, and, in effect, victorious and glorious struggle for himself as king. Daily and hourly vigilant to do so, often enough by soft and even merry methods, — for he was a witty, jocund man, and had a fine ringing laugh in him, and clear pregnant words ever ready, — or if soft methods would not serve, then by hard and even hardest he put down a great deal of miscellaneous anarchy in Norway; was especially busy against heathenism (devil-worship and its rites): this, indeed, may be called the focus and heart of all his royal endeavor in Norway, and of all the troubles he now had with his people there. For this was a serious, vital, all-comprehending matter; devil-worship, a thing not to be tolerated one moment longer than you could by any method help! Olaf's success was intermittent, of varying complexion; but his effort, swift or slow, was strong and continual; and on the whole he did succeed. Take a sample or two of that wonderful conversion process : —

At one of his first Things he found the Bonders all assembled in arms; resolute to the death seemingly, against his proposal and him. Tryggveson said little; waited impassive, "What your reasons are, good men?" One zealous Bonder started up in passionate parliamentary eloquence; but after a sentence or two, broke down; one, and then another, and still another, and remained all three staring in open-mouthed silence there! The peasant-proprietors accepted the phenomenon as ludicrous, perhaps partly as miraculous withal, and consented to baptism this time.

On another occasion of a Thing, which had assembled near some heathen temple to meet him, — temple where Hakon Jarl had done much repairing, and set up many idol figures and sumptuous ornaments, regardless of expense, especially a very big and splendid Thor, with massive gold collar round the neck of him, not the like of it in Norway, — King Olaf Tryggveson was clamorously invited by the Bonders to step in there, enlighten his eyes, and partake of the sacred rites. Instead of which he rushed into the temple with his armed men; smashed down, with his own battle-axe, the god Thor, prostrate on the ground at one stroke, to set an example; and, in a few minutes, had the whole Hakon Pantheon wrecked; packing up meanwhile all the gold and preciosities accumulated there (not forgetting Thor's illustrious gold collar, of which we shall hear again), and victoriously took the plunder home with him for his own royal uses and behoof of the state.

In other cases, though a friend to strong measures, he had to hold in, and await the favorable moment. Thus once, in beginning a parliamentary address, so soon as he came to touch upon Christianity, the Bonders rose in murmurs, in vociferations and jingling of arms, which quite drowned the royal voice; declared, they had taken arms against king Hakon the Good to compel him to desist from his Christian proposals; and they did not think king Olaf a higher man than him (Hakon the Good). The king then said, "He purposed coming to them next Yule to their great sacrificial feast, to see for himself what their customs were," which pacified the Bonders for this time. The appointed place of meeting was again a Hakon-Jarl Temple, not yet done to ruin; chief shrine in those Trondhjem parts, I believe : there should Tryggveson appear at Yule. Well, but before Yule came, Tryggveson made a great banquet in his palace at Trondhjem, and invited far and wide, all manner of important persons out of the district as guests there. Banquet hardly done, Tryggveson gave some slight signal, upon which armed men strode in, seized eleven of these principal persons, and the king said: "Since he himself was to become a heathen again, and do sacrifice, it was his purpose to do it in the highest form, namely, that of Human Sacrifice ; and this time not of slaves and malefactors, but of the best men in the country!" In which stringent circumstances the eleven seized persons, and company at large, gave unanimous consent to baptism; straightway received the same, and abjured their idols; but were not permitted to go home till they had left, in sons, brothers, and other precious relatives, sufficient hostages in the king's hands.

By unwearied industry of this and better kinds, Tryggveson had trampled down idolatry, so far as form went, — how far in substance may be greatly doubted. But it is to be remembered withal, that always on the back of these compulsory adventures there followed English bishops, priests and preachers; whereby to the open-minded, conviction, to all degrees of it, was attainable, while silence and passivity became the duty or necessity of the unconvinced party.

In about two years Norway was all gone over with a rough harrow of conversion. Heathenism at least constrained to be silent and outwardly conformable. Tryggveson next turned his attention to Iceland, sent one Thangbrand, priest from Saxony, of wonderful qualities, military as well as theological, to try and convert Iceland. Thangbrand made a few converts; for Olaf had already many estimable Iceland friends, whom he liked much, and was much liked by; and conversion was the ready road to his favor. Thangbrand, I find, lodged with Hall of Sida (familiar acquaintance of "Burnt Njal," whose Saga has its admirers among us even now). Thangbrand converted Hall and one or two other leading men; but in general he was reckoned quarrelsome and blusterous rather than eloquent and piously convincing. Two skalds of repute made biting lampoons upon Thangbrand, whom Thangbrand, by two opportunities that offered, cut down and did to death because of their skaldic quality. Another he killed with his own hand, I know not for what reason. In brief, after about a year, Thangbrand returned to Norway and king Olaf; declaring the Icelanders to be a perverse, satirical, and inconvertible people, having himself, the record says, "been the death of three men there." King Olaf was in high rage at this result; but was persuaded by the Icelanders about him to try farther, and by a milder instrument. He accordingly chose one Thormod, a pious, patient, and kindly man, who, within the next year or so, did actually accomplish the matter; namely, get Christianity, by open vote, declared at Thingvalla by the general Thing of Iceland there; the roar of a big thunder-clap at the right moment rather helping the conclusion, if I recollect. Whereupon Olaf's joy was no doubt great.

One general result of these successful operations was the discontent, to all manner of degrees, on the part of many Norse individuals, against this glorious and victorious, but peremptory and terrible king of theirs. Tryggveson, I fancy, did not much regard all that; a man of joyful, cheery temper, habitually contemptuous of danger. Another trivial misfortune that befell in these conversion operations, and became important to him, he did not even know of, and would have much despised if he had. It was this: Sigrid, queen dowager of Sweden, thought to be amongst the most shining women of the world, was also known for one of the most imperious, revengeful, and relentless, and had got for herself the name of Sigrid the Proud. In her high widowhood she had naturally many

wooers; but treated them in a manner unexampled. **Two of**
her suitors, a simultaneous Two, were, King Harald Grænske
(a cousin of King Tryggveson's, and kind of king in some
district, by sufferance of the late Hakon's),—this luckless
Grænske and the then Russian Sovereign as well, name not
worth mentioning, were zealous suitors of Queen Dowager
Sigrid, and were perversely slow to accept the negative, which
in her heart was inexorable for both, though the expression
of it could not be quite so emphatic. By ill-luck for them
they came once,—from the far West, Grænske; from the far
East, the Russian;—and arrived both together at Sigrid's court,
to prosecute their importunate, and to her odious and tiresome
suit; much, how very much, to her impatience and disdain.
She lodged them both in some old mansion, which she had
contiguous, and got compendiously furnished for them; and
there, I know not whether on the first or on the second, or on
what following night, this unparalleled Queen Sigrid had the
house surrounded, set on fire, and the two suitors and their
people burnt to ashes! No more of bother from these two at
least! This appears to be a fact; and it could not be unknown
to Tryggveson.

In spite of which, however, there went from Tryggveson,
who was now a widower, some incipient marriage proposals to
this proud widow; by whom they were favorably received; as
from the brightest man in all the world, they might seem worth
being. Now, in one of these anti-heathen onslaughts of King
Olaf's on the idol temples of Hakon — (I think it was that case
where Olaf's own battle-axe struck down the monstrous reful-
gent Thor, and conquered an immense gold ring from the neck
of him, or from the door of his temple),—a huge gold ring, at
any rate, had come into Olaf's hands; and this he bethought
him might be a pretty present to Queen Sigrid, the now favorable, though the proud. Sigrid received the ring with joy;
fancied what a collar it would make for her own fair neck; but
noticed that her two goldsmiths, weighing it on their fingers,
exchanged a glance. "What is that?" exclaimed Queen Sigrid. "Nothing," answered they, or endeavored to answer,
dreading mischief. But Sigrid compelled them to break open

the ring; and there was found, all along the inside of it, an occult ring of copper, not a heart of gold at all! "Ha," said the proud Queen, flinging it away, "he that could deceive in this matter can deceive in many others!" And was in hot wrath with Olaf; though, by degrees, again she took milder thoughts.

Milder thoughts, we say; and consented to a meeting next autumn, at some half-way station, where their great business might be brought to a happy settlement and betrothment. Both Olaf Tryggveson and the high dowager appear to have been tolerably of willing mind at this meeting; but Olaf interposed, what was always one condition with him, "Thou must consent to baptism, and give up thy idol-gods." "They are the gods of all my forefathers," answered the lady; "choose thou what gods thou pleasest, but leave me mine." Whereupon an altercation; and Tryggveson, as was his wont, towered up into shining wrath, and exclaimed at last, "Why should I care about thee then, old faded heathen creature?" And impatiently wagging his glove, hit her, or slightly switched her, on the face with it, and contemptuously turning away, walked out of the adventure. "This is a feat that may cost thee dear one day," said Sigrid. And in the end it came to do so, little as the magnificent Olaf deigned to think of it at the moment.

One of the last scuffles I remember of Olaf's having with his refractory heathens, was at a Thing in Hordaland or Rogaland, far in the North, where the chief opposition hero was one Jaernskaegg ("ironbeard,") *Scottice* ("Airn-shag," as it were!). Here again was a grand heathen temple, Hakon Jarl's building, with a splendid Thor in it and much idol furniture. The king stated what was his constant wish here as elsewhere, but had no sooner entered upon the subject of Christianity than universal murmur, rising into clangor and violent dissent, interrupted him, and Ironbeard took up the discourse in reply. Ironbeard did not break down; on the contrary, he, with great brevity, emphasis, and clearness, signified " that the proposal to reject their old gods was in the highest degree unacceptable to this Thing; that it was contrary to bargain, withal; so that if it were insisted on, they would have to fight with the king about it; and in fact were now ready to do so." In reply to this, Olaf, without word uttered, but merely with some signal to the trusty armed men he had with him, rushed off to the temple close at hand; burst into it, shutting the door behind him; smashed Thor and Co. to destruction; then reappearing victorious, found much confusion outside, and, in particular, what was a most important item, the rugged Ironbeard done to death by Olaf's men in the interim. Which entirely disheartened the Thing from fighting at that moment; having now no leader who dared to head them in so dangerous an enterprise. So that every one departed to digest his rage in silence as he could.

Matters having cooled for a week or two, there was another Thing held; in which King Olaf testified regret for the quarrel that had fallen out, readiness to pay what *mulct* was due by law for that unlucky homicide of Ironbeard by his people; and, withal, to take the fair daughter of Ironbeard to wife, if all would comply and be friends with him in other matters; which was the course resolved on as most convenient: accept baptism, we; marry Jaernskaegg's daughter, you. This bargain held on both sides. The wedding, too, was celebrated, but that took rather a strange turn. On the morning of the bride-night, Olaf, who had not been sleeping, though his fair partner thought he had, opened his eyes, and saw, with astonishment, the fair partner aiming a long knife ready to strike home upon him! Which at once ended their wedded life; poor Demoiselle Ironbeard immediately bundling off with her attendants home again; King Olaf into the apartment of his servants, mentioning there what had happened, and forbidding any of them to follow her.

Olaf Tryggveson, though his kingdom was the smallest of the Norse Three, had risen to a renown over all the Norse world, which neither he of Denmark nor he of Sweden could pretend to rival. A magnificent, far-shining man; more expert in all "bodily exercises" as the Norse call them, than any man had ever been before him, or after was. Could keep five daggers in the air, always catching the proper fifth by its handle, and sending it aloft again; could shoot supremely, throw a

javelin with either hand; and, in fact, in battle usually threw
two together. These, with swimming, climbing, leaping, were
the then admirable Fine Arts of the North; in all which
Tryggveson appears to have been the Raphael and the Michael
Angelo at once. Essentially definable, too, if we look well
into him, as a wild bit of real heroism, in such rude guise and
environment; a high, true, and great human soul. A jovial
burst of laughter in him, withal; a bright, airy, wise way of
speech; dressed beautifully and with care; a man admired and
loved exceedingly by those he liked; dreaded as death by those
he did not like. "Hardly any king," says Snorro, "was ever
so well obeyed; by one class out of zeal and love, by the rest
out of dread." His glorious course, however, was not to last
long.

King Svein of the Double-Beard had not yet completed his
conquest of England, — by no means yet, some thirteen horrid
years of that still before him! — when, over in Denmark, he
found that complaints against him and intricacies had arisen,
on the part principally of one Burislav, King of the Wends
(far up the Baltic), and in a less degree with the King of
Sweden and other minor individuals. Svein earnestly applied
himself to settle these, and have his hands free. Burislav, an
aged heathen gentleman, proved reasonable and conciliatory;
so, too, the King of Sweden, and Dowager Queen Sigrid, his
managing mother. Bargain in both these cases got sealed
and crowned by marriage. Svein, who had become a widower
lately, now wedded Sigrid; and might think, possibly enough,
he had got a proud bargain, though a heathen one. Burislav
also insisted on marriage with Princess Thyri, the Double-
Beard's sister. Thyri, inexpressibly disinclined to wed an
aged heathen of that stamp, pleaded hard with her brother;
but the Double-Bearded was inexorable; Thyri's wailings and
entreaties went for nothing. With some guardian foster-
brother, and a serving-maid or two, she had to go on this hated
journey. Old Burislav, at sight of her, blazed out into mar-
riage-feast of supreme magnificence, and was charmed to see
her; but Thyri would not join the marriage party; refused to
eat with it or sit with it at all. Day after day, for six days,

flatly refused; and after nightfall of the sixth, glided out with
her foster-brother into the woods, into by-paths and inconceivable wanderings ; and, in effect, got home to Denmark. Brother
Svein was not for the moment there ; probably enough gone to
England again. But Thyri knew too well he would not allow
her to stay here, or anywhere that he could help, except with
the old heathen she had just fled from.

Thyri, looking round the world, saw no likely road for her,
but to Olaf Tryggveson in Norway ; to beg protection from the
most heroic man she knew of in the world. Olaf, except by
renown, was not known to her ; but by renown he well was.
Olaf, at sight of her, promised protection and asylum against
all mortals. Nay, in discoursing with Thyri Olaf perceived
more and more clearly what a fine handsome being, soul and
body, Thyri was ; and in a short space of time winded up by
proposing marriage to Thyri ; who, humbly, and we may fancy
with what secret joy, consented to say yes, and become Queen
of Norway. In the due months they had a little son, Harald ;
who, it is credibly recorded, was the joy of both his parents ;
but who, to their inexpressible sorrow, in about a year died,
and vanished from them. This, and one other fact now to be
mentioned, is all the wedded history we have of Thyri.

The other fact is, that Thyri had, by inheritance or covenant, not depending on her marriage with old Burislav, considerable properties in Wendland ; which, she often reflected,
might be not a little behooveful to her here in Norway, where
her civil-list was probably but straitened. She spoke of this
to her husband ; but her husband would take no hold, merely
made her gifts, and said, "Pooh, pooh, can't we live without
old Burislav and his Wendland properties ? " So that the
lady sank into ever deeper anxiety and eagerness about this
Wendland object ; took to weeping ; sat weeping whole days ;
and when Olaf asked, " What ails thee, then ? " would answer, or did answer once, " What a different man my father
Harald Gormson was [vulgarly called Blue-tooth], compared
with some that are now kings ! For no King Svein in the
world would Harald Gormson have given up his own or
his wife's just rights ! " Whereupon Tryggveson started up,

exclaiming in some heat, "Of thy brother Svein I never was afraid; if Svein and I meet in contest, it will not be Svein, I believe, that conquers;" and went off in a towering fume. Consented, however, at last, had to consent, to get his fine fleet equipped and armed, and decide to sail with it to Wendland to have speech and settlement with King Burislav.

Tryggveson had already ships and navies that were the wonder of the North. Especially in building war ships, — the Crane, the Serpent, last of all the Long Serpent,[1] — he had, for size, for outward beauty, and inward perfection of equipment, transcended all example.

This new sea expedition became an object of attention to all neighbors; especially Queen Sigrid the Proud and Svein Double-Beard, her now king, were attentive to it.

"This insolent Tryggveson," Queen Sigrid would often say, and had long been saying, to her Svein, "to marry thy sister without leave had or asked of thee; and now flaunting forth his war navies, as if he, king only of paltry Norway, were the big hero of the North! Why do you suffer it, you kings really great?"

By such persuasions and reiterations, King Svein of Denmark, King Olaf of Sweden, and Jarl Eric, now a great man there, grown rich by prosperous sea robbery and other good management, were brought to take the matter up, and combine strenuously for destruction of King Olaf Tryggveson on this grand Wendland expedition of his. Fleets and forces were with best diligence got ready; and, withal, a certain Jarl Sigwald, of Jomsburg, chieftain of the Jomsvikings, a powerful, plausible, and cunning man, was appointed to find means of joining himself to Tryggveson's grand voyage, of getting into Tryggveson's confidence, and keeping Svein Double-Beard, Eric, and the Swedish King aware of all his movements.

King Olaf Tryggveson, unacquainted with all this, sailed away in summer, with his splendid fleet; went through the Belts with prosperous winds, under bright skies, to the admiration of both shores. Such a fleet, with its shining Serpents,

---

[1] His Long Serpent, judged by some to be of the size of a frigate of forty-five guns (Laing).

long and short, and perfection of equipment and appearance, the Baltic never saw before. Jarl Sigwald joined with new ships by the way: "Had," he too, "a visit to King Burislav to pay; how could he ever do it in better company?" and studiously and skilfully ingratiated himself with King Olaf. Old Burislav, when they arrived, proved altogether courteous, handsome, and amenable; agreed at once to Olaf's claims for his now queen, did the rites of hospitality with a generous plenitude to Olaf; who cheerily renewed acquaintance with that country, known to him in early days (the cradle of his fortunes in the viking line), and found old friends there still surviving, joyful to meet him again. Jarl Sigwald encouraged these delays, King Svein and Co. not being yet quite ready. "Get ready!" Sigwald directed them, and they diligently did. Olaf's men, their business now done, were impatient to be home; and grudged every day of loitering there; but, till Sigwald pleased, such his power of flattering and cajoling Tryggveson, they could not get away.

At length, Sigwald's secret messengers reporting all ready on the part of Svein and Co., Olaf took farewell of Burislav and Wendland, and all gladly sailed away. Svein, Eric, and the Swedish king, with their combined fleets, lay in wait behind some cape in a safe little bay of some island, then called Svolde, but not in our time to be found; the Baltic tumults in the fourteenth century having swallowed it, as some think, and leaving us uncertain whether it was in the neighborhood of Rügen Island or in the Sound of Elsinore. There lay Svein, Eric, and Co. waiting till Tryggveson and his fleet came up, Sigwald's spy messengers daily reporting what progress he and it had made. At length, one bright summer morning, the fleet made appearance, sailing in loose order, Sigwald, as one acquainted with the shoal places, steering ahead, and showing them the way.

Snorro rises into one of his pictorial fits, seized with enthusiasm at the thought of such a fleet, and reports to us largely in what order Tryggveson's winged Coursers of the Deep, in long series, for perhaps an hour or more, came on, and what the three potentates, from their knoll of vantage, said of each as it hove in sight. Svein thrice over guessed this and the other noble vessel to be the Long Serpent; Eric always correcting him, "No, that is not the Long Serpent yet" (and *aside* always), "Nor shall you be lord of it, king, when it does come." The Long Serpent itself did make appearance. Eric, Svein, and the Swedish king hurried on board, and pushed out of their hiding-place into the open sea. Treacherous Sigwald, at the beginning of all this, had suddenly doubled that cape of theirs, and struck into the bay out of sight, leaving the foremost Tryggveson ships astonished, and uncertain what to do, if it were not simply to strike sail and wait till Olaf himself with the Long Serpent arrived.

Olaf's chief captains, seeing the enemy's huge fleet come out, and how the matter lay, strongly advised King Olaf to elude this stroke of treachery, and, with all sail, hold on his course, fight being now on so unequal terms. Snorro says, the king, high on the quarter-deck where he stood, replied, "Strike the sails; never shall men of mine think of flight. I never fled from battle. Let God dispose of my life; but flight I will never take." And so the battle arrangements immediately began, and the battle with all fury went loose; and lasted hour after hour, till almost sunset, if I well recollect. "Olaf stood on the Serpent's quarter-deck," says Snorro, "high over the others. He had a gilt shield and a helmet inlaid with gold; over his armor he had a short red coat, and was easily distinguished from other men." Snorro's account of the battle is altogether animated, graphic, and so minute that antiquaries gather from it, if so disposed (which we but little are), what the methods of Norse sea-fighting were; their shooting of arrows, casting of javelins, pitching of big stones, ultimately boarding, and mutual clashing and smashing, which it would not avail us to speak of here. Olaf stood conspicuous all day, throwing javelins, of deadly aim, with both hands at once; encouraging, fighting and commanding like a highest sea-king.

The Danish fleet, the Swedish fleet, were, both of them, quickly dealt with, and successively withdrew out of shot-range. And then Jarl Eric came up, and fiercely grappled with the Long Serpent, or, rather, with her surrounding comrades; and gradually, as they were beaten empty of men, with the Long Serpent herself. The fight grew ever fiercer, more furious. Eric was supplied with new men from the Swedes and Danes; Olaf had no such resource, except from the crews of his own beaten ships, and at length this also failed him; all his ships, except the Long Serpent, being beaten and emptied. Olaf fought on unyielding. Eric twice boarded him, was twice repulsed. Olaf kept his quarter-deck; unconquerable, though left now more and more hopeless, fatally short of help. A tall young man, called Einar Tamberskelver, very celebrated and important afterwards in Norway, and already the best archer known, kept busy with his bow. Twice he nearly shot Jarl Eric in his ship. "Shoot me that man," said Jarl Eric to a bowman near him; and, just as Tamberskelver was drawing his bow the third time, an arrow hit it in the middle and broke it in two. "What is this that has broken?" asked King Olaf. "Norway from thy hand, king," answered Tamberskelver. Tryggveson's men, he observed with surprise, were striking violently on Eric's; but to no purpose; nobody fell. "How is this?" asked Tryggveson. "Our swords are notched and blunted, king; they do not cut." Olaf stept down to his arm-chest; delivered out new swords; and it was observed as he did it, blood ran trickling from his wrist; but none knew where the wound was. Eric boarded a third time. Olaf, left with hardly more than one man, sprang overboard (one sees that red coat of his still glancing in the evening sun), and sank in the deep waters to his long rest.

Rumor ran among his people that he still was not dead; grounding on some movement by the ships of that traitorous Sigwald, they fancied Olaf had dived beneath the keels of his enemies, and got away with Sigwald, as Sigwald himself evidently did. "Much was hoped, supposed, spoken," says one old mourning Skald; "but the truth was, Olaf Tryggveson was never seen in Norseland more." Strangely he remains still a shining figure to us; the wildly beautifulest man, in body and in soul, that one has ever heard of in the North.

CHAPTER VIII.

JARLS ERIC AND SVEIN.

Jarl Eric, splendent with this victory, not to speak of that over the Jomsburgers with his father long ago, was now made Governor of Norway: Governor or quasi-sovereign, with his brother, Jarl Svein, as partner, who, however, took but little hand in governing; — and, under the patronage of Svein Double-Beard and the then Swedish king (Olaf his name, Sigrid the Proud, his mother's), administered it, they say, with skill and prudence for above fourteen years. Tryggveson's death is understood and laboriously computed to have happened in the year 1000; but there is no exact chronology in these things, but a continual uncertain guessing after such; so that one eye in History as regards them is as if put out; — neither indeed have I yet had the luck to find any decipherable and intelligible map of Norway: so that the other eye of History is much blinded withal, and her path through those wild regions and epochs is an extremely dim and chaotic one. An evil that much demands remedying, and especially wants some first attempt at remedying, by inquirers into English History; the whole period from Egbert, the first Saxon King of England, on to Edward the Confessor, the last, being everywhere completely interwoven with that of their mysterious, continually invasive "Danes," as they call them, and inextricably unintelligible till these also get to be a little understood, and cease to be utterly dark, hideous, and mythical to us as they now are.

King Olaf Tryggveson is the first Norseman who is expressly mentioned to have been in England by our English History books, new or old; and of him it is merely said that he had an interview with King Ethelred II. at Andover, of a pacific and friendly nature, — though it is absurdly added that the noble Olaf was converted to Christianity by that extremely stupid Royal Person. Greater contrast in an interview than in this at Andover, between heroic Olaf Tryggveson and Ethelred the forever Unready, was not perhaps seen in the terrestrial Planet that day. Olaf, or "Olaus," or "Anlaf," as they name him, did "engage on oath to Ethelred not to invade England any more," and kept his promise, they farther say. Essentially a truth, as we already know, though the circumstances were all different; and the promise was to a devout High Priest, not to a crowned Blockhead and cowardly Do-nothing. One other "Olaus" I find mentioned in our Books, two or three centuries before, at a time when there existed no such individual; not to speak of several Anlafs, who sometimes seem to mean Olaf, and still oftener to mean nobody possible. Which occasions not a little obscurity in our early History, says the learned Selden. A thing remediable, too, in which, if any Englishman of due genius (or even capacity for standing labor), who understood the Icelandic and Anglo-Saxon languages, would engage in it, he might do a great deal of good, and bring the matter into a comparatively lucid state. Vain aspirations, — or perhaps not altogether vain.

At the time of Olaf Tryggveson's death, and indeed long before, King Svein Double-Beard had always for chief enterprise the Conquest of England, and followed it by fits with extreme violence and impetus; often advancing largely towards a successful conclusion; but never, for thirteen years yet, getting it concluded. He possessed long since all England north of Watling Street. That is to say, Northumberland, East Anglia (naturally full of Danish settlers by this time), were fixedly his; Mercia, his oftener than not; Wessex itself, with all the coasts, he was free to visit, and to burn and rob in at discretion. There or elsewhere, Ethelred the Unready had no battle in him whatever; and, for a forty years after the beginning of his reign, England excelled in anarchic stupidity, murderous devastation, utter misery, platitude, and sluggish contemptibility, all the countries one has read of. Apparently a very opulent country, too; a ready skill in such arts and fine arts as there were; Svein's very ships, they say, had their gold dragons, top-mast pennons, and other metallic splendors generally wrought for them in England. "Unexampled prosperity" in the manufacture way not unknown there, it would seem! But co-existing with such spiritual bankruptcy as was also unexampled, one would hope. Read *Lupus* (Wulfstan), Archbishop of York's amazing *Sermon* on the subject,[1] addressed to contemporary audiences; setting forth such a state of things, — sons selling their fathers, mothers, and sisters as Slaves to the Danish robber; themselves living in debauchery, blusterous gluttony, and depravity; the details of which are well-nigh incredible, though clearly stated as things generally known, — the humor of these poor wretches sunk to a state of what we may call greasy desperation, "Let us eat and drink, for to-morrow we die." The manner in which they treated their own English nuns, if young, good-looking, and captive to the Danes; buying them on a kind of brutish or subter-brutish "Greatest Happiness Principle" (for the moment), and by a Joint-Stock arrangement, far transcends all human speech or imagination, and awakens in one the momentary red-hot thought, The Danes have served you right, ye accursed! The so-called soldiers, one finds, made not the least fight anywhere; could make none, led and guided as they were: and the "Generals" often enough traitors, always ignorant, and blockheads, were in the habit, when expressly commanded to fight, of taking physic, and declaring that nature was incapable of castor-oil and battle both at once. This ought to be explained a little to the modern English and their War-Secretaries, who undertake the conduct of armies. The undeniable fact is, defeat on defeat was the constant fate of the English; during these forty years not one battle in which they were not beaten. No gleam of victory or real resistance till the noble Edmund Ironside (whom it is always strange to me how such an Ethelred could produce for son) made his appearance and ran his brief course, like a great and far-seen meteor, soon extinguished without result. No remedy for England in that base time, but yearly asking the victorious, plundering, burning and murdering

---

[1] This sermon was printed by Hearne; and is given also by Langebek in his excellent Collection, *Rerum Danicarum Scriptores Medii Ævi.* Hafniæ, 1772–1834.

Danes, "How much money will you take to go away ?" **Thirty**
thousand pounds in silver, which the annual *Danegelt* soon
rose to, continued to be about the average yearly sum, though
generally on the increasing hand; in the last year I think it
had risen to seventy-two thousand pounds in silver, raised
yearly by a tax (Income-Tax of its kind, rudely levied), the
worst of all remedies, good for the day only. Nay, there was
one remedy still worse, which the miserable Ethelred once
tried : that of massacring " all the Danes settled in England "
(practically, of a few thousands or hundreds of them), by
treachery and a kind of Sicilian Vespers. Which issued, as
such things usually do, in terrible monition to you not to try
the like again ! Issued, namely, in redoubled fury on the
Danish part; new fiercer invasion by Svein's Jarl Thorkel;
then by Svein himself; which latter drove the miserable
Æthelred, with wife and family, into Normandy, to wife's
brother, the then Duke there ; and ended that miserable struggle by Svein's becoming King of England himself. Of this
disgraceful massacre, which it would appear has been immensely exaggerated in the English books, we can happily
give the exact date (A.D. 1002) ; and also of Svein's victorious
accession (A.D. 1013),[1] — pretty much the only benefit one gets
out of contemplating such a set of objects.

King Svein's first act was to levy a terribly increased Income-
Tax for the payment of his army. Svein was levying it with
a stronghanded diligence, but had not yet done levying it, when,
at Gainsborough one night, he suddenly died; smitten dead,
once used to be said, by St. Edmund, whilom murdered King
of the East Angles ; who could not bear to see his shrine and
monastery of St. Edmundsbury plundered by the Tyrant's tax-
collectors, as they were on the point of being. In all ways impossible, however, — Edmund's own death did not occur till two
years after Svein's. Svein's death, by whatever cause, befell
1014; his fleet, then lying in the Humber ; and only Knut,[2] his
eldest son (hardly yet eighteen, count some), in charge of it;
who, on short counsel, and arrangement about this questionable

---

[1] Kennet, i. 67 ; Rapin, i. 119, 121 (from the *Saxon Chronicle* both).

[2] Knut born A.D. 988 according to Munch's calculation (ii. 126).

kingdom of his, lifted anchor; made for Sandwich, a safer station at the moment; "cut off the feet and noses" (one shudders, and hopes Not, there being some discrepancy about it!) of his numerous hostages that had been delivered to King Svein; set them ashore;—and made for Denmark, his natural storehouse and stronghold, as the hopefulest first thing he could do.

Knut soon returned from Denmark, with increase of force sufficient for the English problem; which latter he now ended in a victorious, and essentially, for himself and chaotic England, beneficent manner. Became widely known by and by, there and elsewhere, as Knut the Great; and is thought by judges of our day to have really merited that title. A most nimble, sharp-striking, clear-thinking, prudent and effective man, who regulated this dismembered and distracted England in its Church matters, in its State matters, like a real King. Had a Standing Army (*House Carles*), who were well paid, well drilled and disciplined, capable of instantly quenching insurrection or breakage of the peace; and piously endeavored (with a signal earnestness, and even devoutness, if we look well) to do justice to all men, and to make all men rest satisfied with justice. In a word, he successfully strapped up, by every true method and regulation, this miserable, dislocated, and dissevered mass of bleeding Anarchy into something worthy to be called an England again;—only that he died too soon, and a second "Conqueror" of us, still weightier of structure, and under improved auspices, became possible, and was needed here! To appearance, Knut himself was capable of being a Charlemagne of England and the North (as has been already said or quoted), had he only lived twice as long as he did. But his whole sum of years seems not to have exceeded forty. His father Svein of the Forkbeard is reckoned to have been fifty to sixty when St. Edmund finished him at Gainsborough. We now return to Norway, ashamed of this long circuit which has been a truancy more or less.

CHAPTER IX.

KING OLAF THE THICK-SET'S VIKING DAYS.

KING HARALD GRÆNSKE, who, with another from Russia accidentally lodging beside him, got burned to death in Sweden, courting that unspeakable Sigrid the Proud, — was third cousin or so to Tryggve, father of our heroic Olaf. Accurately counted, he is great-grandson of Bjorn the Chapman, first of Haarfagr's sons whom Eric Bloodaxe made away with. His little "kingdom," as he called it, was a district named the Greenland (*Grœneland*); he himself was one of those little Haarfagr kinglets whom Hakon Jarl, much more Olaf Tryggveson, was content to leave reigning, since they would keep the peace with him. Harald had a loving wife of his own, Aasta the name of her, soon expecting the birth of her and his pretty babe, named Olaf, — at the time he went on that deplorable Swedish adventure, the foolish, fated creature, and ended self and kingdom altogether. Aasta was greatly shocked; composed herself however; married a new husband, Sigurd Syr, a kinglet, and a great-grandson of Harald Fairhair, a man of great wealth, prudence, and influence in those countries; in whose house, as favorite and well-beloved stepson, little Olaf was wholesomely and skilfully brought up. In Sigurd's house he had, withal, a special tutor entertained for him, one Rane, known as Rane the Far-travelled, by whom he could be trained, from the earliest basis, in Norse accomplishments and arts. New children came, one or two; but Olaf, from his mother, seems always to have known that he was the distinguished and royal article there. One day his Foster-father, hurrying to leave home on business, hastily bade Olaf, no other being by, saddle his horse for him. Olaf went out with the saddle, chose the biggest he-goat about, saddled that, and brought it to the door by way of horse. Old Sigurd, a most grave man, grinned sardonically at the sight. " Hah, I see thou hast no mind to take commands from me; thou art of too high a humor to take commands." To which, says Snorro, Boy Olaf answered little except by laughing, till Sigurd saddled for himself, and rode away. His mother Aasta appears to have been a thoughtful, prudent woman, though always with a fierce royalism at the bottom of her memory, and a secret implacability on that head.

At the age of twelve Olaf went to sea; furnished with a little fleet, and skilful sea-counsellor, expert old Rane, by his Foster-father, and set out to push his fortune in the world. Rane was a steersman and counsellor in these incipient times; but the crew always called Olaf "King," though at first, as Snorro thinks, except it were in the hour of battle, he merely pulled an oar. He cruised and fought in this capacity on many seas and shores; passed several years, perhaps till the age of nine-teen or twenty, in this wild element and way of life; fighting always in a glorious and distinguished manner. In the hour of battle, diligent enough "to amass property," as the Vikings termed it; and in the long days and nights of sailing, given over, it is likely, to his own thoughts and the unfathomable dialogue with the ever-moaning Sea; not the worst High School a man could have, and indeed infinitely preferable to the most that are going even now, for a high and deep young soul.

His first distinguished expedition was to Sweden: natural to go thither first, to avenge his poor father's death, were it nothing more. Which he did, the Skalds say, in a distinguished manner; making victorious and handsome battle for himself, in entering Mælare Lake; and in getting out of it again, after being frozen there all winter, showing still more surprising, almost miraculous contrivance and dexterity. This was the first of his glorious victories; of which the Skalds reckon up some fourteen or thirteen very glorious indeed, mostly in the Western and Southern countries, most of all in England; till the name of Olaf Haraldson became quite famous in the Vik-ing and strategic world. He seems really to have learned the secrets of his trade, and to have been, then and afterwards, for vigilance, contrivance, valor, and promptitude of execution, a superior fighter. Several exploits recorded of him betoken, in simple forms, what may be called a military genius.

The principal, and to us the alone interesting, of his exploits seem to have lain in England, and, what is further notable, always on the anti-Svein side. English books do not mention him at all that I can find; but it is fairly credible that, as the Norse records report, in the end of Ethelred's reign, he was the ally or hired general of Ethelred, and did a great deal of sea-fighting, watching, sailing, and sieging for this miserable king and Edmund Ironside, his son. Snorro says expressly, London, the impregnable city, had to be besieged again for Ethelred's behoof (in the interval between Svein's death and young Knut's getting back from Denmark), and that our Olaf Haraldson was the great engineer and victorious captor of London on that singular occasion, — London captured for the first time. The Bridge, as usual, Snorro says, offered almost insuperable obstacles. But the engineering genius of Olaf contrived huge "platforms of wainscoting [old walls of wooden houses, in fact], bound together by withes;" these, carried steadily aloft above the ships, will (thinks Olaf) considerably secure them and us from the destructive missiles, big boulder stones, and other mischief profusely showered down on us, till we get under the Bridge with axes and cables, and do some good upon it. Olaf's plan was tried; most of the other ships, in spite of their wainscoting and withes, recoiled on reaching the Bridge, so destructive were the boulder and other missile showers. But Olaf's ships and self got actually under the Bridge; fixed all manner of cables there; and then, with the river current in their favor, and the frightened ships rallying to help in this safer part of the enterprise, tore out the important piles and props, and fairly broke the poor Bridge, wholly or partly, down into the river, and its Danish defenders into immediate surrender. That is Snorro's account.

On a previous occasion, Olaf had been deep in a hopeful combination with Ethelred's two younger sons, Alfred and Edward, afterwards King Edward the Confessor: That they two should sally out from Normandy in strong force, unite with Olaf in ditto, and, landing on the Thames, do something effectual for themselves. But impediments, bad weather or the like, disheartened the poor Princes, and it came to nothing.

Olaf was much in Normandy, what they then called Walland; a man held in honor by those Norman Dukes.

What amount of "property" he had amassed I do not know, but could prove, were it necessary, that he had acquired some tactical or even strategic faculty and real talent for war. At Lymfjord, in Jutland, but some years after this (A.D. 1027), he had a sea-battle with the great Knut himself, — ships combined with flood-gates, with roaring, artificial deluges; right well managed by King Olaf; which were within a hair's-breadth of destroying Knut, now become a King and Great; and did in effect send him instantly running. But of this more particularly by and by.

What still more surprises me is the mystery, where Olaf, in this wandering, fighting, sea-roving life, acquired his deeply religious feeling, his intense adherence to the Christian Faith. I suppose it had been in England, where many pious persons, priestly and other, were still to be met with, that Olaf had gathered these doctrines; and that in those his unfathomable dialogues with the ever-moaning Ocean, they had struck root downwards in the soul of him, and borne fruit upwards to the degree so conspicuous afterwards. It is certain he became a deeply pious man during these long Viking cruises; and directed all his strength, when strength and authority were lent him, to establishing the Christian religion in his country, and suppressing and abolishing Vikingism there; both of which objects, and their respective worth and unworth, he must himself have long known so well.

It was well on in A.D. 1016 that Knut gained his last victory, at Ashdon, in Essex, where the earth pyramids and antique church near by still testify the thankful piety of Knut, — or, at lowest his joy at having *won* instead of lost and perished, as he was near doing there. And it was still this same year when the noble Edmund Ironside, after forced partition-treaty "in the Isle of Alney," got scandalously murdered, and Knut became indisputable sole King of England, and decisively settled himself to his work of governing there. In the year before either of which events, while all still hung uncertain for Knut, and even Eric Jarl of Norway had to be summoned in aid of him, —

in that year 1015, as one might naturally guess, and as all
Icelandic hints and indications lead us to date the thing, Olaf
had decided to give up Vikingism in all its forms; to return to
Norway, and try whether he could not assert the place and
career that belonged to him there. Jarl Eric had vanished
with all his war forces towards England, leaving only a boy,
Hakon, as successor, and Svein, his own brother, — a quiet
man, who had always avoided war. Olaf landed in Norway
without obstacle; but decided to be quiet till he had himself
examined and consulted friends.

His reception by his mother Aasta was of the kindest and
proudest, and is lovingly described by Snorro. A pretty idyllic
or epic piece, of *Norse* Homeric type: How Aasta, hearing of
her son's advent, set all her maids and menials to work at the
top of their speed; despatched a runner to the harvest-field,
where her husband Sigurd was, to warn him to come home
and dress. How Sigurd was standing among his harvest folk,
reapers and binders; and what he had on, — broad slouch hat,
with veil (against the midges), blue kirtle, hose of I forget what
color, with laced boots; and in his hand a stick with silver
head and ditto ring upon it; — a personable old gentleman, of
the eleventh century, in those parts. Sigurd was cautious,
prudentially cunctatory, though heartily friendly in his counsel
to Olaf, as to the King question. Aasta had a Spartan tone in
her wild maternal heart; and assures Olaf that she, with a half-
reproachful glance at Sigurd, will stand by him to the death in
this his just and noble enterprise. Sigurd promises to consult
farther in his neighborhood, and to correspond by messages;
the result is, Olaf, resolutely pushing forward himself, resolves
to call a Thing, and openly claim his kingship there. The
Thing itself was willing enough: opposition parties do here
and there bestir themselves; but Olaf is always swifter than
they. Five kinglets somewhere in the Uplands,[1] — all descendants of Haarfagr; but averse to break the peace, which Jarl
Eric and Hakon Jarl both have always willingly allowed to
peaceable people, — seem to be the main opposition party.
These five take the field against Olaf with what force they

[1] Snorro, Laing's Translation, ii. p. 31 et seq., will minutely specify.

have; Olaf, one night, by beautiful celerity and strategic practice which a Friedrich or a Turenne might have approved,
surrounds these Five; and when morning breaks, there is nothing for them but either death or else instant surrender, and
swearing of fealty to King Olaf. Which latter branch of the
alternative they gladly accept, the whole five of them, and go
home again.

This was a beautiful bit of war-practice by King Olaf on
land. By another stroke still more compendious at sea, he had
already settled poor young Hakon, and made him peaceable for
a long while. Olaf, by diligent quest and spy-messaging, had
ascertained that Hakon, just returning from Denmark and farewell to Papa and Knut, both now under way for England, was
coasting north towards Trondhjem; and intended on or about
such a day to land in such and such a fjord towards the end
of this Trondhjem voyage. Olaf at once mans two big ships,
steers through the narrow mouth of the said fjord, moors one
ship on the north shore, another on the south; fixes a strong
cable, well sunk under water, to the capstans of these two; and
in all quietness waits for Hakon. Before many hours, Hakon's
royal or quasi-royal barge steers gaily into this fjord; is a little
surprised, perhaps, to see within the jaws of it two big ships
at anchor; but steers gallantly along, nothing doubting. Olaf,
with a signal of " All hands," works his two capstans; has the
cable up high enough at the right moment, catches with it the
keel of poor Hakon's barge, upsets it, empties it wholly into
the sea. Wholly into the sea; saves Hakon, however, and his
people from drowning, and brings them on board. His dialogue with poor young Hakon, especially poor young Hakon's
responses, is very pretty. Shall I give it, out of Snorro, and
let the reader take it for as authentic as he can? It is at
least the true image of it in authentic Snorro's *head*, little
more than two centuries later.

"Jarl Hakon was led up to the king's ship. He was the
handsomest man that could be seen. He had long hair as fine
as silk, bound about his head with a gold ornament. When he
sat down in the forehold the king said to him : —

King. " ' It is not false, what is said of your family, that ye are handsome people to look at; but now your luck has deserted you.'

Hakon. "'It has always been the case that success is changeable; and there is no luck in the matter. It has gone with your family as with mine to have by turns the better lot. I am little beyond childhood in years; and at any rate we could not have defended ourselves, as we did not expect any attack on the way. It may turn out better with us another time.'

King. "'Dost thou not apprehend that thou art in such a condition that, hereafter, there can be neither victory nor defeat for thee?'

Hakon. "'That is what only thou canst determine, King, according to thy pleasure.'

King. "'What wilt thou give me, Jarl, if, for this time, I let thee go, whole and unhurt?'

Hakon. "'What wilt thou take, King?'

King. "'Nothing, except that thou shalt leave the country; give up thy kingdom; and take an oath that thou wilt never go into battle against me.'"[1]

Jarl Hakon accepted the generous terms; went to England and King Knut, and kept his bargain for a good few years; though he was at last driven, by pressure of King Knut, to violate it, — little to his profit, as we shall see. One victorious naval battle with Jarl Svein, Hakon's uncle, and his adherents, who fled to Sweden, after his beating, — battle not difficult to a skilful, hard-hitting king, — was pretty much all the actual fighting Olaf had to do in this enterprise. He various times met angry Bonders and refractory Things with arms in their hand; but by skilful, firm management, — perfectly patient, but also perfectly ready to be active, — he mostly managed without coming to strokes; and was universally recognized by Norway as its real king. A promising young man, and fit to be a king, thinks Snorro. Only of middle stature, almost rather shortish; but firm-standing, and stout-built; so that they got to call him Olaf the Thick (meaning Olaf the Thick-*set*, or Stout-built), though his final epithet among them was infinitely higher. For

---

[1] Snorro, ii. pp. 24, 25.

the rest, "a comely, earnest, prepossessing look; beautiful yel-
low hair in quantity; broad, honest face, of a complexion pure
as snow and rose;" and finally (or firstly) "the brightest eyes
in the world; such that, in his anger, no man could stand
them." He had a heavy task ahead, and needed all his qualities and fine gifts to get it done.

CHAPTER X.

REIGN OF KING OLAF THE SAINT.

THE late two Jarls, now gone about their business, had
both been baptized, and called themselves Christians. But
during their government they did nothing in the conversion
way; left every man to choose his own God or Gods; so that
some had actually two, the Christian God by land, and at sea
Thor, whom they considered safer in that element. And in
effect the mass of the people had fallen back into a sluggish
heathenism or half-heathenism, the life-labor of Olaf Tryggveson lying ruinous or almost quite overset. The new Olaf,
son of Harald, set himself with all his strength to mend such
a state of matters; and stood by his enterprise to the end, as
the one highest interest, including all others, for his People and
him. His method was by no means soft; on the contrary, it
was hard, rapid, severe, — somewhat on the model of Tryggveson's, though with more of *bishoping* and preaching superadded. Yet still there was a great deal of mauling, vigorous
punishing, and an entire intolerance of these two things: Heathenism and Sea-robbery, at least of Sea-robbery in the old
style; whether in the style we moderns still practise, and call
privateering, I do not quite know. But Vikingism proper had
to cease in Norway; still more, Heathenism, under penalties
too severe to be borne; death, mutilation of limb, not to mention forfeiture and less rigorous coercion. Olaf was inexorable against violation of the law. "Too severe," cried many;
to whom one answers, "Perhaps in part *yes*, perhaps also in

great part *no ;* depends altogether on the previous question, How far the law was the eternal one of God Almighty in the universe, How far the law merely of Olaf (destitute of right inspiration) left to his own passions and whims ?"

Many were the jangles Olaf had with the refractory Heathen Things and Ironbeards of a new generation: very curious to see. Scarcely ever did it come to fighting between King and Thing, though often enough near it; but the Thing discerning, as it usually did in time, that the King was stronger in men, seemed to say unanimously to itself, "We have lost, then; baptize us, we must burn our old gods and conform." One new feature we do slightly discern: here and there a touch of theological argument on the heathen side. At one wild Thing, far up in the Dovrefjeld, of a very heathen temper, there was much of that; not to be quenched by King Olaf at the moment; so that it had to be adjourned till the morrow, and again till the next day. Here are some traits of it, much abridged from Snorro (who gives a highly punctual account), which vividly represent Olaf's posture and manner of proceeding in such intricacies.

The chief Ironbeard on this occasion was one Gudbrand, a very rugged peasant; who, says Snorro, was like a king in that district. Some days before, King Olaf, intending a religious Thing in those deeply heathen parts, with alternative of Christianity or conflagration, is reported, on looking down into the valley and the beautiful village of Loar standing there, to have said wistfully, "What a pity it is that so beautiful a village should be burnt!" Olaf sent out his message-token all the same, however, and met Gudbrand and an immense assemblage, whose humor towards him was uncompliant to a high degree indeed. Judge by this preliminary speech of Gudbrand to his Thing-people, while Olaf was not yet arrived, but only advancing, hardly got to Breeden on the other side of the hill: "A man has come to Loar who is called Olaf," said Gudbrand, "and will force upon us another faith than we had before, and will break in pieces all our Gods. He says he has a much greater and more powerful God; and it is wonderful that the earth does not burst asunder under him, or that our God lets him go about unpunished when he dares to talk such things. I know this for certain, that if we carry Thor, who has always stood by us, out of our Temple that is standing upon this farm, Olaf's God will melt away, and he and his men be made nothing as soon as Thor looks upon them." Whereupon the Bonders all shouted as one man, "Yea!"

Which tremendous message they even forwarded to Olaf, by Gudbrand's younger son at the head of 700 armed men; but did not terrify Olaf with it, who, on the contrary, drew up his troops, rode himself at the head of them, and began a speech to the Bonders, in which he invited them to adopt Christianity, as the one true faith for mortals.

Far from consenting to this, the Bonders raised a general shout, smiting at the same time their shields with their weapons; but Olaf's men advancing on them swiftly, and flinging spears, they turned and ran, leaving Gudbrand's son behind, a prisoner, to whom Olaf gave his life: "Go home now to thy father, and tell him I mean to be with him soon."

The son goes accordingly, and advises his father not to face Olaf; but Gudbrand angrily replies: "Ha, coward! I see thou, too, art taken by the folly that man is going about with;" and is resolved to fight. That night, however, Gudbrand has a most remarkable Dream, or Vision: a Man surrounded by light, bringing great terror with him, who warns Gudbrand against doing battle with Olaf. "If thou dost, thou and all thy people will fall; wolves will drag away thee and thine, ravens will tear thee in stripes!" And lo, in telling this to Thord Potbelly, a sturdy neighbor of his and henchman in the Thing, it is found that to Thord also has come the self-same terrible Apparition! Better propose truce to Olaf (who seems to have these dreadful Ghostly Powers on his side), and the holding of a Thing, to discuss matters between us. Thing assembles, on a day of heavy rain. Being all seated, uprises King Olaf, and informs them: "The people of Lesso, Loar, and Vaage, have accepted Christianity, and broken down their idol-houses: they believe now in the True God, who has made heaven and earth, and knows all things;" and sits down again without more words.

"Gudbrand replies, 'We know nothing about him of whom thou speakest. Dost thou call him God, whom neither thou nor any one else can see? But we have a God who can be seen every day, although he is not out to-day because the weather is wet; and he will appear to thee terrible and very grand; and I expect that fear will mix with thy very blood when he comes into the Thing. But since thou sayest thy God is so great, let him make it so that to-morrow we have a cloudy day, but without rain, and then let us meet again.'

"The king accordingly returned home to his lodging, taking Gudbrand's son as a hostage; but he gave them a man as hostage in exchange. In the evening the king asked Gudbrand's son What their God was like? He replied that he bore the likeness of Thor; had a hammer in his hand; was of great size, but hollow within; and had a high stand, upon which he stood when he was out. 'Neither gold nor silver are wanting about him, and every day he receives four cakes of bread, besides meat.' They then went to bed; but the king watched all night in prayer. When day dawned the king went to mass; then to table, and from thence to the Thing. The weather was such as Gudbrand desired. Now the Bishop stood up in his choir-robes, with bishop's coif on his head, and bishop's crosier in his hand. He spoke to the Bonders of the true faith, told the many wonderful acts of God, and concluded his speech well.

"Thord Potbelly replies, 'Many things we are told of by this learned man with the staff in his hand, crooked at the top like a ram's horn. But since you say, comrades, that your God is so powerful, and can do so many wonders, tell him to make it clear sunshine to-morrow forenoon, and then we shall meet here again, and do one of two things, — either agree with you about this business, or fight you.' And they separated for the day."

Overnight the king instructed Kolbein the Strong, an immense fellow, the same who killed Gunhild's two brothers, that he, Kolbein, must stand next him to-morrow; people must go down to where the ships of the Bonders lay, and punctually bore holes in every one of them; *item*, to the farms where their horses were, and punctually unhalter the whole of them, and let them loose : all which was done. Snorro continues : —

"Now the king was in prayer all night, beseeching God of his goodness and mercy to release him from evil. When mass was ended, and morning was gray, the king went to the Thing. When he came thither, some Bonders had already arrived, and they saw a great crowd coming along, and bearing among them a huge man's image, glancing with gold and silver. When the Bonders who were at the Thing saw it, they started up, and bowed themselves down before the ugly idol. Thereupon it was set down upon the Thing field; and on the one side of it sat the Bonders, and on the other the King and his people.

"Then Dale Gudbrand stood up and said, 'Where now, king, is thy God? I think he will now carry his head lower; and neither thou, nor the man with the horn, sitting beside thee there, whom thou callest Bishop, are so bold to-day as on the former days. For now our God, who rules over all, is come, and looks on you with an angry eye; and now I see well enough that you are terrified, and scarcely dare raise your eyes. Throw away now all your opposition, and believe in the God who has your fate wholly in his hands.'

"The king now whispers to Kolbein the Strong, without the Bonders perceiving it, 'If it come so in the course of my speech that the Bonders look another way than towards their idol, strike him as hard as thou canst with thy club.'

"The king then stood up and spoke: 'Much hast thou talked to us this morning, and greatly hast thou wondered that thou canst not see our God; but we expect that he will soon come to us. Thou wouldst frighten us with thy God, who is both blind and deaf, and cannot even move about without being carried; but now I expect it will be but a short time before he meets his fate : for turn your eyes towards the east, — behold our God advancing in great light.'

"The sun was rising, and all turned to look. At that moment Kolbein gave their God a stroke, so that he quite burst asunder; and there ran out of him mice as big almost as cats,

and reptiles and adders. The Bonders were so terrified that
some fled to their ships; but when they sprang out upon them
the ships filled with water, and could not get away. Others
ran to their horses, but could not find them. The king then
ordered the Bonders to be called together, saying he wanted
to speak with them; on which the Bonders came back, and
the Thing was again seated.

"The king rose up and said, 'I do not understand what
your noise and running mean. You yourselves see what your
God can do, — the idol you adorned with gold·and silver, and
brought meat and provisions to. You see now that the pro-
tecting powers, who used and got good of all that, were the
mice and adders, the reptiles and lizards; and surely they do
ill who trust to such, and will not abandon this folly. Take
now your gold and ornaments that are lying strewed on the
grass, and give them to your wives and daughters, but never
hang them hereafter upon stocks and stones. Here are two
conditions between us to choose upon : either accept Christianity, or fight this very day, and the victory be to them to
whom the God we worship gives it.'

"Then Dale Gudbrand stood up and said, 'We have sus
tained great damage upon our God; but since he will not
help us, we will believe in the God whom thou believest in.'

"Then all received Christianity. The Bishop baptized
Gudbrand and his son. King Olaf and Bishop Sigurd left
behind them teachers; and they who met as enemies parted
as friends. And afterwards Gudbrand built a church in the
valley."[1]

Olaf was by no means an unmerciful man, — much the reverse where he saw good cause. There was a wicked old King
Rærik, for example, one of those five kinglets whom, with
their bits of armaments, Olaf by stratagem had·surrounded·
one night, and at once bagged and subjected when morning
rose, all of them consenting; all of them except this Rærik,
whom Olaf, as the readiest sure course, took home with him;
blinded, and kept in his own house; finding there was no
alternative but that or death to the obstinate old dog, who

[1] Snorro, ii. pp. 156–161.

was a kind of distant cousin withal, and could not conscientiously be killed. Stone-blind old Rærik was not always in murderous humor. Indeed, for most part he wore a placid, conciliatory aspect, and said shrewd amusing things; but had thrice over tried, with amazing cunning of contrivance, though stone-blind, to thrust a dagger into Olaf, and the last time had all but succeeded. So that, as Olaf still refused to have him killed, it had become a problem what was to be done with him. Olaf's good humor, as well as his quiet, ready sense and practicality, are manifested in his final settlement of this Rærik problem. Olaf's laugh, I can perceive, was not so loud as Tryggveson's, but equally hearty, coming from the bright mind of him!

Besides blind Rærik, Olaf had in his household one Thorarin, an Icelander; a remarkably ugly man, says Snorro, but a far-travelled, shrewdly observant, loyal-minded, and good-humored person, whom Olaf liked to talk with. "Remarkably ugly," says Snorro, "especially in his hands and feet, which were large and ill-shaped to a degree." One morning Thorarin, who, with other trusted ones, slept in Olaf's apartment, was lazily dozing and yawning, and had stretched one of his feet out of the bed before the king awoke. The foot was still there when Olaf did open his bright eyes, which instantly lighted on this foot.

"Well, here is a foot," says Olaf, gayly, "which one seldom sees the match of; I durst venture there is not another so ugly in this city of Nidaros."

"Hah, king!" said Thorarin, "there are few things one cannot match if one seek long and take pains. I would bet, with thy permission, King, to find an uglier."

"Done!" cried Olaf. Upon which Thorarin stretched out the other foot.

"A still uglier," cried he; "for it has lost the little toe."

"Ho, ho!" said Olaf; "but it is I who have gained the bet. The *less* of an ugly thing the less ugly, not the more!"

Loyal Thorarin respectfully submitted.

"What is to be my penalty, then? The king it is that must decide."

"To take me that wicked old Rærik to Leif Ericson in Greenland."

Which the Icelander did; leaving two vacant seats henceforth at Olaf's table. Leif Ericson, son of Eric discoverer of America, quietly managed Rærik henceforth; sent him to Iceland, — I think to father Eric himself; certainly to some safe hand there, in whose house, or in some still quieter neighboring lodging, at his own choice, old Rærik spent the last three years of his life in a perfectly quiescent manner.

Olaf's struggles in the matter of religion had actually settled that question in Norway. By these rough methods of his, whatever we may think of them, Heathenism had got itself smashed dead; and was no more heard of in that country. Olaf himself was evidently a highly devout and pious man; — whosoever is born with Olaf's temper now will still find, as Olaf did, new and infinite field for it! Christianity in Norway had the like fertility as in other countries; or even rose to a higher, and what Dahlmann thinks, exuberant pitch, in the course of the two centuries which followed that of Olaf. Him all testimony represents to us as a most righteous no less than most religious king. Continually vigilant, just, and rigorous was Olaf's administration of the laws; repression of robbery, punishment of injustice, stern repayment of evil-doers, wherever he could lay hold of them.

Among the Bonder or opulent class, and indeed everywhere, for the poor too can be sinners and need punishment, Olaf had, by this course of conduct, naturally made enemies. His severity so visible to all, and the justice and infinite beneficence of it so invisible except to a very few. But, at any rate, his reign for the first ten years was victorious; and might have been so to the end, had it not been intersected, and interfered with, by King Knut in *his* far bigger orbit and current of affairs and interests. Knut's English affairs and Danish being all settled to his mind, he seems, especially after that year of pilgrimage to Rome, and association with the Pontiffs and Kaisers of the world on that occasion, to have turned his more particular attention upon Norway, and the claims he himself had there. Jarl Hakon, too, sister's son of

Knut, and always well seen by him, had long been busy in this direction, much forgetful of that oath to Olaf when his barge got canted over by the cable of two capstans, and his life was given him, not without conditions altogether !

About the year 1026 there arrived two splendid persons out of England, bearing King Knut the Great's letter and seal, with a message, likely enough to be far from welcome to Olaf. For some days Olaf refused to see them or their letter, shrewdly guessing what the purport would be.   Which indeed was couched in mild language, but of sharp meaning enough : a notice to King Olaf, namely, That Norway was properly, by just heritage, Knut the Great's ; and that Olaf must become the great Knut's liegeman, and pay tribute to him, or worse would follow.   King Olaf, listening to these two splendid persons and their letter, in indignant silence till they quite ended, made answer : " I have heard say, by old accounts there are, that King Gorm of Denmark [Blue-tooth's father, Knut's great-grandfather] was considered but a small king; having Denmark only and few people to rule over.   But the kings who succeeded him thought that insufficient for them ; and it has since come so far that King Knut rules over both Denmark and England, and has conquered for himself a part of Scotland.   And now he claims also my paternal bit of heritage ; cannot be contented without that too.   Does he wish to rule over all the countries of the North ?   Can he eat up all the kale in England itself, this Knut the Great ? He shall do that, and reduce his England to a desert, before I lay my head in his hands, or show him any other kind of vassalage.   And so I bid you tell him these my words : I will defend Norway with battle-axe and sword as long as life is given me, and will pay tax to no man for my kingdom." Words which naturally irritated Knut to a high degree.

Next year accordingly (year 1027), tenth or eleventh year of Olaf's reign, there came bad rumors out of England : That Knut was equipping an immense army, — land-army, and such a fleet as had never sailed before ; Knut's own ship in it, — a Gold Dragon with no fewer than sixty benches of oars.   Olaf and Onund King of Sweden, whose sister he had married, well guessed whither this armament was bound.   They were friends withal, they recognized their common peril in this imminence; and had, in repeated consultations, taken measures the best that their united skill (which I find was mainly Olaf's, but loyally accepted by the other) could suggest.   It was in this year that Olaf (with his Swedish king assisting) did his grand feat upon Knut in Lymfjord of Jutland, which was already spoken of.   The special circumstances of which were these : —

Knut's big armament arriving on the Jutish coasts too late in the season, and the coast country lying all plundered into temporary wreck by the two Norse kings, who shrank away on sight of Knut, there was nothing could be done upon them by Knut this year, — or, if anything, what?   Knut's ships ran into Lymfjord, the safe-sheltered frith, or intricate long straggle of friths and straits, which almost cuts Jutland in two in that region; and lay safe, idly rocking on the waters there, uncertain what to do farther.   At last he steered in his big ship and some others, deeper into the interior of Lymfjord, deeper and deeper onwards to the mouth of a big river called the Helge (*Helge-aa*, the Holy River, not discoverable in my poor maps, but certainly enough still existing and still flowing somewhere among those intricate straits and friths), towards the bottom of which Helge river lay, in some safe nook, the small combined Swedish and Norse fleet, under the charge of Onund, the Swedish king, while at the top or source, which is a biggish mountain lake, King Olaf had been doing considerable engineering works, well suited to such an occasion, and was now ready at a moment's notice.   Knut's fleet having idly taken station here, notice from the Swedish king was instantly sent; instantly Olaf's well-engineered flood-gates were thrown open; from the swollen lake a huge deluge of water was let loose; Olaf himself with all his people hastening down to join his Swedish friend, and get on board in time; Helge river all the while alongside of him, with ever-increasing roar, and wider-spreading deluge, hastening down the steeps in the night-watches.   So that, along with Olaf, or some way ahead of him, came immeasurable roaring waste of waters upon Knut's negligent fleet; shattered, broke, and stranded many of his ships, and was within a trifle of destroying the Golden Dragon herself, with Knut on board. Olaf and Onund, we need not say, were promptly there in person, doing their very best; the railings of the Golden Dragon, however, were too high for their little ships; and Jarl Ulf, husband of Knut's sister, at the top of his speed, courageously intervening, spoiled their stratagem, and saved Knut from this very dangerous pass.

Knut did nothing more this winter. The two Norse kings, quite unequal to attack such an armament, except by ambush and engineering, sailed away; again plundering at discretion on the Danish coast; carrying into Sweden great booties and many prisoners; but obliged to lie fixed all winter; and indeed to leave their fleets there for a series of winters, — Knut's fleet, posted at Elsinore on both sides of the Sound, rendering all egress from the Baltic impossible, except at his pleasure. Ulf's opportune deliverance of his royal brother-in-law did not much bestead poor Ulf himself. He had been in disfavor before, pardoned with difficulty, by Queen Emma's intercession; an ambitious, officious, pushing, stirring, and, both in England and Denmark, almost dangerous man; and this conspicuous accidental merit only awoke new jealousy in Knut. . Knut, finding nothing pass the Sound worth much blockading, went ashore; "and the day before Michaelmas," says Snorro, "rode with a great retinue to Roeskilde." Snorro continues his tragic narrative of what befell there: —

"There Knut's brother-in-law, Jarl Ulf, had prepared a great feast for him. The Jarl was the most agreeable of hosts; but the King was silent and sullen. The Jarl talked to him in every way to make him cheerful, and brought forward everything he could think of to amuse him; but the King remained stern, and speaking little. At last the Jarl proposed a game of chess, which he agreed to. A chess-board was produced, and they played together. Jarl Ulf was hasty in temper, stiff, and in nothing yielding; but everything he managed went on well in his hands: and he was a great warrior, about whom there are many stories. He was the most powerful man in Denmark next to the King. Jarl Ulf's sister, Gyda, was married to Jarl Gudin (Godwin) Ulfnadson; and their sons were, Harald King of England, and Jarl Tosti, Jarl Walthiof, Jarl Mauro-Kaare, and Jarl Svein. Gyda was the name of their daughter, who was married to the English King Edward, the Good (whom we call the Confessor).

"When they had played a while, the King made a false move; on which the Jarl took a knight from him; but the King set the piece on the board again, and told the Jarl to make another move. But the Jarl flew angry, tumbled the chess-board over, rose, and went away. The King said, 'Run thy ways, Ulf the Fearful.' The Jarl turned round at the door and said, 'Thou wouldst have run farther at Helge river hadst thou been left to battle there. Thou didst not call me Ulf the Fearful when I hastened to thy help while the Swedes were beating thee like a dog.' The Jarl then went out, and went to bed.

"The following morning, while the King was putting on his clothes, he said to his footboy, 'Go thou to Jarl Ulf and kill him.' The lad went, was away a while, and then came back. The King said, 'Hast thou killed the Jarl?' 'I did not kill him, for he was gone to St. Lucius's church.' There was a man called Ivar the White, a Norwegian by birth, who was the King's courtman and chamberlain. The King said to him, 'Go thou and kill the Jarl.' Ivar went to the church, and in at the choir, and thrust his sword through the Jarl, who died on the spot. Then Ivar went to the King, with the bloody sword in his hand.

"The King said, 'Hast thou killed the Jarl?' 'I have killed him,' said he. 'Thou hast done well,' answered the King."[1]

From a man who built so many churches (one on each battle-field where he had fought, to say nothing of the others), and who had in him such depths of real devotion and other fine cosmic quality, this does seem rather strong! But it is characteristic, withal, — of the man, and perhaps of the times still more. In any case, it is an event worth noting, the slain Jarl Ulf and his connections being of importance in the history of Denmark and of England also. Ulf's wife was Astrid,

[1] Snorro, ii. pp. 252, 253.

sister of Knut, and their only child was Svein, styled afterwards "Svein Estrithson" ("*Astrid*-son") when he became
noted in the world, — at this time a beardless youth, who, on
the back of this tragedy, fled hastily to Sweden, where were
friends of Ulf. After some ten years' eclipse there, Knut and
both his sons being now dead, Svein reappeared in Denmark
under a new and eminent figure, "Jarl of Denmark," highest
Liegeman to the then sovereign there.   Broke his oath to said
sovereign, declared himself, Svein Estrithson, to be real King
of Denmark; and, after much preliminary trouble, and many
beatings and disastrous flights to and fro, became in effect
such, — to the wonder of mankind; for he had not had one
victory to cheer him on, or any good luck or merit that one
sees, except that of surviving longer than some others.   Nevertheless he came to be the Restorer, so called, of Danish inde-
pendence; sole remaining representative of Knut (or Knut's
sister), of Fork-beard, Blue-tooth, and Old Gorm; and ancestor of all the subsequent kings of Denmark for some 400
years; himself coming, as we see, only by the Distaff side,
all of the Sword or male side having died so soon. . Early
death, it has been observed, was the Great Knut's allotment,
and all his posterity's as well; — fatal limit (had there been
no others, which we see there were) to his becoming "Charlemagne of the North" in any considerable degree! Jarl Ulf,
as we have seen, had a sister, Gyda by name, wife to Earl
Godwin ("Gudin Ulfnadsson," as Snorro calls him) a very
memorable Englishman, whose son and hers, King Harald,
Harold in English books, is the memorablest of all.   These
things ought to be better known to English antiquaries, and
will perhaps be alluded to again.

This pretty little victory or affront, gained over Knut in
Lymfjord, was among the last successes of Olaf against that
mighty man.   Olaf, the skilful captain he was, need not have
despaired to defend his Norway against Knut and all the
world.   But he learned henceforth, month by month ever more
tragically, that his own people, seeing softer prospects under
Knut, and in particular the chiefs of them, industriously bribed
by Knut for years past, had fallen away from him; and that

his means of defence were gone. Next summer, Knut's grand fleet sailed, unopposed, along the coast of Norway; Knut summoning a Thing every here and there, and in all of them meeting nothing but sky-high acclamation and acceptance. Olaf, with some twelve little ships, all he now had, lay quiet in some safe fjord, near Lindenæs, what we now call the Naze, behind some little solitary isles on the southeast of Norway there; till triumphant Knut had streamed home again. Home to England again: "Sovereign of Norway" now, with nephew Hakon appointed Jarl and Vice-regent under him! This was the news Olaf met on venturing out; and that his worst anticipations were not beyond the sad truth. All, or almost all, the chief Bonders and men of weight in Norway had declared against him, and stood with triumphant Knut.

Olaf, with his twelve poor ships, steered vigorously along the coast to collect money and force, — if such could now anywhere be had. He himself was resolute to hold out, and try. "Sailing swiftly with a fair wind, morning cloudy with some showers," he passed the coast of Jedderen, which was Erling Skjalgson's country, when he got sure notice of an endless multitude of ships, war-ships, armed merchant ships, all kinds of shipping-craft, down to fishermen's boats, just getting under way against him, under the command of Erling Skjalgson, — the powerfulest of his subjects, once much a friend of Olaf's, but now gone against him to this length, thanks to Olaf's severity of justice, and Knut's abundance in gold and promises for years back. To that complexion had it come with Erling; sailing with this immense assemblage of the naval people and populace of Norway to seize King Olaf, and bring him to the great Knut dead or alive.

Erling had a grand new ship of his own, which far outsailed the general miscellany of rebel ships, and was visibly fast gaining distance on Olaf himself, — who well understood what Erling's puzzle was, between the tail of his game (the miscellany of rebel ships, namely) that could not come up, and the head or general prize of the game which was crowding all sail to get away; and Olaf took advantage of the same. "Lower your sails!" said Olaf to his men (though we must go slower).

" Ho you, we have lost sight of them ! " said Erling to his, and put on all his speed; Olaf going, soon after this, altogether invisible, — behind a little island that he knew of, whence into a certain fjord or bay (Bay of Fungen on the maps), which he thought would suit him. " Halt here, and get out your arms," said Olaf, and had not to wait long till Erling came bounding in, past the rocky promontory, and with astonishment beheld Olaf's fleet of twelve with their battle-axes and their grappling-irons all in perfect readiness. These fell on him, the unready Erling, simultaneous, like a cluster of angry bees ; and in a few minutes cleared his ship of men altogether, except Erling himself. Nobody asked his life, nor probably would have got it if he had. Only Erling still stood erect on a high place on the poop, fiercely defensive, and very difficult to get at. " Could not be reached at all," says Snorro, " except by spears or arrows, and these he warded off with untiring dexterity ; no man in Norway, it was said, had ever defended himself so long alone against many," — an almost invincible Erling, had his cause been good. Olaf himself noticed Erling's behavior, and said to him, from the foredeck below, " Thou hast turned against me to-day, Erling." " The eagles fight breast to breast," answers he. This was a speech of the king's to Erling once long ago, while they stood fighting, not as now, but side by side. The king, with some transient thought of possibility going through his head, rejoins, " Wilt thou surrender, Erling ? " " That will I," answered he ; took the helmet off his head ; laid down sword and shield ; and went forward to the forecastle deck. The king pricked, I think not very harshly, into Erling's chin or beard with the point of his battle-axe, saying, " I must mark thee as traitor to thy Sovereign, though." Whereupon one of the bystanders, Aslak Fitiaskalle, stupidly and fiercely burst up ; smote Erling on the head with his axe ; so that it struck fast in his brain and was instantly the death of Erling. " Ill-luck attend thee for that stroke ; thou hast struck Norway out of my hand by it ! " cried the king to Aslak ; but forgave the poor fellow, who had done it meaning well. The insurrectionary Bonder fleet arriving soon after, as if for certain victory, was struck with astonishment at this Erling catastrophe; and being now without any leader of authority, made not the least attempt at battle; but, full of discouragement and consternation, thankfully allowed Olaf to sail away on his northward voyage, at discretion; and themselves went off lamenting, with Erling's dead body.

This small victory was the last that Olaf had over his many enemies at present.   He sailed along, still northward, day after day; several important people joined him; but the news from landward grew daily more ominous: Bonders busily arming to rear of him; and ahead, Hakon still more busily at Trondhjem, now near by, " — and he will end thy days, King, if he have strength enough!"   Olaf paused; sent scouts to a hill-top: "Hakon's armament visible enough, and under way hitherward, about the Isle of Bjarnö, yonder!"   Soon after, Olaf himself saw the Bonder armament of twenty-five ships, from the southward, sail past in the distance to join that of Hakon; and, worse still, his own ships, one and another (seven in all), were slipping off on a like errand!   He made for the Fjord of Fodrar, mouth of the rugged strath called Valdal, — which I think still knows Olaf, and has now an "Olaf's Highway," where, nine centuries ago, it scarcely had a path.   Olaf entered this fjord, had his land-tent set up, and a cross beside it, on the small level green behind the promontory there.   Finding that his twelve poor ships were now reduced to five, against a world all risen upon him, he could not but see and admit to himself that there was no chance left; and that he must withdraw across the mountains and wait for a better time.

His journey through that wild country, in these forlorn and straitened circumstances, has a mournful dignity and homely pathos, as described by Snorro: how he drew up his five poor ships upon the beach, packed all their furniture away, and with his hundred or so of attendants and their journey-baggage, under guidance of some friendly Bonder, rode up into the desert and foot of the mountains; scaled, after three days' effort (as if by miracle, thought his attendants and thought Snorro), the well-nigh precipitous slope that led across, — never without miraculous aid from Heaven and Olaf, could baggage-wagons have ascended that path!   In short, How he fared along, beset by difficulties and the mournfulest thoughts; but patiently persisted, steadfastly trusted in God; and was fixed to return, and by God's help try again. An evidently very pious and devout man; a good man struggling with adversity, such as the gods, we may still imagine with the ancients, do look down upon as their noblest sight.

He got to Sweden, to the court of his brother-in-law; kindly and nobly enough received there, though gradually, perhaps, ill-seen by the now authorities of Norway. So that, before long, he quitted Sweden; left his queen there with her only daughter, his and hers, the only child they had; he himself had an only son, "by a bondwoman," Magnus by name, who came to great things afterwards; of whom, and of which, by and by. With this bright little boy, and a selected escort of attendants, he moved away to Russia, to King Jarroslav; where he might wait secure against all risk of hurting kind friends by his presence. He seems to have been an exile altogether some two years, — such is one's vague notion; for there is no chronology in Snorro or his Sagas, and one is reduced to guessing and inferring. He had reigned over Norway, reckoning from the first days of his landing there to those last of his leaving it across the Dovrefjeld, about fifteen years, ten of them shiningly victorious.

The news from Norway were naturally agitating to King Olaf; and, in the fluctuation of events there, his purposes and prospects varied much. He sometimes thought of pilgriming to Jerusalem, and a henceforth exclusively religious life; but for most part his pious thoughts themselves gravitated towards Norway, and a stroke for his old place and task there, which he steadily considered to have been committed to him by God. Norway, by the rumors, was evidently not at rest. Jarl Hakon, under the high patronage of his uncle, had lasted there but a little while. I know not that his government was especially unpopular, nor whether he himself much remembered his broken oath. It appears, however, he had left in England a beautiful bride; and considering farther that in England only could bridal ornaments and other wedding outfit of a sufficiently royal kind be found, he set sail thither, to fetch her and them himself. One evening of wildish-looking weather he was seen about the northeast corner of the Pentland Frith; the night rose to be tempestuous; Hakon or any timber of his fleet was never seen more. Had all gone down, — broken oaths, bridal hopes, and all else; mouse and man, — into the roaring waters. There was no farther Opposition-line; the like of which had lasted ever since old heathen Hakon Jarl, down to this his grandson Hakon's *finis* in the Pentland Frith. With this Hakon's disappearance it now disappeared.

Indeed Knut himself, though of an empire suddenly so great, was but a temporary phenomenon. Fate had decided that the grand and wise Knut was to be short-lived; and to leave nothing as successors but an ineffectual young Harald Harefoot, who soon perished, and a still stupider fiercely-drinking Harda-Knut, who rushed down of apoplexy (here in London City, as I guess), with the goblet at his mouth, drinking health and happiness at a wedding-feast, also before long.

Hakon having vanished in this dark way, there ensued a pause, both on Knut's part and on Norway's. Pause or inter-regnum of some months, till it became certain, first, whether Hakon were actually dead, secondly, till Norway, and especially till King Knut himself, could decide what to do. Knut, to the deep disappointment, which had to keep itself silent, of three or four chief Norway men, named none of these three or four Jarl of Norway; but bethought him of a certain Svein, a bastard son of his own, — who, and almost still more his English mother, much desired a career in the world fitter for him, thought they indignantly, than that of captain over Jomsburg, where alone the father had been able to provide for him hitherto. Svein was sent to Norway as king or vice-king for Father Knut; and along with him his fond and vehement mother. Neither of whom gained any favor from the Norse people by the kind of management they ultimately came to show.

Olaf on news of this change, and such uncertainty prevailing everywhere in Norway as to the future course of things, — whether Svein would come, as was rumored of at last, and be able to maintain himself if he did, — thought there might be something in it of a chance for himself and his rights. And, after lengthened hesitation, much prayer, pious invocation, and consideration, decided to go and try it. The final grain that had turned the balance, it appears, was a half-waking morning dream, or almost ocular vision he had of his glorious cousin Olaf Tryggveson, who severely admonished, exhorted, and encouraged him; and disappeared grandly, just in the instant of Olaf's awakening; so that Olaf almost fancied he had seen the very figure of him, as it melted into air. "Let us on, let us on!" thought Olaf always after that. He left his son, not in Russia, but in Sweden with the Queen, who proved very good and carefully helpful in wise ways to him: — in Russia Olaf had now nothing more to do but give his grateful adieus, and get ready.

His march towards Sweden, and from that towards Norway and the passes of the mountains, down Værdal, towards Stickelstad, and the crisis that awaited, is beautifully depicted by Snorro. It has, all of it, the description (and we see clearly, the fact itself had), a kind of pathetic grandeur, simplicity, and rude nobleness; something Epic or Homeric, without the metre or the singing of Homer, but with all the sincerity, rugged truth to nature, and much more of piety, devoutness, reverence for what is forever High in this Universe, than meets us in those old Greek Ballad-mongers. Singularly visual all of it, too, brought home in every particular to one's imagination, so that it stands out almost as a thing one actually saw.

Olaf had about three thousand men with him; gathered mostly as he fared along through Norway. Four hundred, raised by one Dag, a kinsman whom he had found in Sweden and persuaded to come with him, marched usually in a separate body; and were, or might have been, rather an important element. Learning that the Bonders were all arming, especially in Trondhjem country, Olaf streamed down towards them in the closest order he could. By no means very close, subsistence even for three thousand being difficult in such a country. His speech was almost always free and cheerful, though his thoughts always naturally were of a high and earnest, almost sacred tone; devout above all. Stickelstad, a small poor ham-

let still standing where the valley ends, was seen by **Olaf, and**
tacitly by the Bonders as well, to be the natural place for offering battle. There Olaf issued out from the hills one morning :
drew himself up according to the best rules of Norse tactics, —
rules of little complexity, but perspicuously true to the facts.
I think he had a clear open ground still rather raised above the
plain in front; he could see how the Bonder army had not yet
quite arrived, but was pouring forward, in spontaneous rows or
groups, copiously by every path. This was thought to be the
biggest army that ever met in Norway; "certainly not much
fewer than a hundred times a hundred men," according to
Snorro; great Bonders several of them, small Bonders very
many, — all of willing mind, animated with a hot sense of intolerable injuries. "King Olaf had punished great and small
with equal rigor," says Snorro; "which appeared to the chief
people of the country too severe; and animosity rose to the
highest when they lost relatives by the King's just sentence,
although they were in reality guilty. He again would rather renounce his dignity than omit righteous judgment. The accusa-
tion against him, of being stingy with his money, was not just,
for he was a most generous man towards his friends. But that
alone was the cause of the discontent raised against him, that
he appeared hard and severe in his retributions. Besides,
King Knut offered large sums of money, and the great chiefs
were corrupted by this, and by his offering them greater dignities than they had possessed before." On these grounds,
against the intolerable man, great and small were now pouring
along by every path.

Olaf perceived it would still be some time before the Bonder
army was in rank. His own Dag of Sweden, too, was not yet
come up; he was to have the right banner; King Olaf's own
being the middle or grand one; some other person the third or
left banner. All which being perfectly ranked and settled, according to the best rules, and waiting only the arrival of Dag,
Olaf bade his men sit down, and freshen themselves with a
little rest. There were religious services gone through : a
matins-worship such as there have been few; sternly earnest
to the heart of it, and deep as death and eternity, at least on

Olaf's own part. For the rest Thormod sang a stave of the fiercest Skaldic poetry that was in him; all the army straightway sang it in chorus with fiery mind. The Bonder of the nearest farm came up, to tell Olaf that he also wished to fight for him. "Thanks to thee; but don't," said Olaf; "stay at home rather, that the wounded may have some shelter." To this Bonder, Olaf delivered all the money he had, with solemn order to lay out the whole of it in masses and prayers for the souls of such of his enemies as fell. "Such of thy enemies, King?" "Yes, surely," said Olaf, "my friends will all either conquer, or go whither I also am going."

At last the Bonder army too was got ranked; three commanders, one of them with a kind of loose chief command, having settled to take charge of it; and began to shake itself towards actual advance. Olaf, in the mean while, had laid his head on the knees of Finn Arneson, his trustiest man, and fallen fast asleep. Finn's brother, Kalf Arneson, once a warm friend of Olaf, was chief of the three commanders on the opposite side. Finn and he addressed angry speech to one another from the opposite ranks, when they came near enough. Finn, seeing the enemy fairly approach, stirred Olaf from his sleep. "Oh, why hast thou wakened me from such a dream?" said Olaf, in a deeply solemn tone. "What dream was it, then?" asked Finn. "I dreamt that there rose a ladder here reaching up to very Heaven," said Olaf; "I had climbed and climbed, and got to the very last step, and should have entered there hadst thou given me another moment." "King, I doubt thou art *fey;* I do not quite like that dream."

The actual fight began about one of the clock in a most bright last day of July, and was very fierce and hot, especially on the part of Olaf's men, who shook the others back a little, though fierce enough they too; and had Dag been on the ground, which he was n't yet, it was thought victory might have been won. Soon after battle joined, the sky grew of a ghastly brass or copper color, darker and darker, till thick night involved all things; and did not clear away again till battle was near ending. Dag, with his four hundred, arrived in the darkness, and made a furious charge, what was afterwards, in the speech of the people, called "Dag's storm." Which had nearly prevailed, but could not quite; victory again inclining to the so vastly larger party. It is uncertain still how the matter would have gone; for Olaf himself was now fighting with his own hand, and doing deadly execution on his busiest enemies to right and to left. But one of these chief rebels, Thorer Hund (thought to have learnt magic from the Laplanders, whom he long traded with, and made money by), mysteriously would not fall for Olaf's best strokes. Best strokes brought only dust from the (enchanted) deer-skin coat of the fellow, to Olaf's surprise, — when another of the rebel chiefs rushed forward, struck Olaf with his battle-axe, a wild slashing wound, and miserably broke his thigh, so that he staggered or was supported back to the nearest stone; and there sat down, lamentably calling on God to help him in this bad hour. Another rebel of note (the name of him long memorable in Norway) slashed or stabbed Olaf a second time, as did then a third. Upon which the noble Olaf sank dead; and forever quitted this doghole of a world, — little worthy of such men as Olaf, one sometimes thinks. But that too is a mistake, and even an important one, should we persist in it.

With Olaf's death the sky cleared again. Battle, now near done, ended with complete victory to the rebels, and next to no pursuit or result, except the death of Olaf; everybody hastening home, as soon as the big Duel had decided itself. Olaf's body was secretly carried, after dark, to some out-house on the farm near the spot; whither a poor blind beggar, creeping in for shelter that very evening, was miraculously restored to sight. And, truly with a notable, almost miraculous, speed, the feelings of all Norway for King Olaf changed themselves, and were turned upside down, "within a year," or almost within a day. Superlative example of *Extinctus amabitur idem*. Not "Olaf the Thick-set" any longer, but "Olaf the Blessed" or Saint, now clearly in Heaven; such the name and character of him from that time to this. Two churches dedicated to him (out of four that once stood) stand in London at this moment. And the miracles that have been done there, not to speak of Norway and Christendom elsewhere, in his name, were numerous and great for long centuries afterwards. Visibly a Saint Olaf ever since; and, indeed, in *Bollandus* or elsewhere, I have seldom met with better stuff to make a Saint of, or a true World-Hero in all good senses.

Speaking of the London Olaf Churches, I should have added that from one of these the thrice-famous Tooley Street gets its name, — where those Three Tailors, addressing Parliament and the Universe, sublimely styled themselves, "We, the People of England." Saint Olave Street, Saint Oley Street, Stooley Street, Tooley Street; such are the metamorphoses of human fame in the world!

The battle-day of Stickelstad, King Olaf's death-day, is generally believed to have been Wednesday, July 31, 1033. But on investigation, it turns out that there was no total eclipse of the sun visible in Norway that year; though three years before, there was one; but on the 29th instead of the 31st. So that the exact date still remains uncertain; Dahlmann, the latest critic, inclining for 1030, and its indisputable eclipse.[1]

CHAPTER XI.

MAGNUS THE GOOD AND OTHERS.

St. Olaf is the highest of these Norway Kings, and is the last that much attracts us. For this reason, if a reason were not superfluous, we might here end our poor reminiscences of those dim Sovereigns. But we will, nevertheless, for the sake of their connection with bits of English History, still hastily mention the names of one or two who follow, and who throw a momentary gleam of life and illumination on events and epochs that have fallen so extinct among ourselves at present, though once they were so momentous and memorable.

The new King Svein from Jomsburg, Knut's natural son,

---

[1] *Saxon Chronicle* says expressly, under A. D. 1030: "In this year King Olaf was slain in Norway by his own people, and was afterwards sainted."

had no success in Norway, nor seems to have deserved any.
His English mother and he were found to be grasping, oppressive persons; and awoke, almost from the instant that Olaf was
suppressed and crushed away from Norway into Heaven, universal odium more and more in that country. Well-deservedly,
as still appears; for their taxings and extortions of malt, of
herring, of meal, smithwork and every article taxable in
Norway, were extreme; and their service to the country otherwise nearly imperceptible. In brief their one basis there was
the power of Knut the Great; and that, like all earthly
things, was liable to sudden collapse, — and it suffered such
in a notable degree. King Knut, hardly yet of middle age,
and the greatest King in the then world, died at Shaftesbury,
in 1035, as Dahlmann thinks,[1] — leaving two legitimate sons
and a busy, intriguing widow (Norman Emma, widow of Ethelred the Unready), mother of the younger of these two; neither
of whom proved to have any talent or any continuance. In
spite of Emma's utmost efforts, Harald, the elder son of Knut,
not hers, got England for his kingdom; Emma and her Harda-
Knut had to be content with Denmark, and go thither, much
against their will. Harald in England, — light-going little
figure like his father before him, — got the name of Harefoot
here; and might have done good work among his now orderly
and settled people; but he died almost within year and day;
and has left no trace among us, except that of "Harefoot,"
from his swift mode of walking. Emma and her Harda-Knut
now returned joyful to England. But the violent, idle, and
drunken Harda-Knut did no good there; and, happily for
England and him, soon suddenly ended, by stroke of apoplexy
at a marriage festival, as mentioned above. In Denmark he
had done still less good. And indeed, under him, in a year
or two, the grand imperial edifice, laboriously built by Knut's
valor and wisdom, had already tumbled all to the ground, in
a most unexpected and remarkable way. As we are now to
indicate with all brevity.

[1] *Saxon Chronicle* says: "1035. In this year died King Cnut. . . . He
departed at Shaftesbury, November 12, and they conveyed him thence to
Winchester, and there buried him."

Svein's tyrannies in Norway had wrought such fruit that, within the four years after Olaf's death, the chief men in Norway, the very slayers of King Olaf, Kalf Arneson at the head of them, met secretly once or twice; and unanimously agreed that Kalf Arneson must go to Sweden, or to Russia itself; seek young Magnus, son of Olaf, home: excellent Magnus, to be king over all Norway and them, instead of this intolerable Svein. Which was at once done,—Magnus brought home in a kind of triumph, all Norway waiting for him. Intolerable Svein had already been rebelled against: some years before this, a certain young Tryggve out of Ireland, authentic son of Olaf Tryggveson and of that fine Irish Princess who chose him in his low habiliments and low estate, and took him over to her own Green Island,—this royal young Tryggve Olafson had invaded the usurper Svein, in a fierce, valiant, and determined manner; and though with too small a party, showed excellent fight for some time; till Svein, zealously bestirring himself, managed to get him beaten and killed. But that was a couple of years ago; the party still too small, not including one and all as now! Svein, without stroke of sword this time, moved off towards Denmark; never showing face in Norway again. His drunken brother, Harda-Knut, received him brother-like; even gave him some territory to rule over and subsist upon. But he lived only a short while; was gone before Harda-Knut himself; and we will mention him no more.

Magnus was a fine bright young fellow, and proved a valiant, wise, and successful King, known among his people as Magnus the Good. He was only natural son of King Olaf; but that made little difference in those times and there. His strange-looking, unexpected Latin name he got in this way: Alfhild, his mother, a slave through ill-luck of war, though nobly born, was seen to be in a hopeful way; and it was known in the King's house how intimately Olaf was connected with that occurrence, and how much he loved this "King's serving-maid," as she was commonly designated. Alfhild was brought to bed late at night; and all the world, especially King Olaf, was asleep; Olaf's strict rule, then and always, being, Don't awaken me :— seemingly a man sensitive about his sleep. The child was a boy, of rather weakly aspect; no important person present, except Sigvat, the King's Icelandic Skald, who happened to be still awake; and the Bishop of Norway, who, I suppose, had been sent for in hurry. "What is to be done?" said the Bishop: "here is an infant in pressing need of baptism; and we know not what the name is: go, Sigvat, awaken the King, and ask." "I dare not for my life," answered Sigvat; "King's orders are rigorous on that point." "But if the child die unbaptized," said the Bishop, shuddering; too certain, he and everybody, where the child would go in that case! "I will myself give him a name," said Sigvat, with a desperate concentration of all his faculties; "he shall be namesake of the greatest of mankind, — imperial Carolus Magnus; let us call the infant Magnus!" King Olaf, on the morrow, asked rather sharply how Sigvat had dared take such a liberty; but excused Sigvat, seeing what the perilous alternative was. And Magnus, by such accident, this boy was called; and he, not another, is the prime origin and introducer of that name Magnus, which occurs rather frequently, not among the Norman Kings only, but by and by among the Danish and Swedish; and, among the Scandinavian populations, appears to be rather frequent to this day.

Magnus, a youth of great spirit, whose own, and standing at his beck, all Norway now was, immediately smote home on Denmark; desirous naturally of vengeance for what it had done to Norway, and the sacred kindred of Magnus. Denmark, its great Knut gone, and nothing but a drunken Harda-Knut, fugitive Svein and Co., there in his stead, was become a weak dislocated Country. And Magnus plundered in it, burnt it, beat it, as often as he pleased; Harda-Knut struggling what he could to make resistance or reprisals, but never once getting any victory over Magnus. Magnus, I perceive, was, like his Father, a skilful as well as valiant fighter by sea and land; Magnus, with good battalions, and probably backed by immediate alliance with Heaven and St. Olaf, as was then the general belief or surmise about him, could not easily be beaten. And the truth is, he never was, by Harda-Knut or any other. Harda-Knut's last transaction with him was, To make a firm Peace and even Family-treaty sanctioned by all the grandees of both countries, who did indeed mainly themselves make it; their two Kings assenting: That there should be perpetual Peace, and no thought of war more, between Denmark and Norway; and that, if either of the Kings died childless while the other was reigning, the other should succeed him in both Kingdoms. A magnificent arrangement, such as has several times been made in the world's history; but which in this instance, what is very singular, took actual effect; drunken Harda-Knut dying so speedily, and Magnus being the man he was. One would like to give the date of this remarkable Treaty; but cannot with precision. Guess somewhere about 1040 :[1] actual fruition of it came to Magnus, beyond question, in 1042, when Harda-Knut drank that wassail bowl at the wedding in Lambeth, and fell down dead; which in the Saxon Chronicle is dated 3d June of that year. Magnus at once went to Denmark on hearing this event; was joyfully received by the head men there, who indeed, with their fellows in Norway, had been main contrivers of the Treaty; both Countries longing for mutual peace, and the end of such incessant broils.

Magnus was triumphantly received as King in Denmark. The only unfortunate thing was, that Svein Estrithson, the exile son of Ulf, Knut's Brother-in-law, whom Knut, as we saw, had summarily killed twelve years before, emerged from his exile in Sweden in a flattering form; and proposed that Magnus should make him Jarl of Denmark, and general administrator there, in his own stead. To which the sanguine Magnus, in spite of advice to the contrary, insisted on acceding. " Too powerful a Jarl," said Einar Tamberskelver — the same Einar whose bow was heard to break in Olaf Tryggveson's last battle ("Norway breaking from thy hand, King!"), who had now become Magnus's chief man, and had long been among the highest chiefs in Norway; "too powerful a Jarl," said Einar earnestly. But Magnus disregarded it; and a troublesome experience had to teach him that it was true. In about a year, crafty Svein, bringing ends to meet, got himself declared King of Denmark for his own behoof, instead of Jarl for another's:

---

[1] Munch gives the date 1038 (ii. 840), Adam of Bremen 1040.

and had to be beaten and driven out by Magnus. Beaten every year; but almost always returned next year, for a new beating, — almost, though not altogether; having at length got one dreadful smashing-down and half-killing, which held him quiet for a while, — so long as Magnus lived. Nay in the end, he made good his point, as if by mere patience in being beaten; and did become King himself, and progenitor of all the Kings that followed. King Svein Estrithson; so called from Astrid or Estrith, his mother, the great Knut's sister, daughter of Svein Forkbeard by that amazing Sigrid the Proud, who *burnt* those two ineligible suitors of hers both at once, and got a switch on the face from Olaf Tryggveson, which proved the death of that high man.

But all this fine fortune of the often beaten Estrithson was posterior to Magnus's death; who never would have suffered it, had he been alive. Magnus was a mighty fighter; a fiery man; very proud and positive, among other qualities, and had such luck as was never seen before. Luck invariably good, said everybody; never once was beaten, — which proves, continued everybody, that his Father Olaf and the miraculous power of Heaven were with him always. Magnus, I believe, did put down a great deal of anarchy in those countries. One of his earliest enterprises was to abolish Jomsburg, and trample out that nest of pirates. Which he managed so completely that Jomsburg remained a mere reminiscence thenceforth; and its place is not now known to any mortal.

One perverse thing did at last turn up in the course of Magnus: a new Claimant for the Crown of Norway, and he a formidable person withal. This was Harald, half-brother of the late Saint Olaf; uncle or half-uncle, therefore, of Magnus himself. Indisputable son of the Saint's mother by St. Olaf's stepfather, who was himself descended straight from Harald Haarfagr. This new Harald was already much heard of in the world. As an ardent Boy of fifteen he had fought at King Olaf's side at Stickelstad; would not be admonished by **the** Saint to go away. Got smitten down there, not killed; **was** smuggled away that night from the field by friendly help; got cured of his wounds, forwarded to Russia, where he grew to man's estate, under bright auspices and successes.   Fell in love with the Russian Princess, but could not get her to wife; went off thereupon to Constantinople as *Væringer* (Life-Guardsman of the Greek Kaiser); became Chief Captain of the Væringers, invincible champion of the poor Kaisers that then were, and filled all the East with the shine and noise of his exploits.   An authentic *Waring* or *Baring*, such the surname we now have derived from these people; who were an important institution in those Greek countries for several ages: Væringer Life-Guard, consisting of Norsemen, with sometimes a few English among them.   Harald had innumerable adventures, nearly always successful, sing the Skalds; gained a great deal of wealth, gold ornaments, and gold coin; had even Queen Zoe (so they sing, though falsely) enamored of him at one time; and was himself a Skald of eminence; some of whose verses, by no means the worst of their kind, remain to this day.

This character of Waring much distinguishes Harald to me; the only Væringer of whom I could ever get the least biography, true or half-true.   It seems the Greek History-books but indifferently correspond with these Saga records; and scholars say there could have been no considerable romance between Zoe and him, Zoe at that date being 60 years of age! Harald's own lays say nothing of any Zoe, but are still full of longing for his Russian Princess far away.

At last, what with Zoes, what with Greek perversities and perfidies, and troubles that could not fail, he determined on quitting Greece; packed up his immensities of wealth in succinct shape, and actually returned to Russia, where new honors and favors awaited him from old friends, and especially, if I mistake not, the hand of that adorable Princess, crown of all his wishes for the time being.   Before long, however, he decided farther to look after his Norway Royal heritages; and, for that purpose, sailed in force to the Jarl or quasi-King of Denmark, the often-beaten Svein, who was now in Sweden on his usual winter exile after beating.   Svein and he had evidently interests in common.   Svein was charmed to see him, — so warlike, glorious and renowned a man, with masses of money about him, too. Svein did by and by become treacherous; and even attempted, one night, to assassinate Harald in his bed on board ship: but Harald, vigilant of Svein, and a man of quick and sure insight, had providently gone to sleep elsewhere, leaving a log instead of himself among the blankets. In which log, next morning, treacherous Svein's battle-axe was found deeply sticking: and could not be removed without difficulty! But this was after Harald and King Magnus himself had begun treating; with the fairest prospects, — which this of the Svein battle-axe naturally tended to forward, as it altogether ended the other copartnery.

Magnus, on first hearing of Væringer Harald and his intentions, made instant equipment, and determination to fight his uttermost against the same. But wise persons of influence round him, as did the like sort round Væringer Harald, earnestly advised compromise and peaceable agreement. Which, soon after that of Svein's nocturnal battle-axe, was the course adopted; and, to the joy of all parties, did prove a successful solution. Magnus agreed to part his kingdom with Uncle Harald; uncle parting his treasures, or uniting them with Magnus's poverty. Each was to be an independent king, but they were to govern in common; Magnus rather presiding. He, to sit, for example, in the High Seat alone; King Harald opposite him in a seat not quite so high, though if a stranger King came on a visit, both the Norse Kings were to sit in the High Seat. With various other punctilious regulations; which the fiery Magnus was extremely strict with; rendering the mutual relation a very dangerous one, had not both the Kings been honest men, and Harald a much more prudent and tolerant one than Magnus. They, on the whole, never had any weighty quarrel, thanks now and then rather to Harald than to Magnus. Magnus too was very noble; and Harald, with his wide experience and greater length of years, carefully held his heat of temper well covered in.

Prior to Uncle Harald's coming, Magnus had distinguished himself as a Lawgiver. His Code of Laws for the Trondhjem Province was considered a pretty piece of legislation; and in subsequent times got the name of *Gray-goose* (Gràgas); one of

the wonderfulest names ever given to a wise Book. Some say
it came from the gray color of the parchment, some give other
incredible origins; the last guess I have heard is, that the
name merely denotes antiquity; the witty name in Norway for
a man growing old having been, in those times, that he was
now "becoming a gray-goose." Very fantastic indeed; certain,
however, that Gray-goose is the name of that venerable Law
Book; nay, there is another, still more famous, belonging to
Iceland, and not far from a century younger, the Iceland *Gray-
goose*. The Norway one is perhaps of date about 1037, the
other of about 1118; peace be with them both! Or, if any-
body is inclined to such matters let him go to Dahlmann, for
the amplest information and such minuteness of detail as
might almost enable him to be an Advocate, with Silk Gown,
in any Court depending on these Gray-geese.

Magnus did not live long. He had a dream one night of
his Father Olaf's coming to him in shining presence, and an-
nouncing, That a magnificent fortune and world-great renown
was now possible for him; but that perhaps it was his duty
to refuse it; in which case his earthly life would be short.
"Which way wilt thou do, then?" said the shining presence.
"Thou shalt decide for me, Father, thou, not I!" and told his
Uncle Harald on the morrow, adding that he thought he should
now soon die; which proved to be the fact. The magnificent
fortune, so questionable otherwise, has reference, no doubt, to
the Conquest of England; to which country Magnus, as right-
ful and actual King of *Denmark*, as well as undisputed heir to
drunken Harda-Knut, by treaty long ago, had now some evident claim. The enterprise itself was reserved to the patient,
gay, and prudent Uncle Harald; and to him it did prove
fatal,— and merely paved the way for Another, luckier, not
likelier!

Svein Estrithson, always beaten during Magnus's life, by
and by got an agreement from the prudent Harald to *be* King
of Denmark, then; and end these wearisome and ineffectual
brabbles; Harald having other work to do. But in the autumn
of 1066, Tosti, a younger son of our English Earl Godwin, came
to Svein's court with a most important announcement; namely,

that King Edward the Confessor, so called, was dead, and that
Harold, as the English write it, his eldest brother would give
him, Tosti, no sufficient share in the kingship. Which state
of matters, if Svein would go ahead with him to rectify it,
would be greatly to the advantage of Svein. Svein, taught by
many beatings, was too wise for this proposal ; refused Tosti,
who indignantly stepped over into Norway, and proposed it to
King Harald there. Svein really had acquired considerable
teaching, I should guess, from his much beating and hard experience in the world ; one finds him afterwards the esteemed
friend of the famous Historian Adam of Bremen, who reports
various wise humanities, and pleasant discoursings with Svein
Estrithson.

As for Harald Hardrade, " Harald the Hard or Severe," as
he was now called, Tosti's proposal awakened in him all his
old Væringer ambitions and cupidities into blazing vehemence.
He zealously consented ; and at once, with his whole strength,
embarked in the adventure. Fitted out two hundred ships, and
the biggest army he could carry in them ; and sailed with Tosti
towards the dangerous Promised Land. Got into the Tyne,
and took booty ; got into the Humber, thence into the Ouse ;
easily subdued any opposition the official people or their populations could make ; victoriously scattered these, victoriously
took the City of York in a day ; and even got himself homaged
there, " King of Northumberland," as per covenant, — Tosti
proving honorable, — Tosti and he going with faithful strict
copartnery, and all things looking prosperous and glorious.
Except only (an important exception !) that they learnt for certain, English Harold was advancing with all his strength ; and,
in a measurable space of hours, unless care were taken, would
be in York himself. Harald and Tosti hastened off to seize
the post of Stamford Bridge on Derwent River, six or seven
miles east of York City, and there bar this dangerous advent.
Their own ships lay not far off in Ouse River, in case of the
worst. The battle that ensued the next day, September 20,
1066, is forever memorable in English history.

Snorro gives vividly enough his view of it from the Icelandic side : A ring of stalwart Norsemen, close ranked, with

their steel tools in hand; English Harold's Army, mostly
cavalry, prancing and pricking all around; trying to find or
make some opening in that ring. For a long time trying in
vain, till at length, getting them enticed to burst out somewhere in pursuit, they quickly turned round, and quickly made
an end of that matter. Snorro represents English Harold,
with a first party of these horse coming up, and, with preliminary salutations, asking if Tosti were there, and if Harald
were; making generous proposals to Tosti; but, in regard to
Harald and what share of England was to be his, answering
Tosti with the words, "Seven feet of English earth, or more
if he require it, for a grave." Upon which Tosti, like an
honorable man and copartner, said, "No, never; let us fight
you rather till we all die." "Who is this that spoke to you?"
inquired Harald, when the cavaliers had withdrawn. "My
brother Harold," answers Tosti; which looks rather like a
Saga, but may be historical after all. Snorro's history of the
battle is intelligible only after you have premised to it, what
he never hints at, that the scene was on the east side of the
bridge and of the Derwent; the great struggle for the bridge,
one at last finds, was after the fall of Harald; and to the
English Chroniclers, said struggle, which was abundantly
severe, is all they know of the battle.

Enraged at that breaking loose of his steel ring of infantry,
Norse Harald blazed up into true Norse fury, all the old Væringer and Berserkir rage awakening in him; sprang forth into
the front of the fight, and mauled and cut and smashed down,
on both hands of him, everything he met, irresistible by any
horse or man, till an arrow cut him through the windpipe, and
laid him low forever. That was the end of King Harald and
of his workings in this world. The circumstance that he was
a Waring or Baring, and had smitten to pieces so many Ori-
ental cohorts or crowds, and had made love-verses (kind of
iron madrigals) to his Russian Princess, and caught the fancy
of questionable Greek queens, and had amassed such heaps of
money, while poor nephew Magnus had only one gold ring
(which had been his father's, and even his father's *mother's*,
as Uncle Harald noticed), and nothing more whatever of that

precious metal to combine with Harald's treasures : — all this is new to me, naturally no hint of it in any English book; and lends some gleam of romantic splendor to that dim business of Stamford Bridge, now fallen so dull and torpid to most English minds, transcendently important as it once was to all Englishmen. Adam of Bremen says, the English got as much gold plunder from Harald's people as was a heavy burden for twelve men;[1] a thing evidently impossible, which nobody need try to believe. Young Olaf, Harald's son, age about sixteen, steering down the Ouse at the top of his speed, escaped home to Norway with all his ships, and subsequently reigned there with Magnus, his brother. Harald's body did lie in English earth for about a year; but was then brought to Norway for burial. He needed more than seven feet of grave, say some; Laing, interpreting Snorro's measurements, makes Harald eight feet in stature, — I do hope, with some error in excess !

———◆———

CHAPTER XII.

OLAF THE TRANQUIL, MAGNUS BAREFOOT, AND SIGURD THE CRUSADER.

THE new King Olaf, his brother Magnus having soon died, bore rule in Norway for some five-and-twenty years. Rule soft and gentle, not like his father's, and inclining rather to improvement in the arts and elegancies than to anything severe or dangerously laborious. A slim-built, witty-talking, popular and pretty man, with uncommonly bright eyes, and hair like floss silk: they called him Olaf *Kyrre* (the Tranquil or Easy-going).

The ceremonials of the palace were much improved by him. Palace still continued to be built of huge logs pyramidally sloping upwards, with fireplace in the middle of the floor, and no egress for smoke or ingress for light except right overhead,

---

[1] Camden, Rapin, &c. quote.

which, in bad weather, you could shut, or all but shut, with a
lid. Lid originally made of mere opaque board, but changed
latterly into a light frame, covered (*glazed*, so to speak) with
entrails of animals, clarified into something of pellucidity. All
this Olaf, I hope, further perfected, as he did the placing of
the court ladies, court officials, and the like; but I doubt if
the luxury of a glass window were ever known to him, or a
cup to drink from that was not made of metal or horn. In
fact it is chiefly for his son's sake I mention him here; and
with the son, too, I have little real concern, but only a kind
of fantastic.

This son bears the name of Magnus *Barfod* (Barefoot, or
Bareleg); and if you ask why so, the answer is: He was used
to appear in the streets of Nidaros (Trondhjem) now and then
in complete Scotch Highland dress. Authentic tartan plaid
and philibeg, at that epoch, — to the wonder of Trondhjem and
us! The truth is, he had a mighty fancy for those Hebrides
and other Scotch possessions of his; and seeing England now
quite impossible, eagerly speculated on some conquest in Ireland as next best. He did, in fact, go diligently voyaging and
inspecting among those Orkney and Hebridian Isles; putting
everything straight there, appointing stringent authorities,
jarls, — nay, a king, "Kingdom of the Suderöer" (Southern
Isles, now called *Sodor*), — and, as first king, Sigurd, his pretty
little boy of nine years. All which done, and some quarrel
with Sweden fought out, he seriously applied himself to visiting in a still more emphatic manner; namely, to invading,
with his best skill and strength, the considerable virtual or
actual kingdom he had in Ireland, intending fully to enlarge
it to the utmost limits of the Island if possible. He got pros-
perously into Dublin (guess A.D. 1102). Considerable authority he already had, even among those poor Irish Kings, or
kinglets, in their glibs and yellow-saffron gowns; still more,
I suppose, among the numerous Norse Principalities there
"King Murdog, King of Ireland," says the Chronicle of Man,
"had obliged himself, every Yule-day, to take a pair of shoes,
hang them over his shoulder, as your servant does on a

journey, and walk across his court, at bidding and in presence
of Magnus Barefoot's messenger, by way of homage to the said
"King." Murdog on this greater occasion did whatever homage
could be required of him; but that, though comfortable, was
far from satisfying the great King's ambitious mind. The
great King left Murdog; left his own Dublin; marched off
westward on a general conquest of Ireland. Marched easily
victorious for a time; and got, some say, into the wilds of
Connaught, but there saw himself beset by ambuscades and
wild Irish countenances intent on mischief; and had, on the
sudden, to draw up for battle; — place, I regret to say, alto
gether undiscoverable to me; known only that it was boggy in
the extreme. Certain enough, too certain and evident, Magnus
Barefoot, searching eagerly, could find no firm footing there;
nor, fighting furiously up to the knees or deeper, any result
but honorable death! Date is confidently marked " 24 August,
1103," — as if people knew the very day of the month. The
natives did humanely give King Magnus Christian burial. The
remnants of his force, without further molestation, found their
ships on the Coast of Ulster; and sailed home, — without conquest of Ireland; nay perhaps, leaving royal Murdog disposed
to be relieved of his procession with the pair of shoes.

Magnus Barefoot left three sons, all kings at once, reigning
peaceably together. But to us, at present, the only noteworthy
one of them was Sigurd; who, finding nothing special to do at
home, left his brothers to manage for him, and went off on a
far Voyage, which has rendered him distinguishable in the
crowd. Voyage through the Straits of Gibraltar, on to Jerusalem, thence to Constantinople; and so home through Russia,
shining with such renown as filled all Norway for the time
being. A King called Sigurd Jorsalafarer (*Jerusalemer*) or
Sigurd the Crusader henceforth. His voyage had been only
partially of the Viking type; in general it was of the Royal-
Progress kind rather; Vikingism only intervening in cases of
incivility or the like. His reception in the Courts of Portu-
gal, Spain, Sicily, Italy, had been honorable and sumptuous.
The King of Jerusalem broke out into utmost splendor and
effusion at sight of such a pilgrim; and Constantinople did its

highest honors to such a Prince of Væringers. And the truth
is, Sigurd intrinsically was a wise, able, and prudent man;
who, surviving both his brothers, reigned a good while alone
in a solid and successful way. He shows features of an original, independent-thinking man; something of ruggedly strong,
sincere, and honest, with peculiarities that are amiable and
even pathetic in the character and temperament of him; as
certainly, the course of life he took was of his own choosing,
and peculiar enough. He happens furthermore to be, what
he least of all could have chosen or expected, the last of the
Haarfagr Genealogy that had any success, or much deserved
any, in this world. The last of the Haarfagrs, or as good as
the last! So that, singular to say, it is in reality, for one
thing only that Sigurd, after all his crusadings and wonderful
adventures, is memorable to us here: the advent of an Irish
gentleman called "Gylle Krist" (Gil-christ, Servant of Christ),
who, — not over welcome, I should think, but (unconsciously)
big with the above result, — appeared in Norway, while King
Sigurd was supreme. Let us explain a little.

This Gylle Krist, the unconsciously fatal individual, who
"spoke Norse imperfectly," declared himself to be the natural
son of whilom Magnus Barefoot; born to him there while
engaged in that unfortunate "Conquest of Ireland." "Here is
my mother come with me," said Gilchrist, "who declares my
real baptismal name to have been Harald, given me by that
great King; and who will carry the red-hot ploughshares or
do any reasonable ordeal in testimony of these facts. I am
King Sigurd's veritable half-brother: what will King Sigurd
think it fair to do with me?" Sigurd clearly seems to have
believed the man to be speaking truth; and indeed nobody to
have doubted but he was. Sigurd said, "Honorable sustenance
shalt thou have from me here. But, under pain of extirpation,
swear that, neither in my time, nor in that of my young son
Magnus, wilt thou ever claim any share in this Government."
Gylle swore; and punctually kept his promise during Sigurd's
reign. But during Magnus's, he conspicuously broke it; and,
in result, through many reigns, and during three or four
generations afterwards, produced unspeakable contentions,

massacrings, confusions in the country he had adopted. There are reckoned, from the time of Sigurd's death (A.D. 1130), about a hundred years of civil war: no king allowed to distinguish himself by a solid reign of well-doing, or by any continuing reign at all, — sometimes as many as four kings simultaneously fighting; — and in Norway, from sire to son, nothing but sanguinary anarchy, disaster and bewilderment; a Country sinking steadily as if towards absolute ruin. Of all which frightful misery and discord Irish Gylle, styled afterwards King Harald Gylle, was, by ill destiny and otherwise, the visible origin: an illegitimate Irish Haarfagr who proved to be his own destruction, and that of the Haarfagr kindred altogether!

Sigurd himself seems always to have rather favored Gylle, who was a cheerful, shrewd, patient, witty, and effective fellow; and had at first much quizzing to endure, from the younger kind, on account of his Irish way of speaking Norse, and for other reasons. One evening, for example, while the drink was going round, Gylle mentioned that the Irish had a wonderful talent of swift running, and that there were among them people who could keep up with the swiftest horse. At which, especially from young Magnus, there were peals of laughter; and a declaration from the latter that Gylle and he would have it tried to-morrow morning! Gylle in vain urged that he had not himself professed to be so swift a runner as to keep up with the Prince's horses; but only that there were men in Ireland who could. Magnus was positive; and, early next morning, Gylle had to be on the ground; and the race, naturally under heavy bet, actually went off. Gylle started parallel to Magnus's stirrup; ran like a very roe, and was clearly ahead at the goal. "Unfair," said Magnus; "thou must have had hold of my stirrup-leather, and helped thyself along; we must try it again." Gylle ran behind the horse this second time; then at the end, sprang forward; and again was fairly in ahead. "Thou must have held by the tail," said Magnus; "not by fair running was this possible; we must try a third time!" Gylle started ahead of Magnus and his horse, this third time; kept ahead with increasing distance, Magnus galloping his very best; and reached the goal more palpably foremost than ever. So that Magnus had to pay his bet, and other damage and humiliation. And got from his father, who heard of it soon afterwards, scoffing rebuke as a silly fellow, who did not know the worth of men, but only the clothes and rank of them, and well deserved what he had got from Gylle. All the time King Sigurd lived, Gylle seems to have had good recognition and protection from that famous man; and, indeed, to have gained favor all round, by his quiet social demeanor and the qualities he showed.

CHAPTER XIII.

MAGNUS THE BLIND, HARALD GYLLE, AND MUTUAL EXTINCTION OF THE HAARFAGRS.

ON Sigurd the Crusader's death, Magnus naturally came to the throne; Gylle keeping silence and a cheerful face for the time. But it was not long till claim arose on Gylle's part, till war and fight arose between Magnus and him, till the skilful, popular, ever-active and shifty Gylle had entirely beaten Magnus; put out his eyes; mutilated the poor body of him in a horrid and unnamable manner, and shut him up in a convent as out of the game henceforth. There in his dark misery Magnus lived now as a monk; called "Magnus the Blind" by those Norse populations; King Harald Gylle reigning victoriously in his stead. But this also was only for a time. There arose avenging kinsfolk of Magnus, who had no Irish accent in their Norse, and were themselves eager enough to bear rule in their native country. By one of these, — a terribly strong-handed, fighting, violent, and regardless fellow, who also was a Bastard of Magnus Barefoot's, and had been made a Priest, but liked it unbearably ill, and had broken loose from it into the wildest courses at home and abroad; so that his current name got to be "Slembi-diakn," Slim or Ill Deacon, under

which he is much noised of in Snorro and the Sagas : by **this**
Slim-Deacon, Gylle was put an end to (murdered by night,
drunk in his sleep); and poor blind Magnus was brought out,
and again set to act as King, or King's Cloak, in hopes Gylle's
posterity would never rise to victory more.   But Gylle's posterity did, to victory and also to defeat, and were the death of
Magnus and of Slim-Deacon too, in a frightful way ; and all
got their own death by and by in a ditto.   In brief, these two
kindreds (reckoned to be authentic enough Haarfagr people,
both kinds of them) proved now to have become a veritable
crop of dragon's teeth ; who mutually fought, plotted, struggled,
as if it had been their life's business ; never ended fighting,
and seldom long intermitted it, till they had exterminated one
another, and did at last all rest in death.   One of these later
Gylle temporary Kings I remember by the name of Harald
Herdebred, Harald of the Broad Shoulders.   The very last of
them I think was Harald Mund (Harald of the *Wry-Mouth*),
who gave rise to two Impostors, pretending to be Sons of his,
a good while after the poor Wry-Mouth itself and all its troublesome belongings were quietly underground.   What Norway
suffered during that sad century may be imagined.

CHAPTER XIV.

SVERRIR AND DESCENDANTS, TO HAKON THE OLD.

THE end of it was, or rather the first abatement, and *beginning* of the end, That, when all this had gone on ever worsening for some forty years or so, one Sverrir (A.D. 1177), at
the head of an armed mob of poor people called *Birkebeins*,
came upon the scene.   A strange enough figure in History,
this Sverrir and his Birkebeins !   At first a mere mockery
and dismal laughing-stock to the enlightened Norway public.
Nevertheless by unheard-of fighting, hungering, exertion, and
endurance, Sverrir, after ten years of such a death-wrestle

against men and things, got himself accepted as King; and by wonderful expenditure of ingenuity, common cunning, unctuous Parliamentary Eloquence or almost Popular Preaching, and (it must be owned) general human faculty and valor (or value) in the overclouded and distorted state, did victoriously continue such. And founded a new Dynasty in Norway, which ended only with Norway's separate existence, after near three hundred years.

This Sverrir called himself a Son of Harald Wry-Mouth; but was in reality the son of a poor Comb-maker in some little town of Norway; nothing heard of Sonship to Wry-Mouth till after good success otherwise. His Birkebeins (that is to say, *Birchlegs;* the poor rebellious wretches having taken to the woods; and been obliged, besides their intolerable scarcity of food, to thatch their bodies from the cold with whatever covering could be got, and their legs especially with birch bark; sad species of fleecy hosiery; whence their nickname), — his Birkebeins I guess always to have been a kind of Norse *Jacquerie :* desperate rising of thralls and indigent people, driven mad by their unendurable sufferings and famishings, — theirs the *deepest* stratum of misery, and the densest and heaviest, in this the general misery of Norway, which had lasted towards the third generation and looked as if it would last forever : — whereupon they had risen proclaiming, in this furious dumb manner, *un*intelligible except to Heaven, that the same could not, nor would not, be endured any longer! And, by their Sverrir, strange to say, they did attain a kind of permanent success; and, from being a dismal laughing-stock in Norway, came to be important, and for a time all-important there. Their opposition nicknames, " *Baglers* (from Bagall, *baculus,* bishop's staff; Bishop Nicholas being chief Leader)," " *Gold-legs,*" and the like obscure terms (for there was still a considerable course of counter-fighting ahead, and especially of counter-nicknaming), I take to have meant in Norse prefigurement seven centuries ago, "bloated Aristocracy," " tyrannous *Bourgeoisie,*" — till, in the next century, these rents were closed again! —

King Sverrir, not himself bred to comb-making, had, in

his fifth year, gone to an uncle, Bishop in the Faröe Islands; and got some considerable education from him, with a view to Priesthood on the part of Sverrir. But, not liking that career, Sverrir had fled and smuggled himself over to the Birkebeins; who, noticing the learned tongue, and other miraculous qualities of the man, proposed to make him Captain of them; and even threatened to kill him if he would not accept, — which thus at the sword's point, as Sverrir says, he was obliged to do. It was after this that he thought of becoming son of Wry-Mouth and other higher things.

His Birkebeins and he had certainly a talent of campaigning which has hardly ever been equalled. They fought like devils against any odds of number; and before battle they have been known to march six days together without food, except, perhaps, the inner barks of trees, and in such clothing and shoeing as mere birch bark: — at one time, somewhere in the Dovrefjeld, there was serious counsel held among them whether they should not all, as one man, leap down into the frozen gulfs and precipices, or at once massacre one another wholly, and so finish. Of their conduct in battle, fiercer than that of *Baresarks*, where was there ever seen the parallel? In truth they are a dim strange object to one, in that black time; wondrously bringing light into it withal; and proved to be, under such unexpected circumstances, the beginning of better days!

Of Sverrir's public speeches there still exist authentic specimens; wonderful indeed, and much characteristic of such a Sverrir. A comb-maker King, evidently meaning several good and solid things; and effecting them too, athwart such an element of Norwegian chaos-come-again. His descendants and successors were a comparatively respectable kin. The last and greatest of them I shall mention is Hakon VII., or Hakon the Old; whose fame is still lively among us, from the Battle of Largs at least.

CHAPTER XV.

HAKON THE OLD AT LARGS.

In the Norse annals our famous Battle of Largs makes small figure, or almost none at all among Hakon's battles and feats. They do say indeed, these Norse annalists, that the King of Scotland, Alexander III. (who had such a fate among the crags about Kinghorn in time coming), was very anxious to purchase from King Hakon his sovereignty of the Western Isles; but that Hakon pointedly refused; and at length, being again importuned and bothered on the business, decided on giving a refusal that could not be mistaken. Decided, namely, to go with a big expedition, and look thoroughly into that wing of his Dominions; where no doubt much has fallen awry since Magnus Barefoot's grand visit thither, and seems to be inviting the cupidity of bad neighbors! "All this we will put right again," thinks Hakon, "and gird it up into a safe and defensive posture." Hakon sailed accordingly, with a strong fleet; adjusting and rectifying among his Hebrides as he went long, and landing withal on the Scotch coast to plunder and punish as he thought fit. The Scots say he had claimed of them Arran, Bute, and the Two Cumbraes ("given my ancestors by Donald Bain," said Hakon, to the amazement of the Scots) "as part of the Sudöer" (Southern Isles) : — so far from selling that fine kingdom! — and that it was after taking both Arran and Bute that he made his descent at Largs.

Of Largs there is no mention whatever in Norse books. But beyond any doubt, such is the other evidence, Hakon did land there; land and fight, not conquering, probably rather beaten; and very certainly "retiring to his ships," as in either case he behooved to do! It is further certain he was dreadfully maltreated by the weather on those wild coasts; and altogether credible, as the Scotch records bear, that he was so at Largs very specially. The Norse Records or Sagas say merely, he lost many of his ships by the tempests, and many of his men by land fighting in various parts, — tacitly including Largs, no doubt, which was the last of these misfortunes to him. "In the battle here he lost 15,000 men, say the Scots, we 5,000"! Divide these numbers by ten, and the excellently brief and lucid Scottish summary by Buchanan may be taken as the approximately true and exact.[1] Date of the battle is A.D. 1263.

To this day, on a little plain to the south of the village, now town, of Largs, in Ayrshire, there are seen stone cairns and monumental heaps, and, until within a century ago, one huge, solitary, upright stone; still mutely testifying to a battle there, — altogether clearly, to this battle of King Hakon's; who by the Norse records, too, was in these neighborhoods at that same date, and evidently in an aggressive, high kind of humor. For "while his ships and army were doubling the Mull of Cantire, he had his own boat set on wheels, and therein, splendidly enough, had himself drawn across the Promontory at a flatter part," no doubt with horns sounding, banners waving. "All to the left of me is mine and Norway's," exclaimed Hakon in his triumphant boat progress, which such disasters soon followed.

Hakon gathered his wrecks together, and sorrowfully made for Orkney. It is possible enough, as our Guide Books now say, he may have gone by Iona, Mull, and the narrow seas inside of Skye; and that the *Kyle-Akin*, favorably known to sea-bathers in that region, may actually mean the *Kyle* (narrow strait) of Hakon, where Hakon may have dropped anchor, and rested for a little while in smooth water and beautiful environment, safe from equinoctial storms. But poor Hakon's heart was now broken. He went to Orkney; died there in the winter; never beholding Norway more.

He it was who got Iceland, which had been a Republic for four centuries, united to his kingdom of Norway: a long and intricate operation, — much presided over by our Snorro

---

[1] *Buchanani Hist.* i. 130.

Sturleson, so often quoted here, who indeed lost his life (by assassination from his sons-in-law) and out of great wealth sank at once into poverty of zero, — one midnight in his own cellar, in the course of that bad business.   Hakon was a great Politician in his time; and succeeded in many things before he lost Largs.   Snorro's death by murder had happened about twenty years before Hakon's by broken heart.   He is called Hakon the Old, though one finds his age was but fifty-nine, probably a longish life for a Norway King.   Snorro's narrative ceases when Snorro himself was born; that is to say, at the threshold of King Sverrir; of whose exploits and doubtful birth it is guessed by some that Snorro willingly forbore to speak in the hearing of such a Hakon.

CHAPTER XVI.

EPILOGUE.

HAARFAGR's kindred lasted some three centuries in Norway; Sverrir's lasted into its third century there; how long after this, among the neighboring kinships, I did not inquire. For, by regal affinities, consanguinities, and unexpected chances and changes, the three Scandinavian kingdoms fell all peaceably together under Queen Margaret, of the Calmar Union (A.D. 1397); and Norway, incorporated now with Denmark, needed no more kings.

The History of these Haarfagrs has awakened in me many thoughts : Of Despotism and Democracy, arbitrary government by one and self-government (which means no government, or anarchy) by all; of Dictatorship with many faults, and Universal Suffrage with little possibility of any virtue. For the contrast between Olaf Tryggveson and a Universal-Suffrage Parliament or an "Imperial" Copper Captain has, in these nine centuries, grown to be very great.   And the eternal Providence that guides all this, and produces alike

these entities with their epochs, is not *its* course still through
the great deep? Does not it still speak to us, if we have
ears?   Here, clothed in stormy enough passions and instincts,
unconscious of any aim but their own satisfaction, is the blessed
beginning of Human Order, Regulation, and real Government;
there, clothed in a highly different, but again suitable gar-
niture of passions, instincts, and equally unconscious as to
real aim, is the accursed-looking ending (temporary ending) of
Order, Regulation, and Government; — very dismal to the
sane onlooker for the time being; not dismal to him otherwise, his hope, too, being steadfast! But here, at any rate,
in this poor Norse theatre, one looks with interest on the first
transformation, so mysterious and abstruse, of human Chaos
into something of articulate Cosmos; witnesses the wild and
strange birth-pangs of Human Society, and reflects that without something similar (little as men expect such now), no
Cosmos of human society ever was got into existence, nor can
ever again be.

The violences, fightings, crimes — ah yes, these seldom fail,
and they are very lamentable. But always, too, among those
old populations, there was one saving element; the now want
of which, especially the unlamented want, transcends all lamentation. Here is one of those strange, piercing, winged-
words of Ruskin, which has in it a terrible truth for us in
these epochs now come: —

"My friends, the follies of modern Liberalism, many and
great though they be, are practically summed in this denial
or neglect of the quality and intrinsic value of things. Its
rectangular beatitudes, and spherical benevolences, — theology
of universal indulgence, and jurisprudence which will hang
no rogues, mean, one and all of them, in the root, incapacity
of discerning, or refusal to discern, worth and unworth in anything, and least of all in man; whereas Nature and Heaven
command you, at your peril, to discern worth from unworth
in everything, and most of all in man. Your main problem
is that ancient and trite one, 'Who is best man?' and the
Fates forgive much, — forgive the wildest, fiercest, cruelest
experiments, — if fairly made for the determination of that.

Theft and bloodguiltiness are not pleasing in their sight; yet the favoring powers of the spiritual and material world will confirm to you your stolen goods, and their noblest voices applaud the lifting of your spear, and rehearse the sculpture of your shield, if only your robbing and slaying have been in fair arbitrament of that question, 'Who is best man?' But if you refuse such inquiry, and maintain every man for his neighbor's match, — if you give vote to the simple and liberty to the vile, the powers of those spiritual and material worlds in due time present you inevitably with the same problem, soluble now only wrong side upwards; and your robbing and slaying must be done then to find out, 'Who is *worst* man?' Which, in so wide an order of merit, is, indeed, not easy; but a complete Tammany Ring, and lowest circle in the Inferno of Worst, you are sure to find, and to be governed by."[1]

All readers will admit that there was something naturally royal in these Haarfagr Kings. A wildly great kind of kindred; counts in it two Heroes of a high, or almost highest, type : the first two Olafs, Tryggveson and the Saint. And the view of them, withal, as we chance to have it, I have often thought, how essentially Homeric it was : — indeed what is "Homer" himself but the *Rhapsody* of five centuries of Greek Skalds and wandering Ballad-singers, done (*i. e.* "stitched together") by somebody more musical than Snorro was? Olaf Tryggveson and Olaf Saint please me quite as well in their prosaic form; offering me the truth of them as if seen in their real lineaments by some marvellous opening (through the art of Snorro) across the black strata of the ages. Two high, almost among the highest sons of Nature, seen as they veritably were; fairly comparable or superior to god-like Achilleus, goddess-wounding Diomedes, much more to the two Atreidai, Regulators of the Peoples.

I have also thought often what a Book might be made of Snorro, did there but arise a man furnished with due literary insight, and indefatigable diligence; who, faithfully acquaint-

---

[1] *Fors Clavigera,* Letter XIV. pp. 8–10.

ing himself with the topography, the monumental relics and illustrative actualities of Norway, carefully scanning the best testimonies as to place and time which that country can still give him, carefully the best collateral records and chronologies of other countries, and who, himself possessing the highest faculty of a Poet, could, abridging, arranging, elucidating, reduce Snorro to a polished Cosmic state, unweariedly purging away his much chaotic matter! A modern " highest kind of Poet," capable of unlimited slavish labor withal; — who, I fear, is not soon to be expected in this world, or likely to find his task in the *Heimskringla* if he did appear here.

THE LIFE OF

FRIEDRICH SCHILLER.

COMPREHENDING AN EXAMINATION OF HIS WORKS.

[1825.]

FRIEDRICH SCHILLER.

———•———

PART I.

SCHILLER'S YOUTH.

1759–1784.

Among the writers of the concluding part of the last century there is none more deserving of our notice than Friedrich Schiller. Distinguished alike for the splendor of his intellectual faculties, and the elevation of his tastes and feelings, he has left behind him in his works a noble emblem of these great qualities : and the reputation which he thus enjoys, and has merited, excites our attention the more, on considering the circumstances under which it was acquired. Schiller had peculiar difficulties to strive with, and his success has likewise been peculiar. Much of his life was deformed by inquietude and disease, and it terminated at middle age ; he composed in a language then scarcely settled into form, or admitted to a rank among the cultivated languages of Europe: yet his writings are remarkable for their extent and variety as well as their intrinsic excellence ; and his own countrymen are not his only, or perhaps his principal admirers. It is difficult to collect or interpret the general voice ; but the World, no less than Germany, seems already to have dignified him with the reputation of a classic ; to have enrolled him among that select number whose works belong not wholly to any age or nation, but who, having instructed their own contemporaries, are claimed as instructors by the great family of mankind, and set apart

(263)

for many centuries from the common oblivion which soon overtakes the mass of authors, as it does the mass of other men.

Such has been the high destiny of Schiller. His history and character deserve our study for more than one reason. A natural and harmless feeling attracts us towards such a subject; we are anxious to know how so great a man passed through the world, how he lived, and moved, and had his being; and the question, if properly investigated, might yield advantage as well as pleasure. It would be interesting to discover by what gifts and what employment of them he reached the eminence on which we now see him; to follow the steps of his intellectual and moral culture; to gather from his life and works some picture of himself. It is worth inquiring, whether he, who could represent noble actions so well, did himself act nobly; how those powers of intellect, which in philosophy and art achieved so much, applied themselves to the every-day emergencies of life; how the generous ardor, which delights us in his poetry, displayed itself in the common intercourse between man and man. It would at once instruct and gratify us if we could understand him thoroughly, could transport ourselves into his circumstances outward and inward, could see as he saw, and feel as he felt.

But if the various utility of such a task is palpable enough, its difficulties are not less so. We should not lightly think of comprehending the very simplest character, in all its bearings; and it might argue vanity to boast of even a common acquaintance with one like Schiller's. Such men as he are misunderstood by their daily companions, much more by the distant observer, who gleans his information from scanty records, and casual notices of characteristic events, which biographers are often too indolent or injudicious to collect, and which the peaceful life of a man of letters usually supplies in little abundance. The published details of Schiller's history are meagre and insufficient; and his writings, like those of every author, can afford but a dim and dubious copy of his mind. Nor is it easy to decipher even this, with moderate accuracy. The haze of a foreign language, of foreign manners, and modes of thinking strange to us, confuses and obscures the sight, often magnifying what is trivial, softening what is rude, and sometimes hiding or distorting what is beautiful. To take the dimensions of Schiller's mind were a hard enterprise, in any case; harder still with these impediments.

Accordingly we do not, in this place, pretend to attempt it: we have no finished portrait of his character to offer, no formal estimate of his works. It will be enough for us if, in glancing over his life, we can satisfy a simple curiosity, about the fortunes and chief peculiarities of a man connected with us by a bond so kindly as that of the teacher to the taught, the giver to the receiver of mental delight; if, in wandering through his intellectual creation, we can enjoy once more the magnificent and fragrant beauty of that fairy land, and express our feelings, where we do not aim at judging and deciding.

Johann Christoph Friedrich Schiller was a native of Marbach, a small town of Würtemberg, situated on the banks of the Neckar. He was born on the 10th of November, 1759, — a few months later than our own Robert Burns. Schiller's early culture was favored by the dispositions, but obstructed by the outward circumstances of his parents. Though removed above the pressure of poverty, their station was dependent and fluctuating; it involved a frequent change of place and plan. Johann Caspar Schiller, the father, had been a surgeon in the Bavarian army; he served in the Netherlands during the Succession War. After his return home to Würtemberg, he laid aside the medical profession, having obtained a commission of ensign and adjutant under his native Prince. This post he held successively in two regiments; he had changed into the second, and was absent on active duty when Friedrich was born. The Peace of Paris put an end to his military employment; but Caspar had shown himself an intelligent, unassuming and useful man, and the Duke of Würtemberg was willing to retain him in his service. The laying out of various nurseries and plantations in the pleasure-grounds of Ludwigsburg and Solitude was intrusted to the retired soldier, now advanced to the rank of captain: he removed from one establishment to another, from time to time; and continued in the Duke's pay till death. In his latter years he resided chiefly at Ludwigsburg.

This mode of life was not the most propitious for educating such a boy as Friedrich; but the native worth of his parents did more than compensate for the disadvantages of their worldly condition and their limited acquirements in knowledge. The benevolence, the modest and prudent integrity, the true devoutness of these good people shone forth at an after period, expanded and beautified in the character of their son; his heart was nourished by a constant exposure to such influences, and thus the better part of his education prospered well. The mother was a woman of many household virtues; to a warm affection for her children and husband, she joined a degree of taste and intelligence which is of much rarer occurrence. She is said to have been a lover of poetry; in particular an admiring reader of Utz and Gellert, writers whom it is creditable for one in her situation to have relished.[1] Her kindness and tenderness of heart peculiarly endeared her to Friedrich. Her husband appears to have been a person of great probity and meekness of temper, sincerely desirous to approve himself a useful member of society, and to do his duty conscientiously to all men. The seeds of many valuable qualities had been sown in him by nature; and though his early life had been unfavorable for their cultivation, he at a late period labored, not without success, to remedy this disadvantage. Such branches of science and philosophy as lay within his reach, he studied with diligence, whenever his professional employments left him leisure; on a subject connected with the latter he became an author.[2] But what chiefly distinguished him was the practice of a sincere piety, which seems to have diffused itself over all his feelings, and given to his clear and honest character that calm elevation which, in such a case, is its natural result. As his religion mingled itself with every

---

[1] She was of humble descent and little education, the daughter of a baker in Kodweis.

[2] His book is entitled *Die Baumzucht im Grossen* (the Cultivation of Trees on the Grand Scale): it came to a second edition in 1806.

motive and action of his life, the wish which in all his wanderings lay nearest his heart, the wish for the education of his son, was likely to be deeply tinctured with it. There is yet preserved, in his handwriting, a prayer composed in advanced age, wherein he mentions how, at the child's birth, he had entreated the great Father of all, "to supply in strength of spirit what must needs be wanting in outward instruction." The gray-haired man, who had lived to see the maturity of his boy, could now express his solemn thankfulness, that "God had heard the prayer of a mortal."

Friedrich followed the movements of his parents for some time; and had to gather the elements of learning from various masters. Perhaps it was in part owing to this circumstance, that his progress, though respectable, or more, was so little commensurate with what he afterwards became, or with the capacities of which even his earliest years gave symptoms. Thoughtless and gay, as a boy is wont to be, he would now and then dissipate his time in childish sports, forgetful that the stolen charms of ball and leap-frog must be dearly bought by reproaches: but occasionally he was overtaken with feelings of deeper import, and used to express the agitations of his little mind in words and actions, which were first rightly interpreted when they were called to mind long afterwards. His schoolfellows can *now* recollect that even his freaks had sometimes a poetic character; that a certain earnestness of temper, a frank integrity, an appetite for things grand or moving, was discernible across all the caprices of his boyhood. Once, it is said, during a tremendous thunderstorm, his father missed him in the young group within doors; none of the sisters could tell what was become of Fritz, and the old man grew at length so anxious that he was forced to go out in quest of him. Fritz was scarcely past the age of infancy, and knew not the dangers of a scene so awful. His father found him at last, in a solitary place of the neighborhood, perched on the branch of a tree, gazing at the tempestuous face of the sky, and watching the flashes as in succession they spread their lurid gleam over it. To the reprimands of his parent, the whimpering truant pleaded in extenuation, "that the light ning was very beautiful, and that he wished to see where it was coming from!"—Such anecdotes, we have long known, are in themselves of small value : the present one has the additional defect of being somewhat dubious in respect of authenticity. We have ventured to give it, as it came to us, notwithstanding. The picture of the boy Schiller, contemplating the thunder, is not without a certain interest, for such as know the man.

Schiller's first teacher was Moser, pastor and schoolmaster in the village of Lorch, where the parents resided from the sixth to the ninth year of their son. This person deserves mention for the influence he exerted on the early history of his pupil : he seems to have given his name to the Priest "Moser" in the *Robbers ;* his spiritual calling, and the conversation of his son, himself afterwards a preacher, are supposed to have suggested to Schiller the idea of consecrating himself to the clerical profession. This idea, which laid hold of and cherished some predominant though vague propensities of the boy's disposition, suited well with the religious sentiments of his parents, and was soon formed into a settled purpose. In the public school at Ludwigsburg, whither the family had now removed, his studies were regulated with this view; and he underwent, in four successive years, the annual examination before the Stuttgard Commission, to which young men destined for the Church are subjected in that country. Schiller's temper was naturally devout; with a delicacy of feeling which tended towards bashfulness and timidity, there was mingled in him a fervid impetuosity, which was ever struggling through its concealment, and indicating that he felt deeply and strongly, as well as delicately. Such a turn of mind easily took the form of religion, prescribed to it by early example and early affections, as well as nature. Schiller looked forward to the sacred profession with alacrity : it was the serious day-dream of all his boyhood, and much of his youth. As yet, however, the project hovered before him at a great distance, and the path to its fulfilment offered him but little entertainment. His studies did not seize his attention firmly; he followed them from a sense of duty, not of

pleasure. Virgil and Horace he learned to construe accurately;
but is said to have taken no deep interest in their poetry.
The tenderness and meek beauty of the first, the humor and
sagacity and capricious pathos of the last, the matchless ele-
gance of both, would of course escape his inexperienced perception; while the matter of their writings must have appeared
frigid and shallow to a mind so susceptible. He loved rather
to meditate on the splendor of the Ludwigsburg theatre, which
had inflamed his imagination when he first saw it in his ninth
year, and given shape and materials to many of his subsequent
reveries.[1] Under these circumstances, his progress, with all

---

[1] The first display of his poetic gifts occurred also in his ninth year, but
took its rise in a much humbler and less common source than the inspiration
of the stage. His biographers have recorded this small event with a conscientious accuracy, second only to that of Boswell and Hawkins in regard to the
Lichfield *duck*. "The little tale," says one of them, "is worth relating; the
rather that, after an interval of more than twenty years, Schiller himself, on
meeting with his early comrade (the late Dr. Elwert of Kantstadt) for the first
time since their boyhood, reminded him of the adventure, recounting the circumstances with great minuteness and glee. It is as follows. Once in 1768,
Elwert and he had to repeat their catechism together on a certain day publicly
in the church. Their teacher, an ill-conditioned, narrow-minded pietist, had
previously threatened them with a thorough flogging if they missed even a
single word. To make the matter worse, this very teacher chanced to be the
person whose turn it was to catechise on the appointed day. Both the boys
began their answers with dismayed hearts and faltering tongues; yet they
succeeded in accomplishing the task; and were in consequence rewarded by the
mollified pedagogue with two kreutzers apiece. Four kreutzers of ready cash
was a sum of no common magnitude; how it should be disposed of formed a
serious question for the parties interested. Schiller moved that they should
go to Harteneck, a hamlet in the neighborhood, and have a dish of curds-and-
cream: his partner assented; but alas! in Harteneck no particle of curds or
cream was to be had. Schiller then made offer for a quarter-cake of cheese;
but for this four entire kreutzers were demanded, leaving nothing whatever
in reserve for bread! Twice baffled, the little gastronomes, unsatisfied in
stomach, wandered on to Neckarweihingen; where, at length, though not till
after much inquiry, they did obtain a comfortable mess of curds-and-cream,
served up in a gay platter, and silver spoons to eat it with. For all this,
moreover, they were charged but three kreutzers; so that there was still one
left to provide them with a bunch of St. John grapes. Exhilarated by such
liberal cheer, Schiller rose into a glow of inspiration: having left the village,
he mounted with his comrade to the adjacent height, which overlooks both

his natural ability, could not be very striking; the teachers did not fail now and then to visit him with their severities; yet still there was a negligent success in his attempts, which, joined to his honest and vivid temper, made men augur well of him. The Stuttgard Examinators have marked him in their records with the customary formula of approval, or, at worst, of toleration. They usually designate him as "a boy of good hope," *puer bonœ spei.*

This good hope was not, however, destined to be realized in the way they expected: accidents occurred which changed the direction of Schiller's exertions, and threatened for a time to prevent the success of them altogether. The Duke of Würtemberg had lately founded a Free Seminary for certain branches of professional education: it was first set up at Solitude, one of his country residences; and had now been transferred to Stuttgard, where, under an improved form, and with the name of *Karls-schule,* we believe it still exists. The Duke proposed to give the sons of his military officers a preferable claim to the benefits of this institution; and having formed a good opinion both of Schiller and his father, he invited the former to profit by this opportunity. The offer occasioned great embarrassment: the young man and his parents were alike determined in favor of the Church, a project with which this new one was inconsistent. Their embarrassment was but increased, when the Duke, on learning the nature of their scruples, desired them to think well before they decided. It was out of fear, and with reluctance that his proposal was accepted. Schiller enrolled himself in 1773; and turned, with a heavy heart, from freedom and cherished hopes, to Greek, and seclusion, and Law.

His anticipations proved to be but too just: the six years which he spent in this establishment were the most harassing and comfortless of his life. The Stuttgard system of education seems to have been formed on the principle, not of cherish-

Harteneck and Neckarweihingen; and there in a truly poetic effusion he pronounced his malediction on the creamless region, bestowing with the same solemnity his blessing on the one which had afforded him that savory refreshment." *Friedrich von Schillers Leben* (Heidelberg, 1817), p. 11.

FRIEDRICH SCHILLER.

Carlyle, Vol. Nine, p. 263.

ing and correcting nature, but of rooting it out, and supplying its place with something better. The process of teaching and living was conducted with the stiff formality of military drilling; everything went on by statute and ordinance, there was no scope for the exercise of free-will, no allowance for the varieties of original structure. A scholar might possess what instincts or capacities he pleased; the "regulations of the school" took no account of this; he must fit himself into the common mould, which, like the old Giant's bed, stood there, appointed by superior authority, to be filled alike by the great and the little. The same strict and narrow course of reading and composition was marked out for each beforehand, and it was by stealth if he read or wrote anything beside. Their domestic economy was regulated in the same spirit as their preceptorial: it consisted of the same sedulous exclusion of all that could border on pleasure, or give any exercise to choice. The pupils were kept apart from the conversation or sight of any person but their teachers; none ever got beyond the precincts of despotism to snatch even a fearful joy; their very amusements proceeded by the word of command.

How grievous all this must have been, it is easy to conceive. To Schiller it was more grievous than to any other. Of an ardent and impetuous yet delicate nature, whilst his discontentment devoured him internally, he was too modest and timid to give it the relief of utterance by deeds or words. Locked up within himself, he suffered deeply, but without complaining. Some of his letters written during this period have been preserved: they exhibit the ineffectual struggles of a fervid and busy mind veiling its many chagrins under a certain dreary patience, which only shows them more painfully. He pored over his lexicons and grammars, and insipid tasks, with an artificial composure; but his spirit pined within him like a captive's, when he looked forth into the cheerful world, or recollected the affection of parents, the hopes and frolicsome enjoyments of past years. The misery he endured in this severe and lonely mode of existence strengthened or produced in him a habit of constraint and shyness, which clung to his character through life.

The study of Law, for which he had never felt any predilection, naturally grew in his mind to be the representative
of all these evils, and his distaste for it went on increasing.
On this point he made no secret of his feelings. One of the
exercises, yearly prescribed to every scholar, was a written
delineation of his own character, according to his own views
of it, to be delivered publicly at an appointed time: Schiller,
on the first of these exhibitions, ventured to state his persuasion, that he was not made to be a jurist, but called rather by
his inclinations and faculties to the clerical profession. This
statement, of course, produced no effect; he was forced to
continue the accustomed course, and his dislike for Law kept
fast approaching to absolute disgust. In 1775, he was fortunate enough to get it relinquished, though at the expense of
adopting another employment, for which, in different circumstances, he would hardly have declared himself. The study
of Medicine, for which a new institution was about this time
added to the Stuttgard school, had no attractions for Schiller:
he accepted it only as a galling servitude in exchange for one
more galling. His mind was bent on higher objects; and he
still felt all his present vexations aggravated by the thought,
that his fairest expectations from the future had been sacrificed to worldly convenience, and the humblest necessities of
life.

Meanwhile the youth was waxing into manhood, and the
fetters of discipline lay heavier on him, as his powers grew
stronger, and his eyes became open to the stirring and varie-
gated interests of the world, now unfolding itself to him under
new and more glowing colors. As yet he contemplated the
scene only from afar, and it seemed but the more gorgeous on
that account. He longed to mingle in its busy current, and
delighted to view the image of its movements in his favorite
poets and historians. Plutarch and Shakspeare;[1] the writings

[1] The feeling produced in him by Shakspeare he described long afterwards:
it throws light on the general state of his temper and tastes. "When I first,
at a very early age," he says, "became acquainted with this poet, I felt indignant at his coldness, his hardness of heart, which permitted him in the most
melting pathos to utter jests, — to mar, by the introduction of a fool, the soul-

of Klopstock, Lessing, Garve, Herder, Gerstenberg, Goethe, and a multitude of others, which marked the dawning literature of Germany, he had studied with a secret avidity : they gave him vague ideas of men and life, or awakened in him splendid visions of literary glory. Klopstock's *Messias*, combined with his own religious tendencies, had early turned him to sacred poetry : before the end of his fourteenth year, he had finished what he called an " epic poem," entitled *Moses*. The extraordinary popularity of Gerstenberg's *Ugolino*, and Goethe's *Götz von Berlichingen*, next directed his attention to the drama ; and as admiration in a mind like his, full of blind activity and nameless aspirings, naturally issues in imitation, he plunged with equal ardor into this new subject, and produced his first tragedy, *Cosmo von Medicis*, some fragments of which he retained and inserted in his *Robbers*. A mass of minor performances, preserved among his papers, or published in the Magazines of the time, serve sufficiently to show that his mind had already dimly discovered its destination, and was striving with a restless vehemence to reach it, in spite of every obstacle.

Such obstacles were in his case neither few nor small. Schiller felt the mortifying truth, that to arrive at the ideal world, he must first gain a footing in the real ; that he might entertain high thoughts and longings, might reverence the beauties of nature and grandeur of mind, but was born to toil for his daily bread. Poetry he loved with the passionateness of a first affection ; but he could not live by it ; he honored it too highly to wish to live by it. His prudence told him that he must yield to stern necessity, must "forsake the balmy climate of Pindus for the Greenland of a barren and dreary science of terms ; " and he did not hesitate to obey. His professional studies were followed with a rigid though

searching scenes of *Hamlet, Lear*, and other pieces ; which now kept him still where my sensibilities hastened forward, now drove him carelessly onward where I would so gladly have lingered. . . . He was the object of my reverence and zealous study for years before I could love himself. I was not yet capable of comprehending Nature at first-hand : I had but learned to admire her image, reflected in the understanding, and put in order by rules." *Werke*, Bd. viii. 2, p. 77.

reluctant fidelity; it was only in leisure gained by superior diligence that he could yield himself to more favorite pursuits. Genius was to serve as the ornament of his inferior qualities, not as an excuse for the want of them.

But if, when such sacrifices were required, it was painful to comply with the dictates of his own reason, it was still more so to endure the harsh and superfluous restrictions of his teachers. He felt it hard enough to be driven from the enchantments of poetry by the dull realities of duty; but it was intolerable and degrading to be hemmed in still farther by the caprices of severe and formal pedagogues. Schiller brooded gloomily over the constraints and hardships of his situation. Many plans he formed for deliverance. Sometimes he would escape in secret to catch a glimpse of the free and busy world to him forbidden: sometimes he laid schemes for utterly abandoning a place which he abhorred, and trusting to fortune for the rest. Often the sight of his class-books and school-apparatus became irksome beyond endurance; he would feign sickness, that he might be left in his own chamber to write poetry and pursue his darling studies without hindrance. Such artifices did not long avail him; the masters noticed the regularity of his sickness, and sent him tasks to be done while it lasted. Even Schiller's patience could not brook this; his natural timidity gave place to indignation; he threw the paper of exercises at the feet of the messenger, and said sternly that "*here*·he would choose his own studies."

Under such corroding and continual vexations an ordinary spirit would have sunk at length, would have gradually given up its loftier aspirations, and sought refuge in vicious indulgence, or at best have sullenly harnessed itself into the yoke, and plodded through existence, weary, discontented, and broken, ever casting back a hankering look upon the dreams of youth, and ever without power to realize them. But Schiller was no ordinary character, and did not act like one. Beneath a cold and simple exterior, dignified with no artificial attractions, and marred in its native amiableness by the incessant obstruction, the isolation and painful destitutions under which he lived, there was concealed a burning energy of soul, which no obstruction could extinguish. The hard circumstances of his fortune had prevented the natural development of his mind; his faculties had been cramped and misdirected; but they had gathered strength by opposition and the habit of self-dependence which it encouraged. His thoughts, unguided by a teacher, had sounded into the depths of his own nature and the mysteries of his own fate; his feelings and passions, unshared by any other heart, had been driven back upon his own, where, like the volcanic fire that smoulders and fuses in secret, they accumulated till their force grew irresistible.

Hitherto Schiller had passed for an unprofitable, a discontented and a disobedient Boy: but the time was now come when the gyves of school discipline could no longer cripple and distort the giant might of his nature: he stood forth as a Man, and wrenched asunder his fetters with a force that was felt at the extremities of Europe. The publication of the *Robbers* forms an era not only in Schiller's history, but in the Literature of the World; and there seems no doubt that, but for so mean a cause as the perverted discipline of the Stuttgard school, we had never seen this tragedy. Schiller commenced it in his nineteenth year; and the circumstances under which it was composed are to be traced in all its parts. It is the production of a strong untutored spirit, consumed by an activity for which there is no outlet, indignant at the barriers which restrain it, and grappling darkly with the phantoms to which its own energy thus painfully imprisoned gives being. A rude simplicity, combined with a gloomy and overpowering force, are its chief characteristics; they remind us of the defective cultivation, as well as of the fervid and harassed feelings of its author. Above all, the latter quality is visible; the tragic interest of the *Robbers* is deep throughout, so deep that frequently it borders upon horror. A grim inexpiable Fate is made the ruling principle: it envelops and overshadows the whole; and under its lowering influence, the fiercest efforts of human will appear but like flashes that illuminate the wild scene with a brief and terrible splendor, and are lost forever in the darkness. The unsearchable abysses of man's destiny are laid open before us, black and profound and appalling, as they seem to the young mind when it first attempts to explore them : the obstacles that thwart our faculties and wishes, the deceitfulness of hope, the nothingness of existence, are sketched in the sable colors so natural to the enthusiast when he first ventures upon life, and compares the world that is without him to the anticipations that were within.

Karl von Moor is a character such as young poets always delight to contemplate or delineate; to Schiller the analogy of their situations must have peculiarly recommended him. Moor is animated into action by feelings similar to those under which his author was then suffering and longing to act. Gifted with every noble quality of manhood in overflowing abundance, Moor's first expectations of life, and of the part he was to play in it, had been glorious as a poet's dream. But the minor dexterities of management were not among his endowments; in his eagerness to reach the goal, he had forgotten that the course is a labyrinthic maze, beset with difficulties, of which some may be surmounted, some can only be evaded, many can be neither. Hurried on by the headlong impetuosity of his temper, he entangles himself in these perplexities; and thinks to penetrate them, not by skill and patience, but by open force. He is baffled, deceived, and still more deeply involved; but injury and disappointment exasperate rather than instruct him. He had expected heroes, and he finds mean men; friends, and he finds smiling traitors to tempt him aside, to profit by his aberrations, and lead him onward to destruction : he had dreamed of magnanimity and every generous principle, he finds that prudence is the only virtue sure of its reward. Too fiery by nature, the intensity of his sufferings has now maddened him still farther : he is himself incapable of calm reflection, and there is no counsellor at hand to assist him; none, whose sympathy might assuage his miseries, whose wisdom might teach him to remedy or to endure them. He is stung by fury into action, and his activity is at once blind and tremendous. Since the world is not the abode of unmixed integrity, he looks upon it as a den of thieves; since its institutions may obstruct the advancement of worth, and screen delinquency from punishment, he regards the social union as a pestilent nuisance,

the mischiefs of which it is fitting that he in his degree should
do his best to repair, by means however violent. Revenge is
the mainspring of his conduct; but he ennobles it in his own
eyes, by giving it the color of a disinterested concern for the
maintenance of justice, — the abasement of vice from its high
places, and the exaltation of suffering virtue. Single against
the universe, to appeal to the primary law of the stronger, to
"grasp the scales of Providence in a mortal's hand," is frantic
and wicked; but Moor has a force of soul which makes it likewise awful. The interest lies in the conflict of this gigantic
soul against the fearful odds which at length overwhelm it,
and hurry it down to the darkest depths of ruin.

The original conception of such a work as this betrays
the inexperience no less than the vigor of youth: its execution gives a similar testimony. The characters of the piece,
though traced in glowing colors, are outlines more than pictures: the few features we discover in them are drawn with
elaborate minuteness; but the rest are wanting. Everything
indicates the condition of a keen and powerful intellect, which
had studied men in books only; had, by self-examination and
the perusal of history, detected and strongly seized some of
the leading peculiarities of human nature; but was yet ignorant of all the minute and more complex principles which
regulate men's conduct in actual life, and which only a knowledge of living men can unfold. If the hero of the play forms
something like an exception to this remark, he is the sole
exception, and for reasons alluded to above: his character
resembles the author's own. Even with Karl, the success is
incomplete: with the other personages it is far more so.
Franz von Moor, the villain of the Piece, is an amplified
copy of Iago and Richard; but the copy is distorted as well
as amplified. There is no air of reality in Franz: he is a
villain of theory, who studies to accomplish his object by
the most diabolical expedients, and soothes his conscience
by arguing with the priest in favor of atheism and materialism; not the genuine villain of Shakspeare and Nature, who
employs his reasoning powers in creating new schemes and
devising new means, and conquers remorse by avoiding it, —

by fixing his hopes and fears on the more pressing emergencies of worldly business. So reflective a miscreant as
Franz could not exist: his calculations would lead him to
honesty, if merely because it was the best policy.

Amelia, the only female in the piece, is a beautiful creation; but as imaginary as her persecutor Franz. Still and
exalted in her warm enthusiasm, devoted in her love to
Moor, she moves before us as the inhabitant of a higher and
simpler world than ours. "*He* sails on troubled seas," she
exclaims, with a confusion of metaphors, which it is easy to
pardon, "he sails on troubled seas, Amelia's love sails with
him; he wanders in pathless deserts, Amelia's love makes
the burning sand grow green beneath him, and the stunted
shrubs to blossom; the south scorches his bare head, his feet
are pinched by the northern snow, stormy hail beats round
his temples — Amelia's love rocks him to sleep in the storm.
Seas, and hills, and horizons, are between us; but souls escape
from their clay prisons, and meet in the paradise of love!"
She is a fair vision, the *beau idéal* of a poet's first mistress;
but has few mortal lineaments.

Similar defects are visible in almost all the other characters.
Moor, the father, is a weak and fond old man, who could have
arrived at gray hairs in such a state of ignorance nowhere but
in a work of fiction. The inferior banditti are painted with
greater vigor, yet still in rugged and ill-shapen forms; their
individuality is kept up by an extravagant exaggeration of
their several peculiarities. Schiller himself pronounced a
severe but not unfounded censure, when he said of this work,
in a maturer age, that his *chief* fault was in "presuming to
delineate men two years before he had met one."

His skill in the art of composition surpassed his knowledge
of the world; but that too was far from perfection. Schiller's
style in the *Robbers* is partly of a kind with the incidents
and feelings which it represents; strong and astonishing, and
sometimes wildly grand; but likewise inartificial, coarse, and
grotesque. His sentences, in their rude emphasis, come down
like the club of Hercules; the stroke is often of a crushing
force, but its sweep is irregular and awkward. When Moor is

involved in the deepest intricacies of the old question, necessity and free-will, and has convinced himself that he is but an engine in the hands of some dark and irresistible power, he cries out: "Why has my Perillus made of me a brazen bull to roast men in my glowing belly?" The stage-direction says, "shaken with horror:" no wonder that he shook!

Schiller has admitted these faults, and explained their origin, in strong and sincere language, in a passage of which we have already quoted the conclusion. "A singular miscalculation of nature," he says, "had combined my poetical tendencies with the place of my birth. Any disposition to poetry did violence to the laws of the institution where I was educated, and contradicted the plan of its founder. For eight years my enthusiasm struggled with military discipline; but the passion for poetry is vehement and fiery as a first love. What discipline was meant to extinguish, it blew into a flame. To escape from arrangements that tortured me, my heart sought refuge in the world of ideas, when as yet I was unacquainted with the world of realities, from which iron bars excluded me. I was unacquainted with men; for the four hundred that lived with me were but repetitions of the same creature, true casts of one single mould, and of that very mould which plastic nature solemnly disclaimed. . . . Thus circumstanced, a stranger to human characters and human fortunes, to hit the medium line between angels and devils was an enterprise in which I necessarily failed. In attempting it, my pencil necessarily brought out a monster, for which by good fortune the world had no original, and which I would not wish to be immortal, except to perpetuate an example of the offspring which Genius in its unnatural union with Thraldom may give to the world. I allude to the *Robbers*."[1]

Yet with all these excrescences and defects, the unbounded popularity of the *Robbers* is not difficult to account for. To every reader, the excitement of emotion must be a chief consideration; to the mass of readers it is the sole one: and the grand secret of moving others is, that the poet be himself moved. We have seen how well Schiller's temper and circum-

[1] *Deutsches Museum v. Jahr* 1784, cited by Doering.

stances qualified him to fulfil this condition: treatment, not
of his choosing, had raised his own mind into something like
a Pythian frenzy; and his genius, untrained as it was, sufficed
to communicate abundance of the feeling to others. Perhaps
more than abundance: to judge from our individual impression, the perusal of the *Robbers* produces an effect powerful
even to pain; we are absolutely wounded by the catastrophe;
our minds are darkened and distressed, as if we had witnessed
the execution of a criminal. It is in vain that we rebel against
the inconsistencies and crudities of the work: its faults are
redeemed by the living energy that pervades it. We may
exclaim against the blind madness of the hero; but there is
a towering grandeur about him, a whirlwind force of passion
and of will, which catches our hearts, and puts the scruples of
criticism to silence. The most delirious of enterprises is that
of Moor, but the vastness of his mind renders even that interesting. We see him leagued with desperadoes directing their
savage strength to actions more and more audacious; he is in
arms against the conventions of men and the everlasting laws
of Fate: yet we follow him with anxiety through the forests
and desert places, where he wanders, encompassed with peril,
inspired with lofty daring, and torn by unceasing remorse;
and we wait with awe for the doom which he has merited and
cannot avoid. Nor amid all his frightful aberrations do we ever
cease to love him: he is an " archangel though in ruins; " and
the strong agony with which he feels the present, the certainty
of that stern future which awaits him, which his own eye
never loses sight of, makes us lenient to his crimes. When he
pours forth his wild recollections, or still wilder forebodings,
there is a terrible vehemence in his expressions, which over-
powers us, in spite both of his and their extravagance. The
scene on the hills beside the Danube, where he looks at the
setting sun, and thinks of old hopes, and times " when he
could not sleep if his evening prayer had been forgotten," is
one, with all its improprieties, that ever clings to the memory.
" See," he passionately continues, " all things are gone forth
to bask in the peaceful beam of the spring: why must I alone
inhale the torments of hell out of the joys of heaven ? That

all should be so happy, all so married together by the spirit of peace! The whole world one family, its Father above; that Father not *mine!* I alone the castaway, I alone struck out from the company of the just; not for me the sweet name of child, never for me the languishing look of one whom I love; never, never, the embracing of a bosom friend! Encircled with murderers; serpents hissing around me; riveted to vice with iron bonds; leaning on the bending reed of vice over the gulf of perdition; amid the flowers of the glad world, a howling Abaddon! Oh, that I might return into my mother's womb; — that I might be born a beggar! I would never more — O Heaven, that I could be as one of these day-laborers! Oh, I would toil till the blood ran down from my temples, to buy myself the pleasure of one noontide sleep, the blessing of a single tear. There *was* a time too, when I could weep — O ye days of peace, thou castle of my father, ye green lovely valleys! — O all ye Elysian scenes of my childhood! will ye never come again, never with your balmy sighing cool my burning bosom? Mourn with me, Nature! They will never come again, never cool my burning bosom with their balmy sighing. They are gone! gone! and may not return!"

No less strange is the soliloquy where Moor, with the instrument of self-destruction in his hands, the "dread key that is to shut behind him the prison of life, and to unbolt before him the dwelling of eternal night," — meditates on the gloomy enigmas of his future destiny. Soliloquies on this subject are numerous, — from the time of Hamlet, of Cato, and downwards. Perhaps the worst of them has more ingenuity, perhaps the best of them has less awfulness than the present. St. Dominick himself might shudder at such a question, with such an answer as this: "What if thou shouldst send me companionless to some burnt and blasted circle of the universe; which thou hast banished from thy sight; where the lone darkness and the motionless desert were my prospects — forever? I would people the silent wilderness with my fantasies; I should have Eternity for leisure to examine the perplexed image of the universal woe."

Strength, wild impassioned strength, is the distinguishing

quality of Moor. All his history shows it; and his death is of a piece with the fierce splendor of his life. Having finished the bloody work of crime, and magnanimity, and horror, he thinks that, for himself, suicide would be too easy an exit. He has noticed a poor man toiling by the way-side, for eleven children; a great reward has been promised for the head of the Robber; the gold will nourish that poor drudge and his boys, and Moor goes forth to give it them. We part with him in pity and sorrow; looking less at his misdeeds than at their frightful expiation.

The subordinate personages, though diminished in extent and varied in their forms, are of a similar quality with the hero; a strange mixture of extravagance and true energy. In perusing the work which represents their characters and fates, we are alternately shocked and inspired; there is a perpetual conflict between our understanding and our feelings. Yet the latter on the whole come off victorious. The *Robbers* is a tragedy that will long find readers to astonish, and, with all its faults, to move. It stands, in our imagination, like some ancient rugged pile of a barbarous age; irregular, fantastic, useless; but grand in its height and massiveness and black frowning strength. It will long remain a singular monument of the early genius and early fortune of its author.

The publication of such a work as this naturally produced an extraordinary feeling in the literary world. Translations of the *Robbers* soon appeared in almost all the languages of Europe, and were read in all of them with a deep interest, compounded of admiration and aversion, according to the relative proportions of sensibility and judgment in the various minds which contemplated the subject. In Germany, the enthusiasm which the *Robbers* excited was extreme. The young author had burst upon the world like a meteor; and surprise, for a time, suspended the power of cool and rational criticism. In the ferment produced by the universal discussion of this single topic, the poet was magnified above his natural dimensions, great as they were: and though the general sentence was loudly in his favor, yet he found detractors as well as praisers, and both equally beyond the limits of moderation.

One charge brought against him must have damped the joy of literary glory, and stung Schiller's pure and virtuous mind more deeply than any other. He was accused of having injured the cause of morality by his work; of having set up to the impetuous and fiery temperament of youth a model of imitation which the young were too likely to pursue with eagerness, and which could only lead them from the safe and beaten tracks of duty into error and destruction. It has even been stated, and often been repeated since, that a practical exemplification of this doctrine occurred, about this time, in Germany. A young nobleman, it was said, of the fairest gifts and prospects, had cast away all these advantages; betaken himself to the forests, and, copying Moor, had begun a course of active operations, — which, also copying Moor, but less willingly, he had ended by a shameful death.

It can now be hardly necessary to contradict these theories; or to show that none but a candidate for Bedlam as well as Tyburn could be seduced from the substantial comforts of existence, to seek destruction and disgrace, for the sake of such imaginary grandeur. The German nobleman of the fairest gifts and prospects turns out, on investigation, to have been a German blackguard, whom debauchery and riotous extravagance had reduced to want; who took to the highway, when he could take to nothing else, — not allured by an ebullient enthusiasm, or any heroical and misdirected appetite for sublime actions, but driven by the more palpable stimulus of importunate duns, an empty purse, and five craving senses. Perhaps in his later days, this philosopher *may* have referred to Schiller's tragedy, as the source from which he drew his theory of life: but if so, we believe he was mistaken. For characters like him, the great attraction was the charms of revelry, and the great restraint, the gallows, — before the period of Karl von Moor, just as they have been since, and will be to the end of time. Among motives like these, the influence of even the most malignant book could scarcely be discernible, and would be little detrimental, if it were.

Nothing, at any rate, could be farther from Schiller's intention than such a consummation. In his preface, he speaks of the moral effects of the *Robbers* in terms which do honor to his heart, while they show the inexperience of his head. Ridicule, he signifies, has long been tried against the wickedness of the times, whole cargoes of hellebore have been expended, — in vain; and now, he thinks, recourse must be had to more pungent medicines. We may smile at the simplicity of this idea; and safely conclude that, like other specifics, the present one would fail to produce a perceptible effect: but Schiller's vindication rests on higher grounds than these. His work has on the whole furnished nourishment to the more exalted powers of our nature; the sentiments and images which he has shaped and uttered, tend, in spite of their alloy, to elevate the soul to a nobler pitch: and this is a sufficient defence. As to the danger of misapplying the inspiration he communicates, of forgetting the dictates of prudence in our zeal for the dictates of poetry, we have no great cause to fear it. Hitherto, at least, there has always been enough of dull reality, on every side of us, to abate such fervors in good time, and bring us back to the most sober level of prose, if not to sink us below it. We should thank the poet who performs such a service; and forbear to inquire too rigidly whether there is any "moral" in his piece or not. The writer of a work, which interests and excites the spiritual feelings of men, has as little need to justify himself by showing how it exemplifies some wise saw or modern instance, as the doer of a generous action has to demonstrate its merit, by deducing it from the system of Shaftesbury, or Smith, or Paley, or whichever happens to be the favorite system for the age and place. The instructiveness of the one, and the virtue of the other, exist independently of all systems or saws, and in spite of all.

But the tragedy of the *Robbers* produced some inconveniences of a kind much more sensible than these its theoretical mischiefs. We have called it the signal of Schiller's deliverance from school tyranny and military constraint;

but its operation in this respect was not immediate; at first it seemed to involve him more deeply and dangerously than before. He had finished the original sketch of it in 1778; but for fear of offence, he kept it secret till his medical studies were completed.[1] These, in the mean time, he had pursued with sufficient assiduity to merit the usual honors;[2] in 1780, he had, in consequence, obtained the post of surgeon to the regiment *Augé*, in the Würtemberg army. This advancement enabled him to complete his project, to print the *Robbers* at his own expense, not being able to find any bookseller that would undertake it. The nature of the work, and the universal interest it awakened, drew attention to the private circumstances of the author, whom the *Robbers*, as well as other pieces of his writing, that had found their way into the periodical publications of the time, sufficiently showed to be no common man. Many grave persons were offended at the vehement sentiments expressed in the *Robbers;* and the unquestioned ability with which these extravagances were expressed, but made the matter worse. To Schiller's superiors, above all, such things were inconceivable: he might perhaps be a very great genius, but was certainly a dangerous servant for his Highness the Grand Duke of Würtemberg. Officious people mingled themselves in the affair: nay, the graziers of

---

[1] On this subject Doering gives an anecdote, which may perhaps be worth translating. "One of Schiller's teachers surprised him on one occasion reciting a scene from the *Robbers*, before some of his intimate companions. At the words, which Franz von Moor addresses to Moser: *Ha, what! thou knowest none greater? Think again! Death, heaven, eternity, damnation, hovers in the sound of thy voice! Not one greater?* — the door opened, and the master saw Schiller stamping in desperation up and down the room. 'For shame,' said he, 'for shame to get into such a passion, and curse so!' The other scholars tittered covertly at the worthy inspector; and Schiller called after him with a bitter smile, 'A noodle' (*ein confiscirter Kerl*)!"

[2] His Latin Essay on the *Philosophy of Physiology* was written in 1778, and never printed. His concluding *thesis* was published according to custom: the subject is arduous enough, "the connection between the animal and spiritual nature of man," — which Dr. Cabanis has since treated in so offensive a fashion. Schiller's tract we have never seen. Doering says it was long "out of print," till Nasse reproduced it in his Medical Journal (Leipzig, 1820): he is silent respecting its merits.

the Alps were brought to bear upon it. The Grisons magistrates, it appeared, had seen the book: and were mortally huffed at being there spoken of, according to a Swabian adage, as *common highwaymen*.[1] They complained in the *Hamburg Correspondent;* and a sort of Jackal, at Ludwigsburg, one Walter, whose name deserves to be thus kept in mind, volunteered to plead their cause before the Grand Duke.

Informed of all these circumstances, the Grand Duke expressed his disapprobation of Schiller's poetical labors in the most unequivocal terms. Schiller was at length summoned to appear before him; and it then turned out, that his Highness was not only dissatisfied with the moral or political errors of the work, but scandalized moreover at its want of literary merit. In this latter respect, he was kind enough to proffer his own services. But Schiller seems to have received the proposal with no sufficient gratitude; and the interview passed without advantage to either party. It terminated in the Duke's commanding Schiller to abide by medical subjects: or at least to beware of writing any more poetry, without submitting it to *his* inspection.

We need not comment on this portion of the Grand Duke's history: his treatment of Schiller has already been sufficiently avenged. By the great body of mankind, his name will be recollected, chiefly, if at all, for the sake of the unfriended youth whom he now schooled so sharply, and afterwards afflicted so cruelly: it will be recollected also with the angry triumph which we feel against a shallow and despotic "noble of convention," who strains himself to oppress "one of nature's nobility," submitted by blind chance to his dominion, and — finds that he cannot! All this is far more than

---

[1] The obnoxious passage has been carefully expunged from subsequent editions. It was in the third scene of the second act; Spiegelberg discoursing with Razmann, observes, "An honest man you may form of windlestraws; but to make a rascal you must have grist: besides, there is a national genius in it, a certain rascal climate, so to speak." In the first edition, there was added: "*Go to the Grisons, for instance: that is what I call the thief's Athens.*" The patriot who stood forth on this occasion for the honor of the Grisons, to deny this weighty charge, and denounce the crime of making it, was not Dogberry or Verges, but "one of the noble family of Salis."

the Prince of Würtemberg deserves. Of limited faculties, and educated in the French principles of taste, then common to persons of his rank in Germany, he had perused the *Robbers* with unfeigned disgust; he could see in the author only a misguided enthusiast, with talents barely enough to make him dangerous. And though he never fully or formally retracted this injustice, he did not follow it up; when Schiller became known to the world at large, the Duke ceased to persecute him. The father he still kept in his service, and nowise molested.

In the mean time, however, various mortifications awaited Schiller. It was in vain that he discharged the humble duties of his station with the most strict fidelity, and even, it is said, with superior skill: he was a suspected person, and his most innocent actions were misconstrued, his slightest faults were visited with the full measure of official severity. His busy imagination aggravated the evil. He had seen poor Schubart[1] wearing out his tedious eight years of durance in the fortress of Asperg, because he had been "a rock of offence to the powers that were." The fate of this unfortunate author appeared to Schiller a type of his own. His free spirit shrank at the prospect of wasting its strength in strife against the pitiful constraints, the minute and endless persecutions of men who knew him not, yet had his fortune in their hands; the idea of dungeons and jailers haunted and tortured his mind; and the means of escaping them, the renunciation of poetry, the source of all his joy, if likewise of many woes, the radiant guiding-star of his turbid and obscure existence, seemed a sentence of death to all that was dignified, and delightful, and worth retaining, in his character. Totally ignorant of what is called the world; conscious too of the might that slumbered in his soul, and proud of it, as kings are of their sceptres; impetuous when roused, and spurning unjust restraint; yet wavering and timid from the delicacy of his nature, and still more restricted in the freedom of his movements by the circumstances of his father, whose all depended on the pleasure of the court, Schiller felt

---

[1] See Appendix, No. 1.

himself embarrassed, and agitated, and tormented in no common degree. Urged this way and that by the most powerful and conflicting impulses; driven to despair by the paltry shackles that chained him, yet forbidden by the most sacred considerations to break them, he knew not on what he should resolve; he reckoned himself "the most unfortunate of men."

Time at length gave him the solution; circumstances occurred which forced him to decide. The popularity of the *Robbers* had brought him into correspondence with several friends of literature, who wished to patronize the author, or engage him in new undertakings. Among this number was the Freiherr von Dalberg, superintendent of the theatre at Mannheim, under whose encouragement and countenance Schiller remodelled the *Robbers*, altered it in some parts, and had it brought upon the stage in 1781. The correspondence with Dalberg began in literary discussions, but gradually elevated itself into the expression of more interesting sentiments. Dalberg loved and sympathized with the generous enthusiast, involved in troubles and perplexities which his inexperience was so little adequate to thread: he gave him advice and assistance; and Schiller repaid this favor with the gratitude due to his kind, his first, and then almost his only benefactor. His letters to this gentleman have been preserved, and lately published; they exhibit a lively picture of Schiller's painful situation at Stuttgard, and of his unskilful as well as eager anxiety to be delivered from it.[1] His darling project was that Dalberg should bring him to Mannheim, as theatrical poet, by permission of the Duke: at one time he even thought of turning player.

Neither of these projects could take immediate effect, and Schiller's embarrassments became more pressing than ever. With the natural feeling of a young author, he had ventured to go in secret, and witness the first representation of his tragedy, at Mannheim. His incognito did not conceal him; he was put under arrest during a week, for this offence: and as the punishment did not deter him from again transgressing

---

[1] See Appendix, No. 2.

in a similar manner, he learned that it was in contemplation to try more rigorous measures with him. Dark hints were given to him of some exemplary as well as imminent severity: and Dalberg's aid, the sole hope of averting it by quiet means, was distant and dubious. Schiller saw himself reduced to extremities. Beleaguered with present distresses, and the most horrible forebodings, on every side; roused to the highest pitch of indignation, yet forced to keep silence, and wear the face of patience, he could endure this maddening constraint no longer. He resolved to be free, at whatever risk; to abandon advantages which he could not buy at such a price; to quit his stepdame home, and go forth, though friendless and alone, to seek his fortune in the great market of life. Some foreign Duke or Prince was arriving at Stuttgard; and all the people were in movement, occupied with seeing the spectacle of his entrance: Schiller seized this opportunity of retiring from the city, careless whither he went, so he got beyond the reach of turnkeys, and Grand Dukes, and commanding officers. It was in the month of October, 1782.

This last step forms the catastrophe of the publication of the *Robbers:* it completed the deliverance of Schiller from the grating thraldom under which his youth had been passed, and decided his destiny for life. Schiller was in his twenty-third year when he left Stuttgard. He says "he went empty away, — empty in purse and hope." The future was indeed sufficiently dark before him. Without patrons, connections, or country, he had ventured forth to the warfare on his own charges; without means, experience, or settled purpose, it was greatly to be feared that the fight would go against him. Yet his situation, though gloomy enough, was not entirely without its brighter side. He was now a free man, free, however poor; and his strong soul quickened as its fetters dropped off, and gloried within him in the dim anticipation of great and far-extending enterprises. If, cast too rudely among the hardships and bitter disquietudes of the world, his past nursing had not been delicate, he was already taught to look upon privation and discomfort as his daily companions.

If he knew not how to bend his course among the perplexed vicissitudes of society, there was a force within him which would triumph over many difficulties; and a "light from Heaven" was about his path, which, if it failed to conduct him to wealth and preferment, would keep him far from baseness and degrading vices. Literature, and every great and noble thing which the right pursuit of it implies, he loved with all his heart and all his soul: to this inspiring object he was henceforth exclusively devoted; advancing towards this, and possessed of common necessaries on the humblest scale, there was little else to tempt him. His life might be unhappy, but would hardly be disgraceful.

Schiller gradually felt all this, and gathered comfort, while better days began to dawn upon him. Fearful of trusting himself so near Stuttgard as at Mannheim, he had passed into Franconia, and was living painfully at Oggersheim, under the name of Schmidt: but Dalberg, who knew all his distresses, supplied him with money for immediate wants; and a generous lady made him the offer of a home. Madam von Wolzogen lived on her estate of Bauerbach, in the neighborhood of Meinungen; she knew Schiller from his works, and his intimacy with her sons, who had been his fellow-students at Stuttgard. She invited him to her house; and there treated him with an affection which helped him to forget the past, and look cheerfully forward to the future.

Under this hospitable roof, Schiller had leisure to examine calmly the perplexed and dubious aspect of his affairs. Happily his character belonged not to the whining or sentimental sort: he was not of those, in whom the pressure of misfortune produces nothing but unprofitable pain; who spend, in cherishing and investigating and deploring their miseries, the time which should be spent in providing a relief for them. With him, strong feeling was constantly a call to vigorous action: he possessed in a high degree the faculty of conquering his afflictions, by directing his thoughts, not to maxims for enduring them, or modes of expressing them with interest, but to plans for getting rid of them; and to this disposition or habit, — too rare among men of genius, men of a much higher class than mere sentimentalists, but whose sensibility is out of proportion with their inventiveness or activity, — we are to attribute no small influence in the fortunate conduct of his subsequent life. With such a turn of mind, Schiller, now that he was at length master of his own movements, could not long be at a loss for plans or tasks. Once settled at Bauerbach, he immediately resumed his poetical employments; and forgot, in the regions of fancy, the vague uncertainties of his real condition, or saw prospects of amending it in a life of literature. By many safe and sagacious persons, the prudence of his late proceedings might be more than questioned; it was natural for many to forebode that one who left the port so rashly, and sailed with such precipitation, was likely to make shipwreck ere the voyage had extended far: but the lapse of a few months put a stop to such predictions. A year had not passed since his departure, when Schiller sent forth his *Verschwörung des Fiesco* and *Kabale und Liebe;* tragedies which testified that, dangerous and arduous as the life he had selected might be, he possessed resources more than adequate to its emergencies. *Fiesco* he had commenced during the period of his arrest at Stuttgard; it was published, with the other play, in 1783; and soon after brought upon the Mannheim theatre, with universal approbation.

It was now about three years since the composition of the *Robbers* had been finished; five since the first sketch of it had been formed. With what zeal and success Schiller had, in that interval, pursued the work of his mental culture, these two dramas are a striking proof. The first ardor of youth is still to be discerned in them; but it is now chastened by the dictates of a maturer reason, and made to animate the products of a much happier and more skilful invention. Schiller's ideas of art had expanded and grown clearer, his knowledge of life had enlarged. He exhibits more acquaintance with the fundamental principles of human nature, as well as with the circumstances under which it usually displays itself; and far higher and juster views of the manner in which its manifestations should be represented.

In the *Conspiracy of Fiesco* we have to admire not only the energetic animation which the author has infused into all his characters, but the distinctness with which he has discriminated, without aggravating them; and the vividness with which he has contrived to depict the scene where they act and move. The political and personal relations of the Genoese nobility; the luxurious splendor, the intrigues, the feuds, and jarring interests, which occupy them, are made visible before us: we understand and may appreciate the complexities of the conspiracy; we mingle, as among realities, in the pompous and imposing movements which lead to the catastrophe. The catastrophe itself is displayed with peculiar effect. The midnight silence of the sleeping city, interrupted only by the distant sounds of watchmen, by the low hoarse murmur of the sea, or the stealthy footsteps and disguised voice of Fiesco, is conveyed to our imagination by some brief but graphic touches; we seem to stand in the solitude and deep stillness of Genoa, awaiting the signal which is to burst so fearfully upon its slumber. At length the gun is fired; and the wild uproar which ensues is no less strikingly exhibited. The deeds and sounds of violence, astonishment and terror; the volleying cannon, the heavy toll of the alarm-bells, the acclamation of assembled thousands, "the voice of Genoa speaking with Fiesco,"—all is made present to us with a force and clearness, which of itself were enough to show no ordinary power of close and comprehensive conception, no ordinary skill in arranging and expressing its results.

But it is not this felicitous delineation of circumstances and visible scenes that constitutes our principal enjoyment. The faculty of penetrating through obscurity and confusion, to seize the characteristic features of an object, abstract or material; of producing a lively description in the latter case, an accurate and keen scrutiny in the former, is the essential property of intellect, and occupies in its best form a high rank in the scale of mental gifts: but the creative faculty of the poet, and especially of the dramatic poet, is something superadded to this; it is far rarer, and occupies a rank far higher. In this particular, *Fiesco*, without approaching the limits of perfection, yet stands in an elevated range of excellence. The characters, on the whole, are imagined and portrayed with great impressiveness and vigor. Traces of old faults are indeed still to be discovered: there still seems a want of pliancy about the genius of the author; a stiffness and heaviness in his motions. His sublimity is not to be questioned; but it does not always disdain the aid of rude contrasts and mere theatrical effect. He paints in colors deep and glowing, but without sufficient skill to blend them delicately: he amplifies nature more than purifies it; he omits, but does not well conceal the omission. *Fiesco* has not the complete charm of a true though embellished resemblance to reality; its attraction rather lies in a kind of colossal magnitude, which requires it, if seen to advantage, to be viewed from a distance. Yet the prevailing qualities of the piece do more than make us pardon such defects. If the dramatic imitation is not always entirely successful, it is never very distant from success; and a constant flow of powerful thought and sentiment counteracts, or prevents us from noticing, the failure. We find evidence of great philosophic penetration, great resources of invention, directed by a skilful study of history and men; and everywhere a bold grandeur of feeling and imagery gives life to what study has combined. The chief incidents have a dazzling magnificence; the chief characters, an aspect of majesty and force which corresponds to it. Fervor of heart, capaciousness of intellect and imagination, present themselves on all sides: the general effect is powerful and exalting.

Fiesco himself is a personage at once probable and tragically interesting. The luxurious dissipation, in which he veils his daring projects, softens the rudeness of that strength which it half conceals. His immeasurable pride expands itself not only into a disdain of subjection, but also into the most lofty acts of magnanimity: his blind confidence in fortune seems almost warranted by the resources which he finds in his own fearlessness and imperturbable presence of mind. His ambition participates in the nobleness of his other qualities; he is less anxious that his rivals should yield to him in power than in generosity and greatness of character, attributes of which power is with him but the symbol and the fit employment. Ambition in Fiesco is indeed the common wish of every mind to diffuse its individual influence, to see its own activity reflected back from the united minds of millions : but it is the common wish acting on no common man. He does not long to rule, that he may sway other wills, as it were, by the physical exertion of his own : he would lead us captive by the superior grandeur of his qualities, once fairly manifested ; and he aims at dominion, chiefly as it will enable him to manifest these. "It is not the arena that he values, but what lies in that arena : " the sovereignty is enviable, not for its adventitious splendor, not because it is the object of coarse and universal wonder ; but as it offers, in the collected force of a nation, something which the loftiest mortal may find scope for all his powers in guiding. "Spread out the thunder," Fiesco exclaims, "into its single tones, and it becomes a lullaby for children : pour it forth together in *one* quick peal, and the royal sound shall move the heavens." His affections are not less vehement than his other passions : his heart can be melted into powerlessness and tenderness by the mild persuasions of his Leonora ; the idea of exalting this amiable being mingles largely with the other motives to his enterprise. He is, in fact, a great, and might have been a virtuous man ; and though in the pursuit of grandeur he swerves from absolute rectitude, we still respect his splendid qualities, and admit the force of the allurements which have led him astray. It is but faintly that we condemn his sentiments, when, after a night spent in struggles between a rigid and a more accommodating patriotism, he looks out of his chamber, as the sun is rising in its calm beauty, and gilding the waves and mountains, and all the innumerable palaces and domes and spires of Genoa, and exclaims with rapture : "This majestic city — mine ! To flame over it like the kingly Day ; to brood over it with a monarch's power ; all these sleepless longings, all these never satiated wishes to be drowned in that unfathomable ocean !" We admire Fiesco, we disapprove of him, and sympathize with him : he is crushed in the ponderous machinery which himself put in motion and thought to control: we lament his fate, but confess that it was not undeserved. He is a fit "offering of individual free-will to the force of social conventions."

Fiesco is not the only striking character in the play which bears his name. The narrow fanatical republican virtue of Verrina, the mild and venerable wisdom of the old Doria, the unbridled profligacy of his Nephew, even the cold, contented, irreclaimable perversity of the cut-throat Moor, all dwell in our recollections: but what, next to Fiesco, chiefly attracts us, is the character of Leonora his wife. Leonora is of kindred to Amelia in the *Robbers*, but involved in more complicated relations, and brought nearer to the actual condition of humanity. She is such a heroine as Schiller most delights to draw. Meek and retiring by the softness of her nature, yet glowing with an ethereal ardor for all that is illustrious and lovely, she clings about her husband, as if her being were one with his. She dreams of remote and peaceful scenes, where Fiesco should be all to her, she all to Fiesco: her idea of love is, that " *her* name should lie in secret behind every one of his thoughts, should speak to him from every object of Nature; that for him, this bright majestic universe itself were but as the shining jewel, on which her image, only *hers*, stood engraved." Her character seems a reflection of Fiesco's, but refined from his grosser strength, and transfigured into a celestial form of purity, and tenderness, and touching grace. Jealousy cannot move her into anger; she languishes in concealed sorrow, when she thinks herself forgotten. It is affection alone that can rouse her into passion; but under the influence of this, she forgets all weakness and fear. She cannot stay in her palace, on the night when Fiesco's destiny is deciding; she rushes forth, as if inspired, to share in her husband's dangers and sublime deeds, and perishes at last in the tumult.

The death of Leonora, so brought about, and at such a time, is reckoned among the blemishes of the work: that of Fiesco, in which Schiller has ventured to depart from history, is to be more favorably judged of. Ficsco is not here accidentally drowned; but plunged into the waves by the indignant

Verrina, who forgets or stifles the feelings of friendship, in his rage at political apostasy. "The nature of the Drama," we are justly told, "will not suffer the operation of Chance, or of an immediate Providence. Higher spirits can discern the minute fibres of an event stretching through the whole expanse of the system of the world, and hanging, it may be, on the remotest limits of the future and the past, where man discerns nothing save the action itself, hovering unconnected in space. But the artist has to paint for the short view of man, whom he wishes to instruct; not for the piercing eye of superior powers, from whom he learns."

In the composition of *Fiesco*, Schiller derived the main part of his original materials from history; he could increase the effect by gorgeous representations, and ideas pre-existing in the mind of his reader. Enormity of incident and strangeness of situation lent him a similar assistance in the *Robbers*. *Kabale und Liebe* is destitute of these advantages; it is a tragedy of domestic life; its means of interesting are comprised within itself, and rest on very simple feelings, dignified by no very singular action. The name, *Court-Intriguing and Love*, correctly designates its nature; it aims at exhibiting the conflict, the victorious conflict, of political manœuvring, of cold worldly wisdom, with the pure impassioned movements of the young heart, as yet unsullied by the tarnish of everyday life, inexperienced in its calculations, sick of its empty formalities, and indignantly determined to cast off the mean restrictions it imposes, which bind so firmly by their number, though singly so contemptible. The idea is far from original: this is a conflict which most men have figured to themselves, which many men of ardent mind are in some degree constantly waging. To make it, in this simple form, the subject of a drama, seems to be a thought of Schiller's own; but the praise, though not the merit of his undertaking, considerable rather as performed than projected, has been lessened by a multitude of worthless or noxious imitations. The same primary conception has been tortured into a thousand shapes, and tricked out with a thousand tawdry devices and meretricious ornaments, by the Kotzebues, and other "intellectual Jacobins," whose productions have brought what we falsely call the "German Theatre" into such deserved contempt in England. Some portion of the gall, due only to these inflated, flimsy, and fantastic persons, appears to have acted on certain critics in estimating this play of Schiller's. August Wilhelm Schlegel speaks slightingly of the work : he says, "it will hardly move us by its tone of overstrained sensibility, but may well afflict us by the painful impressions which it leaves." Our own experience has been different from that of Schlegel. In the characters of Louisa and Ferdinand Walter we discovered little overstraining; their sensibility we did not reckon very criminal; seeing it united with a clearness of judgment, chastened by a purity of heart, and controlled by a force of virtuous resolution, in full proportion with itself. We rather admired the genius of the poet, which could elevate a poor music-master's daughter to the dignity of a heroine; could represent, without wounding our sense of propriety, the affection of two noble beings, created for each other by nature, and divided by rank; we sympathized in their sentiments enough to feel a proper interest in their fate, and see in them, what the author meant we should see, two pure and lofty minds involved in the meshes of vulgar cunning, and borne to destruction by the excess of their own good qualities and the crimes of others.

Ferdinand is a nobleman, but not convinced that "his patent of nobility is more ancient or of more authority than the primeval scheme of the universe:" he speaks and acts like a young man entertaining such persuasions : disposed to yield everything to reason and true honor, but scarcely anything to mere use and wont. His passion for Louisa is the sign and the nourishment rather than the cause of such a temper : he loves her without limit, as the only creature he has ever met with of a like mind with himself; and this feeling exalts into inspiration what was already the dictate of his nature. We accompany him on his straight and plain path; we rejoice to see him fling aside with a strong arm the artifices and allurements with which a worthless father and more worthless associates assail him at first in vain : there is something attractive in the spectacle of native integrity, fearless though inexperienced, at war with selfishness and craft; something mournful, because the victory will seldom go as we would have it.

Louisa is a meet partner for the generous Ferdinand: the poet has done justice to her character. She is timid and humble; a feeling and richly gifted soul is hid in her by the unkindness of her earthly lot; she is without counsellors except the innate holiness of her heart, and the dictates of her keen though untutored understanding; yet when the hour of trial comes, she can obey the commands of both, and draw from herself a genuine nobleness of conduct, which second-hand prudence, and wealth, and titles, would but render less touching. Her filial affection, her angelic attachment to her lover, her sublime and artless piety, are beautifully contrasted with the bleakness of her external circumstances: she appears before us like the "*one* rose of the wilderness left on its stalk," and we grieve to see it crushed and trodden down so rudely.

The innocence, the enthusiasm, the exalted life and stern fate of Louisa and Ferdinand give a powerful charm to this tragedy: it is everywhere interspersed with pieces of fine eloquence, and scenes which move us by their dignity or pathos. We recollect few passages of a more overpowering nature than the conclusion, where Ferdinand, beguiled by the most diabolical machinations to disbelieve the virtue of his mistress, puts himself and her to death by poison. There is a gloomy and solemn might in his despair; though over-whelmed, he seems invincible: his enemies have blinded and imprisoned him in their deceptions; but only that, like Samson, he may overturn his prison-house, and bury himself, and all that have wronged him, in its ruins.

The other characters of the play, though in general properly sustained, are not sufficiently remarkable to claim much of our attention. Wurm, the chief counsellor and agent of the un-principled, calculating Father, is wicked enough; but there is no great singularity in his wickedness. He is little more than the dry, cool, and now somewhat vulgar miscreant, the villanous Attorney of modern novels. Kalb also is but a worthless subject, and what is worse, but indifferently handled. He is meant for the feather-brained thing of tags and laces, which frequently inhabits courts; but he wants the grace and agility proper to the species; he is less a fool than a blockhead, less perverted than totally inane. Schiller's strength lay not in comedy, but in something far higher. The great merit of the present work consists in the characters of the hero and heroine; and in this respect it ranks at the very head of its class. As a tragedy of common life, we know of few rivals to it, certainly of no superior.

The production of three such pieces as the *Robbers, Fiesco,* and *Kabale und Liebe,* already announced to the world that another great and original mind had appeared, from whose maturity, when such was the promise of its youth, the highest expectations might be formed. These three plays stand related to each other in regard to their nature and form, as well as date: they exhibit the progressive state of Schiller's education; show us the fiery enthusiasm of youth, exasperated into wildness, astonishing in its movements rather than sublime; and the same enthusiasm gradually yielding to the sway of reason, gradually using itself to the constraints prescribed by sound judgment and more extensive knowledge. Of the three, the *Robbers* is doubtless the most singular, and likely perhaps to be the most widely popular: but the latter two are of more real worth in the eye of taste, and will better bear a careful and rigorous study.

With the appearance of *Fiesco* and its companion, the first period of Schiller's literary history may conclude. The stormy confusions of his youth were now subsiding; after all his aberrations, repulses, and perplexed wanderings, he was at length about to reach his true destination, and times of more serenity began to open for him. Two such tragedies as he had lately offered to the world made it easier for his friend Dalberg to second his pretensions. Schiller was at last gratified by the fulfilment of his favorite scheme; in September 1783, he went to Mannheim, as poet to the theatre, a post of respectability and reasonable profit, to the duties of which he forthwith addressed himself with all his heart. He was not long afterwards elected a member of the German Society established for literary objects in Mannheim; and he valued the honor, not only as a testimony of respect from a highly estimable quarter, but also as a means of uniting him more closely with men of kindred pursuits and tempers: and what was more than all, of quieting forever his apprehensions from the government at Stuttgard. Since his arrival at Mannheim, one or two suspicious incidents had again alarmed him on this head; but being now acknowledged as a subject of the Elector Palatine, naturalized by law in his new country, he had nothing more to fear from the Duke of Würtemberg.

Satisfied with his moderate income, safe, free, and surrounded by friends that loved and honored him, Schiller now looked confidently forward to what all his efforts had been a search and hitherto a fruitless search for, an undisturbed life of intellectual labor. What effect this happy aspect of his circumstances must have produced upon him may be easily conjectured. Through many years he had been inured to agitation and distress; now peace and liberty and hope, sweet in themselves, were sweeter for their novelty. For the first time in his life, he saw himself allowed to obey without reluctance the ruling bias of his nature; for the first time inclination and duty went hand in hand. His activity awoke with renovated force in this favorable scene; long-thwarted, half-forgotten projects again kindled into brightness, as the possibility of their accomplishment became apparent: Schiller glowed with a generous pride when he felt his faculties at his own disposal, and thought of the use he meant to make of them. "All my connections," he said, "are now dissolved. The public is now all to me, my study, my sovereign, my confidant. To the public alone I henceforth belong; before this and no other tribunal will I place myself; this alone do I reverence and fear. Something majestic hovers before me, as I determine now to wear no other fetters but the sentence of the world, to appeal to no other throne but the soul of man."

These expressions are extracted from the preface to his

Thalia, a periodical work which he undertook in 1784, devoted to subjects connected with poetry, and chiefly with the drama. In such sentiments we leave him, commencing the arduous and perilous, but also glorious and sublime duties of a life consecrated to the discovery of truth, and the creation of intellectual beauty. He was now exclusively what is called a *Man of Letters,* for the rest of his days.

PART II.

FROM SCHILLER'S SETTLEMENT AT MANNHEIM TO HIS SETTLEMENT AT JENA.

1783–1790.

IF to know wisdom were to practise it; if fame brought true dignity and peace of mind; or happiness consisted in nourishing the intellect with its appropriate food, and surrounding the imagination with ideal beauty, a literary life would be the most enviable which the lot of this world affords. But the truth is far otherwise. The Man of Letters has no immutable, all-conquering volition, more than other men; to understand and to perform are two very different things with him as with every one. His fame rarely exerts a favorable influence on his dignity of character, and never on his peace of mind: its glitter is external, for the eyes of others; within, it is but the aliment of unrest, the oil cast upon the ever-gnawing fire of ambition, quickening into fresh vehemence the blaze which it stills for a moment. Moreover, this Man of Letters is not wholly made of spirit, but of clay and spirit mixed: his thinking faculties may be nobly trained and exercised, but he must have affections as well as thoughts to make him happy, and food and raiment must be given him or he dies. Far from being the most enviable, his way of life is perhaps, among the many modes by which an ardent mind endeavors to express its activity, the most thickly beset with suffering and degradation. Look at the biography of authors! Except the Newgate Calendar, it is the most sickening chapter in the history of man. The calamities of these people are a fertile topic; and too often their faults and vices have kept pace

(302)

with their calamities. Nor is it difficult to see how this has happened. Talent of any sort is generally accompanied with a peculiar fineness of sensibility; of genius this is the most essential constituent; and life in any shape has sorrows enough for hearts so formed. The employments of literature sharpen this natural tendency; the vexations that accompany them frequently exasperate it into morbid soreness. The cares and toils of literature are the business of life; its delights are too ethereal and too transient to furnish that perennial flow of satisfaction, coarse but plenteous and substantial, of which happiness in this world of ours is made. The most finished efforts of the mind give it little pleasure, frequently they give it pain; for men's aims are ever far beyond their strength. And the outward recompense of these undertakings, the distinction they confer, is of still smaller value: the desire for it is insatiable even when successful; and when baffled, it issues in jealousy and envy, and every pitiful and painful feeling. So keen a temperament with so little to restrain or satisfy, so much to distress or tempt it, produces contradictions which few are adequate to reconcile. Hence the unhappiness of literary men, hence their faults and follies.

Thus literature is apt to form a dangerous and discontenting occupation even for the amateur. But for him whose rank and worldly comforts depend on it, who does not live to write, but writes to live, its difficulties and perils are fearfully increased. Few spectacles are more afflicting than that of such a man, so gifted and so fated, so jostled and tossed to and fro in the rude bustle of life, the buffetings of which he is so little fitted to endure. Cherishing, it may be, the loftiest thoughts, and clogged with the meanest wants; of pure and holy purposes, yet ever driven from the straight path by the pressure of necessity, or the impulse of passion; thirsting for glory, and frequently in want of daily bread; hovering between the empyrean of his fancy and the squalid desert of reality; cramped and foiled in his most strenuous exertions; dissatisfied with his best performances, disgusted with his fortune, this Man of Letters too often spends his weary days in conflicts with obscure misery: harassed, chagrined, debased, or maddened; the victim at once of tragedy and farce; the last forlorn outpost in the war of Mind against Matter. Many are the noble souls that have perished bitterly, with their tasks unfinished, under these corroding woes! Some in utter famine, like Otway; some in dark insanity, like Cowper and Collins; some, like Chatterton, have sought out a more stern quietus, and turning their indignant steps away from a world which refused them welcome, have taken refuge in that strong Fortress, where poverty and cold neglect, and the thousand natural shocks which flesh is heir to, could not reach them any more.

Yet among these men are to be found the brightest specimens and the chief benefactors of mankind! It is they that keep awake the finer parts of our souls; that give us better aims than power or pleasure, and withstand the total sovereignty of Mammon in this earth. They are the vanguard in the march of mind; the intellectual Backwoodsmen, reclaiming from the idle wilderness new territories for the thought and the activity of their happier brethren. Pity that from all their conquests, so rich in benefit to others, themselves should reap so little! But it is vain to murmur. They are volunteers in this cause; they weighed the charms of it against the perils: and they must abide the results of their decision, as all must. The hardships of the course they follow are formidable, but not all inevitable; and to such as pursue it rightly, it is not without its great rewards. If an author's life is more agitated and more painful than that of others, it may also be made more spirit-stirring and exalted: fortune may render him unhappy; it is only himself that can make him despicable. The history of genius has, in fact, its bright side as well as its dark. And if it is distressing to survey the misery, and what is worse, the debasement of so many gifted men, it is doubly cheering on the other hand to reflect on the few, who, amid the temptations and sorrows to which life in all its provinces and most in theirs is liable, have travelled through it in calm and virtuous majesty, and are now hallowed in our memories, not less for their conduct than their writings. Such men are the flower of this lower world: to such alone can the epithet of great be applied with its true emphasis. There is a congruity in their proceedings which one loves to contemplate: "he who would write heroic poems, should make his whole life a heroic poem."

So thought our Milton; and, what was more difficult, he acted so. To Milton, the moral king of authors, a heroic multitude, out of many ages and countries, might be joined; a "cloud of witnesses," that encompass the true literary man throughout his pilgrimage, inspiring him to lofty emulation, cheering his solitary thoughts with hope, teaching him to struggle, to endure, to conquer difficulties, or, in failure and heavy sufferings, to

>   .   .   .   "arm th' obdured breast
> With stubborn patience as with triple steel."

To this august series, in his own degree, the name of Schiller may be added.

Schiller lived in more peaceful times than Milton; his history is less distinguished by obstacles surmounted, or sacrifices made to principle; yet he had his share of trials to encounter; and the admirers of his writings need not feel ashamed of the way in which he bore it. One virtue, the parent of many others, and the most essential of any, in his circumstances, he possessed in a supreme degree; he was devoted with entire and unchanging ardor to the cause he had embarked in. The extent of his natural endowments might have served, with a less eager character, as an excuse for long periods of indolence, broken only by fits of casual exertion: with him it was but a new incitement to improve and develop them. The Ideal Man that lay within him, the image of himself as he *should* be, was formed upon a strict and curious standard; and to reach this constantly approached and constantly receding emblem of perfection, was the unwearied effort of his life. This crowning principle of conduct, never ceasing to inspire his energetic mind, introduced a consistency into his actions, a firm coherence into his character, which the changeful condition of his history rendered of peculiar importance. His resources, his place of residence, his associates, his worldly prospects, might vary as they pleased; this purpose did not vary; it was ever present with him to nerve every better faculty of his head and

heart, to invest the chequered vicissitudes of his fortune with
a dignity derived from himself. The zeal of his nature overcame the temptations to that loitering and indecision, that
fluctuation between sloth and consuming toil, that infirmity of
resolution, with all its tormenting and enfeebling consequences,
to which a literary man, working as he does at a solitary task,
uncalled for by any pressing tangible demand, and to be recom-
pensed by distant and dubious advantage, is especially exposed.
Unity of aim, aided by ordinary vigor of character, will generally insure perseverance; a quality not ranked among the
cardinal virtues, but as essential as any of them to the proper
conduct of life. Nine-tenths of the miseries and vices of mankind proceed from idleness : with men of quick minds, to whom
it is especially pernicious, this habit is commonly the fruit of
many disappointments and schemes oft baffled ; and men fail
in their schemes not so much from the want of strength as
from the ill-direction of it. The weakest living creature, by
concentrating his powers on a single object, can accomplish
something : the strongest, by dispersing his over many, may
fail to accomplish anything. The drop, by continual falling,
bores its passage through the hardest rock; the hasty torrent
rushes over it with hideous uproar, and leaves no trace behind.
Few men have applied more steadfastly to the business of
their life, or been more resolutely diligent than Schiller.

The profession of theatrical poet was, in his present circumstances, particularly favorable to the maintenance of this wholesome state of mind. In the fulfilment of its duties, while he
gratified his own dearest predilections, he was likewise warmly
seconded by the prevailing taste of the public. The interest
excited by the stage, and the importance attached to everything connected with it, are greater in Germany than in any
other part of Europe, not excepting France, or even Paris.
Nor, as in Paris, is the stage in German towns considered
merely as a mental recreation, an elegant and pleasant mode
of filling up the vacancy of tedious evenings : in Germany, it
has the advantage of being comparatively new ; and its exhibitions are directed to a class of minds attuned to a far higher
pitch of feeling. The Germans are accused of a proneness to

amplify and systematize, to admire with excess, and to find, in whatever calls forth their applause, an epitome of a thousand excellencies, which no one else can discover in it. Their discussions on the theatre do certainly give color to this charge. Nothing, at least to an English reader, can appear more disproportionate than the influence they impute to the stage, and the quantity of anxious investigation they devote to its concerns.

With us, the question about the moral tendency of theatrical amusements is now very generally consigned to the meditation of debating clubs, and speculative societies of young men under age; with our neighbors it is a weighty subject of inquiry for minds of almost the highest order. With us, the stage is considered as a harmless pastime, wholesome because it occupies the man by occupying his mental, not his sensual faculties; one of the many departments of fictitious representation; perhaps the most exciting; but also the most transitory; sometimes hurtful, generally beneficial, just as the rest are; entitled to no peculiar regard, and far inferior in its effect to many others which have no special apparatus for their application. The Germans, on the contrary, talk of it as of some new organ for refining the hearts and minds of men; a sort of lay pulpit, the worthy ally of the sacred one, and perhaps even better fitted to exalt some of our nobler feelings; because its objects are much more varied, and because it speaks to us through many avenues, addressing the eye by its pomp and decorations, the ear by its harmonies, and the heart and imagination by its poetical embellishments, and heroic acts and sentiments. Influences still more mysterious are hinted at, if not directly announced. An idea seems to lurk obscurely at the bottom of certain of their abstruse and elaborate speculations, as if the stage were destined to replace some of those sublime illusions which the progress of reason is fast driving from the earth; as if its pageantry, and allegories, and figurative shadowing-forth of things, might supply men's nature with much of that quickening nourishment which we once derived from the superstitions and mythologies of darker ages. Viewing the matter in this light, they proceed in the management

of it with all due earnestness. Hence their minute and painful investigations of the origin of dramatic emotion, of its
various kinds and degrees; their subdivisions of romantic and
heroic and romantico-heroic, and the other endless jargon that
encumbers their critical writings. The zeal of the people corresponds with that of their instructors. The want of more
important public interests naturally contributes still farther
to the prominence of this, the discussion of which is not forbidden, or sure to be without effect. Literature attracts nearly
all the powerful thought that circulates in Germany; and the
theatre is the great nucleus of German literature.

It was to be expected that Schiller would participate in a
feeling so universal, and so accordant with his own wishes and
prospects. The theatre of Mannheim was at that period one of
the best in Germany; he felt proud of the share which he had
in conducting it, and exerted himself with his usual alacrity
in promoting its various objects. Connected with the duties
of his office, was the more personal duty of improving his own
faculties, and extending his knowledge of the art which he
had engaged to cultivate. He read much, and studied more.
The perusal of Corneille, Racine, Voltaire, and the other
French classics, could not be without advantage to one whose
exuberance of power, and defect of taste, were the only faults
he had ever been reproached with; and the sounder ideas thus
acquired, he was constantly busy in exemplifying by attempts
of his own. His projected translations from Shakspeare and
the French were postponed for the present: indeed, except in
the instance of *Macbeth*, they were never finished: his *Con-
radin von Schwaben*, and a second part of the *Robbers*, were
likewise abandoned: but a number of minor undertakings
sufficiently evinced his diligence: and *Don Carlos*, which he
had now seriously commenced, was occupying all his poetical
faculties.

Another matter he had much at heart was the setting forth
of a periodical work, devoted to the concerns of the stage. In
this enterprise, Schiller had expected the patronage and co-
operation of the German Society, of which he was a member.
It did not strike him that any other motive than a genuine

love of art, and zeal for its advancement, could have induced
men to join such a body.   But the zeal of the German Society
was more according to knowledge than that of their new associate: they listened with approving ear to his vivid representations, and wide-spreading projects, but declined taking any
part in the execution of them.   Dalberg alone seemed willing
to support him.   Mortified, but not disheartened by their
coldness, Schiller reckoned up his means of succeeding without them.   The plan of his work was contracted within
narrower limits; he determined to commence it on his own
resources.   After much delay, the first number of the *Rhei-
nische Thalia*, enriched by three acts of *Don Carlos*, appeared
in 1785.   It was continued, with one short interruption, till
1794.   The main purpose of the work being the furtherance of
dramatic art, and the extension and improvement of the public
taste for such entertainments, its chief contents are easy to be
guessed at; theatrical criticisms, essays on the nature of the
stage, its history in various countries, its moral and intellectual effects, and the best methods of producing them.   A part
of the publication was open to poetry and miscellaneous
discussion.

Meditating so many subjects so assiduously, Schiller knew
not what it was to be unemployed.   Yet the task of composing dramatic varieties, of training players, and deliberating
in the theatrical senate, or even of expressing philosophically
his opinions on these points, could not wholly occupy such a
mind as his.   There were times when, notwithstanding his
own prior habits, and all the vaunting of dramaturgists, he
felt that their scenic glories were but an empty show, a lying
refuge, where there was no abiding rest for the soul.   His
eager spirit turned away from their paltry world of paste-
board, to dwell among the deep and serious interests of the
living world of men.   The *Thalia*, besides its dramatic speculations and performances, contains several of his poems, which
indicate that his attention, though officially directed else-
whither, was alive to all the common concerns of humanity;
that he looked on life not more as a writer than as a man.
The *Laura*, whom he celebrates, was not a vision of the mind;

but a living fair one, whom he saw daily, and loved in the secrecy of his heart. His *Gruppe aus dem Tartarus* (Group from Tartarus), his *Kindesmörderinn* (Infanticide), are products of a mind brooding over dark and mysterious things. While improving in the art of poetry, in the capability of uttering his thoughts in the form best adapted to express them, he was likewise improving in the more valuable art of thought itself; and applying it not only to the business of the imagination, but also to those profound and solemn inquiries, which every reasonable mortal is called to engage with.

In particular, the *Philosophische Briefe*, written about this period, exhibits Schiller in a new, and to us more interesting point of view. Julius and Raphael are the emblems of his own fears and his own hopes; their *Philosophic Letters* unfold to us many a gloomy conflict that had passed in the secret chambers of their author's soul. Sceptical doubts on the most important of all subjects were natural to such an understanding as Schiller's; but his heart was not of a temper to rest satisfied with doubts; or to draw a sorry compensation for them from the pride of superior acuteness, or the vulgar pleasure of producing an effect on others by assailing their dearest and holiest persuasions. With him the question about the essence of our being was not a subject for shallow speculation, charitably named scientific; still less for vain jangling and polemical victories: it was a fearful mystery, which it concerned all the deepest sympathies and most sublime anticipations of his mind to have explained. It is no idle curiosity, but the shuddering voice of nature that asks: "If our happiness depend on the harmonious play of the sensorium; if our conviction may waver with the beating of the pulse?" What Schiller's ultimate opinions on these points were, we are nowhere specially informed. That his heart was orthodox, that the whole universe was for him a temple, in which he offered up the continual sacrifice of devout adoration, his works and life bear noble testimony; yet, here and there, his fairest visions seem as if suddenly sicklied over with a pale cast of doubt; a withering shadow seems to flit across his soul, and chill it in his loftiest moods. The dark condition of the man who longs to believe and longs in vain, he can represent with a verisimilitude and touching beauty, which shows it to have been familiar to himself. Apart from their ingenuity, there is a certain severe pathos in some of these passages, which affects us with a peculiar emotion. The hero of another work is made to express himself in these terms : —

"What went before and what will follow me, I regard as two black impenetrable curtains, which hang down at the two extremities of human life, and which no living man has yet drawn aside. Many hundreds of generations have already stood before them with their torches, guessing anxiously what lies behind. On the curtain of Futurity, many see their own shadows, the forms of their passions enlarged and put in motion ; they shrink in terror at this image of themselves. Poets, philosophers, and founders of states, have painted this curtain with their dreams, more smiling or more dark, as the sky above them was cheerful or gloomy ; and their pictures deceive the eye when viewed from a distance. Many jugglers too make profit of this our universal curiosity : by their strange mummeries, they have set the outstretched fancy in amazement. A deep silence reigns behind this curtain ; no one once within it will answer those he has left without ; all you can hear is a hollow echo of your question, as if you shouted into a chasm. To the other side of this curtain we are all bound : men grasp hold of it as they pass, trembling, uncertain who may stand within it to receive them, *quid sit id quod tantum morituri vident.* Some unbelieving people there have been, who have asserted that this curtain did but make a mockery of men, and that nothing could be seen because nothing *was* behind it : but to convince these people, the rest have seized them, and hastily pushed them in." [1]

The *Philosophic Letters* paint the struggles of an ardent, enthusiastic, inquisitive spirit to deliver itself from the harassing uncertainties, to penetrate the dread obscurity, which overhangs the lot of man. The first faint scruples of the Doubter are settled by the maxim : "Believe nothing but

[1] *Der Geisterseher,* Schillers Werke, B. iv. p. 350.

thy own reason; there is nothing holier than truth." But Reason, employed in such an inquiry, can do but half the work: she is like the Conjuror that has pronounced the spell of invocation, but has forgot the counter-word; spectres and shadowy forms come crowding at his summons; in endless multitudes they press and hover round his magic circle, and the terror-struck Black-artist cannot lay them. Julius finds that on rejecting the primary dictates of feeling, the system of dogmatical belief, he is driven to the system of materialism. Recoiling in horror from this dead and cheerless creed, he toils and wanders in the labyrinths of pantheism, seeking comfort and rest, but finding none; till, baffled and tired, and sick at heart, he seems inclined, as far as we can judge, to renounce the dreary problem altogether, to shut the eyes of his too keen understanding, and take refuge under the shade of Revelation. The anxieties and errors of Julius are described in glowing terms; his intellectual subtleties are mingled with the eloquence of intense feeling. The answers of his friend are in a similar style; intended not more to convince than to persuade. The whole work is full of passion as well as acuteness; the impress of a philosophic and poetic mind striving with all its vast energies to make its poetry and its philosophy agree. Considered as exhibiting the state of Schiller's thoughts at this period, it possesses a peculiar interest. In other respects there is little in it to allure us. It is short and incomplete; there is little originality in the opinions it expresses, and none in the form of its composition. As an argument on either side, it is too rhetorical to be of much weight; it abandons the inquiry when its difficulties and its value are becoming greatest, and breaks off abruptly without arriving at any conclusion. Schiller has surveyed the dark Serbonian bog of Infidelity: but he has made no causeway through it: the *Philosophic Letters* are a fragment.

Amid employments so varied, with health, and freedom from the coarser hardships of life, Schiller's feelings might be earnest, but could scarcely be unhappy. His mild and amiable manners, united to such goodness of heart, and such height of accomplishment, endeared him to all classes of society in

Mannheim; Dalberg was still his warm friend; Schwann and
Laura he conversed with daily. His genius was fast enlarging
its empire, and fast acquiring more complete command of it;
he was loved and admired, rich in the enjoyment of present
activity and fame, and richer in the hope of what was coming.
Yet in proportion as his faculties and his prospects expanded,
he began to view his actual situation with less and less contentment. For a season after his arrival, it was natural that
Mannheim should appear to him as land does to the ship-
wrecked mariner, full of gladness and beauty, merely because
it is land. It was equally natural that, after a time, this sentiment should abate and pass away; that his place of refuge
should appear but as other places, only with its difficulties and
discomforts aggravated by their nearness. His revenue was
inconsiderable here, and dependent upon accidents for its continuance; a share in directing the concerns of a provincial
theatre, a task not without its irritations, was little adequate
to satisfy the wishes of a mind like his. Schiller longed for
a wider sphere of action; the world was all before him; he
lamented that he should still be lingering on the mere out-
skirts of its business; that he should waste so much time and
effort in contending with the irascible vanity of players, or
watching the ebbs and flows of public taste; in resisting small
grievances, and realizing a small result. He determined upon
leaving Mannheim. If destitute of other holds, his prudence
might still have taught him to smother this unrest, the never-
failing inmate of every human breast, and patiently continue
where he was: but various resources remained to him, and
various hopes invited him from other quarters. The produce
of his works, or even the exercise of his profession, would
insure him a competence anywhere; the former had already
gained him distinction and good-will in every part of Germany.
The first number of his *Thalia* had arrived at the court of
Hessen-Darmstadt while the Duke of Sachsen-Weimar happened to be there: the perusal of the first acts of *Don Carlos* had introduced the author to that enlightened prince,
who expressed his satisfaction and respect by transmitting
him the title of Counsellor. A less splendid but not less

truthful or pleasing testimonial had lately reached him from Leipzig.

"Some days ago," he writes, "I met with a very flattering and agreeable surprise. There came to me, out of Leipzig, from unknown hands, four parcels, and as many letters, written with the highest enthusiasm towards me, and overflowing with poetical devotion. They were accompanied by four miniature portraits, two of which are of very beautiful young ladies, and by a pocket-book sewed in the finest taste. Such a present, from people who can have no interest in it, but to let me know that they wish me well, and thank me for some cheerful hours, I prize extremely; the loudest applause of the world could scarcely have flattered me so agreeably."

Perhaps this incident, trifling as it was, might not be without effect in deciding the choice of his future residence. Leipzig had the more substantial charm of being a centre of activity and commerce of all sorts, that of literature not excepted; and it contained some more effectual friends of Schiller than these his unseen admirers. He resolved on going thither. His wishes and intentions are minutely detailed to Huber, his chief intimate at Leipzig, in a letter written shortly before his removal. We translate it for the hints it gives us of Schiller's tastes and habits at that period of his history.

"This, then, is probably the last letter I shall write to you from Mannheim. The time from the fifteenth of March has hung upon my hands, like a trial for life; and, thank Heaven! I am now ten whole days nearer you. And now, my good friend, as you have already consented to take my entire confidence upon your shoulders, allow me the pleasure of leading you into the interior of my domestic wishes.

"In my new establishment at Leipzig, I purpose to avoid one error, which has plagued me a great deal here in Mannheim. It is this: No longer to conduct my own housekeeping, and also no longer to live alone. The former is not by any means a business I excel in. It costs me less to execute a whole conspiracy, in five acts, than to settle my domestic arrangements for a week; and poetry, you yourself know, is but a dangerous

assistant in calculations of economy.   My mind is drawn different ways; I fall headlong out of my ideal world, if a holed
stocking remind me of the real world.

"As to the other point, I require for my private happiness
to have a true warm friend that would be ever at my hand,
like my better angel; to whom I could communicate my nascent ideas in the very act of conceiving them, not needing to
transmit them, as at present, by letters or long visits.   Nay,
when this friend of mine lives beyond the four corners of my
house, the trifling circumstance, that in order to reach him I
must cross the street, dress myself, and so forth, will of itself
destroy the enjoyment of the moment, and the train of my
thoughts is torn in pieces before I see him.

"Observe you, my good fellow, these are petty matters; but
petty matters often bear the weightiest result in the management of life.   I know myself better than perhaps a thousand
mothers' sons know themselves; I understand how much, and
frequently how little, I require to be completely happy.   The
question therefore is: Can I get this wish of my heart fulfilled
in Leipzig?

"If it were possible that I could make a lodgment with
you, all my cares on that head would be removed.   I am no
bad neighbor, as perhaps you imagine; I have pliancy enough
to suit myself to another, and here and there withal a certain
knack, as Yorick says, at helping to make him merrier and
better.   Failing this, if you could find me any person that
would undertake my small economy, everything would still be
well.

"I want nothing but a bedroom, which might also be my
working room; and another chamber for receiving visits.   The
house-gear necessary for me are a good chest of drawers, a
desk, a bed and sofa, a table, and a few chairs.   With these
conveniences, my accommodation were sufficiently provided
for.

"I cannot live on the ground-floor, nor close by the ridge-
tile; also my windows positively must not look into the
churchyard.   I love men, and therefore like their bustle.
If I cannot so arrange it that we (meaning the *quintuple*

alliance [1]) shall mess together, I would engage at the *table d'hôte* of the inn; for I had rather fast than eat without company, large, or else particularly good.

"I write all this to you, my dearest friend, to forewarn you of my silly tastes; and, at all events, that I may put it in your power to take some preparatory steps, in one place or another, for my settlement. My demands are, in truth, confoundedly naïve, but your goodness has spoiled me.

"The first part of the *Thalia* must already be in your possession; the doom of *Carlos* will ere now be pronounced. Yet I will take it from you orally. Had we five not been acquainted, who knows but we might have become so on occasion of this very *Carlos?* "

Schiller went accordingly to Leipzig; though whether Huber received him, or he found his humble necessaries elsewhere, we have not learned. He arrived in the end of March, 1785, after eighteen months' residence at Mannheim. The reception he met with, his amusements, occupations, and prospects are described in a letter to the Kammerrath Schwann, a bookseller at Mannheim, alluded to above. Except Dalberg, Schwann had been his earliest friend; he was now endeared to him by subsequent familiarity, not of letters and writing, but of daily intercourse; and what was more than all, by the circumstance that *Laura* was his daughter. The letter, it will be seen, was written with a weightier object than the pleasure of describing Leipzig: it is dated 24th April, 1785.

"You have an indubitable right to be angry at my long silence; yet I know your goodness too well to be in doubt that you will pardon me.

"When a man, unskilled as I am in the busy world, visits Leipzig for the first time, during the Fair, it is, if not excusable, at least intelligible, that among the multitude of strange things running through his head, he should for a few days lose recollection of himself. Such, my dearest friend, has till to-day been nearly my case; and even now I have to steal from many avocations the pleasing moments which, in idea, I mean to spend with you at Mannheim.

[1] Who the other three were is nowhere particularly mentioned.

"Our journey hither, of which Herr Götz will give you a circumstantial description, was the most dismal you can well imagine; Bog, Snow and Rain were the three wicked foes that by turns assailed us; and though we used an additional pair of horses all the way from Vach, yet our travelling, which should have ended on Friday, was spun out till Sunday. It is universally maintained that the Fair has visibly suffered by the shocking state of the roads; at all events, even in my eyes, the crowd of sellers and buyers is far *beneath* the description I used to get of it in the Empire.

"In the very first week of my residence here, I made innumerable new acquaintances; among whom, Weisse, Oeser, Hiller, Zollikofer, Professor Huber, Jünger, the famous actor Reinike, a few merchants' families of the place, and some Berlin people, are the most interesting. During Fair-time, as you know well, a person cannot get the *full* enjoyment of any one; our attention to the individual is dissipated in the noisy multitude.

"My most pleasant recreation hitherto has been to visit Richter's coffee-house, where I constantly find half the *world* of Leipzig assembled, and extend my acquaintance with foreigners and natives.

"From various quarters I have had some alluring invitations to Berlin and Dresden; which it will be difficult for me to withstand. It is quite a peculiar case, my friend, to have a literary name. The few men of worth and consideration who offer you their intimacy on that score, and whose regard is really worth coveting, are too disagreeably counterweighed by the baleful swarm of creatures who keep humming round you, like so many flesh-flies; gape at you as if you were a monster, and condescend moreover, on the strength of one or two blotted sheets, to present themselves as colleagues. Many people cannot understand how a man that wrote the *Robbers* should look like another son of Adam. Close-cut hair, at the very least, and postilion's boots, and a hunter's whip, were expected.

"Many families are in the habit here of spending the summer in some of the adjacent villages, and so enjoying the pleasures of the country. I mean to pass a few months in Gohlis, which lies only a quarter of a league from Leipzig, with a very pleasant walk leading to it, through the Rosenthal. Here I purpose being very diligent, working at *Carlos* and the *Thalia;* that so, which perhaps will please you more than anything, I may gradually and silently return to my medical profession. I long impatiently for that epoch of my life, when my prospects may be settled and determined, when I may follow my darling pursuits merely for my own pleasure. At one time I studied medicine *con amore;* could I not do it now with still greater keenness ?

"This, my best friend, might of itself convince you of the truth and firmness of my purpose; but what should offer you the most complete security on that point, what must banish all your doubts about my steadfastness, I have yet kept secret. *Now or never* I must speak it out. Distance alone gives me courage to express the wish of my heart. Frequently enough, when I used to have the happiness of being near you, has this confession hovered on my tongue; but my confidence always forsook me, when I tried to utter it. My best friend! Your goodness, your affection, your generosity of heart, have encouraged me in a hope which I can justify by nothing but the friendship and respect you have always shown me. My free, unconstrained access to your house afforded me the opportunity of intimate acquaintance with your amiable daughter; and the frank, kind treatment with which both you and she honored me, tempted my heart to entertain the bold wish of becoming your son. My prospects have hitherto been dim and vague; they now begin to alter in my favor. I will strive with more continuous vigor when the goal is clear; do you decide whether I can reach it, when the dearest wish of my heart supports my zeal.

"Yet two short years and my whole fortune will be determined. I feel how *much* I ask, how boldly, and with how little right I ask it. A year is past since this thought took possession of my soul; but my esteem for you and your excellent daughter was too high to allow room for a wish, which at that time I could found on no solid basis. I made it a duty

with myself to visit your house less frequently, and to dissi
pate such feelings by absence; but this poor artifice did not
avail me.

"The Duke of Weimar was the first person to whom I disclosed myself. His anticipating goodness, and the declaration
that he took an interest in my happiness, induced me to confess that this happiness depended on a union with your noble
daughter; and he expressed his satisfaction at my choice. I
have reason to hope that he will do more, should it come to
the point of completing my happiness by this union.

"I shall add nothing farther: I know well that hundreds
of others might afford your daughter a more splendid fate
than I at this moment can promise her; but that any other
heart can be more worthy of her, I venture to deny. Your
decision, which I look for with impatience and fearful expectation, will determine whether I may venture to write in
person to your daughter. Fare you well, forever loved by —
Your —

"FRIEDRICH SCHILLER."

Concerning this proposal, we have no farther information
to communicate; except that the parties did not marry, and
did not cease being friends. That Schiller obtained the permission he concludes with requesting, appears from other
sources. Three years afterwards, in writing to the same
person, he alludes emphatically to his eldest daughter; and
what is more ominous, *apologizes* for his silence to her.
Schiller's situation at this period was such as to preclude
the idea of present marriage; perhaps, in the prospect of it,
Laura and he commenced corresponding; and before the
wished-for change of fortune had arrived, both of them,
attracted to other objects, had lost one another in the vor-
tex of life, and ceased to regard their finding one another as
desirable.

Schiller's medical project, like many which he formed, never
came to any issue. In moments of anxiety, amid the fluctu
ations of his lot, the thought of this profession floated through
his mind, as of a distant stronghold, to which, in time of need,

he might retire. But literature was too intimately interwoven with his dispositions and his habits to be seriously interfered with; it was only at brief intervals that the pleasure of pursuing it exclusively seemed over-balanced by its inconveniences. He needed a more certain income than poetry could yield him; but he wished to derive it from some pursuit less alien to his darling study. Medicine he never practised after leaving Stuttgard.

In the mean time, whatever he might afterwards resolve on, he determined to complete his *Carlos*, the half of which, composed a considerable time before, had lately been running the gauntlet of criticism in the *Thalia*.[1] With this for his chief occupation, Gohlis or Leipzig for his residence, and a circle of chosen friends for his entertainment, Schiller's days went happily along. His *Lied an die Freude* (Song to Joy), one of his most spirited and beautiful lyrical productions, was composed here: it bespeaks a mind impetuous even in its gladness, and overflowing with warm and earnest emotions.

But the love of change is grounded on the difference between anticipation and reality, and dwells with man till the age when habit becomes stronger than desire, or anticipation ceases to be hope. Schiller did not find that his establishment at Leipzig, though pleasant while it lasted, would realize his ulterior views: he yielded to some of his "alluring invitations," and went to Dresden in the end of summer. Dresden contained many persons who admired him, more who admired his fame, and a few who loved himself. Among the latter, the Appellationsrath Körner deserves especial mention.[2] Schiller found a true friend in Körner, and made his house a home. He parted his time between Dresden and Löschwitz, near it, where that gentleman resided: it was here that *Don Carlos*, the printing of which was meanwhile

---

[1] Wieland's rather harsh and not too judicious sentence on it may be seen at large in Gruber's *Wieland Geschildert*, B. ii. s. 571.

[2] The well-written life, prefixed to the Stuttgard and Tübingen edition of Schiller's works, is by this Körner. The Theodor Körner, whose *Lyre and Sword* became afterwards famous, was his son.

proceeding at Leipzig, received its completion and last corrections.[1] It was published in 1786.

The story of Don Carlos seems peculiarly adapted for dramatists. The spectacle of a royal youth condemned to death by his father, of which happily our European annals furnish but another example, is among the most tragical that can be figured; the character of that youth, the intermixture of bigotry and jealousy, and love, with the other strong passions, which brought on his fate, afford a combination of circumstances, affecting in themselves, and well calculated for the basis of deeply interesting fiction. Accordingly they have not been neglected: Carlos has often been the theme of poets; particularly since the time when his history, recorded by the Abbé St. Réal, was exposed in more brilliant colors to the inspection of every writer, and almost of every reader.

The Abbé St. Réal was a dexterous artist in that half-illicit species of composition, the historic novel: in the course of his

[1] In vol. x. of the Vienna edition of Schiller are some ludicrous verses, almost his sole attempt in the way of drollery, bearing a title equivalent to this: "To the Right Honorable the Board of Washers, the most humble Memorial of a downcast Tragic Poet, at Löschwitz;" of which Doering gives the following account. "The first part of *Don Carlos* being already printed, by Göschen, in Leipzig, the poet, pressed for the remainder, felt himself obliged to stay behind from an excursion which the Körner family were making, in a fine autumn day. Unluckily, the lady of the house, thinking Schiller was to go along with them, had locked all her cupboards and the cellar. Schiller found himself without meat or drink, or even wood for fuel; still farther exasperated by the dabbling of some washer-maids beneath his window, he produced these lines." The poem is of the kind which cannot be translated; the first three stanzas are as follows:—

> "Die Wäsche klatscht vor meiner Thür,
>   Es plärrt die Küchenzofe,
> Und mich, mich führt das Flügelthier
>   Zu König Philips Hofe.

> "Ich eile durch die Gallerie
>   Mit schnellem Schritt, belausche
> Dort die Prinzessin Eboli
>   Im süssen Liebesrausche.

> "Schon ruft das schöne Weib: Triumph!
>   Schon hör' ich — Tod und Hölle!
> Was hör' ich — einen nassen Strumpf
>   Geworfen in die Welle."

operations, he lighted on these incidents; and, by filling up according to his fancy, what historians had only sketched to him, by amplifying, beautifying, suppressing, and arranging, he worked the whole into a striking little narrative, distinguished by all the symmetry, the sparkling graces, the vigorous description, and keen thought, which characterize his other writings. This French Sallust, as his countrymen have named him, has been of use to many dramatists. His *Conjuraison contre Venise* furnished Otway with the outline of his best tragedy; *Epicaris* has more than once appeared upon the stage; and *Don Carlos* has been dramatized in almost all the languages of Europe. Besides Otway's *Carlos*, so famous at its first appearance, many tragedies on this subject have been written: most of them are gathered to their final rest; some are fast going thither; two bid fair to last for ages. Schiller and Alfieri have both drawn their plot from St. Réal; the former has expanded and added; the latter has compressed and abbreviated.

Schiller's *Carlos* is the first of his plays that bears the stamp of anything like full maturity. The opportunities he had enjoyed for extending his knowledge of men and things, the sedulous practice of the art of composition, the study of purer models, had not been without their full effect. Increase of years had done something for him; diligence had done much more. The ebullience of youth is now chastened into the steadfast energy of manhood; the wild enthusiast, that spurned at the errors of the world, has now become the enlightened moralist, that laments their necessity, or endeavors to find out their remedy. A corresponding alteration is visible in the external form of the work, in its plot and diction. The plot is contrived with great ingenuity, embodying the result of much study, both dramatic and historical. The language is blank verse, not prose, as in the former works; it is more careful and regular, less ambitious in its object, but more certain of attaining it. Schiller's mind had now reached its full stature: he felt and thought more justly; he could better express what he felt and thought.

The merit we noticed in *Fiesco*, the fidelity with which the scene of action is brought before us, is observable to a still greater degree in *Don Carlos*. The Spanish court in the end of the sixteenth century; its rigid, cold formalities; its cruel, bigoted, but proud-spirited grandees; its inquisitors and priests; and Philip, its head, the epitome at once of its good and its bad qualities, in all his complex interests, are exhibited with wonderful distinctness and address. Nor is it at the surface or the outward movements alone that we look; we are taught the mechanism of their characters, as well as shown it in action. The stony-hearted Despot himself must have been an object of peculiar study to the author. Narrow in his understanding, dead in his affections, from his birth the lord of Europe, Philip has existed all his days above men, not among them. Locked up within himself, a stranger to every generous and kindly emotion, his gloomy spirit has had no employment but to strengthen or increase its own elevation, no pleasure but to gratify its own self-will. Superstition, harmonizing with these native tendencies, has added to their force, but scarcely to their hatefulness: it lends them a sort of sacredness in his own eyes, and even a sort of horrid dignity in ours. Philip is not without a certain greatness, the greatness of unlimited external power, and of a will relentless in its dictates, guided by principles, false, but consistent and unalterable. The scene of his existence is haggard, stern and desolate; but it is all his own, and he seems fitted for it. We hate him and fear him; but the poet has taken care to secure him from contempt.

The contrast both of his father's fortune and character are those of Carlos. Few situations of a more affecting kind can be imagined, than the situation of this young, generous and ill-fated prince. From boyhood his heart had been bent on mighty things; he had looked upon the royal grandeur that awaited his maturer years, only as the means of realizing those projects for the good of men, which his beneficent soul was ever busied with. His father's dispositions, and the temper of the court, which admitted no development of such ideas, had given the charm of concealment to his feelings; his life had been in prospect; and we are the more attached to him,

that deserving to be glorious and happy, he had but expected
to be either. Bright days, however, seemed approaching;
shut out from the communion of the Albas and Domingos,
among whom he lived a stranger, the communion of another
and far dearer object was to be granted him; Elizabeth's love
seemed to make him independent even of the future, which
it painted with still richer hues. But in a moment she is
taken from him by the most terrible of all visitations; his
bride becomes his mother; and the stroke that deprives him
of her, while it ruins him forever, is more deadly, because
it cannot be complained of without sacrilege, and cannot be
altered by the power of Fate itself. Carlos, as the poet represents him, calls forth our tenderest sympathies. His soul
seems once to have been rich and glorious, like the garden
of Eden; but the desert-wind has passed over it, and smitten
it with perpetual blight. Despair has overshadowed all the
fair visions of his youth; or if he hopes, it is but the gleam
of delirium, which something sterner than even duty extin-
guishes in the cold darkness of death. His energy survives
but to vent itself in wild gusts of reckless passion, or aimless
indignation. There is a touching poignancy in his expression
of the bitter melancholy that oppresses him, in the fixedness
of misery with which he looks upon the faded dreams of
former years, or the fierce ebullitions and dreary pauses
of resolution, which now prompts him to retrieve what he
has lost, now withers into powerlessness, as nature and reason
tell him that it cannot, must not be retrieved.

Elizabeth, no less moving and attractive, is also depicted
with masterly skill. If she returns the passion of her amiable
and once betrothed lover, we but guess at the fact; for so
horrible a thought has never once been whispered to her own
gentle and spotless mind. Yet her heart bleeds for Carlos;
and we see that did not the most sacred feelings of humanity
forbid her, there is no sacrifice she would not make to restore
his peace of mind. By her soothing influence she strives to
calm the agony of his spirit; by her mild winning eloquence
she would persuade him that for Don Carlos other objects
must remain, when his hopes of personal felicity have been

cut off; she would change his love for her into love for the millions of human beings whose destiny depends on his. A meek vestal, yet with the prudence of a queen, and the courage of a matron, with every graceful and generous quality of womanhood harmoniously blended in her nature, she lives in a scene that is foreign to her; the happiness she should have had is beside her, the misery she must endure is around her; yet she utters no regret, gives way to no complaint, but seeks to draw from duty itself a compensation for the cureless evil which duty has inflicted. Many tragic queens are more imposing and majestic than this Elizabeth of Schiller; but there is none who rules over us with a sway so soft and feminine, none whom we feel so much disposed to love as well as reverence.

The virtues of Elizabeth are heightened by comparison with the principles and actions of her attendant, the Princess Eboli. The character of Eboli is full of pomp and profession; magnanimity and devotedness are on her tongue, some shadow of them even floats in her imagination; but they are not rooted in her heart; pride, selfishness, unlawful passion are the only inmates there. Her lofty boastings of generosity are soon forgotten when the success of her attachment to Carlos becomes hopeless; the fervor of a selfish love once extinguished in her bosom, she regards the object of it with none but vulgar feelings. Virtue no longer according with interest, she ceases to be virtuous; from a rejected mistress the transition to a jealous spy is with her natural and easy. Yet we do not hate the Princess: there is a seductive warmth and grace about her character, which makes us lament her vices rather than condemn them. The poet has drawn her at once false and fair.

In delineating Eboli and Philip, Schiller seems as if struggling against the current of his nature; our feelings towards them are hardly so severe as he intended; their words and deeds, at least those of the latter, are wicked and repulsive enough; but we still have a kind of latent persuasion that they meant better than they spoke or acted. With the Marquis of Posa, he had a more genial task. This Posa, we can

easily perceive, is the representative of Schiller himself. The
ardent love of men, which forms his ruling passion, was likewise the constant feeling of his author; the glowing eloquence
with which he advocates the cause of truth, and justice, and
humanity, was such as Schiller too would have employed in
similar circumstances. In some respects, Posa is the chief
character of the piece; there is a pre-eminent magnificence in
his object, and in the faculties and feelings with which he follows it. Of a splendid intellect, and a daring devoted heart,
his powers are all combined upon a single purpose. Even his
friendship for Carlos, grounded on the likeness of their minds,
and faithful as it is, yet seems to merge in this paramount emotion, zeal for the universal interests of man. Aiming, with all
his force of thought and action, to advance the happiness and
best rights of his fellow-creatures; pursuing this noble aim
with the skill and dignity which it deserves, his mind is at
once unwearied, earnest and serene. He is another Carlos, but
somewhat older, more experienced, and never crossed in hopeless love. There is a calm strength in Posa, which no accident of fortune can shake. Whether cheering the forlorn
Carlos into new activity; whether lifting up his voice in the
ear of tyrants and inquisitors, or taking leave of life amid
his vast unexecuted schemes, there is the same sedate magnanimity, the same fearless composure: when the fatal bullet
strikes him, he dies with the concerns of others, not his own,
upon his lips. He is a reformer, the perfection of reform-
ers; not a revolutionist, but a prudent though determined im-
prover. His enthusiasm does not burst forth in violence, but
in manly and enlightened energy; his eloquence is not more
moving to the heart than his lofty philosophy is convincing to
the head. There is a majestic vastness of thought in his pre-
cepts, which recommends them to the mind independently of
the beauty of their dress. Few passages of poetry are more
spirit-stirring than his last message to Carlos, through the
Queen. The certainty of death seems to surround his spirit
with a kind of martyr glory; he is kindled into transport, and
speaks with a commanding power. The pathetic wisdom of
the line, "Tell him, that when he is a man, he must reverence

the dreams of his youth," has often been admired: that scene has many such.

The interview with Philip is not less excellent. There is something so striking in the idea of confronting the cold solitary tyrant with "the only man in all his states that does not need him;" of raising the voice of true manhood for once within the gloomy chambers of thraldom and priestcraft, that we can forgive the stretch of poetic license by which it is effected. Philip and Posa are antipodes in all respects. Philip thinks his new instructor is "a Protestant;" a charge which Posa rebuts with calm dignity, his object not being separation and contention, but union and peaceful gradual improvement. Posa seems to understand the character of Philip better; not attempting to awaken in his sterile heart any feeling for real glory, or the interests of his fellow-men, he attacks his selfishness and pride, represents to him the intrinsic meanness and misery of a throne, however decked with adventitious pomp, if built on servitude, and isolated from the sympathies and interests of others.

We translate the entire scene; though not by any means the best, it is among the fittest for extraction of any in the piece. Posa has been sent for by the King, and is waiting in a chamber of the palace to know what is required of him; the King enters, unperceived by Posa, whose attention is directed to a picture on the wall: —

Act III. Scene X.

The King and Marquis de Posa.

[*The latter, on noticing the King, advances towards him, and kneels, then rises, and waits without any symptom of embarrassment.*]

KING [*looks at him with surprise*].
    We have met before, then?

MAR.   No.

KING.   You did my crown
Some service: wherefore have you shunn'd my thanks?
Our memory is besieged by crowds of suitors;

Omniscient is none but He in Heaven.
'You should have sought my looks: why did you not?

MAR. 'T is scarcely yet two days, your Majesty,
Since I returned to Spain.

KING.   I am not used
To be my servants' debtor; ask of me
Some favor.

MAR.   I enjoy the laws.

KING.   That right
The very murderer has.

MAR.   And how much more
The honest citizen! — Sire, I 'm content.

KING [*aside*]. Much self-respect indeed, and lofty daring!
But this was to be looked for : I would have·
My Spaniards haughty ; better that the cup
Should overflow than not be full. — I hear
You left my service, Marquis.

MAR.   Making way
For men more worthy. I withdrew.

KING.   'T is wrong:
When spirits such as yours play truant,
My state must suffer. You conceive, perhaps,
Some post unworthy of your merits
Might be offer'd you ?

MAR.   No, Sire, I cannot doubt
But that a judge so skilful, and experienced
In the gifts of men, has at a glance discover'd
Wherein I might do him service, wherein not.
I feel with humble gratitude the favor,
With which your Majesty is loading me
By thoughts so lofty : yet I can —   [*He stops.*

KING.   You pause ?

MAR. Sire, at the moment I am scarce prepar'd
To speak, in phrases of a Spanish subject,
What as a citizen o' th' world I 've thought.
Truth is, in parting from the Court forever,
I held myself discharged from all necessity
Of troubling it with reasons for my absence.

KING. Are your reasons bad, then ? Dare you not risk
Disclosing them ?

MAR.   My life, and joyfully,
Were scope allow'd me to disclose them *all.*

'T is not myself but Truth that I endanger,
Should the King refuse me a full hearing.
Your anger or contempt I fain would shun;
But forced to choose between them, I had rather
Seem to you a man deserving punishment
Than pity.

     KING [*with a look of expectation*].   Well?
     MAR.   The servant of a prince
I cannot be.   [*The King looks at him with astonishment.*
                 I will not cheat my merchant:
If you deign to take me as your servant,
You expect, you wish, my actions only;
You wish my arm in fight, my thought in counsel;
Nothing more you will accept of: not my actions,
Th' approval they might find at Court becomes
The object of my acting.   Now for me
Right conduct has a value of its own:
The happiness my king might cause me plant
I would myself produce; and conscious joy,
And free selection, not the force of duty,
Should impel me.   Is it thus your Majesty
Requires it?   Could you suffer new creators
In your own creation?   Or could I
Consent with patience to become the chisel,
When I hoped to be the statuary?
I love mankind; and in a monarchy,
Myself is all that I can love.

     KING.   This fire
Is laudable.   You would do good to others;
How you do it, patriots, wise men think
Of little moment, so it be but done.
Seek for yourself the office in my kingdoms
That will give you scope to gratify
This noble zeal.

     MAR.   There is not such an office.
     KING.   How?
     MAR.   What the king desires to spread abroad
Through these weak hands, is it the good of men?
That good which my unfetter'd love would wish them?
Pale majesty would tremble to behold it.
No! Policy has fashioned in her courts
Another sort of human good; a sort

Which *she* is rich enough to give away,
Awakening with it in the hearts of men
New cravings, such as *it* can satisfy.
Truth she keeps coining in her mints, such truth
As she can tolerate ; and every die
Except her own she breaks and casts away.
But is the royal bounty wide enough
For me to wish and work in ?   Must the love
I bear my brother pledge itself to be
My brother's jailer ?   Can I call him happy
When he dare not think ?   Sire, choose some other
To dispense the good which *you* have stamped for us. .
With me it tallies not ; a prince's servant
I cannot be.

    KING [*rather quickly*].
         You are a Protestant.
    MAR. [*after some reflection*].
Sire, your creed is also mine.   [*After a pause.*
                  I find.
I am misunderstood : 't is as I feared.
You see me draw the veil from majesty,
And view its mysteries with steadfast eye :
How should you know if I regard as holy
What I no more regard as terrible ?
Dangerous I seem, for bearing thoughts too high :
My King, I am not dangerous : my wishes
Lie buried here.   [*Laying his hand on his breast.*
         The poor and purblind rage
Of innovation, that but aggravates
The weight o' th' fetters which it cannot break,
Will never heat *my* blood.   The century
Admits not my ideas : I live a citizen
Of those that are to come.   Sire, can a picture
Break your rest ?   Your breath obliterates it.
    KING. No other knows you harbor such ideas ?
    MAR. Such, no one.
    KING [*rises, walks a few steps, then stops opposite the Mar-
        quis. — Aside*].   New at least, this dialect !
Flattery exhausts itself : a man of parts
Disdains to imitate.   For once let 's have
A trial of the opposite !   Why not ?
The strange is oft the lucky. — If so be

This is your principle, why let it pass!
I will conform; the crown shall have a servant
New in Spain, — a liberal!

    MAR.   Sire, I see
How very meanly you conceive of men;
How, in the language of the frank true spirit
You find but another deeper artifice
Of a more practis'd coz'ner: I can also
Partly see what causes this.   'T is men;
'T is men that force you to it: they themselves
Have cast away their own nobility,
Themselves have crouch'd to this degraded posture.
Man's innate greatness, like a spectre, frights them;
Their poverty seems safety; with base skill
They ornament their chains, and call it virtue
To wear them with an air of grace.   'T was thus
You found the world; thus from your royal father
Came it to you: how in this distorted,
Mutilated image could you honor man?

    KING. Some truth there is in this.

    MAR.   Pity, however,
That in taking man from the Creator,
And changing him into *your* handiwork,
And setting up yourself to be the god
Of this new-moulded creature, you should have
Forgotten one essential; you yourself
Remained a man, a very child of Adam!
You are still a suffering, longing mortal,
You call for sympathy, and to a god
We can but sacrifice, and pray, and tremble!
O unwise exchange! unbless'd perversion!
When you have sunk your brothers to be play'd
As harp-strings, who will join in harmony
With you the player?

    KING [*aside*].   By Heaven, he touches me!

    MAR. For you, however, this is unimportant;
It but makes you separate, peculiar;
'T is the price you pay for being a god.
And frightful were it if you failed in this!
If for the desolated good of millions,
You the Desolator should gain — nothing!
If the very freedom you have blighted

And kill'd were that alone which could exalt
Yourself! — Sire, pardon me, I must not stay:
The matter makes me rash: my heart is full,
Too strong the charm of looking on the *one*
Of living men to whom I might unfold it.

[*The Count de Lerma enters, and whispers a few words to
the King. The latter beckons to him to withdraw, and
continues sitting in his former posture.*

KING [*to the Marquis, after Lerma is gone*].
Speak on!

MAR. [*after a pause*].   I feel, Sire, all the worth —
KING.   Speak on!
Y' had something more to say.
      MAR.   Not long since, Sire,
I chanced to pass through Flanders and Brabant.
So many rich and flourishing provinces;
A great, a mighty people, and still more,
An honest people! — And this people's Father!
That, thought I, must be divine: so thinking,
I stumbled on a heap of human bones.

[*He pauses; his eyes rest on the King, who endeavors to
return his glance, but with an air of embarrassment is
forced to look upon the ground.*

You are in the right, you *must* proceed so.
That you *could* do, what you saw you *must* do,
Fills me with a shuddering admiration.
Pity that the victim welt'ring in its blood
Should speak so feeble an eulogium
On the spirit of the priest!   That mere men,
Not beings of a calmer essence, write
The annals of the world!   Serener ages
Will displace the age of Philip; these will bring
A milder wisdom; the subject's good will then
Be reconcil'd to th' prince's greatness;
The thrifty State will learn to prize its children,
And necessity no more will be inhuman.

      KING. And when, think you, would those blessed ages
Have come round, had I recoil'd before
The curse of this?   Behold my Spain!   Here blooms
The subject's good, in never-clouded peace:
Such peace will I bestow on Flanders.

      MAR. Peace of a churchyard!   And you hope to end

What you have entered on ?   Hope to withstand
The timeful change of Christendom ; to stop
The universal Spring that shall make young
The countenance o' th' Earth ?   *You* purpose, single
In all Europe, alone, to fling yourself
Against the wheel of Destiny that rolls
For ever its appointed course ; to clutch
Its spokes with mortal arm ?   You may not, Sire !
Already thousands have forsook your kingdoms,
Escaping glad though poor : the citizen
You lost for conscience' sake, he was your noblest.
With mother's arms Elizabeth receives
The fugitives, and rich by foreign skill,
In fertile strength her England blooms.   Forsaken
Of its toilsome people, lies Grenada
Desolate ; and Europe sees with glad surprise
Its enemy faint with self-inflicted wounds.

> [*The King seems moved: the Marquis observes it, and ad-*
> *vances some steps nearer.*

Plant for Eternity and death the seed ?
Your harvest will be nothingness.   The work
Will not survive the spirit of its former ;
It will be in vain that you have labor'd ;
That you have fought the fight with Nature ;
And to plans of Ruin consecrated
A high and royal lifetime.   Man is greater
Than you thought.   The bondage of long slumber
He will break ; his sacred rights he will reclaim.
With Nero and Busiris will he rank
The name of Philip, and — that grieves me, for
You once were good.

  KING.   How know you that ?

  MAR. [*with warm energy*].   You were ;
Yes, by th' All-Merciful !   Yes, I repeat it.
Restore to us what you have taken from us.
Generous as strong, let human happiness
Stream from your horn of plenty, let souls ripen
Round you.   Restore us what you took from us.
Amid a thousand kings become a king.

> [*He approaches him boldly, fixing on him firm and glowing*
> *looks.*

Oh, could the eloquence of all the millions,

Who participate in this great moment,
Hover on my lips, and raise into a flame
That gleam that kindles in your eyes!
Give up this false idolatry of self,
Which makes your brothers nothing!   Be to us
A pattern of the Everlasting and the True!
Never, never, did a mortal hold so much,
To use it so divinely.   All the kings
Of Europe reverence the name of Spain:
Go on in front of all the kings of Europe!
One movement of your pen, and new-created
Is the Earth.   Say but, Let there be freedom!

       [*Throwing himself at his feet.*

 KING [*surprised, turning his face away, then again towards*
   Posa].

Singular enthusiast!   Yet — rise — I —
 MAR. Look round and view God's lordly universe:
On Freedom it is founded, and how rich
Is it with Freedom!   He, the great Creator,
Has giv'n the very worm its sev'ral dewdrop;
Ev'n in the mouldering spaces of Decay,
He leaves Free-will the pleasures of a choice.
This world of *yours!* how narrow and how poor!
The rustling of a leaf alarms the lord
Of Christendom.   You quake at every virtue;
He, not to mar the glorious form of Freedom,
Suffers that the hideous hosts of Evil
Should run riot in his fair Creation.
Him the maker we behold not; calm
He veils himself in everlasting laws,
Which and not Him the sceptic seeing exclaims,
" Wherefore a God?   The World itself is God."
And never did a Christian's adoration
So praise him as this sceptic's blasphemy.
 KING. And such a model you would undertake,
On Earth, in my domains to imitate?
 MAR. You, you can: who else?   To th' people's good
Devote the kingly power, which far too long
Has struggled for the greatness of the throne.
Restore the lost nobility of man.
Once more make of the subject what he was,
The purpose of the Crown; let no tie bind him,

Except his brethren's right, as sacred as
His own.   And when, given back to self-dependence,
Man awakens to the feeling of his worth,
And freedom's proud and lofty virtues blossom,
Then, Sire, having made *your* realms the happiest
In the Earth, it may become your duty
To subdue the realms of others.

  KING [*after a long pause*].
I have heard you to an end.
Not as in common heads, the world is painted
In that head of yours : nor will I mete you
By the common standard.   I am the first
To whom your heart has been disclosed :
I know this, so believe it.   For the sake
Of such forbearance; for your having kept
Ideas, embraced with such devotion, secret
Up to this present moment, for the sake
Of that reserve, young man, I will forget
That I have learned them, and how I learned them.
Arise.   The headlong youth I will set right,
Not as his sovereign, but as his senior.
I will, because I will.   So ! bane itself,
I find, in generous natures may become
Ennobled into something better.   But
Beware my Inquisition !   It would grieve me
If you —
  MAR. Would it ? would it ?
  KING [*gazing at him, and lost in surprise*].
          Such a mortal
Till this hour I never saw.   No, Marquis !
No !   You do me wrong.   To you I will not
Be a Nero, not to you.   *All* happiness
Shall not be blighted by me : you yourself
Shall be permitted to remain a man
Beside me.
  MAR. [*quickly*].   And my fellow-subjects, Sire ?
Oh, not for *me*, not *my* cause was I pleading.
And your subjects, Sire ?
  KING.   You see so clearly
How posterity will judge of me; yourself
Shall teach it how I treated men so soon
As I had found one.

MAR.   O Sire! in being
The most just of kings, at the same instant
Be not the most unjust!   In your Flanders
Are many thousands worthier than I.
'T is but yourself, — shall I confess it, Sire? —
That under this mild form first truly see
What freedom is.
    KING [*with softened earnestness*].
                        Young man, no more of this.
Far differently will you think of men,
When you have seen and studied them as I have.
Yet our first meeting must not be our last;
How shall I try to make you mine?
    MAR.   Sire, let me
Continue as I am.   What good were it
To you, if I like others were corrupted?
    KING.   This pride I will not suffer.   From this moment
You are in my service.   No remonstrance!
I will have it so. . . .

Had the character of Posa been drawn ten years later, it
would have been imputed, as all things are, to the "French
Revolution;" and Schiller himself perhaps might have been
called a Jacobin.   Happily, as matters stand, there is room
for no such imputation.   It is pleasing to behold in Posa the
deliberate expression of a great and good man's sentiments on
these ever-agitated subjects: a noble monument, embodying the
liberal ideas of his age, in a form beautified by his own genius,
and lasting as its other products.[1]

Connected with the superior excellence of Posa, critics have
remarked a dramatic error, which the author himself was the
first to acknowledge and account for.   The magnitude of Posa
throws Carlos into the shade; the hero of the first three acts
is no longer the hero of the other two.   The cause of this, we
are informed, was that Schiller kept the work too long upon
his own hands:

"In composing the piece," he observes, "many interruptions

[1] Jean Paul nevertheless, not without some show of reason, has compared
this Posa to the tower of a lighthouse: "high, far-shining, — empty!" (*Note
of* 1845.)

occurred; so that a considerable time elapsed between beginning and concluding it; and, in the mean while, much within myself had changed. The various alterations which, during this period, my way of thinking and feeling underwent, naturally told upon the work I was engaged with. What parts of it had at first attracted me, began to produce this effect in a weaker degree, and, in the end, scarcely at all. New ideas, springing up in the interim, displaced the former ones; Carlos himself had lost my favor, perhaps for no other reason than because I had become his senior; and, from the opposite cause, Posa had occupied his place. Thus I commenced the fourth and fifth acts with quite an altered heart. But the first three were already in the hands of the public; the plan of the whole could not now be re-formed; nothing therefore remained but to suppress the piece entirely, or to fit the second half to the first the best way I could."

The imperfection alluded to is one of which the general reader will make no great account; the second half is fitted to the first with address enough for his purposes. Intent not upon applying the dramatic gauge, but on being moved and exalted, we may peruse the tragedy without noticing that any such defect exists in it. The pity and love we are first taught to feel for Carlos abide with us to the last; and though Posa rises in importance as the piece proceeds, our admiration of his transcendent virtues does not obstruct the gentler feelings with which we look upon the fate of his friend. A certain confusion and crowding together of events, about the end of the play, is the only fault in its plan that strikes us with any force. Even this is scarcely prominent enough to be offensive.

An intrinsic and weightier defect is the want of ease and lightness in the general composition of the piece; a defect which all its other excellencies will not prevent us from observing. There is action enough in the plot, energy enough in the dialogue, and abundance of individual beauties in both: but there is throughout a certain air of stiffness and effort, which abstracts from the theatrical illusion. The language, in general impressive and magnificent, is now and then inflated into bombast. The characters do not, as it were, verify their human nature, by those thousand little touches and nameless turns, which distinguish the genius essentially dramatic from the genius merely poetical; the Proteus of the stage from the philosophic observer and trained imitator of life. We have not those careless felicities, those varyings from high to low, that air of living freedom which Shakspeare has accustomed us, like spoiled children, to look for in every perfect work of this species. Schiller is too elevated, too regular and sustained in his elevation, to be altogether natural.

Yet with all this, *Carlos* is a noble tragedy. There is a stately massiveness about the structure of it; the incidents are grand and affecting; the characters powerful, vividly conceived, and impressively if not completely delineated. Of wit and its kindred graces Schiller has but a slender share: nor among great poets is he much distinguished for depth or fineness of pathos. But what gives him a place of his own, and the loftiest of its kind, is the vastness and intense vigor of his mind; the splendor of his thoughts and imagery, and the bold vehemence of his passion for the true and the sublime, under all their various forms. He does not thrill, but he exalts us. His genius is impetuous, exuberant, majestic; and a heavenly fire gleams through all his creations. He transports us into a holier and higher world than our own; everything around us breathes of force and solemn beauty. The looks of his heroes may be more staid than those of men, the movements of their minds may be slower and more calculated; but we yield to the potency of their endowments, and the loveliness of the scene which they animate. The enchantments of the poet are strong enough to silence our scepticism; we forbear to inquire whether it is true or false.

The celebrity of Alfieri generally invites the reader of *Don Carlos* to compare it with *Filippo*. Both writers treat the same subject; both borrow their materials from the same source, the *nouvelle historique* of St. Réal: but it is impossible that two powerful minds could have handled one given idea in more diverse manners. Their excellencies are, in fact, so opposite, that they scarcely come in competition. Alfieri's play is short, and the characters are few. He describes no scene: his personages are not the King of Spain and his courtiers, but merely men; their place of action is not the Escurial or Madrid, but a vacant, objectless platform anywhere in space. In all this, Schiller has a manifest advantage. He paints manners and opinions, he sets before us a striking pageant, which interests us of itself, and gives a new interest to whatever is combined with it. The principles of the antique, or perhaps rather of the French drama, upon which Alfieri worked, permitted no such delineation. In the style there is the same diversity. A severe simplicity uniformly marks Alfieri's style; in his whole tragedy there is not a single figure. A hard emphatic brevity is all that distinguishes his language from that of prose. Schiller, we have seen, abounds with noble metaphors, and all the warm exciting eloquence of poetry. It is only in express-ing the character of Philip that Alfieri has a clear superiority. Without the aid of superstition, which his rival, especially in the catastrophe, employs to such advantage, Alfieri has ex-hibited in his Filippo a picture of unequalled power. Ob-scurity is justly said to be essential to terror and sublimity; and Schiller has enfeebled the effect of his Tyrant, by letting us behold the most secret recesses of his spirit: we understand him better, but we fear him less. Alfieri does not show us the internal combination of Filippo: it is from its workings alone that we judge of his nature. Mystery, and the shadow of horrid cruelty, brood over his Filippo: it is only a transient word or act that gives us here and there a glimpse of his fierce, implacable, tremendous soul; a short and dubious glimmer that reveals to us the abysses of his being, dark, lurid, and terrific, "as the throat of the infernal Pool." Alfieri's Filippo is perhaps the most wicked man that human imagination has conceived.

Alfieri and Schiller were again unconscious competitors in the history of Mary Stuart. But the works before us give a truer specimen of their comparative merits. Schiller seems to have the greater genius; Alfieri the more commanding character. Alfieri's greatness rests on the stern concentration of fiery passion, under the dominion of an adamantine will: this was his own make of mind; and he represents it, with strokes in themselves devoid of charm, but in their union terrible as a prophetic scroll. Schiller's moral force is commensurate with his intellectual gifts, and nothing more. The mind of the one is like the ocean, beautiful in its strength, smiling in the radiance of summer, and washing luxuriant and romantic shores: that of the other is like some black unfathomable lake placed far amid the melancholy mountains; bleak, solitary, desolate; but girdled with grim sky-piercing cliffs, overshadowed with storms, and illuminated only by the red glare of the lightning. Schiller is magnificent in his expansion, Alfieri is overpowering in his condensed energy; the first inspires us with greater admiration, the last with greater awe.

This tragedy of *Carlos* was received with immediate and universal approbation. In the closet and on the stage, it excited the warmest applauses equally among the learned and unlearned. Schiller's expectations had not been so high: he knew both the excellencies and the faults of his work; but he had not anticipated that the former would be recognized so instantaneously. The pleasure of this new celebrity came upon him, therefore, heightened by surprise. Had dramatic eminence been his sole object, he might now have slackened his exertions; the public had already ranked him as the first of their writers in that favorite department. But this limited ambition was not his moving principle; nor was his mind of that sort for which rest is provided in this world. The primary disposition of his nature urged him to perpetual toil: the great aim of his life, the unfolding of his mental powers, was one of those which admit but a relative not an absolute progress. New ideas of perfection arise as the former have been reached; the student is always attaining, never has attained.

Schiller's worldly circumstances, too, were of a kind well calculated to prevent excess of quietism. He was still drifting at large on the tide of life; he was crowned with laurels, but without a home. His heart, warm and affectionate, fitted to enjoy the domestic blessings which it longed for,

was allowed to form no permanent attachment: he felt that
he was unconnected, solitary in the world; cut off from the
exercise of his kindlier sympathies; or if tasting such pleasures, it was "snatching them rather than partaking of them
calmly." The vulgar desire of wealth and station never
entered his mind for an instant: but as years were added to
his age, the delights of peace and continuous comfort were
fast becoming more acceptable than any other; and he looked
with anxiety to have a resting-place amid his wanderings, to
be a man among his fellow-men.

For all these wishes, Schiller saw that the only chance of
fulfilment depended on unwearied perseverance in his literary
occupations. Yet though his activity was unabated, and the
calls on it were increasing rather than diminished, its direction
was gradually changing. The Drama had long been stationary, and of late been falling in his estimation: the difficulties
of the art, as he viewed it at present, had been overcome, and
new conquests invited him in other quarters. The latter part
of *Carlos* he had written as a task rather than a pleasure;
he contemplated no farther undertaking connected with the
Stage. For a time, indeed, he seems to have wavered among
a multiplicity of enterprises; now solicited to this, and now
to that, without being able to fix decidedly on any. The restless ardor of his mind is evinced by the number and variety
of his attempts; its fluctuation by the circumstance that all
of them are either short in extent, or left in the state of
fragments. Of the former kind are his lyrical productions,
many of which were composed about this period, during intervals from more serious labors. The character of these performances is such as his former writings gave us reason to
expect. With a deep insight into life, and a keen and comprehensive sympathy with its sorrows and enjoyments, there
is combined that impetuosity of feeling, that pomp of thought
and imagery which belong peculiarly to Schiller. If he had
now left the Drama, it was clear that his mind was still overflowing with the elements of poetry; dwelling among the
grandest conceptions, and the boldest or finest emotions;
thinking intensely and profoundly, but decorating its thoughts

with those graces, which other faculties than the understanding are required to afford them. With these smaller pieces, Schiller occupied himself at intervals of leisure throughout the remainder of his life. Some of them are to be classed among the most finished efforts of his genius. The *Walk*, the *Song of the Bell*, contain exquisite delineations of the fortunes and history of man; his *Ritter Toggenburg*, his *Cranes of Ibycus*, his *Hero and Leander*, are among the most poetical and moving ballads to be found in any language.

Of these poems, the most noted written about this time, the *Freethinking of Passion (Freigeisterei der Leidenschaft)*, is said to have originated in a real attachment. The lady, whom some biographers of Schiller introduce to us by the mysterious designation of the " Fräulein A——, one of the first beauties in Dresden," seems to have made a deep impression on the heart of the poet. They tell us that she sat for the picture of the princess Eboli, in his *Don Carlos ;* that he paid his court to her with the most impassioned fervor, and the extreme of generosity. They add one or two anecdotes of dubious authenticity; which, as they illustrate nothing, but show us only that love could make Schiller crazy, as it is said to make all gods and men, we shall use the freedom to omit.

This enchanting and not inexorable spinster perhaps displaced the Mannheim *Laura* from her throne; but the gallant assiduities, which she required or allowed, seem not to have abated the zeal of her admirer in his more profitable undertakings. Her reign, we suppose, was brief, and without abiding influence. Schiller never wrote or thought with greater diligence than while at Dresden. Partially occupied with conducting his *Thalia*, or with those more slight poetical performances, his mind was hovering among a multitude of weightier plans, and seizing with avidity any hint that might assist in directing its attempts. To this state of feeling we are probably indebted for the *Geisterseher*, a novel, naturalized in our circulating libraries by the title of the *Ghostseer*, two volumes of which were published about this time. The king of quacks, the renowned Cagliostro, was

GOETHE.

Carlyle, Vol. Nine, p. 349,

now playing his dexterous game at Paris: harrowing up the
souls of the curious and gullible of all ranks in that capital,
by various thaumaturgic feats; raising the dead from their
graves; and, what was more to the purpose, raising himself
from the station of a poor Sicilian lacquey to that of a sumptuous and extravagant count. The noise of his exploits appears to have given rise to this work of Schiller's. It is an
attempt to exemplify the process of hoodwinking an acute
but too sensitive man; of working on the latent germ of
superstition, which exists beneath his outward scepticism;
harassing his mind by the terrors of magic, — the magic of
chemistry and natural philosophy and natural cunning; till,
racked by doubts and agonizing fears, and plunging from
one depth of dark uncertainty into another, he is driven at
length to still his scruples in the bosom of the Infallible
Church. The incidents are contrived with considerable address, displaying a familiar acquaintance, not only with
several branches of science, but also with some curious forms
of life and human nature. One or two characters are forcibly
drawn; particularly that of the amiable but feeble Count,
the victim of the operation. The strange Foreigner, with the
visage of stone, who conducts the business of mystification,
strikes us also, though we see but little of him. The work
contains some vivid description, some passages of deep tragical effect: it has a vein of keen observation; in general, a
certain rugged power, which might excite regret that it was
never finished. But Schiller found that his views had been
mistaken: it was thought that he meant only to electrify his
readers, by an accumulation of surprising horrors, in a novel
of the Mrs. Radcliffe fashion. He felt, in consequence, dis-
couraged to proceed; and finally abandoned it.

Schiller was, in fact, growing tired of fictitious writing.
Imagination was with him a strong, not an exclusive, perhaps
not even a predominating faculty: in the sublimest flights of
his genius, intellect is a quality as conspicuous as any other;
we are frequently not more delighted with the grandeur of the
drapery in which he clothes his thoughts, than with the grandeur of the thoughts themselves. To a mind so restless, the

cultivation of all its powers was a peremptory want; in one so
earnest, the love of truth was sure to be among its strongest
passions. Even while revelling, with unworn ardor, in the
dreamy scenes of the Imagination, he had often cast a longing
look, and sometimes made a hurried inroad, into the calmer
provinces of reason: but the first effervescence of youth was
past, and now more than ever, the love of contemplating or
painting things as they should be, began to yield to the love
of knowing things as they are. The tendency of his mind was
gradually changing; he was about to enter on a new field of
enterprise, where new triumphs awaited him.

For a time he had hesitated what to choose; at length he
began to think of History. As a leading object of pursuit,
this promised him peculiar advantages. It was new to him;
and fitted to employ some of his most valuable gifts. It was
grounded on reality, for which, as we have said, his taste was
now becoming stronger; its mighty revolutions and events,
and the commanding characters that figure in it, would likewise present him with things great and moving, for which his
taste had always been strong. As recording the past transactions, and indicating the prospects of nations, it could not fail
to be delightful to one, for whom not only human nature was
a matter of most fascinating speculation, but who looked on
all mankind with the sentiments of a brother, feeling truly
what he often said, that "he had no dearer wish than to see
every living mortal happy and contented with his lot." To all
these advantages another of a humbler sort was added, but
which the nature of his situation forbade him to lose sight of.
The study of History, while it afforded him a subject of continuous and regular exertion, would also afford him, what was
even more essential, the necessary competence of income for
which he felt reluctant any longer to depend on the resources
of poetry, but which the produce of his pen was now the only
means he had of realizing.

For these reasons, he decided on commencing the business
of historian. The composition of *Don Carlos* had already led
him to investigate the state of Spain under Philip II.; and,
being little satisfied with Watson's clear but shallow Work on

that reign, he had turned to the original sources of information, the writings of Grotius, Strada, De Thou, and many others. Investigating these with his usual fidelity and eagerness, the Revolt of the Netherlands had, by degrees, become familiar to his thoughts; distinct in many parts where it was previously obscure; and attractive, as it naturally must be to a temper such as his. He now determined that his first historical performance should be a narrative of that event. He resolved to explore the minutest circumstance of its rise and progress; to arrange the materials he might collect, in a more philosophical order; to interweave with them the general opinions he had formed, or was forming, on many points of polity, and national or individual character; and, if possible, to animate the whole with that warm sympathy, which, in a lover of Freedom, this most glorious of her triumphs naturally called forth.

In the filling-up of such an outline, there was scope enough for diligence. But it was not in Schiller's nature to content himself with ordinary efforts; no sooner did a project take hold of his mind, than, rallying round it all his accomplishments and capabilities, he stretched it out into something so magnificent and comprehensive, that little less than a lifetime would have been sufficient to effect it. This History of the Revolt of the Netherlands, which formed his chief study, he looked upon but as one branch of the great subject he was yet destined to engage with. History at large, in all its bearings, was now his final aim; and his mind was continually occupied with plans for acquiring, improving, and diffusing the knowledge of it.

Of these plans many never reached a describable shape; very few reached even partial execution. One of the latter sort was an intended *History of the most remarkable Conspiracies and Revolutions in the Middle and Later Ages.* A first volume of the work was published in 1787. Schiller's part in it was trifling; scarcely more than that of a translator and editor. St. Réal's *Conspiracy of Bedmar against Venice,* here furnished with an extended introduction, is the best piece in the book. Indeed, St. Réal seems first to have set him on this task: the

Abbé had already signified his predilection for plots and revolutions, and given a fine sample of his powers in treating such
matters. What Schiller did was to expand this idea, and communicate a systematic form to it. His work might have been
curious and valuable, had it been completed; but the pressure
of other engagements, the necessity of limiting his views to
the Netherlands, prevented this for the present; it was afterwards forgotten, and never carried farther.

Such were Schiller's occupations while at Dresden; their
extent and variety are proof enough that idleness was not
among his vices. It was, in truth, the opposite extreme in
which he erred. He wrote and thought with an impetuosity
beyond what nature always could endure. His intolerance of
interruptions first put him on the plan of studying by night;
an alluring but pernicious practice, which began at Dresden,
and was never afterwards forsaken. His recreations breathed
a similar spirit; he loved to be much alone, and strongly
moved. The banks of the Elbe were the favorite resort of his
mornings: here wandering in solitude amid groves and lawns,
and green and beautiful places, he abandoned his mind to delicious musings; watched the fitful current of his thoughts, as
they came sweeping through his soul in their vague, fantastic,
gorgeous forms; pleased himself with the transient images of
memory and hope; or meditated on the cares and studies which
had lately been employing, and were again soon to employ him.
At times, he might be seen floating on the river in a gondola,
feasting himself with the loveliness of earth and sky. He delighted most to be there when tempests were abroad; his unquiet spirit found a solace in the expression of his own unrest
on the face of Nature; danger lent a charm to his situation;
he felt in harmony with the scene, when the rack was sweeping stormfully across the heavens, and the forests were sounding in the breeze, and the river was rolling its chafed waters
into wild eddying heaps.

Yet before the darkness summoned him exclusively to his
tasks, Schiller commonly devoted a portion of his day to the
pleasures of society. Could he have found enjoyment in the

flatteries of admiring hospitality, his present fame would have procured them for him in abundance. But these things were not to Schiller's taste. His opinion of the "flesh-flies" of Leipzig we have already seen: he retained the same sentiments throughout all his life. The idea of being what we call a *lion* is offensive enough to any man, of not more than common vanity, or less than common understanding; it was doubly offensive to him. His pride and his modesty alike forbade it. The delicacy of his nature, aggravated into shyness by his education and his habits, rendered situations of display more than usually painful to him; the *digito prætereuntium* was a sort of celebration he was far from coveting. In the circles of fashion he appeared unwillingly, and seldom to advantage: their glitter and parade were foreign to his disposition; their strict ceremonial cramped the play of his mind. Hemmed in, as by invisible fences, among the intricate barriers of etiquette, so feeble, so inviolable, he felt constrained and helpless; alternately chagrined and indignant. It was the giant among pigmies; Gulliver in Lilliput, tied down by a thousand packthreads. But there were more congenial minds, with whom he could associate; more familiar scenes, in which he found the pleasures he was seeking. Here Schiller was himself; frank, unembarrassed, pliant to the humor of the hour. His conversation was delightful, abounding at once in rare and simple charms. Besides the intellectual riches which it carried with it, there was that flow of kindliness and unaffected good humor, which can render dulness itself agreeable. Schiller had many friends in Dresden, who loved him as a man, while they admired him as a writer. Their intercourse was of the kind he liked, sober, as well as free and mirthful. It was the careless, calm, honest effusion of his feelings that he wanted, not the noisy tumults and coarse delirium of dissipation. For this, under any of its forms, he at no time showed the smallest relish.

A visit to Weimar had long been one of Schiller's projects: he now first accomplished it in 1787. Saxony had been, for ages, the Attica of Germany; and Weimar had, of late, become its Athens. In this literary city, Schiller found what he expected, sympathy and brotherhood with men of kindred minds. To Goethe he was not introduced;[1] but Herder and Wieland received him with a cordial welcome; with the latter he soon formed a most friendly intimacy. Wieland, the Nestor of German letters, was grown gray in the service: Schiller reverenced him as a father, and he was treated by him as a son. "We shall have bright hours," he said; "Wieland is still young, when he loves." Wieland had long edited the *Deutsche Mercur:* in consequence of their connection, Schiller now took part in contributing to that work. Some of his smaller poems, one or two fragments of the History of the Netherlands, and the *Letters on Don Carlos*, first appeared here. His own *Thalia* still continued to come out at Leipzig. With these for his incidental employments, with the Belgian Revolt for his chief study, and the best society in Germany for his leisure, Schiller felt no wish to leave Weimar. The place and what it held contented him so much, that he thought of selecting it for his permanent abode. "You know the men," he writes, "of whom Germany is proud; a Herder, a Wieland, with their brethren; and one wall now encloses me and them. What excellencies are in Weimar! In this city, at least in this territory, I mean to settle for life, and at length once more to get a country."

So occupied and so intentioned, he continued to reside at Weimar. Some months after his arrival, he received an invitation from his early patroness and kind protectress, Madam von Wollzogen, to come and visit her at Bauerbach. Schiller went accordingly to this his ancient city of refuge; he again found all the warm hospitality, which he had of old experienced when its character could less be mistaken; but his excursion thither produced more lasting effects than this. At Rudolstadt, where he stayed for a time on occasion of this journey, he met with a new friend. It was here that he first saw the Fräulein Lengefeld, a lady whose attractions made him loath to leave Rudolstadt, and eager to return.

Next year he did return; he lived from May till November

[1] Doering says, "Goethe was at this time absent in Italy;" an error, as will by and by appear.

there or in the neighborhood. He was busy as usual, and he visited the Lengefeld family almost every day. Schiller's views on marriage, his longing for "a civic and domestic existence," we already know. "To be united with a person," he had said, "that shares our sorrows and our joys, that responds to our feelings, that moulds herself so pliantly, so closely to our humors; reposing on her calm and warm affection, to relax our spirit from a thousand distractions, a thousand wild wishes and tumultuous passions; to dream away all the bitterness of fortune, in the bosom of domestic enjoyment; this the true delight of life." Some years had elapsed since he expressed these sentiments, which time had confirmed, not weakened: the presence of the Fräulein Lengefeld awoke them into fresh activity. He loved this lady; the return of love, with which she honored him, diffused a sunshine over all his troubled world; and, if the wish of being hers excited more impatient thoughts about the settlement of his condition, it also gave him fresh strength to attain it. He was full of occupation, while in Rudolstadt; ardent, serious, but not unhappy. His literary projects were proceeding as before; and, besides the enjoyment of virtuous love, he had that of intercourse with many worthy and some kindred minds.

Among these, the chief in all respects was Goethe. It was during his present visit, that Schiller first met with this illustrious person; concerning whom, both by reading and report, his expectations had been raised so high. No two men, both of exalted genius, could be possessed of more different sorts of excellence, than the two that were now brought together, in a large company of their mutual friends. The English reader may form some approximate conception of the contrast, by figuring an interview between Shakspeare and Milton. How gifted, how diverse in their gifts! The mind of the one plays calmly, in its capricious and inimitable graces, over all the provinces of human interest; the other concentrates powers as vast, but far less various, on a few subjects; the one is catholic, the other is sectarian. The first is endowed with an all-comprehending spirit; skilled, as if by personal experience, in all the modes of human passion and opinion; there-

fore, tolerant of all; peaceful, collected; fighting for no class
of men or principles; rather looking on the world, and the
various battles waging in it, with the quiet eye of one already
reconciled to the futility of their issues; but pouring over all
the forms of many-colored life the light of a deep and subtle
intellect, and the decorations of an overflowing fancy; and
allowing men and things of every shape and hue to have their
own free scope in his conception, as they have it in the world
where Providence has placed them. The other is earnest,
devoted; struggling with a thousand mighty projects of improvement; feeling more intensely as he feels more narrowly;
rejecting vehemently, choosing vehemently; at war with the
one half of things, in love with the other half; hence dissatisfied, impetuous, without internal rest, and scarcely conceiving
the possibility of such a state. Apart from the difference of
their opinions and mental culture, Shakspeare and Milton seem
to have stood in some such relation as this to each other, in
regard to the primary structure of their minds. So likewise,
in many points, was it with Goethe and Schiller. The external circumstances of the two were, moreover, such as to
augment their several peculiarities. Goethe was in his thirty-
ninth year; and had long since found his proper rank and
settlement in life. Schiller was ten years younger, and still
without a fixed destiny; on both of which accounts, his fundamental scheme of thought, the principles by which he
judged and acted, and maintained his individuality, although
they might be settled, were less likely to be sobered and ma-
tured. In these circumstances we can hardly wonder that on
Schiller's part the first impression was not very pleasant.
Goethe sat talking of Italy, and art, and travelling, and a
thousand other subjects, with that flow of brilliant and deep
sense, sarcastic humor, knowledge, fancy and good nature,
which is said to render him the best talker now alive.[1] Schiller looked at him in quite a different mood; he felt his natural constraint increased under the influence of a man so
opposite in character, so potent in resources, so singular and
so expert in using them; a man whom he could not agree with,

---

[1] 1825.

and knew not how to contradict. Soon after their interview, he thus writes :—

"On the whole, this personal meeting has not at all diminished the idea, great as it was, which I had previously formed of Goethe; but I doubt whether we shall ever come into any close communication with each other. Much that still interests me has already had its epoch with him. His whole nature is, from its very origin, otherwise constructed than mine; his world is not my world; our modes of conceiving things appear to be essentially different. From such a combination, no secure, substantial intimacy can result. Time will try."

The aid of time was not, in fact, unnecessary. On the part of Goethe there existed prepossessions no less hostile; and derived from sources older and deeper than the present transitory meeting, to the discontents of which they probably contributed. He himself has lately stated them with his accustomed frankness and good humor, in a paper, part of which some readers may peruse with an interest more than merely biographical.

"On my return from Italy," he says, "where I had been endeavoring to train myself to greater purity and precision in all departments of art, not heeding what meanwhile was going on in Germany, I found here some older and some more recent works of poetry, enjoying high esteem and wide circulation, while unhappily their character to me was utterly offensive. I shall only mention Heinse's *Ardinghello* and Schiller's *Robbers*. The first I hated for its having undertaken to exhibit sensuality and mystical abstruseness, ennobled and supported by creative art: the last, because in it, the very paradoxes moral and dramatic, from which I was struggling to get liberated, had been laid hold of by a powerful though an immature genius, and poured in a boundless rushing flood over all our country.

"Neither of these gifted individuals did I blame for what he had performed or purposed: it is the nature and the privilege of every mortal to attempt working in his own peculiar way; he attempts it first without culture, scarcely with the consciousness of what he is about; and continues it with consciousness increasing as his culture increases; whereby it happens that so many exquisite and so many paltry things are to be found circulating in the world, and one perplexity is seen to rise from the ashes of another.

"But the rumor which these strange productions had excited over Germany, the approbation paid to them by every class of persons, from the wild student to the polished court-lady, frightened me; for I now thought all my labor was to prove in vain; the objects, and the way of handling them, to which I had been exercising all my powers, appeared as if defaced and set aside. And what grieved me still more was, that all the friends connected with me, Heinrich Meyer and Moritz, as well as their fellow-artists Tischbein and Bury, seemed in danger of the like contagion. I was much hurt. Had it been possible, I would have abandoned the study of creative art, and the practice of poetry altogether; for where was the prospect of surpassing those performances of genial worth and wild form, in the qualities which recommended them? Conceive my situation. It had been my object and my task to cherish and impart the purest exhibitions of poetic art; and here was I hemmed in between Ardinghello and Franz von Moor!

"It happened also about this time that Moritz returned from Italy, and stayed with me awhile; during which, he violently confirmed himself and me in these persuasions. I avoided Schiller, who was now at Weimar, in my neighborhood. The appearance of *Don Carlos* was not calculated to approximate us; the attempts of our common friends I resisted; and thus we still continued to go on our way apart."

By degrees, however, both parties found that they had been mistaken. The course of accidents brought many things to light, which had been hidden; the true character of each became unfolded more and more completely to the other; and the cold, measured tribute of respect was on both sides animated and exalted by feelings of kindness, and ultimately of affection. Ere long, Schiller had by gratifying proofs discovered that "this Goethe was a very worthy man;" and Goethe, in his love of genius, and zeal for the interests of literature, was performing for Schiller the essential duties of a friend, even while his personal repugnance continued unabated.

A strict similarity of characters is not necessary, or perhaps very favorable, to friendship. To render it complete, each party must no doubt be competent to understand the other; both must be possessed of dispositions kindred in their great lineaments: but the pleasure of comparing our ideas and emotions is heightened, when there is "likeness in unlikeness." *The same sentiments, different opinions,* Rousseau conceives to be the best material of friendship: reciprocity of kind words and actions is more effectual than all. Luther loved Melancthon; Johnson was not more the friend of Edmund Burke than of poor old Dr. Levitt. Goethe and Schiller met again; as they ultimately came to live together, and to see each other oftener, they liked each other better; they became associates, friends; and the harmony of their intercourse, strengthened by many subsequent communities of object, was never interrupted, till death put an end to it. Goethe, in his time, has done many glorious things; but few on which he should look back with greater pleasure than his treatment of Schiller. Literary friendships are said to be precarious, and of rare occurrence: the rivalry of interest disturbs their continuance; a rivalry greater, where the subject of competition is one so vague, impalpable and fluctuating, as the favor of the public; where the feeling to be gratified is one so nearly allied to vanity, the most irritable, arid and selfish feeling of the human heart. Had Goethe's prime motive been the love of fame, he must have viewed with repugnance, not the misdirection but the talents of the rising genius, advancing with such rapid strides to dispute with him the palm of intellectual primacy, nay as the million thought, already in possession of it; and if a sense of his own dignity had withheld him from offering obstructions, or uttering any whisper of discontent, there is none but a truly patrician spirit that would cordially have offered aid. To

being secretly hostile and openly indifferent, the next resource was to enact the patron; to solace vanity, by helping
the rival whom he could not hinder, and who could do without his help.   Goethe adopted neither of these plans.   It reflects much credit on him that he acted as he did.   Eager to
forward Schiller's views by exerting all the influence within
his power, he succeeded in effecting this; and what was still
more difficult, in suffering the character of benefactor to
merge in that of equal.   They became not friends only, but
fellow-laborers : a connection productive of important consequences in the history of both, particularly of the younger
and more undirected of the two.

Meanwhile the *History of the Revolt of the United Netherlands* was in part before the world; the first volume came
out in 1788.   Schiller's former writings had given proofs of
powers so great and various, such an extent of general intellectual strength, and so deep an acquaintance, both practical
and scientific, with the art of composition, that in a subject
like history, no ordinary work was to be looked for from his
hands.   With diligence in accumulating materials, and patient
care in elaborating them, he could scarcely fail to attain distinguished excellence.   The present volume was well calculated
to fulfil such expectations.   The *Revolt of the Netherlands* possesses all the common requisites of a good history, and many
which are in some degree peculiar to itself.   The information
it conveys is minute and copious; we have all the circumstances of the case, remote and near, set distinctly before us.
Yet, such is the skill of the arrangement, these are at once
briefly and impressively presented.   The work is not stretched
out into a continuous narrative; but gathered up into masses,
which are successively exhibited to view, the minor facts being
grouped around some leading one, to which, as to the central
object, our attention is chiefly directed.   This method of combining the details of events, of proceeding as it were, *per
saltum*, from eminence to eminence, and thence surveying
the surrounding scene, is undoubtedly the most philosophical
of any : but few men are equal to the task of effecting it

rightly. It must be executed by a mind able to look on all its facts at once; to disentangle their perplexities, referring each to its proper head; and to choose, often with extreme address, the station from which the reader is to view them. Without this, or with this inadequately done, a work on such a plan would be intolerable. Schiller has accomplished it in great perfection; the whole scene of affairs was evidently clear before his own eye, and he did not want expertness to discriminate and seize its distinctive features. The bond of cause and consequence he never loses sight of; and over each successive portion of his narrative he pours that flood of intellectual and imaginative brilliancy, which all his prior writings had displayed. His reflections, expressed or implied, are the fruit of strong, comprehensive, penetrating thought. His descriptions are vivid; his characters are studied with a keen sagacity, and set before us in their most striking points of view; those of Egmont and Orange occur to every reader as a rare union of perspicacity and eloquence. The work has a look of order; of beauty joined to calm reposing force. Had it been completed, it might have ranked as the very best of Schiller's prose compositions. But no second volume ever came to light, and the first concludes at the entrance of Alba into Brussels. Two fragments alone, the *Siege of Antwerp*, and the *Passage of Alba's Army*, both living pictures, show us still farther what he might have done had he proceeded. The surpassing and often highly picturesque movements of this War, the devotedness of the Dutch, their heroic achievement of liberty, were not destined to be painted by the glowing pen of Schiller, whose heart and mind were alike so qualified to do them justice.[1]

The accession of reputation, which this work procured its author, was not the only or the principal advantage he

---

[1] If we mistake not, Madame de Staël, in her *Révolution Française*, had this performance of Schiller's in her eye. Her work is constructed on a similar though a rather looser plan of arrangement: the execution of it bears the same relation to that of Schiller; it is less irregular; more ambitious in its rhetoric; inferior in precision, though often not in force of thought and imagery.

derived from it. Eichhorn, Professor of History, was at this
time about to leave the University of Jena: Goethe had
already introduced his new acquaintance Schiller to the special notice of Amelia, the accomplished Regent of Sachsen-
Weimar; he now joined with Voigt, the head Chaplain of the
Court, in soliciting the vacant chair for him. Seconded by
the general voice, and the persuasion of the Princess herself,
he succeeded. Schiller was appointed Professor at Jena; he
went thither in 1789.

With Schiller's removal to Jena begins a new epoch in his
public and private life. His connection with Goethe here first
ripened into friendship, and became secured and cemented by
frequency of intercourse.[1] Jena is but a few miles distant
from Weimar; and the two friends, both settled in public
offices belonging to the same Government, had daily opportunities of interchanging visits. Schiller's wanderings were
now concluded: with a heart tired of so fluctuating an existence, but not despoiled of its capacity for relishing a calmer
one; with a mind experienced by much and varied intercourse
with men; full of knowledge and of plans to turn it to account, he could now repose himself in the haven of domestic
comforts, and look forward to days of more unbroken exertion,
and more wholesome and permanent enjoyment than hitherto
had fallen to his lot. In the February following his settlement at Jena, he obtained the hand of Fräulein Lengefeld;
a happiness, with the prospect of which he had long associated
all the pleasures which he hoped for from the future. A few
months after this event, he thus expresses himself, in writing
to a friend: —

"Life is quite a different thing by the side of a beloved wife,
than so forsaken and alone; even in Summer. Beautiful
Nature! I now for the first time fully enjoy it, live in it. The
world again clothes itself around me in poetic forms; old feel-

---

[1] The obstacles to their union have already been described in the words of
Goethe; the steps by which these were surmounted, are described by him in
the same paper with equal minuteness and effect. It is interesting, but cannot be inserted here. See Appendix, No. 3.

ings are again awakening in my breast. What a life I am leading here ! I look with a glad mind around me ; my heart finds a perennial contentment without it ; my spirit so fine, so refreshing a nourishment. My existence is settled in harmo- nious composure ; not strained and impassioned, but peaceful and clear. I look to my future destiny with a cheerful heart ; now when standing at the wished-for goal, I wonder with myself how it all has happened, so far beyond my expectations. Fate has conquered the difficulties for me ; it has, I may say, forced me to the mark. From the future I expect everything. A few years, and I shall live in the full enjoyment of my spirit ; nay, I think my very youth will be renewed ; an inward poetic life will give it me again."

To what extent these smiling hopes were realized will be seen in the next and concluding Part of this Biography.

PART III.

FROM HIS SETTLEMENT AT JENA TO HIS DEATH.

1790–1805.

THE duties of his new office naturally called upon Schiller to devote himself with double zeal to History: a subject, which from choice he had already entered on with so much eagerness. In the study of it, we have seen above how his strongest faculties and tastes were exercised and gratified: and new opportunities were now combined with new motives for persisting in his efforts. Concerning the plan or the success of his academical prelections, we have scarcely any notice: in his class, it is said, he used most frequently to speak extempore; and his delivery was not distinguished by fluency or grace, a circumstance to be imputed to the agitation of a public appearance; for, as Woltmann assures us, "the beauty, the elegance, ease, and true instructiveness with which he could continuously express himself in private, were acknowledged and admired by all his friends." His matter, we suppose, would make amends for these deficiencies of manner: to judge from his introductory lecture, preserved in his works, with the title, *What is Universal History, and with what views should it be studied,* there perhaps has never been in Europe another course of history sketched out on principles so magnificent and philosophical.[1] But college exercises were far from being his ulti-

---

[1] The paper entitled *Hints on the Origin of Human Society, as indicated in the Mosaic Records, the Mission of Moses, the Laws of Solon and Lycurgus,* are pieces of the very highest order; full of strength and beauty; delicious to the lovers of that plastic philosophy, which employs itself in giving form and life to the "dry bones" of those antique events, that lie before us so inexplicable

mate object, nor did he rest satisfied with mere visions of perfection : the compass of the outline he had traced, for a proper
Historian, was scarcely greater than the assiduity with which
he strove to fill it up. His letters breathe a spirit not only of
diligence but of ardor; he seems intent with all his strength
upon this fresh pursuit; and delighted with the vast prospects
of untouched and attractive speculation, which were opening
around him on every side. He professed himself to be "exceedingly contented with his business;" his ideas on the nature of it were acquiring both extension and distinctness; and
every moment of his leisure was employed in reducing them
to practice. He was now busied with the *History of the
Thirty-Years War.*

This work, which appeared in 1791, is considered by the
German critics as his chief performance in this department
of literature: *The Revolt of the Netherlands,* the only one
which could have vied with it, never was completed; otherwise,
in our opinion, it might have been superior. Either of the
two would have sufficed to secure for Schiller a distinguished
rank among historians, of the class denominated philosophical;
though even both together, they afford but a feeble exemplification of the ideas which he entertained on the manner of composing history. In his view, the business of history is not
merely to record, but to interpret; it involves not only a clear
conception and a lively exposition of events and characters,
but a sound, enlightened theory of individual and national
morality, a general philosophy of human life, whereby to judge
of them, and measure their effects. The historian now stands
on higher ground, takes in a wider range than those that went
before him; he can now survey vast tracts of human action,
and deduce its laws from an experience extending over many
climes and ages. With his ideas, moreover, his feelings ought
to be enlarged: he should regard the interests not of any sect
or state, but of mankind; the progress not of any class of arts

in the brief and enigmatic pages of their chroniclers. The *Glance over Europe
at the period of the first Crusade;* the *Times of the Emperor Frederick I.;* the
Troubles in France, are also masterly sketches, in a simpler and more common
style.

or opinions, but of universal happiness and refinement. His narrative, in short, should be moulded according to the science, and impregnated with the liberal spirit of his time.

Voltaire is generally conceived to have invented and introduced a new method of composing history; the chief historians that have followed him have been by way of eminence denominated philosophical. This is hardly correct. Voltaire wrote history with greater talent, but scarcely with a new species of talent: he applied the ideas of the eighteenth century to the subject; but in this there was nothing radically new. In the hands of a thinking writer history has always been "philosophy teaching by experience;" that is, such philosophy as the age of the historian has afforded. For a Greek or Roman, it was natural to look upon events with an eye to their effect on his own city or country; and to try them by a code of principles, in which the prosperity or extension of this formed a leading object. For a monkish chronicler, it was natural to estimate the progress of affairs by the number of abbeys founded; the virtue of men by the sum-total of donations to the clergy. And for a thinker of the present day, it is equally natural to measure the occurrences of history by quite a different standard: by their influence upon the general destiny of man, their tendency to obstruct or to forward him in his advancement towards liberty, knowledge, true religion and dignity of mind. Each of these narrators simply measures by the scale which is considered for the time as expressing the great concerns and duties of humanity.

Schiller's views on this matter were, as might have been expected, of the most enlarged kind. "It seems to me," said he in one of his letters, "that in writing history for the moderns, we should try to communicate to it such an interest as the History of the Peloponnesian War had for the Greeks. Now this is the problem: to choose and arrange your materials so that, to interest, they shall not need the aid of decoration. We moderns have a source of interest at our disposal, which no Greek or Roman was acquainted with, and which the *patriotic* interest does not nearly equal. This last, in general, is chiefly of importance for unripe nations, for the youth of the world.

But we may excite a very different sort of interest if we represent each remarkable occurrence that happened to *men* as of importance to *man.* It is a poor and little aim to write for one nation; a philosophic spirit cannot tolerate such limits, cannot bound its views to a form of human nature so arbitrary, fluctuating, accidental. The most powerful nation is but a fragment; and thinking minds will not grow warm on its account, except in so far as this nation or its fortunes have been influential on the progress of the species."

That there is not some excess in this comprehensive cosmopolitan philosophy, may perhaps be liable to question. Nature herself has, wisely no doubt, partitioned us into "kindreds, and nations, and tongues:" it is among our instincts to grow warm in behalf of our country, simply for its own sake; and the business of Reason seems to be to chasten and direct our instincts, never to destroy them. We require individuality in our attachments: the sympathy which is expanded over all men will commonly be found so much attenuated by the process, that it cannot be effective on any. And as it is in nature, so it is in art, which ought to be the image of it. Universal philanthropy forms but a precarious and very powerless rule of conduct; and the "progress of the species" will turn out equally unfitted for deeply exciting the imagination. It is not with freedom that we can sympathize, but with free men. There ought, indeed, to be in history a spirit superior to petty distinctions and vulgar partialities; our particular affections ought to be enlightened and purified; but they should not be abandoned, or, such is the condition of humanity, our feelings must evaporate and fade away in that extreme diffusion. Perhaps, in a certain sense, the surest mode of pleasing and instructing all nations *is* to write for one.

This too Schiller was aware of, and had in part attended to. Besides, the Thirty-Years War is a subject in which nationality of feeling may be even wholly spared, better than in almost any other. It is not a German but a European subject; it forms the concluding portion of the Reformation, and this is an event belonging not to any country in particular, but to the human race. Yet, if we mistake not, this

over-tendency to generalization, both in thought and sentiment, has rather hurt the present work. The philosophy,
with which it is imbued, now and then grows vague from
its abstractness, ineffectual from its refinement: the enthusiasm which pervades it, elevated, strong, enlightened, would
have told better on our hearts, had it been confined within
a narrower space, and directed to a more specific class of ob
jects. In his extreme attention to the philosophical aspects
of the period, Schiller has neglected to take advantage of
many interesting circumstances, which it offered under other
points of view. The Thirty-Years War abounds with what
may be called picturesqueness in its events, and still more
in the condition of the people who carried it on. Harte's *History of Gustavus*, a wilderness which mere human patience
seems unable to explore, is yet enlivened here and there
with a cheerful spot, when he tells us of some scalade or
camisado, or speculates on troopers rendered bullet-proof by
art-magic. His chaotic records have, in fact, afforded to our
Novelist the raw materials of Dugald Dalgetty, a cavalier of
the most singular equipment, of character and manners which,
for many reasons, merit study and description. To much of
this, though, as he afterwards proved, it was well known to
him, Schiller paid comparatively small attention; his work
has lost in liveliness by the omission, more than it has gained
in dignity or instructiveness.

Yet, with all its imperfections, this is no ordinary history.
The speculation, it is true, is not always of the kind we wish;
it excludes more moving or enlivening topics, and sometimes
savors of the inexperienced theorist who had passed his days
remote from practical statesmen; the subject has not sufficient unity; in spite of every effort, it breaks into fragments
towards the conclusion: but still there is an energy, a vigorous beauty in the work, which far more than redeems its fail-
ings. Great thoughts at every turn arrest our attention, and
make us pause to confirm or contradict them; happy metaphors,[1] some vivid descriptions of events and men, remind us

---

[1] Yet we scarcely meet with one so happy as that in the *Revolt of the
Netherlands*, where he finishes his picture of the gloomy silence and dismay

of the author of *Fiesco* and *Don Carlos*. The characters of Gustavus and Wallenstein are finely developed in the course of the narrative. Tilly's passage of the Lech, the battles of Leipzig and Lützen figure in our recollection, as if our eyes had witnessed them: the death of Gustavus is described in terms which might draw "iron tears" from the eyes of veterans.[1] If Schiller had inclined to dwell upon the mere visual or imaginative department of his subject, no man could have painted it more graphically, or better called forth our emotions, sympathetic or romantic. But this, we have seen, was not by any means his leading aim.

On the whole, the present work is still the best historical performance which Germany can boast of. Müller's histories are distinguished by merits of another sort; by condensing, in a given space, and frequently in lucid order, a quantity of information, copious and authentic beyond example: but as intellectual productions, they cannot rank with Schiller's. Woltmann of Berlin has added to the *Thirty-Years War* another work of equal size, by way of continuation, entitled *History of the Peace of Munster;* with the first negotiations of which treaty the former concludes. Woltmann is a person of ability; but we dare not say of him, what Wieland said of Schiller, that by his first historical attempt he "has discovered a decided capability of rising to a level with Hume, Robertson and Gibbon." He will rather rise to a level with Belsham or Smollett.

This first complete specimen of Schiller's art in the historical department, though but a small fraction of what he meant to do, and could have done, proved in fact to be the last he ever undertook. At present very different cares awaited him: in 1791, a fit of sickness overtook him; he had to exchange the inspiring labors of literature for the

that reigned in Brussels on the first entrance of Alba, by this striking simile: "Now that the City had received the Spanish General within its walls, it had the air as of a man that has drunk a cup of poison, and with shuddering expectation watches, every moment, for its deadly agency."

[1] See Appendix, No. 4.

disgusts and disquietudes of physical disease. His disorder, which had its seat in the chest, was violent and threatening; and though nature overcame it in the present instance, the blessing of entire health never more returned to him. The cause of this severe affliction seemed to be the unceasing toil and anxiety of mind, in which his days had hitherto been passed: his frame, which, though tall, had never been robust, was too weak for the vehement and sleepless soul that dwelt within it; and the habit of nocturnal study had, no doubt, aggravated all the other mischiefs. Ever since his residence at Dresden, his constitution had been weakened: but this rude shock at once shattered its remaining strength; for a time the strictest precautions were required barely to preserve existence. A total cessation from every intellectual effort was one of the most peremptory laws prescribed to him. Schiller's habits and domestic circumstances equally rebelled against this measure; with a beloved wife depending on him for support, inaction itself could have procured him little rest. His case seemed hard; his prospects of innocent felicity had been too banefully obscured. Yet in this painful and difficult position, he did not yield to despondency; and at length, assistance, and partial deliverance, reached him from a very unexpected quarter. Schiller had not long been sick, when the hereditary Prince, now reigning Duke of Holstein-Augustenburg, jointly with the Count Von Schimmelmann, conferred on him a pension of a thousand crowns for three years.[1] No stipulation was added, but merely that he should be careful of his health, and use every attention to recover. This speedy and generous aid, moreover, was presented with a delicate politeness, which, as Schiller said, touched him more than even the gift itself. We should remember this Count and this Duke; they deserve some admiration and some envy.

This disorder introduced a melancholy change into Schiller's circumstances: he had now another enemy to strive with, a secret and fearful impediment to vanquish, in which much

---

[1] It was to Denmark likewise that Klopstock owed the means of completing his *Messias*.

resolute effort must be sunk without producing any positive result. Pain is not entirely synonymous with Evil; but bodily pain seems less redeemed by good than almost any other kind of it. From the loss of fortune, of fame, or even of friends, Philosophy pretends to draw a certain compensating benefit; but in general the permanent loss of health will bid defiance to her alchemy. It is a universal diminution; the diminution equally of our resources and of our capacity to guide them; a penalty unmitigated, save by love of friends, which then first becomes truly dear and precious to us; or by comforts brought from beyond this earthly sphere, from that serene Fountain of peace and hope, to which our weak Philosophy cannot raise her wing. For all men, in itself, disease is misery; but chiefly for men of finer feelings and endowments, to whom, in return for such superiorities, it seems to be sent most frequently and in its most distressing forms. It is a cruel fate for the poet to have the sunny land of his imagination, often the sole territory he is lord of, disfigured and darkened by the shades of pain; for one whose highest happiness is the exertion of his mental faculties, to have them chained and paralyzed in the imprisonment of a distempered frame. With external activity, with palpable pursuits, above all, with a suitable placidity of nature, much even in certain states of sickness may be performed and enjoyed. But for him whose heart is already over-keen, whose world is of the mind, ideal, internal; when the mildew of lingering disease has struck that world, and begun to blacken and consume its beauty, nothing seems to remain but despondency and bitterness and desolate sorrow, felt and anticipated, to the end.

Woe to him if his will likewise falter, if his resolution fail, and his spirit bend its neck to the yoke of this new enemy! Idleness and a disturbed imagination will gain the mastery of him, and let loose their thousand fiends to harass him, to torment him into madness. Alas! the bondage of Algiers is freedom compared with this of the sick man of genius, whose heart has fainted and sunk beneath its load. His clay dwelling is changed into a gloomy prison; every nerve is become an avenue of disgust or anguish; and the soul sits within, in her

melancholy loneliness, a prey to the spectres of despair, or
stupefied with excess of suffering, doomed as it were to a "life
in death," to a consciousness of agonized existence, without the
consciousness of power which should accompany it.   Happily,
death, or entire fatuity, at length puts an end to such scenes
of ignoble misery; which, however, ignoble as they are, we
ought to view with pity rather than contempt.

Such are frequently the fruits of protracted sickness, in men
otherwise of estimable qualities and gifts, but whose sensibility
exceeds their strength of mind.   In Schiller, its worst effects
were resisted by the only availing antidote, a strenuous determination to neglect them.   His spirit was too vigorous and
ardent to yield even in this emergency : he disdained to dwindle into a pining valetudinarian; in the midst of his infirmities,
he persevered with unabated zeal in the great business of his
life.   As he partially recovered, he returned as strenuously as
ever to his intellectual occupations; and often, in the glow of
poetical conception, he almost forgot his maladies.   By such
resolute and manly conduct, he disarmed sickness of its cruelest power to wound; his frame might be in pain, but his spirit
retained its force, unextinguished, almost unimpeded; he did
not lose his relish for the beautiful, the grand, or the good,
in any of their shapes; he loved his friends as formerly, and
wrote his finest and sublimest works when his health was
gone.   Perhaps no period of his life displayed more heroism
than the present one.

After this severe attack, and the kind provision which he
had received from Denmark, Schiller seems to have relaxed
his connection with the University of Jena : the weightiest
duties of his class appear to have been discharged by proxy,
and his historical studies to have been forsaken.   Yet this was
but a change, not an abatement, in the activity of his mind.
Once partially free from pain, all his former diligence awoke;
and being also free from the more pressing calls of duty and
economy, he was now allowed to turn his attention to objects
which attracted it more.   Among these one of the most alluring was the Philosophy of Kant.

The transcendental system of the Königsberg Professor had,

for the last ten years, been spreading over Germany, which it
had now filled with the most violent contentions. The powers
and accomplishments of Kant were universally acknowledged;
the high pretensions of his system, pretensions, it is true, such
as had been a thousand times put forth, a thousand times found
wanting, still excited notice, when so backed by ability and
reputation. The air of mysticism connected with these doctrines was attractive to the German mind, with which the
vague and the vast are always pleasing qualities; the dreadful
array of first principles, the forest huge of terminology and
definitions, where the panting intellect of weaker men wanders
as in pathless thickets, and at length sinks powerless to the
earth, oppressed with fatigue, and suffocated with scholastic
miasma, seemed sublime rather than appalling to the Germans;
men who shrink not at toil, and to whom a certain degree of
darkness appears a native element, essential for giving play to
that deep meditative enthusiasm which forms so important
a feature in their character. Kant's Philosophy, accordingly,
found numerous disciples, and possessed them with a zeal
unexampled since the days of Pythagoras. This, in fact, resembled spiritual fanaticism rather than a calm ardor in the
cause of science; Kant's warmest admirers seemed to regard
him more in the light of a prophet than of a mere earthly sage.
Such admiration was of course opposed by corresponding censure; the transcendental neophytes had to encounter sceptical
gainsayers as determined as themselves. Of this latter class
the most remarkable were Herder and Wieland. Herder, then
a clergyman of Weimar, seems never to have comprehended
what he fought against so keenly: he denounced and condemned the Kantian metaphysics, because he found them
heterodox. The young divines came back from the University
of Jena with their minds well nigh delirious; full of strange
doctrines, which they explained to the examinators of the
Weimar Consistorium in phrases that excited no idea in the
heads of these reverend persons, but much horror in their
hearts.[1] Hence reprimands, and objurgations, and excessive

---

[1] Schelling has a book on the "Soul of the World:" Fichte's expression
to his students, "To-morrow, gentlemen, I shall create God," is known to most
readers.

bitterness between the applicants for ordination and those appointed to confer it : one young clergyman at Weimar shot himself on this account; heresy, and jarring, and unprofitable logic, were universal. Hence Herder's vehement attacks on this " pernicious quackery ; " this delusive and destructive " system of words." [1] Wieland strove against it for another reason. He had, all his life, been laboring to give currency among his countrymen to a species of diluted epicurism ; to erect a certain smooth, and elegant, and very slender scheme of taste and morals, borrowed from our Shaftesbury and the French. All this feeble edifice the new doctrine was sweeping before it to utter ruin, with the violence of a tornado. It grieved Wieland to see the work of half a century destroyed : he fondly imagined that but for Kant's philosophy it might have been perennial. With scepticism quickened into action by such motives, Herder and he went forth as brother champions against the transcendental metaphysics ; they were not long without a multitude of hot assailants. The uproar produced among thinking men by the conflict, has scarcely been equalled in Germany since the days of Luther. Fields were fought, and victories lost and won ; nearly all the minds of the nation were, in secret or openly, arrayed on this side or on that. Goethe alone seemed altogether to retain his wonted composure ; he was clear for allowing the Kantian scheme to " have its day, as all things have." Goethe has already lived to see the wisdom of this sentiment, so characteristic of his genius and turn of thought.

In these controversies, soon pushed beyond the bounds of temperate or wholesome discussion, Schiller took no part : but the noise they made afforded him a fresh inducement to investigate a set of doctrines, so important in the general estimation. A system which promised, even with a very little plausibility,

---

[1] See *Herder's Leben*, by his Widow. That Herder was not usually troubled with any unphilosophical scepticism, or aversion to novelty, may be inferred from his patronizing Dr. Gall's system of Phrenology, or " Skull-doctrine " as they call it in Germany. But Gall had referred with acknowledgment and admiration to the *Philosophie der Geschichte der Menschheit*. Here lay a difference.

to accomplish all that Kant asserted his complete performance of; to explain the difference between Matter and Spirit, to unravel the perplexities of Necessity and Free-will; to show us the true grounds of our belief in God, and what hope nature gives us of the soul's immortality; and thus at length, after a thousand failures, to interpret the enigma of our being, — hardly needed that additional inducement to make such a man as Schiller grasp at it with eager curiosity.   His progress also was facilitated by his present circumstances; Jena had now become the chief well-spring of Kantian doctrine, a distinction or disgrace it has ever since continued to deserve.   Reinhold, one of Kant's ablest followers, was at this time Schiller's fellow-teacher and daily companion: he did not fail to encourage and assist his friend in a path of study, which, as he believed, conducted to such glorious results.   Under this tuition, Schiller was not long in discovering, that at least the "new philosophy was more poetical than that of Leibnitz, and had a grander character;" persuasions which of course confirmed him in his resolution to examine it.

How far Schiller penetrated into the arcana of transcendentalism it is impossible for us to say.   The metaphysical and logical branches of it seem to have afforded him no solid satisfaction, or taken no firm hold of his thoughts; their influence is scarcely to be traced in any of his subsequent writings. The only department to which he attached himself with his ordinary zeal was that which relates to the principles of the imitative arts, with their moral influences, and which in the Kantian nomenclature has been designated by the term Æsthetics,[1] or the doctrine of sentiments and emotions.   On these subjects he had already amassed a multitude of thoughts; to see which expressed by new symbols, and arranged in systematic form, and held together by some common theory, would necessarily yield enjoyment to his intellect, and inspire him with fresh alacrity in prosecuting such researches.   The new light which dawned, or seemed to dawn, upon him, in the course of these investigations, is reflected, in various treatises,

[1] From the verb αἰσθάνομαι, to feel. — The term is Baumgarten's; prior to Kant (1845).

evincing, at least, the honest diligence with which he studied, and the fertility with which he could produce. Of these the largest and most elaborate are the essays on *Grace and Dignity ;* on *Naïve and Sentimental Poetry ;* and the *Letters on the Æsthetic Culture of Man :* the other pieces are on *Tragic Art ;* on the *Pathetic ;* on the *Cause of our Delight in Tragic Objects ;* on *Employing the Low and Common in Art.*

Being cast in the mould of Kantism, or at least clothed in its garments, these productions, to readers unacquainted with that system, are encumbered here and there with difficulties greater than belong intrinsically to the subject. In perusing them, the uninitiated student is mortified at seeing so much powerful thought distorted, as he thinks, into such fantastic forms : the principles of reasoning, on which they rest, are apparently not those of common logic ; a dimness and doubt overhangs their conclusions ; scarcely anything is proved in a convincing manner. But this is no strange quality in such writings. To an exoteric reader the philosophy of Kant almost always appears to invert the common maxim ; its end and aim seem not to be " to make abstruse things simple, but to make simple things abstruse." Often a proposition of inscrutable and dread aspect, when resolutely grappled with, and torn from its shady den, and its bristling entrenchments of uncouth terminology, and dragged forth into the open light of day, to be seen by the natural eye, and tried by merely human understanding, proves to be a very harmless truth, familiar to us from of old, sometimes so familiar as to be a truism. Too frequently, the anxious novice is reminded of Dryden in the *Battle of the Books :* there is a helmet of rusty iron, dark, grim, gigantic ; and within it, at the farthest corner, is a head no bigger than a walnut. These are the general errors of Kantian criticism ; in the present works, they are by no means of the worst or most pervading kind ; and there is a fundamental merit which does more than counterbalance them. By the aid of study, the doctrine set before us can, in general, at length be comprehended ; and Schiller's fine intellect, recognizable even in its masquerade, is ever and anon peering forth in its native form, which all may understand, which all must relish, and presenting us with passages that show like bright verdant islands in the misty sea of metaphysics.

We have been compelled to offer these remarks on Kant's Philosophy; but it is right to add that they are the result of only very limited acquaintance with the subject. We cannot wish that any influence of ours should add a note, however feeble, to the loud and not at all melodious cry which has been raised against it in this country. When a class of doctrines so involved in difficulties, yet so sanctioned by illustrious names, is set before us, curiosity must have a theory respecting them, and indolence and other humbler feelings are too ready to afford her one. To call Kant's system a laborious dream, and its adherents crazy mystics, is a brief method, brief but false. The critic, whose philosophy includes the *craziness* of men like these, so easily and smoothly in its formulas, should render thanks to Heaven for having gifted him with science and acumen, as few in any age or country have been gifted. Meaner men, however, ought to recollect that where we do not understand, we should postpone deciding, or, at least, keep our decision for our own exclusive benefit. We of England may reject this Kantian system, perhaps with reason; but it ought to be on other grounds than are yet before us. Philosophy is science, and science, as Schiller has observed, cannot always be explained in "conversations by the parlor fire," or in written treatises that resemble such. The *cui bono* of these doctrines may not, it is true, be expressible by arithmetical computations: the subject also is perplexed with obscurities, and probably with manifold delusions; and too often its interpreters with us have been like "tenebrific stars," that "did ray out darkness" on a matter itself sufficiently dark. But what then? Is the jewel always to be found among the common dust of the highway, and always to be estimated by its value in the common judgment? It lies embosomed in the depths of the mine; rocks must be rent before it can be reached; skilful eyes and hands must separate it from the rubbish where it lies concealed, and kingly purchasers alone can prize it and buy it. This law of *ostracism* is as dangerous in science as it was of old in politics. Let us not forget that many things are true which cannot be demonstrated by the rules of *Watt's Logic ;* that many truths are valuable, for which no price is given in Paternoster Row, and no preferment offered at St. Stephen's !　Whoever reads these treatises of Schiller with attention, will perceive that they depend on principles of an immensely higher and more complex character than our "Essays on Taste," and our "Inquiries concerning the Freedom of the Will."　The laws of criticism, which it is their purpose to establish, are derived from the inmost nature of man ; the scheme of morality, which they inculcate, soars into a brighter region, very far beyond the ken of our "Utilities" and "Reflex-senses."　They do not teach us "to judge of poetry and art as we judge of dinner," merely by observing the impressions it produced in us ; and they *do* derive the duties and chief end of man from other grounds than the philosophy of Profit and Loss.　These *Letters on Æsthetic Culture,* without the aid of anything which the most sceptical could designate as superstition, trace out and attempt to sanction for us a system of morality, in which the sublimest feelings of the Stoic and the Christian are represented but as stages in our progress to the pinnacle of true human grandeur ; and man, isolated on this fragment of the universe, encompassed with the boundless desolate Unknown, at war with Fate, without help or the hope of help, is confidently called upon to rise into a calm cloudless height of internal activity and peace, and *be,* what he has fondly named himself, the god of this lower world. When such are the results, who would not make an effort for the steps by which they are attained ?　In Schiller's treatises, it must be owned, the reader, after all exertions, will be fortunate if he can find them.　Yet a second perusal will satisfy him better than the first ; and among the shapeless immensities which fill the Night of Kantism, and the meteoric coruscations, which perplex him rather than enlighten, he will fancy he descries some streaks of a serener radiance, which he will pray devoutly that time may purify and ripen into perfect day. The Philosophy of Kant is probably combined with errors to its very core ; but perhaps also, this ponderous unmanageable dross may bear in it the everlasting gold of truth !　Mighty spirits have already labored in refining it: is it wise in us to take up with the base pewter of Utility, and renounce such projects altogether? We trust, not.[1]

That Schiller's *genius* profited by this laborious and ardent study of Æsthetic Metaphysics, has frequently been doubted, and sometimes denied. That, after such investigations, the process of composition would become more difficult, might be inferred from the nature of the case. That also the principles of this critical theory were in part erroneous, in still greater part too far-fetched and fine-spun for application to the business of writing, we may farther venture to assert. But excellence, not ease of composition, is the thing to be desired; and in a mind like Schiller's, so full of energy, of images and thoughts and creative power, the more sedulous practice of selection was little likely to be detrimental. And though considerable errors might mingle with the rules by which he judged himself, the habit of judging carelessly, or not at all, is far worse than that of sometimes judging wrong. Besides, once accustomed to attend strictly to the operations of his genius, and rigorously to try its products, such a man as Schiller could not fail in time to discover what was false in the principles by which he tried them, and consequently, in the end, to retain the benefits of this procedure without its evils. There is doubtless a purism in taste, a rigid fantastical demand of perfection, a horror at approaching the limits of impropriety, which obstructs the free impulse of the faculties, and if excessive, would altogether deaden them. But the excess on the other side is much more frequent, and, for high endowments, infinitely more pernicious. After the strongest efforts, there may be little realized; without strong efforts, there must be little. That too much care does hurt in any of our tasks is a doctrine so flattering to indolence, that we ought to receive it with extreme caution. In works impressed with the stamp of true genius, their quality, not

---

[1] Are our hopes from Mr. Coleridge always to be fruitless? Sneers at the common-sense philosophy of the Scotch are of little use: it is a poor philosophy, perhaps; but not so poor as none at all, which seems to be the state of matters here at present.

their extent, is what we value : a dull man may spend his
lifetime writing little ; better so than writing much ; but a
man of powerful mind is liable to no such danger. Of all
our authors, Gray is perhaps the only one that from fasti-
diousness of taste has written less than he should have done :
there are thousands that have erred the other way. What
would a Spanish reader give, had Lope de Vega composed a
hundred times as little, and that little a hundred times as
well !

Schiller's own ideas on these points appear to be sufficiently
sound : they are sketched in the following extract of a letter,
interesting also as a record of his purposes and intellectual
condition at this period : —

"Criticism must now make good to me the damage she
herself has done. And damaged me she most certainly has ;
for the boldness, the living glow which I felt before a rule
was known to me, have for several years been wanting. I
now *see* myself *create* and *form* : I watch the play of inspiration ; and my fancy, knowing she is not without witnesses of
her movements, no longer moves with equal freedom. I hope,
however, ultimately to advance so far that *art* shall become a
second *nature*, as polished manners are to well-bred men ;
then Imagination will regain her former freedom, and submit
to none but voluntary limitations."

Schiller's subsequent writings are the best proof that in
these expectations he had not miscalculated.

The historical and critical studies, in which he had been
so extensively and seriously engaged, could not remain without effect on Schiller's general intellectual character. He
had spent five active years in studies directed almost solely
to the understanding, or the faculties connected with it ; and
such industry united to such ardor had produced an immense
accession of ideas. History had furnished him with pictures
of manners and events, of strange conjunctures and conditions
of existence ; it had given him more minute and truer conceptions of human nature in its many forms, new and more accurate opinions on the character and end of man. The domain

of his mind was. both enlarged and enlightened; a multitude of images and detached facts and perceptions had been laid up in his memory; and his intellect was at once enriched by acquired thoughts, and strengthened by increased exercise on a wider circle of knowledge.

But to understand was not enough for Schiller; there were in him faculties which this could not employ, and therefore could not satisfy. The primary vocation of his nature was poetry: the acquisitions of his other faculties served but as the materials for his poetic faculty to act upon, and seemed imperfect till they had been sublimated into the pure and perfect forms of beauty, which it is the business of this to elicit from them. New thoughts gave birth to new feelings: and both of these he was now called upon to body forth, to represent by visible types, to animate and adorn with the magic of creative genius. The first youthful blaze of poetic ardor had long since passed away; but this large increase of knowledge awakened it anew, refined by years and experience into a steadier and clearer flame. Vague shadows of unaccomplished excellence, gleams of ideal beauty, were now hovering fitfully across his mind: he longed to turn them into shape, and give them a local habitation and a name. Criticism, likewise, had exalted his notions of art: the modern writers on subjects of taste, Aristotle, the ancient poets, he had lately studied; he had carefully endeavored to extract the truth from each, and to amalgamate their principles with his own; in choosing, he was now more difficult to satisfy. Minor poems had all along been partly occupying his attention; but they yielded no space for the intensity of his impulses, and the magnificent ideas that were rising in his fancy. Conscious of his strength, he dreaded not engaging with the highest species of his art: the perusal of the Greek tragedians had given rise to some late translations;[1] the perusal of Homer seems now to have suggested the idea of an epic poem. The hero whom he first contemplated was Gustavus Adolphus; he afterwards changed to Frederick the Great of Prussia.

[1] These were a fine version of Euripides' *Iphigenia in Aulide*, and a few scenes of his *Phœnissœ*.

Epic poems, since the time of the *Epigoniad*, and *Leonidas*, and especially since that of some more recent attempts, have with us become a mighty dull affair. That Schiller aimed at something infinitely higher than these faint and superannuated imitations, far higher than even Klopstock has attained, will appear by the following extract from one of his letters : —

"An epic poem in the eighteenth century should be quite a different thing from such a poem in the childhood of the world. And it is that very circumstance which attracts me so much towards this project. Our manners, the finest essence of our philosophies, our politics, economy, arts, in short, of all we know and do, would require to be introduced without constraint, and interwoven in such a composition, to live there in beautiful harmonious freedom, as all the branches of Greek culture live and are made visible in Homer's *Iliad*. Nor am I disinclined to invent a species of machinery for this purpose; being anxious to fulfil, with hairsbreadth accuracy, all the requisitions that are made of epic poets, even on the side of form. Besides, this machinery, which, in a subject so modern, in an age so prosaic, appears to present the greatest difficulty, might exalt the interest in a high degree, were it suitably adapted to this same modern spirit. Crowds of confused ideas on this matter are rolling to and fro within my head; something distinct will come out of them at last.

"As for the sort of metre I would choose, this I think you will hardly guess: no other than *ottave rime*. All the rest, except iambic, are become insufferable to me. And how beautifully might the earnest and the lofty be made to play in these light fetters ! What attractions might the epic *substance* gain by the soft yielding *form* of this fine rhyme ! For, the poem must, not in name only, but in very deed, be capable of being *sung ;* as the *Iliad* was sung by the peasants of Greece, as the stanzas of *Jerusalem Delivered* are still sung by the Venetian gondoliers.

"The epoch of Frederick's life that would fit me best, I have considered also. I should wish to select some unhappy situation; it would allow me to unfold his mind far more poetically. The chief action should, if possible, be very simple, perplexed with no complicated circumstances, that the whole might easily be comprehended at a glance, though the episodes were never so numerous. In this respect there is no better model than the *Iliad*."

Schiller did not execute, or even commence, the project he has here so philosophically sketched : the constraints of his present situation, the greatness of the enterprise compared with the uncertainty of its success, were sufficient to deter him. Besides, he felt that after all his wide excursions, the true home of his genius was the Drama, the department where its powers had first been tried, and were now by habit or nature best qualified to act. To the Drama he accordingly returned. The *History of the Thirty-Years War* had once suggested the idea of Gustavus Adolphus as the hero of an epic poem; the same work afforded him a subject for a tragedy : he now decided on beginning *Wallenstein*. In this undertaking it was no easy task that he contemplated; a common play did not now comprise his aim; he required some magnificent and comprehensive object, in which he could expend to advantage the new poetical and intellectual treasures which he had for years been amassing; something that should at once exemplify his enlarged ideas of art, and give room and shape to his fresh stores of knowledge and sentiment. As he studied the history of Wallenstein, and viewed its capabilities on every side, new ideas gathered round it : the subject grew in magnitude, and often changed in form. His progress in actual composition was, of course, irregular and small. Yet the difficulties of the subject, increasing with his own wider, more ambitious conceptions, did not abate his diligence : *Wallenstein*, with many interruptions and many alterations, sometimes stationary, sometimes retrograde, continued on the whole, though slowly, to advance.

This was for several years his chosen occupation, the task to which he consecrated his brightest hours, and the finest part of his faculties. For humbler employments, demanding rather industry than inspiration, there still remained abundant leisure, of which it was inconsistent with his habits to waste a single

hour. His occasional labors, accordingly, were numerous,
varied, and sometimes of considerable extent. In the end of
1792, a new object seemed to call for his attention; he once
about this time seriously meditated mingling in politics. The
French Revolution had from the first affected him with no
ordinary hopes; which, however, the course of events, particularly the imprisonment of Louis, were now fast converting
into fears. For the ill-fated monarch, and the cause of freedom, which seemed threatened with disgrace in the treatment
he was likely to receive, Schiller felt so deeply interested, that
he had determined, in his case a determination not without
its risks, to address an appeal on these subjects to the French
people and the world at large. The voice of reason advocating
liberty as well as order might still, he conceived, make a
salutary impression in this period of terror and delusion; the
voice of a distinguished man would at first sound like the voice
of the nation, which he seemed to represent. Schiller was
inquiring for a proper French translator, and revolving in his
mind the various arguments that might be used, and the comparative propriety of using or forbearing to use them; but the
progress of things superseded the necessity of such deliberation. In a few months, Louis perished on the scaffold; the
Bourbon family were murdered, or scattered over Europe; and
the French government was changed into a frightful chaos,
amid the tumultuous and bloody horrors of which, calm truth
had no longer a chance to be heard. Schiller turned away
from these repulsive and appalling scenes, into other regions
where his heart was more familiar, and his powers more likely
to produce effect. The French Revolution had distressed and
shocked him; but it did not lessen his attachment to liberty,
the name of which had been so desecrated in its wild con-
vulsions. Perhaps in his subsequent writings we can trace a
more respectful feeling towards old establishments; more
reverence for the majesty of Custom; and with an equal zeal,
a weaker faith in human perfectibility: changes indeed which
are the common fruit of years themselves, in whatever age or
climate of the world our experience may be gathered.

Among the number of fluctuating engagements, one, which

for ten years had been constant with him, was the editing of the *Thalia*. The principles and performances of that work he had long looked upon as insufficient: in particular, ever since his settlement at Jena, it had been among his favorite projects to exchange it for some other, conducted on a more liberal scheme, uniting more ability in its support, and embracing a much wider compass of literary interests. Many of the most distinguished persons in Germany had agreed to assist him in executing such a plan ; Goethe, himself a host, undertook to go hand in hand with him. The *Thalia* was in consequence relinquished at the end of 1793 : and the first number of the *Horen* came out early in the following year. This publication was enriched with many valuable pieces on points of philosophy and criticism ; some of Schiller's finest essays first appeared here : even without the foreign aids which had been promised him, it already bade fair to outdo, as he had meant it should, every previous work of that description.

The *Musen-Almanach*, of which he likewise undertook the superintendence, did not aim so high : like other works of the same title, which are numerous in Germany, it was intended for preserving and annually delivering to the world, a series of short poetical effusions, or other fugitive compositions, collected from various quarters, and often having no connection but their juxtaposition. In this work, as well as in the *Horen*, some of Schiller's finest smaller poems made their first appearance ; many of these pieces being written about this period, especially the greater part of his ballads, the idea of attempting which took its rise in a friendly rivalry with Goethe. But the most noted composition sent forth in the pages of the *Musen-Almanach*, was the *Xenien* ;[1] a collection of epigrams which originated partly, as it seems, in the mean or irritating conduct of various contemporary authors. In spite of the most flattering promises, and of its own intrinsic character, the *Horen*, at its first appearance, instead of being hailed with welcome by the leading minds of the country, for whom it was intended as a rallying point, met in many quarters with no

---

[1] So called from ξένιον, *munus hospitale ;* a title borrowed from Martial, who has thus designated a series of personal epigrams in his Thirteenth Book.

sentiment but coldness or hostility. The controversies of the day had sown discord among literary men; Schiller and Goethe, associating together, had provoked ill-will from a host of persons, who felt the justice of such mutual preference, but liked not the inferences to be drawn from it; and eyed this intellectual duumvirate, however meek in the discharge of its functions and the wearing of its honors, with jealousy and discontent.

The cavilling of these people, awkwardly contrasted with their personal absurdity and insipidity, at length provoked the serious notice of the two illustrious associates : the result was this German Dunciad; a production of which the plan was, that it should comprise an immense multitude of detached couplets, each conveying a complete thought within itself, and furnished by one of the joint operators. The subjects were of unlimited variety; "the most," as Schiller says, "were wild satire, glancing at writers and writings, intermixed with here and there a flash of poetical or philosophic thought." It was at first intended to provide about a thousand of these pointed monodistichs; unity in such a work appearing to consist in a certain boundlessness of size, which should hide the heterogeneous nature of the individual parts : the whole were then to be arranged and elaborated, till they had acquired the proper degree of consistency and symmetry; each sacrificing something of its own peculiar spirit to preserve the spirit of the rest. This number never was completed: and, Goethe being now busy with his *Wilhelm Meister*, the project of completing it was at length renounced; and the *Xenien* were published as unconnected particles, not pretending to constitute a whole. Enough appeared to create unbounded commotion among the parties implicated : the *Xenien* were exclaimed against, abused, and replied to, on all hands; but as they declared war not on persons but on actions; not against Gleim, Nicolai, Manso, but against bad taste, dulness, and affectation, nothing criminal could be sufficiently made out against them.[1] The *Musen-Almanach*, where they appeared in 1797, continued to be pub-

---

[1] This is but a lame account of the far-famed *Xenien* and their results. See more of the matter in Franz Horn's *Poesie und Beredtsamkeit;* in Carlyle's *Miscellanies* (i. 67); &c. (*Note of* 1845.)

lished till the time of Schiller's leaving Jena : the *Horen* ceased some months before.

The co-operation of Goethe, which Schiller had obtained so readily in these pursuits, was of singular use to him in many others. Both possessing minds of the first order, yet constructed and trained in the most opposite modes, each had much that was valuable to learn of the other, and suggest to him. Cultivating different kinds of excellence, they could joyfully admit each other's merit; connected by mutual services, and now by community of literary interests, few unkindly feelings could have place between them. For a man of high qualities, it is rare to find a meet companion; painful and injurious to want one. Solitude exasperates or deadens the heart, perverts or enervates the faculties; association with inferiors leads to dogmatism in thought, and self-will even in affections. Rousseau never should have lived in the Val de Montmorenci; it had been good for Warburton that Hurd had not existed; for Johnson never to have known Boswell or Davies. From such evils Schiller and Goethe were delivered; their intimacy seems to have been equal, frank and cordial; from the contrasts and the endowments of their minds, it must have had peculiar charms. In his critical theories, Schiller had derived much profit from communicating with an intellect as excursive as his own, but far cooler and more sceptical: as he lopped off from his creed the excrescences of Kantism, Goethe and he, on comparing their ideas, often found in them a striking similarity; more striking and more gratifying, when it was considered from what diverse premises these harmonious conclusions had been drawn. On such subjects they often corresponded when absent, and conversed when together. They were in the habit of paying long visits to each other's houses; frequently they used to travel in company between Jena and Weimar. "At Triesnitz, a couple of English miles from Jena, Goethe and he," we are told, "might sometimes be observed sitting at table, beneath the shade of a spreading tree ; talking, and looking at the current of passengers."— There are some who would have "travelled fifty miles on foot" to join the party !

Besides this intercourse with Goethe, he was happy in a kindly connection with many other estimable men, both in literary and in active life. Dalberg, at a distance, was to the last his friend and warmest admirer. At Jena, he had Schütz, Paul, Hufland, Reinhold. Wilhelm von Humboldt, also, brother of the celebrated traveller, had come thither about this time, and was now among his closest associates. At Weimar, excluding less important persons, there were still Herder and Wieland, to divide his attention with Goethe. And what to his affectionate heart must have been the most grateful circumstance of all, his aged parents were yet living to participate in the splendid fortune of the son whom they had once lamented and despaired of, but never ceased to love. In 1793 he paid them a visit in Swabia, and passed nine cheerful months among the scenes dearest to his recollection : enjoying the kindness of those unalterable friends whom Nature had given him; and the admiring deference of those by whom it was most delightful to be honored, — those who had known him in adverse and humbler circumstances, whether they might have respected or contemned him. By the Grand Duke, his ancient censor and patron, he was not interfered with; that prince, in answer to a previous application on the subject, having indirectly engaged to take no notice of this journey. The Grand Duke had already interfered too much with him, and bitterly repented of his interference. Next year he died; an event which Schiller, who had long forgotten past ill-treatment, did not learn without true sorrow, and grateful recollections of bygone kindness. The new sovereign, anxious to repair the injustice of his predecessor, almost instantly made offer of a vacant Tübingen professorship to Schiller; a proposal flattering to the latter, but which, by the persuasion of the Duke of Weimar, he respectfully declined.

Amid labors and amusements so multiplied, amid such variety of intellectual exertion and of intercourse with men, Schiller, it was clear, had not suffered the encroachments of bodily disease to undermine the vigor of his mental or moral powers. No period of his life displayed in stronger colors the lofty and determined zeal of his character. He had already written much; his fame stood upon a firm basis; domestic wants no longer called upon him for incessant effort; and his frame was pining under the slow canker of an incurable malady. Yet he never loitered, never rested; his fervid spirit, which had vanquished opposition and oppression in his youth; which had struggled against harassing uncertainties, and passed unsullied through many temptations, in his earlier manhood, did not now yield to this last and most fatal enemy. The present was the busiest, most productive season of his literary life; and with all its drawbacks, it was probably the happiest. Violent attacks from his disorder were of rare occurrence; and its constant influence, the dark vapors with which it would have overshadowed the faculties of his head and heart, were repelled by diligence and a courageous exertion of his will. In other points, he had little to complain of, and much to rejoice in. He was happy in his family, the chosen scene of his sweetest, most lasting satisfaction; by the world he was honored and admired; his wants were provided for; he had tasks which inspired and occupied him; friends who loved him, and whom he loved. Schiller had much to enjoy, and most of it he owed to himself.

In his mode of life at Jena, simplicity and uniformity were the most conspicuous qualities; the single excess which he admitted being that of zeal in the pursuits of literature, the sin which all his life had most easily beset him. His health had suffered much, and principally, it was thought, from the practice of composing by night: yet the charms of this practice were still too great for his self-denial; and, except in severe fits of sickness, he could not discontinue it. The highest, proudest pleasure of his mind was that glow of intellectual production, that "fine frenzy," which makes the poet, while it lasts, a new and nobler creature; exalting him into brighter regions, adorned by visions of magnificence and beauty, and delighting all his faculties by the intense consciousness of their exerted power. To enjoy this pleasure in perfection, the solitary stillness of night, diffusing its solemn influence over thought as well as earth and air, had at length in Schiller's case grown indispensable. For this purpose, accordingly, he was accustomed, in the present, as in former periods, to invert the common order of things : by day he read, refreshed himself with the aspect of nature, conversed or corresponded with his friends ; but he wrote and studied in the night. And as his bodily feelings were too often those of languor and exhaustion, he adopted, in impatience of such mean impediments, the pernicious expedient of stimulants, which yield a momentary strength, only to waste our remaining fund of it more speedily and surely.

"During summer, his place of study was in a garden, which at length he purchased, in the suburbs of Jena, not far from the Weselhöfts' house, where at that time was the office of the *Allgemeine Litteratur-Zeitung.* Reckoning from the market-place of Jena, it lies on the south-west border of the town, between the Engelgatter and the Neuthor, in a hollow defile, through which a part of the Leutrabach flows round the city. On the top of the acclivity, from which there is a beautiful prospect into the valley of the Saal, and the fir mountains of the neighboring forest, Schiller built himself a small house, with a single chamber.[1] It was his favorite abode during hours of composition; a great part of the works he then wrote were written here. In winter he likewise dwelt apart from the noise of men ; in the Griesbachs' house, on the outside of the city-trench. . . . On sitting down to his desk at night, he was wont to keep some strong coffee, or wine-chocolate, but more frequently a flask of old Rhenish, or Champagne, standing by him, that he might from time to time repair the exhaustion of nature. Often the neighbors used to hear him earnestly declaiming, in the silence of the night: and whoever had an opportunity of watching him on such occasions, a thing very easy to be done from the heights lying opposite his little garden-house, on the other side of the dell, might see him now speaking aloud and walking swiftly to and fro in his chamber, then suddenly throwing himself down into his chair and writing; and drinking the while, sometimes more than once, from the glass stand-

---

[1] "The street leading from Schiller's dwelling-house to this, was by some wags named the *Xenien-gasse;* a name not yet entirely disused."

ing near him. In winter he was to be found at his desk till
four, or even five o'clock in the morning; in summer, till
towards three. He then went to bed, from which he seldom
rose till nine or ten." [1]

Had prudence been the dominant quality in Schiller's character, this practice would undoubtedly have been abandoned,
or rather never taken up. It was an error so to waste his
strength; but one of those which increase rather than diminish
our respect; originating, as it did, in generous ardor for what
was best and grandest, they must be cold censurers that can
condemn it harshly. For ourselves, we but lament and honor
this excess of zeal; its effects were mournful, but its origin
was noble. Who can picture Schiller's feelings in this solitude, without participating in some faint reflection of their
grandeur! The toil-worn but devoted soul, alone, under the
silent starry canopy of Night, offering up the troubled moments of existence on the altar of Eternity! For here the
splendor that gleamed across the spirit of a mortal, transient
as one of us, was made to be perpetual; these images and
thoughts were to pass into other ages and distant lands; to
glow in human hearts, when the heart that conceived them
had long been mouldered into common dust. To the lovers
of genius, this little garden-house might have been a place
to visit as a chosen shrine; nor will they learn without regret that the walls of it, yielding to the hand of time, have
already crumbled into ruin, and are now no longer to be
traced. The piece of ground that it stood on is itself hallowed with a glory that is bright, pure and abiding; but the
literary pilgrim could not have surveyed, without peculiar
emotion, the simple chamber, in which Schiller wrote the
Reich der Schatten, the *Spaziergang*, the *Ideal*, and the immortal scenes of *Wallenstein*.

The last-named work had cost him many an anxious, given
him many a pleasant, hour. For seven years it had continued
in a state of irregular, and oft-suspended progress; sometimes
" lying endless and formless " before him; sometimes on the
point of being given up altogether. The multitude of ideas,

[1] Doering, pp. 118–131.

which he wished to incorporate in the structure of the piece, retarded him; and the difficulty of contenting his taste, respecting the manner of effecting this, retarded him still more. In *Wallenstein* he wished to embody the more enlarged notions which experience had given him of men, especially which history had given him of generals and statesmen; and while putting such characters in action, to represent whatever was, or could be made, poetical, in the stormy period of the Thirty-Years War. As he meditated on the subject, it continued to expand; in his fancy, it assumed successively a thousand forms; and after all due strictness of selection, such was still the extent of materials remaining on his hands, that he found it necessary to divide the play into three parts, distinct in their arrangements, but in truth forming a continuous drama of eleven acts. In this shape it was sent forth to the world, in 1799; a work of labor and persevering anxiety, but of anxiety and labor, as it then appeared, which had not been bestowed in vain. *Wallenstein* is by far the best performance he had yet produced; it merits a long chapter of criticism by itself; and a few hurried pages are all that we can spend on it.

As a porch to the great edifice stands Part first, entitled *Wallenstein's Camp*, a piece in one act. It paints, with much humor and graphical felicity, the manners of that rude tumultuous host which Wallenstein presided over, and had made the engine of his ambitious schemes. Schiller's early experience of a military life seems now to have stood him in good stead: his soldiers are delineated with the distinctness of actual observation; in rugged sharpness of feature, they sometimes remind us of Smollett's seamen. Here are all the wild lawless spirits of Europe assembled within the circuit of a single trench. Violent, tempestuous, unstable is the life they lead. Ishmaelites, their hands against every man, and every man's hand against them; the instruments of rapine; tarnished with almost every vice, and knowing scarcely any virtue but those of reckless bravery and uncalculating obedience to their leader, their situation still presents some aspects which affect or amuse us; and these the poet has seized with his accustomed skill.

Much of the cruelty and repulsive harshness of these soldiers, we are taught to forget in contemplating their forlorn houseless wanderings, and the practical magnanimity, with which even they contrive to wring from Fortune a tolerable scantling of enjoyment. Their manner of existence Wallenstein has, at an after period of the action, rather movingly expressed:

> "Our life was but a battle and a march,
>   And, like the wind's blast, never-resting, homeless,
>   We storm'd across the war-convulsed Earth."

Still farther to soften the asperities of the scene, the dialogue is cast into a rude Hudibrastic metre, full of forced rhymes, and strange double endings, with a rhythm ever changing, ever rough and lively, which might almost be compared to the hard, irregular, fluctuating sound of the regimental drum. In this ludicrous doggerel, with phrases and figures of a correspondent cast, homely, ridiculous, graphic, these men of service paint their hopes and doings. There are ranks and kinds among them; representatives of all the constituent parts of the motley multitude, which followed this prince of *Condottieri.* The solemn pedantry of the ancient Wachtmeister is faithfully given; no less so are the jocund ferocity and heedless daring of Holky's Jägers, or the iron courage and stern camp-philosophy of Pappenheim's Cuirassiers. Of the Jäger the sole principle is military obedience; he does not reflect or calculate; his business is to do whatever he is ordered, and to enjoy whatever he can reach. "Free wished I to live," he says,

> . "Free wished I to live, and easy and gay,
>   And see something new on each new day;
>   In the joys of the moment lustily sharing,
>   'Bout the past or the future not thinking or caring:
>   To the Kaiser, therefore, I sold my bacon,
>   And by him good charge of the whole is taken.
>   Order me on 'mid the whistling fiery shot,
>   Over the Rhine-stream rapid and roaring wide,
>   A third of the troop must go to pot, —
>   Without loss of time, I mount and ride;

> But farther, I beg very much, do you see,
> That in all things else you would leave me free."

The Pappenheimer is an older man, more sedate and more indomitable; he has wandered over Europe, and gathered settled maxims of soldierly principle and soldierly privilege : he is not without a *rationale* of life; the various professions of men have passed in review before him, but no coat that he has seen has pleased him like his own "steel doublet," cased in which, it is his wish,

> "Looking down on the world's poor restless scramble,
> Careless, through it, astride of his nag to ramble."

Yet at times with this military stoicism there is blended a dash of homely pathos; he admits,

> "This sword of ours is no plough or spade,
> You cannot delve or reap with the iron blade;
> For us there falls no seed, no cornfield grows,
> Neither home nor kindred the soldier knows:
> Wandering over the face of the earth,
> Warming his hands at another's hearth :
> From the pomp of towns he must onward roam;
> In the village-green with its cheerful game,
> In the mirth of the vintage or harvest-home,
> No part or lot can the soldier claim.
> Tell me then, in the place of goods or pelf,
> What has he unless to honor himself?
> Leave not even *this* his own, what wonder
> The man should burn and kill and plunder ?"

But the camp of Wallenstein is full of bustle as well as speculation; there are gamblers, peasants, sutlers, soldiers, recruits, capuchin friars, moving to and fro in restless pursuit of their several purposes. The sermon of the Capuchin is an unparalleled composition;[1] a medley of texts, puns,

---

[1] Said to be by Goethe; the materials faithfully extracted from a real sermon (by the Jesuit Santa Clara) of the period it refers to. — There were various Jesuits Santa Clara, of that period: this is the *German* one, Abraham by name; specimens of whose Sermons, a fervent kind of preaching-run-mad, have been reprinted in late years, for dilettante purposes. (*Note of* 1845.)

nicknames, and verbal logic, conglutinated by a stupid judgment, and a fiery catholic zeal. It seems to be delivered with
great unction, and to find fit audience in the camp: towards
the conclusion they rush upon him, and he narrowly escapes
killing or ducking, for having ventured to glance a censure at
the General. The soldiers themselves are jeering, wrangling,
jostling; discussing their wishes and expectations; and, at
last, they combine in a profound deliberation on the state of
their affairs. A vague exaggerated outline of the coming
events and personages is imaged to us in their coarse conceptions. We dimly discover the precarious position of Wallenstein; the plots which threaten him, which he is meditating:
we trace the leading qualities of the principal officers; and
form a high estimate of the potent spirit which binds this
fierce discordant mass together, and seems to be the object of
universal reverence where nothing else is revered.

In the *Two Piccolomini*, the next division of the work, the
generals for whom we have thus been prepared appear in
person on the scene, and spread out before us their plots and
counterplots; Wallenstein, through personal ambition and
evil counsel, slowly resolving to revolt; and Octavio Piccolomini, in secret, undermining his influence among the leaders,
and preparing for him that pit of ruin, into which, in the
third Part, *Wallenstein's Death*, we see him sink with all his
fortunes. The military spirit which pervades the former
piece is here well sustained. The ruling motives of these
captains and colonels are a little more refined, or more disguised, than those of the Cuirassiers and Jägers; but they
are the same in substance; the love of present or future
pleasure, of action, reputation, money, power; selfishness,
but selfishness distinguished by a superficial external propriety, and gilded over with the splendor of military honor,
of courage inflexible, yet light, cool and unassuming. These
are not imaginary heroes, but genuine hired men of war:
we do not love them; yet there is a pomp about their operations, which agreeably fills up the scene. This din of
war, this clash of tumultuous conflicting interests, is felt as
a suitable accompaniment to the affecting or commanding

movements of the chief characters whom it envelops or obeys.

Of the individuals that figure in this world of war, Wallenstein himself, the strong Atlas which supports it all, is by far the most imposing. Wallenstein is the model of a high-souled, great, accomplished man, whose ruling passion is ambition. He is daring to the utmost pitch of manhood; he is enthusiastic and vehement; but the fire of his soul burns hid beneath a deep stratum of prudence, guiding itself by calculations which extend to the extreme limits of his most minute concerns. This prudence, sometimes almost bordering on irresolution, forms the outward rind of his character, and for a while is the only quality which we discover in it. The immense influence which his genius appears to exert on every individual of his many followers, prepares us to expect a great man; and, when Wallenstein, after long delay and much forewarning, is in fine presented to us, we at first experience something like a disappointment. We find him, indeed, possessed of a staid grandeur; yet involved in mystery; wavering between two opinions; and, as it seems, with all his wisdom, blindly credulous in matters of the highest import. It is only when events have forced decision on him, that he rises in his native might, that his giant spirit stands unfolded in its strength before us;

" Night must it be, ere Friedland's star will beam : "

amid difficulties, darkness and impending ruin, at which the boldest of his followers grow pale, he himself is calm, and first in this awful crisis feels the serenity and conscious strength of his soul return. Wallenstein, in fact, though pre-eminent in power, both external and internal, of high intellect and commanding will, skilled in war and statesmanship beyond the best in Europe, the idol of sixty thousand fearless hearts, is not yet removed above our sympathy. We are united with him by feelings which he reckons weak, though they belong to the most generous parts of his nature. His indecision partly takes its rise in the sensibilities of his heart, as well as in the caution of his judgment: his belief in astrology, which gives force and confirmation to this tendency, originates in some soft kindly emotions, and adds a new interest to the spirit of the warrior; it humbles him, to whom the earth is subject, before those mysterious Powers which weigh the destinies of man in their balance, in whose eyes the greatest and the least of mortals scarcely differ in littleness. Wallenstein's confidence in the friendship of Octavio, his disinterested love for Max Piccolomini, his paternal and brotherly kindness, are feelings which cast an affecting lustre over the harsher, more heroic qualities wherewith they are combined. His treason to the Emperor is a crime, for which, provoked and tempted as he was, we do not greatly blame him; it is forgotten in our admiration of his nobleness, or recollected only as a venial trespass. Schiller has succeeded well with Wallenstein, where it was not easy to succeed. The truth of history has been but little violated; yet we are compelled to feel that Wallenstein, whose actions individually are trifling, unsuccessful, and unlawful, is a strong, sublime, commanding character; we look at him with interest, our concern at his fate is tinged with a shade of kindly pity.

In Octavio Piccolomini, his war-companion, we can find less fault, yet we take less pleasure. Octavio's qualities are chiefly negative; he rather walks by the letter of the moral law, than by its spirit; his conduct is externally correct, but there is no touch of generosity within. He is more of the courtier than of the soldier: his weapon is intrigue, not force. Believing firmly that "whatever is, is best," he distrusts all new and extraordinary things; he has no faith in human nature, and seems to be virtuous himself more by calculation than by impulse. We scarcely thank him for his loyalty; serving his Emperor, he ruins and betrays his friend: and, besides, though he does not own it, personal ambition is among his leading motives; he wishes to be general and prince, and Wallenstein is not only a traitor to his sovereign, but a bar to this advancement. It is true, Octavio does not personally tempt him towards his destruction; but neither does he warn him from it; and perhaps he knew that fresh temptation was superfluous. Wallenstein did not deserve such treatment from a man whom he had trusted as a brother, even though such confidence was blind, and guided by visions and starry omens. Octavio is a skilful, prudent, managing statesman; of the kind praised loudly, if not sincerely, by their friends, and detested deeply by their enemies. His object may be lawful or even laudable; but his ways are crooked; we dislike him but the more that we know not positively how to blame him.

Octavio Piccolomini and Wallenstein are, as it were, the two opposing forces by which this whole universe of military politics is kept in motion. The struggle of magnanimity and strength combined with treason, against cunning and apparent virtue, aided by law, gives rise to a series of great actions, which are here vividly presented to our view. We mingle in the clashing interests of these men of war; we see them at their gorgeous festivals and stormy consultations, and participate in the hopes or fears that agitate them. The subject had many capabilities; and Schiller has turned them all to profit. Our minds are kept alert by a constant succession of animating scenes of spectacle, dialogue, incident: the plot thickens and darkens as we advance; the interest deepens and deepens to the very end.

But among the tumults of this busy multitude, there are two forms of celestial beauty that solicit our attention, and whose destiny, involved with that of those around them, gives it an importance in our eyes which it could not otherwise have had. Max Piccolomini, Octavio's son, and Thekla, the daughter of Wallenstein, diffuse an ethereal radiance over all this tragedy; they call forth the finest feelings of the heart, where other feelings had already been aroused; they superadd to the stirring pomp of scenes, which had already kindled our imaginations, the enthusiasm of bright unworn humanity, " the bloom of young desire, the purple light of love." The history of Max and Thekla is not a rare one in poetry; but Schiller has treated it with a skill which is extremely rare. Both of them are represented as combining every excellence; their affection is instantaneous and unbounded; yet the coolest, most sceptical reader is forced to admire them, and believe in them.

Of Max we are taught from the first to form the highest expectations: the common soldiers and their captains speak of him as of a perfect hero; the Cuirassiers had, at Pappenheim's death, on the field of Lützen, appointed him their colonel by unanimous election. His appearance answers these ideas : Max is the very spirit of honor, and integrity, and young ardor, personified. Though but passing into maturer age, he has already seen and suffered much; but the experience of the man has not yet deadened or dulled the enthusiasm of the boy. He has lived, since his very childhood, constantly amid the clang of war, and with few ideas but those of camps; yet here, by a native instinct, his heart has attracted to it all that was noble and graceful in the trade of arms, rejecting all that was repulsive or ferocious. He loves Wallenstein his patron, his gallant and majestic leader : he loves his present way of life, because it is one of peril and excitement, because he knows no other, but chiefly because his young unsullied spirit can shed a resplendent beauty over even the wastest region in the destiny of man. Yet though a soldier, and the bravest of soldiers, he is not this alone. He feels that there are fairer scenes in life, which these scenes of havoc and distress but deform or destroy; his first acquaintance with the Princess Thekla unveils to him another world, which till then he had not dreamed of; a land of peace and serene elysian felicity, the charms of which he paints with simple and unrivalled eloquence. Max is not more daring than affectionate; he is merciful and gentle, though his training has been under tents; modest and altogether unpretending, though young and universally admired. We conceive his aspect to be thoughtful but fervid, dauntless but mild : he is the very poetry of war, the essence of a youthful hero. We should have loved him anywhere; but here, amid barren scenes of strife and danger, he is doubly dear to us.

His first appearance wins our favor; his eloquence in sentiment prepares us to expect no common magnanimity in action. It is as follows : *Octavio* and *Questenberg* are consulting on

affairs of state; *Max* enters : he is just returned from convoy-
ing the *Princess Thekla* and her mother, the daughter and the
wife of *Friedland,* to the camp at Pilsen.

ACT I. SCENE IV.

MAX PICCOLOMINI, OCTAVIO PICCOLOMINI, QUESTENBERG.

MAX 'T is he himself! My father, welcome, welcome!
> [*He embraces him: on turning round, he observes Questenberg,
>   and draws coldly back.*

Busied, I perceive? I will not interrupt you.

OCT. How now, Max? View this stranger better!
An old friend deserves regard and kindness ;
The Kaiser's messenger should be rever'd!

MAX [*drily*]. Von Questenberg! If it is good that brings you
To our head-quarters, welcome!

QUEST. [*has taken his hand*]. Nay, draw not
Your hand away, Count Piccolomini!
Not on mine own account alone I grasp it,
And nothing common will I say therewith.
Octavio, Max, Piccolomini!   [*Taking both their hands*
Names of benignant solemn import! Never
Can Austria's fortune fail while two such stars,
To guide and guard her, gleam above our hosts.

MAX. You play it wrong, Sir Minister! To praise,
I wot, you come not hither; to blame and censure
You are come. Let me be no exception.

OCT. [*to Max*]. He comes from Court, where every one is not
So well conteuted with the Duke as here.

MAX. And what new fault have they to charge him with?
That he alone decides what he alone
Can understand? Well! Should it not be so?
It should and must! This man was never made
To ply and mould himself like wax to others:
It goes against his heart; he cannot do it,
He has the spirit of a ruler, and
The station of a ruler. Well for us
It is so! Few can rule themselves, can use
Their wisdom wisely: happy for the whole
Where there is one among them that can be
A centre and a hold for many thousands;

That can plant himself like a firm column,
For the whole to lean on safely! Such a one
Is Wallenstein; some other man might better
Serve the Court, none else could serve the Army.

QUEST. The Army, truly!

MAX.   And it is a pleasure
To behold how all awakes and strengthens
And revives around him; how men's faculties
Come forth; their gifts grow plainer to themselves!
From each he can elicit his endowment,
His peculiar power; and does it wisely;
Leaving each to be the man he found him,
Watching only that he always be so.
I' th' proper place: and thus he makes the talents
Of all mankind his own.

QUEST.   No one denies him
Skill in men, and skill to use them. His fault is
That in the ruler he forgets the servant,
As if he had been born to be commander.

MAX. And is he not? By birth he is invested
With all gifts for it, and with the farther gift
Of finding scope to use them; of acquiring
For the ruler's faculties the ruler's office.

QUEST. So that how far the rest of us have rights
Or influence, if any, lies with Friedland?

MAX. He is no common person; he requires
No common confidence: allow him space;
The proper limit he himself will set.

QUEST. The trial shows it!

MAX.   Ay! Thus it is with them!
Still so! All frights them that has any depth;
Nowhere are they at ease but in the shallows.

OCT. [to Quest.]. Let him have his way, my friend! The argu-
          ment
Will not avail us.

MAX.   They invoke the spirit
I' th' hour of need, and shudder when he rises.
The great, the wonderful, must be accomplished
Like a thing of course!— In war, in battle,
A moment is decisive; on the spot
Must be determin'd, in the instant done.
With ev'ry noble quality of nature

The leader must be gifted: let him live, then,
In their noble sphere! The oracle within him,
The living spirit, not dead books, old forms,
Not mould'ring parchments must he take to counsel.

OCT. My Son! despise not these old narrow forms!
They are as barriers, precious walls and fences,
Which oppressed mortals have erected
To mod'rate the rash will of their oppressors.
For the uncontrolled has ever been destructive.
The way of Order, though it lead through windings,
Is the best. Right forward goes the lightning
And the cannon-ball: quick, by the nearest path.
They come, op'ning with murderous crash their way,
To blast and ruin! My Son! the quiet road
Which men frequent, where peace and blessings travel,
Follows the river's course, the valley's bendings;
Modest skirts the cornfield and the vineyard,
Revering property's appointed bounds;
And leading safe though slower to the mark.

QUEST. Oh, hear your Father! him who is at once
A hero and a man!

OCT.   It is the child
O' th' camp that speaks in thee, my Son: a war
Of fifteen years has nursed and taught thee; peace
Thou hast never seen. My Son, there is a worth
Beyond the worth of warriors: ev'n in war itself
The object is not war. The rapid deeds
Of power, th' astounding wonders of the moment —
It is not these that minister to man
Aught useful, aught benignant or enduring.
In haste the wandering soldier comes, and builds
With canvas his light town: here in a moment
Is a rushing concourse; markets open;
Roads and rivers crowd with merchandise
And people; Traffic stirs his hundred arms.
Ere long, some morning, look, — and it is gone!
The tents are struck, the host has marched away;
Dead as a churchyard lies the trampled seed-field,
And wasted is the harvest of the year.

MAX. O Father! that the Kaiser *would* make peace!
The bloody laurel I would gladly change
For the first violet Spring should offer us,

The tiny pledge that Earth again was young!

OCT. How's this?   What is it that affects thee so?

MAX. Peace I have never seen?   Yes, I have seen it!
Ev'n now I come from it: my journey led me
Through lands as yet unvisited by war.
O Father! life has charms, of which we know not:
We have but seen the barren coasts of life;
Like some wild roving crew of lawless pirates,
Who, crowded in their narrow noisome ship,
Upon the rude sea, with rude manners dwell;
Naught of the fair land knowing but the bays,
Where they may risk their hurried thievish landing.
Of the loveliness that, in its peaceful dales,
The land conceals — O Father! — Oh, of this,
In our wild voyage we have seen no glimpse.

OCT. [*gives increased attention*].
And did this journey show thee much of it?

MAX. 'T was the first holiday of my existence.
Tell me, where's the end of all this labor,
This grinding labor that has stolen my youth,
And left my heart uncheer'd and void, my spirit
Uncultivated as a wilderness?
This camp's unceasing din; the neighing steeds;
The trumpet's clang; the never-changing round
Of service, discipline, parade, give nothing
To the heart, the heart that longs for nourishment.
There is no soul in this insipid bus'ness;
Life has another fate and other joys.

OCT. Much hast thou learn'd, my Son, in this short journey!

MAX. O blessed bright day, when at last the soldier
Shall turn back to life, and be again a man!
Through th' merry lines the colors are unfurl'd,
And homeward beats the thrilling soft peace-march;
All hats and helmets deck'd with leafy sprays,
The last spoil of the fields!   The city's gates
Fly up; now needs not the petard to burst them:
The walls are crowded with rejoicing people;
Their shouts ring through the air: from every tower
Blithe bells are pealing forth the merry vesper
Of that bloody day.   From town and hamlet
Flow the jocund thousands; with their hearty
Kind impetuosity our march impeding.

The old man, weeping that he sees this day,
Embraces his long-lost son : a stranger
He revisits his old home ; with spreading boughs
The tree o'ershadows him at his return,
Which waver'd as a twig when he departed ;
  And modest blushing comes a maid to meet him,
Whom on her nurse's breast he left. O happy,
For whom some kindly door like this, for whom
Soft arms to clasp him shall be open'd !—
    QUEST. [*with emotion*].   O that
The times you speak of should be so far distant !
Should not be to-morrow, be to-day !
    MAX. And who's to blame for it but you at Court ?
I will deal plainly with you, Questenberg :
When I observ'd you here, a twinge of spleen
And bitterness went through me. It is you
That hinder peace ; yes, you. The General
Must force it, and you ever keep tormenting him,
Obstructing all his steps, abusing him ;
For what ? Because the good of Europe lies
Nearer his heart, than whether certain acres
More or less of dirty land be Austria's !
You call him traitor, rebel, God knows what,
Because he spares the Saxons ; as if that
Were not the only way to peace ; for how
If during war, war end not, *can* peace follow ?
Go to ! go to ! As I love goodness, so I hate
This paltry work of yours : and here I vow to God,
For him, this rebel, traitor Wallenstein,
To shed my blood, my heart's blood, drop by drop,
Ere I will see you triumph in his fall !

The Princess Thekla is perhaps still dearer to us. Thekla,
just entering on life, with " timid steps," with the brilliant
visions of a cloister yet undisturbed by the contradictions of
reality, beholds in Max, not merely her protector and escort
to her father's camp, but the living emblem of her shapeless
yet glowing dreams. She knows not deception, she trusts and
is trusted : their spirits meet and mingle, and " clasp each
other firmly and forever." All this is described by the poet
with a quiet inspiration, which finds its way into our deepest

sympathies. Such beautiful simplicity is irresistible. "How long," the Countess Terzky asks,

How long is it since you disclosed your heart?
   MAX.   This morning first I risked a word of it.
   COUN.   Not till this morning during twenty days?
   MAX.   'T was at the castle where you met us, 'twixt this
And Nepomuk, the last stage of the journey.
On a balcony she and I were standing, our looks
In silence turn'd upon the vacant landscape ;
And before us the dragoons were riding,
Whom the Duke had sent to be her escort.
Heavy on my heart lay thoughts of parting,
And with a faltering voice at last I said :
All this reminds me, Fräulein, that to-day
I must be parted from my happiness;
In few hours you will find a father,
Will see yourself encircled by new friends ;
And I shall be to you nought but a stranger,
Forgotten in the crowd — "Speak with Aunt Terzky!"
Quick she interrupted me; I noticed
A quiv'ring in her voice; a glowing blush
Spread o'er her cheeks ; slow rising from the ground,
Her eyes met mine: I could control myself
No longer —
     [*The Princess appears at the door, and stops; the Countess,*
        but not Piccolomini, observing her.
          — I clasp'd her wildly in my arms,
My lips were join'd with hers. Some footsteps stirring
I' th' next room parted us ; 't was you ; what then
Took place, you know.
   COUN.   And can you be so modest,
Or incurious, as not once to ask me
For *my* secret, in return?
   MAX.   Your secret?
   COUN.   Yes, sure! On coming in the moment after,
How my niece receiv'd me, what i' th' instant
Of her first surprise she —
   MAX.   Ha?
   THEKLA [*enters hastily*].   Spare yourself
The trouble, Aunt! That he can learn from me.

    .   .   .   .   .   .

We rejoice in the ardent, pure and confiding affection of these two angelic beings: but our feeling is changed and made more poignant, when we think that the inexorable hand of Destiny is already lifted to smite their world with blackness and desolation. Thekla has enjoyed "two little hours of heavenly beauty;" but her native gayety gives place to serious anticipations and alarms; she feels that the camp of Wallenstein is not a place for hope to dwell in. The instructions and explanations of her aunt disclose the secret: she is not to love Max; a higher, it may be a royal, fate awaits her; but she is to tempt him from his duty, and make him lend his influence to her father, whose daring projects she now for the first time discovers. From that moment her hopes of happiness have vanished, never more to return. Yet her own sorrows touch her less than the ruin which she sees about to overwhelm her tender and affectionate mother. For herself, she waits with gloomy patience the stroke that is to crush her. She is meek, and soft, and maiden-like; but she is Friedland's daughter, and does not shrink from what is unavoidable. There is often a rectitude, and quick inflexibility of resolution about Theklas which contrasts beautifully with her inexperience and timorou, acuteness of feeling: on discovering her father's treason, she herself decides that Max "shall obey his first impulse," and forsake her.

There are few scenes in poetry more sublimely pathetic than this. We behold the sinking but still fiery glory of Wallenstein, opposed to the impetuous despair of Max Piccolomini, torn asunder by the claims of duty and of love; the calm but broken-hearted Thekla, beside her broken-hearted mother, and surrounded by the blank faces of Wallenstein's desponding followers. There is a physical pomp corresponding to the moral grandeur of the action; the successive revolt and departure of the troops is heard without the walls of the Palace; the trumpets of the Pappenheimers re-echo the wild feelings of their leader. What follows too is equally affecting. Max being forced away by his soldiers from the side of Thekla, rides forth at their head in a state bordering on frenzy. Next day come tidings of his fate, which no heart is hard enough to hear unmoved. The effect it produces upon Thekla displays all the hidden energies of her soul. The first accidental hearing of the news had almost overwhelmed her; but she summons up her strength: she sends for the messenger, that she may question him more closely, and listen to his stern details with the heroism of a Spartan virgin.

Act IV. Scene X.

THEKLA; the SWEDISH CAPTAIN; FRÄULEIN NEUBRUNN.

CAPT. [*approaches respectfully*].
Princess — I — must pray you to forgive me
My most rash unthinking words: I could not —
    THEKLA [*with noble dignity*].
You saw me in my grief; a sad chance made you
At once my confidant, who were a stranger.
    CAPT. I fear the sight of me is hateful to you:
They were mournful tidings I brought hither.
    THEKLA.   The blame was mine! 'T was I that forced them from
                you;
Your voice was but the voice of Destiny.
My terror interrupted your recital:
Finish it, I pray you.
    CAPT.   'T will renew your grief!
    THEKLA.   I am prepared for 't, I will be prepared.
Proceed! How went the action? Let me hear.
    CAPT.   At Neustadt, dreading no surprise, we lay
Slightly entrench'd; when towards night a cloud
Of dust rose from the forest, and our outposts
Rush'd into the camp, and cried: The foe was there!
Scarce had we time to spring on horseback, when
The Pappenheimers, coming at full gallop,
Dash'd o'er the palisado, and next moment
These fierce troopers pass'd our camp-trench also.
But thoughtlessly their courage had impelled them
To advance without support; their infantry
Was far behind; only the Pappenheimers
Boldly following their bold leader —
            [*Thekla makes a movement. The Captain pauses for a
            moment, till she beckons him to proceed.*
On front and flank with all our horse we charged them;

And ere long forc'd them back upon the trench,
Where rank'd in haste our infantry presented
An iron hedge of pikes to stop their passage.
Advance they could not, nor retreat a step,
Wedg'd in this narrow prison, death on all sides.
Then the Rheingraf call'd upon their leader,
In fair battle, fairly to surrender:
But Colonel Piccolomini —   [*Thekla, tottering, catches by a seat.*
               — We knew him

By 's helmet-plume and his long flowing hair,
The rapid ride had loosen'd it : to th' trench
He points ; leaps first himself his gallant steed
Clean over it ; the troop plunge after him :
But — in a twinkle it was done ! — his horse
Run through the body by a partisan,
Rears in its agony, and pitches far
Its rider ; and fierce o'er him tramp the steeds
O' th' rest, now heeding neither bit nor bridle.

    [*Thekla, who has listened to the last words with increasing an-*
       guish, falls into a violent tremor; she is sinking to the ground;
       Fräulein Neubrunn hastens to her, and receives her in her arms.

NEU. Lady, dearest mistress —
CAPT. [*moved*].   Let me begone.
THEKLA. 'T is past ; conclude it.
CAPT.   Seeing their leader fall,
A grim inexorable desperation
Seiz'd the troops : their own escape forgotten,
Like wild tigers they attack us ; their fury
Provokes our soldiers, and the battle ends not
Till the last man of the Pappenheimers falls.

    THEKLA [*with a quivering voice*].
And where — where is — You have not told me all.
    CAPT. [*after a pause*].
This morning we interr'd him. He was borne
By twelve youths of the noblest families,
And all our host accompanied the bier.
A laurel deck'd his coffin ; and upon it
The Rheingraf laid his own victorious sword.
Nor were tears wanting to his fate : for many
Of us had known his noble-mindedness.
And gentleness of manners ; and all hearts
Were mov'd at his sad end. Fain would the Rheingraf

Have sav'd him ; but himself prevented it ;
'T is said he wish'd to die

NEU. [*with emotion, to Thekla, who hides her face*].

               O dearest mistress,

Look up ! Oh, why would you insist on this ?

THEKLA. Where is his grave ?

CAPT.   I' th' chapel of a cloister

At Neustadt is he laid, till we receive
Directions from his father.

THEKLA.   What is its name ?

CAPT. St. Catharine's.

THEKLA.   Is 't far from this ?

CAPT.   Seven leagues.

THEKLA. How goes the way ?

CAPT.   You come by Tirschenreit

And Falkenberg, and through our farthest outposts.

THEKLA. Who commands them ?

CAPT.   Colonel Seckendorf.

THEKLA [*steps to a table, and takes a ring from her jewel-box*].

You have seen me in my grief, and shown me
A sympathizing heart : accept a small
Memorial of this hour [*giving him the ring*]. Now leave me.

CAPT. [*overpowered*].   Princess !

    [*Thekla silently makes him a sign to go, and turns from him.
      He lingers, and attempts to speak; Neubrunn repeats the
      sign; he goes.*

SCENE XI.

NEUBRUNN; THEKLA.

THEKLA [*falls on Neubrunn's neck*].

Now, good Neubrunn, is the time to show the love
Which thou hast always vow'd me. Prove thyself
A true friend and attendant ! We must go,
This very night.

NEU.   Go ! This very night ! And whither ?

THEKLA. Whither ? There is but one place in the world,
The place where he lies buried : to his grave.

NEU. Alas, what would you there, my dearest mistress ?

THEKLA. What there ? Unhappy girl ! Thou would'st not ask
If thou hadst ever lov'd. There, there, is all
That yet remains of him; that one small spot

Is all the earth to me.   Do not detain me!

Oh, come!   Prepare, think how we may escape.

    NEU. Have you reflected on your father's anger?

    THEKLA. I dread no mortal's anger now.

    NEU.   The mockery

Of the world, the wicked tongue of slander!

    THEKLA. I go to seek one that is cold and low:

Am I, then, hast'ning to my lover's arms?

O God! I am but hast'ning to his grave!

    NEU. And we alone? Two feeble, helpless women?

    THEKLA. We will arm ourselves; my hand shall guard thee.

    NEU. In the gloomy night-time?

    THEKLA.   Night will hide us.

    NEU. In this rude storm?

    THEKLA.   Was *his* bed made of down,

When the horses' hoofs went o'er him?

    NEU.   O Heaven!

And then the many Swedish posts! They will not

Let us pass.

    THEKLA. Are they not men? Misfortune

Passes free through all the earth.

    NEU.   So far! So —

    THEKLA. Does the pilgrim count the miles, when journeying

To the distant shrine of grace?

    NEU.   How shall we

Even get out of Eger?

    THEKLA.   Gold opens gates.

Go! Do go!

    NEU.   If they should recognize us?

    THEKLA. In a fugitive despairing woman

No one will look to meet with Friedland's daughter.

    NEU. And where shall we get horses for our flight?

    THEKLA. My Equerry will find them.   Go and call him.

    NEU. Will he venture without his master's knowledge?

    THEKLA. He will, I tell thee.   Go! Oh, linger not!

    NEU. Ah! And what will your mother do when you

Are vanish'd?

    THEKLA [*recollecting this, and gazing with a look of anguish*].

          O my mother!

    NEU.   Your good mother!

She has already had so much to suffer.

Must this last heaviest stroke too fall on her?

THEKLA. I cannot help it. Go, I prithee, go!

NEU. Think well what you are doing.

THEKLA.   All is thought
That can be thought, already.

NEU.   *Were* we there,
What would you do?

THEKLA.   God will direct me, there.

NEU. Your heart is full of trouble: O my lady!
This way leads *not* to peace.

THEKLA.   To that deep peace
Which he has found. Oh, hasten! Go! No words!
There is some force, I know not what to call it,
Pulls me irresistibly, and drags me
On to his grave: there I shall find some solace
Instantly: the strangling band of sorrow
Will be loosen'd; tears will flow. Oh, hasten!
Long time ago we might have been o' th' road.
No rest for me till I have fled these walls:
They fall upon me, some dark power repels me
From them — Ha! What's this? The chamber's filling
With pale gaunt shapes! No room is left for me!
More! more! The crowding spectres press on me,
And push me forth from this accursed house.

NEU. You frighten me, my lady: I dare stay
No longer; quickly I'll call Rosenberg.

SCENE XII.

THEKLA.

It is his spirit calls me! 'T is the host
Of faithful souls that sacrificed themselves
In fiery vengeance for him. They upbraid me
For this loit'ring: *they* in death forsook him not,
Who in their life had led them; their rude hearts
Were capable of this: and *I* can live?
No! No! That laurel-garland which they laid
Upon his bier was twined for both of us!
What is this life without the light of love?
I cast it from me, since its worth is gone.
Yes, when we found and lov'd each other, life

> WAS something!   Glittering lay before me
> The golden morn : I had two hours of Heaven.
>
>   Thou stoodest at the threshold of the scene
> Of busy life; with timid steps I cross'd it:
> How fair it lay in solemn shade and sheen!
> And thou beside me, like some angel, posted
> To lead me out of childhood's fairy land
> On to life's glancing summit, hand in hand!
> My first thought was of joy no tongue can tell,
> My first look on *thy* spotless spirit fell.
>   [*She sinks into a reverie, then with signs of horror proceeds.*
> And Fate put forth his hand : inexorable, cold,
> My friend it grasp'd and clutch'd with iron hold,
> And — under th' hoofs of their wild horses hurl'd:
> Such is the lot of loveliness i' th' world!

Thekla has yet another pang to encounter; the parting with her mother: but she persists in her determination, and goes forth to die beside her lover's grave.   The heart-rending emotions, which this amiable creature has to undergo, are described with an almost painful effect: the fate of Max and Thekla might draw tears from the eyes of a stoic.

Less tender, but not less sublimely poetical, is the fate of Wallenstein himself.   We do not pity Wallenstein; even in ruin he seems too great for pity.   His daughter having vanished like a fair vision from the scene, we look forward to Wallenstein's inevitable fate with little feeling save expectant awe : —

> This kingly Wallenstein, whene'er he falls,
> Will drag a world to ruin down with him;
> And as a ship that in the midst of ocean
> Catches fire, and shiv'ring springs into the air,
> And in a moment scatters between sea and sky
> The crew it bore, so will he hurry to destruction
> Ev'ry one whose fate was join'd with his.

Yet still there is some touch of pathos in his gloomy fall; some visitings of nature in the austere grandeur of his slowly coming, but inevitable and annihilating doom.   The last scene of his life is among the finest which poetry can boast of. Thekla's death is still unknown to him; but he thinks of Max, and almost weeps. He looks at the stars: dim shadows of superstitious dread pass fitfully across his spirit, as he views these fountains of light, and compares their glorious and enduring existence with the fleeting troubled life of man. The strong spirit of his sister is subdued by dark forebodings; omens are against him; his astrologer entreats, one of the relenting conspirators entreats, his own feelings call upon him, to watch and beware. But he refuses to let the resolution of his mind be overmastered; he casts away these warnings, and goes cheerfully to sleep, with dreams of hope about his pillow, unconscious that the javelins are already grasped which will send him to his long and dreamless sleep. The death of Wallenstein does not cause tears; but it is perhaps the most high-wrought scene of the play. A shade of horror, of fateful dreariness, hangs over it, and gives additional effect to the fire of that brilliant poetry, which glows in every line of it. Except in *Macbeth* or the conclusion of *Othello*, we know not where to match it. Schiller's genius is of a kind much narrower than Shakspeare's; but in his own peculiar province, the exciting of lofty, earnest, strong emotion, he admits of no superior. Others are finer, more piercing, varied, thrilling, in their influence: Schiller, in his finest mood, is overwhelming.

This tragedy of *Wallenstein*, published at the close of the eighteenth century, may safely be rated as the greatest dramatic work of which that century can boast. France never rose into the sphere of Schiller, even in the days of her Corneille: nor can our own country, since the times of Elizabeth, name any dramatist to be compared with him in general strength of mind, and feeling, and acquired accomplishment. About the time of *Wallenstein's* appearance, we of this gifted land were shuddering at *The Castle Spectre!* Germany, indeed, boasts of Goethe: and on some rare occasions, it must be owned that Goethe, has shown talents of a higher order than are here manifested; but he has made no equally regular or powerful exertion of them: *Faust* is but a careless effusion compared with *Wallenstein*. The latter is in truth a vast and magnificent work. What an assemblage of images, ideas, emotions, disposed in the most felicitous and impressive order! We have conquerors, statesmen, ambitious generals, marauding soldiers, heroes, and heroines, all acting and feeling as they would in nature, all faithfully depicted, yet all embellished by the spirit of poetry, and all made conducive to heighten one paramount impression, our sympathy with the three chief characters of the piece.[1]

Soon after the publication of *Wallenstein*, Schiller once more changed his abode. The "mountain air of Jena" was conceived by his physicians to be prejudicial in disorders of the lungs; and partly in consequence of this opinion, he determined henceforth to spend his winters in Weimar. Perhaps a weightier reason in favor of this new arrangement was the opportunity it gave him of being near the theatre, a constant attendance on which, now that he had once more become a dramatist, seemed highly useful for his farther improvement. The summer he, for several years, continued still to spend in Jena; to which, especially its beautiful environs, he declared himself particularly attached. His little garden-house was still his place of study during summer;· till at last he settled constantly at Weimar. Even then he used frequently to visit Jena; to which there was a fresh attraction in later years, when Goethe chose it for his residence, which, we understand, it still occasionally is. With Goethe he often stayed for months.

This change of place produced little change in Schiller's habits or employment: he was now as formerly in the pay of

---

[1] *Wallenstein* has been translated into French by M. Benjamin Constant; and the last two parts of it have been faithfully rendered into English by Mr. Coleridge. As to the French version, we know nothing, save that it is an *improved* one; but that little is enough: Schiller, as a dramatist, improved by M. Constant, is a spectacle we feel no wish to witness. Mr. Coleridge's translation is also, as a whole, unknown to us: but judging from many large specimens, we should pronounce it, excepting Sotheby's *Oberon*, to be the best, indeed the only sufferable, translation from the German with which our literature has yet been enriched.

the Duke of Weimar; now as formerly engaged in dramatic composition as the great object of his life. What the amount of his pension was, we know not: that the Prince behaved to him in a princely manner, we have proof sufficient. Four years before, when invited to the University of Tübingen, Schiller had received a promise, that, in case of sickness or any other cause preventing the continuance of his literary labor, his salary should be doubled. It was actually increased on occasion of the present removal; and again still farther in 1804, some advantageous offers being made to him from Berlin. Schiller seems to have been, what he might have wished to be, neither poor nor rich: his simple unostentatious economy went on without embarrassment: and this was all that he required. To avoid pecuniary perplexities was constantly among his aims: to amass wealth, never. We ought also to add that, in 1802, by the voluntary solicitation of the Duke, he was ennobled; a fact which we mention, for his sake by whose kindness this honor was procured; not for the sake of Schiller, who accepted it with gratitude, but had neither needed nor desired it.

The official services expected of him in return for so much kindness seem to have been slight, if any. Chiefly or altogether of his own accord, he appears to have applied himself to a close inspection of the theatre, and to have shared with Goethe the task of superintending its concerns. The rehearsals of new pieces commonly took place at the house of one of these friends; they consulted together on all such subjects, frankly and copiously. Schiller was not slow to profit by the means of improvement thus afforded him; in the mechanical details of his art he grew more skilful: by a constant observation of the stage, he became more acquainted with its capabilities and its laws. It was not long till, with his characteristic expansiveness of enterprise, he set about turning this new knowledge to account. In conjunction with Goethe, he remodelled his own *Don Carlos* and his friend's *Count Egmont*, altering both according to his latest views of scenic propriety. It was farther intended to treat, in the same manner, the whole series of leading German plays, and thus to produce a national stock of dramatic pieces, formed according to the best rules; a vast project, in which some progress continued to be made, though other labors often interrupted it. For the present, Schiller was engaged with his *Maria Stuart:* it appeared in 1800.

This tragedy will not detain us long. It is upon a subject, the incidents of which are now getting trite, and the moral of which has little that can peculiarly recommend it. To exhibit the repentance of a lovely but erring woman, to show us how her soul may be restored to its primitive nobleness, by sufferings, devotion and death, is the object of *Maria Stuart.* It is a tragedy of sombre and mournful feelings; with an air of melancholy and obstruction pervading it; a looking backward on objects of remorse, around on imprisonment, and forward on the grave. Its object is undoubtedly attained. We are forced to pardon and to love the heroine; she is beautiful, and miserable, and lofty-minded; and her crimes, however dark, have been expiated by long years of weeping and woe. Considering also that they were the fruit not of calculation, but of passion acting on a heart not dead, though blinded for a time, to their enormity, they seem less hateful than the cold premeditated villany of which she is the victim. Elizabeth is selfish, heartless, envious; she violates no law, but she has no virtue, and she lives triumphant: her arid, artificial character serves by contrast to heighten our sympathy with her warm-hearted, forlorn, ill-fated rival. These two Queens, particularly Mary, are well delineated: their respective qualities are vividly brought out, and the feelings they were meant to excite arise within us. There is also Mortimer, a fierce, impetuous, impassioned lover; driven onward chiefly by the heat of his blood, but still interesting by his vehemence and unbounded daring. The dialogue, moreover, has many beauties; there are scenes which have merited peculiar commendation. Of this kind is the interview between the Queens; and more especially the first entrance of Mary, when, after long seclusion, she is once more permitted to behold the cheerful sky. In the joy of a momentary freedom, she forgets that she is still a captive; she addresses the clouds, the "sailors of the air," who "are not subjects of Elizabeth," and bids them carry tidings of her to the hearts that love her in other lands. Without doubt, in all that he intended, Schiller has succeeded; *Maria Stuart* is a beautiful tragedy; it would have formed the glory of a meaner man, but it cannot materially alter his. Compared with *Wallenstein*, its purpose is narrow, and its result is common. We have no manners or true historical delineation. The figure of the English court is not given; and Elizabeth is depicted more like one of the French Medici, than like our own politic, capricious, coquettish, imperious, yet on the whole true-hearted, "good Queen Bess." With abundant proofs of genius, this tragedy produces a comparatively small effect, especially on English readers. We have already wept enough for Mary Stuart, both over prose and verse; and the persons likely to be deeply touched with the moral or the interest of her story, as it is recorded here, are rather a separate class than men in general. Madame de Staël, we observe, is her principal admirer.

Next year, Schiller took possession of a province more peculiarly his own: in 1801, appeared his *Maid of Orleans (Jungfrau von Orleans)*; the first hint of which was suggested to him by a series of documents, relating to the sentence of Jeanne d'Arc, and its reversal, first published about this time by De l'Averdy of the *Académie des Inscriptions*. Schiller had been moved in perusing them: this tragedy gave voice to his feelings.

Considered as an object of poetry or history, Jeanne d'Arc, the most singular personage of modern times, presents a character capable of being viewed under a great variety of aspects, and with a corresponding variety of emotions. To the English of her own age, bigoted in their creed, and baffled by her prowess, she appeared inspired by the Devil, and was naturally burnt as a sorceress. In this light, too, she is painted in the poems of Shakspeare. To Voltaire, again, whose trade it was to war with every kind of superstition, this child of fanatic ardor seemed no better than a moonstruck zealot; and the people who followed her, and believed in her, something worse than lunatics. The glory of what she had achieved was for-

gotten, when the means of achieving it were recollected; and
the Maid of Orleans was deemed the fit subject of a poem, the
wittiest and most profligate for which literature has to blush.
Our illustrious *Don Juan* hides his head when contrasted with
Voltaire's *Pucelle:* Juan's biographer, with all his zeal, is but
an innocent, and a novice, by the side of this arch-scorner.

Such a manner of considering the Maid of Orleans is evidently not the right one. Feelings so deep and earnest as
hers can never be an object of ridicule: whoever pursues a
purpose of any sort with such fervid devotedness, is entitled
to awaken emotions, at least of a serious kind, in the hearts
of others. Enthusiasm puts on a different shape in every
different age: always in some degree sublime, often it is dangerous; its very essence is a tendency to error and exaggeration; yet it is the fundamental quality of strong souls; the
true nobility of blood, in which all greatness of thought or
action has its rise. *Quicquid vult valdè vult* is ever the first
and surest test of mental capability. This peasant girl, who
felt within her such fiery vehemence of resolution, that she
could subdue the minds of kings and captains to her will, and
lead armies on to battle, conquering, till her country was
cleared of its invaders, must evidently have possessed the elements of a majestic character. Benevolent feelings, sublime
ideas, and above all an overpowering will, are here indubitably
marked. Nor does the form, which her activity assumed, seem
less adapted for displaying these qualities, than many other
forms in which we praise them. The gorgeous inspirations of
the Catholic religion are as real as the phantom of posthumous
renown; the love of our native soil is as laudable as ambition, or the principle of military honor. Jeanne d'Arc must
have been a creature of shadowy yet far-glancing dreams, of
unutterable feelings, of "thoughts that wandered through
Eternity." Who can tell the trials and the triumphs, the
splendors and the terrors, of which her simple spirit was the
scene! "Heartless, sneering, god-forgetting French!" as old
Suwarrow called them, — they are not worthy of this noble
maiden. Hers were errors, but errors which a generous soul
alone could have committed, and which generous souls would

have done more than pardon. Her darkness and delusions were of the understanding only; they but make the radiance of her heart more touching and apparent; as clouds are gilded by the orient light into something more beautiful than azure itself.

It is under this aspect that Schiller has contemplated the Maid of Orleans, and endeavored to make us contemplate her. For the latter purpose, it appears that more than one plan had occurred to him. His first idea was, to represent Joanna, and the times she lived in, as they actually were: to exhibit the superstition, ferocity, and wretchedness of the period, in all their aggravation; and to show us this patriotic and religious enthusiast beautifying the tempestuous scene by her presence; swaying the fierce passions of her countrymen; directing their fury against the invaders of France; till at length, forsaken and condemned to die, she perished at the stake, retaining the same steadfast and lofty faith, which had ennobled and re-deemed the errors of her life, and was now to glorify the ignominy of her death. This project, after much deliberation, he relinquished, as too difficult. By a new mode of manage-ment, much of the homeliness and rude horror, that defaced and encumbered the reality, is thrown away. The Dauphin is not here a voluptuous weakling, nor is his court the centre of vice and cruelty and imbecility: the misery of the time is touched but lightly, and the Maid of Arc herself is invested with a certain faint degree of mysterious dignity, ultimately represented as being in truth a preternatural gift; though whether preternatural, and if so, whether sent from above or from below, neither we nor she, except by faith, are absolutely sure, till the conclusion.

The propriety of this arrangement is liable to question; indeed, it has been more than questioned. But external blemishes are lost in the intrinsic grandeur of the piece: the spirit of Joanna is presented to us with an exalting and pathetic force sufficient to make us blind to far greater im-proprieties. Joanna is a pure creation, of half-celestial origin, combining the mild charms of female loveliness with the awful majesty of a prophetess, and a sacrifice doomed to perish for

her country. She resembled, in Schiller's view, the Iphigenia
of the Greeks; and as such, in some respects, he has treated
her.

The woes and desolation of the land have kindled in
Joanna's keen and fervent heart a fire, which the loneliness
of her life, and her deep feelings of religion, have nourished
and fanned into a holy flame. She sits in solitude with her
flocks, beside the mountain chapel of the Virgin, under the
ancient Druid oak, a wizard spot, the haunt of evil spirits as
well as of good; and visions are revealed to her such as human
eyes behold not. It seems the force of her own spirit, expressing its feelings in forms which react upon itself. The
strength of her impulses persuades her that she is called from
on high to deliver her native France; the intensity of her
own faith persuades others; she goes forth on her mission;
all bends to the fiery vehemence of her will; she is inspired
because she thinks herself so. There is something beautiful
and moving in the aspect of a noble enthusiasm, fostered in
the secret soul, amid obstructions and depressions, and at
length bursting forth with an overwhelming force to accomplish its appointed end: the impediments which long hid it
are now become testimonies of its power; the very ignorance,
and meanness, and error, which still in part adhere to it, increase our sympathy without diminishing our admiration; it
seems the triumph, hardly contested, and not wholly carried,
but still the triumph, of Mind over Fate, of human volition
over material necessity.

All this Schiller felt, and has presented with even more
than his usual skill. The secret mechanism of Joanna's mind
is concealed from us in a dim religious obscurity; but its
active movements are distinct; we behold the lofty heroism
of her feelings; she affects us to the very heart. The quiet,
devout innocence of her early years, when she lived silent,
shrouded in herself, meek and kindly though not communing
with others, makes us love her: the celestial splendor which
illuminates her after-life adds reverence to our love. Her
words and actions combine an overpowering force with a
calm unpretending dignity: we seem to understand how they

must have carried in their favor the universal conviction.
Joanna is the most noble being in tragedy. We figure her
with her slender lovely form, her mild but spirit-speaking
countenance; "beautiful and terrible;" bearing the banner of
the Virgin before the hosts of her country; travelling in the
strength of a rapt soul; irresistible by faith; "the lowly herdsmaid," greater in the grandeur of her simple spirit than the
kings and queens of this world. Yet her breast is not entirely
insensible to human feeling, nor her faith never liable to waver.
When that inexorable vengeance, which had shut her ear
against the voice of mercy to the enemies of France, is suspended at the sight of Lionel, and her heart experiences the
first touch of mortal affection, a baleful cloud overspreads the
serene of her mind; it seems as if Heaven had forsaken her,
or from the beginning permitted demons or earthly dreams
to deceive her. The agony of her spirit, involved in endless
and horrid labyrinths of doubt, is powerfully portrayed. She
has crowned the king at Rheims; and all is joy, and pomp,
and jubilee, and almost adoration of Joanna: but Joanna's
thoughts are not of joy. The sight of her poor but kind and
true-hearted sisters in the crowd, moves her to the soul. Amid
the tumult and magnificence of this royal pageant, she sinks
into a reverie; her small native dale of Arc, between its quiet
hills, rises on her mind's eye, with its straw-roofed huts, and
its clear greensward; where the sun is even then shining so
brightly, and the sky is so blue, and all is so calm and motherly
and safe. She sighs for the peace of that sequestered home;
then shudders to think that she shall never see it more. Accused of witchcraft, by her own ascetic melancholic father, she
utters no word of denial to the charge; for her heart is dark,
it is tarnished by earthly love, she dare not raise her thoughts
to Heaven. Parted from her sisters; cast out with horror by
the people she had lately saved from despair, she wanders forth,
desolate, forlorn, not knowing whither. Yet she does not sink
under this sore trial: as she suffers from without, and is forsaken of men, her mind grows clear and strong, her confidence
returns. She is now more firmly fixed in our admiration than
before; tenderness is united to our other feelings; and her

faith has been proved by sharp vicissitudes. Her countrymen recognize their error; Joanna closes her career by a glorious death; we take farewell of her in a solemn mood of heroic pity.

Joanna is the animating principle of this tragedy; the scenes employed in developing her character and feelings constitute its great charm. Yet there are other personages in it, that leave a distinct and pleasing impression of themselves in our memory. Agnes Sorel, the soft, languishing, generous mistress of the Dauphin, relieves and heightens by comparison the sterner beauty of the Maid. Dunois, the Bastard of Orleans, the lover of Joanna, is a blunt, frank, sagacious soldier, and well described. And Talbot, the gray veteran, delineates his dark, unbelieving, indomitable soul, by a few slight but expressive touches: he sternly passes down to the land, as he thinks, of utter nothingness, contemptuous even of the fate that destroys him, and

> " On the soil of France he sleeps, as does
> A hero on the shield he would not quit."

A few scattered extracts may in part exhibit some of these inferior personages to our readers, though they can afford us no impression of the Maid herself. Joanna's character, like every finished piece of art, to be judged of must be seen in all its bearings. It is not in parts, but as a whole, that the delineation moves us; by light and manifold touches, it works upon our hearts, till they melt before it into that mild rapture, free alike from the violence and the impurities of Nature, which it is the highest triumph of the Artist to communicate.

ACT III. SCENE IV.

[*The* DAUPHIN CHARLES, *with his suite: afterwards* JOANNA. *She is in armor, but without her helmet; and wears a garland in her hair.*

DUNOIS [*steps forward*].
My heart made choice of her while she was lowly;
This new honor raises not her merit
Or my love. Here, in the presence of my King

And of this holy Archbishop, I offer her
My hand and princely rank, if she regard me
As worthy to be hers.

CHARLES.   Resistless Maid,
Thou addest miracle to miracle !
Henceforward I believe that nothing is
Impossible to thee.   Thou hast subdued
This haughty spirit, that till now defied
Th' omnipotence of Love.

LA HIRE [steps forward].   If I mistake not
Joanna's form of mind, what most adorns her
Is her modest heart.   The rev'rence of the great
She merits: but her thoughts will never rise
So high.   She strives not after giddy splendors:
The true affection of a faithful soul
Contents her; and the still, sequester'd lot
Which with this hand I offer her.

CHARLES.   Thou too,
La Hire ?   Two valiant suitors, equal in
Heroic virtue and renown of war !
— Wilt thou, that hast united my dominions,
Soften'd my opposers, part my firmest friends ?
Both may not gain thee, each deserving thee :
Speak, then !   Thy heart must here be arbiter.

AGNES SOREL [approaches].
Joanna is embarrass'd and surprised ;
I see the bashful crimson tinge her cheeks.
Let her have time to ask her heart, to open
Her clos'd bosom in trustful confidence
With me.   The moment is arriv'd when I
In sisterly communion also may
Approach the rigorous Maid, and offer her
The solace of my faithful, silent breast.
First let us women sit in secret judgment
On this matter that concerns us ; then expect
What we shall have decided.

CHARLES [about to go].   Be it so, then !
JOANNA.   Not so, Sire !   'T was not the embarrassment
Of virgin shame that dy'd my cheeks in crimson :
To this lady I have nothing to confide,
Which I need blush to speak of before men.
Much am I honor'd by the preference

Of these two noble Knights; but it was not
To chase vain worldly grandeurs, that I left
The shepherd moors; not in my hair to bind
The bridal garland, that I girt myself
With warlike armor.   To far other work
Am I appointed: and the spotless virgin
Alone can do it.   I am the soldier
Of the God of Battles; to no living man
Can I be wife.

    ARCHBISHOP. As kindly help to man
Was woman born; and in obeying Nature
She best obeys and reverences Heaven.
When the command of God who summon'd thee
To battle is fulfill'd, thou wilt lay down
Thy weapons, and return to that soft sex
Which thou deny'st, which is not call'd to do
The bloody work of war.

    JOANNA.   Father, as yet
I know not how the Spirit will direct me:
When the needful time comes round, His voice
Will not be silent, and I will obey it.
For the present, I am bid complete the task
He gave me.   My sov'reign's brow is yet uncrown'd,
His head unwetted by the holy oil,
He is not yet a King.

    CHARLES.   We are journeying
Towards Rheims.

    JOANNA.   Let us not linger by the way.
Our foes are busy round us, shutting up
Thy passage: I will lead thee through them all.

    DUNOIS. And when the work shall be fulfill'd, when we
Have marched in triumph into Rheims,
Will not Joanna then —

    JOANNA.   If God see meet
That I return with life and vict'ry from
These broils, my task is ended, and the herdsmaid
Has nothing more to do in her King's palace.

    CHARLES [*taking her hand*].
It is the Spirit's voice impels thee now,
And Love is mute in thy inspired bosom.
Believe me, it will not be always mute!
Our swords will rest; and Victory will lead

Meek Peace by th' hand, and Joy will come again
To ev'ry breast, and softer feelings waken
In every heart: in thy heart also waken;
And tears of sweetest longing wilt thou weep,
Such as thine eyes have never shed.   This heart,
Now fill'd by Heav'n, will softly open
To some terrestrial heart.   Thou hast begun
By blessing thousands; but thou wilt conclude
By blessing one.

JOANNA.   Dauphin!   Art thou weary
Of the heavenly vision, that thou seekest
To deface its chosen vessel, wouldst degrade
To common dust the Maid whom God has sent thee?
Ye blind of heart!   O ye of little faith!
Heaven's brightness is about you, before your eyes
Unveils its wonders; and ye see in me
Nought but a woman.   Dare a woman, think ye,
Clothe herself in iron harness, and mingle
In the wreck of battle?   Woe, woe to me,
If bearing in my hand th' avenging sword
Of God; I bore in my vain heart a love
To earthly man!   Woe to me!   It were better
That I never had been born.   No more,
No more of this!   Unless ye would awake the wrath
Of HIM that dwells in me!   The eye of man
Desiring me is an abomination
And a horror.

CHARLES.   Cease!   'Tis vain to urge her.

JOANNA.   Bid the trumpets sound!   This loit'ring grieves
And harasses me.   Something chases me
From sloth, and drives me forth to do my mission,
Stern beck'ning me to my appointed doom.

SCENE V.

A KNIGHT [in haste].

CHARLES. How now?
        KNIGHT.   The enemy has pass'd the Marne:
Is forming as for battle.
        JOANNA [as if inspired].   Arms and battle!

My soul has cast away its bonds !   To arms !
Prepare yourselves, while I prepare the rest !   [*She hastens out.*

.   .   .   .   .

[*Trumpets sound with a piercing tone, and while the scene is changing
pass into a wild tumultuous sound of battle.*]

Scene VI.

[*The scene changes to an open space encircled with trees. During the
music, soldiers are seen hastily retreating across the background.*]

TALBOT, *leaning upon* FASTOLF, *and accompanied by* Soldiers. *Soon
after,* LIONEL.

    TALBOT.   Here set me down beneath this tree, and you
Betake yourselves again to battle : quick !
I need no help to die.
    FASTOLF.   O day of woe !   [*Lionel enters.*
Look, what a sight awaits you, Lionel !
Our General expiring of his wounds !
    LIONEL.   Now God forbid !   Rise, noble Talbot !   This
Is not a time for you to faint and sink.
Yield not to Death; force faltering Nature
By your strength of soul, that life depart not !
    TALBOT.   In vain !   The day of Destiny is come
That prostrates with the dust our power in France.
In vain, in the fierce clash of desp'rate battle,
Have I risk'd our utmost to withstand it:
The bolt has smote and crush'd me, and I lie
To rise no more forever.   Rheims is lost ;
Make haste to rescue Paris.
    LIONEL.   Paris has surrender'd
To the Dauphin: an express is just arriv'd
With tidings.
    TALBOT [*tears away his bandages*].
             Then flow out, ye life-streams ;
I am grown to loathe this Sun.
    LIONEL.   They want me !
Fastolf, bear him to a place of safety :
We can hold this post few instants longer,
The coward knaves are giving way on all sides,
Irresistible the Witch is pressing on.

TALBOT. Madness, thou conquerest, and I must **yield:**
Stupidity can baffle the very gods.
High Reason, radiant Daughter of God's Head,
Wise Foundress of the system of the Universe,
Conductress of the stars, who art thou, then,
If, tied to th' tail o' th' wild horse Superstition,
Thou must plunge, eyes open, vainly shrieking,
Sheer down with that drunk Beast to the Abyss?
Cursed who sets his life upon the great
And dignified; and with forecasting spirit
Forms wise projects! The Fool-king rules this world.

    LIONEL. Oh, Death is near you! Think of your **Creator!**

    TALBOT. Had we as brave men been defeated
By brave men, we might have consoled ourselves
With common thoughts of Fortune's fickleness:
But that a sorry farce should be our ruin! —
Did our earnest toilsome struggle merit
No graver end than this?

    LIONEL [*grasps his hand*]. Talbot, farewell!
The meed of bitter tears I'll duly pay you,
When the fight is done, should I outlive it.
Now Fate calls me to the field, where yet
She wav'ring sits, and shakes her doubtful urn.
Farewell! we meet beyond the unseen shore.
Brief parting for long friendship! God be with you!   [*Exit.*

    TALBOT. Soon it is over, and to th' Earth I render,
To the everlasting Sun, the atoms,
Which for pain and pleasure join'd to form me;
And of the mighty Talbot, whose renown
Once fill'd the world, remains nought but a handful
Of light dust. Thus man comes to his end;
And our one conquest in this fight of life
Is the conviction of life's nothingness,
And deep disdain of all that sorry stuff
We once thought lofty and desirable.

SCENE VII.

Enter CHARLES; BURGUNDY; DUNOIS; DU CHATEL; *and* Soldiers.

    BURGUN. The trench is storm'd.
    DUNOIS.   The victory is ours.

CHARLES [*observing Talbot*].

Ha! who is this that to the light of day
Is bidding his constrained and sad farewell?
His bearing speaks no common man: go, haste,
Assist him, if assistance yet avail.

[*Soldiers from the Dauphin's suite step forward.*

FASTOLF. Back! Keep away! Approach not the Departing,
Whom in life ye never wish'd too near you.

BURGUN. What do I see? Lord Talbot in his blood!

[*He goes towards him. Talbot gazes fixedly at him,
and dies.*

FASTOLF. Off, Burgundy! With th' aspect of a traitor
Poison not the last look of a hero.

DUNOIS. Dreaded Talbot! stern, unconquerable!
Dost thou content thee with a space so narrow,
And the wide domains of France once could not
Stay the striving of thy giant spirit? —
Now for the first time, Sire, I call you King:
The crown but totter'd on your head, so long
As in this body dwelt a soul.

CHARLES [*after looking at the dead in silence*]. It was
A higher hand that conquer'd him, not we.
Here on the soil of France he sleeps, as does
A hero on the shield he would not quit.
Bring him away.   [*Soldiers lift the corpse, and carry it off.*
And peace be with his dust!
A fair memorial shall arise to him
I' th' midst of France: here, where the hero's course
And life were finished, let his bones repose.
Thus far no other foe has e'er advanced.
His epitaph shall be the place he fell on.

. . . . .

SCENE IX.

*Another empty space in the field of battle. In the distance are seen the
towers of Rheims illuminated by the sun.*

*A Knight, cased in black armor, with his visor shut. JOANNA follows
him to the front of the scene, where he stops and awaits her.*

JOANNA. Deceiver! Now I see thy craft. Thou hast,
By seeming flight, enticed me from the battle,

And warded death and destiny from off the head
Of many a Briton.   Now they reach thy own.

KNIGHT.   Why dost thou follow me, and track my steps
With murd'rous fury?   I am not appointed
To die by thee.

JOANNA.   Deep in my lowest soul
I hate thee as the Night, which is thy color.
To sweep thee from the face of Earth, I feel
Some irresistible desire impelling me.
Who art thou?   Lift thy visor: had not I
Seen Talbot fall, I should have named thee Talbot.

KNIGHT.   Speaks not the prophesying Spirit in thee?

JOANNA.   It tells me loudly, in my inmost bosom,
That Misfortune is at hand.

KNIGHT.   Joanna d'Arc!
Up to the gates of Rheims hast thou advanced,
Led on by victory.   Let the renown
Already gain'd suffice thee!   As a slave
Has Fortune serv'd thee: emancipate her,
Ere in wrath she free herself; fidelity
She hates; no one obeys she to the end.

JOANNA.   How say'st thou, in the middle of my course,
That I should pause and leave my work unfinish'd?
I will conclude it, and fulfil my vow.

KNIGHT.   Nothing can withstand thee; thou art most strong;
In ev'ry battle thou prevailest.   But go
Into no other battle.   Hear my warning!

JOANNA.   This sword I quit not, till the English yield.

KNIGHT.   Look!   Yonder rise the towers of Rheims, the goal
And purpose of thy march; thou seest the dome
Of the cathedral glittering in the sun:
There wouldst thou enter in triumphal pomp,
To crown thy sov'reign and fulfil thy vow.
Enter not there.   Turn homewards.   Hear my warning!

JOANNA.   Who art thou, false, double-tongued betrayer,
That wouldst frighten and perplex me?   Dar'st thou
Utter lying oracles to me?

[*The Black Knight attempts to go ; she steps in his way.*
No!
Thou shalt answer me, or perish by me!

[*She lifts her arm to strike him.*

KNIGHT [*touches her with his hand: she stands immovable*].
Kill what is mortal!
                    [*Darkness, lightning and thunder.   The Knight sinks.*
    JOANNA. [*stands at first amazed: but soon recovers herself*].
                    It was nothing earthly.
Some delusive form of Hell, some spirit
Of Falsehood, sent from th' everlasting Pool
To tempt and terrify my fervent soul!
Bearing the sword of God, what do I fear?
Victorious will I end my fated course;
Though Hell itself with all its fiends assail me,
My heart and faith shall never faint or fail me.   [*She is going.*

SCENE X.

LIONEL, JOANNA.

    LIONEL.   Accursed Sorceress, prepare for battle:
Not both of us shall leave the place alive.
Thou hast destroyed the chosen of my host;
Brave Talbot has breath'd out his mighty spirit
In my bosom.   I will avenge the Dead,
Or share his fate.   And wouldst thou know the man
Who brings thee glory, let him die or conquer,
I am Lionel, the last survivor
Of our chiefs; and still unvanquish'd is this arm.
            [*He rushes towards her; after a short contest, she strikes
            the sword from his hand.*
Faithless fortune!   [*He struggles with her.*
    JOANNA [*seizes him by the plume from behind, and tears his hel-
            met violently down, so that his face is exposed: at
            the same time she lifts her sword with the right
            hand*].
                    Suffer what thou soughtest
The Virgin sacrifices thee through me!
            [*At this moment she looks in his face; his aspect touches
            her; she stands immovable, and then slowly drops her
            arm.*
    LIONEL.   Why lingerest thou, and stayest the stroke of death?
My honor thou hast taken, take my life:
'T is in thy hands to take it; I want not mercy.
            [*She gives him a sign with her hand to depart.*

Fly from *thee?* Owe *thee* my life? Die rather!

JOANNA [*her face turned away*].

I will not remember that thou owedst
Thy life to me.

LIONEL.   I hate thee and thy gift.
I want not mercy.   Kill thy enemy,
Who meant to kill thee, who abhors thee!

JOANNA.   Kill me, and fly!

LIONEL.   Ha!   How is this?

JOANNA [*hides her face*].   Woe's me!

LIONEL [*approaches her*].

Thou killest every Briton, I have heard,
Whom thou subdu'st in battle : why spare me?

JOANNA [*lifts her sword with a rapid movement against him, but
          quickly lets it sink again, when she observes his face*].
          O Holy Virgin!

LIONEL.   Wherefore namest thou
The Virgin?   *She* knows nothing of thee; Heaven
Has nought to say to thee.

JOANNA [*in violent anguish*].   What have I done!
My vow, my vow is broke!   [*Wrings her hands in despair.*

LIONEL [*looks at her with sympathy, and comes nearer*].
                              Unhappy girl!
I pity thee; thou touchest me; thou showedst
Mercy to me alone.   My hate is going :
I am constrain'd to feel for thee.   Who art thou?
Whence comest thou?

JOANNA.   Away!   Begone!

LIONEL.   Thy youth,
Thy beauty melt and sadden me; thy look
Goes to my heart: I could wish much to save thee;
Tell me how I may!   Come, come with me!   Forsake
This horrid business; cast away those arms!

JOANNA.   I no more deserve to bear them!

LIONEL.   Cast them
Away, then, and come with me!

JOANNA [*with horror*].   Come with thee!

LIONEL.   Thou mayst be sav'd: come with me!   I will save thee.
But delay not.   A strange sorrow for thee
Seizes me, and an unspeakable desire
To save thee.   [*Seizes her arm.*

JOANNA. Ha! Dunois! 'T is they!
If they should find thee! —
    LIONEL.   Fear not; I will guard thee.
    JOANNA. I should die, were they to kill thee.
    LIONEL.   Am I
Dear to thee?
    JOANNA.   Saints of Heaven!
    LIONEL.   Shall I ever
See thee, hear of thee, again?
    JOANNA.   Never! Never!
    LIONEL. This sword for pledge that I will see thee!
             [*He wrests the sword from her.*
    JOANNA.   Madman!
Thou dar'st?
    LIONEL. I yield to force; again I'll see thee.   [*Exit.*

The introduction of supernatural agency in this play, and the final aberration from the truth of history, have been considerably censured by the German critics: Schlegel, we recollect, calls Joanna's end a "rosy death." In this dramaturgic discussion, the mere reader need take no great interest. To require our belief in apparitions and miracles, things which we cannot now believe, no doubt for a moment disturbs our submission to the poet's illusions: but the miracles in this story are rare and transient, and of small account in the general result: they give our reason little trouble, and perhaps contribute to exalt the heroine in our imaginations. It is still the mere human grandeur of Joanna's spirit that we love and reverence; the lofty devotedness with which she is transported, the generous benevolence, the irresistible determination. The heavenly mandate is but the means of unfolding these qualities, and furnishing them with a proper passport to the minds of her age. To have produced, without the aid of fictions like these, a Joanna so beautified and exalted, would undoubtedly have yielded greater satisfaction: but it may be questioned whether the difficulty would not have increased in a still higher ratio. The sentiments, the characters, are not only accurate, but exquisitely beautiful; the incidents, excepting the very last, are possible, or even probable: what remains is but a very slender evil.

After all objections have been urged, and this among others has certainly a little weight, the *Maid of Orleans* will remain one of the very finest of modern dramas. Perhaps, among all Schiller's plays, it is the one which evinces most of that quality denominated *genius* in the strictest meaning of the word. *Wallenstein* embodies more thought, more knowledge, more conception; but it is only in parts illuminated by that ethereal brightness, which shines over every part of this. The spirit of the romantic ages is here imaged forth; but the whole is exalted, embellished, ennobled. It is what the critics call idealized. The heart must be cold, the imagination dull, which the *Jungfrau von Orleans* will not move.

In Germany this case did not occur: the reception of the work was beyond example flattering. The leading idea suited the German mind; the execution of it inflamed the hearts and imaginations of the people; they felt proud of their great poet, and delighted to enthusiasm with his poetry. At the first exhibition of the play in Leipzig, Schiller being in the theatre, though not among the audience, this feeling was displayed in a rather singular manner. When the curtain dropped at the end of the first act, there arose on all sides a shout of "*Es lebe Friedrich Schiller!*" accompanied by the sound of trumpets and other military music: at the conclusion of the piece, the whole assembly left their places, went out, and crowded round the door through which the poet was expected to come; and no sooner did he show himself, than his admiring spectators, uncovering their heads, made an avenue for him to pass; and as he walked along, many, we are told, held up their children, and exclaimed, "*That is he!*"[1]

This must have been a proud moment for Schiller; but also

- Doering (p. 176); — who adds as follows: "Another testimony of approval, very different in its nature, he received at the first production of the play in Weimar. Knowing and valuing, as he did, the public of that city, it could not but surprise him greatly, when a certain young Doctor S—— called out to him, '*Bravo, Schiller!*' from the gallery, in a very loud tone of voice. Offended at such impertinence, the poet hissed strongly, in which the audience joined him. He likewise expressed in words his displeasure at this conduct; and the youthful sprig of medicine was, by direction of the Court, farther punished for his indiscreet applause, by some admonitions from the police."

an agitating, painful one; and perhaps on the whole, the latter feeling, for the time, prevailed. Such noisy, formal, and tumultuous plaudits were little to his taste: the triumph they confer, though plentiful, is coarse; and Schiller's modest nature made him shun the public gaze, not seek it. He loved men, and did not affect to despise their approbation; but neither did this form his leading motive. To him art, like virtue, was its own reward; he delighted in his tasks for the sake of the fascinating feelings which they yielded him in their performance. Poetry was the chosen gift of his mind, which his pleasure lay in cultivating: in other things he wished not that his habits or enjoyments should be different from those of other men.

At Weimar his present way of life was like his former one at Jena: his business was to study and compose; his recreations were in the circle of his family, where he could abandon himself to affections, grave or trifling, and in frank and cheerful intercourse with a few friends. Of the latter he had lately formed a social club, the meetings of which afforded him a regular and innocent amusement. He still loved solitary walks: in the Park at Weimar he might frequently be seen wandering among the groves and remote avenues, with a note-book in his hand; now loitering slowly along, now standing still, now moving rapidly on; if any one appeared in sight, he would dart into another alley, that his dream might not be broken.[1] "One of his favorite resorts," we are told, "was the thickly overshadowed rocky path which leads to the *Römische Haus*, a pleasure-house of the Duke's, built under the direction of Goethe. There he would often sit in the gloom of the crags, overgrown with cypresses and boxwood; shady hedges before him; not far from the murmur of a little brook, which there gushes in a smooth slaty channel, and where some verses of Goethe are cut upon a brown plate of stone, and fixed in

---

[1] "Whatever he intended to write, he first composed in his head, before putting down a line of it on paper. He used to call a work *ready* so soon as its existence in his spirit was complete: hence in the public there often were reports that such and such a piece of his was finished, when, in the common sense, it was not even begun." — *Jördens Lexicon*, § SCHILLER.

the rock." He still continued to study in the night: the morning was spent with his children and his wife, or in pastimes such as we have noticed; in the afternoon he revised what had been last composed, wrote letters, or visited his friends. His evenings were often passed in the theatre; it was the only public place of amusement which he ever visited; nor was it for the purpose of amusement that he visited this: it was his observatory, where he watched the effect of scenes and situations; devised new schemes of art, or corrected old ones. To the players he was kind, friendly: on nights when any of his pieces had been acted successfully or for the first time, he used to invite the leaders of the company to a supper in the Stadthaus, where the time was spent in mirthful diversions, one of which was frequently a recitation, by Genast, of the Capuchin's sermon in *Wallenstein's Camp*. Except on such rare occasions, he returned home directly from the theatre, to light his midnight lamp, and commence the most earnest of his labors.

The assiduity, with which he struggled for improvement in dramatic composition, had now produced its natural result: the requisitions of his taste no longer hindered the operation of his genius; art had at length become a second nature. A new proof at once of his fertility, and of his solicitude for farther improvement, appeared in 1803. The *Braut von Messina* was an experiment; an attempt to exhibit a modern subject and modern sentiments in an antique garb. The principle on which the interest of this play rests is the Fatalism of the ancients: the plot is of extreme simplicity; a Chorus also is introduced, an elaborate discussion of the nature and uses of that accompaniment being prefixed by way of preface. The experiment was not successful: with a multitude of individual beauties this *Bride of Messina* is found to be ineffectual as a whole: it does not move us; the great object of every tragedy is not attained. The Chorus, which Schiller, swerving from the Greek models, has divided into two contending parts, and made to enter and depart with the principals to whom they are attached, has in his hands become the medium of conveying many beautiful effusions of poetry; but it retards the progress of the plot; it dissipates and diffuses our sympathies; the interest we should take in the fate and prospects of Manuel and Cæsar, is expended on the fate and prospects of man. For beautiful and touching delineations of life; for pensive and pathetic reflections, sentiments, and images, conveyed in language simple but nervous and emphatic, this tragedy stands high in the rank of modern compositions. There is in it a breath of young tenderness and ardor, mingled impressively with the feelings of gray-haired experience, whose recollections are darkened with melancholy, whose very hopes are chequered and solemn. The implacable Destiny which consigns the brothers to mutual enmity and mutual destruction, for the guilt of a past generation, involving a Mother and a Sister in their ruin, spreads a sombre hue over all the poem; we are not unmoved by the characters of the hostile Brothers, and we pity the hapless and amiable Beatrice, the victim of their feud. Still there is too little action in the play; the incidents are too abundantly diluted with reflection; the interest pauses, flags, and fails to produce its full effect. For its specimens of lyrical poetry, tender, affecting, sometimes exquisitely beautiful, the *Bride of Messina* will long deserve a careful perusal; but as exemplifying a new form of the drama, it has found no imitators, and is likely to find none.

The slight degree of failure or miscalculation which occurred in the present instance, was next year abundantly redeemed. *Wilhelm Tell*, sent out in 1804, is one of Schiller's very finest dramas; it exhibits some of the highest triumphs which his genius, combined with his art, ever realized. The first descent of Freedom to our modern world, the first unfurling of her standard on the rocky pinnacle of Europe, is here celebrated in the style which it deserved. There is no false tinsel-decoration about *Tell*, no sickly refinement, no declamatory sentimentality. All is downright, simple, and agreeable to Nature; yet all is adorned and purified and rendered beautiful, without losing its resemblance. An air of freshness and wholesomeness breathes over it; we are among honest, inoffensive, yet fearless peasants, untainted by the vices, undazzled by the theories, of

more complex and perverted conditions of society. The opening of the first scene sets us down among the Alps. It is "a
high rocky shore of the Luzern Lake, opposite to Schwytz.
The lake makes a little bight in the land, a hut stands at a
short distance from the bank, the fisher-boy is rowing himself
about in his boat. Beyond the lake, on the other side, we see
the green meadows, the hamlets and farms of Schywtz, lying
in the clear sunshine. On our left are observed the peaks of
the Hacken surrounded with clouds: to the right, and far in
the distance, appear the glaciers. We hear the *rance des vaches*
and the tinkling of cattle-bells." This first impression never
leaves us; we are in a scene where all is grand and lovely;
but it is the loveliness and grandeur of unpretending, unadul-
terated Nature. These Switzers are not Arcadian shepherds
or speculative patriots; there is not one crook or beechen bowl
among them, and they never mention the Social Contract, or
the Rights of Man. They are honest people, driven by oppression to assert their privileges; and they go to work like men
in earnest, bent on the despatch of business, not on the display
of sentiment. They are not philosophers or tribunes; but
frank, stalwart landmen: even in the field of Rütli, they do
not forget their common feelings; the party that arrive first
indulge in a harmless little ebullition of parish vanity: " *We*
are first here!" they say, "we Unterwaldeners!" They have
not charters or written laws to which they can appeal; but
they have the traditionary rights of their fathers, and bold
hearts and strong arms to make them good. The rules by
which they steer are not deduced from remote premises, by a
fine process of thought; they are the accumulated result of
experience, transmitted from peasant sire to peasant son.
There is something singularly pleasing in this exhibition of
genuine humanity; of wisdom, embodied in old adages and
practical maxims of prudence; of magnanimity, displayed in
the quiet unpretending discharge of the humblest every-day
duties. Truth is superior to Fiction: we feel at home among
these brave good people; their fortune interests us more than
that of all the brawling, vapid, sentimental heroes in creation.
Yet to make them interest us was the very highest problem

of art; it was to copy lowly Nature, to give us a copy of it
embellished and refined by the agency of genius, yet preserving the likeness in every lineament. The highest quality of
art is to conceal itself: these peasants of Schiller's are what
every one imagines he could imitate successfully; yet in the
hands of any but a true and strong-minded poet they dwindle
into repulsive coarseness or mawkish insipidity. Among our
own writers, who have tried such subjects, we remember none
that has succeeded equally with Schiller. One potent but ill
fated genius has, in far different circumstances and with far
other means, shown that he could have equalled him: the
Cotter's Saturday Night of Burns is, in its own humble way,
as quietly beautiful, as *simplex munditiis*, as the scenes of *Tell*.
No other has even approached them; though some gifted persons have attempted it. Mr. Wordsworth is no ordinary man;
nor are his pedlers, and leech-gatherers, and dalesmen, without
their attractions and their moral; but they sink into whining
drivellers beside *Rösselmann the Priest, Ulric the Smith, Hans
of the Wall*, and the other sturdy confederates of Rütli.

The skill with which the events are concatenated in this
play corresponds to the truth of its delineation of character.
The incidents of the Swiss Revolution, as detailed in Tschudi
or Müller, are here faithfully preserved, even to their minutest
branches. The beauty of Schiller's descriptions all can relish;
their fidelity is what surprises every reader who has been in
Switzerland. Schiller never saw the scene of his play; but
his diligence, his quickness and intensity of conception, supplied this defect. Mountain and mountaineer, conspiracy and
action, are all brought before us in their true forms, all glowing in the mild sunshine of the poet's fancy. The tyranny of
Gessler, and the misery to which it has reduced the land; the
exasperation, yet patient courage of the people; their characters, and those of their leaders, Fürst, Stauffacher, and
Melchthal; their exertions and ultimate success, described as
they are here, keep up a constant interest in the piece. It
abounds in action, as much as the *Bride of Messina* is defective in that point.

But the finest delineation is undoubtedly the character of

Wilhelm Tell, the hero of the Swiss Revolt, and of the present drama. In Tell are combined all the attributes of a great man, without the help of education or of great occasions to develop them. His knowledge has been gathered chiefly from his own experience, and this is bounded by his native mountains: he has had no lessons or examples of splendid virtue, no wish or opportunity to earn renown: he has grown up to manhood, a simple yeoman of the Alps, among simple yeomen; and has never aimed at being more. Yet we trace in him a deep, reflective, earnest spirit, thirsting for activity, yet bound in by the wholesome dictates of prudence; a heart benevolent, generous, unconscious alike of boasting or of fear. It is this salubrious air of rustic, unpretending honesty that forms the great beauty in Tell's character: all is native, all is genuine; he does not declaim: he dislikes to talk of noble conduct, he exhibits it. He speaks little of his freedom, because he has always enjoyed it, and feels that he can always defend it. His reasons for destroying Gessler are not drawn from jurisconsults and writers on morality, but from the everlasting instincts of Nature: the Austrian Vogt must die; because if not, the wife and children of Tell will be destroyed by him. The scene, where the peaceful but indomitable archer sits waiting for Gessler in the hollow way among the rocks of Küssnacht, presents him in a striking light. Former scenes had shown us Tell under many amiable and attractive aspects; we knew that he was tender as well as brave, that he loved to haunt the mountain tops, and inhale in silent dreams the influence of their wild and magnificent beauty: we had seen him the most manly and warm-hearted of fathers and husbands; intrepid, modest, and decisive in the midst of peril, and venturing his life to bring help to the oppressed. But here his mind is exalted into stern solemnity; its principles of action come before us with greater clearness, in this its fiery contest. The name of murder strikes a damp across his frank and fearless spirit; while the recollection of his children and their mother proclaims emphatically that there is no remedy. Gessler must perish: Tell swore it darkly in his secret soul, when the monster forced him to aim at the head of his boy; and he will keep his oath. His thoughts wander to and fro, but his volition is unalterable; the free and peaceful mountaineer is to become a shedder of blood: woe to them that have made him so!

Travellers come along the pass; the unconcern of their every-day existence is strikingly contrasted with the dark and fateful purposes of Tell. The shallow innocent garrulity of Stüssi the Forester, the maternal vehemence of Armgart's Wife, the hard-hearted haughtiness of Gessler, successively presented to us, give an air of truth to the delineation, and deepen the impressiveness of the result.

ACT IV. SCENE III.

The hollow way at Küssnacht. You descend from behind amid rocks; and travellers, before appearing on the scene, are seen from the height above. Rocks encircle the whole space; on one of the foremost is a projecting crag overgrown with brushwood.

TELL [*enters with his bow*].

Here through the hollow way he'll pass; there is.
No other road to Küssnacht: here I'll do it!
The opportunity is good; the bushes
Of alder there will hide me; from that point
My arrow hits him; the strait pass prevents
Pursuit. Now, Gessler, balance thy account
With Heaven! Thou must be gone: thy sand is run.

　　Remote and harmless I have liv'd; my bow
Ne'er bent save on the wild beast of the forest;
My thoughts were free of murder. Thou hast scar'd me
From my peace; to fell asp-poison hast thou
Changed the milk of kindly temper in me;
Thou hast accustom'd me to horrors. Gessler!
The archer who could aim at his boy's head
Can send an arrow to his enemy's heart.

　　Poor little boys! My kind true wife! I will
Protect them from thee, Landvogt! When I drew
That bowstring, and my hand was quiv'ring,

And with devilish joy thou mad'st me point it
At the child, and I in fainting anguish
Entreated thee in vain; then with a grim
Irrevocable oath, deep in my soul,
I vow'd to God in Heav'n, that the *next* aim
I took should be thy heart.   The vow I made
In that despairing moment's agony
Became a holy debt; and I will pay it.

   Thou art my master, and my Kaiser's Vogt;
Yet would the Kaiser not have suffer'd thee
To do as thou hast done.   He sent thee hither
To judge us; rigorously, for he is angry;
But not to glut thy savage appetite
With murder, and thyself be safe, among us:
There is a God to punish them that wrong us.

   Come forth, thou bringer once of bitter sorrow,
My precious jewel now, my trusty yew!
A mark I 'll set thee, which the cry of woe
Could never penetrate: to *thee* it shall not
Be impenetrable.   And, good bowstring,
Which so oft in sport hast serv'd me truly,
Forsake me not in this last awful earnest;
Yet once hold fast, thou faithful cord; thou oft
For me hast wing'd the biting arrow;
Now send it sure and piercing, now or never!
Fail this, there is no second in my quiver.
                  [*Travellers cross the scene.*

   Here let me sit on this stone bench, set up
For brief rest to the wayfarer; for here
There is no home.   Each pushes on quick, transient,
Regarding not the other or his sorrows.
Here goes the anxious merchant, and the light·
Unmoneyed pilgrim; the pale pious monk,
The gloomy robber, and the mirthful showman;
The carrier with his heavy-laden horse,
Who comes from far-off lands; for every road
Will lead one to the end o' th' World.
They pass; each hastening forward on his path,
Pursuing his own business: mine is death!	[*Sits down.*

Erewhile, my children, were your father out,
There was a merriment at his return;
For still, on coming home, he brought you somewhat,
Might be an Alpine flower, rare bird, or elf-bolt,
Such as the wand'rer finds upon the mountains:
Now he is gone in quest of other spoil.
On the wild way he sits with thoughts of murder:
'T is for his enemy's life he lies in wait.
And yet on you, dear children, you alone
He thinks as then: for your sake is he here;
To guard you from the Tyrant's vengeful mood,
He bends his peaceful bow for work of blood.　　　　[*Rises.*

No common game I watch for.　Does the hunter
Think it nought to roam the livelong day,
In winter's cold; to risk the desp'rate leap
From crag to crag, to climb the slipp'ry face
O' to' dizzy steep, gluing his steps in 's blood;
And all to catch a pitiful chamois?
Here is a richer prize afield: the heart
Of my sworn enemy, that would destroy me.
　　　　　　[*A sound of gay music is heard in the distance; it*
　　　　　　　　approaches.

All my days, the bow has been my comrade,
I have trained myself to archery; oft
Have I took the bull's-eye, many a prize
Brought home from merry shooting; but to-day
I will perform my master-feat, and win me
The best prize in the circuit of the hills.
　　　　　　[*A wedding company crosses the scene, and mounts up*
　　　　　　　　through the Pass.　Tell looks at them, leaning on his
　　　　　　　　bow; Stüssi the Forester joins him.
STÜSSI.　'T is Klostermey'r of Morlischachen holds
His bridal feast to-day: a wealthy man;
Has half a score of glens i' th' Alps.　They're going
To fetch the bride from Imisee; to-night
There will be mirth and wassail down at Küssnacht.
Come you!　All honest people are invited.
　　TELL.　A serious guest befits not bridal feasts.
　　STÜSSI.　If sorrow press you, dash it from your heart!

Seize what you can ; the times are hard ; one needs
To snatch enjoyment nimbly while it passes.
Here 't is a bridal, there 't will be a burial.

TELL. And oftentimes the one leads to the other.

STÜSSI. The way o' th' world at present! There is nought
But mischief everywhere : an avalanche
Has come away in Glarus; and, they tell me,
A side o' th' Glärnish has sunk under ground.

TELL. Do, then, the very hills give way ! On earth
Is nothing that endures.

STÜSSI.   In foreign parts, too,
Are strange wonders. I was speaking with a man
From Baden : a Knight, it seems, was riding
To the King ; a swarm of hornets met him
By the way, and fell on 's horse, and stung it
Till it dropt down dead of very torment,
And the poor Knight was forced to go afoot.

TELL. Weak creatures too have stings.

*[Armgart's Wife enters with several children, and places
herself at the entrance of the Pass.*

STÜSSI.   'T is thought to bode
Some great misfortune to the land ; some black
Unnatural action.

TELL.   Ev'ry day such actions
Occur in plenty : needs no sign or wonder
To foreshow them.

STÜSSI.   Ay, truly ! Well for him
That tills his field in peace, and undisturb'd
Sits by his own fireside !

TELL.   The peacefulest
Dwells not in peace, if wicked neighbors hinder.

*[Tell looks often, with restless expectation, towards the top
of the Pass.*

STÜSSI. Too true. — Good b'ye ! — You 're waiting here for some
one ?

TELL. That am I.

STÜSSI.   Glad meeting with your friends !
You are from Uri ? His Grace the Landvogt
Is expected thence to-day.

TRAVELLER [*enters*]. Expect not
The Landvogt now. The waters, from the rain,
Are flooded, and have swept down all the bridges. *[Tell stands up.*

ARMGART [*coming forward*].

The Vogt not come!

   STÜSSI.   Did you want aught with him?

   ARMGART. Ah! yes, indeed!

   STÜSSI.   Why have you placed yourself

In this strait pass to meet him?

   ARMGART.   In the pass

He cannot turn aside from me, must hear me.

   FRIESSHARDT [*comes hastily down the Pass, and calls into the
Scene*].

Make way! make way! My lord the Landvogt

Is riding close at hand.

   ARMGART.   The Landvogt coming!

      [*She goes with her children to the front of the Scene. Gess-
ler and Rudolph der Harras appear on horseback at the
top of the Pass.*

   STÜSSI [*to Friesshardt*].

How got you through the water, when the flood

Had carried down the bridges?

   FRIESS.   We have battled

With the billows, friend; we heed no Alp-flood.

   STÜSSI. Were you o' board i' th' storm?

   FRIESS.   That were we;

While I live, I shall remember 't.

   STÜSSI.   Stay, stay!

Oh, tell me!

   FRIESS.   Cannot; must run on t' announce

His lordship in the Castle.   [*Exit.*

   STÜSSI.   Had these fellows

I' th' boat been honest people, 't would have sunk

With ev'ry soul of them. But for such rakehells,

Neither fire nor flood will kill them. [*He looks round.*] Whither

Went the Mountain-man was talking with me?   [*Exit.*

       GESSLER *and* RUDOLPH DER HARRAS *on horseback.*

   GESSLER. Say what you like, I am the Kaiser's servant,

And must think of pleasing him. He sent me

Not to caress these hinds, to soothe or nurse them:

Obedience is the word! The point at issue is

Shall Boor or Kaiser here be lord o' th' land.

WILLIAM TELL

ARMGART. Now is the moment! Now for my petition!

                   [*Approaches timidly.*

     GESSLER. This Hat at Aldorf, mark you, I set up
Not for the joke's sake, or to try the hearts
O' th' people; these I know of old: but that
They might be taught to bend their necks to me,
Which are too straight and stiff: and in the way
Where they are hourly passing, I have planted
This offence, that so their eyes may fall on 't,
And remind them of their lord, whom they forget.

     RUDOLPH. But yet the people have some rights —
     GESSLER.   **Which now**
Is not a time for settling or admitting.
Mighty things are on the anvil. The house
Of Hapsburg must wax powerful; what the Father
Gloriously began, the Son must forward:
This people is a stone of stumbling, which
One way or t' other must be put aside.

           [*They are about to pass along. The Woman throws her-
                self before the Landvogt.*

     ARMGART. Mercy, gracious Landvogt! Justice! Justice!
     GESSLER. Why do you plague me here, and stop my way,
I' th' open road? Off! Let me pass!
     ARMGART.   My husband
Is in prison; these orphans cry for bread.
Have pity, good your Grace, have pity on us!

     RUDOLPH. Who or what are you, then? Who is your husband?
     ARMGART. A poor wild-hay-man of the Rigiberg,
Whose trade is, on the brow of the abyss,
To mow the common grass from craggy shelves
And nooks to which the cattle dare not climb.

     RUDOLPH [*to Gessler*]. By Heaven, a wild and miserable life!
Do now! do let the poor drudge free, I pray you!
Whatever be his crime, that horrid trade
Is punishment enough.

          [*To the Woman*] You shall have justice:
In the Castle there, make your petition;
This is not the place.

     ARMGART.   No, no! I stir not
From the spot till you give up my husband!
'T is the sixth month he has lain i' th' dungeon,

Waiting for the sentence of some judge, in vain.

GESSLER. Woman! Would'st lay hands on me? Begone!

ARMGART.   Justice, Landvogt! thou art judge o' th' land here,
I' th' Kaiser's stead and God's.   Perform thy duty!
As thou expectest justice from above,
Show it to us.

GESSLER.   Off!   Take the mutinous rabble
From my sight.

ARMGART [*catches the bridle of the horse*].
                    No, no!   I now have nothing
More to lose.   Thou shalt not move a step, Vogt,
Till thou hast done me right.   Ay, knit thy brows,
And roll thy eyes as sternly as thou wilt;
We are so wretched, wretched now, we care not
Aught more for thy anger.

GESSLER.   Woman, make way!
Or else my horse shall crush thee.

ARMGART.   Let it! there —

    [*She pulls her children to the ground, and throws herself*
        along with them in his way.

Here am I with my children : let the orphans
Be trodden underneath thy horse's hoofs!
'T is not the worst that thou hast done.

RUDOLPH.   Woman!   Art mad?

ARMGART [*with still greater violence*].
                    'T is long that thou hast trodden
The Kaiser's people under foot.   Too long!
Oh, I am but a woman; were I a man,
I should find something else to do than lie
Here crying in the dust.

    [*The music of the Wedding is heard again, at the top of the*
      Pass, but softened by distance.

GESSLER.   Where are my servants?
Quick!   Take her hence!   I may forget myself,
And do the thing I shall repent.

RUDOLPH.   My lord,
The servants cannot pass; the place above
Is crowded by a bridal company.

GESSLER.   I 've been too mild a ruler to this people;
They are not tamed as they should be; their tongues
Are still at liberty.   This shall be-alter'd!

I will break that stubborn humor; Freedom
With its pert vauntings shall no-more be heard of:
I will enforce a new law in these lands;
There shall not —

[*An arrow pierces him; he claps his hand upon his heart, and is about to sink. With a faint voice.*

God be merciful to me!

RUDOLPH. Herr Landvogt — God! What is it? Whence came it?

ARMGART [*springing up*].

Dead! dead! He totters, sinks! 'T has hit him!

RUDOLPH [*springs from his horse*].

Horrible! — O God of Heaven! — Herr Ritter,
Cry to God for mercy! You are dying.

GESSLER. 'T is Tell's arrow.

[*Has slid down from his horse into Rudolph's arms, who sets him on the stone bench.*

TELL [*appears above, on the point of the rock*].

Thou hast found the archer;

Seek no other. Free are the cottages,
Secure is innocence from thee; thou wilt
Torment the land no more.

[*Disappears from the height. The people rush in.*

STÜSSI [*foremost*].   What? What has happen'd?

ARMGART. The Landvogt shot, kill'd by an arrow.

PEOPLE [*rushing in*].   Who?
Who is shot?

[*Whilst the foremost of the wedding company enter on the Scene, the hindmost are still on the height, and the music continues.*

RUDOLPH. He's bleeding, bleeding to death.
Away! Seek help; pursue the murderer!
Lost man! Must it so end with thee? Thou wouldst not
Hear my warning!

STÜSSI.   Sure enough! There lies he
Pale and going fast.

MANY VOICES.   Who was it killed him?

RUDOLPH. Are the people mad, that they make music
Over murder? Stop it, I say!

[*The music ceases suddenly; more people come crowding round.*

Herr Landvogt,

Can you not speak to me?   Is there nothing
You would entrust me with?

> [*Gessler makes signs with his hand, and vehemently repeats
> them, as they are not understood.*·

Where shall I run?

To Küssnacht!   I cannot understand you:
Oh, grow not angry!   Leave the things of Earth,
And think how you shall make your peace with Heaven!

> [*The whole bridal company surround the dying man with an
> expression of unsympathizing horror.*

STÜSSI.   Look there!   How pale he grows!   Now!   Death is
          coming
Round his heart: his eyes grow dim and fixed.

ARMGART [*lifts up one of her children*].
See, children, how a miscreant departs!

RUDOLPH.   Out on you, crazy hags!   Have ye no touch
Of feeling in you, that ye feast your eyes
On such an object?   Help me, lend your hands!
Will no one help to pull the tort'ring arrow
From his breast?

WOMEN [*start back*].   *We* touch him whom God has smote!

RUDOLPH. My curse upon you!   [*Draws his sword.*

STÜSSI [*lays his hand on Rudolph's arm*].

                            Softly, my good Sir!
Your government is at an end.   The Tyrant
Is fallen: we will endure no farther violence:
We are free.

ALL [*tumultuously*].   The land is free!

RUDOLPH.   Ha! runs it so?
Are rev'rence and obedience gone already?

> [*To the armed Attendants, who press in.*

You see the murd'rous deed that has been done.
Our help is vain, vain to pursue the murd'rer;
Other cares demand us.   On!   To Küssnacht!
To save the Kaiser's fortress!   For at present
All bonds of order, duty, are unloosed,
No man's fidelity is to be trusted.

> [*Whilst he departs with the Attendants, appear six Fratres
> Misericordiæ.*

ARMGART. Room!   Room!   Here come the Friars of Mercy.

STÜSSI. The victim slain, the ravens are assembling!

FRATRES MISERICORDIÆ [*form a half-circle round the dead body, and sing in a deep tone*].

> With noiseless tread death comes on man,
>> No plea, no prayer delivers him ;
> From midst of busy life's unfinished plan,
>> With sudden hand, it severs him :
> And ready or not ready, — no delay,
>> Forth to his Judge's bar he must away !

The death of Gessler, which forms the leading object of the plot, happens at the end of the fourth act; the fifth, occupied with representing the expulsion of his satellites, and the final triumph and liberation of the Swiss, though diversified with occurrences and spectacles, moves on with inferior animation. A certain want of unity is, indeed, distinctly felt throughout all the piece ; the incidents do not point one way ; there is no connection, or a very slight one, between the enterprise of Tell and that of the men of Rütli. This is the principal, or rather sole, deficiency of the present work; a deficiency inseparable from the faithful display of the historical event, and far more than compensated by the deeper interest and the wider range of action and delineation, which a strict adherence to the facts allows. By the present mode of management, Alpine life in all its length and breadth is placed before us : from the feudal halls of Attinghausen to Ruodi the Fisher of the Luzern Lake, and Armgart, —

> " The poor wild-hay-man of the Rigiberg,
>> Whose trade is, on the brow of the abyss,
> To mow the common grass from craggy shelves
> And nooks to which the cattle dare not climb," —

we stand as if in presence of the Swiss, beholding the achievement of their freedom in its minutest circumstances, with all its simplicity and unaffected greatness. The light of the poet's genius is upon the Four Forest Cantons, at the opening of the Fourteenth Century : the whole time and scene shine as with the brightness, the truth, and more than the beauty, of reality.

The tragedy of *Tell* wants unity of interest and of action; but in spite of this, it may justly claim the high dignity of ranking with the very best of Schiller's plays. Less comprehensive and ambitious than *Wallenstein*, less ethereal than the *Jungfrau*, it has a look of nature and substantial truth, which neither of its rivals can boast of. The feelings it inculcates and appeals to are those of universal human nature, and presented in their purest, most unpretending form. There is no high-wrought sentiment, no poetic love. Tell loves his wife as honest men love their wives; and the episode of Bertha and Rudenz, though beautiful, is very brief, and without effect on the general result. It is delightful and salutary to the heart to wander among the scenes of *Tell:* all is lovely, yet all is real. Physical and moral grandeur are united; yet both are the unadorned grandeur of Nature. There are the lakes and green valleys beside us, the Schreckhorn, the Jungfrau, and their sister peaks, with their avalanches and their palaces of ice, all glowing in the southern sun; and dwelling among them are a race of manly husbandmen, heroic without ceasing to be homely, poetical without ceasing to be genuine.

We have dwelt the longer on this play, not only on account of its peculiar fascinations, but also — as it is our last! Schiller's faculties had never been more brilliant than at present: strong in mature age, in rare and varied accomplishments, he was now reaping the full fruit of his studious vigils; the rapidity with which he wrote such noble poems, at once betokened the exuberant riches of his mind and the prompt command which he enjoyed of them. Still all that he had done seemed but a fraction of his appointed task: a bold imagination was carrying him forward into distant untouched fields of thought and poetry, where triumphs yet more glorious were to be gained. Schemes of new writings, new kinds of writing, were budding in his fancy; he was yet, as he had ever been, surrounded by a multitude of projects, and full of ardor to labor in fulfilling them. But Schiller's labors and triumphs were drawing to a close. The invisible Messenger was already near, which overtakes alike the busy and the idle, which arrests man in the midst of his pleasures or his occupations, *and changes his countenance and sends him away.*

In 1804, having been at Berlin witnessing the exhibition of his *Wilhelm Tell,* he was seized, while returning, with a paroxysm of that malady which for many years had never wholly left him. The attack was fierce and violent; it brought him to the verge of the grave; but he escaped once more; was considered out of danger, and again resumed his poetical employments. Besides various translations from the French and Italian, he had sketched a tragedy on the history of Perkin Warbeck, and finished two acts of one on that of a kindred but more fortunate impostor, Dimitri of Russia. His mind, it would appear, was also frequently engaged with more solemn and sublime ideas. The universe of human thought he had now explored and enjoyed; but he seems to have found no permanent contentment in any of its provinces. Many of his later poems indicate an incessant and increasing longing for some solution of the mystery of life; at times it is a gloomy resignation to the want and the despair of any. His ardent spirit could not satisfy itself with things seen, though gilded with all the glories of intellect and imagination; it soared away in search of other lands, looking with unutterable desire for some surer and brighter home beyond the horizon of this world. Death he had no reason to regard as probably a near event; but we easily perceive that the awful secrets connected with it had long been familiar to his contemplation. The veil which hid them from his eyes was now shortly, when he looked not for it, to be rent asunder.

The spring of 1805, which Schiller had anticipated with no ordinary hopes of enjoyment and activity, came on in its course, cold, bleak, and stormy; and along with it his sickness returned. The help of physicians was vain; the unwearied services of trembling affection were vain: his disorder kept increasing; on the 9th of May it reached a crisis. Early in the morning of that day, he grew insensible, and by degrees delirious. Among his expressions, the word *Lichtenberg* was frequently noticed; a word of no import; indicating, as some thought, the writer of that name, whose works he had lately been reading; according to others, the castle of Leuchtenberg, which, a few days before his sickness, he had been proposing to visit. The poet and the sage was soon to lie low; but his friends were spared the farther pain of seeing him depart in madness. The fiery canopy of physical suffering, which had bewildered and blinded his thinking faculties, was drawn aside; and the spirit of Schiller looked forth in its wonted serenity, once again before it passed away forever. After noon his delirium abated; about four o'clock he fell into a soft sleep, from which he erelong awoke in full possession of his senses. Restored to consciousness in that hour, when the soul is cut off from human help, and man must front the King of Terrors on his own strength, Schiller did not faint or fail in this his last and sharpest trial. Feeling that his end was come, he addressed himself to meet it as became him; not with affected carelessness or superstitious fear, but with the quiet unpretending manliness which had marked the tenor of his life. Of his friends and family he took a touching but a tranquil farewell: he ordered that his funeral should be private, without pomp or parade. Some one inquiring how he felt, he said *"Calmer and calmer;"* simple but memorable words, expressive of the mild heroism of the man. About six he sank into a deep sleep; once for a moment he looked up with a lively air, and said, *"Many things were growing plain and clear to him!"* Again he closed his eyes; and his sleep deepened and deepened, till it changed into the sleep from which there is no awakening; and all that remained of Schiller was a lifeless form, soon to be mingled with the clods of the valley.

The news of Schiller's death fell cold on many a heart : not in Germany alone, but over Europe, it was regarded as a public loss, by all who understood its meaning. In Weimar especially, the scene of his noblest efforts, the abode of his chosen friends, the sensation it produced was deep and universal. The public places of amusement were shut; all ranks made haste to testify their feelings, to honor themselves and the deceased by tributes to his memory. It was Friday when Schiller died; his funeral was meant to be on Sunday; but the state of his remains made it necessary to proceed before. Doering thus describes the ceremony : —

"According to his own directions, the bier was to be borne by private burghers of the city; but several young artists and students, out of reverence for the deceased, took it from them. It was between midnight and one in the morning, when they approached the churchyard. The overclouded heaven threatened rain. But as the bier was set down beside the grave, the clouds suddenly split asunder, and the moon, coming forth in peaceful clearness, threw her first rays on the coffin of the Departed. They lowered him into the grave; and the moon again retired behind her clouds. A fierce tempest of wind began to howl, as if it were reminding the bystanders of their great, irreparable loss. At this moment who could have applied without emotion the poet's own words : —

> 'Alas, the ruddy morning tinges
>   A silent, cold, sepulchral stone ;
> And evening throws her crimson fringes
>   But round his slumber dark and lone!' "

So lived and so died Friedrich Schiller; a man on whose history other men will long dwell with a mingled feeling of reverence and love. Our humble record of his life and writings is drawing to an end : yet we still linger, loath to part with a spirit so dear to us. From the scanty and too much neglected field of his biography, a few slight facts and indications may still be gleaned; slight, but distinctive of him as an individual, and not to be despised in a penury so great and so unmerited.

Schiller's age was forty-five years and a few months when he died.[1] Sickness had long wasted his form, which at no time could boast of faultless symmetry. He was tall and strongly boned; but unmuscular and lean : his body, it might be perceived, was wasting under the energy of a spirit too keen for it. His face was pale, the cheeks and temples rather

[1] "He left a widow, two sons, and two daughters," of whom we regret to say that we have learned nothing. "Of his three sisters, the youngest died before him; the eldest is married to the Hofrath Reinwald, in Meinungen; the second to Herr Frankh, the clergyman of Meckmühl, in Würtemberg." *Doering.*

hollow, the chin somewhat deep and slightly projecting, the
nose irregularly aquiline, his hair inclined to auburn. Withal
his countenance was attractive, and had a certain manly beauty.
The lips were curved together in a line, expressing delicate
and honest sensibility; a silent enthusiasm, impetuosity not
unchecked by melancholy, gleamed in his softly kindled eyes
and pale cheeks, and the brow was high and thoughtful. To
judge from his portraits, Schiller's face expressed well the
features of his mind : it is mildness tempering strength; fiery
ardor shining through the clouds of suffering and disappointment, deep but patiently endured. Pale was its proper tint;
the cheeks and temples were best hollow. There are few
faces that affect us more than Schiller's; it is at once meek,
tender, unpretending, and heroic.

In his dress and manner, as in all things, he was plain and
unaffected. Among strangers, something shy and retiring
might occasionally be observed in him : in his own family, or
among his select friends, he was kind-hearted, free, and gay
as a little child. In public, his external appearance had nothing in it to strike or attract. Of an unpresuming aspect, wearing plain apparel, his looks as he walked were constantly bent
on the ground; so that frequently, as we are told, "he failed
to notice the salutation of a passing acquaintance; but if he
heard it, he would catch hastily at his hat, and give his cordial
'Guten Tag.'" Modesty, simplicity, a total want of all parade
or affectation were conspicuous in him. These are the usual
concomitants of true greatness, and serve to mitigate its splendor. Common things he did as a common man. His conduct
in such matters was uncalculated, spontaneous; and therefore
natural and pleasing.

Concerning his mental character, the greater part of what
we had to say has been already said, in speaking of his works.
The most cursory perusal of these will satisfy us that he had
a mind of the highest order; grand by nature, and cultivated
by the assiduous study of a lifetime. It is not the predominating force of any one faculty that impresses us in Schiller;
but the general force of all. Every page of his writings bears
the stamp of internal vigor; new truths, new aspects of known

truth, bold thought, happy imagery, lofty emotion. Schiller would have been no common man, though he had altogether wanted the qualities peculiar to poets. His intellect is clear, deep, and comprehensive; its deductions, frequently elicited from numerous and distant premises, are presented under a magnificent aspect, in the shape of theorems, embracing an immense multitude of minor propositions. Yet it seems powerful and vast, rather than quick or keen; for Schiller is not notable for wit, though his fancy is ever prompt with its metaphors, illustrations, comparisons, to decorate and point the perceptions of his reason. The earnestness of his temper farther disqualified him for this: his tendency was rather to adore the grand and the lofty than to despise the little and the mean. Perhaps his greatest faculty was a half-poetical, half-philosophical imagination: a faculty teeming with magnificence and brilliancy; now adorning, or aiding to erect, a stately pyramid of scientific speculation; now brooding over the abysses of thought and feeling, till thoughts and feelings, else unutterable, were embodied in expressive forms, and palaces and landscapes glowing in ethereal beauty rose like exhalations from the bosom of the deep.

Combined and partly of kindred with these intellectual faculties was that vehemence of temperament which is necessary for their full development. Schiller's heart was at once fiery and tender; impetuous, soft, affectionate, his enthusiasm clothed the universe with grandeur, and sent his spirit forth to explore its secrets and mingle warmly in its interests. Thus poetry in Schiller was not one but many gifts. It was not the "lean and flashy song" of an ear apt for harmony, combined with a maudlin sensibility, or a mere animal ferocity of passion, and an imagination creative chiefly because unbridled: it was, what true poetry is always, the quintessence of general mental riches, the purified result of strong thought and conception, and of refined as well as powerful emotion. In his writings, we behold him a moralist, a philosopher, a man of universal knowledge: in each of these capacities he is great, but also in more; for all that he achieves in these is brightened and gilded with the touch of another quality; his maxims, his feelings, his opinions are transformed from the lifeless shape of didactic truths, into living shapes that address faculties far finer than the understanding.

The gifts by which such transformation is effected, the gift of pure, ardent, tender sensibility, joined to those of fancy and imagination, are perhaps not wholly denied to any man endowed with the power of reason; possessed in various degrees of strength, they add to the products of mere intellect corresponding tints of new attractiveness; in a degree great enough to be remarkable they constitute a poet. Of this peculiar faculty how much had fallen to Schiller's lot, we need not attempt too minutely to explain. Without injuring his reputation, it may be admitted that, in general, his works exhibit rather extraordinary strength than extraordinary fineness or versatility. His power of dramatic imitation is perhaps never of the very highest, the Shakspearean kind; and in its best state, it is farther limited to a certain range of characters. It is with the grave, the earnest, the exalted, the affectionate, the mournful, that he succeeds: he is not destitute of humor, as his *Wallenstein's Camp* will show, but neither is he rich in it; and for sprightly ridicule in any of its forms he has seldom shown either taste or talent. Chance principally made the drama his department; he might have shone equally in many others. The vigorous and copious invention, the knowledge of life, of men and things, displayed in his theatrical pieces, might have been available in very different pursuits; frequently the charm of his works has little to distinguish it from the charm of intellectual and moral force in general; it is often the capacious thought, the vivid imagery, the impetuous feeling of the orator, rather than the wild pathos and capricious enchantment of the poet. Yet that he was capable of rising to the loftiest regions of poetry, no reader of his *Maid of Orleans*, his character of Thekla, or many other of his pieces, will hesitate to grant. Sometimes we suspect that it is the very grandeur of his general powers which prevents us from exclusively admiring his poetic genius. We are not lulled by the syren song of poetry, because her melodies are blended with the clearer, manlier tones of serious reason, and of honest though exalted feeling.

Much laborious discussion has been wasted in defining genius, particularly by the countrymen of Schiller, some of whom have narrowed the conditions of the term so far, as to find but three *men of genius* since the world was created: Homer, Shakspeare, and Goethe! From such rigid precision, applied to a matter in itself indefinite, there may be an apparent, but there is no real, increase of accuracy. The creative power, the faculty not only of imitating given forms of being, but of imagining and representing new ones, which is here attributed with such distinctness and so sparingly, has been given by nature in complete perfection to no man, nor entirely denied to any. The shades of it cannot be distinguished by so loose a scale as language. A definition of genius which excludes such a mind as Schiller's will scarcely be agreeable to philosophical correctness, and it will tend rather to lower than to exalt the dignity of the word. Possessing all the general mental faculties in their highest degree of strength, an intellect ever active, vast, powerful, far-sighted; an imagination never weary of producing grand or beautiful forms; a heart of the noblest temper, sympathies comprehensive yet ardent, feelings vehement, impetuous, yet full of love and kindliness and tender pity; conscious of the rapid and fervid exercise of all these powers within him, and able farther to present their products refined and harmonized, and "married to immortal verse," Schiller may or may not be called a man of genius by his critics; but his mind in either case will remain one of the most enviable which can fall to the share of a mortal.

In a poet worthy of that name, the powers of the intellect are indissolubly interwoven with the moral feelings; and the exercise of his art depends not more on the perfection of the one than of the other. The poet, who does not feel nobly and justly, as well as passionately, will never permanently succeed in making others feel: the forms of error and falseness, infinite in number, are transitory in duration; truth, of thought and sentiment, but chiefly of sentiment, truth alone is eternal and unchangeable. But, happily, a delight in the products of reason and imagination can scarcely ever be divided from, at least, a love for virtue and genuine greatness. Our feelings are in favor of heroism; we *wish* to be pure and perfect. Happy he whose resolutions are so strong, or whose temptations are so weak, that he can convert these feelings into action! The severest pang, of which a proud and sensitive nature can be conscious, is the perception of its own debasement. The sources of misery in life are many : vice is one of the surest. Any human creature, tarnished with guilt, will in general be wretched; a man of genius in that case will be doubly so, for his ideas of excellence are higher, his sense of failure is more keen. In such miseries, Schiller had no share. The sentiments, which animated his poetry, were converted into principles of conduct; his actions were as blameless as his writings were pure. With his simple and high predilections, with his strong devotedness to a noble cause, he contrived to steer through life, unsullied by its meanness, unsubdued by any of its difficulties or allurements. With the world, in fact, he had not much to do; without effort, he dwelt apart from it; its prizes were not the wealth which could enrich him. His great, almost his single aim, was to unfold his spiritual faculties, to study and contemplate and improve their intellectual creations. Bent upon this, with the steadfastness of an apostle, the more sordid temptations of the world passed harmlessly over him. Wishing not to seem, but to be, envy was a feeling of which he knew but little, even before he rose above its level. Wealth or rank he regarded as a means, not an end; his own humble fortune supplying him with all the essential conveniences of life, the world had nothing more that he chose to covet, nothing more that it could give him. He was not rich; but his habits were simple, and, except by reason of his sickness and its consequences, unexpensive. At all times he was far above the meanness of self-interest, particularly in its meanest shape, a love of money. Doering tells us, that a bookseller having travelled from a distance expressly to offer him a higher price for the copyright of *Wallenstein*, at that time in the press, and for which he was on terms with Cotta of Tübingen, Schiller answering, "Cotta deals steadily, with me, and I with him," sent away this new merchant, without even the hope of a future bargain. The anecdote is small; but it seems to paint the integrity of the man, careless of pecuniary concerns in comparison with the strictest uprightness in his conduct. In fact, his real wealth lay in being able to pursue his darling studies, and to live in the sunshine of friendship and domestic love. This he had always longed for; this he at last enjoyed. And though sickness and many vexations annoyed him, the intrinsic excellence of his nature chequered the darkest portions of their gloom with an effulgence derived from himself. The ardor of his feelings, tempered by benevolence, was equable and placid: his temper, though overflowing with generous warmth, seems almost never to have shown any hastiness or anger. To all men he was humane and sympathizing; among his friends, open-hearted, generous, helpful; in the circle of his family, kind, tender, sportive. And what gave an especial charm to all this was, the unobtrusiveness with which it was attended: there was no parade, no display, no particle of affectation; rating and conducting himself simply as an honest man and citizen, he became greater by forgetting that he was great.

Such were the prevailing habits of Schiller. That in the mild and beautiful brilliancy of their aspect there must have been some specks and imperfections, the common lot of poor humanity, who knows not? That these were small and transient, we judge from the circumstance that scarcely any hint of them has reached us: nor are we anxious to obtain a full description of them. For practical uses, we can sufficiently conjecture what they were; and the heart desires not to dwell upon them. This man is passed away from our dim and tarnished world: let him have the benefit of departed friends; let him be transfigured in our thoughts, and shine there without the little blemishes that clung to him in life.

Schiller gives a fine example of the German character: he has all its good qualities in a high degree, with very few of its defects. We trace in him all that downrightness and simplicity, that sincerity of heart and mind, for which the Germans are remarked; their enthusiasm, their patient, long-continuing, earnest devotedness; their imagination, delighting in the lofty and magnificent; their intellect, rising into refined abstractions, stretching itself into comprehensive generalizations. But the excesses to which such a character is liable are, in him, prevented by a firm and watchful sense of propriety. His simplicity never degenerates into ineptitude or insipidity; his enthusiasm must be based on reason; he rarely suffers his love of the vast to betray him into toleration of the vague. The boy Schiller was extravagant; but the man admits no bombast in his style, no inflation in his thoughts or actions. He is the poet of truth; our understandings and consciences are satisfied, while our hearts and imaginations are moved. His fictions are emphatically nature copied and embellished; his sentiments are refined and touchingly beautiful, but they are likewise manly and correct; they exalt and inspire, but they do not mislead.   Above all, he has no cant; in any of its thousand branches, ridiculous or hateful, none.   He does not distort his character or genius into shapes, which he thinks more becoming than their natural one : he does not hang out principles which are not his, or harbor beloved persuasions which he half or wholly knows to be false.   He did not often speak of wholesome prejudices; he did not "embrace the Roman Catholic religion because it was the grandest and most comfortable."   Truth with Schiller, or what seemed such, was an indispensable requisite : if he but suspected an opinion to be false, however dear it may have been, he seems to have examined it with rigid scrutiny, and if he found it guilty, to have plucked it out, and resolutely cast it forth.   The sacrifice might cause him pain, permanent pain; real damage, he imagined, it could hardly cause him.   It is irksome and dangerous to travel in the dark; but better so, than with an *Ignisfatuus* to guide us.   Considering the warmth of his sensibilities, Schiller's merit on this point is greater than we might at first suppose.   For a man with whom intellect is the ruling or exclusive faculty, whose sympathies, loves, hatreds, are comparatively coarse and dull, it may be easy to avoid this half-wilful entertainment of error, and this cant which is the consequence and sign of it.   But for a man of keen tastes, a large fund of innate probity is necessary to prevent his aping the excellence which he loves so much, yet is unable to attain. Among persons of the latter sort, it is extremely rare to meet with one completely unaffected. Schiller's other noble qualities would not have justice, did we neglect to notice this, the truest proof of their nobility. Honest, unpretending, manly simplicity pervades all parts of his character and genius and habits of life. We not only admire him, we trust him and love him.

"The character of child-like simplicity," he has himself observed,[1] "which genius impresses on its works, it shows also in its private life and manners. It is bashful, for nature is ever so; but it is not prudish, for only corruption is prudish. It is clear-sighted, for nature can never be the contrary; but it is not cunning, for this only art can be. It is faithful to its character and inclinations; but not so much because it is directed by principles, as because after all vibrations nature constantly reverts to her original position, constantly renews her primitive demand. It is modest, nay timid, for genius is always a secret to itself; but it is not anxious, for it knows not the dangers of the way which it travels. Of the private habits of the persons who have been peculiarly distinguished by their genius, our information is small; but the little that has been recorded for us of the chief of them, — of Sophocles, Archimedes, Hippocrates; and in modern times, of Dante and Tasso, of Rafaelle, Albrecht Dürer, Cervantes, Shakspeare, Fielding, and others, — confirms this observation." Schiller himself confirms it; perhaps more strongly than most of the examples here adduced. No man ever wore his faculties more meekly, or performed great works with less consciousness of their greatness. Abstracted from the contemplation of himself, his eye was turned upon the objects of his labor, and he pursued them with the eagerness, the entireness, the spontaneous sincerity, of a boy pursuing sport. Hence this "child-like simplicity," the last perfection of his other excellencies. His was a mighty spirit unheedful of its might. He walked the earth in calm power: "the staff of his

[1] *Naive und sentimentalische Dichtung.*

spear was like a weaver's beam;" but he wielded it like a
wand.

Such, so far as we can represent it, is the form in which
Schiller's life and works have gradually painted their character in the mind of a secluded individual, whose solitude
he has often charmed, whom he has instructed, and cheered,
and moved. The original impression, we know, was faint and
inadequate, the present copy of it is still more so; yet we
have sketched it as we could: the figure of Schiller, and of
the figures he conceived and drew are there; himself, "and
in his hand a glass which shows us many more." To those
who look on him as we have wished to make them, Schiller
will not need a farther panegyric. For the sake of Literature,
it may still be remarked, that his merit was peculiarly due to
her. Literature was his creed, the dictate of his conscience;
he was an Apostle of the Sublime and Beautiful, and this his
calling made a hero of him. For it was in the spirit of a true
man that he viewed it, and undertook to cultivate it; and its
inspirations constantly maintained the noblest temper in his
soul. The end of Literature was not, in Schiller's judgment,
to amuse the idle, or to recreate the busy, by showy spectacles
for the imagination, or quaint paradoxes and epigrammatic
disquisitions for the understanding: least of all was it to
gratify in any shape the selfishness of its professors, to minister to their malignity, their love of money, or even of fame.
For persons who degrade it to such purposes, the deepest contempt of which his kindly nature could admit was at all times
in store. "Unhappy mortal!" says he to the literary trades-
man, the man who writes for gain, "Unhappy mortal, who
with science and art, the noblest of all instruments, effectest
and attemptest nothing more than the day-drudge with the
meanest; who, in the domain of perfect Freedom, bearest
about in thee the spirit of Slave!" As Schiller viewed it,
genuine Literature includes the essence of philosophy, religion, art; whatever speaks to the immortal part of man.
The daughter, she is likewise the nurse of all that is spiritual
and exalted in our character. The boon she bestows is truth;

innate probity is necessary to prevent his aping the excellence which he loves so much, yet is unable to attain. Among persons of the latter sort, it is extremely rare to meet with one completely unaffected. Schiller's other noble qualities would not have justice, did we neglect to notice this, the truest proof of their nobility. Honest, unpretending, manly simplicity pervades all parts of his character and genius and habits of life. We not only admire him, we trust him and love him.

"The character of child-like simplicity," he has himself observed,[1] "which genius impresses on its works, it shows also in its private life and manners. It is bashful, for nature is ever so; but it is not prudish, for only corruption is prudish. It is clear-sighted, for nature can never be the contrary; but it is not cunning, for this only art can be. It is faithful to its character and inclinations; but not so much because it is directed by principles, as because after all vibrations nature constantly reverts to her original position, constantly renews her primitive demand. It is modest, nay timid, for genius is always a secret to itself; but it is not anxious, for it knows not the dangers of the way which it travels. Of the private habits of the persons who have been peculiarly distinguished by their genius, our information is small; but the little that has been recorded for us of the chief of them, — of Sophocles, Archimedes, Hippocrates; and in modern times, of Dante and Tasso, of Rafaelle, Albrecht Dürer, Cervantes, Shakspeare, Fielding, and others, — confirms this observation." Schiller himself confirms it; perhaps more strongly than most of the examples here adduced. No man ever wore his faculties more meekly, or performed great works with less consciousness of their greatness. Abstracted from the contemplation of himself, his eye was turned upon the objects of his labor, and he pursued them with the eagerness, the entireness, the spontaneous sincerity, of a boy pursuing sport. Hence this "child-like simplicity," the last perfection of his other excellencies. His was a mighty spirit unheedful of its might. He walked the earth in calm power: "the staff of his

---

[1] *Naive und sentimentalische Dichtung.*

it. His Matter caprice can dishonor as she has ennobled it; but the chaste Form is withdrawn from her mutations. The Roman of the first century had long bent the knee before his Cæsars, when the statues of Rome were still standing erect; the temples continued holy to the eye, when their gods had long been a laughing-stock; and the abominations of a Nero and a Commodus were silently rebuked by the style of the edifice which lent them its concealment. Man has lost his dignity, but Art has saved it, and preserved it for him in expressive marbles. Truth still lives in fiction, and from the copy the original will be restored.

"But how is the Artist to guard himself from the corruptions of his time, which on every side assail him? By despising its decisions. Let him look upwards to his dignity and his mission, not downwards to his happiness and his wants. Free alike from the vain activity, that longs to impress its traces on the fleeting instant; and from the discontented spirit of enthusiasm, that measures by the scale of perfection the meagre product of reality, let him leave to *common sense*, which is here at home, the province of the actual; while *he* strives from the union of the possible with the necessary to bring out the ideal. This let him imprint and express in fiction and truth, imprint it in the sport of his imagination and the earnest of his actions, imprint it in all sensible and spiritual forms, and cast it silently into everlasting Time."[1]

Nor were these sentiments, be it remembered, the mere boasting manifesto of a hot-brained inexperienced youth, entering on literature with feelings of heroic ardor, which its difficulties and temptations would soon deaden or pervert: they are the calm principles of a man, expressed with honest manfulness, at a period when the world could compare them with a long course of conduct. In this just and lofty spirit, Schiller undertook the business of literature; in the same spirit he pursued it with unflinching energy all the days of his life. The common, and some uncommon, difficulties of a fluctuating and dependent existence could not quench or abate

---

[1] *Über die æsthetische Erziehung des Menschen.*

his zeal: sickness itself seemed hardly to affect him. During his last fifteen years, he wrote his noblest works; yet, as it has been proved too well, no day of that period could have passed without its load of pain.[1] Pain could not turn him from his purpose, or shake his equanimity: in death itself he was *calmer and calmer.* Nor has he gone without his recompense. To the credit of the world it can be recorded, that their suffrages, which he never courted, were liberally bestowed on him: happier than the mighty Milton, he found "fit hearers," even in his lifetime, and they were not "few." His effect on the mind of his own country has been deep and universal, and bids fair to be abiding: his effect on other countries must in time be equally decided; for such nobleness of heart and soul shadowed forth in beautiful imperishable emblems, is a treasure which belongs not to one nation, but to all. In another age, this Schiller will stand forth in the foremost rank among the master-spirits of his century; and be admitted to a place among the chosen of all centuries. His works, the memory of what he did and was, will rise afar off like a towering landmark in the solitude of the Past, when distance shall have dwarfed into invisibility the lesser people that encompassed him, and hid him from the near beholder.

On the whole, we may pronounce him happy. His days passed in the contemplation of ideal grandeurs, he lived among the glories and solemnities of universal Nature; his thoughts were of sages and heroes, and scenes of elysian beauty. It is true, he had no rest, no peace; but he enjoyed the fiery consciousness of his own activity, which stands in place of it for men like him. It is true, he was long sickly; but did he not even then conceive and body forth Max Piccolomini, and Thekla, and the Maid of Orleans, and the scenes of *Wilhelm Tell?* It is true, he died early; but the student will exclaim with Charles XII. in another case, "Was

---

[1] On a surgical inspection of his body after death, the most vital organs were found totally deranged. "The structure of the lungs was in great part destroyed, the cavities of the heart were nearly grown up, the liver had become hard, and the gall-bladder was extended to an extraordinary size." *Doering.*

it not enough of life when he had conquered kingdoms?"
These kingdoms which Schiller conquered were not for one
nation at the expense of suffering to another; they were
soiled by no patriot's blood, no widow's, no orphan's tear:
they are kingdoms conquered from the barren realms of
Darkness, to increase the happiness, and dignity, and power,
of all men; new forms of Truth, new maxims of Wisdom,
new images and scenes of Beauty, won from the "void and
formless Infinite;" a κτῆμα ἐς αἰεί, "a possession forever,"
to all the generations of the Earth.

SUPPLEMENT OF 1872.

HERR SAUPE'S BOOK.

[NOTE IN PEOPLE'S EDITION.]

In the end of Autumn last a considerately kind old Friend of mine brought home to me, from his Tour in Germany, a small Book by a Herr Saupe, one of the Head-masters of Gera High-School, — Book entitled "Schiller and His Father's Household,"[1] — of which, though it has been before the world these twenty years and more, I had not heard till then. The good little Book, — an altogether modest, lucid, exact and amiable, though not very lively performance, offering new little facts about the Schiller world, or elucidations and once or twice a slight correction of the old, — proved really interesting and instructive; awoke, in me especially, multifarious reflections, mournfully beautiful old memories; — and led to farther readings in other Books touching on the same subject, particularly in these three mentioned below,[2] — the first two of them earlier than Saupe's, the third later and slightly corrective of him once or twice; — all which agreeably employed me for some weeks, and continued to be rather a pious recreation than any labor.

To this accident of Saupe's little Book there was, meanwhile, added another not less unexpected: a message, namely, from Bibliopolic Head-quarters that my own poor old Book on Schiller was to be reprinted, and that in this "*People's Edition*" it would want (on deduction of the German Piece by Goethe, which had gone into the "*Library Edition*," but which had no fitness here) some sixty or seventy pages for the proper size of the volume. *Saupe*, which I was still reading, or idly reading about, offered the ready expedient: — and here accordingly *Saupe* is. I have had him faithfully translated, and with

---

[1] *Schiller und sein Väterliches Haus.* Von Ernst Julius Saupe, Subconrector am Gymnasium zu Gera. Leipzig: Verlagsbuchhandlung von J. J. Weber, 1851.

[2] *Schiller's Leben von Gustav Schwab* (Stuttgart, 1841).

Schiller's Leben, verfasst aus, &c. By Caroline von Wolzogen, *born* von Lengefeld (Schiller's Sister-in-law): Stuttgart und Tübingen, 1845.

Schiller's Beziehungen zu Eltern, Geschwistern und der Familie von Wolzogen, aus den Familien-Papieren. By Baroness von Gleichen (Schiller's youngest Daughter) and Baron von Wolzogen (her Cousin): Stuttgart, 1859.

some small omissions or abridgments, slight transposals here and there for clearness' sake, and one or two elucidative patches, gathered from the three subsidiary Books already named, all duly distinguished from Saupe's text;—whereby the gap or deficit of pages is well filled up, almost of its own accord. And thus I can now certify that, in all essential respects, the authentic *Saupe* is here made accessible to English readers as to German; and hope that to many lovers of Schiller among us, who are likely to be lovers also of humbly beautiful Human Worth, and of such an unconsciously noble scene of Poverty made *richer* than any California, as that of the elder Schiller Household here manifests, it may be a welcome and even profitable bit of reading.

                                                                    T. C.

CHELSEA, Nov. 1872.

SAUPE'S

"SCHILLER AND HIS FATHER'S HOUSEHOLD."

———◆————

I. THE FATHER.

"SCHILLER'S Father, Johann Caspar Schiller, was born at Bittenfeld, a parish hamlet in the ancient part of Würtemberg, a little north of Waiblingen, on the 27th October, 1723. He had not yet completed his tenth year when his Father, Johannes Schiller, *Schultheiss*, 'Petty Magistrate,' of the Village, and by trade a Baker, died, at the age of fifty-one. Soon after which the fatherless Boy, hardly fitted out with the most essential elements of education, had to quit school, and was apprenticed to a Surgeon; with whom, according to the then custom, he was to learn the art of 'Surgery;' but in reality had little more to do than follow the common employment of a Barber.

"After completing his apprenticeship and proof-time, the pushing young lad, eager to get forward in the world, went, during the Austrian-Succession War, in the year 1745, with a Bavarian Hussar Regiment, as 'Army-Doctor,' into the Netherlands. Here, as his active mind found no full employment in the practice of his Art, he willingly undertook, withal, the duties of a sub-officer in small military enterprises. On the Peace of Aix-la-Chapelle, 1748, when a part of this Regiment was disbanded, and Schiller with them, he returned to his homeland; and set himself down in Marbach, a pleasant little country town on the Neckar, as practical Surgeon there. Here, in 1749, he married the Poet's Mother; then a young girl of sixteen: Elisabetha Dorothea, born at Marbach in the

(463)

year 1733, the daughter of a respectable townsman, Georg Friedrich Kodweis, who, to his trade of Baker adding that of Innkeeper and Woodmeasurer, had gathered a little fortune, and was at this time counted well-off, though afterwards, by some great inundation of the Neckar," date not given, "he was again reduced to poverty. The brave man by this unavoidable mischance came, by degrees, so low that he had to give up his house in the Market-Place, and in the end to dwell in a poor hut, as Porter at one of the Toll-Gates of Marbach. Elisabetha was a comely girl to look upon; slender, well-formed, without quite being tall; the neck long, hair high-blond, almost red, brow broad, eyes as if a little sorish, face covered with freckles; but with all these features enlivened by a soft expression of kindliness and good-nature.

"This marriage, for the first eight years, was childless; after that, they gradually had six children, two of whom died soon after birth; the Poet Schiller was the second of these six, and the only Boy. The young couple had to live in a very narrow, almost needy condition, as neither of them had any fortune; and the Husband's business could hardly support a household. There is still in existence a legal Marriage Record and Inventory, such as is usual in these cases, which estimates the money and money's worth brought together by the young people at a little over 700 gulden (£70). Out of the same Inventory, one sees, by the small value put upon the surgical instruments, and the outstanding debts of patients, distinctly enough, that Caspar Schiller's practice, at that point of time, did not much exceed that of a third-class Surgeon, and was scarcely adequate, as above stated, to support the thriftiest household. And therefore it is not surprising that Schiller, intent on improving so bare a position, should, at the breaking-out of the Seven-Years War, have anew sought a military appointment, as withal more fit for employing his young strength and ambitions.

"In the beginning of the year 1757 he went, accordingly, as Ensign and Adjutant, into the Würtemberg Regiment Prince Louis; which in several of the campaigns in the Seven-Years War belonged to an auxiliary corps of the Austrian Army."

—Was he at the *Ball of Fulda,* one wonders? Yes, for certain! He was at the Ball of Fulda (tragicomical Explosion of a Ball, *not* yet got to the dancing point); and had to run for life, as his Duke, in a highly ridiculous manner, had already done. And, again, tragically, it is certain that he stood on the fated Austrian left-wing at the *Battle of Leuthen;* had his horse shot under him there, and was himself nearly drowned in a quagmire, struggling towards Breslau that night.[1]

"In Bohemia this Corps was visited by an infectious fever, and suffered by the almost pestilential disorder a good deal of loss. In this bad time, Schiller, who by his temperance and frequent movement in the open air had managed to retain perfect health, showed himself very active and helpful; and cheerfully undertook every kind of business in which he could be of use. He attended the sick, there being a scarcity of Doctors; and served at the same time as Chaplain to the Regiment, so far as to lead the Psalmody, and read the Prayers. When, after this, he was changed into another Würtemberg Regiment, which served in Hessen and Thüringen, he employed every free hour in filling up, by his own industrious study, the many deeply felt defects in his young schooling; and was earnestly studious. By his perseverant zeal and diligence, he succeeded in the course of these war-years in acquiring not only many medical, military and agricultural branches of knowledge, but also, as his Letters prove, in amassing a considerable amount of general culture. Nor did his praiseworthy efforts remain without recognition and external reward. At the end of the Seven-Years War, he had risen to be a Captain, and had even saved a little money.

"His Wife, who, during these War times, lived, on money sent by him, in her Father's house at Marbach, he could only visit seldom, and for short periods in winter-quarters, much as he longed for his faithful Wife; who, after the birth of a Daughter, in September, 1757, was dearer to him than ever.

---

[1] See *Life of Friedrich* (Book xix. chap. 8; Book xviii. chap. 10), and Schiller Senior's rough bit of Autobiography, called "*Meine Lebensgeschichte,*" in *Schiller's Beziehungen zu Eltern, Geschwistern und der Familie von Wolzogen* (mentioned above), p. 1. et seqq.

But never had the rigid fetters of War-discipline appeared more oppressive than when, two years later, in November, 1759, a Son, the Poet, was born. With joyful thanks to God, he saluted this dear Gift of Heaven; in daily prayer commended Mother and Child to 'the Being of all Beings;' and waited now with impatience the time when he should revisit his home, and those that were his there. Yet there still passed four years before Father Schiller, on conclusion of the Hubertsburg Peace, 1763, could return home from the War, and again take up his permanent residence in his home-country. Where, on his return, his first Garrison quarters were, whether at Ludwigsburg, Cannstadt or what other place, is not known. On the other hand, all likelihoods are, that, so soon as he could find it possible, he carried over his Wife and his two Children, the little Daughter Christophine six, and the little Friedrich now four, out of Marbach to his own quarters, wherever these were."

There is no date to the Neckar Inundation above mentioned; but we have elsewhere evidence that the worthy Father Kodweis with his Wife, at this time, still dwelt in their comfortable house in the Market-Place. We know also, though it is not mentioned in the text, that their pious Daughter struggled zealously to the last to alleviate their sore poverty; and the small effect, so far as money goes, may testify how poor and straitened the Schiller Family itself then was.

"With the Father's return out of War, there came a new element into the Family, which had so long been deprived of its natural Guardian and Counsellor. To be House-Father in the full sense of the word was now all the more Captain Schiller's need and duty, the longer his War-service had kept him excluded from the sacred vocation of Husband and Father. For he was throughout a rational and just man, simple, strong, expert, active for practical life, if also somewhat quick and rough. This announced itself even in the outward make and look of him; for he was of short stout stature and powerful make of limbs; the brow high-arched, eyes sharp and keen. Withal, his erect carriage, his firm step, his neat clothing, as well as his clear and decisive mode of speech, all testified of strict military training; which also extended itself over his whole domestic life, and even over the daily devotions of the Family. For although the shallow Illuminationism of that period had produced some influence on his religious convictions, he held fast by the pious principles of his forebeers; read regularly to his household out of the Bible; and pronounced aloud, each day, the Morning and Evening Prayer. And this was, in his case, not merely an outward decorous bit of discipline, but in fact the faithful expression of his Christian conviction, that man's true worth and true happiness can alone be found in the fear of the Lord, and the moral purity of his heart and conduct. He himself had even, in the manner of those days, composed a long Prayer, which he in later years addressed to God every morning, and which began with the following lines: —

> 'True Watcher of Israel!
> To Thee be praise, thanks and honor.
> Praying aloud I praise Thee,
> That earth and Heaven may hear.'[1]

"If, therefore, a certain otherwise accredited Witness calls him a kind of crotchety, fantastic person, mostly brooding over strange thoughts and enterprises, this can only have meant that Caspar Schiller in earlier years appeared such, namely at the time when, as incipient Surgeon at Marbach, he saw himself forced into a circle of activity which corresponded neither to his inclination, strength nor necessities.

" On the spiritual development of his Son this conscientious Father employed his warmest interest and activities; and appears to have been for some time assisted herein by a near relation, a certain Johann Friedrich Schiller from Bittenfeld; the same who, as *Studiosus Philosophiæ*, was, in 1759, God-father to the Boy. He is said to have given the little Godson

---

[1] *Treuer Wächter Israels !*
Dir sei Preis und Dank und Ehren;
Laut betend lob' ich Dich,
Dass es Erd' und Himmel hören &c.

Fritz his first lessons in Writing, Natural-History and Geography. A more effective assistance in this matter the Father soon after met with on removing to Lorch.

"In the year 1765, the reigning Duke, Karl of Würtemberg, sent Captain Schiller as Recruiting Officer to the Imperial Free-Town Schwäbish-Gmünd; with permission to live with his Family in the nearest Würtemberg place, the Village and Cloister of Lorch. Lorch lies in a green meadow-ground, surrounded by beech-woods, at the foot of a hill, which is crowned by the weird buildings of the Cloister, where the Hohenstaufen graves are; opposite the Cloister and Hamlet, rise the venerable ruins of Hohenstaufen itself, with a series of hills; at the bottom winds the Rems," a branch of the Neckar, "towards still fruitfuler regions. In this attractive rural spot the Schiller Family resided for several years; and found from the pious and kindly people of the Hamlet, and especially from a friend of the house, Moser, the worthy Parish-Parson there, the kindliest reception. The Schiller children soon felt themselves at home and happy in Lorch, especially Fritz did, who, in the Parson's Son, Christoph Ferdinand Moser, a soft gentle child, met with his first boy-friend. In this worthy Parson's house he also received, along with the Parson's own Sons, the first regular and accurate instruction in reading and writing, as also in the elements of Latin and Greek. This arrangement pleased and comforted Captain Schiller not a little: for the more distinctly he, with his clear and candid character, recognized the insufficiency of his own instruction and stock of knowledge, the more impressively it lay on him that his Son should early acquire a good foundation in Languages and Science, and learn something solid and effective. What he could himself do in that particular he faithfully did; bringing out, with this purpose, partly the grand historical memorials of that neighborhood, partly his own life-experiences, in instructive and exciting dialogues with his children. He would point out to the listening little pair the venerable remains of the Hohenstaufen Ancestral Castle, or tell them of his own soldier-career. He took the Boy with him into the Exercise Camp, to the Woodmen in the Forest, and even into the farther distant pleasure-castle of Hohenheim; and thereby led their youthful imagination into many changeful imaginings of life.[1]

"Externally little Fritz and his Sister were not like; Christophine more resembling the Father, whilst Friedrich was the image of the Mother. On the other hand, they had internally very much in common; both possessed a lively apprehension for whatever was true, beautiful or good. Both had a temper capable of enthusiasm, which early and chiefly turned towards the sublime and grand: in short, the strings of their souls were tuned on a cognate tone. Add to this, that both, in the beautifulest, happiest period of their life, had been under the sole care and direction of the pious genial Mother; and that Fritz, at least till his sixth year, was exclusively limited to Christophine's society, and had no other companion. They two had to be, and were, all to each other. Christophine on this account stood nearer to her Brother throughout all his life than the Sisters who were born later.

"In rural stillness, and in almost uninterrupted converse with outdoor nature, flowed by for Fritz and her the greatest part of their childhood and youth. Especially dear to them was their abode in this romantic region. Every hour that was free from teaching or other task, they employed in roaming about in the neighborhood; and they knew no higher joy than a ramble into the neighboring hills. In particular they liked to make pilgrimages together to a chapel on the Calvary Hill at Gmünd, a few miles off, to which the way was still through the old monkish grief-stations, on to the Cloister of Lorch noticed above. Often they would sit with closely grasped hands, under the thousand-years-old Linden, which stood on a projection before the Cloister-walls, and seemed to whisper to them long-silent tales of past ages. On these walks the hearts of the two clasped each other ever closer and more firmly, and they faithfully shared their little childish joys and sorrows. Christophine would bitterly weep when her vivacious Brother had committed some small misdeed and was punished for it. In such cases, she often enough confessed Fritz's faults as her own, and was punished when she had in

[1] *Saupe*, p. 11.

reality had no complicity in them. It was with great sorrow
that they two parted from their little Paradise; and both of
them always retained a great affection for Lorch and its neighborhood. Christophine, who lived to be ninety, often even in
her latter days looked back with tender affection to their abode
there.[1]

"In his family circle, the otherwise hard-mannered Father
showed always to Mother and Daughters the tenderest respect
and the affectionate tone which the heart suggests. Thus, if
at table a dish had chanced to be especially prepared for him,
he would never eat of it without first inviting the Daughters
to be helped. As little could he ever, in the long-run, withstand the requests of his gentle Wife; so that not seldom she
managed to soften his rough severity. The Children learned
to make use of this feature in his character; and would thereby
save themselves from the first outburst of his anger. They
confessed beforehand to the Mother their bits of misdoings,
and begged her to inflict the punishment, and prevent their
falling into the heavier paternal hand. Towards the Son
again, whose moral development his Father anxiously watched
over, his wrath was at times disarmed by touches of courage
and fearlessness on the Boy's part. Thus little Fritz, once on
a visit at Hohenheim, in the house where his Father was calling, and which formed part of the side-buildings of the Castle,
whilst his Father followed his business within doors, had, un-
observed, clambered out of a saloon window, and undertaken
a voyage of discovery over the roofs. The Boy, who had been
missed and painfully sought after, was discovered just on the
point of trying to have a nearer view of the Lion's Head, by
which one of the roof-gutters discharges itself, when the terrified Father got eye on him, and called out aloud. Cunning
Fritz, however, stood motionless where he was on the roof, till
his Father's anger had stilled itself, and pardon was promised
him." — Here farther is a vague anecdote made authentic:
"Another time the little fellow was not to be found at the
evening meal, while, withal, there was a heavy thunderstorm

[1] *Saupe*, pp. 106-108.

in the sky, and fiery bolts were blazing through the black clouds. He was searched for in vain, all over the house; and at every new thunder-clap the misery of his Parents increased. At last they found him, not far from the house, on the top of the highest lime-tree, which he was just preparing to descend, under the crashing of a very loud peal. 'In God's name, what hast thou been doing there?' cried the agitated Father. 'I wanted to know,' answered Fritz, 'where all that fire in the sky was coming from!'

"Three full years the Schiller Family lived at Lorch; and this in rather narrow circumstances, as the Father, though in the service of his Prince, could not, during the whole of this time, receive the smallest part of his pay, but had to live on the little savings he had made during War-time. Not till 1768, after the most impressive petitioning to the Duke, was he at last called away from his post of Recruiting Officer, and transferred to the Garrison of Ludwigsburg, where he, by little and little, squeezed out the pay owing him.

"Upon his removal, the Father's first care was to establish his little Boy, now nine years old, — who, stirred on probably by the impressions he had got in the Parsonage at Lorch, and the visible wish of his Parents, had decided for the Clerical Profession, — in the Latin school at Ludwigsburg. This done, he made it his chief care that his Son's progress should be swift and satisfying there. But on that side, Fritz could never come up to his expectations, though the Teachers were well enough contented. But out of school-time, Fritz was not so zealous and diligent as could be wished; liked rather to spring about and sport in the garden. The arid, stony, philological instruction of his teacher, Johann Friedrich Jahn, who was a solid Latiner, and nothing more, was not calculated to make a specially alluring impression on the clever and lively Boy; thus it was nothing but the reverence and awe of his Father that could drive him on to diligence.

"To this time belongs the oldest completely preserved Poem of Schiller's; it is in the form of a little Hymn, in which, on New Year's Day, 1769, the Boy, now hardly over nine years old, presents to his Parents the wishes of the season. It may stand here by way of glimpse into the position of the Son towards his Parents, especially towards his Father.

'MUCH-LOVED PARENTS.[1]'

'Parents, whom I lovingly honor,
  To-day my heart is full of thankfulness!
  This Year may a gracious God increase
  What is at all times your support!

·'The Lord, the Fountain of all joy,
  Remain always your comfort and portion;
  His Word be the nourishment of your heart,
  And Jesus your wished-for salvation.

'I thank you for all your proofs of love,
  For all your care and patience;
  My heart shall praise all your goodness,
  And ever comfort itself in your favor.

---

[1] HERZGELIEBTE ELTERN.

Eltern, die ich zärtlich ehre,
Mein Herz ist heut' voll Dankbarkeit!
Der treue Gott dies Jahr vermehre
Was Sie erquickt zu jeder Zeit!

Der Herr, die Quelle aller Freude,
Verbleibe stets Ihr Trost und Theil;
Sein Wort sei Ihres Herzens Weide,
Und Jesus Ihr erwunschtes Heil.

Ich dank' von alle Liebes-Proben,
Von alle Sorgfalt und Geduld,
Mein Herz soll alle Güte loben,
Und trösten sich stets Ihrer Huld.

Gehorsam, Fleiss und zarte Liebe
Verspreche ich auf dieses Jahr.
Der Herr schenk' mir nur gute Treibe,
Und mache all' mein Wunsch... wahr.   Amen.

       JOHANN CHRISTOPH FRIEDRICH SCHILLER.

Den 1 Januarii, Anno 1769.

'Obedience, diligence and tender love
I promise you for this Year.
God send me only good inclinations,
And make true all my wishes! Amen.

'JOHANN FRIEDRICH SCHILLER.

'1 January, 1769.'

"According to the pious wish of their Son, this year, 1769, did bring somewhat which 'comforted' them. Captain Schiller, from of old a lover of rural occupations, and skilful in gardening and nursery affairs, had, at Ludwigsburg, laid out for himself a little Nursery. It was managed on the same principles which he afterwards made public in his Book, *Die Baumzucht im Grossen* (Neustrelitz, 1795, and second edition, Giessen, 1806); and was prospering beautifully. The Duke, who had noticed this, signified satisfaction in the thing; and he appointed him, in 1770, to shift to his beautiful Forest-Castle, Die Solitüde, near Stuttgard, as overseer of all his Forest operations there. Hereby to the active man was one of his dearest wishes fulfilled; and a sphere of activity opened, corresponding to his acquirements and his inclination. At Solitüde, by the Duke's order, he laid out a Model Nursery for all Würtemberg, which he managed with perfect care and fidelity; and in this post he so completely satisfied the expectations entertained of him, that his Prince by and by raised him to the rank of Major." He is reckoned to have raised from seeds, and successfully planted, 60,000 trees, in discharge of this function, which continued for the rest of his life.

"His Family, which already at Lorch, in 1766, had been increased by the birth of a Daughter, Luise, waited but a short time in Ludwigsburg till the Father brought them over to the new dwelling at Solitüde. Fritz, on the removal of his Parents, was given over as boarder to his actual Teacher, the rigorous pedant Jahn; and remained yet two years at the Latin school in Ludwigsburg. During this time, the lively, and perhaps also sometimes mischievous Boy, was kept in the strictest fetters; and, by the continual admonitions, exhortations, and manually practical corrections of Father and of Teacher, not a little held down and kept in fear. The fact, for instance, that

he liked more the potent Bible-words and pious songs of a
Luther, a Paul Gerhard, and Gellert, than he did the frozen
lifeless catechism-drill of the Ludwigsburg Institute, gave
surly strait-laced Jahn occasion to lament from time to time
to the alarmed Parents, that 'their Son had no feeling whatever for religion.' In this respect, however, the otherwise so
irritable Father easily satisfied himself, not only by his own
observations of an opposite tendency, but chiefly by stricter
investigation of one little incident that was reported to him.
The teacher of religion in the Latin school, Superintendent
Zilling, whose name is yet scornfully remembered, had once,
in his dull awkwardness, introduced even Solomon's Song as
an element of nurture for his class; and was droning out, in
an old-fashioned way, his interpretation of it as symbolical of
the Christian Church and its Bridegroom Christ, when he was,
on the sudden, to his no small surprise and anger, interrupted
by the audible inquiry of little Schiller, 'But was this Song,
then, actually sung to the Church?' Schiller Senior took the
little heretic to task for this rash act; and got as justification
the innocent question, 'Has the Church really got teeth of
ivory?' The Father was enlightened enough to take the Boy's
opposition for a natural expression of sound human sense;
nay, he could scarcely forbear a laugh; whirled swiftly round,
and murmured to himself, 'Occasionally she has Wolf's teeth.'
And so the thing was finished.[1]

"At Ludwigsburg Schiller and Christophine first saw a
Theatre; where at that time, in the sumptuous Duke's love of
splendor, only pompous operas and ballets were given. The
first effect of this new enjoyment, which Fritz and his Sister
strove to repeat as often as they could, was that at home, with
little clipped and twisted paper dolls, they set about representing scenes; and on Christophine's part it had the more important result of awakening and nourishing, at an early age, her
æsthetic taste. Schiller considered her, ever after these youthful sports, as a true and faithful companion in his poetic dreams
and attempts; and constantly not only told his Sister, whose
silence on such points could be perfect, of all that he secretly

[1] *Saupe*, p. 18.

did in the way of verse-making in the Karl's School, — which, as we shall see, he entered in 1773, — but if possible brought it upon the scene with her. Scenes from the lyrical operetta of *Semele* were acted by Schiller and Christophine, on those terms; which appears in a complete shape for the first time in Schiller's *Anthology*, printed 1782.[1]

"So soon as Friedrich had gone through the Latin school at Ludwigsburg, which was in 1772, he was, according to the standing regulation, to enter one of the four Lower Cloister-schools; and go through the farther curriculum for a Würtemberg clergyman. But now there came suddenly from the Duke to Captain Schiller an offer to take his Son, who had been represented to him as a clever boy, into the new Military Training-School, founded by his Highness at Solitüde, in 1771; where he would be brought up, and taken charge of, free of cost.

"In the Schiller Family this offer caused great consternation and painful embarrassment. The Father was grieved to be obliged to sacrifice a long-cherished paternal plan to the whim of an arbitrary ruler; and the Son felt himself cruelly hurt to be torn away so rudely from his hope and inclination. Accordingly, how dangerous soever for the position of the Family a declining of the Ducal grace might seem, the straightforward Father ventured nevertheless to lay open to the Duke, in a clear and distinct statement, how his purpose had always been to devote his Son, in respect both of his inclination and his hitherto studies, to the Clerical Profession; for which in the new Training-School he could not be prepared. The Duke showed no anger at this step of the elder Schiller's; but was just as little of intention to let a capable and hopeful scholar, who was also the Son of one of his Officers and Dependents, escape him. He simply, with brevity, repeated his wish, and required the choice of another study, in which the Boy would have a better career and outlook than in the Theological Department. Nill they, will they, there was nothing for the Parents but compliance with the so plainly intimated will

[1] *Saupe*, p. 109.

of this Duke, on whom their Family's welfare so much depended.

"Accordingly, 17th January, 1773, Friedrich Schiller, then
in his fourteenth year, stept over to the Military Training-
School at Solitüde.

"In September of the following year, Schiller's Parents had,
conformably to a fundamental law of the Institution, to acknowledge and engage by a written Bond, 'That their Son, in
virtue of his entrance into this Ducal Institution, did wholly
devote himself to the service of the Würtemberg Ducal House;
that he, without special Ducal permission, was not empowered
to go out of it; and that he had, with his best care, to observe
not only this, but all other regulations of the Institute.' By this
time, indeed directly upon signature of this strict Bond, young
Schiller had begun to study Jurisprudence; — which, however,
when next year, 1775, the Training-School, raised now to be a
'Military Academy,' had been transferred to Stuttgard, he
either of his own accord, or in consequence of a discourse and
interview of the Duke with his Father, exchanged for the
Study of Medicine.

"From the time when Schiller entered this 'Karl's School'
[Military Academy, in official style], he was nearly altogether
withdrawn from any tutelage of his Father; for it was only
to Mothers, and to Sisters still under age, that the privilege of
visiting their Sons and Brothers, and this on the Sunday only,
was granted: beyond this, the Karl's Scholars, within their
monastic cells, were cut off from family and the world, by iron
doors and sentries guarding them. This rigorous seclusion from
actual life and all its friendly impressions, still more the spiritual constraint of the Institution, excluding every free activity,
and all will of your own, appeared to the Son in a more hateful
light than to the Father, who, himself an old soldier, found it
quite according to order that the young people should be kept
in strict military discipline and subordination. What filled
the Son with bitter discontent and indignation, and at length
brought him to a kind of poetic outburst of revolution in the
Robbers, therein the Father saw only a wholesome regularity,
and indispensable substitute for paternal discipline. Transient

complaints of individual teachers and superiors little disturbed
the Father's mind; for, on the whole, the official testimonies
concerning his Son were steadily favorable. The Duke too
treated young Schiller, whose talents had not escaped his
sharpness of insight, with particular good-will, nay distinction.
To this Prince, used to the accurate discernment of spiritual
gifts, the complaints of certain Teachers, that Schiller's slow
progress in Jurisprudence proceeded from want of head, were
of no weight whatever; and he answered expressly, 'Leave
me that one alone; he will come to something yet!' But that
Schiller gave his main strength to what in the Karl's School
was a strictly forbidden object, to poetry namely, this I believe
was entirely hidden from his Father, or appeared to him,
on occasional small indications, the less questionable, as he
saw that, in spite of this, the Marketable-Sciences were not
neglected.

" At the same age, viz. about twenty-two, at which Captain
Schiller had made his first military sally into the Netherlands
and the Austrian-Succession War, his Son issued from the
Karl's School, 15th December, 1780; and was immediately appointed Regimental-Doctor at Stuttgard, with a monthly pay
of twenty-three gulden [£2 6s.=11s. and a fraction per week].
With this appointment, Schiller had, as it were, openly altogether outgrown all special paternal guardianship or guidance;
and was, from this time, treated by his Father as come to ma-
jority, and standing on his own feet. If he came out, as frequently happened, with a comrade to Solitüde, he was heartily
welcome there, and the Father's looks often dwelt on him with
visible satisfaction. If in the conscientious and rigorous old
man, with his instructive and serious experiences of life, there
might yet various anxieties and doubts arise when he heard of
the exuberantly genial ways of his hopeful Son at Stuttgard,
he still looked upon him with joyful pride, in remarking how
those so promising Karl's Scholars, who had entered into the
world along with him, recognized his superiority of mind, and
willingly ranked themselves under him. Nor could it be otherwise than highly gratifying to his old heart to remark always

with what deep love the gifted Son constantly regarded his Parents and Sisters." [1] — Of Schiller's first procedures in Stuttgard, after his emancipation from the Karl's School, and appointment as Regimental-Surgeon, or rather of his general behavior and way of life there, which are said to have been somewhat wild, genially, or even *ungenially* extravagant, and to have involved him in many paltry entanglements of debts, as one bad consequence, — there will be some notice in the next Section, headed *"The Mother."* His Regimental Doctorship, and stay in Stuttgard altogether, lasted twenty-two months.

This is Schiller's bodily appearance, as it first presented itself to an old School-fellow, who, after an interval of eighteen months, saw him again on Parade, as Doctor of the Regiment Augé, — more to his astonishment than admiration.

" Crushed into the stiff tasteless Old-Prussian Uniform ; on each of his temples three stiff rolls as if done with gypsum ; the tiny three-cocked hat scarcely covering his crown ; so much the thicker the long pigtail, with the slender neck crammed into a very narrow horsehair stock ; the felt put under the white spatterdashes, smirched by traces of shoe-blacking, giving to the legs a bigger diameter than the thighs, squeezed into their tight-fitting breeches, could boast of. Hardly, or not at all, able to bend his knees, the whole man moved like a stork."

" The Poet's form," says this Witness elsewhere, a bit of a dilettante artist it seems, " had somewhat the following appearance: Long straight stature ; long in the legs, long in the arms ; pigeon-breasted ; his neck very long ; something rigorously stiff ; in gait and carriage not the smallest elegance. His brow was broad ; the nose thin, cartilaginous, white of color, springing out at a notably sharp angle, much bent, — a parrot-nose, and very sharp in the point (according to Dannecker the Sculptor, Schiller, who took snuff, had pulled it out so with his hand). The red eyebrows, over the deep-lying dark-gray eyes, were bent too close together at the nose, which gave him a pathetic expression. The lips were thin, energetic ; the under-

[1] *Saupe*, p. 25.

lip protruding, as if pushed forward by the inspiration of his feelings; the chin strong; cheeks pale, rather hollow than full, freckly; the eyelids a little inflamed; the bushy hair of the head dark red; the whole head rather ghostlike than manlike, but impressive even in repose, and all expression when Schiller declaimed. Neither the features nor the somewhat shrieky voice could he subdue. Dannecker," adds the satirical Witness, "has unsurpassably cut this head in marble for us." [1]

"The publication of the *Robbers* [Autumn, 1781], — which Schiller, driven on by rage and desperation, had composed in the fetters of the Karl's School, — raised him on the sudden to a phenomenon on which all eyes in Stuttgard were turned. What, with careless exaggeration, he had said to a friend some months before, on setting forth his *Elegy on the Death of a Young Man*, 'The thing has made my name hereabouts more famous than twenty years of practice would have done; but it is a name like that of him who burnt the Temple of Ephesus: God be merciful to me a sinner!' might now with all seriousness be said of the impression his *Robbers* made on the harmless townsfolk of Stuttgard. But how did Father Schiller at first take up this eccentric product of his Son, which openly declared war on all existing order? Astonishment and terror, anger and detestation, boundless anxiety, with touches of admiration and pride, stormed alternately through the solid honest man's paternal breast, as he saw the frank picture of a Prodigal Son rolled out before him; and had to gaze into the most revolting deeps of the passions and vices. Yet he felt himself irresistibly dragged along by the uncommon vivacity of action in this wild Drama; and at the same time powerfully attracted by the depth, the tenderness and fulness of true feeling manifested in it: so that, at last, out of those contradictory emotions of his, a clear admiration and pride for his Son's bold and rich spirit maintained the upper hand. By Schiller's friends and closer connections, especially by his Mother and Sisters, all pains were of course taken to keep up this favorable humor in the Father, and carefully to hide from him all

[1] Schwab, *Schiller's Leben* (Stuttgard, 1841), p. 68.

disadvantageous or disquieting tidings about the Piece and its consequences and practical effects. Thus he heard sufficiently of the huge excitement and noise which the *Robbers* was making all over Germany, and of the seductive approval which came streaming in on the youthful Poet, even out of distant provinces; but heard nothing either of the Duke's offended and angry feelings over the *Robbers*, a production horrible to him; nor of the Son's secret journeys to Mannheim, and the next consequences of these [his brief arrest, namely], nor of the rumor circulating in spiteful quarters, that this young Doctor was neglecting his own province of medicine, and meaning to become a play-actor. How could the old man, in these circumstances, have a thought that the *Robbers* would be the loss of Family and Country to his poor Fritz! And yet so it proved.

"Excited by all kinds of messagings, informings and insinuations, the imperious Prince, in spite of his secret pleasure in this sudden renown of his Pupil, could in nowise be persuaded to revoke or soften his harsh Order, which 'forbade the Poet henceforth, under pain of military imprisonment, either to write anything poetic or to communicate the same to foreign persons' [non-Würtembergers]. In vain were all attempts of Schiller to obtain his discharge from Military Service and his ' *Entschwäbung* ' (Un-*Swabian*-ing); such petitions had only for result new sharper rebukes and hard threatening expressions, to which the mournful fate of Schubart in the Castle of Hohenasperg[1] formed a too questionable background.

"Thus by degrees there ripened in the strong soul of this young man the determination to burst these laming fetters of his genius, by flight from despotic Würtemberg altogether; and, in some friendlier country, gain for himself the freedom without which his spiritual development was impossible. Only to one friend, who clung to him with almost enthusiastic devotion, did he impart his secret. This was Johann Andreas Streicher of Stuttgard, who intended to go next year to Hamburg, and there, under Bach's guidance, study music; but declared himself ready to accompany Schiller even now, since

---

[1] See Appendix ii. *infrà*.

it had become urgent. Except to this trustworthy friend, Schiller had imparted his plan to his elder Sister Christophine alone; and she had not only approved of the sad measure, but had undertaken also to prepare their Mother for it. The Father naturally had to be kept dark on the subject; all the more that, if need were, he might pledge his word as an Officer that he had known nothing of his Son's intention.

" Schiller went out, in company of Madam Meier, Wife of the *Regisseur* (Theatre-manager) at Mannheim, a native of Stuttgard, and of this Streicher, one last time to Solitüde, to have one more look of it and of his dear ones there; especially to soothe and calm his Mother. On the way, which they travelled on foot, Schiller kept up a continual discourse about the Mannheim Theatre and its interests, without betraying his secret to Madam Meier. The Father received these welcome guests with frank joy; and gave to the conversation, which at first hung rather embarrassed, a happy turn by getting into talk, with cheery circumstantiality, of the grand Pleasure-Hunt, of the Play and of the Illumination, which were to take place, in honor of the Russian Grand-Prince, afterwards Czar Paul, and his Bride, the Duke of Würtemberg's Niece, on the 17th September instant, at Solitüde. Far other was the poor Mother's mood; she was on the edge of betraying herself, in seeing the sad eyes of her Son; and she could not speak for emotion. The presence of Streicher and a Stranger with whom the elder Schiller was carrying on a, to him, attractive conversation, permitted Mother and Son to withdraw speedily and unremarked. Not till after an hour did Schiller reappear, alone now, to the company; neither this circumstance, nor Schiller's expression of face, yet striking the preoccupied Father. Though to the observant Streicher, his wet red eyes betrayed how painful the parting must have been. Gradually on the way back to Stuttgard, amid general talk of the three, Schiller regained some composure and cheerfulness.

" The bitter sorrow of this hour of parting renewed itself yet once in Schiller's soul, when on the flight itself, about midnight of the 17th. In effect it was these same festivities that had decided the young men's time and scheme of journey; and under the sheltering noise of which their plan was luckily executed. Towards midnight of the abovesaid day, when the Castle of Solitüde, with all its surroundings, was beaming in full splendor of illumination, there rolled past, almost rubbing elbows with it, the humble Schiller Vehicle from Stuttgard, which bore the fugitive Poet with his true Friend on their way. Schiller pointed out to his Friend the spot where his Parents lived, and, with a half-suppressed sigh and a woe-begone exclamation, 'Oh, my Mother!' sank back upon his seat."

Mannheim, the goal of their flight, is in Baden-Baden, under another Sovereign; lies about 80 miles to N.W. of Stuttgard. Their dreary journey lasted two days, — arrival not till deep in the night of the second. Their united stock of money amounted to 51 gulden, — Schiller 23, Streicher 28, — £5 6s. in all. Streicher subsequently squeezed out from home £3 more; and that appears to have been their sum-total.[1]

"Great was the astonishment and great the wrath of the Father, when at length he understood that his Son had broken the paternal, written Bond, and withdrawn himself by flight from the Ducal Service. He dreaded, not without reason, the heavy consequences of so rash an action; and a thousand gnawing anxieties bestormed the heart of the worthy man. Might not the Duke, in the first outburst of his indignation, overwhelm forever the happiness of their Family, which there was nothing but the income of his post that supported in humble competence? And what a lot stood before the Son himself, if he were caught in flight, or if, what was nowise improbable, his delivery back was required and obtained? Sure enough, there had risen on the otherwise serene heaven of the Schiller Family a threatening thundercloud; which, any day, might discharge itself, bringing destruction on their heads.

"The thing, however, passed away in merciful peace. Whatever may have been the Duke's motives or inducements to let the matter, in spite of his embitterment, silently drop,

---

[1] Schwab, *Schiller's Leben.*

—whether his bright festal humor in presence of those high kinsfolk, or the noble frankness with which the Runaway first of all, to save his Family, had in a respectful missive, dated from Mannheim, explained to his Princely Educator the necessity of his flight; or the expectation, flattering to the Ducal pride, that the future greatness of his Pupil might be a source of glory to him and his Karl's School: enough, on his part, there took place no kind of hostile step against the Poet, and still less against his Family. Captain Schiller again breathed freer when he saw himself delivered from his most crushing anxiety on this side; but there remained still a sharp sting in his wounded heart. His military feeling of honor was painfully hurt by the thought that they might now look upon his Son as a deserter; and withal the future of this voluntary Exile appeared so uncertain and wavering, that it did not offer the smallest justification of so great a risk. By degrees, however, instead of anger and blame there rose in him the most sympathetic anxiety for the poor Son's fate; to whom, from want of a free, firm and assuring position in life, all manner of contradictions and difficulties must needs arise.

"And Schiller did actually, at Mannheim, find himself in a bad and difficult position. The Superintendent of the celebrated Mannheim Theatre, the greatly powerful Imperial Baron von Dalberg, with whom Schiller, since the bringing out of his *Robbers*, had stood in lively correspondence, drew back when Schiller himself was here; and kept the Poet at a distance as a political Fugitive; leaving him to shift as he could. In vain had Schiller explained to him, in manly open words, his economic straits, and begged from him a loan of 300 gulden [£30] to pay therewith a pressing debt in Stuttgard, and drag himself along, and try to get started in the world. Dalberg returned the *Fiesco*, Schiller's new republican Tragedy, which had been sent him, with the declaration that he could advance no money on the *Fiesco*, in its present form; the Piece must first be remodelled to suit the stage. During this remodelling, which the otherwise so passionately vivid and hopeful Poet began without murmur, he lived entirely on the journey-money that had been saved up by the faithful Streicher, who would on no account leave him."

What became of this good Streicher afterwards, I have inquired considerably, but with very little success. On the total exhaustion of their finance, Schiller and he had to part company, — Schiller for refuge at Bauerbach, as will soon be seen. Streicher continued about Mannheim, not as Schiller's fellow-lodger any longer, but always at his hand, passionately eager to serve him with all his faculties by night or by day; and they did not part finally till Schiller quitted Mannheim, two years hence, for Leipzig. After which they never met again. Streicher, in Mannheim, seems to have subsisted by his musical talent; and to have had some connection with the theatre in that capacity. In similar dim positions, with what shiftings, adventures and vicissitudes is quite unknown to me, he long survived Schiller, and, at least fifty years after these Mannheim struggles, wrote some Book of bright and loving Reminiscences concerning him, the exact *title* of which I can nowhere find, — though passages from it are copied by Biographer Schwab here and there. His affection for Schiller is of the nature of worship rather, of constant adoration; and probably formed the sunshine to poor Streicher's life. Schiller nowhere mentions him in his writings or correspondences, after that final parting at Mannheim, 1784.

"The necessities of the two Friends reached by and by such a height that Schiller had to sell his Watch, although they had already for several weeks been subsisting on loans. To all which now came Dalberg's overwhelming message, that even this Remodelling of *Fiesco* could not be serviceable; and of course could not have money paid for it. Schiller thereupon, at once resolute what to do, walked off to the worthy Bookseller Schwann," with whom he was already on a trustful, even grateful footing; "and sold him his MS. at one louis-d'or the sheet. At the same time, too, he recognized the necessity of quitting Mannheim, and finding a new asylum in Saxony; seeing, withal, his farther continuance here might be as dangerous for him as it was a matter of apprehension to his Friends. For although the

Duke of Würtemberg undertook nothing that was hostile to him, and his Family at Solitüde experienced no annoyance, yet the impetuous Prince might, any day, take it into his head to have him put in prison. In the ever livelier desire after a securely hidden place of abode, where he might execute in peace his poetic plans and enterprises, Schiller suddenly took up an earlier purpose, which had been laid aside.

"In the Stuttgard time he had known Wilhelm von Wolzogen, by and by his Brother-in-law [they married two sisters], who, with three Brothers, had been bred in the Karl's School. The two had, indeed, during the academic time, Wolzogen being some years younger, had few points of contact, and were not intimate. But now on the appearance of the *Robbers,* Wolzogen took a cordial affection and enthusiasm for the widely celebrated Poet, and on closer acquaintance with Schiller, also affected his Mother, — who, as Widow, for her three Sons' sake, lived frequently at Stuttgard, — with a deep and zealous sympathy in Schiller's fate. Schiller had, with a truly childlike trust, confided himself to this excellent Lady, and after his Arrest, — a bitter consequence of his secret visit to Mannheim, — had confessed to her his purpose to run away. Frau von Wolzogen, who feared no sacrifice when the question was of the fortune of her friends, had then offered him her family mansion, Bauerbach, near Meiningen, as a place of refuge. Schiller's notion had also been to fly thither; though, deceived by false hopes, he changed that purpose. He now wrote at once to Stuttgard, and announced to Frau von Wolzogen his wish to withdraw for some time to Bauerbach." To which, as is well known, the assent was ready and zealous.

"Before quitting Mannheim, Schiller could not resist the longing wish to see his Parents yet one time; and wrote to them accordingly, 19 Nov. 1782, in visible haste and excitement : —

' BEST PARENTS, — As I am at present in Mannheim, and am to go away forever in five days, I wished to prepare for myself and you the one remaining satisfaction of seeing one another once more. To-day is the 19th, on the 21st you receive this Letter; — if you therefore,

without the least delay (that is indispensable), leave Stuttgard, you
might on the 22d be at the Post-house in Bretten, which is about half
way from Mannheim, and where you would find me. I think it would
be best if Mamma and Christophine, under the pretext of going to Ludwigsburg to Wolzogen, should make this journey. Take the Frau
Vischerin [a Captain's Widow, sung of under the name of "Laura,"
with whom he had last lodged in Stuttgard] and also Wolzogen with
you, as I wish to speak with both of them, perhaps for the last time,
Wolzogen excepted. I will give you a Karolin as journey-money; but
not till I see you at Bretten. By the prompt fulfilment of my Prayer,
I will perceive whether is still dear to you,

'Your ever-grateful Son,

'SCHILLER.'"

From Mannheim, Bauerbach or Meiningen lies about 120
miles N.E.; and from Stuttgard almost as far straight North.
Bretten, "a little town on a hill, celebrated as Melancthon's
Birthplace, his Father's house still standing there," is some
35 miles S.E. of Mannheim, and as far N.W. from Stuttgard.
From Mannheim, in this wise, it is not at all on the road to
Meiningen, though only a few miles more remote in direct
distance. Schiller's purpose had been, after this affectionate
interview, to turn at once leftward and make for Meiningen,
by what road or roads there were from Bretten thither.
Schiller's poor guinea (Karolin) was not needed on this occasion; the rendezvous at Bretten being found impossible
or inexpedient at the Stuttgard end of it. Our Author
continues:—

"Although this meeting, on which the loving Son and
Brother wished to spend his last penny, did not take effect;
yet this mournful longing of his, evident from the Letter, and
from the purpose itself, must have touched the Father's heart
with somewhat of a reconciliatory feeling. Schiller Senior
writes accordingly, 8 December, 1782, the very day after his
Son's arrival at Bauerbach, to Bookseller Schwann in Mannheim: 'I have not noticed here the smallest symptom that his
Ducal Durchlaucht has any thought of having my Son searched
for and prosecuted; and indeed his post here has long since
been filled up; a circumstance which visibly indicates that
they can do without him.' This Letter to Schwann concludes

in the following words, which are characteristic: 'He (my Son) has, by his untimely withdrawal, against the advice of his true friends, plunged himself into this difficult position; and it will profit him in soul and body that he feel the pain of it, and thereby become wiser for the future. I am not afraid, however, that want of actual necessaries should come upon him, for in such case I should feel myself obliged to lend a hand.'

" And in effect Schiller, during his abode in Bauerbach, did once or twice receive little subventions of money from his Father, although never without earnest and not superfluous admonition to become more frugal, and take better heed in laying out his money. For economics were, by Schiller's own confession, 'not at all his talent; it cost him less,' he says, 'to execute a whole conspiracy and tragedy-plot than to adjust his scheme of housekeeping.' — At this time it was never the Father himself who wrote to Schiller, but always Christophine, by his commission; and on the other hand, Schiller too never risked writing directly to his Father, as he felt but too well how little on his part had been done to justify the flight in his Father's eyes. He writes accordingly, likewise on that 8th December 1782, to his Publisher Schwann: 'If you can accelerate the printing of my *Fiesco*, you will very much oblige me by doing so. You know that nothing but the prohibition to become an Author drove me out of the Würtemberg service. If I now, on this side, don't soon let my native country hear of me, they will say the step I took was useless and without real motive.'

" In Bauerbach Schiller lived about eight months, under the name of Doctor Ritter, unknown to everybody; and only the Court-Librarian, Reinwald, in Meiningen, afterwards his Brother-in-law," as we shall see, "in whom he found a solid friend, had been trusted by Frau von Wolzogen with the name and true situation of the mysterious stranger. The most of Schiller's time here was spent in dramatic labors, enterprises and dreams. The outcome of all these were his third civic Tragedy, *Louise Miller*, or *Kabale und Liebe*, which was finished in February, 1783, and the settling on *Don Carlos* as

a new tragic subject. Many reasons, meanwhile, in the last
eight months, had been pushing Schiller into the determination to leave his asylum, and anew turn towards Mannheim.
A passionate, though unreturned attachment to Charlotte von
Wolzogen at that time filled Schiller's soul; and his removal
therefore must both to Frau von Wolzogen for her own and
her Daughter's sake, and to Schiller himself, have appeared
desirable. It was Frau von Wolzogen's own advice to him to
go for a short time to Mannheim, there to get into clear terms
with Dalberg, who had again begun corresponding with him:
so, in July, 1783, Schiller bade his solitary, and, by this time
dear and loved, abode a hasty adieu; and, much contrary to
fond hope, never saw it again.

"In September, 1783, his bargainings with Dalberg had
come to this result, That for a fixed salary of 500 gulden
[£50 a year] he was appointed Theatre-Poet here. By this
means, to use his own words, the way was open to him gradually to pay off a considerable portion of his debts, and so
escape from the drowning whirlpool, and remain an honest
man. Now, furthermore, he thought it permissible to show
himself to his Family with a certain composure of attitude;
and opened straightway a regular correspondence with his
Parents again. And Captain Schiller volunteers a stiff-starched
but true and earnest Letter to the Baron Dalberg himself;
most humbly thanking that gracious nobleman for such beneficent favor shown my poor Son; and begs withal the far
stranger favor that Dalberg would have the extreme goodness
to appoint the then inexperienced young man some true friend
who might help him to arrange his housekeeping, and in moral
things might be his Mentor!

"Soon after this, an intermittent fever threw the Poet on
a sick-bed; and lamed him above five weeks from all capacity
of mental labor. Not even in June of the following year was
the disease quite overcome. Visits, acquaintanceships, all
kinds of amusements, and more than anything else, over-
hasty attempts at work, delayed his cure; — so that his
Father had a perfect right to bring before him his, Schiller's,
own blame in the matter: 'That thou [*Er*, He; the then usual

tone towards servants and children] for eight whole months hast weltered about with intermittent fever, surely that does little honor to thy study of medicine; and thou wouldst, with great justice, have poured the bitterest reproaches on any Patient who, in a case like thine, had not held himself to the diet and regimen that were prescribed to him!' —

"In Autumn, 1783, there seized Schiller so irresistible a longing to see his kindred again, that he repeatedly expressed to his Father the great wish he had for a meeting, either at Mannheim or some other place outside the Würtemberg borders. To the fulfilment of this scheme there were, however, in the sickness which his Mother had fallen into, in the fettered position of the Father, and in the rigorously frugal economies of the Family, insuperable obstacles. Whereupon his Father made him the proposal, that he, Friedrich, either himself or by him, the Captain, should apply to the Duke Karl's Serene Highness; and petition him for permission to return to his country and kindred. As Schiller to this answered nothing, Christophine time after time pressingly repeated to him the Father's proposal. At the risk of again angering his Father, Schiller gave, in his answer to Christophine, of 1st January, 1784, the decisive declaration that his honor would frightfully suffer if he, without connection with any other Prince, without character and lasting means of support, after his forceful withdrawal from Würtemberg, should again show face there. 'That my Father,' adds he, as ground of this refusal, 'give his name to such a petition can help me little; for every one will at once, so long as I cannot make it plain that I no longer need the Duke of Würtemberg, suspect in a return, obtained on petition (by myself or by another is all one), a desire to get settled in Würtemberg again. Sister, consider with serious attention these circumstances; for the happiness of thy Brother may, by rash haste in this matter, suffer an incurable wound. Great part of Germany knows of my relations to your Duke and of the way I left him. People have interested themselves for me at the expense of this Duke; how horribly would the respect of the public (and on this depends my whole future fortune), how miserably would

my own honor sink by the suspicion that I had sought this
return; that my circumstances had forced me to repent my
former step; that the support which I had sought in the wide
world had misgone, and I was seeking it anew in my Birth-
land! The open manlike boldness, which I showed in my
forceful withdrawal, would get the name of a childish outburst of mutiny, a stupid bit of impotent bluster, if I do not
make it good. Love for my dear ones, longing for my Father-
land might perhaps excuse me in the heart of this or the
other candid man; but the world makes no account of all
that.

"'For the rest, if my Father is determined to do it, I cannot
hinder him; only this I say to thee, Sister, that in case even
the Duke would permit it, I will not show myself on Würtemberg ground till I have at least a character (for which object
I shall zealously labor); and that in case the Duke refuses, I
shall not be able to restrain myself from avenging the affront
thereby put upon me by open fooleries (*sottisen*) and expressions of myself in print.'

"The intended Petition to the Duke was not drawn out, —
and Father Schiller overcame his anger on the matter; as, on
closer consideration of the Son's aversion to this step, he
could not wholly disapprove him. Yet he did not hide from
Schiller-Junior the steadfast wish that he would in some way
or other try to draw near to the Duke; at any-rate he, Father
Schiller, 'hoped to God that their parting would not last forever; and that, in fine, he might still live to see his only Son
near him again.'

"In Mannheim Schiller's financial position, in spite of his
earnest purpose to manage wisely, grew by degrees worse
rather than better. Owing to the many little expenses laid
upon him by his connections in society, his income would not
suffice; and the cash-box was not seldom run so low that he
had not wherewithal to support himself next day. Of assistance from home, with the rigorous income of his Father,
which scarcely amounted to £40 a year, there could nothing
be expected; and over and above, the Father himself had, in
this respect, very clearly spoken his mind. 'Parents and

Sisters,' said Schiller Senior, 'have as just a right as they have a confidence, in cases of necessity, to expect help and support from a Son.' To fill to overflowing the measure of the Poet's economical distress, there now stept forth suddenly some secret creditors of his in Stuttgard, demanding immediate payment. Whereupon, in quick succession, there came to Captain Schiller, to his great terror, two drafts from the Son, requiring of him, the one £10, the other £5. The Captain, after stern reflection, determined at last to be good for both demands; but wrote to the Son that he only did so in order that his, the Son's, labor might not be disturbed; and in the confident anticipation that the Son, regardful of his poor Sisters and their bit of portion, would not leave him in the lurch.

"But Schiller, whom still other debts in Stuttgard, unknown to his Father, were pressing hard, could only repay the smaller of these drafts; and thus the worthy Father saw himself compelled to pay the larger, the £10, out of the savings he had made for outfit of his Daughters. Whereupon, as was not undeserved, he took his Son tightly to task, and wrote to him: 'As long as thou, my Son, shalt make thy reckoning on resources that are still to come, and therefore are still subject to chance and mischance, so long wilt thou continue in thy mess of embarrassments. Furthermore, as long as thou thinkest, This gulden or batzen [shilling or farthing] can't help me to get over it; so long will thy debts become never the smaller: and, what were a sorrow to me, thou wilt not be able, after a heavy labor of head got done, to recreate thyself in the society of other good men. But, withal, to make recreation-days of that kind more numerous than work-days, that surely will not turn out well. Best Son, thy abode in Bauerbach has been of that latter kind. *Hinc illæ lacrymæ!* For these thou art now suffering, and that not by accident. The embarrassment thou now art in is verily a work of Higher Providence, to lead thee off from too great trust in thy own force; to make thee soft and contrite; that, laying aside all self-will, thou mayest follow more the counsel of thy Father and other true friends; must meet every one with due respectful courtesy and readiness to oblige; and become ever more convinced that our most gracious Duke, in his restrictive plans, meant well with thee; and that altogether thy position and outlooks had now been better, hadst thou complied, and continued in thy country. Many a time I find thou hast wayward humors, that make thee to thy truest friend scarcely endurable; stiff ways which repel the best wishing man; — for example, when I sent thee my excellent old friend Herr Amtmann Cramer from Altdorf near Speier, who had come to Herr Hofrath Schwann's in the end of last year, thy reception of him was altogether dry and stingy, though by my Letter I had given thee so good an opportunity to seek the friendship of this honorable, rational, and influential man (who has no children of his own), and to try whether he might not have been of help to thee. Thou wilt do well, I think, to try and make good this fault on another opportunity.'

"At the same time the old man repeatedly pressed him to return to Medicine, and graduate in Heidelberg: 'a theatre-poet in Germany,' he signified, 'was but a small light; and as he, the Son, with all his Three Pieces, had not made any footing for himself, what was to be expected of the future ones, which might not be of equal strength! Doctorship, on the other hand, would give him a sure income and reputation as well.' — Schiller himself was actually determined to follow his Father's advice as to Medicine; but this project and others of the same, which were sometimes taken up, went to nothing, now and always, for want of money to begin with.

"Amid these old tormenting hindrances, affronts and embarrassments, Schiller had also many joyful experiences, to which even his Father was not wholly indifferent. To these belong, besides many others, his reception into the *Kurpfälzische Deutsche Gesellschaft*," German Society of the Electoral Palatinate, "of this year; which he himself calls a great step for his establishment; as well as the stormy applause with which his third Piece, *Kabale und Liebe*, came upon the boards, in March following. His Father acknowledged receipt of this latter Work with the words, 'That I possess a copy of thy new Tragedy I tell nobody; for I dare not, on account of certain passages, let any one notice that it has pleased me.' Nevertheless the Piece, as already the *Robbers* had done, came in Stuttgard also to the acting point; and was received with loud approval. Schiller now, with new pleasure and inspiration, laid hands on his *Don Carlos ;* and with the happy progress of this Work, there began for him a more confident temper of mind, and a clearing up of horizon and outlook; which henceforth only transiently yielded to embarrassments in his outer life.

"Soon after this, however, there came upon him an unexpected event so suddenly and painfully that, in his extremest excitement and misery, he fairly hurt the feelings of his Father by unreasonable requirements of him, and reproaches on their being refused. A principal Stuttgard Cautioner of his, incessantly pressed upon by the stringent measures of the creditors there, had fairly run off, saved himself by flight, from Stuttgard, and been seized in Mannheim, and there put in jail. Were not this Prisoner at once got out, Schiller's honor and peace of conscience were at stake. And so, before his (properly Streicher's) Landlord, the Architect Hölzel, could get together the required 300 gulden, and save this unlucky friend, the half-desperate Poet had written home, and begged from his Father that indispensable sum. And on the Father's clear refusal, had answered him with a very unfilial Letter. Not till after the lapse of seven weeks, did the Father reply; in a Letter, which, as a luminous memorial of his faithful honest father-heart and of his considerate just character as a man, deserves insertion here : —

" 'Very unwilling,' writes he, 'am I to proceed to the answering of thy last Letter, 21st November of the past year; which I could rather wish never to have read than now to taste again the bitterness contained there. Not enough that thou, in the beginning of the said Letter, very undeservedly reproachest me, as if I could and should have raised the 300 gulden for thee, — thou continuest to blame me, in a very painful way, for my inquiries about thee on this occasion. Dear Son, the relation between a good Father and his Son fallen into such a strait, who, although gifted with many faculties of mind, is still, in all that belongs to true greatness and contentment, much mistaken and astray, can never justify the Son in taking up as an injury what the Father has said out of love, out of consideration and experience of his own, and meant only for his Son's good. As to what concerns those 300 gulden, every one, alas, who knows my position here, knows that it cannot be possible for me to have even 50 gulden, not to speak of 300, before me in store; and that I should borrow such a sum, to the still farther disadvantage of my other children, for a Son, who of the much that he has promised me has been able to perform so little, — there, for certain, were I an unjust Father.' Farther on, the old man takes him up on another side, a private family affair. Schiller had, directly and through others, in reference to the prospect of a marriage between his elder Sister Christophine and his friend Reinwald the Court Librarian of Meiningen, expressed himself in a doubting manner, and thereby delayed the settlement of this affair. In regard to which his Father tells him : —

" ' And now I have something to remark in respect of thy Sister. As thou, my Son, partly straight out, and partly through Frau von Kalb, hast pictured Reinwald in a way to deter both me and thy Sister in counselling and negotiating in the way we intended, the affair seems to have become quite retrograde : for Reinwald, these two months past, has not written a word more. Whether thou, my Son, didst well to hinder a match not unsuitable for the age, and the narrow pecuniary circumstances of thy Sister, God, who sees into futurity, knows. As I am now sixty-one years of age, and can leave little fortune when I die; and as thou, my Son, how happily soever thy hopes be fulfilled, wilt yet have to struggle, years long, to get out of these present embarrassments, and arrange thyself suitably; and as, after that, thy own probable marriage will always require thee to have more thy own advantages in view, than to be able to trouble thyself much about those of thy Sisters; — it would not, all things considered, have been ill if Christophine had got a settlement. She would quite certainly, with her apparent regard for Reinwald, have been able to fit herself into his ways and him; all the better as she,

God be thanked, is not yet smit with ambition, and the wish for great things, and can suit herself to all conditions.' "

The Reinwald marriage did take place by and by, in spite of Schiller Junior's doubts; and had not Christophine been the paragon of Wives, might have ended very ill for all parties.

"After these incidents, Schiller bent his whole strength to disengage himself from the crushing burden of his debts, and to attain the goal marked out for him by his Parents' wishes, — an enduring settlement and steady way of life. Two things essentially contributed to enliven his activity, and brighten his prospects into the future. One was, the original beginning, which falls in next June, 1784, of his friendly intimacy with the excellent Körner; in whom he was to find not only the first founder of his outer fortune in life, but also a kindred spirit, and cordial friend such as he had never before had. The second was, that he made, what shaped his future lot, acquaintance with Duke Karl August of Weimar; who, after hearing him read the first act of *Don Carlos* at the Court of Darmstadt, had a long conversation with the Poet, and officially, in consequence of the same, bestowed on him the title of Rath. This new relation to a noble German Prince gave him a certain standing-ground for the future; and at the same time improved his present condition, by completely securing him in respect of any risk from Würtemberg. The now Schiller, as Court-Counsellor (*Hofrath*) to the Duke of Weimar; distinguished in this way by a Prince, who was acquainted with the Muses, and accustomed only to what was excellent, — stept forth in much freer attitude, secure of his position and himself, than the poor fugitive under ban of law had done.

"Out of this, however, and the fact resulting from it, that he now assumed a more decisive form of speech in the Periodical '*Thalia*' founded by him, and therein spared the players as little as the public, there grew for him so many and such irritating brabbles and annoyances that he determined to quit his connection with the Theatre, leave Mannheim altogether; and, at Leipzig with his new title of Rath, to begin a new honorable career. So soon as the necessary moneys

and advices from his friend [Körner] had arrived, he repaired thither, end of March 1785; and remained there all
the summer. In October of the same year, he followed his
friend Körner to Dresden; and found in the family of this
just-minded, clear-seeing man the purest and warmest sympathy for himself and his fortunes. The year 1787 led him at
last to Weimar. But here too he had still long to struggle,
under the pressure of poverty and want of many things, while
the world, in ever-increasing admiration, was resounding with
his name, till, in 1789, his longing for a civic existence, and
therewith the intensest wish of his Parents, was fulfilled.

"Inexpressible was the joy of the now elderly Father to
see his deeply beloved Son, after so many roamings, mis-
chances and battles, at last settled as Professor in Jena;
and soon thereafter, at the side of an excellent Wife, happy
at a hearth of his own. The economic circumstances of the
Son were now also shaped to the Father's satisfaction. If his
College salary was small, his literary labors, added thereto,
yielded him a sufficient income; his Wife moreover had come
to him quite fitted out, and her Mother had given all that
belongs to a household. 'Our economical adjustment,' writes
Schiller to his Father, some weeks after their marriage, 'has
fallen out, beyond all my wishes, well; and the order, the
dignity which I see around me here serves greatly to exhila-
rate my mind. Could you but for a moment get to me, you
would rejoice at the happiness of your Son.'

" Well satisfied and joyful of heart, from this time, the
Father's eye followed his Son's career of greatness and renown upon which the admired Poet every year stepped onwards, powerfuler, and richer in results, without ever, even
transiently, becoming strange to his Father's house and his
kindred there. Quite otherwise, all letters of the Son to
Father and Mother bear the evident stamp of true-hearted,
grateful and pious filial love. He took, throughout, the
heartiest share in all, even the smallest, events that befell
in his Father's house; and in return communicated to his
loved ones all of his own history that could soothe and
gratify them. Of this the following Letter, written by him,

26th October, 1791, on receipt of a case of wine sent from home, furnishes a convincing proof : —

'DEAREST FATHER, — I have just returned with my dear Lotte from Rudolstadt [her native place], where I was passing part of my holidays; and find your Letter. Thousand thanks for the thrice-welcome news you give me there, of the improving health of our dear Mother, and of the general welfare of you all. The conviction that it goes well with you, and that none of my dear loved ones is suffering, heightens for me the happiness which I enjoy here at the side of my dear Lotte.

' You are careful, even at this great distance, for your children, and gladden our little household with gifts. Heartiest thanks from us both for the Wine you have sent; and with the earliest carriage-post the Reinwalds shall have their share. Day after to-morrow we will celebrate your Birthday as if you were present, and with our whole heart drink your health.

' Here I send you a little production of my pen, which may perhaps give pleasure to my dear Mother and Sisters; for it should be at least written for ladies. In the year 1790 Wieland edited the *Historical Calendar*, and in this of 1791 and in the 1792 that will follow, I have undertaken the task. Insignificant as a *Calendar* seems to be, it is that kind of book which the Publishers can circulate the most extensively, and which accordingly brings them the best payment. To the Authors also they can, accordingly, offer much more. For this Essay on the *Thirty-Years War* they have given me 80 Louis-d'or, and I have in the middle of my Lectures written it in four weeks. Print, copper-plates, binding, Author's honorarium cost the Publisher 4,500 *reichs-thaler* [£675], and he counts on a sale of 7,000 copies or more.

' *28th*. To-day,' so he continues, after some remarks on a good old friend of his Father's, written after interruption, — ' To-day is your Birthday, dearest Father, which we both celebrate with a pious joy that Heaven has still preserved you sound and happy for us thus far. May Heaven still watch over your dear life and your health, and pre-serve your days to the latest age, that so your grateful Son may be able to spread, with all the power he has, joy and contentment over the evening of your life, and pay the debts of filial duty to you !

' Farewell, my dearest Father; loving kisses to our dearest Mother and my dear Sisters. We will soon write again.

' The Wine has arrived in good condition; once more receive our hearty thanks. — Your greatful and obedient Son

' FRIEDRICH.'

"In the beginning of this year (1791) the Poet had been seized with a violent and dangerous affection of the chest. The immediate danger was now over; but his bodily health was, for the rest of his life, shattered to ruin, and required, for the time coming, especially for the time just come, all manner of soft treatment and repose. The worst, therefore, was to be feared if his friends and he could not manage to place him, for the next few years, in a position freer from economic cares than now. Unexpectedly, in this difficulty, help appeared out of Denmark. Two warm admirers of Schiller's genius, the then hereditary Prince of Holstein-Augustenburg [Grandfather of the Prince Christian now, 1872, conspicuous in our English Court], and Count von Schimmelmann, offered the Poet a pension of 1,000 thalers [£150] for three years; and this with a fineness and delicacy of manner, which touched the recipient more even than the offer itself did, and moved him to immediate assent. The Pension was to remain a secret; but how could Schiller prevail on himself to be silent of it to his Parents? With tears of thankfulness the Parents received this glad message; in their pious minds they gathered out of this the beneficent conviction that their Son's heavy sorrows, and the danger in which his life hung, had only been decreed by Providence to set in its right light the love and veneration which he far and near enjoyed. Schiller himself this altogether unexpected proof of tenderest sympathy in his fate visibly cheered, and strengthened ·even in health; at lowest, the strength of his spirit, which now felt itself free from outward embarrassments, subdued under it the weakness of his body.

"In the middle of the year 1793, the love of his native country, and the longing after his kindred, became so lively in him that he determined, with his Wife, to visit Swabia. He writes to Körner: 'The Swabian, whom I thought I had altogether got done with, stirs himself strongly in me; but indeed I have been eleven years parted from Swabia; and Thüringen is not the country in which I can forget it.' In August he set out, and halted first in the then *Reichstadt*

[Imperial Free-town] Heilbronn, where he found the friend-liest reception; and enjoyed the first indescribable emotion in seeing again his Parents, Sisters and early friends. 'My dear ones,' writes he to Körner, 27th August, from Heilbronn, 'I found well to do, and, as thou canst suppose, greatly re-joiced to meet me again. My Father, in his seventieth year, is the image of a healthy old age; and any one who did not know his years would not count them above sixty. He is in continual activity, and this it is which keeps him healthy and youthful.' In large draughts the robust old man enjoyed the pleasure, long forborne, of gazing into the eyes of his Son, who now stood before him a completed man. He knew not whether more to admire than love him; for, in his whole ap-pearance, and all his speeches and doings, there stamped itself a powerful lofty spirit, a tender loving heart, and a pure noble character. His youthful fire was softened, a mild seriousness and a friendly dignity did not leave him even in jest; instead of his old neglect in dress, there had come a dignified ele-gance; and his lean figure and his pale face completed the interest of his look. To this was yet added the almost wonderful gift of conversation upon the objects that were dear to him, whenever he was not borne down by attacks of illness.

"From Heilbronn, soon after his arrival, Schiller wrote to Duke Karl, in the style of a grateful former Pupil, whom con-tradictory circumstances had pushed away from his native country. He got no answer from the Duke; but from Stutt-gard friends he did get sure tidings that the Duke, on receipt of this Letter, had publicly said, If Schiller came into Wür-temberg Territory, he, the Duke, would take no notice. To Schiller Senior, too, he had at the same time granted the humble petition that he might have leave to visit his Son in Heilbronn now and then.

"Under these circumstances, Schiller, perfectly secure, visited Ludwigsburg and even Solitüde, without, as he him-self expressed it, asking permission of the 'Schwabenkönig.' And, in September, in the near prospect of his Wife's confine-ment, he went altogether to Ludwigsburg, where he was a

good deal nearer to his kindred; and moreover, in the clever
Court-Doctor von Hoven, a friend of his youth, hoped to find
counsel, help and enjoyment.   Soon after his removal, Schiller
had, in the birth of his eldest Son, Karl, the sweet happiness
of first paternal joy; and with delight saw fulfilled what he
had written to a friend shortly before his departure from
Jena: 'I shall taste the joys of a Son and of a Father, and
it will, between these two feelings of Nature, go right well
with me.'

"The Duke, ill of gout, and perhaps feeling that death was
nigh, seemed to make a point of strictly ignoring Schiller; and
laid not the least hindrance in his way.   On the contrary,
he granted Schiller Senior, on petition, the permission to make
use of a certain Bath as long as he liked; and this Bath lay
so near Ludwigsburg that he could not but think the meaning merely was, that the Father wished to be nearer his Son.
Absence was at once granted by the Duke, useful and necessary as the elder Schiller always was to him at home.   For
the old man, now Major Schiller, still carried on his over-
seeing of the Ducal Gardens and Nurseries at Solitüde, and
his punctual diligence, fidelity, intelligence and other excel-
lences in that function had long been recognized.

"In a few weeks after, 24th October, 1793, Duke Karl
died; and was, by his illustrious Pupil, regarded as in some
sort a paternal friend.   Schiller thought only of the great
qualities of the deceased, and of the good he had done him;
not of the great faults which as Sovereign, and as man, he had
manifested.   Only to his most familiar friend did he write:
'The death of old Herod has had no influence either on me or
my Family, — except indeed that all men who had immediately
to do with that Sovereign Herr, as my Father had, are glad
now to have the prospect of a man before them.   That the
new Duke is, in every good, and also in every bad meaning of
the word.'   Withal, however, his Father, to whom naturally
the favor of the new Duke, Ludwig Eugen, was of importance,
could not persuade Schiller to welcome him to the Sovereignty
with a poem.   To Schiller's feelings it was unendurable to
awaken, for the sake of an external advantage from the

new Lord, any suspicions as if he welcomed the death of the old." [1]

Christophine, Schiller's eldest Sister, whom he always loved the most, was not here in Swabia; — long hundred miles away, poor Christophine, with her sickly and gloomy Husband at Meiningen, these ten years past! — but the younger two, Luise and Nanette, were with him, the former daily at his hand. Luise was then twenty-seven, and is described as an excellent domestic creature, amiable, affectionate, even enthusiastic; yet who at an early period, though full of admiration about her Brother and his affairs, had turned all her faculties and tendencies upon domestic practicality, and the satisfaction of being useful to her loved ones in their daily life and wants. [2] "Her element was altogether house-management; the aim of her endeavor to attain the virtues by which she saw her pious Mother made happy herself, in making others happy in the narrow indoor kingdom. This quiet household vocation, with its manifold labors and its simple joys, was Luise's world; beyond which she needed nothing and demanded nothing. From her Father she had inherited this feeling for the practical, and this restless activity; from the Mother her piety, compassion and kindliness; from both, the love of order, regularity and contentment. Luise, in the weak state of Schiller's Wife's health, was right glad to take charge of her Brother's housekeeping; and, first at Heilbronn and then at Ludwigsburg, did it to the complete satisfaction both of Brother and Sister-in-law. Schiller himself gives to Körner the grateful testimony, that she 'very well understands household management.'

"In this daily relation with her delicate and loving Brother, to whom Luise looked up with a sort of timid adoration, he became ever dearer to her; with a silent delight, she would often look into the soft eyes of the great and wonderful man; from whose powerful spirit she stood so distant, and to whose rich heart so near. All too rapidly for her flew by the bright days of his abode in his homeland, and long she looked after

[1] *Saupe*, p. 60.   [2] Ibid. p. 136 et seqq.

the vanished one with sad longing; and Schiller also felt himself drawn closer to his Sister than before; by whose silent faithful working his abode in Swabia had been made so smooth and agreeable."

Nanette he had, as will by and by appear, seen at Jena, on her Mother's visit there, the year before;—with admiration and surprise he then saw the little creature whom he had left a pretty child of five years old, now become a blooming maiden, beautiful to eye and heart, and had often thought of her since. She too was often in his house, at present; a loved and interesting object always. She had been a great success in the foreign Jena circle, last year; and had left bright memories there. This is what Saupe says afterwards, of her appearance at Jena, and now in Schiller's temporary Swabian home:—

"She evinced the finest faculties of mind, and an uncommon receptivity and docility, and soon became to all that got acquainted with her a dear and precious object. To declaim passages from her Brother's Poems was her greatest joy; she did her recitation well; and her Swabian accent and naïvete of manner gave her an additional charm for her new relatives, and even exercised a beneficent influence on the Poet's own feelings. With hearty pleasure his beaming eyes rested often on the dear Swabian girl, who understood how to awaken in his heart the sweet tones of childhood and home. 'She is good,' writes he of her to his friend Körner, 'and it seems as if something could be made of her. She is yet much the child of nature, and that is still the best she could be, never having been able to acquire any reasonable culture.' With Schiller's abode in Swabia, from August, 1793, till May, 1794, Nanette grew still closer to his heart, and in his enlivening and inspiring neighborhood her spirit and character shot out so many rich blossoms, that Schiller on quitting his Father's house felt justified in the fairest hopes for the future." Just before her visit to Jena, Schiller Senior writes to his Son: "It is a great pity for Nanette that I cannot give her a better education. She has sense and talent and the best of hearts; much too of my dear Fritz's turn of mind, as he will himself see, and be able to judge." [1]

"For the rest, on what childlike confidential terms Schiller lived with his Parents at this time, one may see by the following Letter, of 8th November, 1793, from Ludwigsburg: —

'Right sorry am I, dearest Parents, that I shall not be able to celebrate my Birthday, 11th November, along with you. But I see well that good Papa cannot rightly risk just now to leave Solitüde at all, — a visit from the Duke being expected there every day. On the whole, it does not altogether depend on the day on which one is to be merry with loved souls; and every day on which I can be where my dear Parents are shall be festal and welcome to me like a Birthday.

'About the precious little one here Mamma is not to be uneasy. [Here follow some more precise details about the health of this little Gold Son; omitted.] Of watching and nursing he has no lack; that you may believe; and he is indeed, a little leanness excepted, very lively and has a good appetite.

'I have been, since I made an excursion to Stuttgard, tolerably well; and have employed this favorable time to get a little forward in my various employments which have been lying waste so long. For this whole week, I have been very diligent, and getting on briskly. This is also the cause that I have not written to you. I am always supremely happy when I am busy and my labor speeds.

'For your so precious Portrait I thank you a thousand times, dearest Father: yet glad as I am to possess this memorial of you, much gladder still am I that Providence has granted me to have you yourself, and to live in your neighborhood. But we must profit better by this good time, and no longer make such pauses before coming together again. If you once had seen the Duke at Solitüde and known how you stand with him, there would be, I think, no difficulty in a short absence of a few days, especially at this season of the year. I will send up the carriage [hired at Jena for the visit thither and back] at the very first opportunity, and leave it with you, to be ready always when you can come.

'My and all our hearty and childlike salutations to you both, and to the good Nane [Nanette] my brotherly salutation.

'Hoping soon for a joyful meeting, — Your obedient Son,

'FRIEDRICH SCHILLER.'

[1] *Saupe,* pp. 149, 150.

"In the new-year time, 1794, Schiller spent several agreeable weeks in Stuttgard; whither he had gone primarily on
account of some family matter which had required settling
there. At least he informs his friend Körner, on the 17th
March, from Stuttgard, 'I hope to be not quite useless to my
Father here, though, from the connections in which I stand, I
can expect nothing for myself.'

"By degrees, however, the sickly, often-ailing Poet began to
long again for a quiet, uniform way of life; and this feeling,
daily strengthened by the want of intellectual conversation,
which had become a necessary for him, grew at length so
strong, that he, with an alleviated heart, thought of departure
from his Birth-land, and of quitting his loved ones; glad that
Providence had granted him again to possess his Parents and
Sisters for months long, and to live in their neighborhood.
He gathered himself into readiness for the journey back; and
returned, first to his original quarters at Heilbronn, and, in
May, 1794, with Wife and Child, to Jena.

"Major Schiller, whom the joy to see his Son and Grandson seemed to have made young again, lived with fresh pleasure
in his idyllic calling; and in free hours busied himself with
writing down his twenty years' experiences in the domain of
garden- and tree-culture, — in a Work, the printing and publication of which were got managed for him by his renowned
Son. In November, 1794, he was informed that the young
Publisher of the first *Musen-Almanach* had accepted his MS.
for an honorarium of twenty-four Karolins; and that the same
was already gone to press. Along with this, the good old Major was valued by his Prince, and by all who knew him. His
subordinates loved him as a just impartial man; feared him,
too, however, in his stringent love of order. Wife and children
showed him the most reverent regard and tender love; but the
Son was the ornament of his old age. He lived to see the
full renown of the Poet, and his close connection with Goethe,
through which he was to attain complete mastership and lasting composure. With hands quivering for joy the old man
grasped the MSS. of his dear Son; which from Jena, *viâ*

Cotta's Stuttgard Warehouses, were before all things transmitted to him. In a paper from his hand, which is still in existence, there is found a touching expression of thanks, That God had given him such a joy in his Son. 'And Thou Being of all beings,' says he in the same, 'to Thee did I pray, at the birth of my one Son, that Thou wouldst supply to him in strength of intellect and faculty what I, from want of learning, could not furnish; and Thou hast heard me. Thanks to Thee, most merciful Being, that Thou hast heard the prayer of a mortal!'

"Schiller had left his loved ones at Solitüde whole and well; and with the firm hope that he would see them all again. And the next-following years did pass untroubled over the prosperous Family. But 'ill-luck,' as the proverb says, 'comes with a long stride.' In the Spring of 1796, when the French, under Jourdan and Moreau, had overrun South Germany, there reached Schiller, on a sudden, alarming tidings from Solitüde. In the Austrian chief Hospital, which had been established in the Castle there, an epidemic fever had broken out; and had visited the Schiller Family among others. The youngest Daughter Nanette had sunk under this pestilence, in the flower of her years; and whilst the second Daughter Luise lay like to die of the same, the Father also was laid bedrid with gout. For fear of infection, nobody except the Doctors would risk himself at Solitüde; and so the poor weakly Mother stood forsaken there, and had, for months long, to bear alone the whole burden of the household distress. Schiller felt it painfully that he was unable to help his loved ones, in so terrible a posture of affairs; and it cost him great effort to hide these feelings from his friends. In his pain and anxiety, he turned himself at last to his eldest Sister Christophine, Wife of Hofrath Reinwald in Meiningen; and persuaded her to go to Solitüde to comfort and support her people there. Had not the true Sister-heart at once acceded to her Brother's wishes, he had himself taken the firm determination to go in person to Swabia, in the middle of May, and bring his Family away from Solitüde, and make arrangements for their nursing and accommodation. The news of his Sister's setting out relieved him of a great and continual anxiety. 'Heaven bless thee,' writes he to her on the 6th May, 'for this proof of thy filial love.' He earnestly entreats her to prevent his dear Parents from delaying, out of thrift, any wholesome means of improvement to their health; and declares himself ready, with joy, to bear all costs, those of travelling included: she is to draw on Cotta in Tübingen for whatever money she needs. . Her Husband also he thanks, in a cordial Letter, for his consent to this journey of his Wife.

"July 11, 1796, was born to the Poet, who had been in much trouble about his own household for some time, his second Son, Ernst. Great fears had been entertained for the Mother; which proving groundless, the happy event lifted a heavy burden from his heart; and he again took courage and hope. But soon after, on the 15th August, he writes again to the faithful Körner about his kinsfolk in Swabia: 'From the War we have not suffered so much; but all the more from the condition of my Father, who, broken down under an obstinate and painful disease, is slowly wending towards death. How sad this fact is, thou mayest think.'

"Within few weeks after, 7th September, 1796, the Father died; in his seventy-third year, after a sick-bed of eight months. Though his departure could not be reckoned other than a blessing, yet the good Son was deeply shattered by the news of it. What his filially faithful soul suffered, in these painful days, is touchingly imaged in two Letters, which may here make a fitting close to this Life-sketch of Schiller's Father. It was twelve days after his Father's death when he wrote to his Brother-in-law, Reinwald, in Meiningen: —

'Thou hast here news, dear Brother, of the release of our good Father; which, much as it had to be expected, nay wished, has deeply affected us all. The conclusion of so long and withal so active a life is, even for bystanders, a touching object: what must it be to those whom it so nearly concerns? I have to tear myself away from thinking of this painful loss, since it is my part to help the dear remaining ones. It is a great comfort to thy Wife that she has been able to continue and fulfil her daughterly duty till her Father's last release. She would never have consoled herself, had he died a few days after her departure home.

'Thou understandest how in the first days of this fatal breach among us, while so many painful things storm in upon our good Mother, thy Christophine could not have left, even had the Post been in free course. But this still remains stopped, and we must wait the War-events on the Franconian, Swabian and Palatinate borders. How much this absence of thy Wife must afflict, I feel along with thee; but who can fight against such a chain of inevitable destinies? Alas, public and universal disorder rolls up into itself our private events too, in the fatalest way.

'Thy Wife longs from her heart for home; and she only the more deserves our regard that she, against her inclination and her interest, resolved to be led only by the thought of her filial duties. Now, however, she certainly will not delay an hour longer with her return, the instant it can be entered upon without danger and impossibility. Comfort her too when thou writest to her; it grieves her to know thee forsaken, and to have no power to help thee.

'Fare right well, dear Brother. — Thine, SCHILLER.'

"Nearly at the same time he wrote to his Mother: —

'Grieved to the heart, I take up the pen to lament with you and my dear Sisters the loss we have just sustained. In truth, for a good while past I have expected nothing else: but when the inevitable actually comes, it is always a sad and overwhelming stroke. To think that one who was so dear to us, whom we hung upon with the feelings of early childhood, and also in later years were bound to by respect and love, that such an object is gone from the world, that with all our striving we cannot bring it back, — to think of this is always something frightful. And when, like you, my dearest best Mother, one has shared with the lost Friend and Husband joy and sorrow for so many long years, the parting is all the painfuler. Even when I look away from what the good Father that is gone was to myself and to us all, I cannot without mournful emotion contemplate the close of so steadfast and active a life, which God continued to him so long, in such soundness of body and mind, and which he managed so honorably and well. Yes truly, it is not a small thing to hold out so faithfully upon so long and toilsome a course; and like him, in his seventy-third year, to part from the world in so childlike and pure a mood. Might I but, if it cost me all his sorrows, pass away from my life as innocently as he from his! Life is so severe a trial; and the advantages which Providence, in some

respects, may have granted me compared with him, are joined with so
many dangers for the heart and for its true peace!

'I will not attempt to comfort you and my dear Sisters. You all
feel, like me, how much we have lost; but you feel also that Death
alone could end these long sorrows. With our dear Father it is now
well; and we shall all follow him ere long. Never shall the image of
him fade from our hearts; and our grief for him can only unite us still
closer together.

'Five or six years ago it did not seem likely that you, my dear
ones, should, after such a loss, find a Friend in your Brother, — that I
should survive our dear Father. God has ordered it otherwise; and
He grants me the joy to feel that I may still be something to you.
How ready I am thereto, I need not assure you. We all of us know
one another in this respect, and are our dear Father's not unworthy
children.' "

This earnest and manful lamentation, which contains also
a just recognition of the object lamented, may serve to prove,
think Saupe and others, what is very evident, that Caspar
Schiller, with his stiff, military regulations, spirit of discipline
and rugged, angular ways, was, after all, the proper Father
for a wide-flowing, sensitive, enthusiastic, somewhat lawless
Friedrich Schiller; and did beneficently compress him into
something of the shape necessary for his task in this world.

———•———

II. THE MOTHER.

OF Schiller's Mother, Elisabetha Dorothea Kodweis, born at
Marbach, 1733, the preliminary particulars have been given
above: That she was the daughter of an Innkeeper, Woodmeasurer and Baker; prosperous in the place when Schiller
Senior first arrived there. We should have added, what Saupe
omits, that the young Surgeon boarded in their house; and
that by the term Woodmeasurer (*Holzmesser*, Measurer of
Wood) is signified an Official Person appointed not only to
measure and divide into portions the wood supplied as fuel

from the Ducal or Royal Forests, but to be responsible also
for payment of the same. In which latter capacity, Kodweis,
as Father Schiller insinuates, was rash, imprudent and unlucky, and at one time had like to have involved that prudent, parsimonious Son-in-law in his disastrous economics.
We have also said what Elisabetha's comely looks were,
and particular features; pleasing and hopeful, more and
more, to the strict young Surgeon, daily observant of her and
them.

"In her circle," Saupe continues, "she was thought by her
early playmates a kind of enthusiast; because she, with average faculties of understanding combined deep feeling, true
piety and love of Nature, a talent for Music, nay even for
Poetry. But perhaps it was the very reverse qualities in her,
the fact namely that what she wanted in culture, and it may
be also in clearness and sharpness of understanding, was so
richly compensated by warmth and lovingness of character, —
perhaps it was this which most attracted to her the heart of
her deeply reasonable Husband. And never had he cause to
repent his choice. For she was, and remained, as is unanimously testified of her by trustworthy witnesses, an unpretending, soft and dutiful Wife; and, as all her Letters testify,
had the tenderest mother-heart. She read a good deal, even
after her marriage, little as she had of time for reading.
Favorite Books with her were those on Natural History; but
she liked best of all to study the Biographies of famous men,
or to dwell in the spiritual poetizing of an Utz, a Gellert and
Klopstock. She also liked, and in some measure had the
power, to express her own feelings in verses; which, with all
their simplicity, show a sense for rhythm and some expertness
in diction. Here is one instance; her salutation to the Husband who was her First-love, on New Year's Day, 1757, the
ninth year of their as yet childless marriage: —

'Oh, could I but have found forget-me-not in the Valley,
   And roses beside it! Then had I plaited thee
   In fragrant blossoms the garland for this New Year,
   Which is still brighter to me than that of our Marriage was.

'I grumble, in truth, that the cold North now governs us,
And every flowret's bud is freezing in the cold earth!
Yet one thing does not freeze, I mean my loving heart;
Thine that is, and shares with thee its joys and sorrows.'[1]

"The Seven-Years War threw the young Wife into manifold anxiety and agitation; especially since she had become a Mother, and in fear for the life of her tenderly loved Husband, had to tremble for the Father of her children too. To this circumstance Christophine ascribes, certainly with some ground, the world-important fact that her Brother had a much weaker constitution than herself. He had in fact been almost born in a camp. In late Autumn, 1759, the Infantry Regiment of Major-General Romann, in which Caspar Schiller was then a Lieutenant, had, for sake of the Autumn Manœuvres of the Würtemberg Soldiery, taken Camp in its native region. The Mother had thereupon set out from Marbach to visit her long-absent Husband in the Camp; and it was in his tent that she felt the first symptoms of her travail. She rapidly hastened back to Marbach; and by good luck still reached her Father's house in the Market-place there, near by the great Fountain; where she, on the 11th November, was delivered of a Boy. For almost four years the little Friedrich with Christophine and Mother continued in the house of the well-contented Grandparents (who had not yet fallen poor), under her exclusive care. With self-sacrificing love and careful fidelity, she nursed her little Boy; whose tender body had to suffer not only from the common ailments of children, but was heavily visited with fits of cramp. In a beautiful region, on the bosom of a tender Mother, and in these first years far from the over-

---

[1] *O hätt ich doch im Thal Vergissmeinnicht gefunden*
Und Rosen nebenbei! Dann hät' ich Dir gewunden
In Blüthenduft den Kranz zu diesem neuen Jahr,
Der schöner noch als der am Hochzeittage war.

Ich zürne, traun, dass itzt der kalte Nord regieret,
Und jedes Blümchens Keim in kalter Erde frieret!
Doch eines frieret nicht, es ist mein liebend Herz;
Dein ist es, theilt mit Dir die Freuden und den Schmerz.

sight of a rigorous Father, the Child grew up, and unfolded himself under cheerful and harmonious impressions.

"On the return of his Father from the War, little Fritz, now four years old, was quite the image of his Mother; long-necked, freckled and reddish-haired like her. It was the pious Mother's work, too, that a feeling of religion, early and vivid, displayed itself in him. The easily receptive Boy was indeed keenly attentive to all that his Father, in their Family-circle, read to them, and inexhaustible in questions till he had rightly caught the meaning of it : but he listened with most eagerness when his Father read passages from the Bible, or vocally uttered them in prayer. 'It was a touching sight,' says his eldest Sister, 'the expression of devotion on the dear little Child's countenance. With its blue eyes directed towards Heaven, its high-blond hair about the clear brow, and its fast-clasped little hands. It was like an angel's head to look upon.'

"With Father's return, the happy Mother conscientiously shared with him the difficult and important business of bringing up their Son; and both in union worked highly beneficially for his spiritual development. The practical and rigorous Father directed his chief aim to developing the Boy's intellect and character; the mild, pious, poetic-minded Mother, on the other hand, strove for the ennobling nurture of his temper and his imagination. It was almost exclusively owing to her that his religious feeling, his tender sense of all that was good and beautiful, his love of mankind, tolerance, and capability of self-sacrifice, in the circle of his Sisters and playmates, distinguished the Boy.

"On Sunday afternoons, when she went to walk with both the Children, she was wont to explain to them the Church-Gospel of the day. 'Once,' so stands it in Christophine's Memorials, 'when we two, as children, had set out walking with dear Mamma to see our Grandparents, she took the way from Ludwigsburg to Marbach, which leads straight over the Hill,' a walk of some four miles. 'It was a beautiful Easter Monday, and our Mother related to us the history of the two Disciples to whom, on their journey to Emmaus, Jesus had joined himself. Her speech and narrative grew ever more

inspired; and when we got upon the Hill, we were all so much
affected that we knelt down and prayed. This Hill became
a Tabor to us.'

"At other times she entertained the children with fairy-tales
and magic histories. Already while in Lorch she had likewise
led the Boy, so far as his power of comprehension and her
own knowledge permitted, into the domains of German Poetry.
Klopstock's *Messias,* Opitz's Poems, Paul Gerhard's and Gellert's pious Songs, were made known to him in this tender age,
through his Mother; and were, for that reason, doubly dear.
At one time also the artless Mother made an attempt on him
with Hofmannswaldau;[1] but the sugary and windy tone of him
hurt the tender poet-feeling of the Boy. With smiling dislike
he pushed the Book away; and afterwards was wont to remark,
when, at the new year, rustic congratulants with their foolish
rhymes would too liberally present themselves, 'Mother, there
is a new Hofmannswaldau at the door!' Thus did the excellent Mother guide forward the soul of her docile Boy, with
Bible-passages and Church-symbols, with tales, histories and
poems, into gradual form and stature. Never forgetting,
withal, to awaken and nourish his sense for the beauties of
Nature. Before long, Nature had become his dearest abode;
and only love of that could sometimes tempt him to little
abridgments of school-hours. Often, in the pretty region of
Lorch, he wished the Sun good-night in open song; or with
childish pathos summoned Stuttgard's Painters to represent
the wondrous formation and glorious coloring of the sunset
clouds. If, in such a humor, a poor man met him, his overflowing little heart would impel him to the most active pity;
and he liberally gave away whatever he had by him and thought
he could dispense with. The Father, who, as above indicated,
never could approve or even endure such unreasonable giving
up of one's feelings to effeminate impressions, was apt to intervene on these occasions, even with manual punishment, — unless
the Mother were at hand to plead the little culprit off.

[1] A once celebrated Silesian of the 17th century, distinguished for his blusterous exaggerations, numb-footed caprioles, and tearing of a passion to rags;
— now extinct.

"But nothing did the Mother forward with more eagerness, by every opportunity, than the kindling inclination of her Son to become a Preacher; which even showed itself in his sports. Mother or Sister had to put a little cowl on his head, and pin round him by way of surplice a bit of black apron; then would he mount a chair and begin earnestly to preach; ranging together in his own way, not without some traces of coherency, all that he had retained from teaching and church-visiting in this kind, and interweaving it with verses of songs. The Mother, who listened attentively and with silent joy, put a higher meaning into this childish play; and, in thought, saw her Son already stand in the Pulpit, and work, rich in blessings, in a spiritual office. The spiritual profession was at that time greatly esteemed, and gave promise of an honorable existence. Add to this, that the course of studies settled for young Würtemberg Theologians not only offered important pecuniary furtherances and advantages, but also morally the fewest dangers. And thus the prudent and withal pious Father, too, saw no reason to object to this inclination of the Son and wish of the Mother.

"It had almost happened, however, that the Latin School in Ludwigsburg (where our Fritz received the immediately preparatory teaching for his calling) had quite disgusted him with his destination for theology. The Teacher of Religion in the Institute, a narrow-minded, angry-tempered Pietist," as we have seen, "used the sad method of tormenting his scholars with continual rigorous, altogether soulless, drillings and trainings in matters of mere creed; nay he threatened often to whip them thoroughly, if, in the repetition of the catechism, a single word were wrong. And thus to the finely sensitive Boy instruction was making hateful to him what domestic influences had made dear. Yet these latter did outweigh and overcome, in the end; and he remained faithful to his purpose of following a spiritual career.

"When young Schiller, after the completion of his course at the Latin School, 1777, was to be confirmed, his Mother and her Husband came across to Ludwigsburg the day before that solemn ceremony. Just on their arrival, she saw her Son wandering idle and unconcerned about the streets; and impressively represented to him how greatly his indifference to the highest and most solemn transaction of his young life troubled her. Struck and affected hereby, the Boy withdrew; and, after a few hours, handed to his Parents a German Poem, expressive of his feelings over the approaching renewal of his baptismal covenant. The Father, who either had n't known the occasion of this, or had looked upon his Son's idling on the street with less severe eyes, was highly astonished, and received him mockingly with the question, 'Hast thou lost thy senses, Fritz?' The Mother, on the other hand, was visibly rejoiced at that poetic outpouring, and with good cause. For, apart from all other views of the matter, she recognized in it how firmly her Son's inclination was fixed on the study of Theology. — [This anecdote, if it were of any moment whatever, appears to be a little doubtful.]

"The painfuler, therefore, was it to the Mother's heart when her Son, at the inevitable entrance into the Karl's School, had to give up Theology; and renounce withal, for a long time, if not forever, her farther guidance and influence. But she was too pious not to recognize by degrees, in this change also, a Higher Hand; and could trustfully expect the workings of the same. Besides, her Son clung so tenderly to her, that at least there was no separation of him from the Mother's heart to be dreaded. The heart-warm attachment of childish years to the creed taught him by his Mother might, and did, vanish; but not the attachment to his Mother herself, whose dear image often enough charmed back the pious sounds and forms of early days, and for a time scared away doubts and unbelief.

"Years came and went; and Schiller, at last, about the end of 1780, stept out of the Academy, into the actual world, which he as yet knew only by hearsay. Delivered from that long unnatural constraint of body and spirit, he gave free course to his fettered inclinations; and sought, as in Poetry so also in Life, unlimited freedom! The tumults of passion and youthful buoyancy, after so long an imprisonment, had their sway; and embarrassments in money, their natural consequence, often brought him into very sad moods.

"In this season of time, so dangerous for the moral purity of the young man, his Mother again was his good Genius: a warning and request, in her soft tone of love sufficed to recall youthful levity within the barriers again, and restore the balance. She anxiously contrived, too, that the Son, often and willingly, visited his Father's house. Whenever Schiller had decided to give himself a good day, he wandered out with some friend as far as Solitüde. [Only some four or five miles.] 'What a baking and a roasting then went on by that good soul,' says one who witnessed it, 'for the dear Prodigy of a Son and the comrade who had come with him; for whom the good Mother never could do enough! Never have I seen a better maternal heart, a more excellent, more domestic, more womanly woman.'

"The admiring recognition which the Son had already found among his youthful friends, and in wider circles, was no less grateful to her heart than the gradual perception that his powerful soul, welling forth from the interior to the outward man, diffused itself into his very features, and by degrees even advantageously altered the curvatures and the form of his body. His face about this time got rid of its freckles and irregularities of skin; and strikingly improved, moreover, by the circumstance that the hitherto rather drooping nose gradually acquired its later aquiline form. And withal, the youthful Poet, with the growing consciousness of his strength and of his worth, assumed an imposing outward attitude; so that a witty Stuttgard Lady, whose house Schiller often walked past, said of him: 'Regiment's Dr. Schiller steps out as if the Duke were one of his inferior servants!'

"The indescribable impression which the *Robbers*, the gigantic first-born of a Karl's Scholar, made in Stuttgard, communicated itself to the Mother too; innocently she gave herself up to the delight of seeing her Son's name wondered at and celebrated; and was, in her Mother-love, inventive enough to overcome all doubts and risks which threatened to dash her joy. By Christophine's mediations, and from the Son himself as well, she learned many a disquieting circumstance, which for the present had to be carefully concealed from her

Husband; but nothing whatever could shake her belief in her Son and his talent. Without murmur, with faithful trust in God, she resigned herself even to the bitter necessity of losing for a long time her only Son; having once got to see, beyond disputing, that his purpose was firm to withdraw himself by flight from the Duke's despotic interference with his poetical activity as well as with his practical procedures; and that this purpose of his was rigorously demanded by the circum. stances. Yet a sword went through her soul when Schiller, for the last time, appeared at Solitüde, secretly to take leave of her." Her feelings on this tragic occasion have been de- scribed above; and may well be pictured as among the pain. fulest, tenderest and saddest that a Mother's heart could have to bear. Our Author continues : —

" In reality, it was to the poor Mother a hard and lament- able time. Remembrance of the lately bright and safe-looking situation, now suddenly rent asunder and committed to the dubious unknown; anxiety about their own household and the fate of her Son; the Father's just anger, and perhaps some tacit self-reproach that she had favored a dangerous game by keeping it concealed from her honest-hearted Husband, — lay like crushing burdens on her heart. And if many a thing did smooth itself, and many a thing, which at first was to be feared, did not take place, one thing remained fixed continu- ally, — painful anxiety about her Son. To the afflicted Mother, in this heavy time, Frau von Wolzogen devoted the most sin- cere and beneficent sympathy; a Lady of singular goodness of heart, who, during Schiller's eight hidden months at Bauer- bach, frequently went out to see his Family at Solitüde. By her oral reports about Schiller, whom she herself several times visited at Bauerbach, his Parents were more soothed than by his own somewhat excited Letters. With reference to this magnanimous service of friendship, Schiller wrote to her at Stuttgard in February, 1783: ' A Letter to my Parents is get- ting on its way; yet, much as I had to speak of you, I have said nothing whatever [from prudent motives] of your late appearance here, or of the joyful moments of our conversa- tion together. You yourself still, therefore, have all that to

tell, and you will presumably find a pair of attentive hearers.'
Frau von Wolzogen ventured also to apply to a high court lady,
Countess von Hohenheim [Duke's *finale* in the *illicit* way,
whom he at length wedded], personally favorable to Schiller,
and to direct her attention, before all, upon the heavy-laden
Parents. Nor was this without effect. For the Countess's
persuasion seems essentially to have contributed to the result
that Duke Karl, out of respect for the deserving Father, left
the evasion of his own Pupil unpunished.

"It must, therefore, have appeared to the still agitated
Mother, who reverenced the Frau von Wolzogen as her helpful guardian, a flagrant piece of ingratitude, when she learnt
that her Son was allowing himself to be led into a passionate
love for the blooming young Daughter of his Benefactress.
She grieved and mourned in secret to see him exposed to new
storms; foreseeing clearly, in this passion, a ready cause for
his removal from Bauerbach. To such agitations her body
was no longer equal; a creeping, eating misery undermined
her health. She wrote to her Son at Mannheim, with a soft
shadow of reproof, that in this year, since his absence, she had
become ten years older in health and looks. Not long after,
she had actually to take to bed, because of painful cramps,
which, proceeding from the stomach, spread themselves over
breast, head, back and loins. The medicines which the Son,
upon express account of symptoms by the Father, prescribed
for her, had no effect. By degrees, indeed, these cramps
abated or left off; but she tottered about in a state of sickness, years long: the suffering mind would not let the body
come to strength. For though her true heart was filled with
a pious love, which hopes all, believes and suffers all, yet she
was neither blind to the faults of her Son, nor indifferent to
the thought of seeing her Family's good repute and well-being
threatened by his non-performances and financial confusions.

"With the repose and peace which the news of her Son's
appointment to Jena, and intended marriage, had restored
to his Family, there appeared also (beginning of 1790) an
improvement to be taking place in the Mother's health.
Learning this by a Letter from his Father, Schiller wrote

back with lightened heart : ' How welcome, dearest Father,
was your last Letter to me, and how necessary ! I had, the
very day before, got from Christophine the sad news that my
dearest Mother's state had grown so much worse ; and what
a blessed turn now has this weary sickness taken ! If in the
future *regimen vitæ* (diet arrangements) of my dearest Mother,
there is strict care taken, her long and many sufferings, with
the source of them, may be removed. Thanks to a merciful
Providence, which saves and preserves for us the dear Mother
of our youth. My soul is moved with tenderness and gratitude. I had to think of her as lost to us forever ; and she has
now been given back.' In reference to his approaching marriage with Lottchen von Lengefeld, he adds, ' How did it lacer-
ate my heart to think that my dearest Mother might not live
to see the happiness of her Son ! Heaven bless you with
thousand-fold blessings, best Father, and grant to my dear
Mother a cheerful and painless life ! '

"Soon, however, his Mother again fell sick, and lay in great
danger. Not till August following could the Father announce
that she was saved, and from day to day growing stronger.
The annexed history of the disorder seemed so remarkable to
Schiller, that he thought of preparing it for the public ; unless
the Physician, Court-Doctor Consbruch, liked better to send it
out in print himself. ' On this point,' says Schiller, ' I will
write to him by the first post ; and give him my warmest
thanks for the inestimable service he has done us all, by his
masterly cure of our dear Mamma ; and for his generous and
friendly behavior throughout.' ' How heartily, my dearest
Parents,' writes he farther, ' did it rejoice us both [this Letter
is of 29th December ; on the 20th February of that year he
had been wedded to his Lotte], this good news of the still-
continuing improvement of our dearest Mother ! With full
soul we both of us join in the thanks which you give to gracious Heaven for this recovery ; and our heart now gives way
to the fairest hopes that Providence, which herein overtops
our expectations, will surely yet prepare a joyful meeting for
us all once more.'

"Two years afterwards this hope passed into fulfilment.

The Mother being now completely cured of her last disorder, there seized her so irresistible a longing for her Son, that even her hesitating Husband, anxious lest her very health should suffer, at last gave his consent to the far and difficult journey to Jena. On the 3d September, 1792, Schiller, in joyful humor, announces to his friend in Dresden, 'To-day I have received from home the very welcome tidings that my good Mother, with one of my Sisters, is to visit us here this month. Her arrival falls at a good time, when I hope to be free and loose from labor; and then we have ahead of us mere joyful undertakings.' The Mother came in company with her youngest Daughter, bright little Nane, or Nanette; and surprised him two days sooner than, by the Letters from Solitüde, he had expected her. Unspeakable joy and sweet sorrow seized Mother and Son to feel themselves, after ten years of separation, once more in each other's arms. The long journey, bad weather and roads had done her no harm. 'She has altered a little, in truth,' writes he to Körner, 'from what she was ten years ago; but after so many sicknesses and sorrows, she still has a healthy look. It rejoices me much that things have so come about, that I have her with me again, and can be a joy to her.'

"The Mother likewise soon felt herself at home and happy in the trusted circle of her children; only too fast flew by the beautiful and happy days, which seemed to her richly to make amends for so many years of sorrows and cares. Especially it did her heart good to see for herself what a beneficent influence the real and beautiful womanhood of her Daughter-in-law exercised upon her Son. Daily she learnt to know the great advantages of mind and heart in her; daily she more deeply thanked God that for her Son, who, on account even of his weak health, was not an altogether convenient Husband, there had been so tender-hearted and so finely cultivated a Wife given him as life-companion. The conviction that the domestic happiness of her Son was secure contributed essentially also to alleviate the pain of departure.

"Still happier days fell to her when Schiller, stirred up by her visit, came the year after, with his Wife, to Swabia; and

lived there from August, 1793, till May, 1794. It was a singular and as if providential circumstance, which did not escape
the pious Mother, that Schiller, in the same month in which
he had, eleven years ago, hurried and in danger, fled out of
Stuttgard to Ludwigsburg, should now in peace and without
obstruction come, from Heilbronn by the same Ludwigsburg,
to the near neighborhood of his Parents. With bitter tears of
sorrow, her eye had then followed the fugitive, in his dark
trouble and want of everything; with sweet tears of joy she
now received her fame-crowned Son, whom God, through sufferings and mistakes and wanderings, had led to happiness and
wisdom. The birth of the Grandson gave to her life a new
charm, as if of youth returned. She felt herself highly favored
that God had spared her life to see her dear Son's first-born
with her own eyes. It was a touching spectacle to see the
Grandmother as she sat by the cradle of the little ' Gold Son,'
and listened to every breath-drawing of the child; or when,
with swelling heart, she watched the approaching steps of her
Son, and observed his true paternal pleasure over his first-
born.

 " Well did the excellent Grandmother deserve such refreshment of heart; for all too soon there came again upon her
troublous and dark days. Schiller had found her stronger and
cheerfuler than on her prior visit to Jena; and had quitted
his Home-land with the soothing hope that his good Mother
would reach a long and happy age. Nor could he have the
least presentiment of the events which, three years later,
burst in, desolating and destroying, upon his family, and
brought the health and life of his dear Mother again into
peril. It is above stated, in our sketch of the Husband, in
what extraordinary form the universal public misery, under
which, in 1796, all South Germany was groaning, struck the
Schiller Family at Solitüde. Already on the 21st March of this
year, Schiller had written to his Father, 'How grieved I am
for our good dear Mother, on whom all manner of sorrows
have stormed down in this manner! But what a mercy of
God it is, too, that she still has strength left not to sink under
these circumstances, but to be able still to afford you so much

help! Who would have thought, six or seven years ago, that she, who was so infirm and exhausted, would now be serving you all as support and nurse? In such traits I recognize a good Providence which watches over us; and my heart is touched by it to the core.'

"Meanwhile the poor Mother's situation grew ever frightfuler from day to day; and it needed her extraordinary strength of religious faith to keep her from altogether sinking under the pains, sorrows and toils, which she had for so many weeks to bear all alone, with the help only of a hired maid. The news of such misery threw Schiller into the deepest grief. He saw only one way of sending comfort and help to his poor Mother, and immediately adopted it; writing to his eldest Sister in Meiningen, as follows : —

'Thou too wilt have heard, dearest Sister, that Luise has fallen seriously ill; and that our poor dear Mother is thereby robbed of all consolation. If Luise's case were to grow worse, or our Father's even, our poor Mother would be left entirely forsaken. Such misery would be unspeakable. Canst thou make it possible, think'st thou, that thy strength could accomplish such a thing? If so, at once make the journey thither. What it costs I will pay with joy. Reinwald might accompany thee; or, if he did not like that, come over to me here, where I would brotherlike take care of him.

'Consider, my dear Sister, that Parents, in such extremity of need, have the justest claim upon their children for help. O God, why am not I myself in such health as in my journey thither three years ago! Nothing should have hindered me from hastening to them; but that I have scarcely gone over the threshold for a year past makes me so weak that I either could not stand the journey, or should fall down into sickness myself in that afflicted house. Alas, I can do nothing for them but help with money; and, God knows, I do that with joy. Consider that our dear Mother, who has held up hitherto with an admirable courage, must at last break down under so many sorrows. I know thy childlike loving heart, I know the perfect fairness and equitable probity of my Brother-in-law. Both these facts will teach you better than I under the circumstances. Salute him cordially. — Thy faithful Brother,

'SCHILLER.'"

Christophine failed not to go, as we saw above. "From the time of her arrival there, no week passed without Schiller's writing home; and his Letters much contributed to strengthen and support the heavy-laden Mother. The assurance of being tenderly loved by such a Son was infinitely grateful to her; she considered him as a tried faithful friend, to whom one, without reluctance, yields his part in one's own sorrows. Schiller thus expressed himself on this matter in a Letter to Christophine of 9th May. 'The last Letter of my dear good Mother has deeply affected me. Ah, how much has this good Mother already undergone; and with what patience and courage has she borne it! How touching is it that she opened her heart to me; and what woe was mine that I cannot immediately comfort and soothe her! Hadst thou not gone, I could not have stayed here. The situation of our dear ones was horrible; so solitary, without help from loving friends, and as if forsaken by their two children, living far away! I dare not think of it. What did not our good Mother do for *her* Parents; and how greatly has she deserved the like from us! Thou wilt comfort her, dear Sister; and me thou wilt find heartily ready for all that thou canst propose to me. Salute our dear Parents in the tenderest way, and tell them that their Son feels their sorrows.'

"The excellent Christophine did her utmost in these days of sorrow. She comforted her Mother, and faithfully nursed her Father to his last breath; nay she saved him and the house, with great presence of mind, on a sudden inburst of French soldiers. Nor did she return to Meiningen till all tumult of affairs was past, and the Mother was again a little composed. And composure the Mother truly needed; for in a short space she had seen a hopeful Daughter and a faithful Husband laid in their graves; and by the death of her Husband a union severed which, originating in mutual affection, had for forty-seven years been blessed with the same mutual feeling. To all which in her position was now added the doubly pressing care about her future days. Here, however, the Son so dear to her interposed with loving readiness, and the tender manner natural to him : —

"'You, dear Mother,' he writes, 'must now choose wholly for yourself what your way of life is to be; and let there be,

I charge you, no care about me or others in your choice. Ask yourself where you would like best to live, — here with me, or with Christophine, or in our native country with Luise. Whithersoever your choice falls, there will we provide the means. For the present, of course, in the circumstances given, you would remain in Würtemberg a little while; and in that time all would be arranged. I think you might pass the winter months most easily at Leonberg [pleasant Village nearest to Solitüde]; and then with the Spring you would come with Luise to Meiningen; where, however, I would expressly advise that you had a household of your own. But of all this, more next time. I would insist upon your coming here to me, if I did not fear things would be too foreign and too unquiet for you. But were you once in Meiningen, we will find means enough to see each other, and to bring your dear Grandchildren to you. It were a great comfort, dearest Mother, at least to know you, for the first three or four weeks after Christophine's departure, among people of your acquaintance; as the sole company of our Luise would too much remind you of times that are gone. But should there be no Pension granted by the Duke, and the Sale of Furniture, &c. did not detain you too long, you might perhaps travel with both the Sisters to Meiningen; and there compose yourself in the new world so much the sooner. All that you need for a convenient life must and shall be yours, dear Mother. It shall be henceforth my care that no anxiety on that head be left you. After so many sorrows, the evening of your life must be rendered cheerful, or at least peaceful; and I hope you will still, in the bosom of your Children and Grandchildren, enjoy many a good day.' In conclusion, he bids her send him everything of Letters and MSS. which his dear Father left; hereby to fulfil his last wish; which also shall have its uses to his dear Mother.

"The Widow had a Pension granted by the Duke, of 200 gulden [near £20]; and therein a comfortable proof that official people recognized the worth of her late Husband, and held him in honor. She remained in her native country; and lived the next three years, according to her Son's counsel, with Luise in the little village of Leonberg, near to Solitüde, where

an arrangement had been made for her.   Here a certain Herr
Roos, a native of Würtemberg, had made some acquaintance
with her, in the winter 1797–8 ; to whom we owe the following sketch of portraiture. 'She was a still agreeable old person of sixty-five or six, whose lean wrinkly face still bespoke
cheerfulness and kindliness.   Her thin hair was all gray ; she
was of short [middle] stature, and her attitude slightly stoop-
ing; she had a pleasant tone of voice ; and her speech flowed
light and cheerful.   Her bearing generally showed native grace,
and practical acquaintance with social life.'

"Towards the end of 1799, there opened to the Mother a
new friendly outlook in the marriage of her Luise to the
young Parson, M. Frankh, in Clever-Sulzbach, a little town
near Heilbronn.   The rather as the worthy Son-in-law
would on no account have the Daughter separated from the
Mother." Error on Saupe's part.   The Mother Schiller continued to occupy her own house at Leonberg till near the
end of her life; she naturally made frequent little visits to
Clever-Sulzbach; and her death took place there.[1] "Shortly
before the marriage, Schiller wrote, heartily wishing Mother
and Sister happiness in this event.   It would be no small
satisfaction to his Sister, he said, that she could lodge and
wait upon her good dear Mother in a well-appointed house
of her own ; to his Mother also it must be a great comfort
to see her children all settled, and to live up again in a new
generation.

"Almost contemporary with the removal of the Son from
Jena to Weimar was the Mother's with her Daughter to
Clever-Sulzbach.   The peaceful silence which now environed
them in their rural abode had the most salutary influence
both on her temper of mind and on her health; all the more
as Daughter and Son-in-law vied with each other in respectful attention to her.   The considerable distance from her
Son, when at times it fell heavy on her, she forgot in reading his Letters; which were ever the unaltered expression
of the purest and truest child-love.   She forgot it too, as
often, over the immortal works out of which his powerful

---

[1] *Beziehungen*, p. 197 n.

spirit spoke to her. She lived to hear the name of Fried-rich Schiller celebrated over all Germany with reverent enthusiasm; and ennobled by the German People sooner and more gloriously than an Imperial Patent could do it. Truly a Mother that has had such joys in her Son is a happy one; and can and may say, 'Lord, now let me depart in peace; I have lived enough!'

"In the beginning of the year 1802, Schiller's Mother again fell ill. Her Daughter Luise hastened at once to Stuttgard, where she then chanced to be, and carried her home to Clever-Sulzbach, to be under her own nursing. So soon as Schiller heard of this, he wrote, in well-meant consideration of his Sister's frugal economies, to Dr. Hoven, a friend of his youth at Ludwigsburg; and empowered him to take his Mother over thither, under his own medical care: he, Schiller, would with pleasure pay all that was necessary for lodging and attendance. But the Mother stayed with her Daughter; wrote, however, in her last Letter to Schiller: 'Thy unwearied love and care for me God reward with thousand-fold love and blessings! Ah me! another such Son there is not in the world!' Schiller, in his continual anxiety about the dear Patient, had his chief solace in knowing her to be in such tender hands; and he wrote at once, withal, to his Sister: 'Thou wilt permit me also that on my side I try to do something to lighten these burdens for thee. I therefore make this agreement with my Bookseller Cotta that he shall furnish my dear Mother with the necessary money to make good, in a convenient way, the extra outlays which her illness requires.'

"Schiller's hope, supported by earlier experiences, that kind Nature would again help his Mother, did not find fulfilment. On the contrary, her case grew worse; she suffered for months the most violent pains; and was visibly travelling towards Death. Two days before her departure, she had the Medallion of her Son handed down to her from the wall; and pressed it to her heart; and, with tears, thanked God, who had given her such good children. On the 29th April, 1802, she passed away, in the 69th year of her age.

Schiller, from the tenor of the last news received, had given up all hope; and wrote, in presentiment of the bitter loss, to his Sister Frankh at Clever-Sulzbach:—

'Thy last letter, dearest Sister, leaves me without hope of our dear Mother. For a fortnight past I have looked with terror for the tidings of her departure; and the fact that thou hast not written in that time, is a ground of fear, not of comfort. Alas! under her late circumstances, life was no good to her more; a speedy and soft departure was the one thing that could be wished and prayed for. But write me, dear Sister, when thou hast recovered thyself a little from these mournful days. Write me minutely of her condition and her utterances in the last hours of her life. It comforts and composes me to busy myself with her, and to keep the dear image of my Mother living before me.

'And so they are both gone from us, our dear Parents; and we Three alone remain. Let us be all the nearer to each other, dear Sister; and believe always that thy Brother, though so far away from thee and thy Sister, carries you both warmly in his heart; and in all the accidents of this life will eagerly meet you with his brotherly love.

'But I can write no more to-day. Write me a few words soon. I embrace thee and thy dear Husband with my whole heart; and thank him again for all the love he has shown our departed Mother.

'Your true Brother,

'SCHILLER.'

"Soon after this Letter, he received from Frankh, his Brother-in-law, the confirmation of his sad anticipations. From his answer to Frankh we extract the following passage: 'May Heaven repay with rich interest the dear Departed One all that she has suffered in life, and done for her children! Of a truth she deserved to have loving children; for she was a good Daughter to her suffering necessitous Parents; and the childlike solicitude she always had for them well deserved the like from us. You, my dear Brother-in-law, have shared the assiduous care of my Sister for Her that is gone; and acquired thereby the justest claim upon my brotherly love. Alas, you had already given your spiritual support and filial service to my late Father, and taken on yourself the duties of his absent Son. How cordially I thank you! Never shall I think of my departed Mother without, at the same time, blessing the memory of him who alleviated so kindly the last days of her life.' He then signifies the wish to have, from the effects of his dear Mother, something that, without other worth, will remain a continual memorial of her. And was in effect heartily obliged to his Brother, who sent him a ring which had been hers. 'It is the most precious thing that he could have chosen for me,' writes he to Luise; 'and I will keep it as a sacred inheritance.' Painfully had it touched him, withal, that the day of his entering his new house at Weimar had been the death-day of his Mother. He noticed this singular coincidence, as if in mournful presentiment of his own early decease, as a singular concatenation of events by the hand of Destiny.

"A Tree and a plain stone Cross, with the greatly comprehensive short inscription, 'Here rests Schiller's Mother,' now mark her grave in Clever-Sulzbach Church-yard."

———◆———

III. THE SISTERS.

SAUPE has a separate Chapter on each of the three Sisters of Schiller; but most of what concerns them, especially in relation to their Brother, has been introduced incidentally above. Besides which, Saupe's flowing pages are too long for our space; so that instead of translating, henceforth, we shall have mainly to compile from Saupe and others, and faithfully abridge.

Christophine (born 4 Sept. 1757; married " June, 1786;"
died 31 August, 1847).[1]

Till Schiller's flight, in which what endless interest and industries Christophine had we have already seen, the young

[1] Here, from Schiller Senior himself (*Autobiography,* called " *Curriculum Vitæ*," in *Beziehungen,* pp. 15–18) is a List of his six Children; — the two that died so young we have marked in italics:

1. " ELISABETH CHRISTOPHINE FRIEDERICKE, born 4 September, 1757, at Marbach.

2. " JOHANN CHRISTOPH FRIEDRICH, born 10 November, 1759, at Marbach.

girls, — Christophine 25, Luise 16, Nanette a rosy little creature of 5, — had known no misfortune; nor, except Christophine's feelings on the death of the two little Sisters, years
ago, no heavy sorrow. At Solitüde, but for the general cloud
of anxiety and grief about their loved and gifted Brother and
his exile, their lives were of the peaceablest description : diligence in household business, sewing, spinning, contented punc-
tuality in all things; in leisure hours eager reading (or at times,
on Christophine's part, drawing and painting, in which she
attained considerable excellence), and, as choicest recreation,
walks amid the flourishing Nurseries, Tree-avenues, and fine
solid industries and forest achievements of Papa. Mention is
made of a Cavalry Regiment stationed at Solitüde; the young
officers of which, without society in that dull place, and with
no employment except parade, were considerably awake to the
comely Jungfers Schiller and their promenadings in those
pleasant woods : one Lieutenant of them (afterwards a Colonel,
"Obrist von Miller of Stuttgard") is said to have manifested
honorable aspirations and intentions towards Christophine, —
which, however, and all connection with whom or his comrades,
the rigorously prudent Father strictly forbade; his piously
obedient Daughters, Christophine it is rather thought with
some regret, immediately conforming. A Portrait of this Von
Miller, painted by Christophine, still exists, it would appear,
among the papers of the Schillers.[1]

The great transaction of her life, her marriage with Reinwald, Court Librarian of Meiningen, had its origin in 1783;
the fruit of that forced retreat of Schiller's to Bauerbach, and
of the eight months he spent there, under covert, anonymously
and in secret, as "Dr. Ritter," with Reinwald for his one friend
and adviser. Reinwald, who commanded the resources of an

---

3. "LUISE DOROTHEA KATHARINA, born 24 January, 1766, at Lorch.

4. "*Maria Charlotte, born 20 November, 1768, at Ludwigsburg : died 29 March,
1774; age 5 gone.*

5. "*Beata Friedericke, born 4 May, 1773, at Ludwigsburg : died 22 December,
same year.*

6. "CAROLINE CHRISTIANE, born 8 September, 1777, at Solitüde;" — (this
is she they call, in fond diminutive, *Nane* or *Nanette*).

[1] *Beziehungen*, p. 217 n.

excellent Library, and of a sound understanding, long seriously and painfully cultivated, was of essential use to Schiller; and is reckoned to be the first real guide or useful counsellor he ever had in regard to Literature. One of Christophine's Letters to her Brother, written at her Father's order, fell by accident on Reinwald's floor, and was read by him, — awakening in his over-clouded, heavy-laden mind a gleam of hope and aspiration. "This wise, prudent, loving-hearted and judicious young woman, of such clear and salutary principles of wisdom as to economics too, what a blessing she might be to me as Wife in this dark, lonely home of mine!" Upon which hint he spake; and Schiller, as we saw above, who loved him well, but knew him to be within a year or two of fifty, always ailing in health, taciturn, surly, melancholy, and miserably poor, was rebuked by Papa for thinking it questionable. We said, it came about all the same. Schiller had not yet left Mannheim for the second and last time, when, in 1784, Christophine paid him a visit, escorted thither by Reinwald; who had begged to have that honor allowed him; having been at Solitüde, and, either there or on his road to Mannheim, concluded his affair. Streicher, an eye-witness of this visit, says, "The healthy, cheerful and blooming Maiden had determined to share her future lot with a man whose small income and uncertain health seemed to promise little joy. Nevertheless her reasons were of so noble a sort, that she never repented, in times following, this sacrifice of her fancy to her understanding, and to a Husband of real worth."[1] They were married "June, 1786;" and for the next thirty, or indeed, in all, sixty years, Christophine lived in her dark new home at Meiningen; and never, except in that melancholy time of sickness, mortality and war, appears to have seen Native Land and Parents again.

What could have induced, in the calm and well-discerning Christophine, such a resolution, is by no means clear; Saupe, with hesitation, seems to assign a religious motive, "the desire of doing good." Had that abrupt and peremptory dismissal of Lieutenant Miller perhaps something to do with it? Prob-

[1] *Schwab*, p. 173, citing Streicher's words.

ably her Father's humor on the matter, at all times so anxious
and zealous to see his Daughters settled, had a chief effect.
It is certain, Christophine consulted her Parish Clergyman on
the affair; and got from him, as Saupe shows us, an affirmatory
or at least permissive response. Certain also that she summoned her own best insight of all kinds to the subject, and
settled it calmly and irrevocably with whatever faculty was
in her.

To the candid observer Reinwald's gloomy ways were not
without their excuse. Scarcely above once before this, in his
now longish life, had any gleam of joy or success shone on
him, to cheer the strenuous and never-abated struggle. His
father had been Tutor to the Prince of Meiningen, who became Duke afterwards, and always continued to hold him in
honor. Father's death had taken place in 1751, young Reinwald then in his fourteenth year. After passing with distinction his three years' curriculum at Jena, Reinwald returned
to Meiningen, expecting employment and preferment; — the
rather perhaps as his Mother's bit of property got much
ruined in the Seven-Years War then raging. Employment
Reinwald got, but of the meanest *Kanzlist* (Clerkship) kind;
and year after year, in spite of his merits, patient faithfulness
and undeniable talent, no preferment whatever. At length,
however, in 1762, the Duke, perhaps enlightened by experience
as to Reinwald, or by personal need of such a talent, did send
him as *Geheimer Kanzlist* (kind of Private Secretary) to
Vienna, with a view to have from him reports "about politics
and literary objects" there. This was an extremely enjoyable
position for the young man; but it lasted only till the Duke's
death, which followed within two years. Reinwald was then
immediately recalled by the new Duke (who, I think, had
rather been in controversy with his Predecessor), and thrown
back to nearly his old position; where, without any regard
had to his real talents and merits, he continued thirteen years,
under the title of *Consistorial Kanzlist;* and, with the mis-
erablest fraction of yearly pay, "carried on the slavish, spirit-
killing labors required of him." In 1776, — uncertain whether
as promotion or as mere abridgment of labor, — he was

placed in the Library as now; that is to say, had become *Sub*-Librarian, at a salary of about £15, with all the Library duties to do; an older and more favored gentleman, perhaps in lieu of pension, enjoying the Upper Office, and doing none of the work.

Under these continual pressures and discouragements poor Reinwald's heart had got hardened into mutinous indignation, and his health had broken down: so that, by this time, he was noted in his little world as a solitary, taciturn, morose and gloomy man; but greatly respected by the few who knew him better, as a clear-headed, true and faithful person, much distinguished by intellectual clearness and veracity, by solid scholarly acquirements and sterling worth of character. To bring a little help or cheerful alleviation to such a down-pressed man, if a wise and gentle Christophine could accomplish it, would surely be a bit of well-doing; but it was an extremely difficult one!

The marriage was childless; not, in the first, or in any times of it, to be called unhappy; but, as the weight of years was added, Christophine's problem grew ever more difficult. She was of a compassionate nature, and had a loving, patient and noble heart; prudent she was; the skilfulest and thriftiest of financiers; could well keep silence, too, and with a gentle stoicism endure much small unreason. Saupe says withal, "Nobody liked a laugh better, or could laugh more heartily than she, even in her extreme old age." — Christophine herself makes no complaint, on looking back upon her poor Reinwald, thirty years after all was over. Her final record of it is: "for twenty-nine years we lived contentedly together." But her rugged hypochondriac of a Husband, morbidly sensitive to the least interruption of his whims and habitudes, never absent from their one dim sitting-room, except on the days in which he had to attend at the Library, was in practice infinitely difficult to deal with; and seems to have kept her matchless qualities in continual exercise. He belonged to the class called in Germany *Stubengelehrten* (Closet Literary-men), who publish little or nothing that brings them profit, but are continually poring and studying. Study was the one consolation he had in life; and formed his continual employment to the end of his days. He was deep in various departments, Antiquarian, Philological, Historical; deep especially in Gothic philology, in which last he did what is reckoned a real feat, — he, Reinwald, though again it was another who got the reward. He had procured somewhere, "a Transcript of the famous Anglo-Saxon Poem *Heliand* (Saviour) from the Cotton Library in England," this he, with unwearied labor and to great perfection, had at last got ready for the press; Translation, Glossary, Original all in readiness; — but could find no Publisher, nobody that would print without a premium. Not to earn *less* than nothing by his labor, he sent the Work to the München Library; where, in after years, one Schmeller found it, and used it for an *editio princeps* of his own. *Sic vos non vobis;* heavy-laden Reinwald![1] —

To Reinwald himself Christophine's presence and presidency in his dim household were an infinite benefit, — though not much recognized by him, but accepted rather as a natural tribute due to unfortunate down-pressed worth, till towards the very end, when the singular merit of it began to dawn upon him, like the brightness of the Sun when it is setting. Poor man, he anxiously spent the last two weeks of his life in purchasing and settling about a neat little cottage for Christophine; where accordingly she passed her long widowhood, on stiller terms, though not on less beneficent and humbly beautiful, than her marriage had offered.

Christophine, by pious prudence, faith in Heaven, and in the good fruits of real goodness even on Earth, had greatly comforted the gloomy, disappointed, pain-stricken man; enlightened his darkness, and made his poverty noble. *Simplex munditiis* might have been her motto in all things. Her beautiful Letters to her Brother are full of cheerful, though also, it is true, sad enough, allusions to her difficulties with Reinwald, and partial successes. Poor soul, her hopes, too, are gently turned sometimes on a blessed future, which might still lie ahead: of her at last coming, as a Widow, to live with her

---

[1] *Schiller's Beziehungen* (where many of Christophine's *Letters*, beautiful all of them, are given).

Brother, in serene affection, like that of their childhood together; in a calm blessedness such as the world held no other for her! But gloomy Reinwald survived bright Schiller for above ten years; and she had thirty more of lone widowhood, under limited conditions, to spend after him, still in a noble, humbly-admirable, and even happy and contented manner. She was the flower of the Schiller Sisterhood, though all three are beautiful to us; and in poor Nane, there is even something of poetic, and tragically pathetic. For one blessing, Christophine "lived almost always in good health." Through life it may be said of her, she was helpful to all about her, never hindersome to any; and merited, and had, the universal esteem, from high and low, of those she had lived among. At Meiningen, 31st August, 1847, within a few days of her ninety-first year, without almost one day's sickness, a gentle stroke of apoplexy took her suddenly away, and so ended what may be called a *Secular* Saintlike existence, mournfully beautiful, wise and noble to all that had beheld it.

Nanette (born 8th September, 1777, died 23d March, 1796; age not yet 19).

Of Nanette we were told how, in 1792, she charmed her Brother and his Jena circle, by her recitations and her amiable enthusiastic nature; and how, next year, on Schiller's Swabian visit, his love of her grew to something of admiration, and practical hope of helping such a rich talent and noble heart into some clear development, — when, two years afterwards, death put, to the dear Nanette and his hopes about her, a cruel end. We are now to give the first budding out of those fine talents and tendencies of poor Nanette, and that is all the history the dear little Being has. Saupe proceeds: —

"Some two years after Schiller's flight, Nanette as a child of six or seven had, with her elder Sister Luise, witnessed the first representation of Schiller's *Kabale und Liebe* in the Stuttgard theatre. With great excitement, and breath held in, she had watched the rolling up of the curtain; and during the whole play no word escaped her lips; but the excited glance of her eyes, and her heightened color, from act to act, testified her intense emotion. The stormy applause with which her Brother's Play was received by the audience made an indelible impression on her.

" The Players, in particular, had shone before her as in a magic light; the splendor of which, in the course of years, rather increased than diminished. The child's bright fancy loved to linger on those never-to-be-forgotten people, by whom her Brother's Poem had been led into her sight and under-standing. The dawning thought, how glorious it might be to work such wonders herself, gradually settled, the more she read and heard of her dear Brother's poetic achievements, into the ardent but secret wish of being herself able to represent his Tragedies upon the stage. On her visit to Jena, and dur-ing her Brother's abode in Swabia, she was never more atten-tive than when Schiller spoke occasionally of the acting of his Pieces, or unfolded his opinion of the Player's Art.

" The wish of Nanette, secretly nourished in this manner, to be able, on the stage, which represents the world, to con-tribute to the glory of her Brother, seized her now after his return with such force and constancy, that Schiller's Sister-in-law, Caroline von Wolzogen, urged him to yield to the same ; to try his Sister's talent; and if it was really distinguished, to let her enter this longed-for career. Schiller had no love for the Player Profession ; but as, in his then influential con-nections in Weimar, he might steer clear of many a danger, he promised to think the thing over. And thus this kind and amiable protectress had the satisfaction of cheering Nanette's last months with the friendly prospect that her wishes might be fulfilled. — Schiller's hope, after a dialogue with Goethe on the subject, had risen to certainty, when with the liveliest sorrow he learnt that Nanette was ill of that contagious Hospital Fever, and, in a few days more, that she was gone forever." [1]

Beautiful Nanette; with such a softly glowing soul, and such a brief tragically beautiful little life ! Like a Daughter of the rosy-fingered Morn; her existence all a sun-gilt soft

[1] *Saupe*, pp. 150–155.

auroral cloud, and no sultry Day, with its dusts and disfigurements, permitted to follow. Father Schiller seems, in his rugged way, to have loved Nanette best of them all; in an embarrassed manner, we find him more than once recommending her to Schiller's help, and intimating what a glorious thing for her, were it a possible one, education might be. He followed her in few months to her long home; and, by his own direction, " was buried in the Churchyard at Gerlingen by her side."

Luise (born 24th January, 1766; married 20th October, 1799; died 14th September, 1836).

Of Luise's life too, except what was shown above, there need little be said. In the dismal pestilential days at Solitüde, while her Father lay dying, and poor Nanette caught the infection, Luise, with all her tender assiduities and household talent, was there; but, soon after Nanette's death, the fever seized her too; and she long lay dangerously ill in that forlorn household; still weak, but slowly recovering, when Christophine arrived.

The Father, a short while before his death, summoned to him that excellent young Clergyman, Frankh, who had been so unweariedly kind to them in this time of sickness when all neighbors feared to look in, To ask him what his intentions towards Luise were. It was in presence of the good old man that they made solemn promise to each other; and at Leonberg, where thenceforth the now widowed Mother's dwelling was, they were formally betrothed; and some two years after that were married.

Her Mother's death, so tenderly watched over, took place at their Parsonage at Clever-Sulzbach, as we saw above. Frankh, about two years after, was promoted to a better living, Möckmühl by name; and lived there, a well-doing and respected Parson, till his death, in 1834; which Luise's followed in September of the second year afterwards. Their marriage lasted thirty-five years. Luise had brought him three children; and seems to have been, in all respects, an excellent Wife. She was ingenious in intellectuals as well as economics; had a taste for poetry; a boundless enthusiasm for her Brother; seems to have been an anxious Mother, often ailing herself, but strenuously doing her best at all times.

A touching memorial of Luise is Schiller's last Letter to her, Letter of affectionate apology for long silence, — apology, and hope of doing better, — written only a few weeks before his own death. It is as follows : —

"WEIMAR, 27th March, 1805.

" Yes, it is a long time indeed, good dear Luise, since I have written to thee; but it was not for amusements that I forgot thee; it was because in this time I have had so many hard illnesses to suffer, which put me altogether out of my regular way; for many months I had lost all courage and cheerfulness, and given up all hope of my recovery. In such a humor one does not like to speak; and since then, on feeling myself again better, there was, after the long silence, a kind of embarrassment; and so it was still put off. But now, when I have been anew encouraged by thy sisterly love, I gladly join the thread again; and it shall, if God will, not again be broken.

"Thy dear Husband's promotion to Möckmühl, which I learned eight days ago from our Sister [Christophine], has given us great joy, not only because it so much improves your position, but also because it is so honorable a testimony for my dear Brother-in-law's deserts. May you feel yourselves right happy in these new relations, and right long enjoy them! We too are got thereby a few miles nearer you; and on a future journey to Franconia, which we are every year projecting, we may the more easily get over to you.

"How sorry am I, dear Sister, that thy health has suffered so much; and that thou wert again so unfortunate with thy confinement! Perhaps your new situation might permit you, this summer, to visit some tonic watering-place, which might do thee a great deal of good. —

"Of our Family here, my Wife will write thee more at large. Our Children, this winter, have all had chicken-pox; and poor little Emilie [a babe of four months] had much to suffer in the affair. Thank God, things are all come round with us again, and my own health too begins to confirm itself.

"A thousand times I embrace thee, dear Sister, and my dear Brother-in-law as well, whom I always wish from the heart to have more acquaintance with. Kiss thy Children in my name; may all go right happily with you, and much joy be in store! How would our dear Parents have rejoiced in your good fortune; and especially our dear Mother, had she been spared to see it! Adieu, dear Luise. With my whole soul,

"Thy faithful Brother,

"SCHILLER."

Schiller's tone and behavior to his Sisters is always beautifully human and brotherlike, as here. Full of affection, sincerity and the warmest truest desire to help and cheer. The noble loving Schiller; so mindful always of the lowly, from his own wildly dangerous and lofty path! He was never rich, poor rather always; but of a spirit royally munificent in these respects; never forgets the poor "birthdays" of his Sisters, whom one finds afterwards gratefully recognizing their "beautiful dress" or the like!—

Of date some six weeks after this Letter to Luise, let us take from Eye-witnesses one glimpse of Schiller's own deathbed. It is the eighth day of his illness; his last day but one in this world:—

"*Morning of 8th May*, 1805. — Schiller, on awakening from sleep, asked to see his youngest Child. The Baby" Emilie, spoken of above, "was brought. He turned his head round; took the little hand in his, and, with an inexpressible look of love and sorrow, gazed into the little face; then burst into bitter weeping, hid his face among the pillows; and made a sign to take the child away." — This little Emilie is now the Baroness von Gleichen, Co-editress with her Cousin Wolzogen of the clear and useful Book, *Beziehungen*, often quoted above.

It was to that same Cousin Wolzogen's Mother (Caroline von Wolzogen, Authoress of the Biography), and in the course of this same day, that Schiller made the memorable response, "Calmer, and calmer." — "Towards evening he asked to see the Sun once more. The curtain was opened; with bright eyes and face he gazed into the beautiful sunset. It was his last farewell to Nature.

"*Thursday, 9th May.* All the morning, his mind was wandering; he spoke incoherent words, mostly in Latin. About three in the afternoon, complete weakness came on; his breathing began to be interrupted. About four, he asked for naphtha, but the last syllable died on his tongue. He tried to write, but produced only three letters; in which, however, the character of his hand was still visible. Till towards six, no change. His Wife was kneeling at the bedside; he still pressed her offered hand. His Sister-in-law stood, with the Doctor, at the foot of the bed, and laid warm pillows on his feet, which were growing cold. There now darted, as it were, an electrical spasm over all his countenance; the head sank back; the profoundest repose transfigured his face. His features were as those of one softly sleeping," — wrapt in hard-won Victory and Peace forevermore! [1] —

[1] *Schwab*, p. 627, citing Voss, an eye-witness; and Caroline von Wolzogen herself.

APPENDIX.

No. 1. Page 27.

DANIEL SCHUBART.

THE enthusiastic discontent so manifest in the *Robbers* has by some been in part attributed to Schiller's intercourse with Schubart. This seems as wise as the hypothesis of Gray's Alderman, who, after half a century of turtle-soup, imputed the ruin of his health to eating two unripe grapes: "he felt them cold upon his stomach, the moment they were over'; he never got the better of them." Schiller, it appears, saw Schubart only once, and their conversation was not of a confidential kind. For any influence this interview could have produced upon the former, the latter could have merited no mention here: it is on other grounds that we refer to him. Schubart's history, not devoid of interest in itself, unfolds in a striking light the circumstances under which Schiller stood at present; and may serve to justify the violence of his alarms, which to the happy natives of our Island might otherwise appear pusillanimous and excessive. For these reasons we subjoin a sketch of it.

Schubart's character is not a new one in literature; nor is it strange that his life should have been unfortunate. A warm genial spirit; a glowing fancy, and a friendly heart; every faculty but diligence, and every virtue but "the understrapping virtue of discretion:" such is frequently the constitution of the poet; the natural result of it also has frequently been pointed out, and sufficiently bewailed. This man was one of the many who navigate the ocean of life with "more sail than ballast;" his voyage contradicted every rule of seamanship, and necessarily ended in a wreck.

Christian Friedrich Daniel Schubart was born at Obersontheim in Swabia, on the 26th of April, 1739. His father, a well-meaning soul, officiated there in the multiple capacity of schoolmaster, precentor, and curate; dignities which, with various mutations and improvements, he subsequently held in several successive villages of the same district. Daniel, from the first, was a thing of inconsistencies; his life proceeded as if by fits and starts. At school, for a while, he lay dormant: at the age of seven he could not read, and had acquired the reputation of a perfect dunce. But "all at once," says his biographer, "the rind which enclosed his spirit started asunder;" and Daniel became the prodigy of the school! His good father determined to make a learned man of him: he sent him at the age of fourteen to the Nördlingen Lyceum, and two years afterwards to a similar establishment at Nürnberg. Here Schubart began to flourish with all his natural luxuriance; read classical and domestic poets; spouted, speculated; wrote flowing songs; discôvered "a decided turn for music," and even composed tunes for the harpsichord! In short, he became an acknowledged *genius*: and his parents consented that he should go to Jena, and perform his *cursus* of Theology.

Schubart's purposes were not at all like the decrees of Fate: he set out towards Jena; and on arriving at Erlangen, resolved to proceed no farther, but perform his *cursus* where he was. For a time he studied well; but afterwards "tumultuously," that is, in violent fits, alternating with fits as violent of idleness and debauchery. He became a *Bursche* of the first water; drank and declaimed, rioted and ran in debt; till his parents, unable any longer to support such expenses, were glad to seize the first opening in his *cursus*, and recall him. He returned to them with a miud fevered by intemperance, and a constitution permanently injured; his heart burning with regret, and vanity, and love of pleasure; his head without habits of activity or principles of judgment, a whirlpool where fantasies and hallucinations and "fragments of science" were chaotically jumbled to and fro. But he could babble college-latin; and talk with a trenchant tone about the "revolutions of Philosophy." Such accomplishments procured him pardon from his parents: the precentorial spirit of his father was more than reconciled on discovering that Daniel could also preach and play upon the organ. The good old people still loved their prodigal, and would not cease to hope in him.

As a preacher Schubart was at first very popular; he imitated Cramer; but at the same time manifested first-rate pulpit talents of his own. These, however, he entirely neglected to improve: presuming on his gifts and their acceptance, he began to "play such fantastic tricks before high Heaven," as made his audience sink to yawning, or explode in downright laughter. He often preached extempore; once he preached in verse! His love of company and ease diverted him from study; his musical propensities diverted him still farther. He had special gifts as an organist; but to handle the concordance and to make " the heaving bellows learn to blow" were inconsistent things.

Yet withal it was impossible to hate poor Schubart, or even seriously to dislike him. A joyful, piping, guileless mortal, good nature, innocence of heart, and love of frolic beamed from every feature of his countenance ; he wished no ill to any son of Adam. He was musical and poetical, a maker and a singer of sweet songs; humorous also, speculative, discursive ; his speech, though aimless and redundant, glittered with the hues of fancy, and here and there with the keenest rays of intellect. He was vain, but had no touch of pride ; and the excellencies which he loved in himself, he acknowledged and as warmly loved in others. He was a man of few or no principles, but his nervous system was very good. Amid his chosen comrades, a jug of indifferent beer and a pipe of tobacco could change the earth into elysium for him, and make his brethren demi-gods. To look at his laughing eyes, and his effulgent honest face, you were tempted to forget that he was a perjured priest, that the world had duties for him which he was neglecting. Had life been all a May-game, Schubart was the best of men, and the wisest of philosophers.

Unluckily it was not : the voice of Duty had addressed him in vain ; but that of Want was more impressive. He left his father's house, and engaged himself as tutor in a family at Königsbronn. To teach the young idea how to shoot had few delights for Schubart : he soon gave up this place in favor of a younger brother ; and endeavored to subsist, for some time, by affording miscellaneous assistance to the clergy of the neighboring villages. Ere long, preferring even pedagogy to starvation, he again became a teacher. The bitter morsel was sweetened with a seasoning of music ; he was appointed not only schoolmaster but also organist of Geisslingen. A fit of diligence now seized him : his late difficulties had impressed him ; and the parson of the place, who subsequently married Schubart's sister, was friendly and skilful enough to turn the impression to account. Had poor Schubart always been in such hands, the epithet " poor " could never have belonged to him. In this little village-school he introduced some important reforms and improvements, and in consequence attracted several valuable scholars. Also for his own behoof, he studied honestly. His conduct here, if not irreprehensible, was at least very much amended. His marriage, in his twenty-fifth year, might have improved it still farther ; for his wife was a good, soft-hearted, amiable creature, who loved him with her whole heart, and would have died to serve him.

But new preferments awaited Schubart, and with them new temptations. His fame as a musician was deservedly extending : in time it reached Ludwigsburg, and the Grand Duke of Würtemberg himself heard Schubart spoken of! The schoolmaster of Geisslingen was, in 1768, promoted to be organist and band-director in this gay and pompous court. With a bounding heart, he tossed away his ferula, and hastened to the scene, where joys forevermore seemed calling on him. He plunged into the heart of business and amusement. Besides the music which he taught and played, publicly and privately, with great applause, he gave the military officers instruction in various branches of science; he talked and feasted; he indited songs and rhapsodies; he lectured on History and the Belles Lettres. All this was more than Schubart's head could stand. In a little time he fell in debt; took up with virtuosi; began to read Voltaire, and talk against religion in his drink. From the rank of genius, he was fast degenerating into that of profligate: his affairs grew more and more embarrassed; and he had no gift of putting any order in them. Prudence was not one of Schubart's virtues; the nearest approximation he could make to it was now and then a little touch of cunning. His wife still loved him; loved him with that perverseness of affection, which increases in the inverse ratio of its requital: she had long patiently endured his follies and neglect, happy if she could obtain a transient hour of kindness from him. But his endless course of riot, and the straits to which it had reduced their hapless family, at length overcame her spirits: she grew melancholy, almost broken-hearted; and her father took her home to him, with her children, from the spendthrift who had been her ruin. Schubart's course in Ludwigsburg was verging to its close; his extravagance increased, and debts pressed heavier and heavier on him: for some scandal with a young woman of the place, he was cast into prison; and let out of it, with an injunction forthwith to quit the dominions of the Grand Duke.

Forlorn and homeless, here then was Schubart footing the hard highway, with a staff in his hand, and one solitary *thaler* in his purse, not knowing whither he should go. At Heilbronn, the Bürgermeister Wachs permitted him to teach his Bürgermeisterinn the harpsichord; and Schubart did not die of hunger. For a space of time he wandered to and fro, with numerous impracticable plans; now talking for his victuals; now lecturing or teaching music; kind people now attracted to him by his genius and misfortunes, and anon repelled from him by the faults which had abased him. Once a gleam of court-preferment revisited his path: the Elector Palatine was made acquainted with his gifts, and sent for him to Schwetzingen to play before him. His playing gratified the Electoral ear; he would have been provided for, had he not in conversation with his Highness happened to express a rather free opinion of the Mannheim Academy, which at that time was his Highness's hobby. On the instant of this luckless oversight, the door of patronage was slammed in Schubart's face, and he stood solitary on the pavement as before.

One Count Schmettau took pity on him; offered him his purse and home; both of which the way-worn wanderer was happy to accept. At Schmettau's he fell in with Baron Leiden, the Bavarian envoy, who advised him to turn Catholic, and accompany the returning embassy to Munich. Schubart hesitated to become a renegade; but departed with his new patron, upon trial. In the way, he played before the Bishop of Würzburg; was rewarded by his Princely Reverence with gold as well as praise; and arrived under happy omens at Munich. Here for a while fortune seemed to smile on him again. The houses of the great were thrown open to him; he talked and played, and fared sumptuously every day. He took serious counsel with himself about the great Popish question; now inclining this way, now that: he was puzzling which to choose, when Chance entirely relieved him of the trouble. "A person of respectability" in Munich wrote to Würtemberg to make inquiries who or what this general favorite was; and received for answer, that the general favorite was a villain, and had been banished from Ludwigsburg for denying that there was a Holy Ghost! — Schubart was happy to evacuate Munich without tap of drum.

Once more upon the road without an aim, the wanderer turned to Augsburg, simply as the nearest city, and — set up a Newspaper! The *Deutsche Chronik* flourished in his hands; in a little while it had acquired a decided character for sprightliness and talent; in time it became the most widely circulated journal of the country. Schubart was again a prosperous man: his writings, stamped with the vigorous impress of his own genius, travelled over Europe; artists and men of letters gathered round him; he had money, he had fame; the rich and noble threw their parlors open to him, and listened with delight to his overflowing, many-colored conversation. He wrote paragraphs and poetry; he taught music and gave concerts; he set up a spouting establishment, recited newly published poems, read Klopstock's *Messias* to crowded and enraptured audiences. Schubart's evil genius seemed asleep, but Schubart himself awoke it. He had borne a grudge against the clergy, ever since his banishment from Ludwigsburg; and he now employed the facilities of his journal for giving vent to it. He criticised the priesthood of Augsburg; speculated on their selfishness and cant, and took every opportunity of turning them and their proceedings into ridicule. The Jesuits especially, whom he regarded as a fallen body, he treated with extreme freedom; exposing their deceptions, and holding up to public contumely certain quacks whom they patronized. The Jesuitic Beast was prostrate, but not dead : it had still strength enough to lend a dangerous kick to any one who came too near it. One evening an official person waited upon Schubart, and mentioned an *arrest* by virtue of a warrant from the Catholic Bürgermeister ! Schubart was obliged to go to prison. The heads of the Protestant party made an effort in his favor : they procured his liberty, but not without a stipulation that he should immediately depart from Augsburg. Schubart asked to know his crime ; but the Council answered him : " We have our reasons ; let that satisfy you : " and with this very moderate satisfaction he was forced to leave their city.

But Schubart was now grown an adept in banishment ; so trifling an event could not unhinge his equanimity. Driven out of Augsburg, the philosophic editor sought refuge in Ulm, where the publication of his journal had, for other reasons, already been appointed to take place. The *Deutsche Chronik* was as brilliant here as ever : it extended more and more through Germany ; " copies of it even came to London, Paris, Amsterdam, and Petersburg." Nor had its author's fortune altered much ; he had still the same employments, and remunerations, and extravagances ; the same sort of friends, the same sort of enemies. The latter were a little busier than formerly : they propagated scandals ; engraved caricatures, indited lampoons against him ; but this he thought a very small matter. A man that has been three or four times banished, and as often put in prison, and for many years on the point of starving, will not trouble himself much about a gross or two of pasquinades. Schubart had his wife and family again beside him, he had money also to support them ; so he sang and fiddled, talked and wrote, and " built the lofty rhyme," and cared no fig for any one.

But enemies, more fell than these, were lurking for the thoughtless Man of Paragraphs. The Jesuits had still their feline eyes upon him, and longed to have their talons in his flesh. They found a certain General Ried, who joined them on a quarrel of his own. This General Ried, the Austrian Agent at Ulm, had vowed inexpiable hatred against Schubart, it would seem, for a very slight cause indeed : once Schubart had engaged to play before him, and then finding that the harpsichord was out of order, had refused, flatly refused ! The General's elevated spirit called for vengeance on this impudent plebeian ; the Jesuits encouraged him ; and thus all lay in eager watch. An opportunity ere long occurred. One week in 1778, there appeared in Schubart's newspaper an Extract of a Letter from Vienna, stating that " the Empress Maria Theresa had been struck by apoplexy." On reading which, the General made instant application to his Ducal Highness, requesting that the publisher of this " atrocious libel" should be given up to him, and " sent to expiate his crime in Hungary," by imprisonment — for life. The Duke desired his gallant friend to be at ease, for that *he* had long had his own eye on this man, and would himself take charge of him. Accordingly, a few days afterwards, Herr von Scholl, Comptroller of the Convent of Blaubeuren, came to Schubart with a multitude of compliments, inviting him to dinner, " as there was a stranger wishing to be introduced to him." Schubart sprang into the *Schlitten* with this wolf in sheep's clothing, and away they drove to Blaubeuren. Arrived here, the honorable Herr von Scholl left him in a private room, and soon returned with a posse of official Majors and Amtmen, the chief of whom advanced to Schubart, and declared him — *an arrested man!* The hapless Schubart thought it was a jest; but alas here was no jesting! Schubart then said with a composure scarcely to be looked for, that " he hoped the Duke would not condemn him unheard." In this too he was deceived; the men of office made him mount a carriage with them, and set off without delay for Hohenasperg. The Duke himself was there with his Duchess, when these bloodhounds and their prey arrived : the princely couple gazed from a window as the group went past them, and a fellow-creature took his farewell look of sun and sky !

If hitherto the follies of this man have cast an air of farce upon his sufferings, even when in part unmerited, such sentiments must now give place to that of indignation at his cruel and cold-blooded persecutors. Schubart, who never had the heart to hurt a fly, and with all his indiscretions, had been no man's enemy but his own, was conducted to a narrow subterraneous dungeon, and left, without book or pen, or any sort of occupation or society, to chew the cud of bitter thought, and count the leaden months as they passed over him, and brought no mitigation of his misery. His Serene Transparency of Würtemberg, nay the heroic General himself, might have been satisfied, could they have seen him : physical squalor, combined with moral agony, were at work on Schubart; at the end of a year, he was grown so weak, that he could not stand except by leaning on the walls of his cell. A little while, and he bade fair to get beyond the reach of all his tyrants. This, however, was not what they wanted. The prisoner was removed to a wholesome upper room ; allowed the use of certain books, the sight of certain company, and had, at least, the privilege to think and breathe without obstruction. He was farther gratified by hearing that his wife and children had been treated kindly: the boys had been admitted to the Stuttgard school, where Schiller was now studying ; to their mother there had been assigned a pension of two hundred gulden. Charles of

Würtemberg was undoubtedly a weak and heartless man, but we know not that he was a savage one: in the punishment of Schubart, it is possible enough that he believed himself to be discharging an important duty to the world. The only subject of regret is, that any duty to the world, beyond the duty of existing inoffensively, should be committed to such hands; that men like Charles and Ried, endowed with so very small a fraction of the common faculties of manhood, should have the destiny of any living thing at their control.

Another mitigating circumstance in Schubart's lot was the character of his gaoler. This humane person had himself tasted the tender mercies of "paternal" government; he knew the nature of a dungeon better even than his prisoner. "For four years," we are told, "he had seen no human face; his scanty food had been lowered to him through a trap-door; neither chair nor table were allowed him, his cell was never swept, his beard and nails were left to grow, the humblest conveniences of civilized humanity were denied him!"[1] On this man affliction had produced its softening, not its hardening influence: he had grown religious, and merciful in heart; he studied to alleviate Schubart's hard fate by every means within his power. He spoke comfortingly to him; ministered to his infirmities, and, in spite of orders, lent him all his books. These, it is true, were only treatises on theosophy and mystical devotion; but they were the best he had; and to Schubart, in his first lonely dungeon, they afforded occupation and solace.

Human nature will accommodate itself to anything. The King of Pontus taught himself to eat poison: Schubart, cut out from intemperance and jollity, did not pine away in confinement and abstemiousness; he had lost Voltaire and gay company, he found delight in solitude and Jacob Böhm. Nature had been too good to him to let his misery in any case be unalloyed. The vague unguided ebullience of spirit, which had so often set the table in a roar, and made him the most fascinating of debauchees, was now mellowed into a cloudy enthusiasm, the sable of which was still copiously blended with rainbow colors. His brain had received a slight though incurable crack; there was a certain exasperation mixed with his unsettled fervor; but he was not wretched, often even not uncomfortable. His religion was not real; but it had reality enough for present purposes; he was at once a sceptic and a mystic, a true disciple of Böhm as well as of Voltaire. For afflicted, irresolute, imaginative men like Schubart, this is not a rare or altogether ineffectual resource: at the bottom of their minds they doubt or disbelieve, but

---

[1] And yet Mr. Fox is reported to have said: *There was one* FREE *Government on the Continent, and that one was — Würtemberg.* They had a parliament and " three estates " like the English. — So much for paper Constitutions !

their hearts exclaim against the slightest whisper of it; they dare not look into the fathomless abyss of Infidelity, so they cover it over with the dense and strangely-tinted smoke of Theosophy. Schubart henceforth now and then employed the phrases and figures of religion; but its principles had made no change in his theory of human duties: it was not food to strengthen the weakness of his spirit, but an opiate to stay its craving.

Schubart had still farther resources: like other great men in captivity, he set about composing the history of his life. It is true, he had no pens or paper; but this could not deter him. A fellow-prisoner, to whom, as he one day saw him pass by the grating of his window, he had communicated his desire, entered eagerly into the scheme: the two contrived to unfasten a stone in a wall that divided their apartments; when the prison-doors were bolted for the night, this volunteer amanuensis took his place, Schubart trailed his mattress to the friendly orifice, and there lay down, and dictated in whispers the record of his fitful story. These memoirs have been preserved; they were published and completed by a son of Schubart's: we have often wished to see them, but in vain.

By day, Schubart had liberty to speak with certain visitors. One of these, as we have said above, was Schiller. That Schubart, in their single interview, was pleased with the enthusiastic friendly boy, we could have conjectured, and he has himself informed us. "Excepting Schiller," said the veteran garreteer, in writing afterwards to Gleim, "I scarcely know of any German youth in whom the sacred spark of genius has mounted up within the soul like flame upon the altar of a Deity. We are fallen into the shameful times, when women bear rule over men; and make the toilet a tribunal before which the most gigantic minds must plead. Hence the stunted spirit of our poets; hence the dwarf products of their imagination; hence the frivolous witticism, the heartless sentiment, crippled and ricketed by soups, ragouts and sweetmeats, which you find in fashionable ballad-mongers."

Time and hours wear out the roughest day. The world began to feel an interest in Schubart, and to take some pity on him: his songs and poems were collected and published; their merit and their author's misery exhibited a shocking contrast. His Highness of Würtemberg at length condescended to remember that a mortal, of wants and feelings like his own, had been forced by him to spend, in sorrow and inaction, the third part of an ordinary lifetime; to waste, and worse than waste, ten years of precious time; time, of which not all the dukes and princes in the universe could give him back one instant. He commanded Schubart to be liberated; and the rejoicing Editor (unacquitted, unjudged, unaccused!) once more beheld the blue zenith and the full ring of the horizon.   He joined his wife at Stuttgard, and recommenced his newspaper.   The *Deutsche Chronik* was again popular ; the notoriety of its conductor made amends for the decay which critics did not fail to notice in his faculties.   Schubart's sufferings had in fact permanently injured him ; his mind was warped and weakened by theosophy and solitude ; bleak northern vapors often flitted over it, and chilled its tropical luxuriance.   Yet he wrote and rhymed ; discoursed on the corruption of the times, and on the means of their improvement.   He published the first portion of his Life, and often talked amazingly about the Wandering Jew, and a romance of which he was to form the subject.   The idea of making old *Joannes a temporibus*, the " Wandering," or as Schubart's countrymen denominate him, the " Eternal Jew," into a novel hero, was a mighty favorite with him.   In this antique cordwainer, as on a raft at anchor in the stream of time, he would survey the changes and wonders of two thousand years : the Roman and the Arab were to figure there ; the Crusader and the Circumnavigator, the Eremite of the Thebaid and the Pope of Rome.   Joannes himself, the Man existing out of Time and Space, Joannes the unresting and undying, was to be a deeply tragic personage.   Schubart warmed himself with this idea ; and talked about it in his cups, to the astonishment of simple souls.   He even wrote a certain rhapsody connected with it, which is published in his poems. But here he rested ; and the project of the Wandering Jew, which Goethe likewise meditated in his youth, is still unexecuted.   Goethe turned to other objects : and poor Schubart was surprised by death, in the midst of his schemes, on the 10th of October, 1791.

Of Schubart's character as a man, this record of his life leaves but a mean impression.   Unstable in his goings, without principle or plan, he flickered through existence like an *ignis-fatuus ;* now shooting into momentary gleams of happiness and generosity, now quenched in the mephitic marshes over which his zig-zag path conducted him.   He had many amiable qualities, but scarcely any moral worth.   From first to last his circumstances were against him ; his education was unfortunate, its fluctuating aimless wanderings enhanced its ill effects.   The thrall of the passing moment, he had no will ; the fine endowments of his heart were left to riot in chaotic turbulence, and their forces cancelled one another.   With better models and advisers, with more rigid habits, and a happier fortune, he might have been an admirable man : as it is, he is far from admirable.

The same defects have told with equal influence on his character as a writer.   Schubart had a quick sense of the beautiful, the moving, and the true; his nature was susceptible and fervid; he had a keen intellect, a fiery imagination; and his "iron memory" secured forever the various produce of so many gifts. But he had no diligence, no power of self-denial. His knowledge lay around him like the plunder of a sacked city. Like this too, it was squandered in pursuit of casual objects. He wrote in gusts; the *labor limæ et mora* was a thing he did not know. Yet his writings have great merit. His newspaper essays abound in happy illustration and brilliant careless thought. His songs, excluding those of a devotional and theosophic cast, are often full of nature, heartiness and true simplicity. "From his youth upwards," we are told, "he studied the true Old-German *Volkslied;* he watched the artisan on the street, the craftsman in his workshop, the soldier in his guardhouse, the maid by the spinning-wheel; and transferred the genuine spirit of primeval Germanism, which he found in them, to his own songs." Hence their popularity, which many of them still retain. "In his larger lyrical pieces," observes the same not injudicious critic, "we discover fearless singularity; wild imagination, dwelling rather on the grand and frightful than on the beautiful and soft; deep, but seldom long-continued feeling; at times far-darting thoughts, original images, stormy vehemence; and generally a glowing, self-created, figurative diction. He never wrote to show his art; but poured forth, from the inward call of his nature, the thought or feeling which happened for the hour to have dominion in him."[1]

Such were Schubart and his works and fortunes; the *disjecta membra* of a richly gifted but ill-starred and infatuated poet! The image of his persecutions added speed to Schiller's flight from Stuttgard; may the image of his wasted talents and ineffectual life add strength to our resolves of living otherwise!

———◆———

No. 2. Page 28.

LETTERS OF SCHILLER.

A FEW Extracts from Schiller's correspondence may be gratifying to some readers. The *Letters to Dalberg,* which constitute the chief part of it as yet before the public, are on the whole less interesting than might have been expected, if we did not recollect that the writer

---

[1] *Jördens Lexicon:* from which most part of the above details are taken. — There exists now a decidedly compact, intelligent and intelligible *Life of Schubart,* done, in three little volumes, by Strauss, some years ago. (*Note of* 1857.)

of them was still an inexperienced youth, overawed by his idea of
Dalberg, to whom he could communicate with freedom only on a
single topic; and besides oppressed with grievances, which of themselves would have weighed down his spirit, and prevented any frank
or cordial exposition of its feelings.

Of the Reichsfreiherr von Dalberg himself, this correspondence gives
us little information, and we have gleaned little elsewhere. He is
mentioned incidentally in almost every literary history connected with
his time; and generally as a mild gentlemanly person, a judicious
critic, and a warm lover of the arts and their cultivators. The following notice of his death is extracted from the *Conversations Lexicon*,
Part III. p. 12: "Died at Mannheim, on the 27th of December, 1806,
in his 85th year, Wolfgang Heribert, Reichsfreiherr von Dalberg;
knighted by the Emperor Leopold on his coronation at Frankfort.
A warm friend and patron of the arts and sciences; while the German
Society flourished at Mannheim, he was its first President; and the
theatre of that town, the school of the best actors in Germany, of
Iffland, Beck, Beil, and many others, owes to him its foundation, and
its maintenance throughout his long Intendancy, which he held till
1803. As a writer and a poet, he is no less favorably known. We
need only refer to his *Cora*, a musical drama, and to the *Mönch von
Carmel*." — These letters of Schiller were found among his papers at
his death; rescued from destruction by two of his executors, and published at Carlsruhe, in a small duodecimo, in the year 1819. There
is a verbose preface, but no note or comment, though some such aid is
now and then a little wanted.

The letters most worthy of our notice are those relating to the
exhibition of the *Robbers* on the Mannheim stage, and to Schiller's
consequent embarrassments and flight. From these, accordingly, the
most of our selections shall be taken. It is curious to see with what
timidity the intercourse on Schiller's part commences; and how this
awkward shyness gradually gives place to some degree of confidence,
as he becomes acquainted with his patron, or is called to treat of subjects where he feels that he himself has a dignity, and rights of his
own, forlorn and humble as he is. At first he never mentions Dalberg but with all his titles, some of which to our unceremonious ears
seem ludicrous enough. Thus in the full style of German reverence,
he avoids directly naming his correspondent, but uses the oblique designation of "your Excellency," or something equally exalted: and he
begins his two earliest letters with an address, which, literally interpreted, runs thus: "Empire-free, Highly-wellborn, Particularly-much-
to-be-venerated, Lord Privy Counsellor!" Such sounding phrases

make us smile: but they entirely depend on custom for their import,· and the smile which they excite is not by any means a philosophic one. It is but fair that in our version we omit them, or render them by some more grave equivalent.

The first letter is as follows:—

[No date.]

"The proud judgment, passed upon me in the flattering letter which I had the honor to receive from your Excellency, is enough to set the prudence of an Author on a very slippery eminence. The authority of the quarter it proceeds from, would almost communicate to that sentence the stamp of infallibility, if I could regard it as anything but a mere encouragement of my Muse. More than this a deep feeling of my weakness will not let me think it; but if my strength shall ever climb to the height of a masterpiece, I certainly shall have this warm approval of your Excellency alone to thank for it, and so will the world. For several years I have had the happiness to know you from the public papers: long ago the splendor of the Mannheim theatre attracted my attention. And, I confess, ever since I felt any touch of dramatic talent in myself, it has been among my darling projects some time or other to remove to Mannheim, the true temple of Thalia; a project, however, which my *closer* connection with Würtemberg might possibly impede.

"Your Excellency's very kind proposal on the subject of the *Robbers*, and such other pieces as I may produce in future, is infinitely precious to me; the maturing of it well deserves a narrower investigation of your Excellency's theatre, its special mode of management, its actors, the *non plus ultra* of its machinery; in a word, a full conception of it, such as I shall never get while my only scale of estimation is this Stuttgard theatre of ours, an establishment still in its minority. Unhappily my *economical* circumstances render it impossible for me to travel much; though I could travel now with the greater happiness and confidence, as I have still some *pregnant ideas* for the Mannheim theatre, which I could wish to have the honor of communicating to your Excellency. For the rest, I remain," &c.

From the second letter we learn that Schiller had engaged to *theatrilize* his original edition of the *Robbers*, and still wished much to be connected in some shape with Mannheim. The third explains itself:

"STUTTGARD, 6th October, 1781.

"Here then at last returns the luckless prodigal, the remodelled *Robbers!* I am sorry that I have not kept the time, appointed by myself; but a transitory glance at the number and extent of the changes I have made, will, I trust, be sufficient to excuse me. Add to this, that a contagious epidemic was at work in our military Hospital, which, of course, interfered very often with my *otia poetica*. After finishing my work, I may assure you I could engage with less effort of mind, and certainly with far more contentment, to compose a new piece, than to undergo the labor I have just concluded. The task was complicated and tedious. Here I had to correct an error, which naturally was rooted in the very groundwork of the play; there perhaps to sacrifice a beauty to the limits of the stage, the humor of the pit, the stupidity of the gallery, or some such sorrowful convention; and I need not tell you, that as in nature, so on the stage, an idea, an emotion, can have only one suitable expression, one proper tone. A single alteration in a trait of character may give a new tendency to the whole personage, and, consequently, to his actions, and the mechanism of the piece which depends on them.

" In the original, the Robbers are exhibited in strong contrast with each other ; and I dare maintain that it is difficult to draw half a dozen robbers in strong contrast, without in some of them offending the delicacy of the stage. In my first conception of the piece, I excluded the idea of its ever being represented in a theatre; hence came it that Franz was planned as a *reasoning* villain; a plan which, though it may content the thinking Reader, cannot fail to vex and weary the Spectator, who does not come to think, and who wants not philosophy, but action.

" In the new edition, I could not overturn this arrangement without breaking down the whole economy of the piece. Accordingly I can predict, with tolerable certainty, that Franz when he appears on the stage, will not play the part which he has played with the reader. And, at all events, the rushing stream of the action will hurry the spectator over all the finer shadings, and rob him of a third part of the whole character.

" Karl von Moor might chance to form an era on the stage; except a few speculations, which, however, work as indispensable colors in the general picture, he is all action, all visible life. Spiegelberg, Schweitzer, Hermann, are, in the strictest sense, personages for the stage; in a less degree, Amelia and the Father.

" Written and oral criticisms I have endeavored to turn to advantage. The alterations are important; certain scenes are altogether new. Of this number, are Hermann's counter-plots to undermine the schemes of Franz; his interview with that personage, which, in the first composition of the work, was entirely and very unhappily forgotten.

His interview with Amelia in the garden has been postponed to the succeeding act; and my friends tell me that I could have fixed upon no better act than this, no better time than a few moments prior to the meeting of Amelia with Moor. Franz is brought a little nearer human nature; but the mode of it is rather strange. A scene like his condemnation in the fifth act has never, to my knowledge, been exhibited on any stage; and the same may be said of the scene where Amelia is sacrificed by her lover.

"If the piece should be too long, it stands at the discretion of the manager to abbreviate the speculative parts of it, or here and there, without prejudice to the general impression, to omit them altogether. But in the *printing*, I use the freedom humbly to protest against the leaving out of anything. I had satisfactory reasons of my own for all that I allowed to pass; and my submission to the stage does not extend so far, that I can leave *holes* in my work, and mutilate the characters of men for the convenience of actors.

"In regard to the selection of costume, without wishing to prescribe any rules, I may be permitted to remark, that though in nature dress is unimportant, on the stage it is never so. In this particular, the taste of my Robber Moor will not be difficult to hit. He wears a plume; for this is mentioned expressly in the play, at the time when he abdicates his office. I have also given him a baton. His dress should always be noble without ornament, unstudied but not negligent.

"A young but excellent composer is working at a symphony for my unhappy prodigal: I know it will be masterly. So soon as it is finished, I shall take the liberty of offering it to you.

"I must also beg you to excuse the irregular state of the manuscript, the incorrectness of the penmanship. I was in haste to get the piece ready for you; hence the double sort of handwriting in it; hence also my forbearing to correct it. My copyist, according to the custom of all *reforming* caligraphers, I find, has wofully abused the spelling. To conclude, I recommend myself and my endeavors to the kindness of an honored judge. I am," &c.

"STUTTGARD, 12th December, 1781.

"With the change projected by your Excellency, in regard to the publishing of my play, I feel entirely contented, especially as I perceive that by this means two interests that had become very alien, are again made one, without, as I hope, any prejudice to the results and the success of my work. Your Excellency, however, touches on some other *very* weighty changes, which the piece has undergone from your hands; and these, in respect of myself, I feel to be so important, that I shall beg to explain my mind at some length regarding them. At the outset, then, I must honestly confess to you, I hold the projected transference of the action represented in my play to the epoch of the *Landfried*, and the Suppression of Private Wars, with the whole accompaniment which it gains by this new position, as infinitely better than mine; and must hold it so, although the whole piece should go to ruin thereby. Doubtless it is an objection, that in our enlightened century, with our watchful police and fixedness of statute, such a reckless gang should have arisen in the very bosom of the laws, and still more, have taken root and subsisted for years: doubtless the objection is well founded, and I have nothing to allege against it, but the license of Poetry to raise the probabilities of the real world to the rank of true, and its possibilities to the rank of probable.

"This excuse, it must be owned, is little adequate to the objection it opposes. But when I grant your Excellency so much (and I grant it honestly, and with complete conviction), what will follow? Simply that my play has got an ugly fault at its birth, which fault, if I may say so, it must carry with it to its grave, the fault being interwoven with its very nature, and not to be removed without destruction of the whole.

"In the first place, all my personages speak in a style too modern, too enlightened for that ancient time. The dialect is not the right one. That simplicity so vividly presented to us by the author of *Götz von Berlichingen*, is altogether wanting. Many long tirades, touches great and small, nay entire characters, are taken from the aspect of the present world, and would not answer for the age of Maximilian. In a word, this change would reduce the piece into something like a certain woodcut which I remember meeting with in an edition of Virgil. The Trojans wore hussar boots, and King Agamemnon had a pair of pistols in his belt. I should commit a *crime* against the age of Maximilian, to avoid an *error* against the age of Frederick the Second.

"Again, my whole episode of Amelia's love would make a frightful contrast with the simple chivalry attachment of that period. Amelia would, at all hazards, need to be remoulded into a chivalry maiden; and I need not tell you that this character, and the sort of love which reigns in my work, are so deeply and broadly tinted into the whole picture of the Robber Moor, nay, into the whole piece, that every part of the delineation would require to be repainted, before those tints could be removed. So likewise is it with the character of Franz, that speculative, metaphysico-refining knave.

"In a word, I think I may affirm, that this projected transposition of my work, which, prior to the commencement, would have lent it the highest splendor and completeness, could not fail now, when the piece is planned and finished, to change it into a defective *quodlibet*, a crow with peacock's feathers.

"Your Excellency will forgive a father this earnest pleading in behalf of his son. These are but words, and in the long-run every theatre can make of any piece what they think proper; the author must content himself. In the present case, he looks upon it as a happiness that he has fallen into such hands. With Herr Schwann, however, I will make it a condition that, at least, he *print* the piece according to the first plan. In the theatre I pretend to no vote whatever.

"That other change relating to Amelia's death was perhaps even more interesting to me. Believe me, your Excellency, this was the portion of my play which cost me the greatest effort and deliberation, of all which the result was nothing else than this, that Moor *must* kill his Amelia, and that the action is even a *positive beauty*, in his character; on the one hand painting the ardent lover, on the other the Bandit Captain, with the liveliest colors. But the vindication of this part is not to be exhausted in a single letter. For the rest, the few words which you propose to substitute in place of this scene, are truly exquisite, and altogether worthy of the situation. I should be proud of having written them.

"As Herr Schwann informs me that the piece, with the music and indispensably necessary pauses, will last about five hours (too long for any piece!), a second curtailment of it will be called for. I should not wish that any but myself undertook this task, and I myself, *without the sight of a rehearsal, or of the first representation*, cannot undertake it.

"If it were possible that your Excellency could fix the general rehearsal of the piece some time between the twentieth and the thirtieth of this month, and make good to me the main expenses of a journey to you, I should hope, in some few days, I might unite the interest of the stage with my own, and give the piece that proper rounding-off, which, without an actual view of the representation, cannot well be given it. On this point, may I request the favor of your Excellency's decision soon, that I may be prepared for the event.

"Herr Schwann writes me that a Baron von Gemmingen has given himself the trouble and done me the honor to read my piece. This Herr von Gemmingen, I also hear, is author of the *Deutsche Hausvater*. I long to have the honor of assuring him that I liked his *Hausvater* uncommonly, and admired in it the traces of a most accomplished man and

writer.   But what does the author of the *Deutsche Hausvater* care about
the babble of a young apprentice ?   If I should ever have the honor of
meeting Dalberg at Mannheim, and testifying the affection and reverence I bear him, I will then also press into the arms of that other, and
tell him how dear to me such souls are as Dalberg and Gemmingen.

"Your thought about the small Advertisement, before our production
of the piece, I exceedingly approve of ; along with this I have enclosed
a sketch of one.   For the rest, I have the honor, with perfect respect,
to be always," &c.

This is the enclosed scheme of an Advertisement ; which was afterwards adopted : —

"THE ROBBERS,

"A PLAY.

"THE picture of a great, misguided soul, furnished with every gift
for excellence, and lost in spite of all its gifts : unchecked ardor and bad
companionship contaminate his heart ; hurry him from vice to vice, till
at last he stands at the head of a gang of murderers, heaps horror upon
horror, plunges from abyss to abyss into all the depths of desperation.
Great and majestic in misfortune ; and by misfortune improved, led back
to virtue.   Such a man in the Robber Moor you shall bewail and hate,
abhor and love.   A hypocritical, malicious deceiver, you shall likewise
see unmasked, and blown to pieces in his own mines.   A feeble, fond,
and too indulgent father.   The sorrows of enthusiastic love, and the tor-
ture of ungoverned passion.   Here also, not without abhorrence, you
shall cast a look into the interior economy of vice, and from the stage be
taught how all the gilding of fortune cannot kill the inward worm ; how
terror, anguish, remorse, and despair follow close upon the heels of the
wicked.   Let the spectator weep to-day before our scene, and shudder,
and learn to bend his passions under the laws of reason and religion.
Let the youth behold with affright the end of unbridled extravagance ;
nor let the man depart from our theatre, without a feeling that Providence makes even villains instruments of His purposes and judgments,
and can marvellously unravel the most intricate perplexities of fate."

Whatever reverence Schiller entertained for Dalberg as a critic and a
patron, and however ready to adopt his alterations when they seemed
judicious, it is plain, from various passages of these extracts, that in regard
to writing, he had also firm persuasions of his own, and conscientiousness
enough to adhere to them while they continued such.   In regard to the

conducting of his life, his views as yet were far less clear. The following fragments serve to trace him from the first exhibition of his play at Mannheim to his flight from Stuttgard : —

"STUTTGARD, 17th January, 1782.

"I here in writing repeat my warmest thanks for the courtesies received from your Excellency, for your attention to my slender efforts, for the dignity and splendor you bestowed upon my piece, for all your Excellency did to exalt its little merits and hide its weaknesses by the greatest outlay of theatric art. The shortness of my stay at Mannheim would not allow me to go into details respecting the play or its representation; and as I could not say all, my time being meted out to me so sparingly, I thought it better to say absolutely nothing. I observed much, I learned much; and I believe, if Germany shall ever find in me a true dramatic poet, I must reckon the date of my commencement from the past week." . . .

"STUTTGARD, 24th May, 1782.

. . . "My impatient wish to see the piece played a second time, and the absence of my Sovereign favoring that purpose, have induced me, with some ladies and male friends as full of curiosity respecting Dalberg's theatre and *Robbers* as myself, to undertake a little journey to Mannheim, which we are to set about to-morrow. As this is the principal aim of our journey, and to me a more perfect enjoyment of my play is an exceedingly important object, especially since this would put it in my power to set about *Fiesco* under better auspices, I make it my earnest request of your Excellency, if possible, to procure me this enjoyment on Tuesday the 28th current." . . .

"STUTTGARD, 4th June, 1782.

"The satisfaction I enjoyed at Mannheim in such copious fulness, I have paid, since my return, by this epidemical disorder, which has made me till to-day entirely unfit to thank your Excellency for so much regard and kindness. And yet I am forced almost to repent the happiest journey of my life; for by a truly mortifying contrast of Mannheim with my native country, it has pained me so much, that Stuttgard and all Swabian scenes are become intolerable to me. Unhappier than I am can no one be. I have feeling enough of my bad condition, perhaps also feeling enough of my meriting a better; and in both points of view but *one* prospect of relief.

"May I dare to cast myself into your arms, my generous benefactor? I know how soon your noble heart inflames when sympathy and humanity appeal to it; I know how strong your courage is to undertake a noble action, and how warm your zeal to finish it. My new friends in Mannheim, whose respect for you is boundless, told me this: but their assurance was not necessary; I myself in that hour of your time, which I had the happiness exclusively to enjoy, read in your countenance far more than they had told me. It is this which makes me bold to *give* myself without reserve to you, to put my whole fate into your hands, and look to you for the happiness of my life. As yet I am little or nothing. In this Arctic Zone of taste, I shall never grow to anything, unless happier stars and a *Grecian climate* warm me into genuine poetry. Need I say more, to expect from Dalberg all support?

" Your Excellency gave me every hope to this effect; the squeeze of the hand that sealed your promise, I shall forever feel. If your Excellency will adopt the two or three hints I have subjoined, and use them in a letter to the Duke, I have no very great misgivings as to the result.

" And now with a burning heart, I repeat the request, the soul of all this letter. Could you look into the interior of my soul, could you see what feelings agitate it, could I paint to you in proper colors how my spirit strains against the grievances of my condition, you would not, I know you would not, delay one hour the aid which an application from you to the Duke might procure me.

" Again I throw myself into your arms, and wish nothing more than soon, very soon, to have it in my power to show by personal exertions in your service, the reverence with which I could devote to you myself and all that I am."

The " hints " above alluded to, are given in a separate enclosure, the main part of which is this : —

" I earnestly desire that you could secure my union with the Mannheim Theatre for a specified period (which at your request might be lengthened), at the end of which I might again belong to the Duke. It will thus have the air rather of an excursion than a final abdication of my country, and will not strike them so ungraciously. In this case, however, it would be useful to suggest that means of practising and studying medicine might be afforded me at Mannheim. This will be peculiarly necessary, lest they sham, and higgle about letting me away."

———

" STUTTGARD, 15th July, 1782.

" My long silence must have almost drawn upon me the reproach of folly from your Excellency, especially as I have not only delayed answering your last kind letter, but also retained the two books by me. All this was occasioned by a harassing affair which I have had to do with here. Your Excellency will doubtless be surprised when you learn that, for my last journey to you, I have been confined a fortnight under arrest. Everything was punctually communicated to the Duke. On this matter I have had an interview with him.

"If your Excellency think my prospects of coming to you anywise attainable, my only prayer is to *accelerate the fulfilment of them.* The reason why I now wish this with double earnestness, is one which I dare trust no whisper of to paper. This alone I can declare for certain, that within a month or two, if I have not the happiness of being with you, there will remain no further hope of my ever being there. Ere that time, I shall be forced to take a *step*, which will render it impossible for me to stay at Mannheim." . . .

The next two extracts are from letters to another correspondent. Doering quotes them without name or date: their purport sufficiently points out their place.

"I must haste to get away from this: in the end they might find me an apartment in the Hohenasperg, as they have found the honest and ill-fated Schubart. They talk of better culture that I need. It is possible enough, they might cultivate me differently in Hohenasperg : but I had rather try to make shift with what culture I have got, or may still get, by my unassisted efforts. This at least I owe to no one but my own free choice, and volition that disdains constraint."

"In regard to those affairs, concerning which they wish to put my spirit under wardship, I have long reckoned my minority to be concluded. The best of it is, that one can cast away such clumsy manacles : me at least they shall not fetter."

[No date.]

"Your Excellency will have learned from my friends at Mannheim, what the history of my affairs was up to your arrival, which unhappily I could not wait for. When I tell you *that I am flying my country*, I have painted my whole fortune. But the worst is yet behind. I have not the necessary *means* of setting my mishap at defiance. For the sake of safety, I had to withdraw from Stuttgard with the utmost speed, at the time of the Prince's arrival. Thus were my economical arrangements suddenly snapped asunder: I could not even pay my debts. My hopes had been set on a removal to Mannheim; there I trusted, by your Excellency's assistance, that my new play might not only have cleared me of debt, but have permanently put me into better circumstances. All this was frustrated by the necessity for hastening my removal. I went empty away; empty in purse and hope. I blush at being forced to make such disclosures to you; though I know they do not disgrace me. Sad enough for me to see realized in myself the hateful saying, that mental growth and full stature are things denied to every Swabian!

"If my former conduct, if all that your Excellency knows of my character, inspires you with confidence in my love of honor, permit me frankly to ask your assistance. Pressingly as I now need the profit I expect from my *Fiesco*, it will be impossible for me to have the piece in readiness before three weeks: my heart was oppressed; the feeling of my own situation drove me back from my poetic dreams. But if at the specified period, I could make the play not only *ready*, but, as I also hope, *worthy*, I take courage from that persuasion, respectfully to ask that your Excellency would be so obliging as *advance* for me the price that will then become due. I need it now, perhaps more than I shall ever do again throughout my life. I had near 200 florins of debt in Stuttgard, which I could not pay. I may confess to you, that this gives me more uneasiness than anything about my future destiny. I shall have no rest till I am free on *that* side.

"In eight days, too, my travelling purse will be exhausted. It is yet utterly impossible for me to labor with my mind. In my hand, therefore, are at present no resources.

"My actual situation being clear enough from what I have already said, I hold it needless to afflict your Excellency with any *importuning picture* of my want. Speedy aid is all that I can now think of or wish. Herr Meyer has been requested to communicate your Excellency's resolution to me, and to save you from the task of writing to me in person at all. With peculiar respect, I call myself," &c.

It is pleasing to record that the humble aid so earnestly and modestly solicited by Schiller, was afforded him; and that he never forgot to love the man who had afforded it; who had assisted him, when assistance was of such essential value. In the first fervor of his gratitude, for this and other favors, the poet warmly declared that "he owed all, all to Dalberg;" and in a state of society where Patronage, as Miss Edgeworth has observed, directly the antipodes of Mercy, is in general "twice cursed," cursing him that gives and him that takes, it says not a little for the character both of the obliged and the obliger in the present instance, that neither of them ever ceased to remember their connection with pleasure. Schiller's first play had been introduced to the Stage by Dalberg, and his last was dedicated to him.[1] The venerable critic, in his eighty-third year, must have received with a calm joy the tragedy of *Tell*, accompanied by an address so full of kindness and respect: it must have gratified him to think that the youth who was once his, and had now become the world's, could, after long experience, still say of him,

> "And fearlessly to thee may *Tell* be shown,
> For every noble feeling is thy own."

Except this early correspondence, very few of Schiller's letters have been given to the world.[2] In Doering's Appendix, we have found one written six years after the poet's voluntary exile, and agreeably contrasted in its purport with the agitation and despondency of that unhappy period. We translate it for the sake of those who, along with us, regret that while the world is deluged with insipid correspondences, and "pictures of mind" that were not worth drawing, the correspondence of a man who never wrote unwisely should lie mouldering in private repositories, ere long to be irretrievably destroyed; that the "picture of a mind" who was among the conscript fathers of the human race should still be

---

[1] It clearly appears I am wrong here; I have confounded the Freiherr Wolfgang Heribert von Dalberg, Director of the Mannheim Theatre, with Archduke and *Fürst Primas* Karl Theodor Dalberg, his younger Brother, — a man justly eminent in the Politico-Ecclesiastical world of his time, and still more distinguished for his patronage of letters, and other benefactions to his country, than the Freiherr was. Neither is the play of *Tell* "dedicated" to him, as stated in the text; there is merely a copy presented, with some verses by the Author inscribed in it; at which time Karl Theodor was in his *sixtieth* year. A man of conspicuous station, of wide activity, and high influence and esteem in Germany. He was the personal friend of Herder, Goethe, Schiller, Wieland; by Napoleon he was made *Fürst Primas*, Prince Primate of the Confederation of the Rhine, being already Archbishop, Elector of Mentz, &c. The good and brave deeds he did in his time appear to have been many, public and private. Pensions to deserving men of letters were among the number: Zacharias Werner, I remember, had a pension from him, — and still more to the purpose, Jean Paul. He died in 1817. There was a third Brother also memorable for his encouragement of Letters and Arts. "*Ist kein Dalberg da*, Is there no Dalberg here?" the Herald cries on a certain occasion. (See *Conv. Lexicon*, b. iii.)
To Sir Edward Bulwer, in his *Sketch of the Life of Schiller* (p. c.), I am indebted for very kindly pointing out this error; as well as for much other satisfaction derived from that work. (*Note of* 1845.)
[2] There have since been copious contributions: *Correspondence with Goethe, Correspondence with Madam von Wollzogen*, and perhaps others which I have not seen. (*Note of* 1845.)

left so vague and dim. This letter is addressed to Schwann, during Schiller's first residence in Weimar: it has already been referred to in the Text.

<hr>

"WEIMAR, 2d May, 1788.

"You apologize for your long silence to spare *me* the pain of an apology. I feel this kindness, and thank you for it. You do not impute my silence to decay of friendship; a proof that you have read my heart more justly than my evil conscience allowed me to hope. Continue to believe that the memory of you lives ineffaceably in my mind, and needs not to be brightened up by the routine of visits, or letters of assurance. So no more of this.

"The peace and calmness of existence which breathes throughout your letter, gives me joy; I who am yet drifting to and fro between wind and waves, am forced to envy you that uniformity, that health of soul and body. To me also in time it will be granted, as a recompense for labors I have yet to undergo.

"I have now been in Weimar nearly three quarters of a year: after finishing my *Carlos*, I at last accomplished this long-projected journey. To speak honestly, I cannot say but that I am exceedingly contented with the place; and my reasons are not difficult to see.

"The utmost political tranquillity and freedom, a very tolerable disposition in the people, little constraint in social intercourse, a select circle of interesting persons and thinking heads, the respect paid to literary diligence: add to this the unexpensiveness to me of such a town as Weimar. Why should I not be satisfied?

"With Wieland I am pretty intimate, and to him I must attribute no small influence on my present happiness; for I like him, and have reason to believe that he likes me in return. My intercourse with Herder is more limited, though I esteem him highly as a writer and a man. It is the caprice of chance alone which causes this; for we opened our acquaintance under happy enough omens. Besides, I have not always time to act according to my likings. With Bode no one can be very friendly. I know not whether you think here as I do. Goethe is still but *expected* out of Italy. The Duchess Dowager is a lady of sense and talent, in whose society one does not feel constrained.

"I thank you for your tidings of the fate of *Carlos* on your stage. To speak candidly, my hopes of its success on any stage were not high; and I know my reasons. It is but fair that the Goddess of the Theatre avenge herself on me, for the little gallantry with which I was inspired in writing. In the mean time, though *Carlos* prove a never so decided failure on the stage, I engage for it, our public shall see it ten times acted, before they understand and fully estimate the merit that should counterbalance it defects. When one has seen the beauty of a work, and not till then, I think one is entitled to pronounce on its deformity. I hear, however, that the second representation succeeded better than the first. This arises either from the changes made upon the piece by Dalberg, or from the fact, that on a second view, the public comprehended certain things, which on a first, they — did not comprehend.

"For the rest, no one can be more satisfied than I am that *Carlos*, from causes honorable as well as causes dishonorable to it, is no speculation for the stage. Its very length were enough to banish it. Nor was it out of confidence or self-love that I forced the piece on such a trial; perhaps out of self-interest rather. If in the affair my vanity played any part, it was in this, that I thought the work had solid stuff in it sufficient to outweigh its sorry fortune on the boards.

"The present of your portrait gives me true pleasure. I think it a striking likeness; that of Schubart a little less so, though this opinion may proceed from my faulty memory as much as from the faultiness of Lobauer's drawing. The engraver merits all attention and encouragement; what I can do for the extension of his good repute shall not be wanting.

"To your dear children present my warmest love. At Wieland's I hear much and often of *your eldest daughter;* there in a few days she has won no little estimation and affection. Do I still hold any place in her remembrance? Indeed, I ought to blush, that by my long silence I so ill deserve it.

"That you are going to my dear native country, and will not pass my Father without seeing him, was most welcome news to me. The Swabians are a good people; this I more and more discover, the more I grow acquainted with the other provinces of Germany. To my family you will be cordially welcome. Will you take a pack of compliments from me to them? Salute my Father in my name; to my Mother and my Sisters *your daughter* will take my kiss."

"And with these hearty words," as Doering says, "we shall conclude this paper."

No. 3. Page 96.

FRIENDSHIP WITH GOETHE.

THE history of Schiller's first intercourse with Goethe has been recorded by the latter in a paper published a few years ago in the *Morphologie*, a periodical work, which we believe he still occasionally continues, or purposes to continue. The paper is entitled *Happy Incident ;* and may be found in Part I. Volume 1 (pp. 90–96) of the work referred to. The introductory portion of it we have inserted in the text at page 91 ; the remainder, relating to certain scientific matters, and anticipating some facts of our narrative, we judged it better to reserve for the Appendix. After mentioning the publication of *Don Carlos*, and adding that " each continued to go on his way apart," he proceeds : —

" His Essay on *Grace and Dignity* was yet less of a kind to reconcile me. The Philosophy of Kant, which exalts the dignity of mind so highly, while appearing to restrict it, Schiller had joyfully embraced : it unfolded the extraordinary qualities which Nature had implanted in him ; and in the lively feeling of freedom and self-direction, he showed himself unthankful to the Great Mother, who surely had not acted like a stepdame towards him. Instead of viewing her as self-subsisting, as producing with a living force, and according to appointed laws, alike the highest and the lowest of her works, he took her up under the aspect of some empirical native qualities of the human mind. Certain harsh passages I could even directly apply to myself : they exhibited my confession of faith in a false light ; and I felt that if written without particular attention to me, they were still worse ; for in that case, the vast chasm which lay between us gaped but so much the more distinctly.

" There was no union to be dreamed of. Even the mild persuasion of Dalberg, who valued Schiller as he ought, was fruitless : indeed the reasons I set forth against any project of a union were difficult to contradict. No one could deny that between two spiritual antipodes there was more intervening than a simple diameter of the sphere : antipodes of that sort act as a sort of poles, and so can never coalesce. But that some relation may exist between them will appear from what follows.

" Schiller went to live at Jena, where I still continued unacquainted with him. About this time Batsch had set in motion a Society for Natural History, aided by some handsome collections, and an extensive apparatus. I used to attend their periodical meetings: one day I found Schiller there; we happened to go out together; some discourse arose between us. He appeared to take an interest in what had been exhibited; but observed, with great acuteness and good sense, and much to my satisfaction, that such a disconnected way of treating Nature was by no means grateful to the exoteric, who desired to penetrate her mysteries.

" I answered, that perhaps the initiated themselves were never rightly at their ease in it, and that there surely was another way of representing Nature, not separated and disunited, but active and alive, and expanding from the whole into the parts. On this point he requested explanations, but did not hide his doubts; he would not allow that such a mode, as I was recommending, had been already pointed out by experiment.

" We reached his house; the talk induced me to go in. I then expounded to him with as much vivacity as possible, the *Metamorphosis of Plants*,[1] drawing out on paper, with many characteristic strokes, a symbolic Plant for him, as I proceeded. He heard and saw all this with much interest and distinct comprehension; but when I had done, he shook his head and said: 'This is no experiment, this is an idea.' I stopped with some degree of irritation; for the point which separated us was most luminously marked by this expression. The opinions in *Dignity and Grace* again occurred to me; the old grudge was just awakening; but I smothered it, and merely said: 'I was happy to find that I had got ideas without knowing it, nay that I saw them before my eyes.'

" Schiller had much more prudence and dexterity of management than I: he was also thinking of his periodical the *Horen*, about this time, and of course rather wished to attract than repel me. Accordingly he answered me like an accomplished Kantito; and as my stiff-necked Realism gave occasion to many contradictions, much battling took place between us, and at last a truce, in which neither party would consent to yield the victory, but each held himself invincible. Positions like the following grieved me to the very soul: *How can there ever be an experiment that shall correspond with an idea? The specific quality of an idea is, that no experiment can reach it or agree with it.*

---

[1] A curious physiologico-botanical theory by Goethe, which appears to be entirely unknown in this country; though several eminent continental botanists have noticed it with commendation. It is explained at considerable length in this same *Morphologie*.

Yet if he held as an idea the same thing which I looked upon as an experiment, there must certainly, I thought, be some community between us, some ground whereon both of us might meet! The first step was now taken; Schiller's attractive power was great, he held all firmly to him that came within his reach: I expressed an interest in his purposes, and promised to give out in the *Horen* many notions that were lying in my head; his wife, whom I had loved and valued since her childhood, did her part to strengthen our reciprocal intelligence; all friends on both sides rejoiced in it; and thus by means of that mighty and interminable controversy between *object* and *subject,* we two concluded an alliance, which remained unbroken, and produced much benefit to ourselves and others."

The friendship of Schiller and Goethe forms so delightful a chapter in their history, that we long for more and more details respecting it. Sincerity, true estimation of each other's merit, true sympathy in each other's character and purposes appear to have formed the basis of it, and maintained it unimpaired to the end. Goethe, we are told, was minute and sedulous in his attention to Schiller, whom he venerated as a good man and sympathized with as an afflicted one: when in mixed companies together, he constantly endeavored to draw out the stores of his modest and retiring friend; or to guard his sick and sensitive mind from annoyances that might have irritated him; now softening, now exciting conversation, guiding it with the address of a gifted and polished man, or lashing out of it with the scorpion-whip of his satire much that would have vexed the more soft and simple spirit of the valetudinarian. These are things which it is good to think of: it is good to know that there *are* literary men, who have other principles besides vanity; who can divide the approbation of their fellow mortals, without quarrelling over the lots; who in their solicitude about their "fame" do not forget the common charities of nature, in exchange for which the "fame" of most authors were but a poor bargain.

No. 4.   Page 103.

DEATH OF GUSTAVUS ADOLPHUS.

As a specimen of Schiller's historical style, we have extracted a few scenes from his masterly description of the Battle of Lützen. The whole forms a picture, executed in the spirit of Salvator; and though this is but a fragment, the importance of the figure represented in it will perhaps counterbalance that deficiency.

"At last the dreaded morning dawned; but a thick fog, which lay brooding over all the field, delayed the attack till noon. Kneeling in front of his lines, the King offered up his devotions; the whole army, at the same moment, dropping on their right knees, uplifted a moving hymn, and the field-music accompanied their singing. The King then mounted his horse; dressed in a jerkin of buff, with a surtout (for a late wound hindered him from wearing armor), he rode through the ranks, rousing the courage of his troops to a cheerful confidence, which his own forecasting bosom contradicted. *God with us* was the battle-word of the Swedes; that of the Imperialists was *Jesus Maria.* About eleven o'clock, the fog began to break, and Wallenstein's lines became visible. At the same time, too, were seen the flames of Lützen, which the Duke had ordered to be set on fire, that he might not be outflanked on this side. At length the signal pealed; the horse dashed forward on the enemy; the infantry advanced against his trenches.

"Meanwhile the right wing, led on by the King in person, had fallen on the left wing of the Friedlanders. The first strong onset of the heavy Finland Cuirassiers scattered the light-mounted Poles and Croats, who were stationed here, and their tumultuous flight spread fear and disorder over the rest of the cavalry. At this moment notice reached the King that his infantry were losing ground, and likely to be driven back from the trenches they had stormed; and also that his left, exposed to a tremendous fire from the Windmills behind Lützen, could no longer keep their place. With quick decision, he committed to Von Horn the task of pursuing the already beaten left wing of the enemy; and himself hastened, at the head of Steinbock's regiment, to restore the confusion of his own. His gallant horse bore him over the trenches with the speed of lightning; but the squadrons that came after him could not pass so rapidly; and none but a few horsemen, among whom Franz Albert, Duke of Sachsen-Lauenburg, is mentioned, were alert enough to keep beside him. He galloped right to the place where his infantry was most oppressed; and while looking round to spy out some weak point, on which his attack might be directed, his short-sightedness led him too near the enemy's lines. An Imperial sergeant (*gefreiter*), observing that every one respectfully made room for the advancing horseman, ordered a musketeer to fire on him. 'Aim at *him* there,' cried he; 'that must be a man of consequence.' The soldier drew his trigger; and the King's left arm was shattered by the ball. At this instant, his cavalry came galloping up, and a confused cry of '*The King bleeds! The King is shot!*' spread horror and dismay through their ranks. 'It is nothing: follow me!' exclaimed the King, collecting all his strength; but overcome with pain, and on the point of fainting, he desired the Duke of Lauenburg, in French, to take him without notice from the tumult. The Duke then turned with him to the right wing, making a wide circuit to conceal this accident from the desponding infantry; but as they rode along, the King received a second bullet through the back, which took from him the last remainder of his strength. 'I have got enough, brother,' said he with a dying voice: 'haste, save thyself.' With these words he sank from his horse; and here, struck by several other bullets, far from his attendants, he breathed out his life beneath the plundering hands of a troop of Croats. His horse flying on without its rider, and bathed in blood, soon announced to the Swedish cavalry the fall of their King; with wild yells they rush to the spot, to snatch that sacred spoil from the enemy. A deadly fight ensues around the corpse, and the mangled remains are buried under a hill of slain men.

"The dreadful tidings hasten in a few minutes over all the Swedish army: but instead of deadening the courage of these hardy troops, they rouse it to a fierce consuming fire. Life falls in value, since the holiest of all lives is gone; and death has now no terror for the lowly, since it has not spared the anointed head. With the grim fury of lions, the Upland, Småland, Finnish, East and West Gothland regiments dash a second time upon the left wing of the enemy, which, already making but a feeble opposition to Von Horn, is now utterly driven from the field.

"But how dear a victory, how sad a triumph! Now first when the rage of battle has grown cold, do they feel the whole greatness of their loss, and the shout of the conqueror dies in a mute and gloomy despair. He who led them on to battle has not returned with them. Apart he lies, in his victorious field, confounded with the common heaps of humble dead. After long fruitless searching, they found the royal corpse, not far from the great stone, which had already stood for centuries between Lützen and the Merseburg Canal, but which, ever since this memorable incident, has borne the name of *Schwedenstein*, the Stone of the Swede. Defaced with wounds and blood, so as scarcely to be recognized, trodden under the hoofs of horses, stripped of his ornaments, even of his clothes, he is drawn from beneath a heap of dead bodies, brought to Weissenfels, and there delivered to the lamentations of his troops and the last embraces of his Queen. Vengeance had first required its tribute, and blood must **flow** as an offering to the Monarch ; now Love assumes its rights, and mild tears are shed for the Man. Individual grief is lost in the universal sorrow. Astounded by this overwhelming stroke, the generals in blank despondency stand round his bier, and none yet ventures to conceive the full extent of his loss."

The descriptive powers of the Historian, though the most popular, are among the lowest of his endowments. That Schiller was not wanting in the nobler requisites of his art, might be proved from his reflections on this very incident, " striking like a hand from the clouds into the calculated horologe of men's affairs, and directing the considerate mind to a higher plan of things." But the limits of our Work are already reached. Of Schiller's histories and dramas we can give no farther specimens : of his lyrical, didactic, moral poems we must take our leave without giving any. Perhaps the time may come, when all his writings, transplanted to our own soil, may be offered in their entire dimensions to the thinkers of these Islands ; a conquest by which our literature, rich as it is, might be enriched still farther.

Printed in the United Kingdom
by Lightning Source UK Ltd.
102078UKS00001B/129